PC
Repair and Troubleshooting Guide

By
Mark Edward Soper

BPB PUBLICATIONS

FIRST EDITION 2017
Copyright © BPB Publications, India
ISBN: 978-81-8333-509-6

Reprinted in India under arrangement with Pearson Education Inc., USA
Authorized reprint from the English language edition, entitled The PC and Gadget Help Desk, 1st Edition, 9780789753458 by Mark Edward Soper, Published by Pearson Eduction, Inc., publishing as QUE Publishing, Copyright © 2017 Pearson Education, Inc.

Distributors:

BPB PUBLICATIONS
20, Ansari Road, Darya Ganj
New Delhi-110002
Ph: 23254990/23254991

DECCAN AGENCIES
4-3-329, Bank Street,
Hyderabad-500195
Ph: 24756967/24756400

MICRO MEDIA
Shop No. 5, Mahendra Chambers,
150 DN Rd. Next to Capital Cinema,
V.T. (C.S.T.) Station, MUMBAI-400 001
Ph: 22078296/22078297

BPB BOOK CENTRE
376 Old Lajpat Rai Market,
Delhi-110006
Ph: 23861747

COMPUTER BOOK CENTRE
12, Shrungar Shopping Centre,
M.G.Road, BENGALURU–560001
Ph: 25587923/25584641

Published by Manish Jain for BPB Publications, 20, Ansari Road, Darya Ganj, New Delhi-110002 and Printed at Akash Press, New Delhi

CONTENTS

6 Keeping Devices Powered Up 155

7 Desktop Power Supply Troubleshooting 167

18 Upgrading and Troubleshooting Storage Devices 445

ABOUT THE AUTHOR

Mark Edward Soper has helped users deal with problems with computers, digital cameras, and other personal tech devices for more than 25 years. He is the author of *PC Help Desk in a Book* and co-author of *Leo Laporte's PC Help Desk*, as well as more than two dozen other books on Windows, digital photography, networking, broadband Internet, CompTIA A+ Certification, and computer troubleshooting and upgrading. With this level of experience, Mark is experienced at helping readers understand and use creative solutions to connectivity, configuration issues, data recovery, and other types of problems that can beset users of personal technology. Mark is also the creator of *Building and Repairing PCs* (Que Video), which provides more than two hours of detailed, hands-on help for building, repairing, and upgrading desktop and laptop computers.

Dedication

For Jim K. and Connie E. Thanks to each of you for the opportunities to sell, train, and learn about computers and personal tech "back in the day."

WE WANT TO HEAR FROM YOU!

As the reader of this book, you are our most important critic and commentator. We value your opinion and want to know what we're doing right, what we could do better, what areas you'd like to see us publish in, and any other words of wisdom you're willing to pass our way.

We welcome your comments. You can email or write to let us know what you did or didn't like about this book—as well as what we can do to make our books better.

Please note that we cannot help you with technical problems related to the topic of this book.

When you write, please be sure to include this book's title and author as well as your name and email address. We will carefully review your comments and share them with the author and editors who worked on the book.

Email: sales@bpbonline.com

Introduction

Why You Need This Book

If you're a typical electronics user, you have a PC (maybe more than one), a smartphone, a tablet or two, and a printer. You probably also have a home theater system with an HDTV, a sound bar or receiver, and a Blu-ray player. Add a digital camera or HD camcorder, and you have a home full of devices that are supposed to work nicely with each other—if you're an expert.

If you said to yourself, "Hey, I'm no expert," that's OK. This book is the expert you've been looking for. I've spent years using, writing about, and learning about these technologies, and I'm here to help.

If you've ever been frustrated by long hold times for "help" that didn't help much, unnecessary service calls, or problems you just can't fix, this book is for you. It isn't written for technology geniuses, but for people who just want their home and personal technology tools to do the jobs they're supposed to—and a little bit more.

This is my third *PC Help Desk* book, and I'm very glad to be covering this topic again. When I wrote my first *PC Help Desk* book and teamed up with Leo Laporte for a sequel about a decade ago, the emphasis was on computers (mainly desktops).

Things have changed a lot since then: a lot more users have laptops than desktops; Windows, Apple, and Android are fighting over the mobile device space; getting devices to play nicely with each other across operating systems and device types is essential; digital cameras, HD camcorders, and action camcorders are part of the action; and home theater systems dominate living rooms and dens in many parts of the world. This book is written for this diverse, exciting, and frustrating world.

We want to help you get your devices working properly, help you solve problems when they occur, and show you how to get your devices to work together and play together.

Technology problems can be divided into three categories:

- Hardware problems
- Software problems
- Internet/networking problems

Sometimes, a technology problem involves two or more of these areas, making the solution even tougher. Fortunately, *The PC and Gadget Help Desk* is designed to solve the most common problems you'll encounter in all three areas, even if multiple problems are plaguing your system.

This book is designed to give you the answers you need to your computer problems—fast! Our goal is to take you directly from symptoms to solutions.

You can count on the solutions in this book. This book is the product of countless hours discovering problems with home and personal electronics (sometimes even creating problems on purpose), discovering solutions, and testing solutions to those problems. In this process, I've used some of the latest products on the market, but I never forget that we're all living on budgets and need help with devices that might not be the newest but still need to work.

I know what it's like to have problems finding answers to technology questions. I've spent more than 25 years as a teacher, trainer, consultant, writer, and filmmaker on technology topics to answer those questions. Read this book and you get the benefits of that experience. This book is based on facts, not fantasy, so you can rely on it.

How to Use This Book

When you have a technology question or problem, you don't need to stuff your brain with huge numbers of facts that you must to sift through to find the answers. *The PC and Gadget Help Desk* is designed to provide you with fast access to practical solutions you can apply right away. I hope you'll find it fascinating reading, but it's really designed as a quick reference you'll turn to when your computer has a problem, and one you can put aside until you have another problem or another question.

Some troubleshooting books tell you *what* do to without telling you *why*. Again, *The PC and Gadget Help Desk* is different. I love to explain why things are the way they are inside your computer, commiserate with you when things don't make sense, and show you solutions that make sense. You deserve an explanation of technology problems and their solutions, and we make sure you get what you deserve.

Some books are designed to be read just once; again, *The PC and Gadget Help Desk* is different. Because of its broad and deep coverage of technology problems and solutions, you'll turn to it as a valuable reference again and again to solve problems at home, at the office, or at the corporate help desk.

Here's how to get the most from this book:

1. Take a look at the chapters: they're discussed in detail later in this introduction. Go to the chapter that most closely matches your general problem area. For example, if you're having a problem

getting your PC or devices to connect with your HDTV, go to Chapter 12, "Troubleshooting Home Theater, HDTVs, and Projectors."

2. Starting with Chapter 3, "Troubleshooting Internet Problems," each chapter starts with a feature we call Fast Track to Solutions, a table of symptoms and solutions. Use this table to point you toward underlying problems and their solutions. Start here when you need help fast. Each table lists symptoms common to the parts of your computer or peripherals discussed in that chapter.

3. As soon as you have located the appropriate Fast Track to Solutions symptoms table, look up the symptom. Each symptom sends you directly to a troubleshooting flowchart or book section that covers your problem and its solution.

4. If you are directed to a particular book section, use the text, screen shots, and equipment photos to learn more about how your hardware and software work and to learn the troubleshooting steps needed to solve your problem.

5. If you are directed to a flowchart, each flowchart provides step-by-step solutions with ample cross-references to the text that provide detailed information about the problem and how to find the solution.

6. Use the special elements in each chapter to find valuable tips and shortcuts, discover useful websites, and avoid potential dangers.

Here's an example of how to use this book to solve a problem.

1. Assume that you can't start your computer. Chapter 8 covers problems with starting Windows computers and tablets, so turn to the beginning of Chapter 8 to get started. The Fast Track to Solutions symptoms table at the beginning of this chapter offers a flowchart called "Troubleshooting a System That Won't Start."

2. Go to the flowchart and follow the solutions given in order. For example, in this flowchart, the first question is, "Is your computer beeping?" If you answer Yes, follow the recommendations to use the beep codes to find and solve the problem. If the answer is No, go to the next question.

3. Read the recommended text sections or view the figures provided as references.

4. Continue through the flowchart until you find the solution that matches your hardware and situation.

5. Use the pictures and screenshots provided to help you locate and use similar features on your system. For many problems, you will use a combination of a flowchart and particular book sections to find the right solution.

How This Book Is Organized

The PC and Gadget Help Desk includes the following sections:

- The first 23 chapters cover all the important hardware and software components of your computer and peripherals.

- Chapter 24 includes a guide to troubleshooting methods and tools and 11 flowcharts to help you solve technology problems.
- The Glossary defines personal technology terms and acronyms.

The following sections explain the book sections in greater detail.

Chapter 1, "PC, Tablet, Mobile Device, Home Theater, Digital Camera, and Camcorder Anatomy 101"

Whatever type of technology problem you're facing, read this chapter first. It explains the major features of the technology devices this book covers. Wondering what a subsystem is? Confused about software, hardware, and firmware? Want to avoid frying your PC when you upgrade it? Not sure what the ports on your PC, tablet, or digital camera are for? Want to protect the information on your Windows computer? This chapter answers these and many other essential questions.

Chapter 2, "Upgrade, Repair, or Replace?"

When a technology device has a problem, what should you do? This chapter gives you guidelines and case studies to help you figure out whether it's better to repair or replace a broken device, or whether you should buy upgrades or replace a device that needs a speed or capacity boost.

Chapter 3, "Troubleshooting Internet Problems"

Wi-Fi adapters, routers, switches, cables—there are a lot of components between your device and the Internet. If your network is too slow, if you're not sure it's secure enough, or if you need to "borrow" your smartphone's cellular connection so your other devices can connect to the Internet, this chapter is ready to help.

Chapter 4, "Curing Malware and Stopping Scams"

Viruses, worms, Trojan horses, email scams—malware's the name, and trouble is its game. Learn how to protect your PCs and mobile devices from threats and discover the clues to scams that threaten your financial and personal information.

Chapter 5, "Solving Problems with Viewing Your Photos and Videos"

Can't view your photos or videos on your Windows PC, tablet, or mobile device? Discover the software and settings that will help you enjoy your photos, your videos, and your favorite downloads.

Chapter 6, "Keeping Devices Powered Up"

Laptops, tablets, and smartphones all rely on rechargeable batteries. Come to think of it, so do digital cameras and camcorders. Learn how to choose the best charging methods, shop for replacement batteries, and troubleshoot laptop charger problems.

Chapter 7, "Desktop Power Supply Troubleshooting"

If you use a desktop computer, the power supply is one of the components you probably don't worry about. However, when your system starts crashing or it's time to add more hardware, the power supply needs your attention. Learn how to test a power supply, select a new power supply that's good enough for the work it needs to do, and install it. Keep your desktop and mobile devices safe from power problems by discovering how to choose and use surge suppression and battery backup devices.

Chapter 8, "Fixing Windows Devices That Can't Start"

Even if your computer's power supply is working flawlessly, problems with BIOS configuration (the BIOS controls how drives and other devices work at startup), Windows configuration, drive problems, and loose cables can keep your laptop, desktop, or Windows tablet from working. Learn how to recognize common hardware and BIOS problems, and use Windows repair tools such as System Restore and Refresh to get your system back in working order.

Chapter 9, "Solving File Sharing Problems"

Windows 7, 8, and 8.1 use HomeGroup as their preferred network method. Learn how to set it up, troubleshoot symptoms, and fix problems with it. Go beyond HomeGroup networking to stream media and share files with Windows XP, Android, and iOS systems.

Chapter 10, "Troubleshooting Device Sharing"

Networks aren't just for Internet access and folder sharing anymore. Learn how to connect your PC to a wireless printer and use network attached drives with your PC, Android, or iOS device.

Chapter 11, "Troubleshooting Printing"

Whether you use an inkjet or laser printer at home or in the office, problems with print quality, finding the correct printer driver, and using your printer with Android or iOS devices can give you headaches. For fast relief, read this chapter.

Chapter 12, "Troubleshooting Home Theater, HDTVs, and Projectors"

The incredible information and media resources available to your PC or mobile device are limited by small screens and tinny speakers. Connect your PC and mobile devices to home theater systems,

HDTVs, and projectors to fully enjoy music, movies, video, and photos. Learn how to solve problems with cables and configurations.

Chapter 13, "Fixing Slow 3D Gaming"

Nobody likes to lose, and slow 3D performance is a sure way to stay out of the winner's circle. Learn how to update and tweak AMD and NVIDIA drivers, enable CrossFireX and SLI, find speed plus stability when you overclock your system, and get a better display for gaming.

Chapter 14, "Keeping Your Devices Updated"

From malware threats and hackers to improved drivers, there are plenty of reasons to keep your system updated. Learn how to optimize Windows Update, add support for updating Microsoft Office, install updates manually when necessary, update third-party apps, and update and roll back device drivers. You'll also discover how to update iOS and Android devices without breaking your bandwidth budget.

Chapter 15, "Dealing with Contrary Memory"

RAM is the fuel that enables your computer to juggle multiple apps at high speed. Learn how to figure out how much you need, choose the right RAM upgrade for your computer, install it, and test it.

Chapter 16, "Keeping Devices Cool"

The CPU, graphics card, and RAM produce a lot of heat inside your computer, and heat can shorten the life of your computer. Learn how to monitor temperatures, keep your desktop or laptop cool, replace defective fans, and what to do if your mobile device is getting warm.

Chapter 17, "Troubleshooting Touchscreens, Keyboards, and Mice"

Whether you enter data and select files with your finger, a keyboard, or a mouse, you need reliable performance from your Windows PC, Android, or iOS device. Learn how to test touchscreens for problems, clean them, choose a stylus, troubleshoot wired and wireless keyboards and mice, use a single receiver with multiple input devices, solve problems with Bluetooth, and customize your mouse's or touchpad's behavior.

Chapter 18, "Upgrading and Troubleshooting Storage Devices"

If your hard disk or SSD stops working, you're on the road to a very bad day. Learn how to get early warnings of storage problems, test your drives for errors, and use Format to try to fix a problem drive. If you've deleted important files, learn how to recover them using Windows' own backup and retrieval tools and third-party data-recovery apps. Running short of space? Discover tips, tricks, and strategies for freeing up space and using cloud storage with Windows, Android, and iOS devices.

Chapter 19, "Software Troubleshooting"

Software that stops working turns your computer into an expensive paperweight. Discover when and how to use an app on a different computer, how to convert a trial mode app into a licensed app without reinstalling it, how to activate an app, how to repair a program (app), and how to trick an old program into running properly on a new version of Windows.

Chapter 20, "Digital Camera Troubleshooting"

Whether you prefer to use a smartphone, point-and-shoot camera, or a camera with interchangeable lenses (digital SLR or compact system camera), problems with exposure, lighting, and white balance can make getting good pictures harder. This chapter shows you how to use your device or camera's semi-automatic and manual settings to get better pictures around the clock, day or night.

Chapter 21, "HD Camcorder and Video Troubleshooting"

You can shoot video with a smartphone, a tablet, most digital cameras, an action camcorder, or a general-purpose HD camcorder. Whichever device you choose, this chapter gives you the guidance you need for clearer, sharper, and better-sounding video.

Chapter 22, "iOS Troubleshooting"

Your iPhone needs to make phone calls, and it, along with your iPad and iPod Touch, is designed to give you mobile access to the Internet and the world. When you can't connect to the Internet, make phone calls, or use FaceTime, it might be time to restart or reset your device. We're here to help you back up your stuff and get your device back into good working order.

Chapter 23, "Android Troubleshooting"

If you can't make a phone call with your Android smartphone or it has stopped working, it might be time for a Factory Reset. Learn how to perform one, why you need to run a third-party backup as well, and find quick references to other Android problems and solutions throughout the book.

Chapter 24, "Troubleshooting Flowcharts"

Whether you've arrived at the flowcharts from a symptoms table or headed straight to the back, you'll find 11 flowcharts to help you with major PC and peripheral problems.

If you're an experienced troubleshooter, the flowcharts might be all you need. However, if you're new to solving your own computer problems, be sure to read the section called "Troubleshooting Methodology." We've placed it at the front of Chapter 24 so you won't miss it. This section puts our recommendations for tools, techniques, and general troubleshooting philosophy at your fingertips.

Glossary

It's easy to get lost in an ocean of acronyms and terms when you're trying to understand, upgrade, or troubleshoot personal technology. Use the Glossary to explain the unfamiliar and refresh your knowledge.

ACKNOWLEDGMENTS

A successful author has many people to thank, so I'd better get started! Whether this is the first one of my books you've tried or you're back for more, thank you so very much for your support, your encouragement, and your suggestions.

Each of us has been entrusted by the Almighty with talents and gifts. I thank Him, the ultimate source of all goodness and wisdom, for the opportunity to share what I have learned and encourage you to learn with me.

My wife Cheryl deserves much of the credit for this book. Not only has she exemplified the love of God in my life, but as a librarian, she saw the urgent need for this book and encouraged me to write it.

Thousands of students across the country, as well as clients here at home, have provided me with case studies and opportunities to put these tips, techniques, and tools to work. My extended family's mixture of Windows PCs and mobile devices of both the iOS and Android families, digital cameras, and home theater systems has also provided plenty of opportunities to learn how everything (sometimes) can work together.

I also want to thank the editorial and design team that Que Publishing put together for this book: Many thanks to Rick Kughen (ably assisted by Todd Brakke) for bringing me back for a third generation of *PC Help Desk*. Thanks also to Greg Wiegand for giving this project the green light, Brandon Cackowski-Schnell for developing the book, Karen Weinstein for checking technical issues, Sandra Schroeder for managing this project, Seth Kerney for supervising the final production stages, Barbara Hacha for making the grammar behave itself, Kristin Watterson for coordinating the project, and Mark Shirar for a great cover and interior design. It's been more than 15 years since I teamed up with Que Publishing, and I look forward to many more years of working together to bring you technical information that teaches, informs, and inspires.

1

PC, TABLET, MOBILE DEVICE, HOME THEATER, DIGITAL CAMERA, AND CAMCORDER ANATOMY 101

One Device = Many Subsystems

You can't troubleshoot a technology device very well unless you understand what it's supposed to do, what connections it has on the outside, and what connections and components it has on the inside.

Whether you're trying to solve a problem with a Windows computer, a home theater system, a digital camera, or a smartphone, you need to understand the principle of subsystems.

What's a subsystem? A *subsystem* is the portion of a device that does a particular task. For example, a smartphone or tablet's Wi-Fi subsystem includes the Wi-Fi antenna, the Wi-Fi radio, and the menu settings that enable, disable, and configure the Wi-Fi radio to connect to a particular Wi-Fi source (SSID). A laptop computer's Wi-Fi subsystem includes the Wi-Fi antenna, the Wi-Fi radio, driver files to enable the computer's operating system to use the Wi-Fi hardware, and a configuration program to enable, disable, and configure the Wi-Fi radio.

When you consider that most devices covered in this book are designed to send and receive Wi-Fi or Bluetooth signals, store information, perform calculations on information, share information over a network, and output information to displays, speakers, or printers, you can see that even the "simplest" device includes several subsystems.

In this chapter, we'll outline the subsystems that are found in each type of device discussed in this book and show you common sources of problems.

Hardware, Software, and Firmware

Each subsystem in a device covered in this book typically has at least two of the following three types of components:

- **Hardware**—This is the physical part of the subsystem (such as the Wi-Fi radio and antenna in the smartphone, tablet, or PC). It has components that can be damaged or broken and repaired or replaced.
- **Software**—This is the instructions that tell the subsystem what to do. Software can be downloaded from the Internet, installed from a USB flash drive or CD, or can be included in a device. Software that is built in to a chip is called firmware.
- **Firmware**—Firmware is "software on a chip" that enables a device to perform functions without the installation of additional software. Most devices have firmware, and many devices' firmware can be updated with improved or additional instructions so the device can perform new tasks, work with newer types of hardware, or work more reliably.

Desktop and Laptop PC Subsystems

You can't troubleshoot a computer very well unless you understand what a computer is and how it's put together. Although your "personal confuser" might look like a big (or not-so-big) box on your desk, it's not really a single unit. Instead, it's a collection of hardware subsystems:

- Video
- Storage
- Input devices
- Printers and other output devices
- Audio
- Networking
- Processor
- Memory
- Power

Computer hardware can't do a thing for you (or to you) without software. As it turns out, these subsystems are controlled by two types of software:

- **A system BIOS (basic input/output system) chip on the motherboard**—A BIOS chip is an example of "software on a chip," or firmware.

- **The operating system and its device drivers**—These are the files that tell Windows how to use your PC's hardware. In this book, we concentrate on Microsoft Windows 7 and Windows 8/8.1.

Application programs such as Microsoft Office, Adobe Photoshop Elements, Quicken, and innumerable others (we didn't take time to count them) communicate with hardware through the operating system and its device drivers and the system BIOS. The end result? You create, change, store, print, and transmit documents, photos, videos, and other digital masterpieces.

There are plenty of ways the whole process can fail, and with the greater demands we place on our computers today, more is at stake than ever before. A few years ago, a computer failure might have meant that you'd lose your home budget or customer records. Now, a computer failure could also wipe out your digital photo collection or gigabytes of digital music files. That's scary!

We're here to help take the fright out of computer problems and help you keep your PC running. The first step to handling computer problems is learning what's inside a typical computer. If you don't understand your PC, troubleshooting it is just about impossible.

This section introduces you to the major components in typical computers, including those prone to being a point of failure. Think of this as an anatomy lesson, but without the formaldehyde and nasty smells.

What Is a Point of Failure?

In the following sections, we use the term *point of failure* to refer to a component or BIOS configuration that could cause problems for your system. This term isn't meant to suggest that computers are constantly on the verge of having a problem, but that some parts of the computer are more likely to cause problems than others.

Before you start exploring your computer, especially before you open it, be sure to protect your equipment from electrostatic discharge.

Stop ESD—Don't Fry Your PC!

Electrostatic discharge (ESD) is a hidden danger to your data and your computer hardware, particularly when you open your computer to install new hardware or to troubleshoot a problem inside your system. ESD takes place when two items with different electrical potentials come close to each other or touch each other. ESD can happen even if you don't see a spark or feel a shock, and it takes very little ESD to damage or destroy computer parts. About 800 volts of ESD will give you a tingle or shock, but it takes less than 100 volts (an amount you can't even feel) to ruin a CPU, a memory module, or other computer part. Low-power construction makes these parts very vulnerable to ESD.

You can avoid ESD damage when you're working inside your computer by following these tips:

- Use antistatic cleaning wipes to clean cases and monitors.
- Wear cotton or other natural fibers when you work on your PC; if you're working at home, ditch those synthetic-soled shoes and work in your stocking feet (cotton socks, please!) to avoid generating static electricity.

- Buy and use anti-ESD devices, such as a wrist strap with an alligator clip and an antistatic mat. Connect the alligator clip to the computer *after* you disconnect it from power; this equalizes the electrical potential between you and the computer to prevent ESD. Figure 1.1 shows you how a wrist strap works to protect your PC.
- Hold components by the case or card bracket—never by the circuit board or data/power connector.

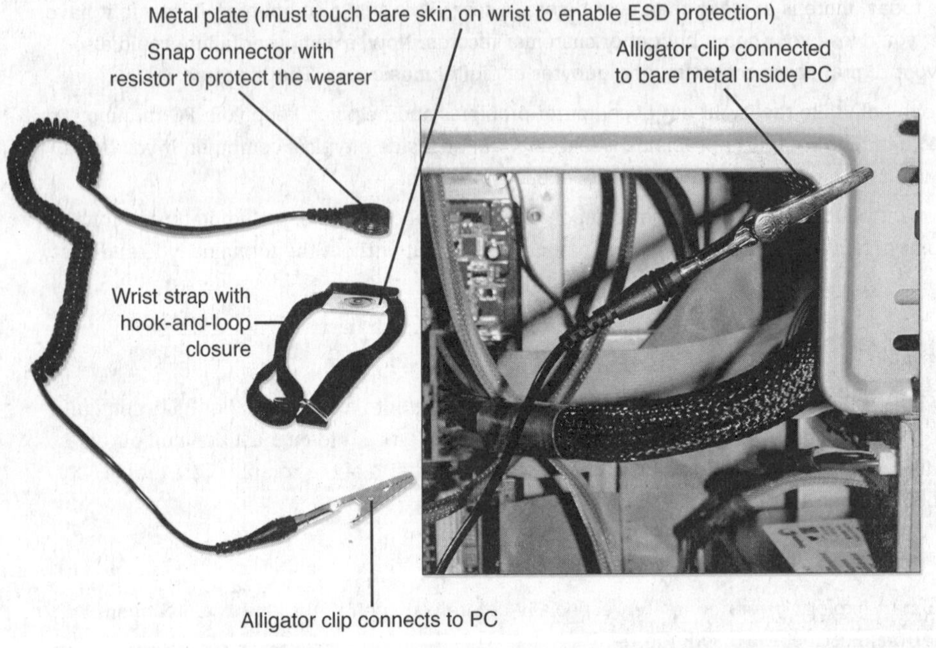

Figure 1.1 A wrist strap reduces ESD potential when you connect the alligator clip to bare metal inside your PC and wear it properly.

Don't Commit These ESD Goofs

ESD protection is only as good as the user. To make sure a wrist strap works, take off the wristwatch or dangly bracelets on the wrist you want to use for the strap. Adjust the strap so the metal plate is snug against the inside of your wrist (so that hair won't interfere with ESD protection). Make sure you snap the cable with the alligator clip to the wrist strap. Make sure you attach the alligator clip to a metal part of the PC's chassis. You could use the power supply grill or the drive bay frame, as in Figure 1.1.

If you wear your wrist strap over your shirt, sweater, or blouse—or don't connect it to the alligator clip—you're wasting your time.

If you want to keep parts you remove from the computer safe as well as prevent ESD when you're inside the PC, look for a *field service kit*, which combines a grounding strap for your body with a grounded parts mat for the components you are removing (or installing).

Tracking Down ESD Protection

Try your local computer component store for ESD protection, but if you can't find protective devices locally, try these online sources:

- **e-Mat**—www.anti-staticmat.com
- **Fry's Electronics**—www.frys.com (search for "anti-static")
- **Radio Shack**—www.radioshack.com (search for "anti-static")

Desktop PC Anatomy

Desktops aren't as popular as laptops these days, but that's OK. Laptops make sense for people who are satisfied with keeping a computer for a couple of years and then moving on to another one. However, if you like building things yourself, having complete control over what's inside your PC, upgrading your system as leading-edge technology changes, or at least want to buy a prebuilt PC that has serious expansion options, desktop PCs still make sense.

A desktop PC is a PC that has separate display, keyboard, and drives/processor/memory components. The drives, the processor (aka the CPU), and memory (RAM) are built into a box known as a case or chassis. The outside of the computer case is where you'll find the following items:

- Cable connections for external peripherals, such as cable or DSL modems, printers, displays, all-in-one units, and external drives
- Drive bays for removable-media and optical drives
- The power supply fan and voltage switch
- The power switch, reset button, and signal lights

No matter what you think the source of a computer problem might be, it pays to start with the outside. From systems that won't start to speakers that are "quiet—maybe too quiet," external ports and devices are worth investigating for the answers.

Front Views of Typical Desktop Computers

Most typical "desktop" computers use a tower form factor that is sometimes too bulky for your desk, so they're often placed on the floor. Figure 1.2 shows the front-mounted drives and ports found on a typical desktop computer built from standard components.

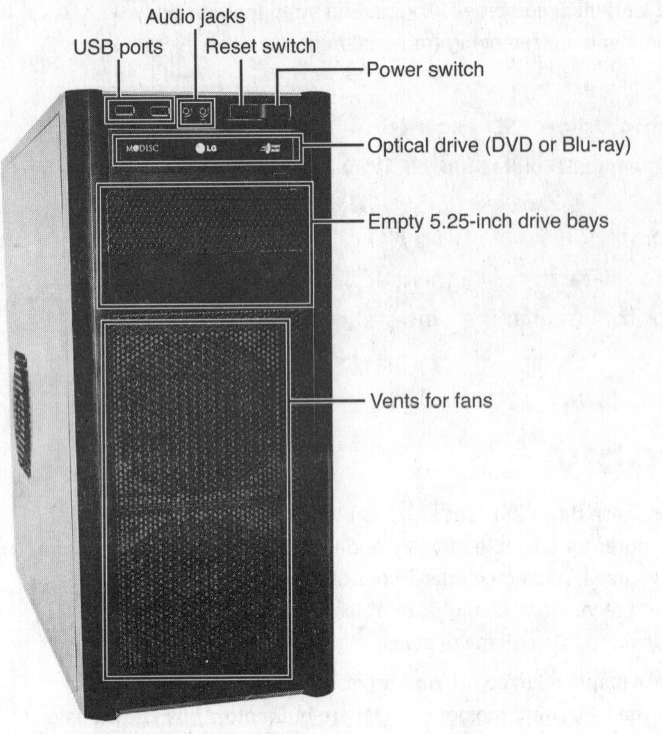

Figure 1.2
Most recent desktop computers feature built-in AV and USB ports on the case front.

What Makes a "Desktop" Computer a Desktop Computer?

Today, a "desktop computer" (like the one shown in Figure 1.2) is often found on the floor. Back in the 1980s, though, when the first IBM PCs were battling the Apple IIs for desktop dominance, a PC did sit on the desk. These days, the term *desktop computer* usually describes computers that have the following features:

- They use standard internal components such as motherboards, processors, memory, drives, sound cards, and video cards.
- They are too bulky to be moved around frequently. In other words, they lack mobility, unlike a laptop or tablet.
- They can be upgraded and rebuilt by the user without special tools.
- They use a separate display.
- They use separate input devices (keyboard, mouse, or other pointing device).

The case shown in Figure 1.2 is sometimes referred to as a "full-tower" case. Typical cases in this category have room for eight or more internal drives (three in 5.25-inch bays and up to five or more in 3.5-inch bays; some of these also have one or two bays for 2.5-inch SSDs). Smaller tower cases have fewer drive bays and use smaller motherboards with fewer expansion slots.

Where Should I Put My Computer?

If you have a desktop PC in a tower case, you might be wondering where to put it. Traditionally, users placed them on the floor, but the problem is that a PC that's on the floor can be kicked, bumped by the vacuum cleaner, might inhale pet hairs into its air intakes, and suffer other indignities. If you don't want your PC sitting on your desk, but don't want it resting on the floor, get a computer desk with a shelf for the case, or put wheels on the bottom of the case to raise it above the floor. Just make sure you put it someplace where you can get to the internal drives and front-mounted ports easily. In some cases, you might need to add extension cables to your mouse, keyboard, or video cables to enable them to reach to your system. If you have pets, make sure you can easily open your system every few months so a computer-grade vacuum cleaner and canned air can be used to remove pet hair: too much pet hair can kill your PC by causing it to overheat! Refer to Figure 1.3.

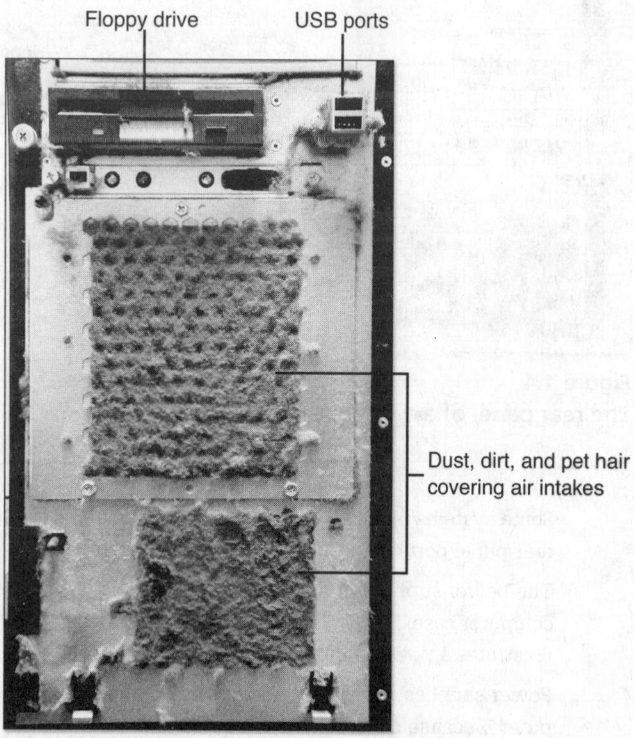

Figure 1.3
Remove the front panel of a desktop computer to determine if the air intakes need cleaning.

Rear Views of Typical Desktop Computers

If you're trying to fix a problem with a balky external peripheral, you need to look for the port to which it's connected. Although more and more PCs have front-mounted ports, most PCs connect some or all external peripherals to rear-mounted ports.

Almost all desktop computers built since the late 1990s use a motherboard design based on the ATX standard. These motherboards use a port cluster, which usually places the mouse and keyboard ports to the left, followed by some USB ports and additional I/O or audio ports to the right, as shown in Figures 1.4 and 1.5.

Figure 1.4 shows the rear of a typical desktop computer before power or data cables are connected.

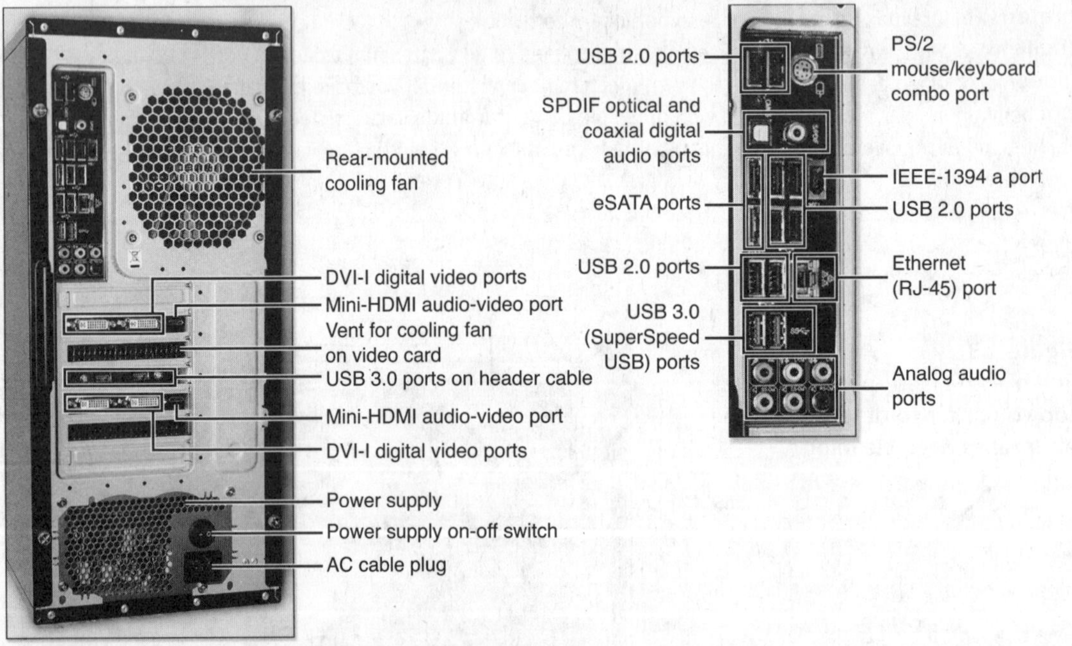

Figure 1.4
The rear panel of a typical desktop computer.

Some systems include built-in video rather than relying on video cards. Figure 1.5 illustrates the rear-panel port cluster from this type of system.

The power supply can be located at either the top or the bottom of a typical tower-type desktop computer case. Figure 1.4 illustrates a system with a bottom-mounted power supply, and Figure 1.6 illustrates a power supply located at the top of the case.

Power supplies convert high-voltage AC power into the low-voltage DC power used inside the computer. Because conversions of this type create heat, the power supply has a fan to cool itself and also help overall system cooling. The fan is often found on the rear of the unit, as in Figure 1.6, but some use a fan that faces the inside of the PC, and a few have both types of fans.

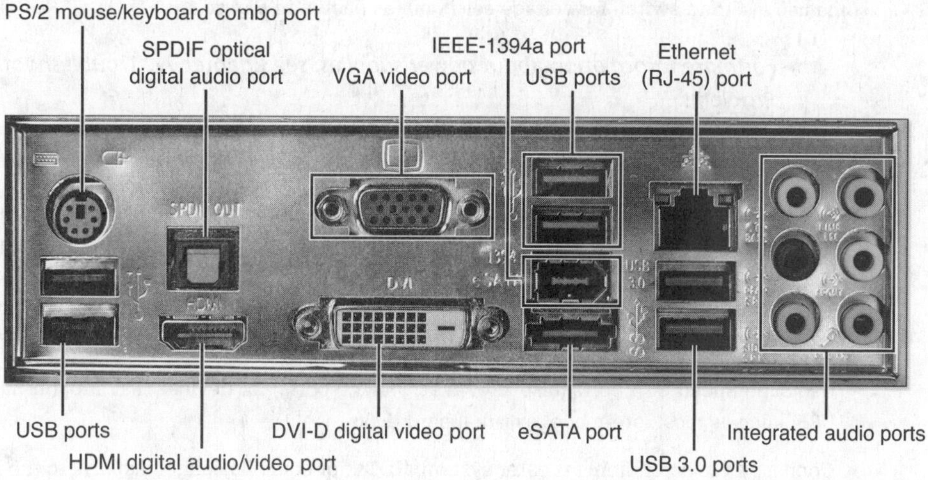

Figure 1.5 The port cluster of a typical desktop computer with integrated (built-in) video ports.

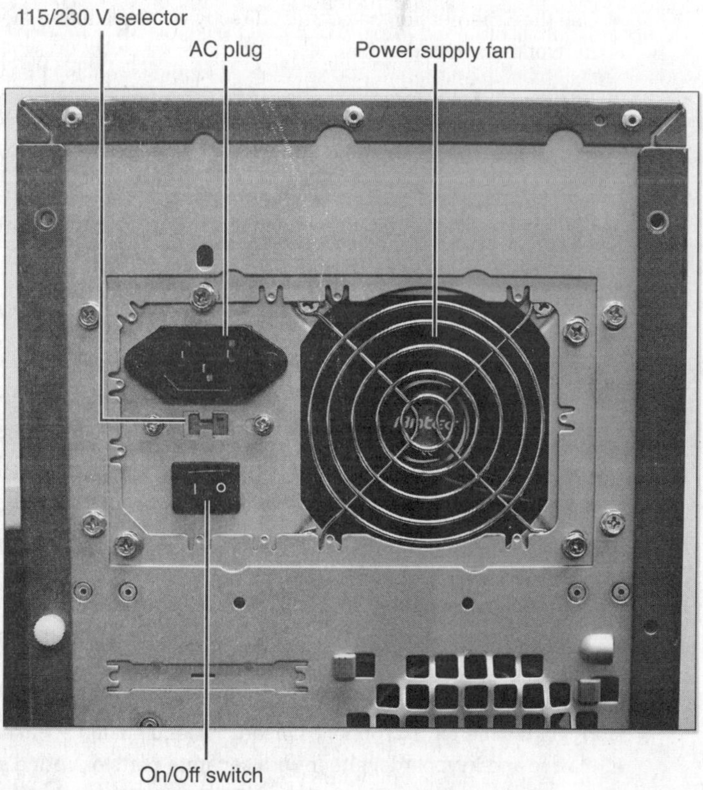

Figure 1.6 A typical power supply mounted in a computer.

Although many power supplies can switch between 115-volt and 230-volt services automatically, some use a sliding switch for voltage selection, as shown in Figure 1.6.

➡ *For more information about power supplies, see Chapter 7, "Troubleshooting Power Problems."*

Ports and Their Uses

As you can see, typical desktop computers have a lot of connections. Here's what you use them for:

- Plug your PC into an AC power source with the AC power jack.
- You can attach almost any external device (drives, all-in-one devices, printers, TV tuners, modems, Wi-Fi adapters, mice, keyboards, and so on) into your system's USB ports.
- Use SuperSpeed USB ports (also known as USB 3.0 ports) for devices that support SuperSpeed USB, such as most late-model external hard disks.
- Connect a projector, home theater system, HDTV, or some flat-panel displays to the HDMI port to put your laptop on the "big screen."
- The VGA and DVI ports support older displays and some HDTVs.
- Use the Ethernet port to connect directly to a broadband modem or to a switch or router for easy networking.
- Use the IEEE-1394a port to connect to some types of external devices, including some DV camcorders, drives, and scanners.
- Use the SPDIF ports to connect to home theater systems or HDTVs.
- Use the mini-jack audio ports to connect to headphones, earbuds, or PC speakers.

Points of Failure on the Rear of Your Computer

The most likely point of failure on the rear of your computer is peripheral cabling. Fortunately, most devices other than displays now use USB cables instead of older and bulkier types of cables, such as serial and parallel (see Figure 1.8). Although VGA cables (see Figure 1.7) are still used for many displays and some projectors, most late-model PCs use other types of cables.

Note that serial, parallel, and VGA cables all use thumbscrews. If you don't fasten the thumbscrews to the connector on the computer, your cables won't connect tightly, and this could cause intermittent or complete failure of your peripherals.

USB 3.0 cables resemble USB 2.0 cables but have additional power and data leads; you can plug a USB 3.0 device into a USB 2.0 port, but it will it run at USB 2.0 speeds only. Other types of external cables include IEEE-1394a, HDMI and DVI (for HDTV and HD-compatible displays), RJ-45 cables used for Ethernet networking, SPDIF coaxial and optical cables for digital audio, and 3.5mm mini-jack cables used for microphones, headsets, and analog speakers. Some systems also still support PS/2 mice and keyboards, either with separate ports or with a single combo port. Figure 1.8 illustrates these cables (see Figures 1.4 and 1.5 for the corresponding ports).

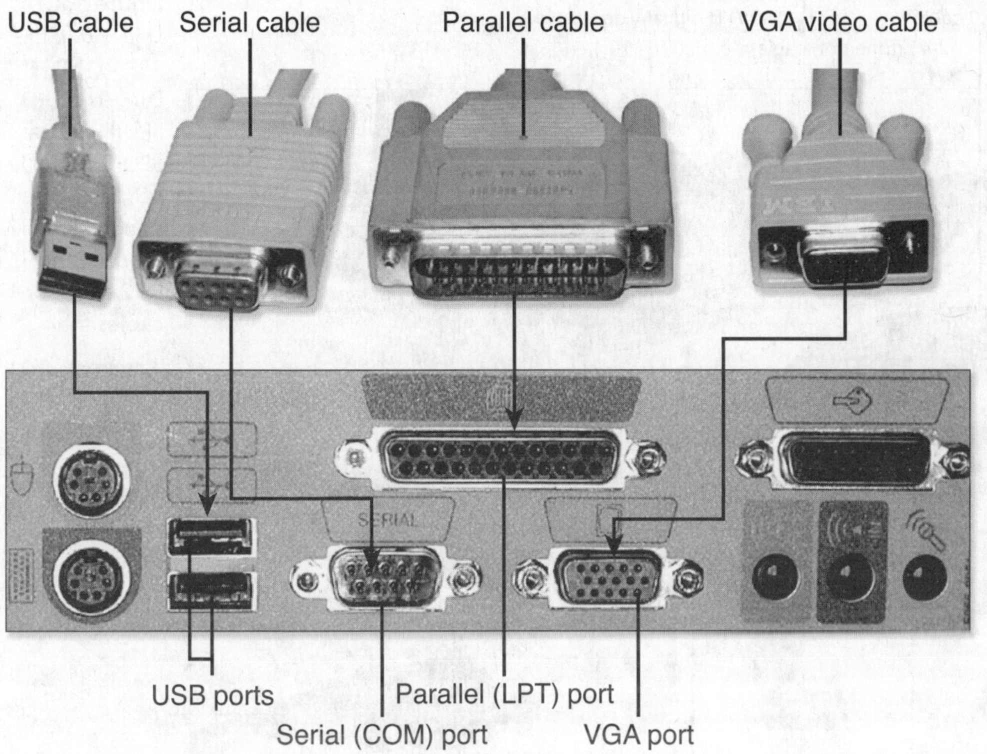

Figure 1.7
USB, serial, parallel, and VGA cables (top) and the ports they connect to (bottom).

Peripheral cables such as the PS/2 mouse and keyboard, audio, and newer types of cables such as USB and IEEE-1394a are pushed into place and are very lightweight. No thumbscrews or other locking devices are needed. However, these cables can also be pulled out of the socket easily, precisely because they are lightweight. You can disconnect and reconnect USB and IEEE-1394 devices while the power is on because they support hot swapping.

When you attach cables to the ports at the rear of the computer, avoid tangling them together. Tangled cables could cause electrical interference with each other, leading to erratic performance of external devices such as your printer and monitor. Also, tangled cables put extra stress on ports, which could cause malfunctions or port failures.

The power supply shown previously in Figure 1.5 is another likely point of failure. If the three-prong power cable is not plugged all the way into the computer, the system might not start up at all, or it might shut down unexpectedly. If the voltage selector switch is not set correctly, the computer will not start at all, and if the power supply is set for 115V and is plugged into a 230V supply, the power supply and possibly other parts of the computer will be destroyed.

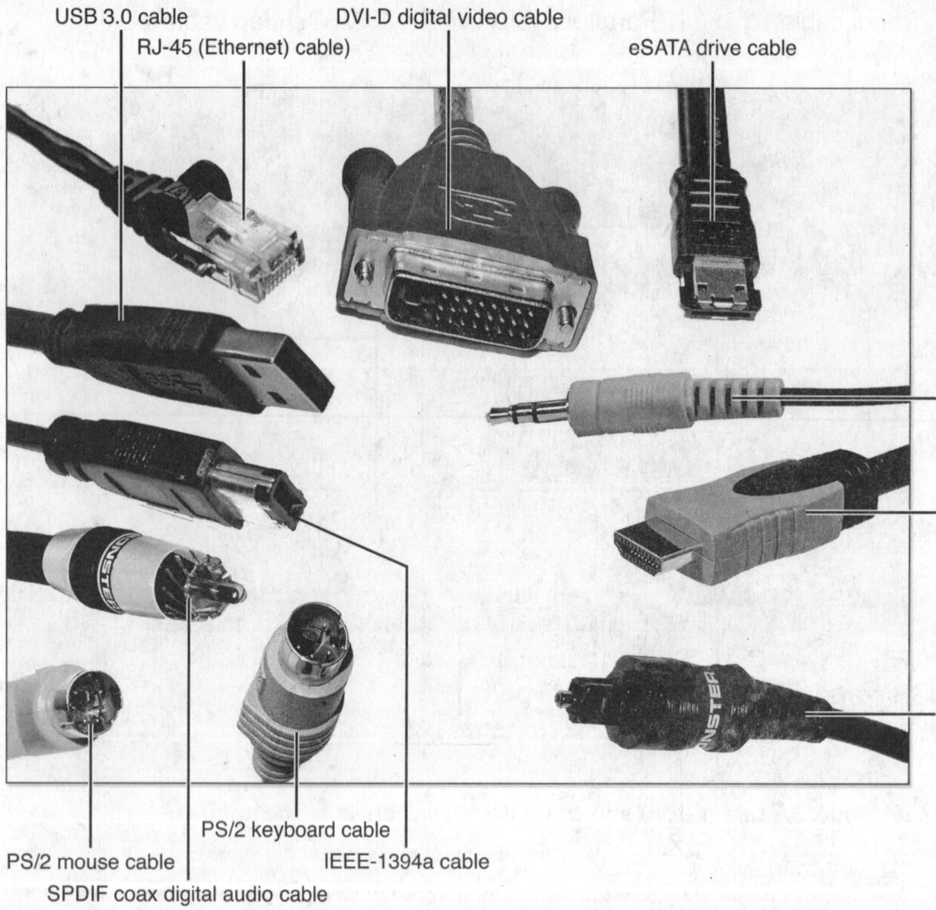

Figure 1.8 USB 3.0, IEEE-1394a, HDMI, DVI, RJ-45, SPDIF coaxial, SPDIF optical, 3.5mm mini-jack, PS/2 mouse, and PS/2 keyboard cables.

Internal Components

You can replace almost any component in a desktop computer, including its motherboard (which connects the processor or CPU to all other components) and the CPU itself. It's no surprise, then, that the interior of a typical desktop computer is a busy place.

As you have already learned, some problems that manifest themselves on the outside of the computer come from problems inside the computer. If you add memory, add an internal drive, upgrade your processor or motherboard, or add a card to your computer, you will need to work with the interior of the computer to complete the task. The interior of a typical desktop computer is a crowded place, as Figure 1.9 shows.

Each of the devices highlighted in Figure 1.9, as well as the data, signal, and power cables that connect these devices to the motherboard and power supply, can cause significant system problems if they fail.

In the following sections, we'll take a closer look at the major features of typical desktop motherboards.

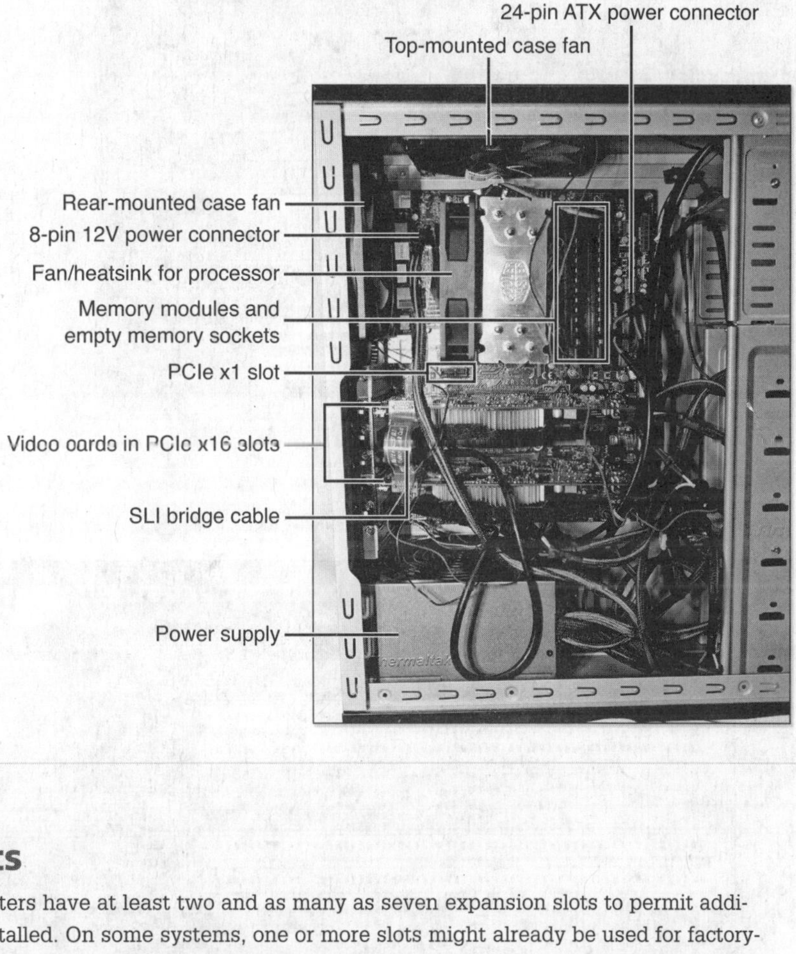

Figure 1.9
The interior of a typical PC using an ATX motherboard.

Expansion Slots

Typical desktop computers have at least two and as many as seven expansion slots to permit additional devices to be installed. On some systems, one or more slots might already be used for factory-installed devices, such as video cards. Most computers have several PCI slots, and many also have one or more PCIe (PCI—Express) x16 slots for high-speed video. Figure 1.10 compares PCIe and PCI slots on a typical system.

A few old systems have an AGP slot for high-speed video along with some PCI slots. Figure 1.11 compares PCI and AGP slots.

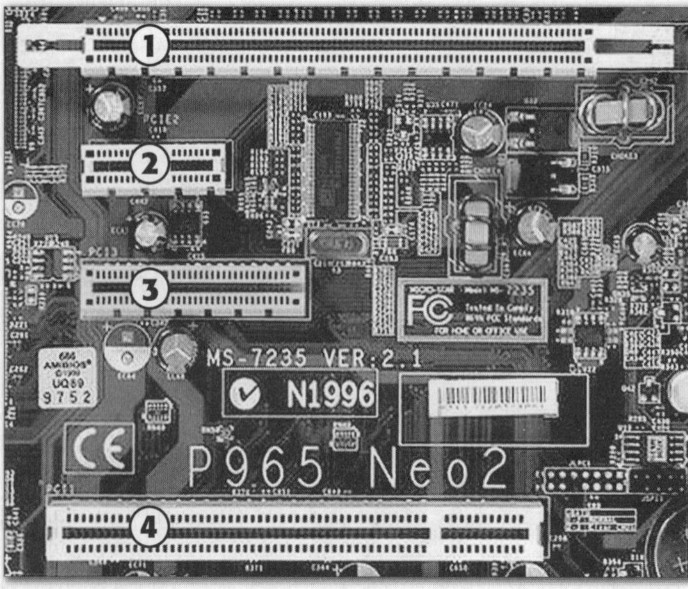

Figure 1.10
PCIe and PCI slots compared. The front of the motherboard is to the right.

1. PCI Express x16 slot
2. PCI Express x1 slot
3. PCI Express x4 slot
4. PCI slot (32-bit, 33MHz)

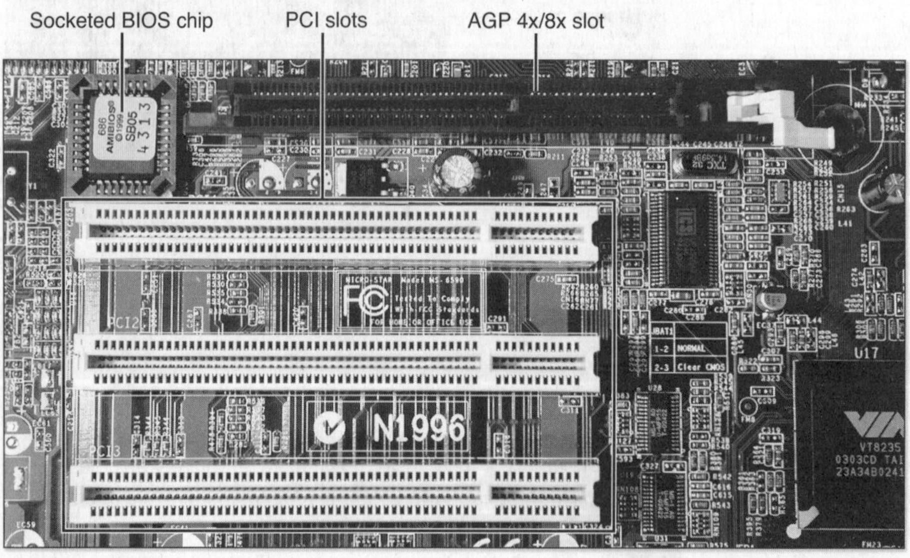

Figure 1.11
AGP and PCI slots compared. The front of the motherboard is to the right. Note how the AGP slot is offset toward the front of the motherboard.

Regardless of the type of expansion slot your add-on card uses, you need to push the card connector all the way into the expansion slot when you install a card, as shown in Figure 1.12.

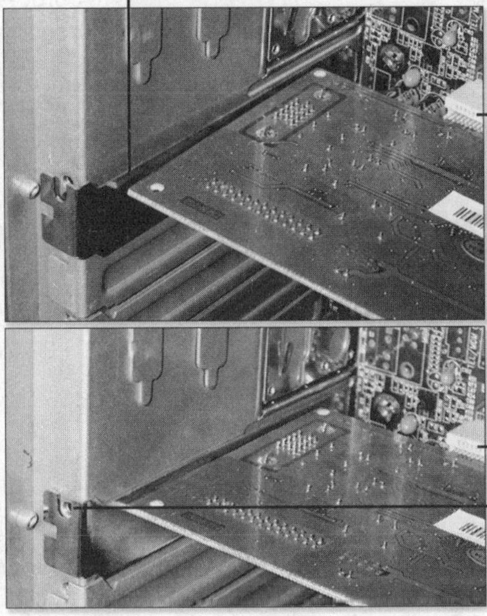

Figure 1.12
A video card partly inserted into the slot (top) and fully inserted into the slot (bottom).

After the card is properly inserted into the expansion slot, you need to fasten the card bracket to the case with a screw.

Points of Failure Inside the Computer

Some of the problems you could encounter because of devices inside your computer include the following:

- **Overheating**—Clogged air vents (refer to Figure 1.3), failure of the fans in the power supply or case or those attached to the processor or video card can cause overheating and can lead to component damage. The CPU fan shown in Figure 1.9 is connected to the motherboard to obtain power. Some case-mounted fans use a standard Molex four-wire drive power connector instead (shown in Figure 1.15).
- **Computer not starting**—An improperly installed video or other add-on card (refer to Figure 1.12), processor (see Figure 1.13), or memory module (see Figure 1.14) can prevent the computer from starting.

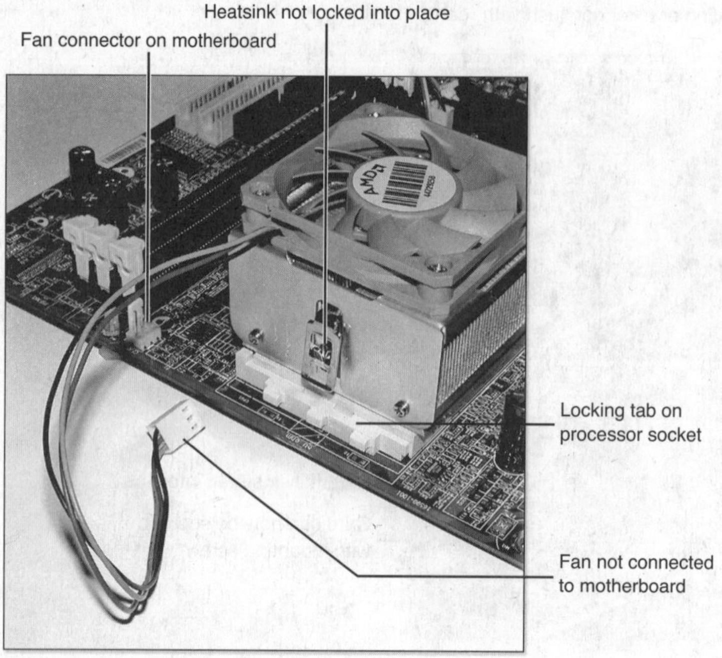

Figure 1.13
A processor that is not properly installed.

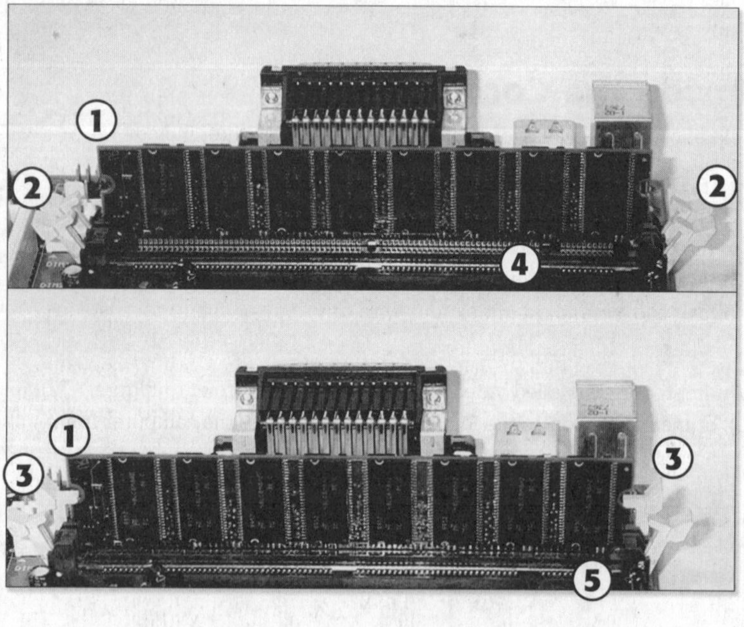

Figure 1.14
A memory module before (top) and after (bottom) being locked into its socket.

1. DIMM memory module
2. Module locks in open position
3. Module locks in closed position
4. Memory module edge connector before module fully inserted
5. Memory module edge connector after module fully inserted

- **Multimedia failures**—If the cables for front-mounted headphone and microphone jacks are not properly attached to the corresponding cable header on the motherboard, audio hardware connected to these ports will not function (see Figure 1.15).

AC'97 Versus HDA Audio

Most systems are designed to support the High Definition Audio (HDA) standard originally developed by Intel. This standard is also called *Azalia*. Some cases have two types of front-panel audio header cables: one for HDA/Azalia and the other for the older AC'97 standard. Unless your motherboard does not support HDA/Azalia, use the HDA audio cable.

Figure 1.15
AC'97 and HDA front-panel audio cables compared to a typical motherboard audio header.

- **Switch and status light failures**—The tiny cables that connect the case power switch, reset switch, and status lights are easy to disconnect accidentally if you are working near the edges of the motherboard (see Figures 1.16 through 1.18).
- **Internal drive failures**—Internal drives are typically connected to Serial ATA (SATA) headers on the motherboard; some older systems also use Parallel ATA (PATA or ATA/IDE) headers. If the cables are not properly attached to the headers, the drives will fail. See "Loose Drive Data and Power Cables," p.208, in Chapter 8, "Fixing Windows Devices That Can't Start," for examples.
- **External drive and device failures**—External drives are usually connected to USB ports. If a USB port is connected to a header cable but the header cable is installed incorrectly, a drive or any other device connected to that port will fail (see Figure 1.19).

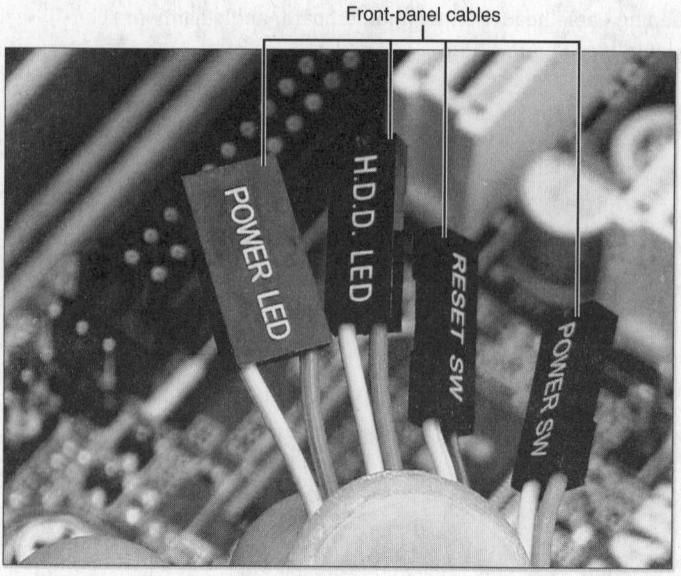

Figure 1.16
Front-panel switch and status light cables before installation.

Figure 1.17
The front-panel header.

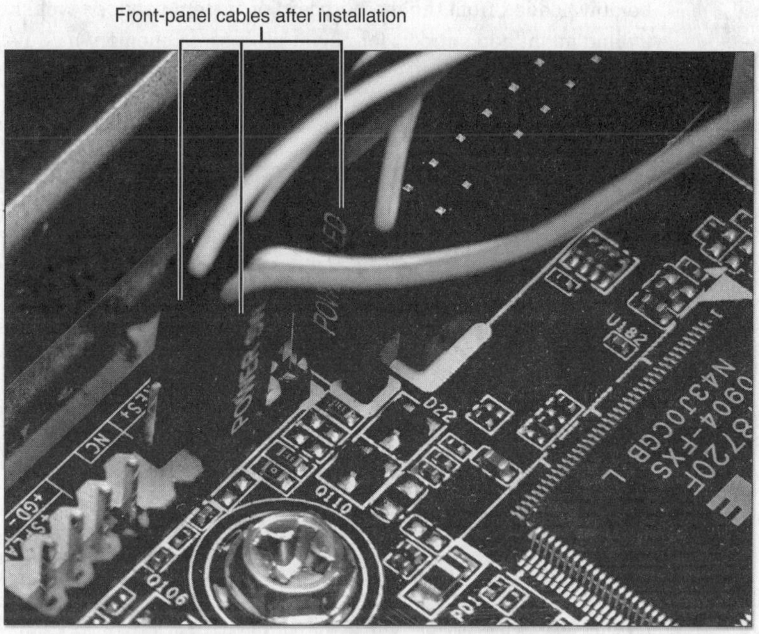

Figure 1.18
The cables after installation.

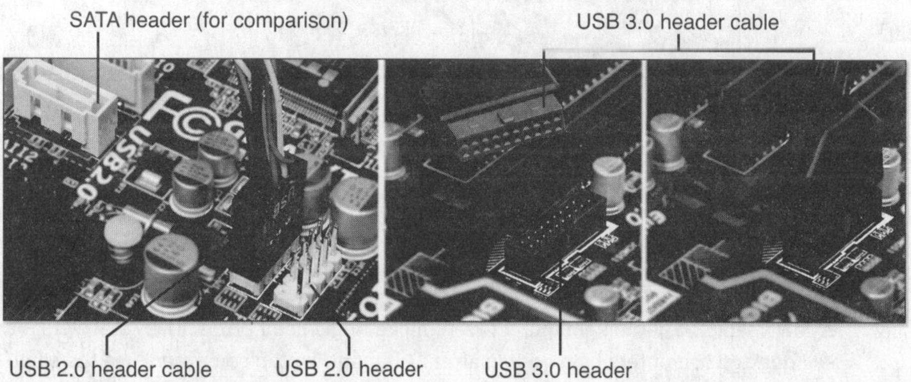

Figure 1.19
USB 2.0 and USB 3.0 headers on typical motherboards.

- **Battery failure**—The battery (see Figure 1.20) maintains the system settings that are configured by the system BIOS. The settings are stored in a part of the computer called the CMOS (more formally known as the *nonvolatile RAM/real-time clock*, or *NVRAM/RTC*). If the battery dies (the average life is about 2–3 years), these settings will be lost and your system cannot start.
- **BIOS chip failure**—The system BIOS chip (see Figure 1.20) can be destroyed by electrostatic discharge (ESD) or lightning strikes. However, BIOS chips can also become outdated. Although

some BIOS chips are socketed, BIOS updates for both socketed and surface-mounted chips can be downloaded from the motherboard or system vendor's website. Updates can improve reliability and might add support for newer processors, memory modules, and other hardware.

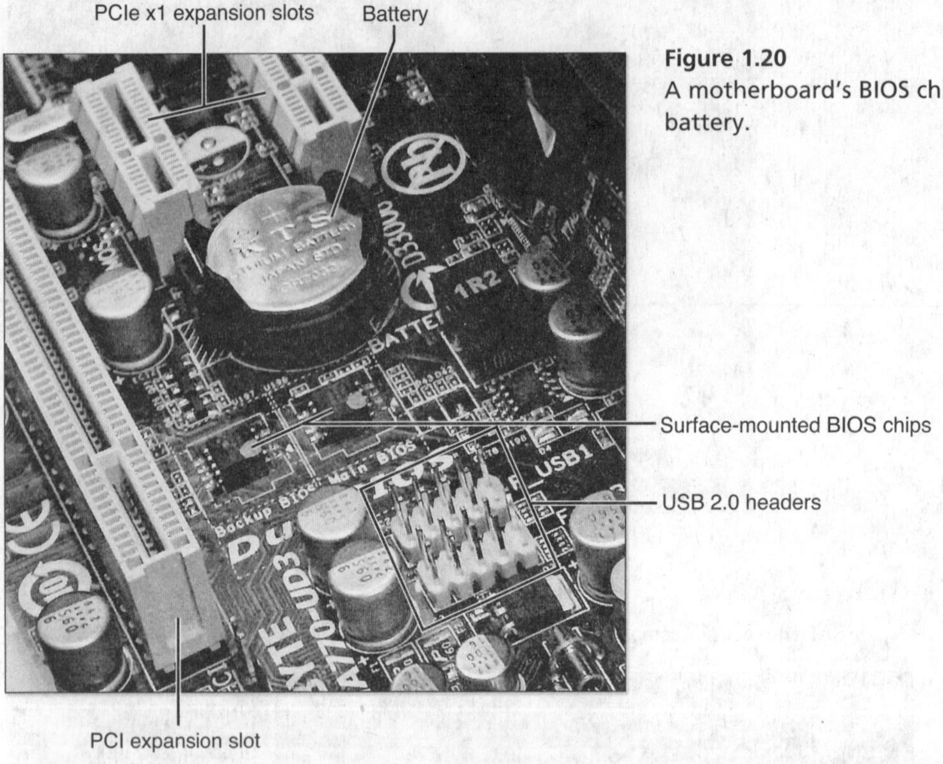

Figure 1.20
A motherboard's BIOS chips and battery.

Laptop and Netbook PC Anatomy

A few years ago, laptop computers were niche items used primarily by travelers, but today they outsell desktop computers by a wide margin. Although laptop computers use the same types of peripherals, operating system, and application software as desktop computers use, in addition to being lightweight and mobile, they differ in several ways from desktop computers:

- Laptop computers feature integrated keyboards, pointing devices, wireless network hardware, and flat-panel displays.
- Laptop keyboards tend to be smaller than desktop keyboards, and some lack integrated keypads.
- Laptop computers can run on either rechargeable battery or AC power.

- Keyboards feature dual-purpose function and other keys to control built-in speakers, Wi-Fi and Bluetooth radios, and display functions.
- Some include ExpressCard slots for adding additional ports, cellular modems, or TV tuners.
- Most include a single hard disk and a single optical (DVD, combo Blu-ray/DVD, or rewriteable BD) drive.
- Some include an SSD (solid-state drive) instead of a hard disk.
- Laptop computers have integrated pointing devices built in to their keyboards; most use a touch-pad, but a few feature a pointing stick. (Which one is better is a matter of personal preference.)

Laptops Versus Netbooks

Netbooks are essentially low-powered, smaller versions of laptops. They typically feature smaller screens and keyboards, fewer ports, and slower processors. Netbooks have largely been replaced by tablets with detachable keyboards.

Laptop External Ports and Features

Figures 1.21 through 1.23 show you the ports on typical laptop computers.

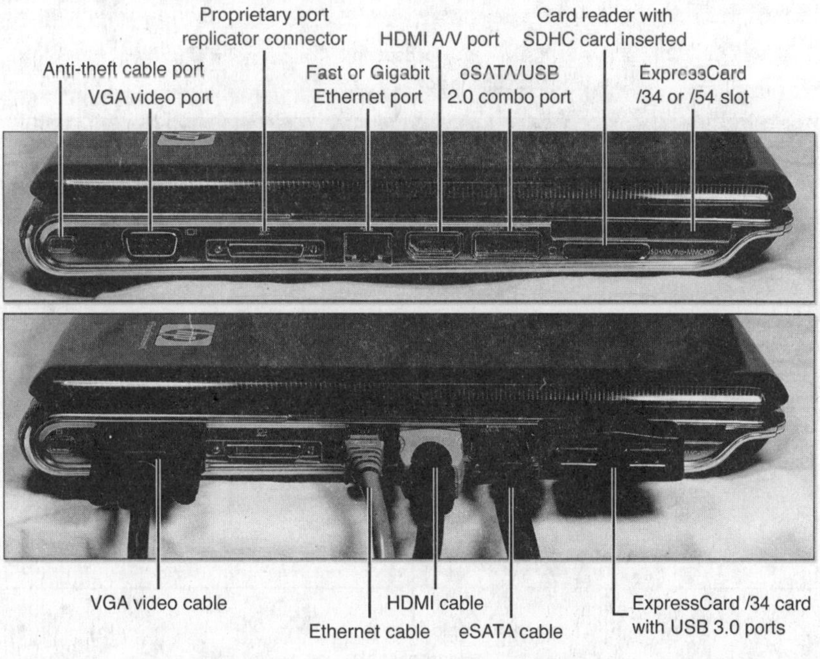

Figure 1.21 Typical laptop ports and cables.

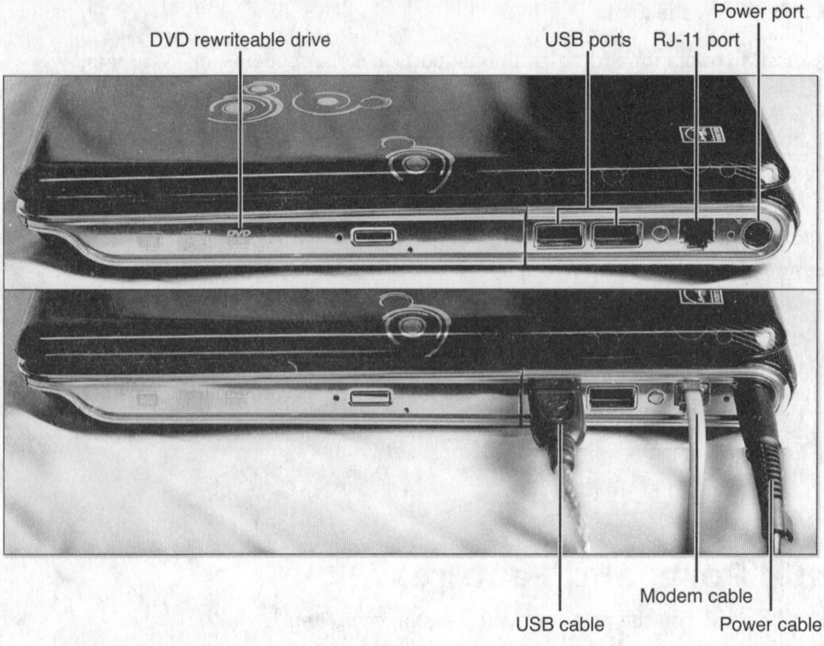

Figure 1.22
Typical laptop ports and cables.

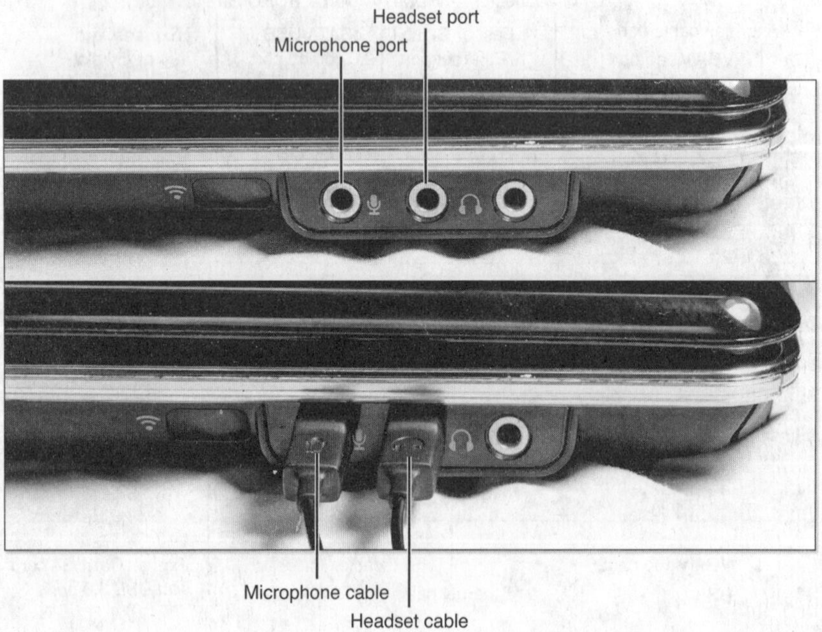

Figure 1.23
Typical laptop ports and cables.

Some laptops, such as the Acer V5 laptop shown in Figure 1.24, use a proprietary dongle to provide VGA and Ethernet connections. By using a dongle, a laptop can use a slimmer design without losing connectivity.

Figure 1.24
Proprietary VGA/ Ethernet dongle.

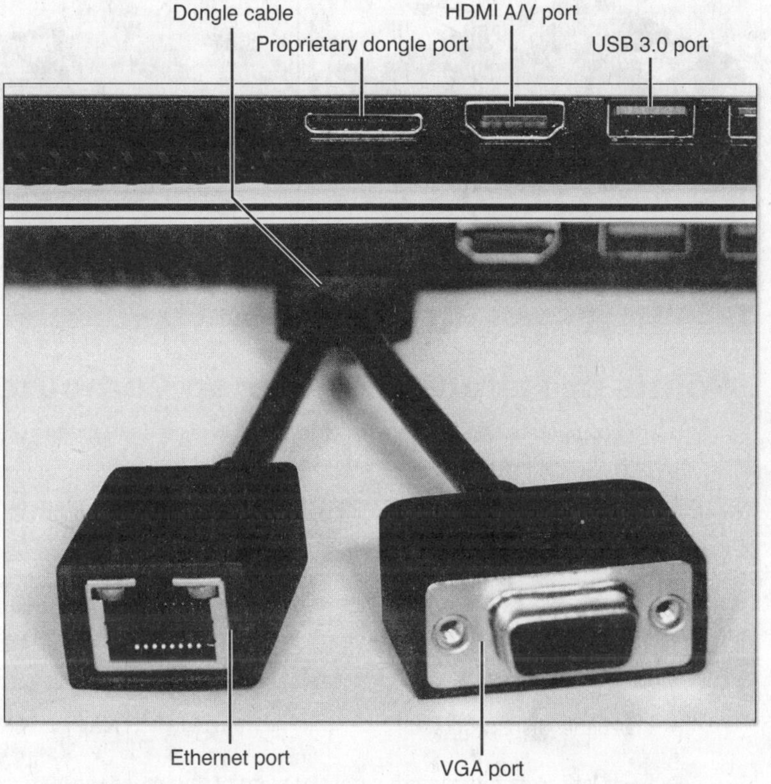

Most laptop features are the same as on desktop computers, but the ExpressCard shown in Figure 1.21 is an exception. ExpressCard enables you to install high-speed ports, such as USB 3.0 ports shown in Figure 1.21 or a cellular modem, in any laptop with an ExpressCard slot.

Laptop Internal Features

If you want to add RAM to a laptop or replace its hard disk or SSD, you'll need to open the device. Most laptops, as in Figure 1.25, have access to these components from the bottom.

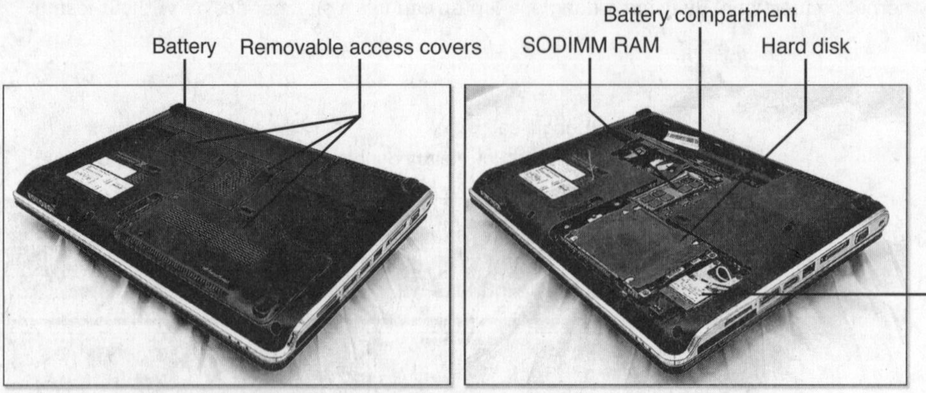

Figure 1.25 Typical laptop component access.

Points of Failure on a Laptop Computer

Laptop computers don't have a lot of internal wires, which means that if you add memory or replace a drive, there's not much chance of causing problems.

As with desktop computers, external cabling can be a major point of failure on laptop computers. However, laptop computers also have a few unique points of failure:

- ExpressCard devices
- Internal drives
- Keyboards
- Flat-panel display screens

ExpressCard slots represent a potential point of failure for these reasons:

- If an ExpressCard is not pushed completely into the ExpressCard slot, it will not work.
- If an ExpressCard is ejected without being stopped by using the Eject Hardware system tray control, it could be damaged.

Although a laptop computer's drives are much more rugged than those found in desktop computers, they can be more expensive to replace if damaged. You can perform an upgrade to a hard disk or an optical drive without special tools on many models.

Keyboards on a laptop computer can be damaged by spilled drinks or by impact damage. If they stop working, keep in mind that keyboard modules are proprietary and vary by brand and model.

The biggest potential expense is the flat-panel LCD or LED/LCD display. However, the most common display failure on laptops with a fluorescent backlight display is the power inverter (refer to Figure 1.27).

Workarounds for Laptop Component Failures

In the event that your laptop screen or keyboard is damaged, you can usually plug in an external screen or a standard USB keyboard and use your laptop on your desk.

All-in-One PC Anatomy

An all-in-one PC's design is a compromise between the complete integration of a laptop computer and the completely modular design of a desktop computer. With an all-in-one PC, it's easy to swap the mouse (or other pointing device) and keyboard if you don't like the items supplied with your system, but it's difficult to swap other components. A typical all-in-one PC looks like a large display with a mouse and keyboard. The "brains" of the unit are on the back side of the display. The optical drive, audio ports, and USB ports are accessed on the sides of the unit.

External Ports and Features

An all-in-one PC typically has a laptop-style slim optical drive, a card reader, some audio ports and USB ports on the sides of the display, and a rear panel with additional USB ports, an audio (speaker) port, a power connector, and an Ethernet port on the rear (see Figure 1.26).

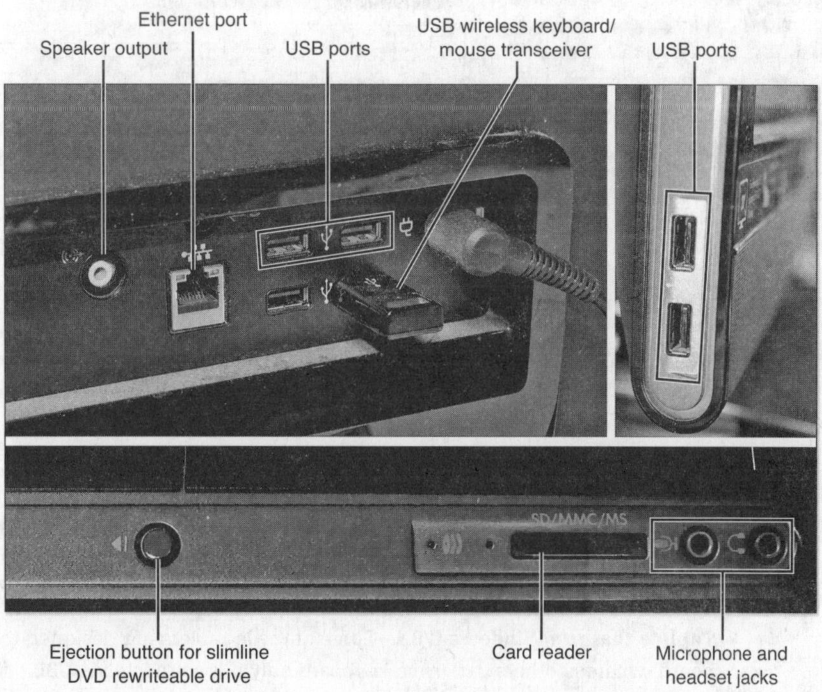

Figure 1.26
Typical all-in-one computer ports and features.

Internal Components

Because of its size, an all-in-one computer typically resembles a laptop internally. Figure 1.27 shows the interior of a typical all-in-one unit after partial disassembly, rotated 180 degrees from the rear detail shown in Figure 1.26.

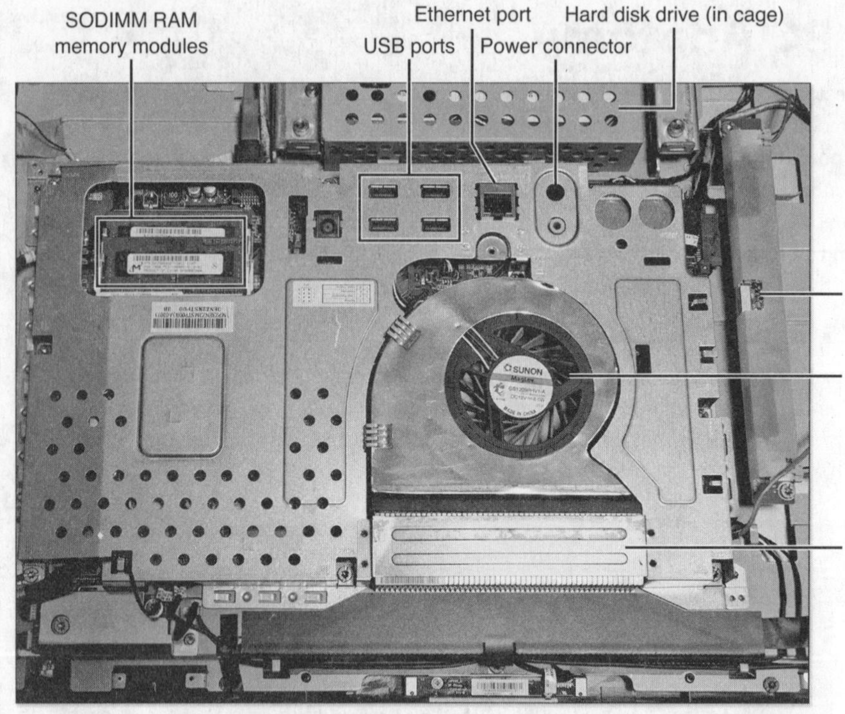

Figure 1.23 Interior of an all-in-one PC.

Points of Failure

An all-in-one computer can suffer similar failures as a laptop computer, except that it uses a desktop keyboard and mouse. The memory, hard disk, and optical drives used by all-in-one computers are similar to those used by laptop computers.

Windows Tablet Anatomy

Tablets are much simpler than either laptop PCs or desktop PCs in both external ports and features and in accessible internal components. Windows tablets are available in two variations:

- **Tablets that run Windows 8/8.1**—Some of these tablets are designed to use a dockable keyboard, whereas others can use a keyboard only if it connects via USB or Bluetooth. Some tablets are full-blown laptops that convert to tablets using faster processors than the Intel ATOM used by most Windows 8/8.1 tablets. These tablets run the same versions of Windows 8/8.1 that desktop and laptop computers can use. Some older versions of these tablets were originally shipped with Windows 7, but can be upgraded to Windows 8/8.1.

- **Tablets that run Windows 8/8.1 RT**—These tablets use some version of the low-powered ARM processor also used by most Android tablets. They use a special version of Windows that looks like Windows 8/8.1 but is made especially for ARM processors. The Microsoft Surface is one example of this type of tablet.

External Ports and Features

Because tablets are designed primarily for media consumption (viewing websites, reading email, watching or listening to media), they typically have fewer ports than laptop computers:

- One USB 2.0 or USB 3.0 port
- Micro-SD/SDHC/SDXC slot
- Micro-HDMI port or Mini DisplayPort for HD audio/video
- 3.5mm mini-jack for stereo speakers or headphones
- Proprietary keyboard dock or cover connector

Figures 1.28 through 1.30 illustrate some of these ports on a typical Windows tablet, the Samsung ATIV-500.

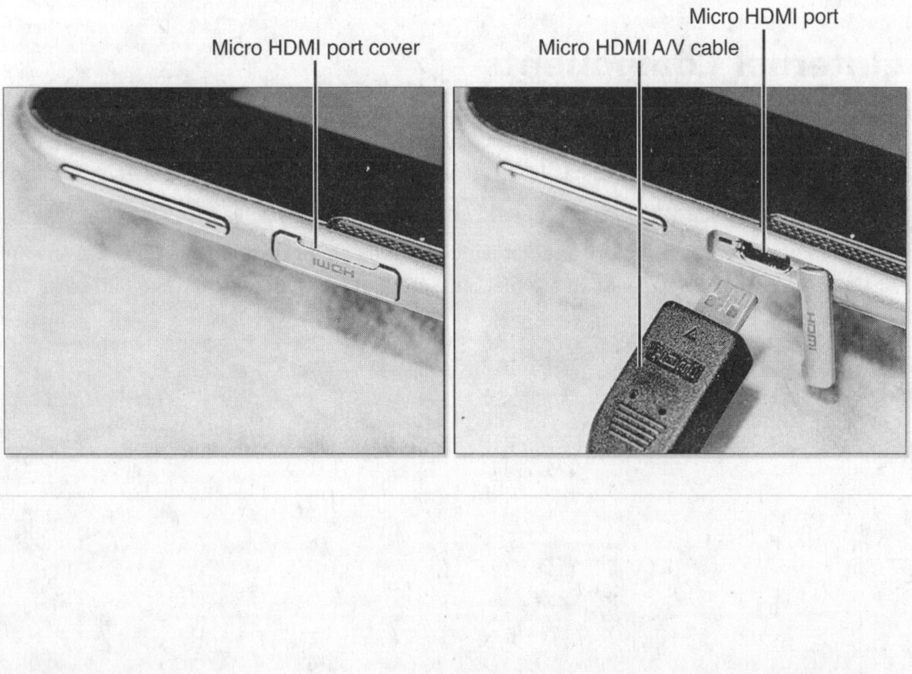

Figure 1.28 Typical Windows tablet Micro HDMI ports and cables.

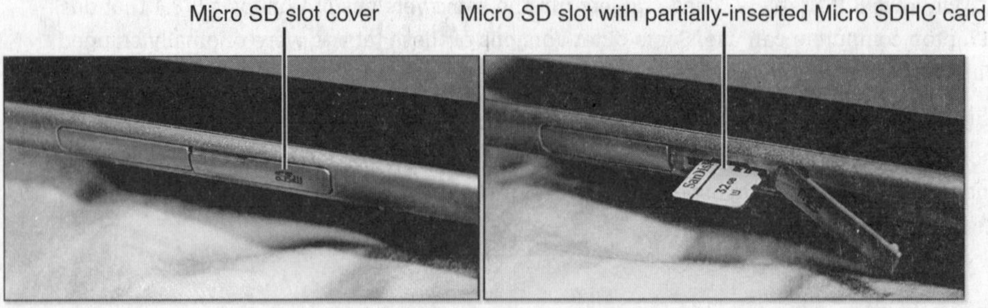

Figure 1.29 Typical Windows tablet Micro SD slot.

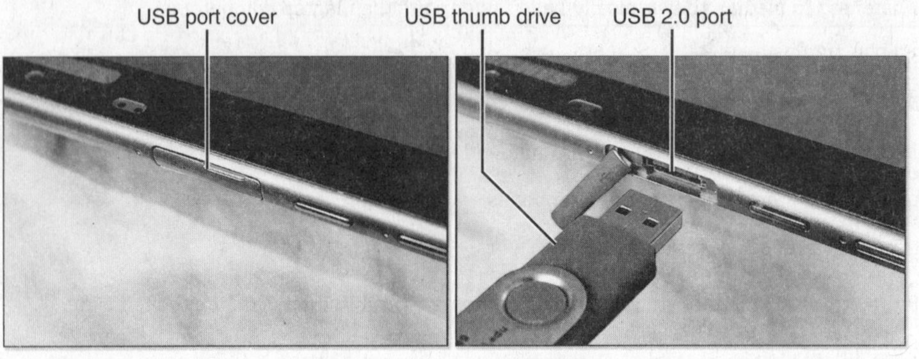

Figure 1.30 Typical Windows tablet USB port.

Internal Components

Although a Windows tablet has a CPU with integrated 3D graphics and memory (RAM), other components differ. Instead of a hard disk, a tablet has an internal solid state drive (SSD) that might range in size from as little as 32GB to as much as 512GB (sizes of 128GB or less are most common).

Tablets include Wi-Fi and Bluetooth, enabling wireless access to a variety of networks and devices.

However, unlike a laptop, a tablet isn't designed as an upgradeable device. You cannot increase the RAM or the SSD capacity in a tablet, and a tablet lacks an optical drive (although you can connect one via USB).

Points of Failure

A tablet is designed to be rugged and durable. The major risk is screen breakage, so keeping the tablet in a sleeve or custom-designed case when not in use is a good idea.

Battery rundown can cause a tablet to fail temporarily until it is recharged. To help prevent premature battery rundown, disable unnecessary services (for example, Bluetooth can be disabled if you don't use Bluetooth keyboards or exchange data via Bluetooth).

Preparing a Windows-Based Computer or Tablet for Easier Troubleshooting

Problems with a Windows-based computer or tablet can have three major causes:

- Misconfiguration of onboard hardware in the computer's BIOS or UEFI firmware setup dialogs
- Hardware failure
- Problems with Windows or applications (apps, software)

If you want to make troubleshooting startup problems a lot easier, you need to know two things:

- How the drives are configured
- If Windows won't start, what the error is

This takes a little work on your part, but the amount of time you can save later is immense.

Taking Pictures of Your BIOS Settings

To determine how your drives are configured in the system BIOS or UEFI firmware, you need a digital camera, tablet, or smartphone that can take close-up photos of your computer screen.

1. Restart your computer.
2. Press the key that starts the BIOS or UEFI firmware setup program (see Figure 1.31). You might need to press a key to open the startup menu and a second key to select how to start the computer.
3. Navigate to the dialogs that include the drive boot order (see Figures 1.32 and 1.33), the drive configuration (see Figure 1.34), and your built-in port configurations (see Figure 1.35).
4. Take pictures of the settings. Use the playback and zoom features in your digital camera to make sure you have good photos.
5. When you exit the setup screen, choose the option to exit without saving changes (on most systems, press the ESC key, then answer N to saving changes). Your computer will restart.

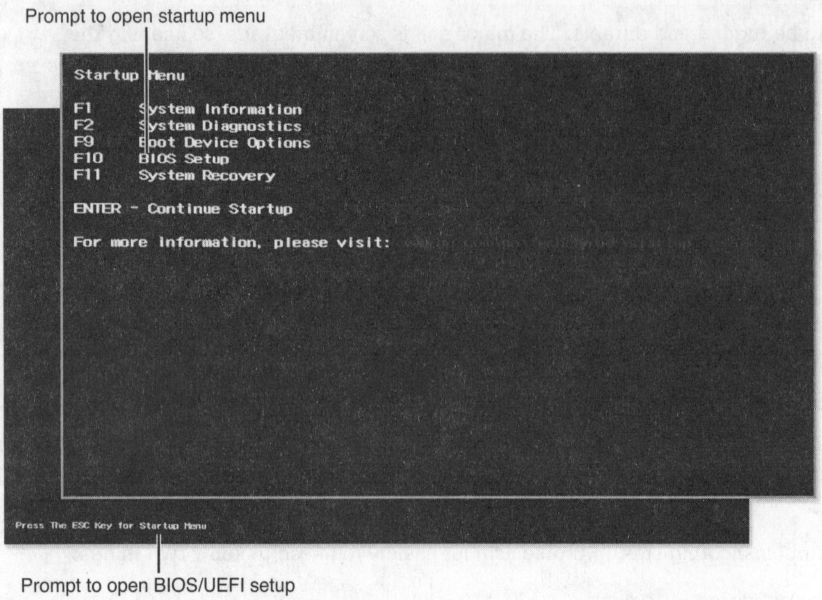

Figure 1.31 Preparing to open the BIOS configuration dialog at system startup.

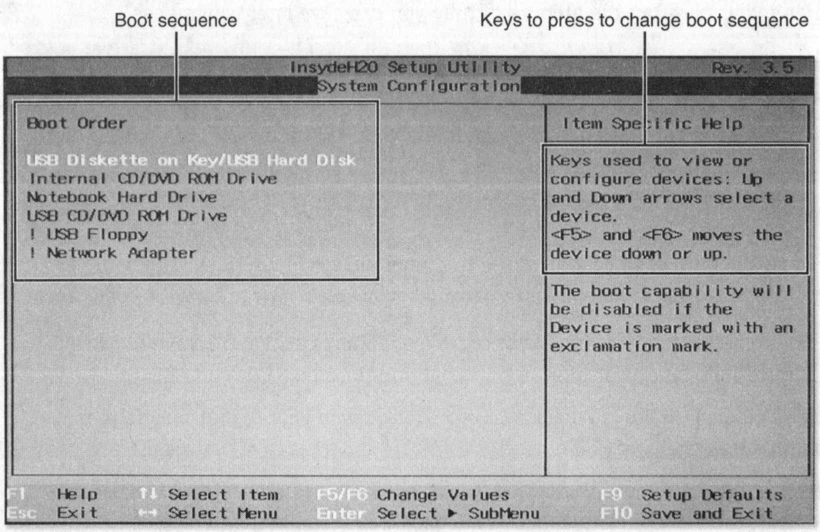

Figure 1.32 Typical boot order dialogs from a text-based BIOS.

Figure 1.33
Typical boot order dialog for UEFI graphical firmware.

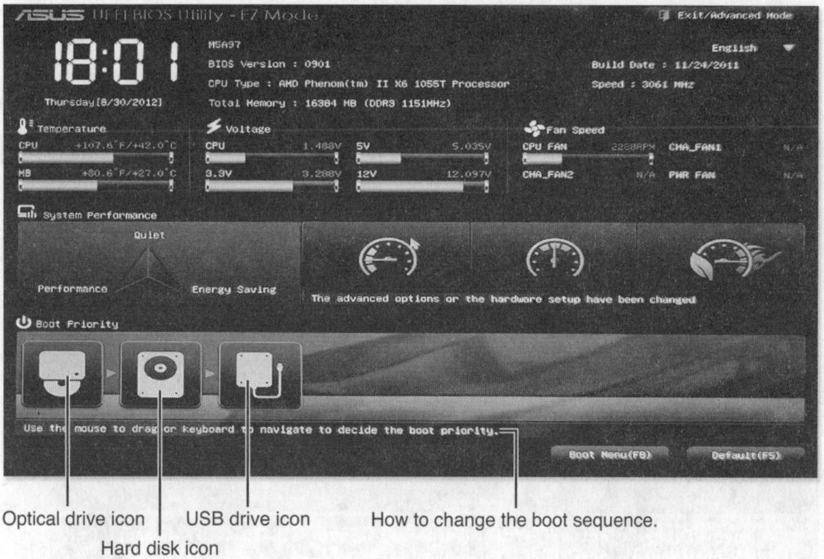

Figure 1.34
A typical hard disk/SSD/optical drive configuration dialog.

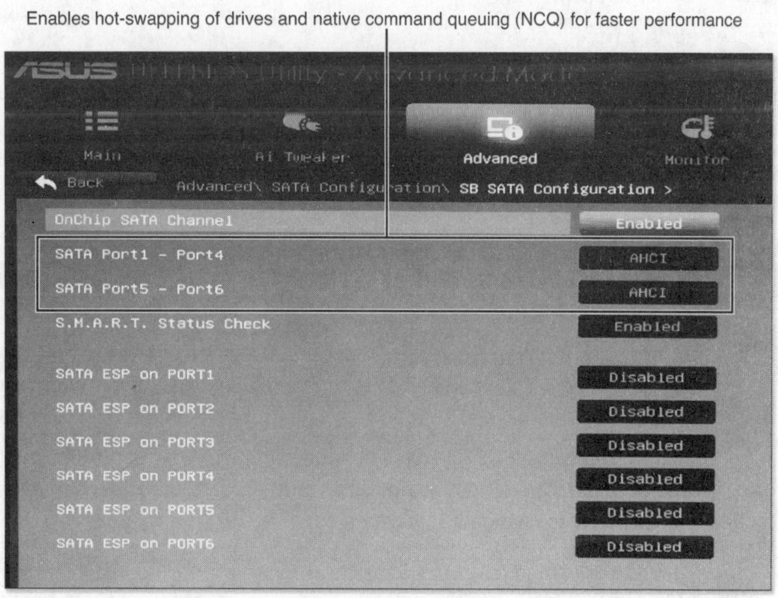

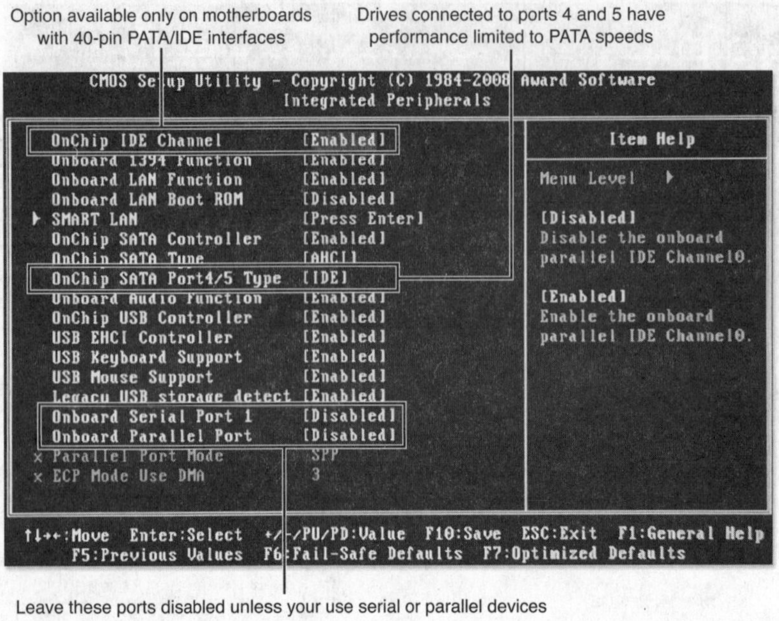

Figure 1.35
A typical integrated port and drive (SATA) configuration dialog.

Tip

You will get the best results with a simple camera if you set the camera for P mode and set the ISO to 400 or 800. If you can set the aperture (f-stop) and shutter speed manually (M mode), use f/2.8 to f/4.0 for the aperture and about 1/125 second for the shutter speed with an ISO of 400 or 800. Adjust these settings as needed to get the best possible photos. Turn off your camera or device's flash.

Recovering from Firmware Settings Failure

If your system BIOS or UEFI firmware settings are corrupted by failure of the motherboard's onboard battery or by a power surge, you will see a message at startup that the computer has reverted to default settings. You will need to start the BIOS or UEFI setup program, make any changes needed, and save those changes. Your system will probably not be able to start until you do this.

Most systems use a CR2032 coin-shaped lithium 3V battery (refer to Figure 1.20) to maintain BIOS/UEFI settings. Check your computer or motherboard instruction manual for the location of the battery and how to change it if it wears out.

Tip

If you need to reset BIOS or firmware settings, select Optimized or Standard Defaults first, then make any additional changes manually. If your BIOS or firmware dialogs are graphical (as in Figures 1.32 or 1.33, you can use your mouse or keyboard to move around the menus and select the option to save changes. If your BIOS or firmware dialogs are text-based (Figures 1.34 or 1.35), use the keyboard to move around the menus and select the option to save changes.

Configuring Windows to Keep STOP (Blue Screen) Errors Displayed

STOP (also called Blue Screen of Death, or BSOD) errors stop your computer in its tracks. The easiest way to learn how a STOP error happened is to read the error message and then research possible causes. Unfortunately, most Windows computers are configured to restart immediately when this happens.

Here's how to change your computer's configuration so that a STOP error does not automatically reboot the computer. These steps work for Windows 7 and Windows 8/8.1:

> **Note**
> To learn more about STOP errors, see "STOP (Blue Screen) Errors at Startup," p.203, in Chapter 8, "Fixing Windows Devices That Can't Start."

1. Open Control Panel.
2. Click or tap **System and Security**.
3. Click or tap **System** to open the System properties sheet.
4. Click or tap the **Advanced System Settings** link in the left pane.
5. Click or tap the **Settings** button in the Startup and Recovery portion of the Advanced tab (see Figure 1.36).

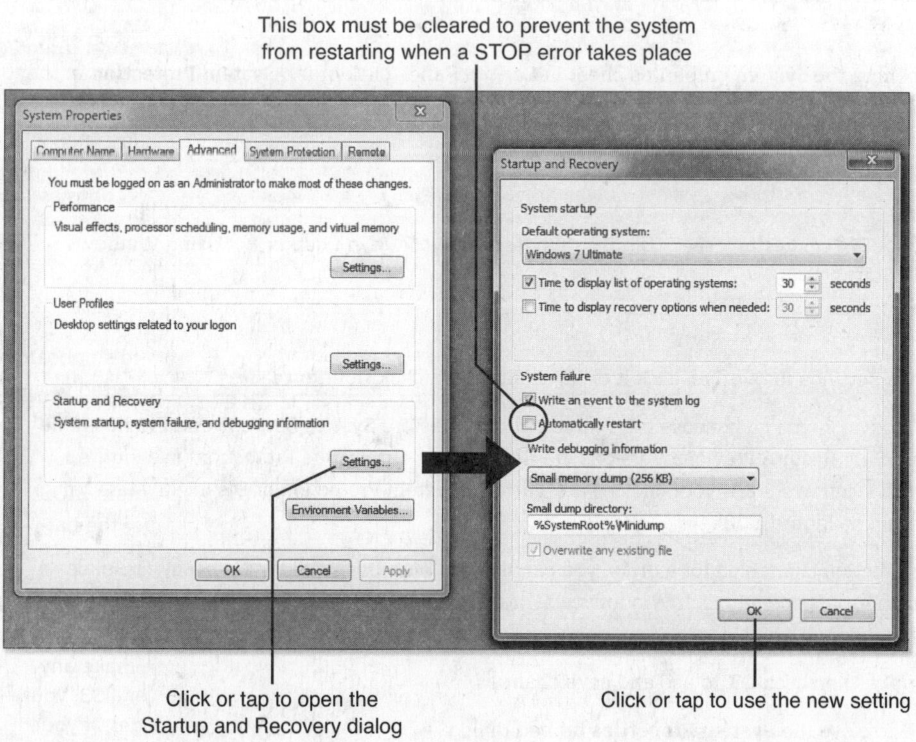

Figure 1.36 Disabling automatic startup when a STOP error occurs.

6. If the Automatically Restart box is checked, click the box to clear it.
7. Click **OK** twice.
8. Restart the computer if prompted.

Setting Up System Protection

The System Protection feature in Windows is used to create restore points. A restore point is a special file that records Windows, software, and hardware configurations as of a specified time. Restore points are typically created after Windows installs a critical update.

> **Note**
> To learn how to restore a previous version of a file, see "Restoring a Previous Version in Windows 7," p.460, in Chapter 18, "Upgrading and Troubleshooting Storage Devices."

In Windows 7, restore points also store previous versions of files.

System Protection is automatically enabled for your system (C:) drive. To enable system protection for other hard disk drives or SSDs, or to change how it works, use the System Protection tab of System Properties.

1. After opening the System properties sheet in Control Panel, click or tap **System Protection** in the left pane. The protection settings for each eligible drive are listed.

> **Note**
> To learn more about System Restore, see "Using System Restore," p.218, in Chapter 8, "Fixing Windows Devices That Can't Start."

2. To change settings for a drive, click it or tap it, and then click **Configure.**
3. With Windows 7, you can choose from three options: Restore System Settings and Previous File Versions, Only Restore Previous Versions of Files, or Turn Off System Protection (see Figure 1.37). With Windows 8/8.1, your choices are Turn On System Protection or Disable System Protection (see Figure 1.38).
4. When protection is enabled for a drive, you can use the **Max Usage** slider to specify the maximum amount of space to use. If Windows attempts to create a restore point that would use more than the maximum, the oldest restore points are deleted until enough space is available.
5. Click **Apply**, then click **OK** to use and save changes.
6. Click **OK** to close the **System Properties** tabbed dialog.

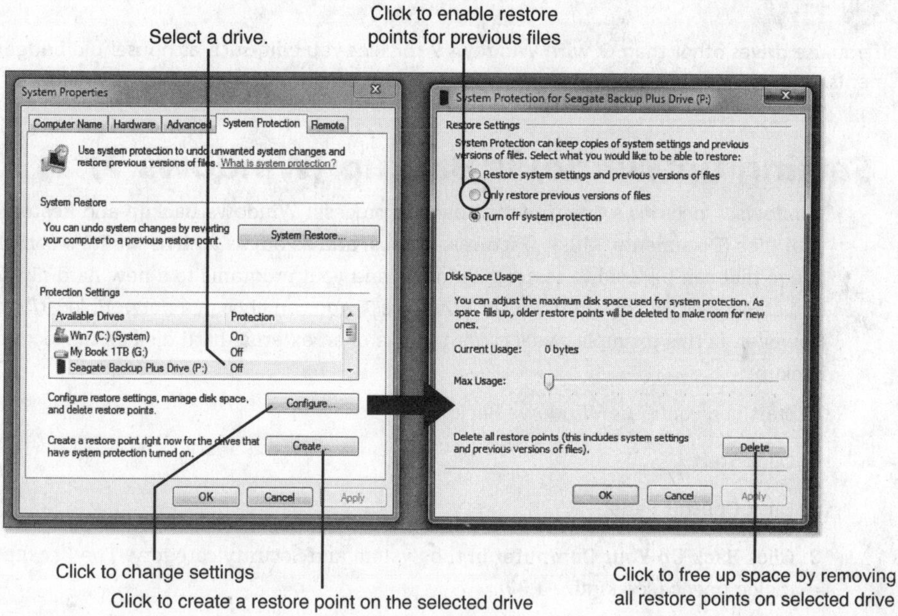

Figure 1.37 System Protection settings in Windows 7.

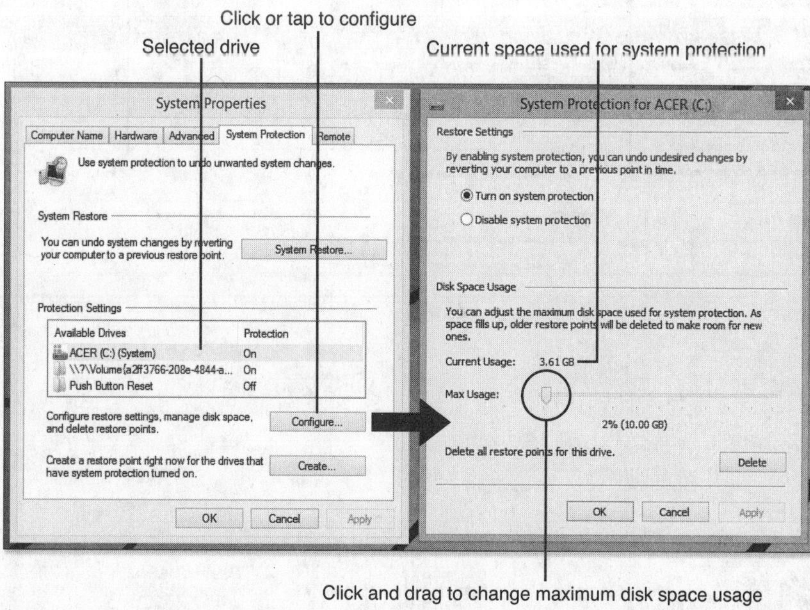

Figure 1.38 System Protection settings in Windows 8/8.1.

Tip

If you use drives other than C: with Windows 7 for files you edit, such as household budgets, business documents, photos, and so, enable protection for previous versions of files for those drives.

Setting Up Windows Backup (Windows 7)

Windows 7 includes a dual-function backup process: Windows Backup and Restore can back up your files (Documents, Music, Pictures, Videos, and so on) as well as create a complete system image that can be used to restore Windows and your programs to a new hard disk in case the system crashes. With some editions of Windows 7, you can choose a network location for your backup. However, in this example, we'll cover the use of an external hard disk as the location for your backup.

To start and configure Windows Backup:

1. Click **Start**.
2. Click **Control Panel**.
3. Click **Back Up Your Computer** in the System and Security category. The Backup and Restore dialog opens (see Figure 1.39).

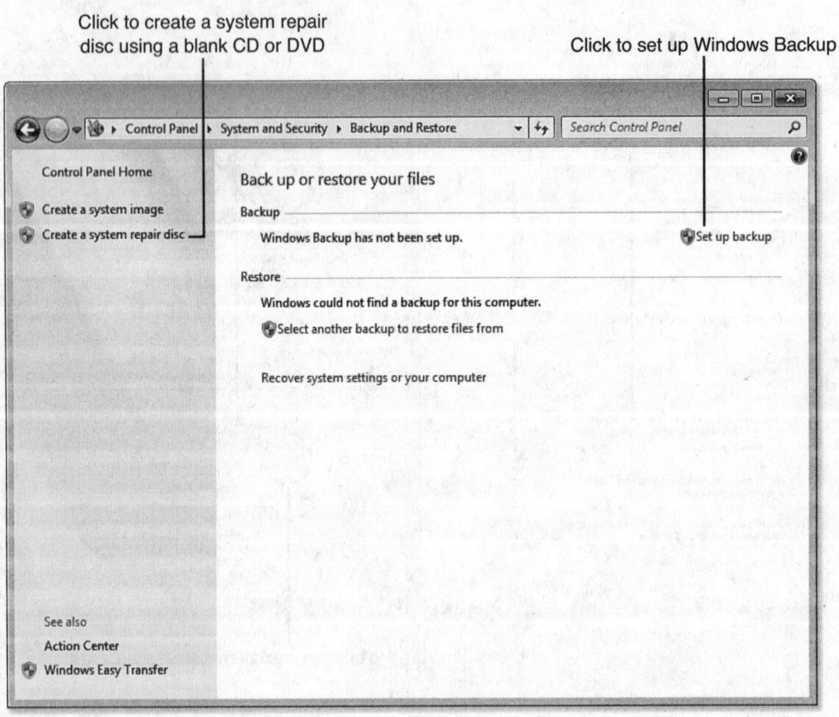

Figure 1.39 The Backup and Restore dialog in Windows 7 before you run your first backup.

4. Connect the drive you want to use to store your backups to your system and turn it on.
5. Click **Set Up Backup**. This opens the Select Where You Want to Save Your Backup (see Figure 1.40) dialog.
6. Choose a location to store your backup. Select the external hard disk drive you connected in step 4.
7. Click **Next**. The What Do You Want to Back Up dialog appears.
8. Click **Let Windows Choose**.
9. Click **Next**.
10. After you review your backup settings (see Figure 1.41), click **Save Settings and Run Backup**.

Caution

Although you can use your Windows 7 installation disc as an emergency disc if you need to restore a system image created with Backup and Restore, we recommend making a separate emergency disc. This is especially important if you have a preinstalled version of Windows 7. You can use a recordable CD or DVD disc.

Tip

If you use locations other than Windows libraries for your files, select **Let Me Choose** in step 8. This option enables you to select the files and folders you want to back up.

Figure 1.40
Selecting a location for your backup.

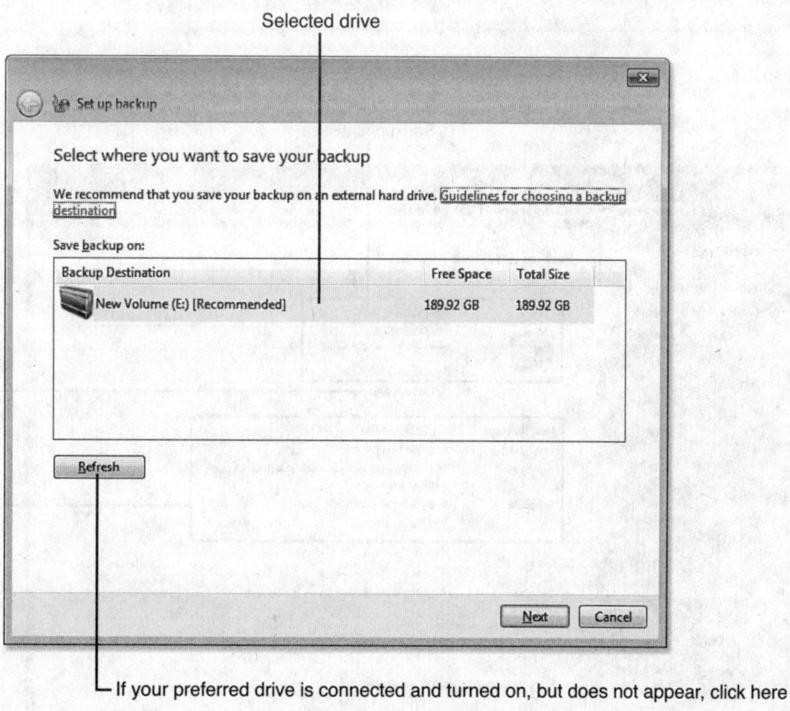

11. The backup runs. At the end of the backup, the backup size, remaining space on the backup drive, and other information is displayed (see Figure 1.42).

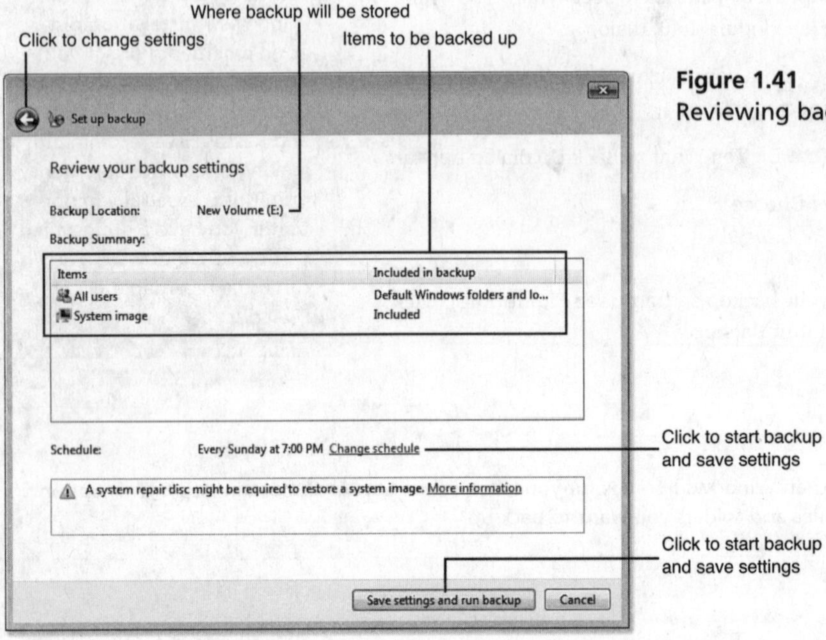

Figure 1.41
Reviewing backup settings.

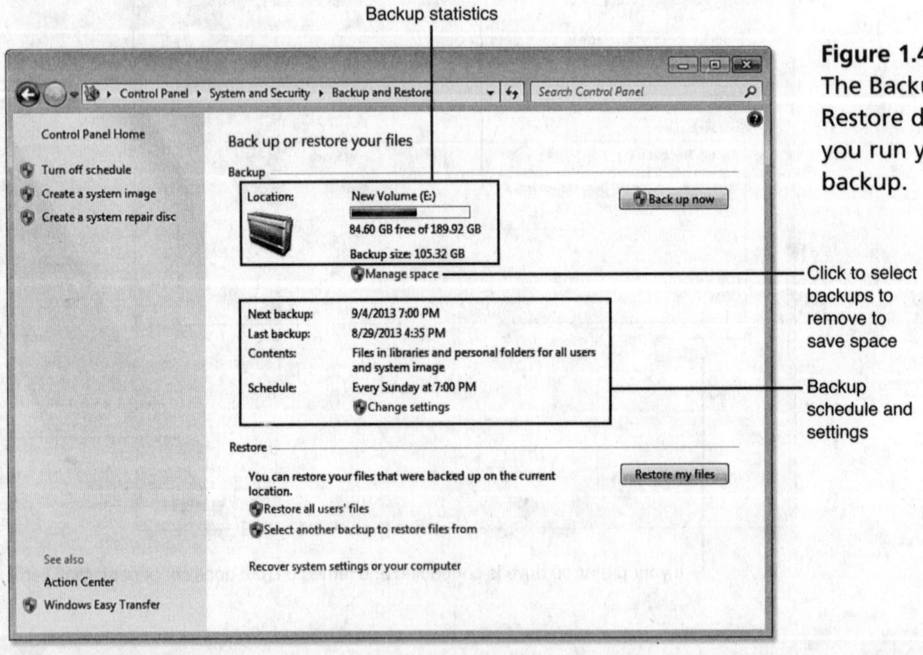

Figure 1.42
The Backup and Restore dialog after you run your first backup.

Note

To learn how to restore a file from a backup, see "Retrieving Files from a Backup (Windows 7)" p.466, in Chapter 18, "Upgrading and Troubleshooting Storage Devices."

Setting Up File History (Windows 8/8.1)

Windows 8/8.1's File History is designed to be easier and simpler to use than Windows 7's Backup and Restore. File History has two goals:

- Easy backup of different versions of your files as you create and edit them
- Easy selection of the file and version you want to restore if anything goes wrong

File History copies files from your libraries, your desktop, your contacts, your favorites, and your offline files (files stored on your system) on OneDrive (Windows 8.1 only). File History won't back up library files that are encrypted with EFS, library files on a network drive, or files stored on drives that don't use the NTFS file system (such as optical drives, some external hard disk drives, or USB flash drives).

To set up and run File History, follow these steps:

1. Connect an external hard disk to your computer.
2. Open Control Panel.
3. Click or tap **Save Backup Copies of Your Files with File History**. File History displays an external drive (typically the one you connected in step 1).
4. If you have more than one external drive, click or tap **Select Drive** to choose the drive to use for File History.
5. Click or tap **Turn On**. File History backs up your drives (see Figure 1.43).
6. File History runs on a schedule, but you can run it again at any time by clicking **Run Now**.

Use the Advanced Settings link in the left pane of File History to adjust settings for how often to save files, how long to keep files, and how much disk space (offline cache) to use (see Figure 1.44).

Note

To learn how to restore a file with File History, see "Restoring a Previous Version or Deleted File in Windows 8/8.1," p.462, in Chapter 18, "Upgrading and Troubleshooting Storage Devices."

Note

If you have a very large backup drive, you might want to let other users of your homegroup use it. If so, click Yes when prompted to recommend the drive to others in the homegroup. Click No if you expect to need the drive's capacity for the computer to which it is connected.

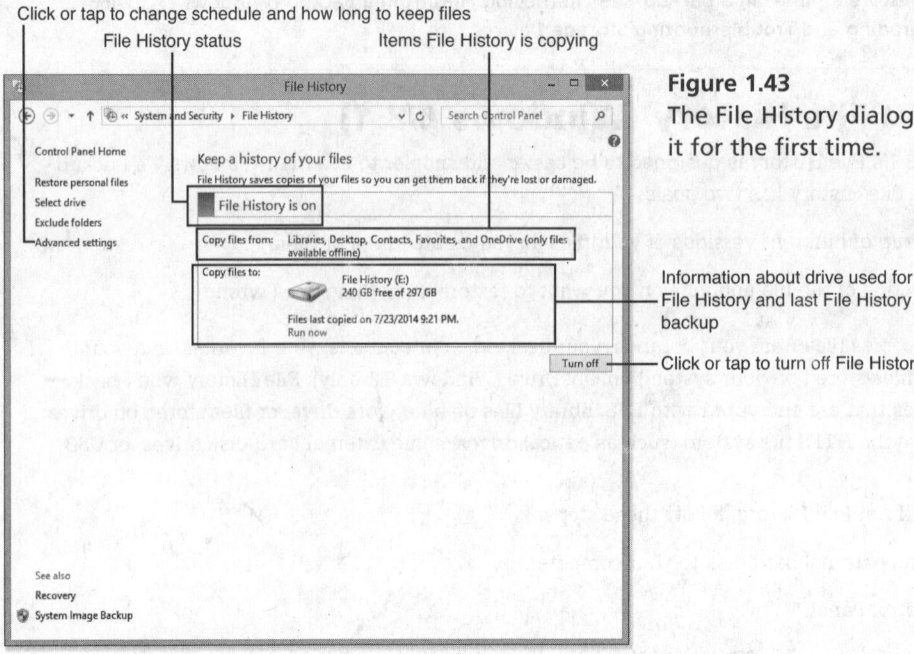

Figure 1.43
The File History dialog after you use it for the first time.

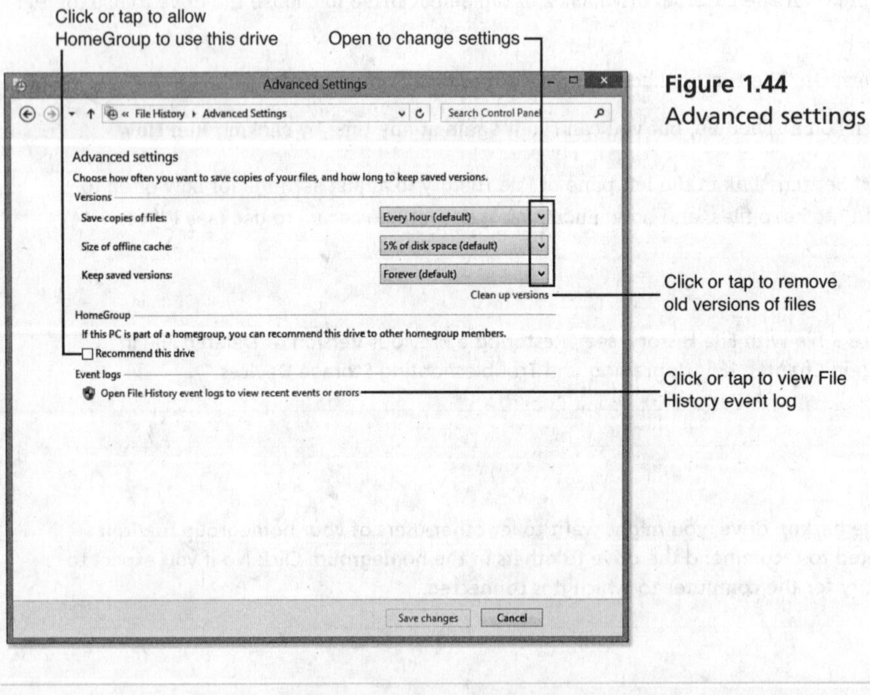

Figure 1.44
Advanced settings for File History.

Android Tablet and Smartphone Anatomy

Android tablets and smartphones run some version of Google's Android operating system. Unlike Apple's iOS devices, Android devices often include internal and external expansion options.

Android External Ports and Features

Android tablets typically feature a mini-jack audio port, a micro-USB or proprietary charging/interface port, and a micro-SD card reader (refer to Figure 1.28). Some also feature a mini-HDMI A/V port (also see Figure 1.28). Speakers and front-facing and rear-facing cameras with microphones and speakers round out the typical feature list. Resolutions on rear-facing webcams typically range from 3MP to 5MP.

External controls typically include an on/off switch, a volume control, and a HD touchscreen with a resolution of 720p or higher.

Android smartphones usually have similar features, except that virtually all of them use the now-standard micro-USB charging and interface port, and some have rear-facing cameras with resolutions exceeding 10MP.

Android Internal Components

Android tablets use low power multicore processors. Some use low-power Intel ATOM processors that also support Windows, whereas others use some type of ARM-compatible processor. Storage capacity typically ranges from 16GB to 64GB.

Android smartphones use only ARM-compatible processors and typically feature storage capacity of 8GB to 16GB.

Android devices, unlike their iOS counterparts, typically include removable batteries. SIM cards are typically removable on tablets with cellular radios (as well as all smartphones), and Wi-Fi 802.11n and Bluetooth 4.0 wireless networking round out communication options.

Points of Failure

Tablets and smartphones are designed to be rugged and durable. The major risk of permanent damage is screen breakage, so keeping tablets in a sleeve or custom-designed case when not in use is a good idea. To protect a smartphone, use a custom-designed screen protector.

Charging cables, whether OEM or third-party, tend to be easy to damage. Keep spares on hand.

Battery rundown can cause a tablet or smartphone to fail temporarily until it is recharged. To help prevent premature battery rundown, disable unnecessary services (for example, Bluetooth can be disabled if you don't use Bluetooth keyboards or exchange data via Bluetooth). On a smartphone, leave Wi-Fi disabled when you are not near a Wi-Fi hotspot.

If the battery fails or if you need to swap to a charged battery in the field, most Android devices are easy to open so you can replace the battery.

iOS Device Anatomy

IOS devices (iPhone, iPad, and iPod Touch) share many features in common. Let's take a closer look.

iOS External Ports and Features

The latest generation of iOS devices uses the Lightning compact data/charging port, compared to older versions that use the long-time iOS standard 30-pin port. Both types of cables plug into a USB port on a computer or charger.

All these devices feature front-facing HD and rear-facing multi-megapixel cameras, HD touch-screens, volume control, rotation control, and menu buttons. Unlike Android devices, iOS devices don't have expandable storage and rely exclusively on wireless (Wi-Fi or Bluetooth) connections for video playback.

Internal Components

IOS devices are not designed for user serviceability, so the battery is not interchangeable. A special tool or a bent paperclip is needed to remove the SIM card in case it needs to be swapped out.

Caution

If you are considering a refurbished iOS device, keep in mind that Apple replaces the battery as part of its standard refurbishing policy. Third-party vendors typically do not.

Points of Failure

Tablets and smartphones are designed to be rugged and durable. The major risk of permanent damage is screen breakage, so keeping tablets in a sleeve or custom-designed case when not in use is a good idea. To protect a smartphone, use a custom-designed screen protector.

Charging cables, whether Apple or third-party, tend to be easy to damage. Keep spares on hand.

Battery rundown can cause a tablet or smartphone to fail temporarily until it is recharged. To help prevent premature battery rundown, disable unnecessary services (for example, Bluetooth can be disabled if you don't use Bluetooth keyboards or exchange data via Bluetooth). On a smartphone, leave Wi-Fi disabled when you are not near a Wi-Fi hotspot.

If the battery fails, you will need to have your device serviced.

HDTV Anatomy

High-definition TVs (HDTVs) display TV and video sources at 720p or higher resolutions (1080i, 1080p, and 4K). HDTVs typically use one of the following designs:

- Liquid crystal display with LED backlight (LCD/LED or so-called "LED" HDTVs)
- Liquid-crystal display with fluorescent backlight (now obsolete)
- Plasma display

Note

The first HDTVs used CRTs, and some very large HDTVs built in 2012 used Texas Instruments digital light processing (DLP) technology, but these display technologies are no longer used for HDTVs. DLP continues to be a popular choice for HD projectors.

Video Ports

HDTVs typically include two or more HDMI A/V ports, one VGA port, and some combination of Component (HD analog), S-Video, or Composite (standard TV and video) ports.

> **Note**
> For photos and more information, see "Troubleshooting TV and Video Inputs," p.310, in Chapter 12, "Troubleshooting Home Theater, HDTVs, and Projectors."

Audio Ports

HDTVs can receive both video and audio through HDMI ports. Other audio ports typically featured are S/PDIF ports for digital stereo signals and RCA analog stereo audio jacks.

Attachment Points

Most HDTVs can be wall mounted using one of several sizes of VESA wall mounts. VESA wall mounts attach to the rear of an HDTV by means of four bolts in a square or rectangular pattern. See the instruction manual for your HDTV and wall mount for details.

Points of Failure

The fluorescent backlight assembly used in many older HDTVs is a common source of failure. In the event that the backlight fails, be sure to check the inverter powering the backlight for failure, because it is more likely to fail than the backlight itself and is less expensive to replace. Plasma HDTVs are subject to screen burn-in, and you should take precautions and perform maintenance tasks as recommended in the instruction manual for a plasma HDTV.

If you use a wall mount, be sure the wall mount is securely fastened to the wall using the recommended type of screws or bolts. Make certain the wall mount is designed for the size and weight of your HDTV and that the bolts used to fasten the wall mount to the rear of the HDTV are properly installed. If you are not sure of your ability to install or properly secure a wall mount, have an HDTV installation professional do it for you. Cable damage is also a possibility, but cables can be easily replaced.

> **Note**
> Officially, the VESA wall mount is known as the flat display mounting interface (FDMI). It is also known as the VESA mounting interface standard (MIS). Many HDTV vendors deviate from official FDMI standards, but HDTV wall mounts can usually be adjusted to match the most common deviations. For more information, see http://en.wikipedia.org/wiki/Flat_Display_Mounting_Interface and its sources.

Projector Anatomy

Projectors vary widely in features, such as ANSI lumens (the higher the better in bright light), zoom lens picture size and throw (the ability to fill a screen at short distances), projector bulb cost, capability to be wall or ceiling mounted, capability to run upside down, and the video and PC resolutions supported. Some projectors now support wireless (Wi-Fi) data sources.

Video and Signal Ports

Typical video ports on late-model projectors include the following:

- Composite video
- VGA
- HDMI

Some projectors might include DVI digital video or S-video (analog video that is better than composite). Some projectors can be adapted to use component video.

Many projectors also include a USB type A port you can use to attach a thumb drive, a digital camera, or a USB hard disk, and some include a USB type B port you can use as a video source. To use the USB type B port for video, connect the projector via USB, turn it on, and install the software provided in the projector.

Audio Ports

Projectors support stereo audio via RCA ports or an HDMI port. Figure 1.45 illustrates typical audio and video ports on a late-model Epson projector.

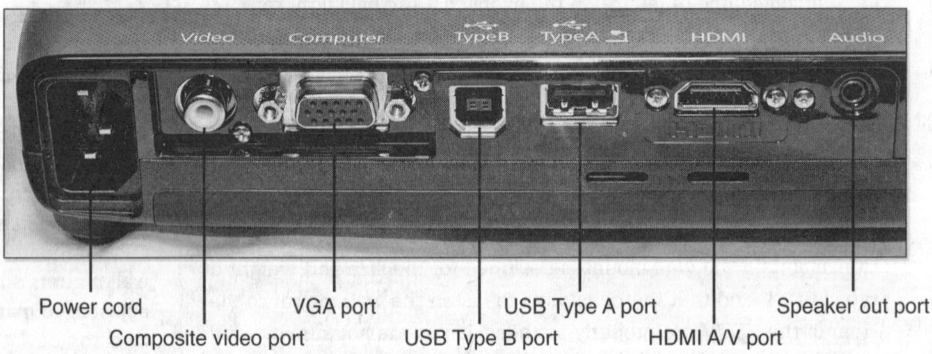

Figure 1.45 A/V ports on a typical late-model LCD projector.

Projector Controls

Projector controls enable the user to adjust for keystoning (a non-square image caused by the projector not being lined up with the middle of the projection surface), select a video source, turn the projector on and off, select bulb brightness, adjust colors, temporarily shut off the projector bulb, adjust focus, and adjust zoom. Figure 1.46 shows some typical controls on a late-model Epson projector.

> **Note**
>
> Use the remote control for easier access to menu selections.

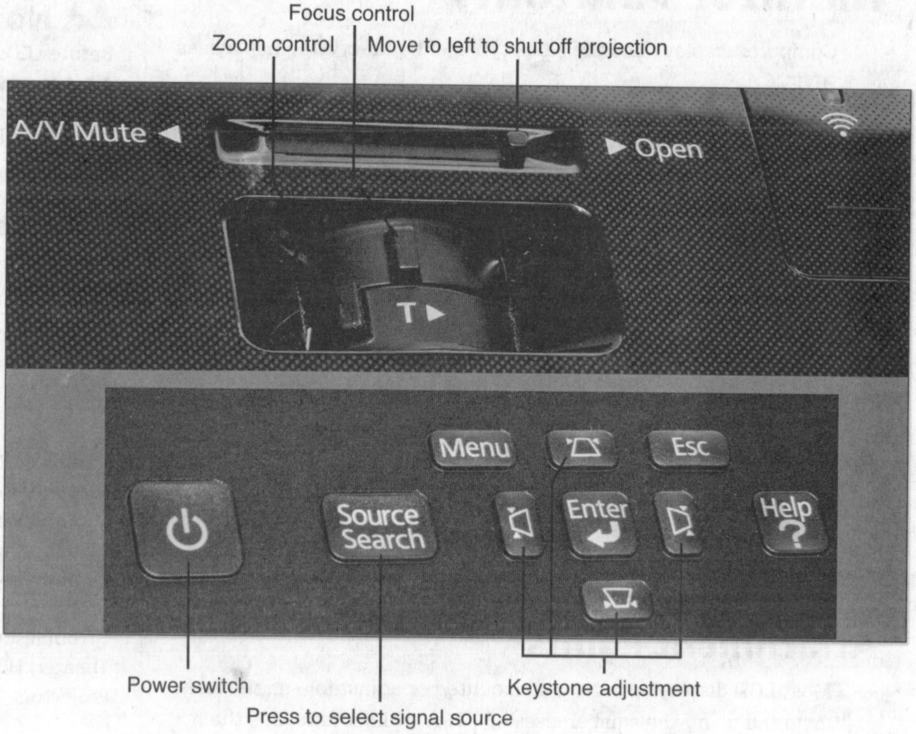

Figure 1.46 Controls on a typical late-model LCD projector.

Internal Components

Most projectors include three separate LCD light sources (one each for red, green, and blue) or a DLP (which uses a spinning transparent disk with alternating RGB and clear panels).

In either case, a single projector bulb provides the light needed to display the picture. As projector bulbs age, their light output drops as material from the filament is deposited inside the bulb. A cooling fan helps the projector shed excess heat during operation.

Points of Failure

A projector is vulnerable to impact damage (dropping it can shatter the bulb, misalign the DLP wheel, or damage the LCD array), projector bulb failure, and fan failure.

Be sure to let the projector cool down before putting it away to avoid undue stress on the bulb and other internal components.

Monitor Anatomy

Computer displays use the same types of liquid-crystal displays as HDTVs do:

- Liquid crystal display with LED backlight (LCD/LED or so-called "LED" HDTVs)
- Liquid-crystal display with fluorescent backlight (now obsolete)

Note

Before LCDs were common, most computers used CRTs, but these are limited in screen size (most are 17-inch diagonal measure or less), limited in resolution (most are 1280x1024 or less), very bulky, very heavy, used much more power than LCD displays, and produced much more heat.

Video Ports

Most displays typically include one HDMI or DVI port and one VGA port. Use the front-panel control to select a signal source.

Note

For more information about video ports, see "Troubleshooting TV and Video Inputs," p.310, in Chapter 12, "Troubleshooting Home Theater, HDTVs, and Projectors."

Audio Ports

Monitors with built-in speakers might have a stereo mini-jack port (used when DVI or VGA is the video source) or HDMI (supports both audio and video).

Attachment Points

Most LCD displays can be wall mounted or adjustable-angle desk mounted using the smaller sizes of VESA wall mounts. See the instruction manual for your monitor and wall or desk mount for details.

Points of Failure

The fluorescent backlight assembly used in many older monitors is a common source of failure. In the event that the backlight fails, be sure to check the inverter powering the backlight for failure, because it is more likely to fail than the backlight itself and is less expensive to replace. If you use a VESA desk mount, be sure the mount is securely fastened to the desk, make certain the desk mount is designed for the size and weight of your LCD display, and that the bolts used to fasten the desk mount to the rear of the monitor are properly installed. If you're not sure you can do this properly, ask a professional for help.

Receiver/Sound Bar Anatomy

Receivers provide surround audio capabilities for home theater systems. Sound bars are essentially simplified receivers that provide stereo audio or simulated surround sound for an HDTV.

Audio and Video Ports

A/V receivers include multiple HDMI ports to enable devices such as cable boxes, streaming media boxes, HDTVs, and computers to provide HD audio and video. To support older devices, A/V receivers also include stereo analog and S/PDIF digital audio ports. A/V receivers use two-wire connections to speakers and might support either two-wire passive subwoofers or active (powered) subwoofers that connect via RCA subwoofer cables. See Figure 12.19 (Chapter 12) for a typical example.

Audio receivers and sound bars include stereo analog, S/PDIF digital audio, and subwoofer connections. A/V and audio receivers also include AM/FM tuners and external antenna leads.

> **Note**
>
> For more information about audio ports, see "Can't Hear Computer Audio Through AV Receiver," p.322, in Chapter 12, "Troubleshooting Home Theater, HDTVs, and Projectors."

Points of Failure

Receivers and sound bars can overheat, so keeping their air vents clean is very important. When you place a receiver in a cabinet, make sure the unit has adequate airflow for cooling.

If the wrong input is selected, the device will appear to fail. Check inputs carefully and select the correct input for the signal type needed. If the receiver uses assignable ports and a power failure takes place, it might be necessary to use the receiver's setup program again to reassign the ports to the desired functions.

Digital Camera Anatomy

Although compact point-and-shoot digital cameras are rapidly being replaced by smartphones and tablets with rear-facing cameras for casual picture-taking, cameras with long zoom lenses as well as digital SLR and compact system cameras with interchangeable lenses are popular with photographers. Although details vary, most cameras have the features discussed in the following sections.

Control Buttons and Switches

Press the Menu button to display options for the current shooting or viewing mode. Press the Playback button to view photos or videos you've taken on the camera's LCD display or to transfer photos or videos when the camera is connected to your computer via USB. Press the Shutter button to take a photo or to shoot video. Press the zoom (W & T) buttons to shoot a wider view or get closer to your subject. While viewing a photo or video you don't want to keep, press the Delete (Trash Can) button to discard it. Use the shooting mode selector switch to choose between photos and videos. Use the Flash button to enable/disable/select flash modes.

Digital SLR and other cameras that support user-selected settings will also have a control dial with options for shooting in full automatic, scene, or creative modes where you control some or all settings. These types of cameras have buttons or menu options for ISO (light sensitivity), EV/AV adjustment (overriding normal exposure), and white balance (adjusts for light that's bluer or redder than normal daylight).

External Features

All digital cameras have an LCD display that is used for selecting shooting and setup options. The LCD display on some cameras swivels for easier shooting at a greater number of angles.

A cover protects the USB port, AV port, and connections for remote control devices available for some cameras.

Any digital camera that can shoot video also includes a microphone port for recording audio, and some also support add-on microphones.

Digital SLRs and some other cameras have a hot shoe designed for electronic flash units. A *hot shoe* has contacts that control the functions of the flash, such as a zooming head or automatic exposure. Figures 1.47 and 1.48 illustrate typical cameras and features.

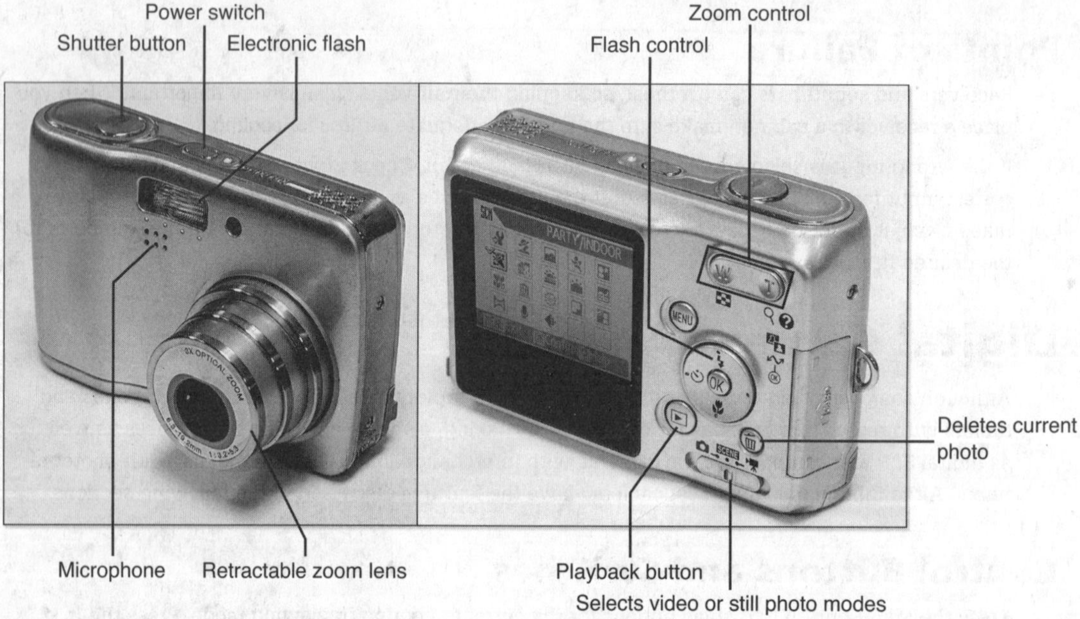

Figure 1.47
Features of a typical point-and-shoot compact digital camera.

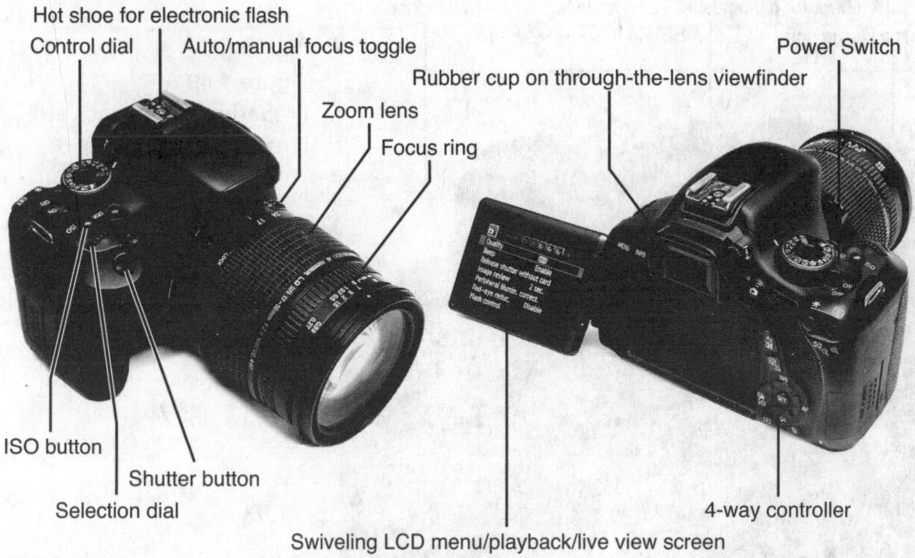

Figure 1.48
Features of a typical digital SLR camera.

Interchangeable Components

Digital SLR and compact system cameras have several interchangeable components and accessories. These include the following:

- **Lenses**—Replace lenses with zoom lenses that provide a wider field of view or longer reach than the "kit" lens included with the camera, or add a prime (nonzoom) lens for better performance in dim light. See Figure 1.49.
- **Add-on electronic flash**—Use the hot shoe at the top of the camera for more powerful flash units with tilt-swivel heads (see Figure 1.50).
- **Microphones**—Many cameras in these categories can use external microphones for better audio quality when recording video.

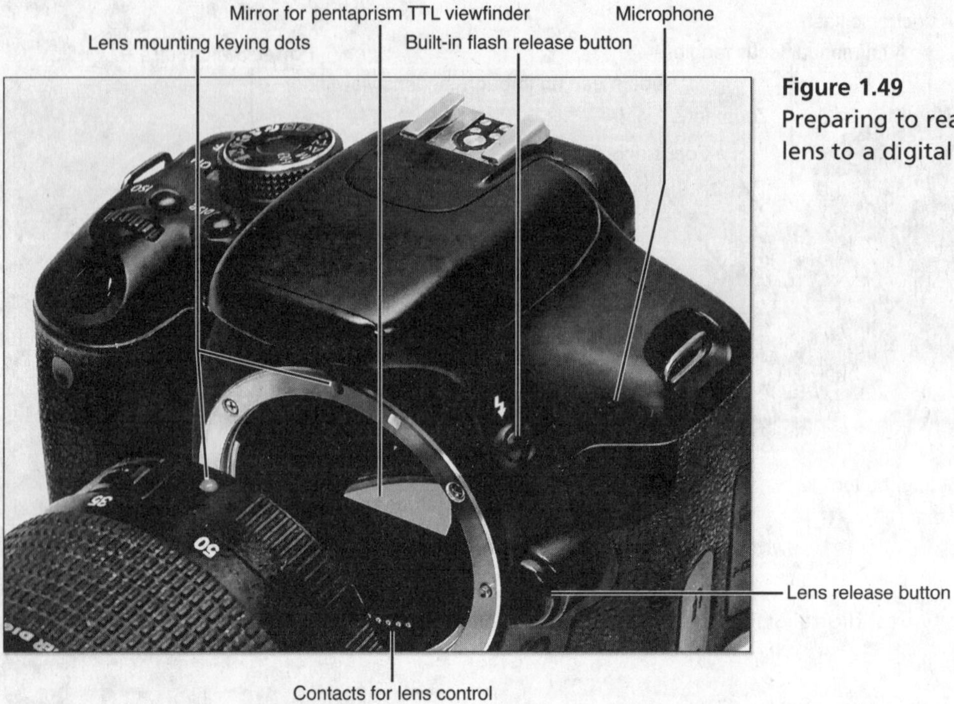

Figure 1.49
Preparing to reattach a lens to a digital SLR.

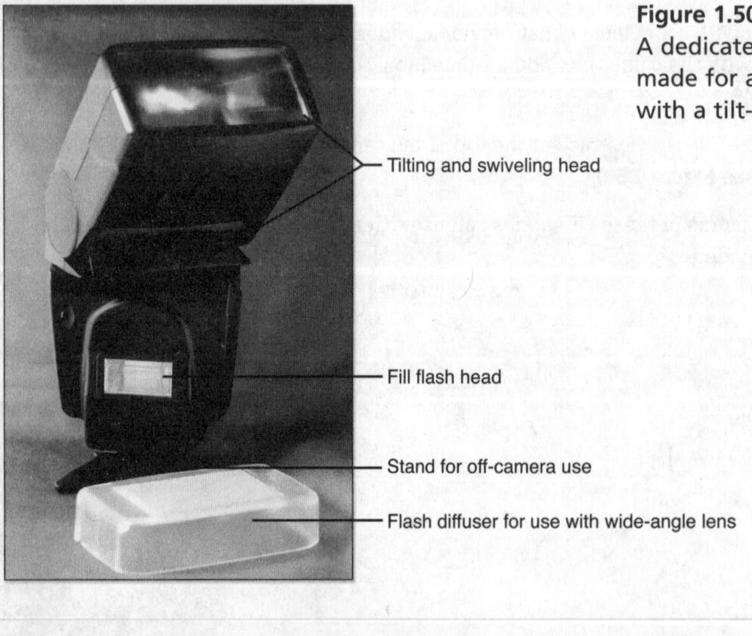

Figure 1.50
A dedicated electronic flash (a flash made for a particular camera model) with a tilt-swivel head and fill flash.

Internal Components

Digital SLR cameras such as the one shown in Figure 1.49 feature mirrors that reflect the light coming through the lens into a five-sided prism (pentaprism) that the photographer uses to frame the photo. Compact system cameras use electronic viewfinders or the LCD display at the back for this task.

All digital cameras have image sensors at the back of the device and in line with the lens. Image sensors are rated in megapixels (MP), which refers to the number of individual dots in the image recorded to the camera's memory card or other storage. The size of the image sensor has a direct effect on the camera's ability to shoot in low light. Generally, full-frame digital SLR cameras (those with a sensor size the same as a 35mm film frame) produce the least amount of image noise (false color dots) when shooting in low light, followed by digital SLR cameras with APS sensors, compact system cameras, and point-and-shoot cameras.

Almost all digital cameras of all types use memory cards, most often from the Secure Digital (SD) family.

Note

For more information about choosing SD cards, see "Choosing Fast Flash-Memory Cards," p.541, in Chapter 20, "Digital Camera Troubleshooting."

Points of Failure

Digital cameras can have numerous points of failure. Dirt on lenses causes poor-quality shooting. LCD screen and lenses can be scratched. Impact damage can throw a lens out of alignment, requiring a trip to the repair shop. Unless a camera is water sealed, you should avoid shooting in damp or rainy conditions. Dirt and dust in a camera with a retractable lens or lens cover can cause the lens to get stuck in the open or closed position.

A digital camera is a useless paperweight without working batteries. However, don't store batteries in a camera that will not be used over a long time, because they might leak or corrode and ruin your camera.

When you change lenses, turn off your camera, be sure to use front and rear lens caps on lenses not attached to the camera, and avoid swapping lenses in dirty or dusty environments because the image sensor can become dirty.

Caution

Color runs, a popular 5k race in which groups of runners run through clouds of dyed cornstarch, can be dangerous to any type of digital camera or camcorder. See http://petapixel.com/2013/05/08/photographing-a-color-run-will-destroy-your-camera-gear-dont-do-it/ for details and photos of gear damage.

Camcorder Anatomy

Camcorders no longer use videotape for storage. Instead, they use built-in or add-on flash memory. Although camcorders vary widely in price and features, most have at least some of the features covered in this section.

Control Buttons

Most camcorders, except for so-called "action" or "sports" models, have motorized zoom lenses. Some also have a custom control button in addition to the normal on/off button and snapshot (still photo) button.

Other buttons found on some models are used to switch the LCD display between shooting and playback modes, switching between battery information and live display, and shooting short videos (sometimes known as video snapshots).

External Features

Camcorders typically feature a fixed or adjustable-angle LCD display for composing the scene, viewing video after shooting, and for configuring the camcorder.

Some low-cost camcorders use AA batteries, but most camcorders use proprietary rechargeable batteries. Some models can use both standard- and high-capacity batteries for longer shooting times.

Figure 1.51 illustrates a typical camcorder and its features.

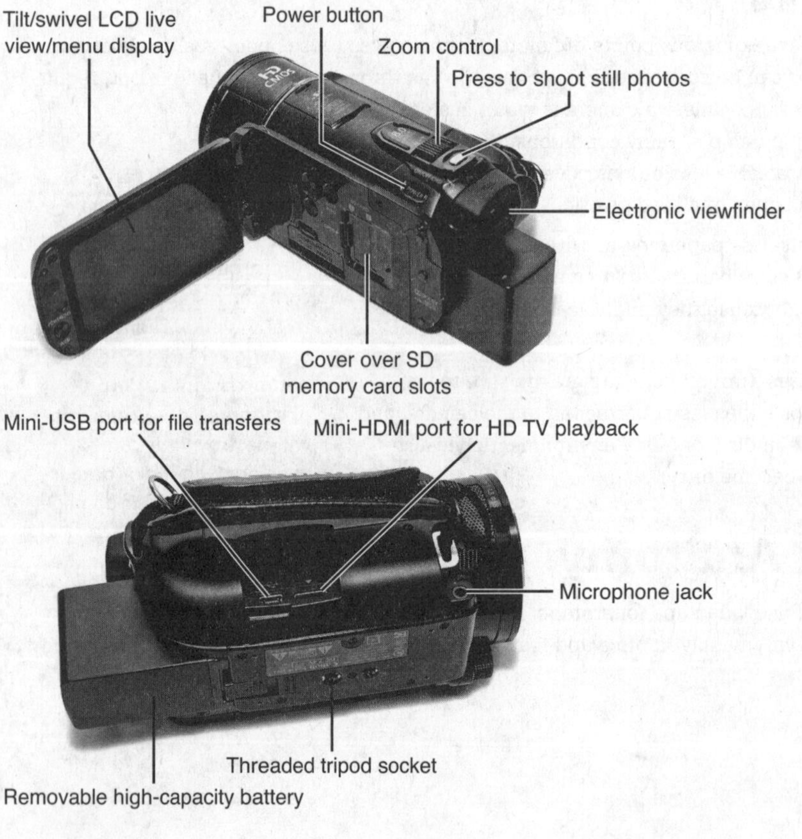

Figure 1.51 A typical HD camcorder.

Connection and Add-ons

Older DV camcorders used the FireWire (IEEE-1394) port for video transfer. However, today's HD camcorders connect via USB. For direct playback to an HDTV, look for models that have an HDMI or DisplayPort connection (usually of a reduced size). Some also have proprietary headers for component HD video as well as a standard mini-jack for stereo audio.

Camcorders with a mini advanced shoe can use add-ons such as microphones and movie lights to help improve audio and video quality.

Points of Failure

HD camcorders are vulnerable to the same types of threats as digital cameras: dust, dirt, impact damage, scratches to lens or LCD display, weak batteries, and battery corrosion and leakage.

2

UPGRADE, REPAIR, OR REPLACE?

The 50% Rule

Sooner or later, you will have a personal technology failure. It could be a digital camera that takes a bath, a smartphone that gets stepped on, or a tablet that gets dropped. But whatever it is, you're going to ask yourself, "What do I do now? Should I repair it or replace it?"

Enter the 50% rule. It's pretty simple: if it costs more than 50% of a comparable new item to repair your existing device, it's time to send it to the electronics recyclers and get a new (or refurbished) one.

Here's why:

- If you repair your existing item, you're locked into the technology it includes. Newer computers feature more and faster USB ports you can use for almost all upgrades; newer smartphones and tablets have bigger, sharper screens; newer receivers support streaming media services, and so on. However, if you replace your existing device, you can move your personal tech into the future.
- If you repair one problem with your existing item, another problem could happen later. This is more of an issue with complex devices, especially those with multiple replaceable components, such as laptop and desktop computers, digital cameras, HDTVs, and receivers. Devices such as smartphones and tablets typically feature single-board, system-on-a-chip (SoC) construction: replace the main board, and you've replaced everything.
- Although most desktop and laptop computers have upgradeable memory (RAM) and hard disk or SSD (storage), upgrading memory

and storage can sometimes cost more than half of what a new computer would cost. I typically upgrade the RAM and hard disk in my computers (these are easy upgrades to perform and I do them myself). The costs for these components are relatively low when new parts use the same technology as the parts in my computer. However, if you wanted to upgrade a computer that uses an older memory technology (DDR2, for example, compared with today's DDR3), you would pay much more per GB.

Applying the Rule

Here's how it works:

You have a $700 digital SLR camera you purchased two years ago. It needs major repair to the tune of $350. However, a camera with comparable features now costs only $500. It makes more sense to replace your old camera because the 50% rule recommends that you pay no more than $250 for a repair. If you choose a camera of the same brand, most of your accessories (except for spare batteries) will probably work with the new camera.

You have a $600 (actual noncontract price) smartphone that you purchased a year ago. You purchased insurance for it in case of damage, but you must pay a $200 deductible. If it is damaged, unless you can buy the same model for less than $200 new or refurbished, get it repaired and pay the $200 deductible.

You have a two-year-old $500 laptop that needs a new hard disk and more RAM. You want to install a 1TB drive and 16GB of RAM. As of mid-2014, you'd probably pay about $200–220 for those upgrades (if you can do the work yourself). The price of the parts is less than 50% of the original cost of your computer.

However, if you cannot install these upgrades yourself, you will need to include the cost of labor. For example, Best Buy's Geek Squad would charge $200 for installation of these upgrades and data transfer from the old drive to the new drive. Thus, the total price of these upgrades would exceed $400 in parts and labor, which is well above the 50% threshold for considering a replacement. Before you decide to replace your computer, check the cost of a new laptop with this amount of drive capacity and RAM.

Here are some other factors to consider if you are considering buying a replacement computer:

- Can you reuse your existing software on your new computer? If you are moving from Windows 7 to Windows 8.1, for example, much but not necessarily all of your software is likely to be compatible. However, you must determine whether your software can be legally transferred to another computer. If you must replace it, be sure to factor in the cost as you calculate the 50% rule.
- If you can transfer an app or program, be sure to factor in the time necessary to deactivate it and uninstall it from the old computer, install it and reactivate it on the new computer.
- If you are not comfortable transferring data files from your old computer yourself or with the assistance of a transfer program, expect to pay about $100 for a technician to do it for you.
- Finally, consider the cost of your time. Time is money, and you might prefer to pay a technician to do these tasks rather than take your own time to learn how to perform these transfers and do them yourself.

Note

As an alternative to manually transferring programs and data, consider using one of the PCMover programs available from LapLink (www.laplink.com/index.php). PCMover transfers programs and settings from your old computer to your new computer, and free technical support is included. The time savings when using PCMover compared with manual transfers is considerable.

So, now that we have a clearer picture of the total cost of a computer upgrade, let's run the numbers (see Table 2.1).

Table 2.1 Upgrade or Replace—Laptop

Component or Service Cost	Upgrade Laptop Yourself	Upgrade Laptop Using a Tech	Replace Laptop
1TB hard disk	$100	$100	Included in cost
16GB RAM	$120	$120	Included in cost
Installation	Free	$200	Included in cost
Data Transfer	Free	Included in installation cost	$100
App and data transfer using PCMover	$60	$60	$60
New Laptop with 1TB RAM, 16GB RAM			$1250.00 (average of multiple models)
Totals	$280.00	$480.00	$1,410.00

Assuming the processor speed and other features of the existing laptop are suitable, either upgrading it yourself or having a tech upgrade the unit will be considerably cheaper than buying a new laptop.

The older an item gets, the less sense it makes to pay for a repair or component upgrades, especially as the price approaches or exceeds 50% replacement cost. A replacement item might offer more features, faster performance, larger screen size, and so on.

Note

One way to make replacing an existing unit more attractive to your wallet is to look for factory-refurbished or factory-reconditioned items. Many electronics vendors offer these through their own online outlet stores, major online retailers, and some big-box electronics or office-supply stores.

Some have the same warranty as new, and others might have a shorter warranty or no warranty at all. Check recent reviews for the seller and the product, but skip units that don't have any warranty. Full disclosure: I've been buying factory-refurbished products for years from several major vendors and have always been satisfied.

Exceptions

The main reason to spend more than 50% of replacement cost on a repair or upgrade is if you cannot find a suitable replacement for an item. Whether for compatibility reasons, user interface, screen size, or some other reason—it doesn't matter. If you prefer to stay with your current device, it's your money.

OEM Versus Third-Party Components

If you need to buy replacement parts for a laptop or desktop computer, a tablet, a smartphone, or a digital camera, you have two choices:

- Original equipment manufacturer (OEM)
- Third-party replacements

From chargers to cables, from batteries to drives and lenses, you can choose from items from the original product vendor or items from other suppliers. Which should you choose? Let's look at the benefits of each approach.

When to Use OEM Repair/Replacement Parts

OEM repair/replacement parts are going to work with your device. Period. They aren't designed to work with any other brand or type of product, they fully support your device, and they have a warranty from the same company that supplied your device.

If you value reliability, single sourcing, and warranty coverage above price, stick with OEM. This is particularly the case if you need to replace a computer motherboard on a system with a preinstalled version of Windows. Although you could install a third-party motherboard (depending on the chassis and power supply used in the original system), only the same model motherboard from the OEM supplier will work with a preinstalled version of Windows.

Benefits of Third-Party Repair/Replacement Parts

The number one reason to use third-party repair/replacement parts is money—saving money, that is. You can save up to 50% or more by buying replacement chargers, batteries, lenses, and other repair/replacement parts for your electronics device from third-party vendors.

The second reason to use third-party repair/replacement parts is to get more features. For example, if you buy an OEM charger for your laptop, it might work only on the model you bought, or possibly a narrow range of models from the same vendor. Buy a universal model and you might pay about the same price (or less), but you can use it with many brands and models. Some include a USB charging port for a smartphone or tablet.

The third reason is that many OEM parts, such as memory modules and hard disk drives, are actually sourced from third-party vendors. By using a memory vendor's compatibility database, you can find memory that will fit your computer, often for less than your system vendor changes.

Finding the Best Values in Third-Party Components

Some third-party products are terrific, others are merely adequate, and a few are truly terrible. To find the winners and avoid the losers, check online reviews carefully. Look for products from major third-party accessory vendors, and when you read reviews, I recommend that you look not only at the so-called "most helpful" reviews, but sort reviews so that the newest reviews appear first.

Why? If recent reviews for a product are better than older reviews, this might indicate that the product has been improved. However, if older reviews are better than newer reviews, product quality might have slipped.

How can you avoid fake reviews? Reviews that are mostly emotion based ("Loved it! Hated it!") aren't useful and are easy to fake. Look for reviews that emphasize details and look also at the reviewers themselves to help sort out honest reviews from those that are simply pushing the product.

You can help other users find the best products by posting reviews yourself.

3

TROUBLESHOOTING INTERNET PROBLEMS

Fast Track to Solutions

Table 3.1 Symptom Table

Symptom	Flowchart or Book Section	Page #
I'm not sure which channel is the best for my wireless router.	Choosing an Uncluttered Channel	71
I use a Wireless-N router and adapters, but my network is no faster than when I used Wireless-G. I am using WPA encryption.	Wireless-N or Wireless-AC+WPA2 Encryption – Speed and Better Security	74
I have older devices. How can I make sure they don't slow down my network?	Why WEP and WPA's Time is Over	75
I see references to N150 and N600 routers and adapters. Which ones are faster?	Why Some Wireless-N and AC Devices Run Faster Than Others	76
I need to figure out what's slowing down my wireless network.	Troubleshooting Wireless Network Performance (flowchart)	Chapter 24
I have a Wireless-AC router, but my laptop's wireless connection is still slow.	Old Computer, New Router? Boosting Wi-Fi Speed	77

Symptom	Flowchart or Book Section	Page #
When my friends come over, I'd like to let them use my wireless network, but I don't want them checking out my shared folders.	Using Guest Mode	79
I'm trying to create a long encryption key, but I can't remember it and it's hard to type in.	Encryption Keys Problems and Solutions	81
I can't get a wireless signal in some parts of my house or office.	Solving Signal Strength Problems	82
My home has concrete or brick walls, and a wireless repeater still can't cover some rooms.	Installing and Using Powerline Adapters	93
My computer has a Gigabit Ethernet port, but my network only runs at Fast Ethernet (100Mbps) speeds.	Speeding Up a Slow Wired Network	88
I need to figure out where the slowdowns are in my Ethernet network.	Ethernet Performance Troubleshooting (flowchart)	Chapter 24
I want to share my cellular data connection with a single PC.	Using USB Tethering	97
I want to share my cellular data connection with several devices.	Using a Wi-Fi Hotspot	97
I have upgraded my router's firmware, but I want more features. Do I need to buy a new router?	DD-WRT and Other Third-Party Router Firmware	104

Speeding Up a Slow Wireless Network

Does your wireless (Wi-Fi) network have a bad case of the slows? Have you replaced an aging Wireless-G, Wireless-A, or Wireless-B router with a brand-new Wireless-N or Wireless-AC router, only to discover little or no change in performance? Here are the keys to boosting performance (and improving security, too):

- Choose an uncluttered channel.
- Encryption matters, both for security and for speed.

- Wireless-N loves WPA2 encryption.
- WEP and WPA are old; it's time for an upgrade.
- Some Wireless-N devices are faster than others.
- Old laptop, new router—how to boost your connection speed.

Let's take a closer look at each of these.

> **Note**
> Some broadband modems also include a wireless router. Whether your router is separate from your broadband modem or they are a single unit, the issues discussed in this chapter are the same.

Choosing an Uncluttered Channel

If you are using Wireless-G or standard Wireless-N networking, the 2.4GHz frequency band these networks use is a busy one: you're competing with other wireless networks in your area, some types of wireless phones, and older versions of Bluetooth (a wireless network used for smartphone headsets and other very short-range wireless connections).

To make matters worse, although 2.4GHz wireless has 11 channels, most of them have significant overlap. The only three that have minimal overlap are channel 1, channel 6, and channel 11. If you use a wireless channel that is already in use nearby, your effective range and signal strength are lower than they should be, and so is your network performance.

Fortunately, you don't need to knock on doors to ask your neighbors the intimate details of their wireless networks. Instead, you can see this information in real time. The InSSIDer Wi-Fi diagnostic utility (www.inssider.com) from MetaGeek provides an easy-to-use view of both 2.4GHz and 5.0GHz wireless networks in your area. Although InSSIDer is now a commercial product as of version 4 ($19.95), free downloads of the previous 3.x version are still available from some download sites, such as MajorGeeks (www.majorgeeks.com) and Softpedia (www.softpedia.com).

Use InSSIDer to see which channels are in use (it also advises which channel to switch to if your current choice is too crowded), which networks are secured, and which are unencrypted ("open"). See Figure 3.1 for a typical example in a residential neighborhood.

In this example, channel 36 is recommended over the current channel in use (channels 149+153).

To change the channel used by your wireless network:

1. Log in to your router.
2. Navigate to the Wireless Configuration dialog.
3. Select a different channel (when using 2.4GHz networking, channels 1, 6, and 11 have less interference than others).
4. Save your changes and exit the router configuration dialog.

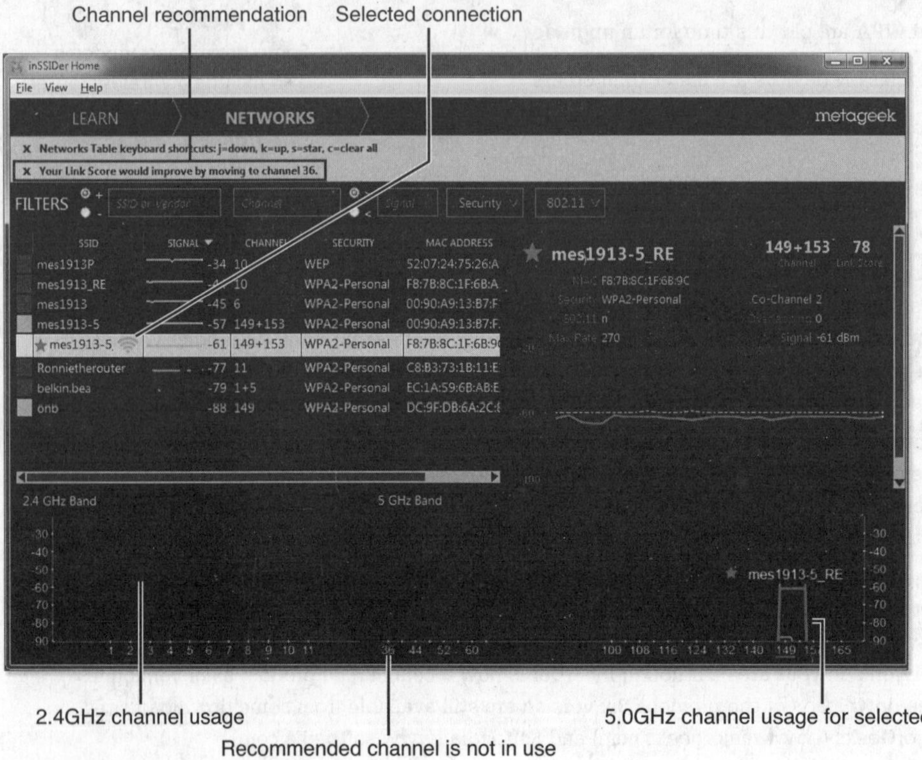

Figure 3.1 Using InSSIDer to detect information about your and other nearby wireless networks.

Figure 3.2 illustrates a typical wireless channel configuration dialog on a dual-frequency (2.4GHz and 5.0GHz) Wireless-N router from Western Digital.

Note

Some routers use Auto as the default channel setting, as in Figure 3.2. The router changes the channel according to the settings of nearby routers. If you are satisfied with your network's performance, leave the setting as is. However, if InSSIDer recommends a different channel that is not in use (or is not used as much), manually select the recommended channel.

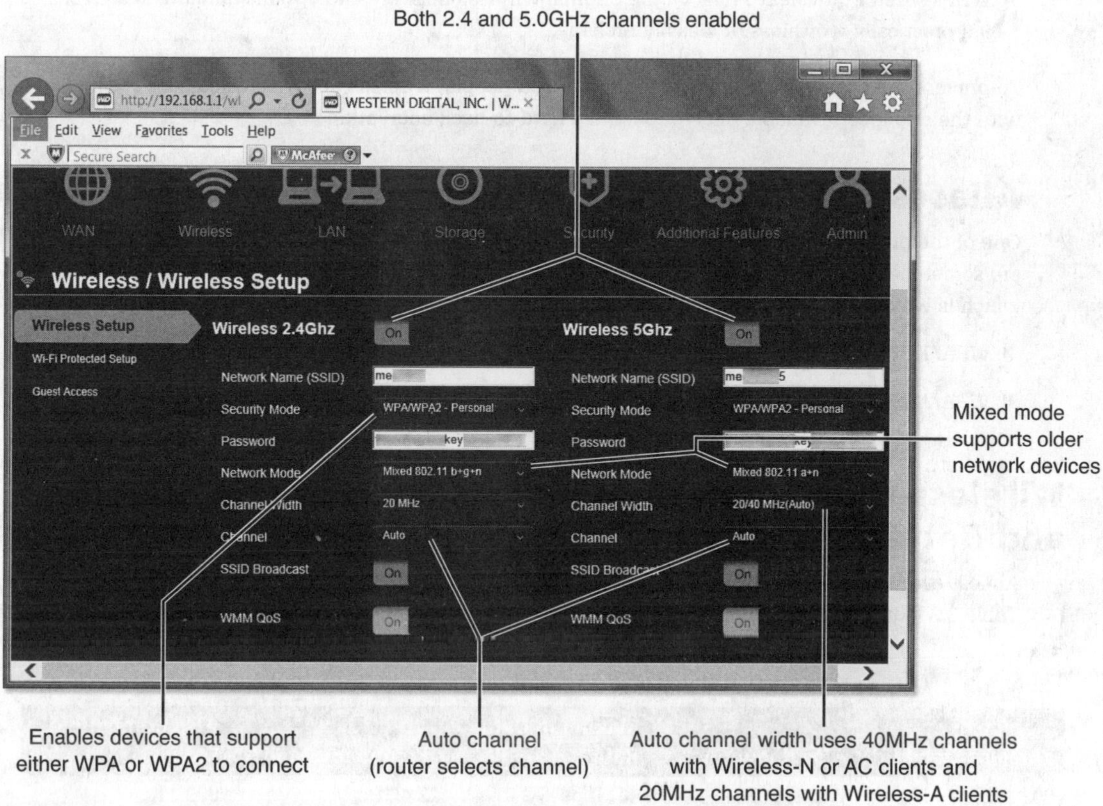

Figure 3.2
Setting up a dual-frequency wireless router.

Understanding Encryption

An unsecured home or office network is an invitation to data thieves and other assorted criminals to "borrow" your network, steal or distribute illicit information, and leave you facing charges when they disappear. Your home or office network needs to be secure.

There are three standards for Wi-Fi encryption:

- WPA2 (Wi-Fi Protected Access 2) is the newest and most powerful encryption method. It's designed to give your wireless network maximum protection. As you'll see later, it's also important to wireless network performance.
- WPA (Wi-Fi Protected Access) is an older, weaker version that should be used only if WPA2 is not supported by your devices (for example, if you are still using Wireless-B and Wireless-G devices that don't support WPA2).

- WEP (Wired Equivalent Privacy), the original wireless network encryption standard, is so weak it's practically worthless. It's easily broken.

To prevent the possibilities of use by unauthorized people, wireless networks should be secured with the strongest available encryption and a hard-to-hack encryption key.

Aliases for WPA and WPA2 Encryption

One of the problems with setting up WPA2 encryption on your router and devices is that both types are sometimes referred to as WPA. In those cases, the encryption type listed is the key to knowing which is which:

- WPA/TKIP=WPA
- WPA/AES=WPA2

Wireless-N or Wireless-AC+WPA2 Encryption—Speed and Better Security

Almost every wireless router on the market today supports 802.11n or its successor, 802.11ac. As Table 3.2 indicates, Wireless-N and Wireless-AC can run much more quickly than their predecessors.

Table 3.2 Wireless Network (Wi-Fi) Standards

Wireless Standard	Also Known As	Maximum Data Rate	Frequency Band	Also Compatible With
802.11b	Wireless-B	11Mbps	2.4GHz	802.11g
802.11a	Wireless-A	54Mbps	5.0GHz	802.11n *
802.11g	Wireless-G	54Mbps	2.4GHz	802.11b, 802.11n
	Wireless-N	150Mbps per stream^	2.4GHz 5.0GHz (optional)	802.11b 802.11g 802.11a*
802.11ac	Wireless-AC	433Mbps per stream&	5.0GHz	802.11a 802.11n#@ 802.11b@ 802.11g@

*Only 802.11n hardware that supports the optional 5.0GHz frequency band is compatible with 802.11a hardware.

^Up to four streams supported. Most devices support one, two, or three streams.

&Up to eight streams supported, 80MHz and 160MHz channels supported.

#Native support for 5.0GHz version only.

@802.11ac devices also support older 2.4GHz standards.

Because all laptops and tablets now include Wireless-N support, it looks as if you can give a big boost to your network by retiring your old Wireless-G router and replacing it with a Wireless-N or, even better, a Wireless-AC router.

However, if you replaced an old Wireless-G router with a Wireless-N or Wireless-AC router but didn't see any speed improvements, here's why: Wireless-N and Wireless-AC can run at speeds faster than Wireless-G and Wireless-A if, *and only if,* you use WPA2 encryption (or no encryption at all) on your network. Wireless-N and Wireless-AC require the use of WPA2 encryption. If you use older encryption standards, your network runs as if it's a Wireless-G network.

Why WEP and WPA's Time Is Over

At this time, Wireless-N routers and devices dominate, and Wireless-AC is coming up fast. But because a lot of older devices are still connecting to those routers, you might have a mixture of Wireless-N or Wireless-AC and older-standard devices on your wireless network. If that sounds like your wireless network, you may have two challenges:

- Getting maximum performance
- Protecting your wireless network

As you've already learned, WPA2 encryption is the secret to maximum 802.11n and 802.11ac performance and maximum safety. However, what are your alternatives if you suspect (or know) that some of your hardware doesn't support WPA2 encryption? Here's what you can do:

- Install driver or firmware upgrades to enable existing devices to use WPA2 encryption. This is the least expensive route to take *if* your devices can be upgraded.
- Downgrade the security of your network to a lower standard supported by all of your devices. If you're still using a Wireless-G router, this is acceptable. However, if you configure a Wireless-N or Wireless-AC router to use WPA or WEP encryption, it runs at Wireless-G speeds only. That means you lose out on most of your potential network speed.
- Drop encryption completely. Use this option, and you might as well put a welcome mat on your router, inviting data thieves, media pirates, pornographers, and spies to use your wireless connection. Law enforcement and digital media rights enforcement can trace illicit traffic back to your router, so you'll be blamed for any misdeeds performed using your Internet connection.
- Replace devices or adapters that don't support WPA2 wireless networking with newer, compatible devices that do. If you have a lot of older hardware around, this could cost some bucks, but it makes your network faster and more secure.
- Set up two separate wireless networks: one with WPA2 support for maximum security and the other with weaker security for older devices.

Tip

To help support older types of wireless hardware that don't support WPA2, some routers (refer to Figure 3.2) support WPA/WPA2 encryption. This setting uses WPA encryption on devices that don't support WPA2 and uses WPA2 encryption on devices that support it. This provides better security than using WPA only, but it can slow down your network.

However, even if you upgrade or replace older devices with devices that support WPA2 encryption, you might still be disappointed with the performance of your network.

Why Some Wireless-N and AC Devices Run Faster Than Others

Although Wireless-N and Wireless-AC networks support the same 2.4GHz frequencies as Wireless-B and Wireless-G (and many Wireless-N routers and some adapters and all Wireless-AC devices also support the 5.0GHz frequencies used by Wireless-A), devices on these networks can vary widely in performance. Why?

Unlike its predecessors, Wireless-N is designed to support multiple data streams with multiple send-and-receive antennas and two different channel widths (20MHz, as with older Wi-Fi standards, and 40MHz). Wireless-AC also supports multiple data streams with even wider (and faster) 80MHz and 160MHz channels.

Although Wireless-N is capable of providing as much as 150Mbps per data stream, that assumes the use of wide (40MHz) channels and short transmission times. In reality, you'll probably get about half that speed, especially if your devices and router support only 2.4GHz signaling.

Wireless-AC's big speed improvements are based on using the wider 80MHz and 160MHz channels that are available only if you use Wireless-AC routers and adapters; if a Wireless-AC router is connecting to Wireless-N 5.0GHz adapters, or vice versa, the connection acts like a Wireless-N connection. If you have a mixture of device speeds, the speed of the slower device determines the speed of the connection.

Another factor that has a big impact on Wireless-N and AC speeds is the number of antennas supported by the router and the adapters (either built-in or add-on devices). This is typically expressed in this way:

- 1x1—one transmit, one receive antenna
- 2x2—two transmit, two receive antennas
- 2x3—two transmit, three receive antennas
- 3x2—three transmit, two receive antennas
- 3x3—three transmit, three receive antennas

The number of transmit antennas generally corresponds to the number of spatial streams (data streams) the device can support. In the case of a router that supports both 2.4GHz and 5GHz signals, the specifications include this information for each band.

Note

When a device has a different number of receiving and sending antennas, the device might be identified by the number of spatial (data) streams it can send and receive. For example, a device with a 2x3 antenna configuration can also be identified as having a 2x3:2 configuration (two send antennas, three receive antennas, two spatial [data] streams send/receive support). Some smartphones and tablets simply use the term MIMO (multiple input, multiple output) if they support two or more wireless N streams.

It can be difficult to determine exactly what the antenna and stream support is on some devices. Fortunately, almost all Wireless-N and Wireless-AC routers and devices identify their performance potential by their class designation.

For example, a Wireless-N device with N150 performance has a maximum link rate of 150Mbps and supports only the 2.4GHz band. A Wireless-N device with N600 performance has a maximum link rate of 300Mbps for 2.4GHz and 300Mbps for 5.0GHz (300+300=600).

A Wireless-AC device with AC750 performance has a 300Mbps maximum link rate for 2.4GHz and 433Mbps for 5.0GHz, whereas an AC1900 model has a 600Mbps link rate for 2.4GHz and 1300Mbps link rate for 5.0GHz.

> **Note**
> For much more about N and AC router classes, see www.smallnetbuilder.com/wireless/wireless-basics/32316-how-to-buy-a-wireless-router-2014-edition.

To achieve maximum speed and maximum flexibility for your network:

- Choose a router that supports 2.4GHz and 5.0GHz frequencies.
- Configure your router to use WPA2 encryption.
- Use the fastest available dual-band Wireless-N or Wireless-AC wireless adapters.

Old Computer, New Router? Boosting Wi-Fi Speed

If you have a laptop or desktop computer with a Wireless-G adapter or a simple 1x1 (150Mbps) Wireless-N adapter and a Wireless-N router rated for higher speeds, you can improve your wireless connection speed by upgrading to a better Wireless-N adapter or a Wireless-AC adapter. Here's a case in point:

My HP Pavilion DV6-series laptop has a Broadcom 4313GN 802.11bgn wireless adapter, as shown in Device Manager (see Figure 3.3). It connects to an N900 router, but it has a connection speed of only 72Mbps. Multiply this value by 2 to get the rating (144Mbps rounds up to N150).

I connected a Netgear N600 adapter to my laptop's USB port after installing its drivers. Then I disabled the onboard wireless adapter:

To disable the onboard adapter, follow these steps:

1. Open Device Manager.
2. Expand the Network Adapters listing.
3. Right-click the existing adapter.
4. Select **Disable** from the right-click menu.
5. Click **Yes** to disable it.

(To enable it, follow steps 1–3, and then select **Enable** in step 4 and confirm this choice.)

After I connected to my router using the 2.4GHz channel, the connection status of the new adapter shows twice the speed of the old adapter. The best speed, though, was achieved when I connected to the 5GHz channel in which I achieved a speed that was more than 3.3 times faster than with the original adapter (see Figure 3.4). Multiply the speed shown by 2x to determine the rating.

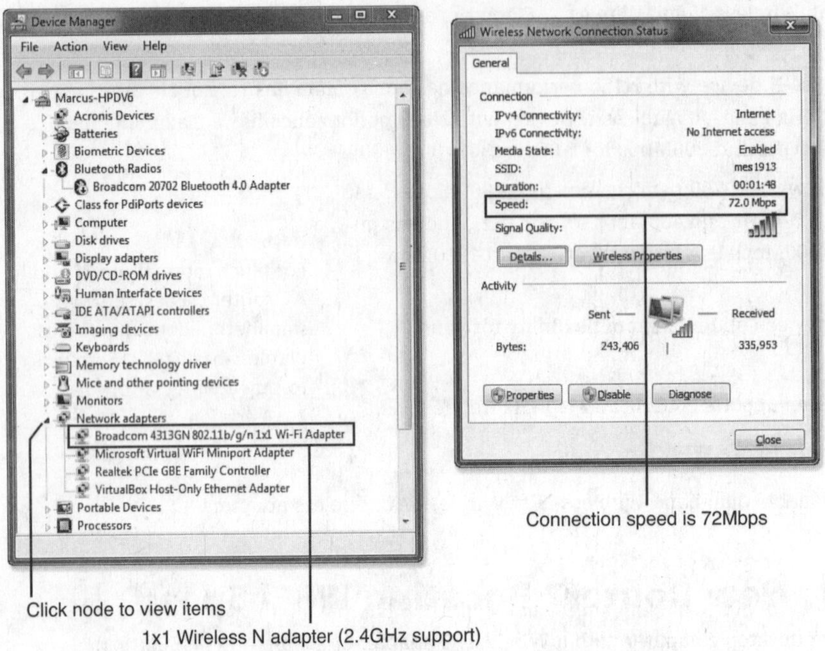

Figure 3.3 The author's laptop has a built-in 2.4GHz-only Wireless-N adapter from Broadcom.

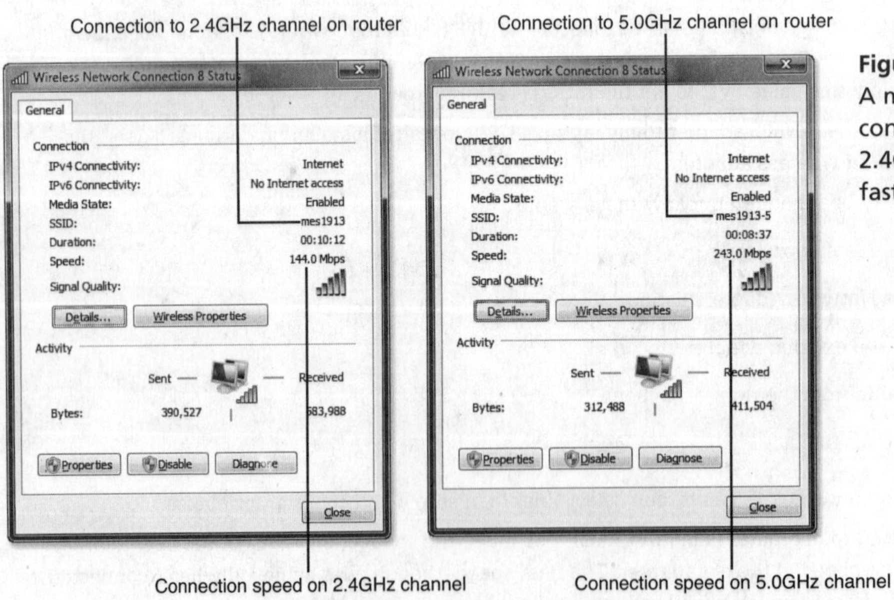

Figure 3.4 A much faster connection using 2.4GHz and even faster at 5GHz.

The faster speeds made an obvious difference when using streaming video from services such as Netflix or YouTube and when transferring files between computers on the home network.

Dealing with Slow, Insecure Devices on Your Home Network

Network security is only as strong as its weakest link. Because wireless networking has been around for more than 10 years, you might have a wide range of devices on your wireless network, and some of them won't support WPA2–the strongest Wi-Fi encryption and the one that's necessary to get maximum speed from Wireless-N and Wireless-AC routers and devices. The most likely offenders include the following:

- Early Wireless-G (802.11g) routers or network adapters
- Older portable game systems

It's easy to replace old routers and network adapters, including those that connect to games. For example, the original Microsoft Xbox 360 Wireless Network Adapter supported Wireless a/b/g. You can replace it with the Xbox 360 Wireless N Network Adapter.

However, older portable game systems can be more difficult to replace. For example, although Nintendo's current crop of portable systems (2DS, 3DS, and 3DS XL) use WPA2 encryption, they support DS online games that work only with WEP encryption. If you're still playing online DS games, you can't change encryption types.

To keep the gamers in the family happy, you can use one of these alternatives: Guest mode or weaker encryption for older devices.

Using Guest Mode

If your wireless router supports a Guest mode, you can use it to provide devices that can't support the newest security settings (or don't use security at all) an Internet connection without reducing the security settings used by newer devices on your network. It's also handy for letting friends and family get on your network safely: Guest mode prevents access to network printers or shares. Depending on the router, Guest mode might be available for only 2.4GHz channels or for both 2.4 and 5.0GHz channels. Although it does not use encryption, it requires that users open their browsers and enter the password you provide during setup. Figure 3.5 illustrates a router configuration screen for Guest mode. If Security mode is enabled, this dialog also prompts the user to set up a password (encryption key).

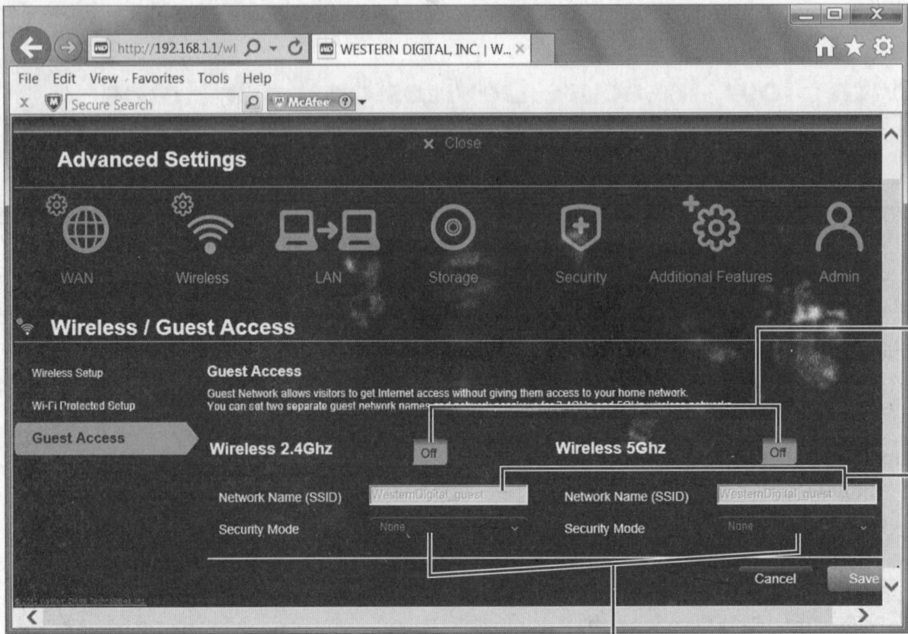

Figure 3.5 This router supports Guest mode for both 2.4GHz and 5.0GHz networks.

2.4GHz for Older Devices

If your router doesn't support Guest mode, configure the 2.4GHz channel in your router to use WEP encryption for devices that must use this encryption type, and use the 5GHz frequency with WPA2 encryption for PCs, tablets, portable game systems, and smartphones that support this encryption type and frequency. To make this strategy work, upgrade to dual-band Wireless-N or any Wireless-AC adapters and routers.

Setting Up a Secure Wireless Network

If you read the preceding sections of this chapter and nodded along, saying, "Guess I'd better secure my network," or are preparing to set up a brand-new wireless network, these tips are for you.

Your first challenge is how to set up a secure network. You typically have two choices:

- Select and enter encryption keys manually.
- Use Wi-Fi Protected Setup (WPS).

Which is a better choice?

Encryption Keys Problems and Solutions

With WPA2 (preferred) or WPA encryption, you have three options when you configure your router and your network devices:

- You can use up to 63 ASCII characters (letters, numbers, and symbols)
- You can use up to 63 ASCII letters and numbers characters only
- You can use 64 hex characters (numbers 0–9, letters A–F only), such as 41 69 3a 5e, and so on.

Naturally, whatever you use when you set up the router has to be used for each and every device that will connect to the wireless network.

Tip

Instead of retyping the encryption key at every device you want to add to your wireless network, copy the encryption key into a text (Notepad) file, preferably on a USB thumb drive you can put away for emergencies.

If you need to enter the encryption key on a device that has a USB port, you can insert the thumb drive and copy the encryption key from the file into the appropriate dialog in the connection setup. To set up a smartphone or tablet, send the encryption key via email or messaging and then copy it from the file.

Why ASCII Works for Encryption Keys

With three choices, which is best? Unfortunately, limitations in some devices prevent you from entering some symbol keys (for example, a device with a limited onscreen keyboard, such as a smartphone), and some devices don't support hex characters.

I recommend that you use a long (a 30- to 50-character ASCII text/numeric) encryption key so that PCs, tablets, smartphones, and portable game systems can all connect to your wireless network. You may have problems with some devices as you approach 60 characters.

Creating a Hard-to-Break, Easy-to-Remember Encryption Key

An encryption key (passphrase) that's just a few characters long can be easy to break, so the longer the better. However, if you use a random password generator to create a key such as: OE03zI7tAG48BcAiR2U5R1XiFD2X4l5higMWoxN0DwJUAiO3NcIkqFc6YrnvnZL (key generated by GRC's Perfect Passwords generator at https://www.grc.com/passwords.htm), you won't be able to remember it. Instead, consider creating a long encryption key from a combination of words and numbers that you can remember. Here's a made-up example that uses characters and numbers from the movie *Star Wars, Episode 4 (A New Hope)* to create a 60-character encryption key:

LukeSkywalker3Jawas2Wookie1DeathStar0LeiaOrgana5snubfighter

Wi-Fi Protected Setup Problems and Solutions

If you've been through the process of entering encryption keys before, you know that a secure encryption key is more than a few characters long and can be hard to type. To make network setup easier, most router and PC adapter vendors support a technology called Wi-Fi Protected Setup (WPS). With WPS, you have three setup options, depending on your equipment:

- Press a button on the router and the adapter. On some routers, the button might be an onscreen clickable button in the router configuration program.
- Enter a PIN number from the device into the router's WPS setup dialog.
- Enter a PIN number from the router into the device's setup dialog.

> **Note**
> The PIN number is typically found on a label on the router or device. Some routers might also list it in their configuration program dialog.

Although WPS is easy, it is not always the best way to set up your device. Here are some reasons why:

- **WPS is not as secure as other methods**—WPS encryption can be overcome with a brute-force attack. For this reason, many wireless router vendors now offer options to disable WPS.
- **Be sure to check any warnings on new wireless devices before you use WPS to add them to an existing network**—For example, Epson states that WPS should *not* be used to set up its wireless printers if it was not used to set up other devices on the network. Using WPS in this situation could disrupt existing wireless connections. A good general rule is: if you've been using WPS for wireless network setup, keep using it. However, if you've been using manual wireless network setup, don't change to WPS.
- **Some devices don't support WPS**—Both the router and the device must support WPS, or you will need to enter the encryption key as discussed earlier.

> **Note**
> The newest version of Wi-Fi Protected Setup supports NFC (near field communication). This is also known as tap-to-connect technology. This technology, first developed for smartphones, enables a connection when devices are moved next to each other. NFC makes it easier to add new devices, such as smartphones and tablets, to a Wi-Fi–encrypted network. NFC support must be present in both the router and the device in order to use this WPS setup method.

Solving Signal Strength Problems

As with any radio-frequency device, the further your Wi-Fi adapter is from a wireless router or access point, the weaker the signal is likely to be. Wireless-N and Wireless-AC routers and adapters are designed to use reflected signals to help overcome this problem (two or more antennas improve range and performance), and 2.4GHz channels have a longer range than 5.0GHz channels.

Are you wondering if this problem affects you? Try this simple test. If you have a dual-band device (one that can use both 2.4GHz and 5.0GHz signals) and a dual-band router that is set up to use both types of signals, look at the signal strength as you move your device around your home or office. As Figure 3.6 illustrates, the signal strength of a 2.4GHz radio is typically stronger than that of a 5.0GHz radio at medium to longer distances.

Figure 3.6
2.4GHz has its uses, such as a longer effective range than 5.0GHz.

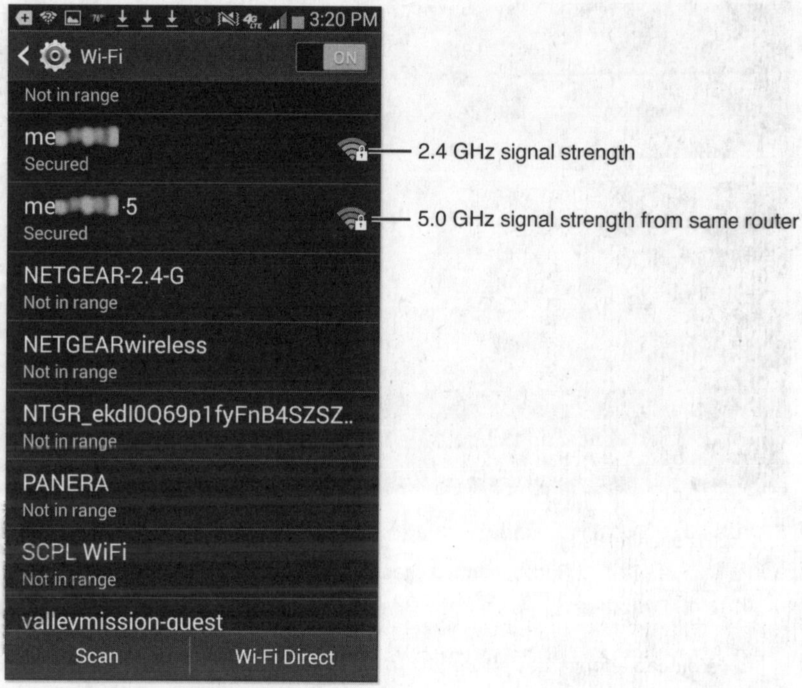

For a more precise view of signal strength, channels, and potential interference from other networks, install the free Wifi Analyzer app on your Android smartphones or tablet (it's available from Google Play). Wifi Analyzer displays signal strength for wireless networks in real time, so as you walk around your home or office, you can see changes in signal strength in your network and other detected networks (see Figure 3.7).

In some parts of your home or business, you might discover that you have hardly any signal. Even if you upgrade your router to a three- or four-antenna device and replace your single-antenna adapters in your PCs to multi-antenna adapters, you might still have range problems with non-PC devices such as smartphones (such as the Galaxy S III shown in Figure 3.6), tablets, and portable gaming systems.

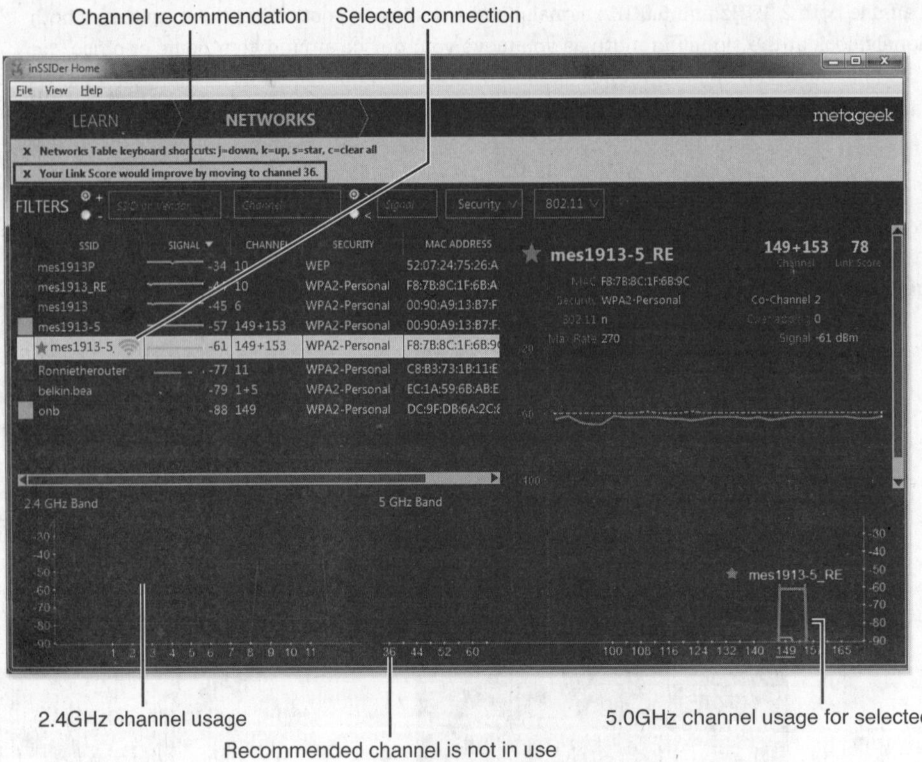

Figure 3.7 Wifi Analyzer showed big changes in signal strength as I moved around my home.

You can adopt three strategies to extend the range of your wireless network:

- Improve antenna positioning.
- Install wireless repeaters or signal boosters.
- Use powerline adapters.

Caution

Some older wireless routers (primarily Wireless-G models) have removable antennas, enabling you to replace stock antennas with higher-gain antennas. However, results are mixed, and with many new routers lacking provision for replacement antennas, it's best to look at other methods for extending the range of your network.

Improving Antenna Positioning

The antennas in your wireless router and the adapters your computers use to connect to the router are the first keys to better range and signal strength.

- If your router has external antennas, adjust them to different angles to help improve signal quality.
- If your router has internal antennas, consider hanging the router on the wall or turning it 90 degrees to improve signal quality.
- Putting your router in a central position in your home or office helps you get maximum useful range, as it broadcasts signals in a 3D "bubble." If your router is located on an outside wall, much of the signal is being broadcast outside of your home or work area.

If you use a USB wireless adapter, consider using a USB extension cable to help get a better signal to your computer. Some USB wireless adapters include this type of cable (see Figure 3.8), or you can buy one from a local or online vendor.

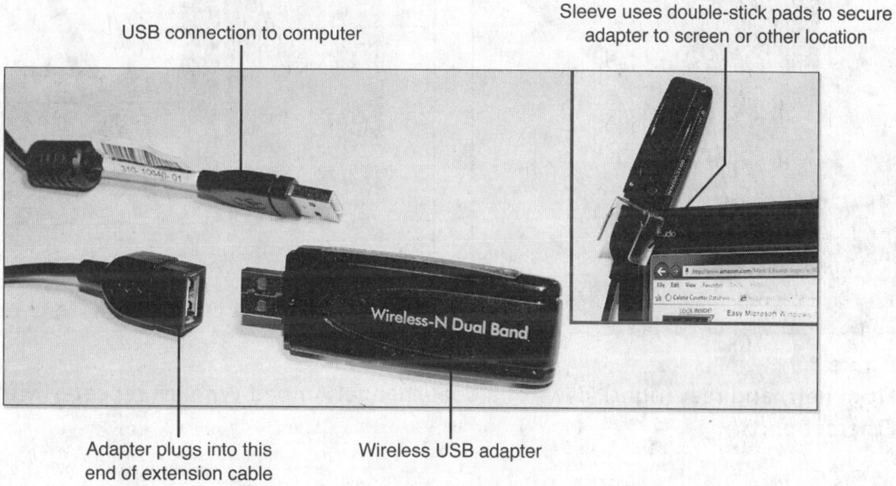

Figure 3.8 Connect your USB wireless adapter to an extension cable and move it away from your desk, and you might get a better signal.

Installing and Using a Signal Repeater

If changing router or antenna positions isn't giving you a strong enough signal in some parts of your home or office, repeat your wireless signal.

A signal repeater is a special type of wireless access point that receives a wireless signal from a router and rebroadcasts it. Some signal repeaters plug directly into an AC wall outlet, and others use a separate AC adapter and resemble a router. Some also include Fast or Gigabit Ethernet ports (see Figure 3.9).

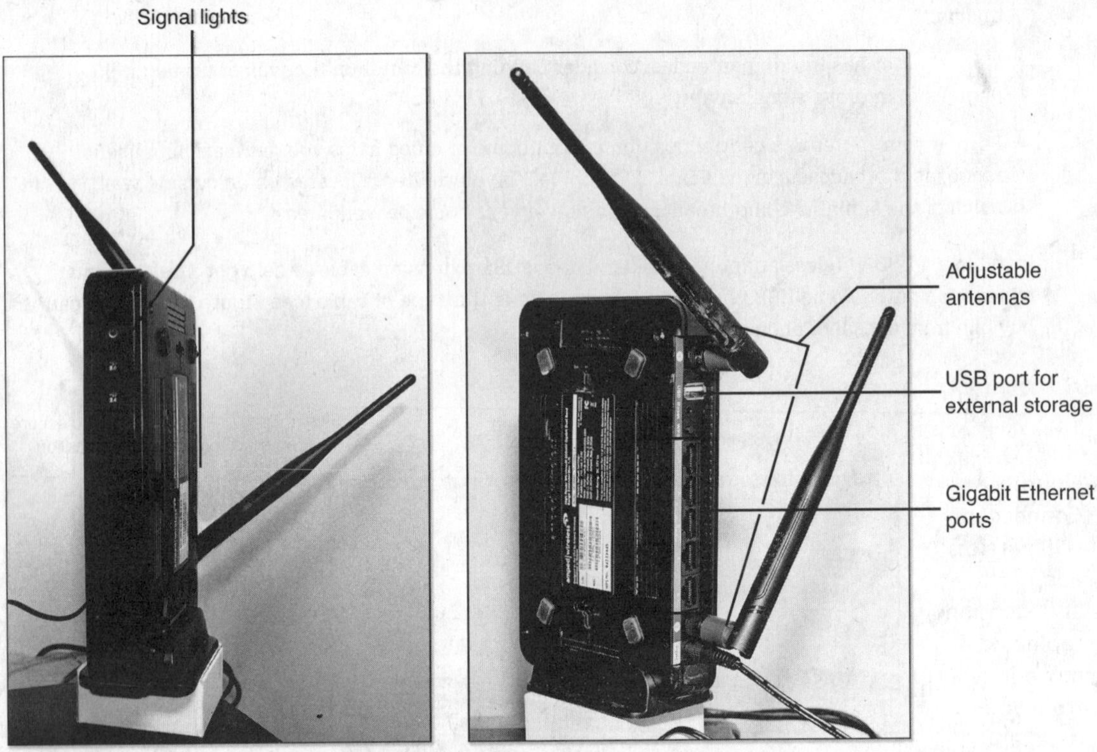

Figure 3.9
Front (left) and rear (right) views of a dual-channel Amped Wireless repeater with built-in Gigabit Ethernet ports.

Here's how to set up a typical unit using WPS:

1. Determine where you want to place the repeater.
2. Plug the repeater into AC power (on some models, the repeater itself plugs into the wall).
3. If you are using Wi-Fi Protected Setup (WPS), press the WPS button on the router and on the repeater or use the PIN number method (depending upon your router and repeater's features). Refer to Figure 3.24.
4. To connect to the repeater, select it from the list of available networks and enter the encryption key (if prompted).

With some models, the instructions are a little different:

1. Determine where you want to place the repeater.
2. Plug the repeater into AC power.

3. Log in to the repeater's web interface with your browser (see the instructions for the correct IP address to use).
4. If the repeater includes a signal-strength analyzer, use it to make sure the repeater is getting a strong enough signal from the router. Move the repeater or adjust its antennas as needed.
5. Specify the desired SSID(s) for each channel (2.4GHz and 5.0GHz). In Figures 3.10 and 3.11, I added the suffix "_RE" to my original router name to indicate the SSID is a repeater.
6. Specify whether to use the same encryption key(s) or enter new encryption keys.
7. Save changes and exit.
8. To connect to the repeater, select it from the list of available networks and enter the encryption key (if prompted).

Figure 3.10 illustrates how a router and repeater might appear in the Windows 7 wireless network connection dialog.

Figure 3.10
Router and repeater signals as shown in a typical Windows 7 wireless connection dialog.

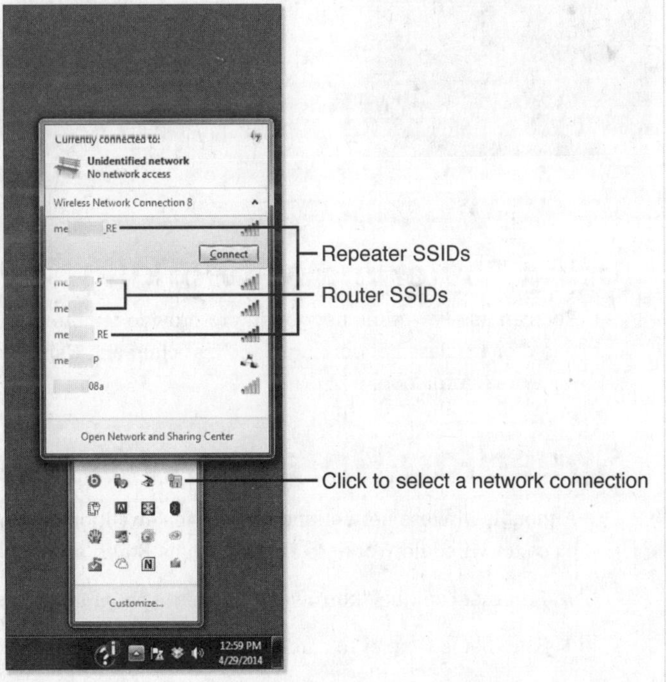

Figure 3.11 illustrates the same devices as shown in Windows 8/8.1.

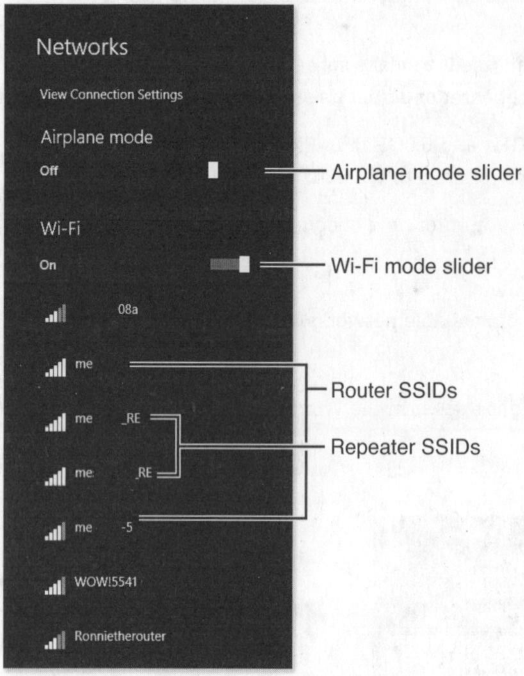

Figure 3.11
Router and repeater signals as shown in a typical Windows 8/8.1 wireless connection dialog.

Using Powerline Networking

You can use Powerline networking to provide remote portions of your home or office with either wired or wireless networking. See "Installing and Using Powerline Adapters," later in this chapter, for more information.

Speeding Up a Slow Wired Network

Although wireless networking gets all the attention in home and office networking, there's still a place for wired networking, also known as Ethernet:

- Ethernet can't be "borrowed" by neighbors or strangers the way Wi-Fi can be.
- Ethernet is simpler to configure than Wi-Fi: just plug it in!
- Gigabit Ethernet is faster than all wireless networks except Wireless-AC.

If you already have wiring in place or have short cable runs you can hide behind furniture or with cable management devices, wired networking can make more sense than wireless. This is especially true if you have brick or concrete walls or other obstacles that make wireless networking slow or that give it limited range.

Gigabit Ethernet (1000Mbps) is the fastest wired Ethernet standard available for home use. It's faster than most wireless networks, making for maximum-speed file sharing, streaming media downloads, and network printing. Here's how to determine whether you're already enjoying Gigabit Ethernet speeds:

1. Go to a Windows computer that is using a wired Ethernet connection in your home or office.
2. Open the Network and Sharing Center (available from Control Panel or from the Network menu).
3. Double-click the Local Area Connection shortcut (see Figure 3.12).

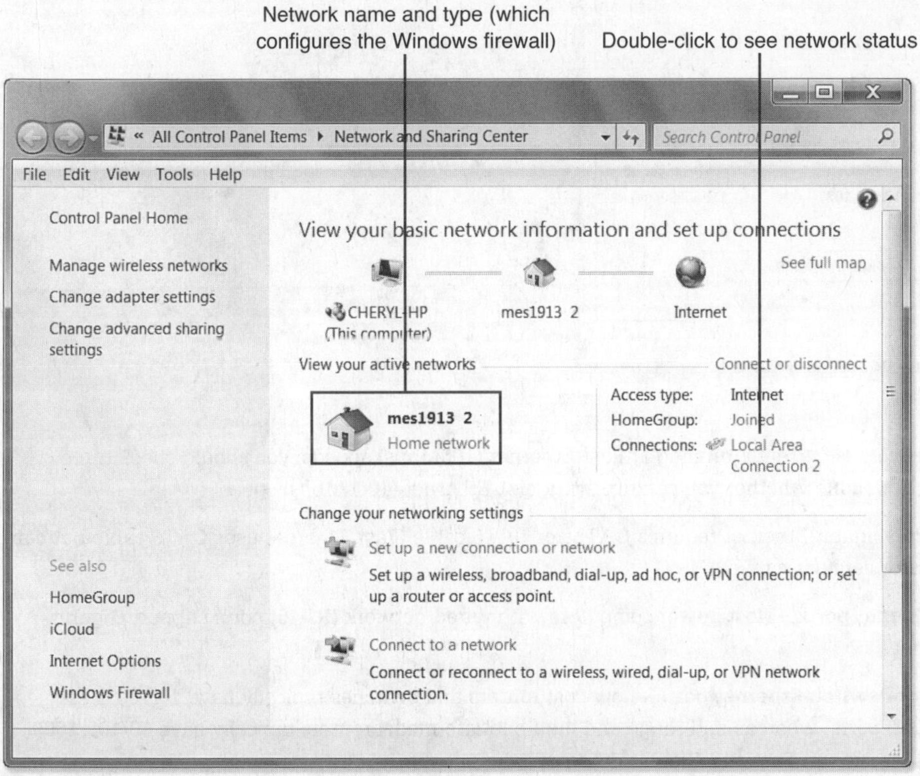

Figure 3.12
The Network and Sharing Center displaying a wired Ethernet (local area) connection.

4. The connection speed is shown in the status box that appears (see Figure 3.13).
5. Close the Status, Network and Sharing, and Control Panel or Network dialogs.

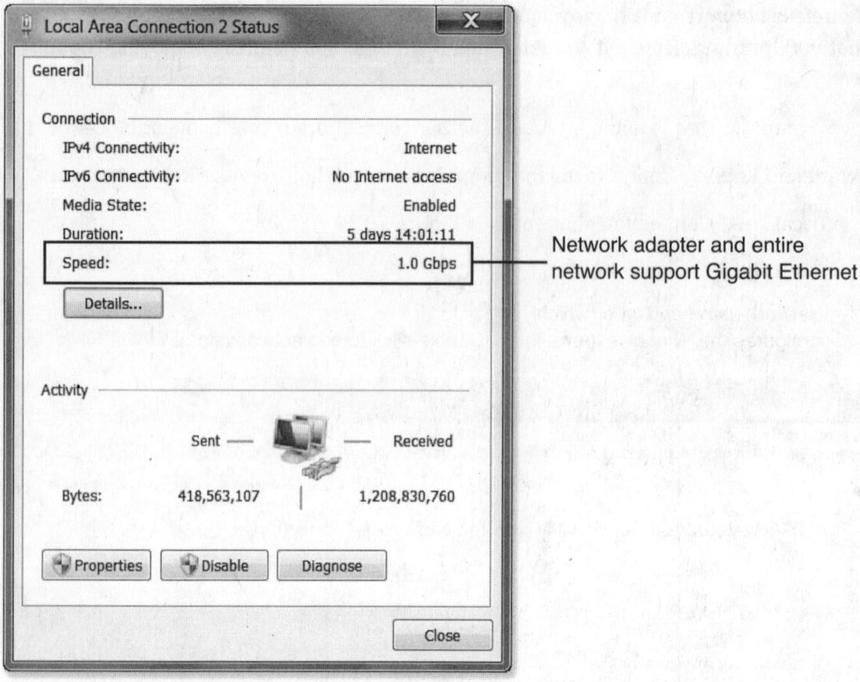

Figure 3.13
This computer is connected to a Gigabit Ethernet network.

If your network is currently running at Fast Ethernet (100Mbps) speeds, you should check three things to determine whether you can run at Gigabit Ethernet (1000Mbps) speeds:

- **Wiring**—Gigabit Ethernet requires CAT5e or CAT6 cable (Fast Ethernet uses CAT5 cable but can use faster versions as well).
- **PC Ethernet ports**—Most newer computers with wired network (RJ-45) ports support Gigabit Ethernet.
- **Router or switch Ethernet ports**—Low-cost routers and switches typically have 10/100 (Fast Ethernet) ports, whereas mid-range and high-end late-model routers typically have 10/100/1000 ports that support Fast and Gigabit Ethernet.

How can you check the specifications for each of these potential bottlenecks? Read on for the answers.

Checking Your Network Cable

To see what type of network cable you have, examine the cables themselves. Figure 3.14 illustrates a typical CAT5e cable and its markings.

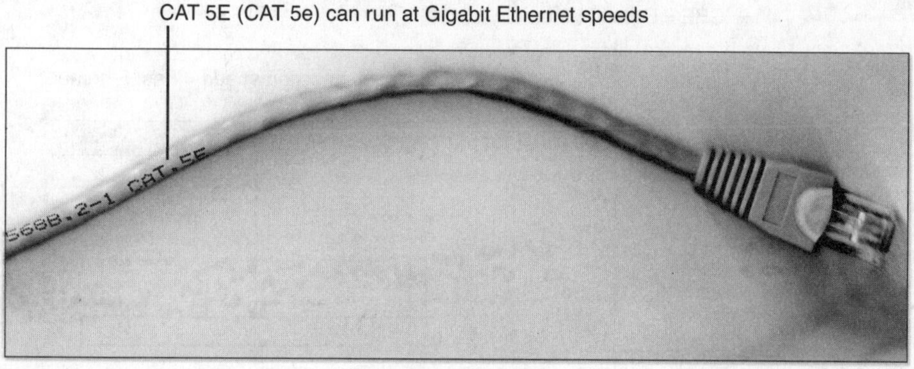

Figure 3.14 Typical markings on a CAT5e cable.

> **Note**
> If your Ethernet cabling is built in to the wall, you might be able to see the cable markings by removing the cover of an RJ-45 wall jack. You can also hire a network cable installer to test your network for Gigabit Ethernet compatibility. If your cable was installed as part of new construction, check with your builder to determine what type of network cable was used.

If all the cables between your wireless router, wired router, or switches and your computers are CAT5e or CAT6, your network has the potential to run at Gigabit speeds. However, if you find CAT5 cable, don't replace it until you determine which of your computers or devices have Gigabit Ethernet ports.

Checking Your Computers for Gigabit Ports

To determine whether the network port(s) in your computers support Gigabit Ethernet, follow this procedure in Windows 7 or from the Windows 8/8.1 desktop:

1. Open Windows Explorer (Windows 7) or File Explorer (Windows 8/8.1).
2. Right-click **Computer** (Windows 7) or This PC (Windows 8/8.1). and select **Properties**.
3. Open Device Manager.
4. Expand the Network Adapters category.
5. Look for an entry that reads Gigabit Ethernet, GBE, or similar (see Figure 3.15).
6. Close Device Manager and System properties.

> **Note**
> If you cannot determine the network type supported from Device Manager, search for the network adapter name online to determine what speed of Ethernet it supports.

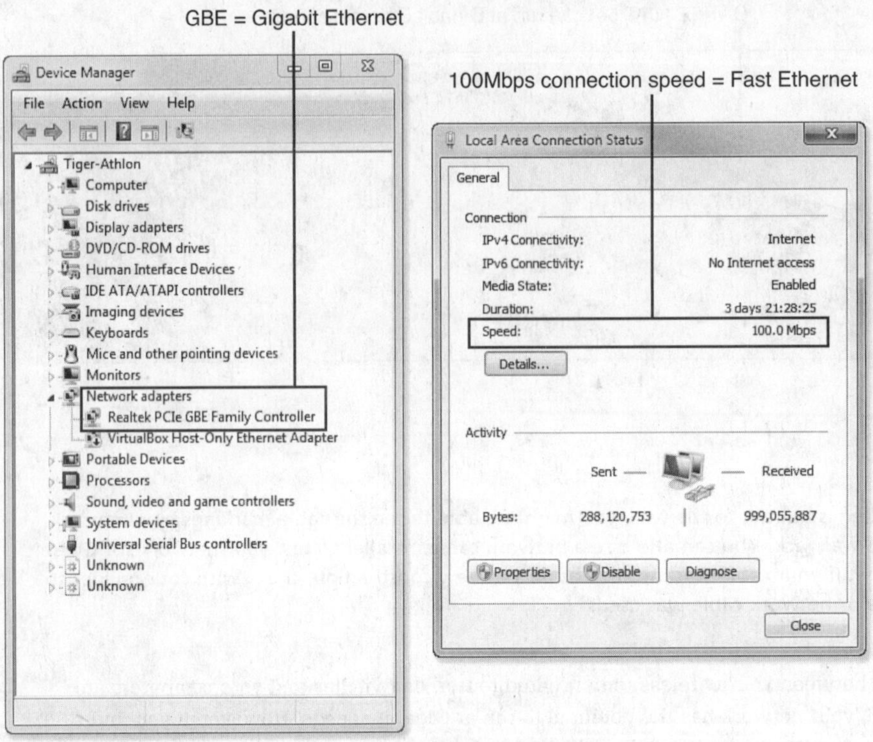

Figure 3.15 This computer has a Gigabit Ethernet port, but connects to the router only at Fast Ethernet speeds.

Checking Your Router or Switch

To determine whether your router or switch supports Gigabit Ethernet, use one of the following methods:

- If you can get access to the router or switch, determine its name and revision number, and then look up the router's specifications online. Many current-model routers, including those with 802.11ac support (the fastest Wireless standard), support Fast Ethernet (100Mbps) rather than Gigabit Ethernet.
- If you cannot access the router or switch, compare the speeds supported to the status of the network connection (refer to Figure 3.15). If the wiring used between the adapter and router or switch is CAT5e or CAT6, and the network adapter supports Gigabit Ethernet, the router supports only Fast Ethernet speeds.

> **Note**
> Three other factors can slow down your network: the presence of sub-standard keystone jacks (the wall plugs used for Ethernet connections), female/female Ethernet adapters (used to connect two cables together for longer runs), or the use of one or more Ethernet hubs.
>
> If your wired network contains one or more Ethernet hubs, replace them with Ethernet switches. A hub resembles a switch physically, but it subdivides the total bandwidth of the connection among the connected ports. For example, if you have a Fast Ethernet (100Mbps) hub with four ports in use, each port gets only 25Mbps connection speed.

Installing and Using Powerline Adapters

Although HomePlug (which transmits network signals through your home power lines) is not as well known as Ethernet or Wi-Fi, it represents a useful way to extend a network when it's not feasible to repeat a wireless signal to other parts of your home or office.

> **Note**
> The original 85Mbps HomePlug standard has been replaced by faster HomePlug AV (200Mbps) and HomePlug AV2 (500Mbps) standards. You can determine the version of HomePlug supported by the rated speed of the adapter.

A HomePlug network includes two transceivers:

- One plugs into an AC wall outlet and connects to a wired Ethernet port on a router or switch.
- The other transceiver plugs into another AC wall outlet, enabling you to connect your device via Ethernet.
- In some kits, the second transceiver includes a Wi-Fi transceiver. If the transceiver includes both an Ethernet port and a Wi-Fi transceiver, you can use either wired or wireless Ethernet (Wi-Fi) connections for the remote device.

To add an additional device, buy a compatible adapter. If the devices are just a few feet away from the remote adapter, you can connect the adapter to the uplink port on a Fast or Gigabit Ethernet switch to share the connection among multiple devices.

To make the connection between the transceivers, just plug them in and push a button on each adapter to pair them (you can use more than two adapters on most HomePlug networks). Figure 3.16 illustrates a typical setup using two adapters and an Ethernet switch.

HomePlug is a good choice for masonry or concrete construction because it is not affected by solid walls or heavy ceilings.

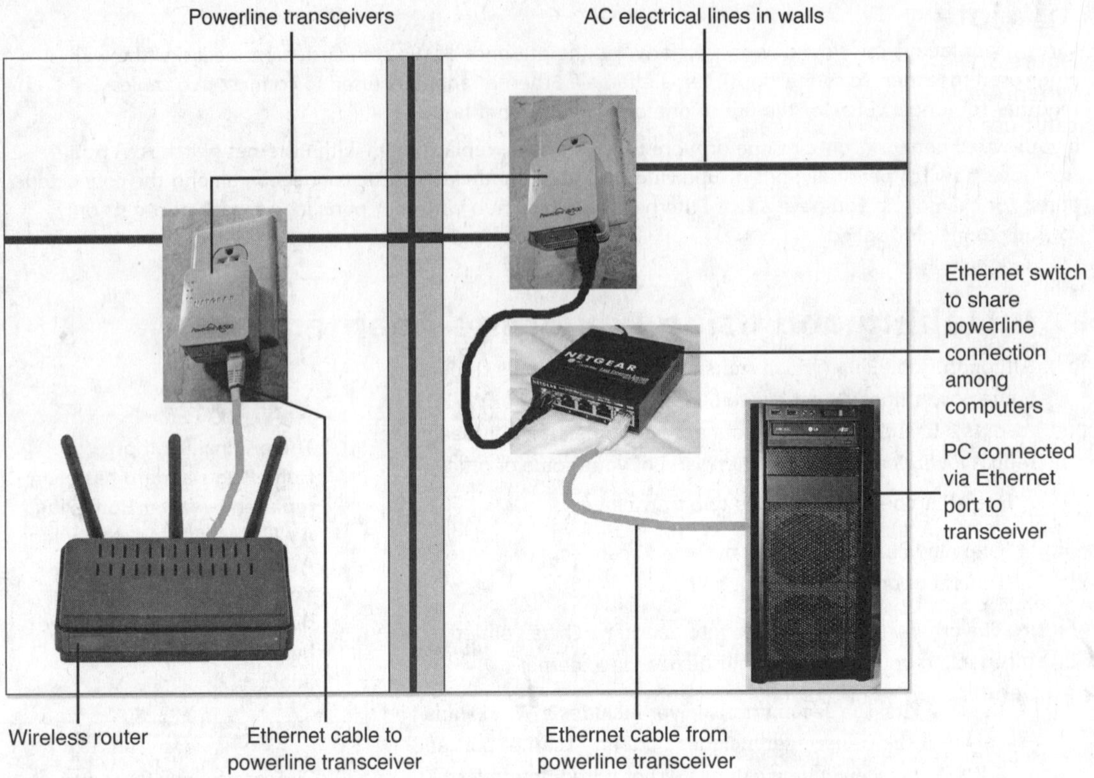

Figure 3.16
A typical HomePlug AV2 network.

Airplane Mode Versus Wi-Fi Mode

If you are unable to connect your mobile device to a wireless network or to a cellular network, your device might be set to Airplane mode. Airplane mode (see Figure 3.17) shuts off all radios in your device, including Wi-Fi, Bluetooth, and cellular. This setting, originally developed to enable mobile device users to use their devices during airplane takeoffs and landings, has other benefits:

- Longer battery life.
- Privacy.
- Mobile devices typically display a small airplane icon in their notification area when Airplane mode is enabled.

To enable Airplane mode, use the Settings menu in your mobile device (see Figure 3.18). On Windows 8/8.1, you can enable Airplane mode from the Networks menu (refer to Figure 3.11).

Figure 3.17
When Airplane mode is enabled, you can't use Google or other data services.

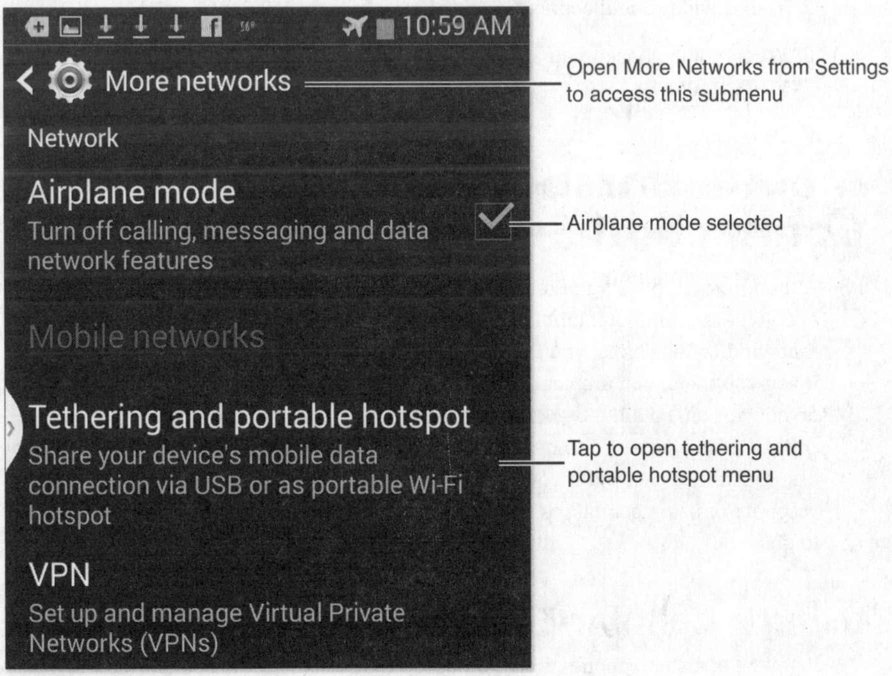

Figure 3.18
Enabling Airplane mode on a Samsung Android-based smartphone.

Tip

By default, Airplane mode disables all communication to and from your device. However, you can selectively enable Wi-Fi or Bluetooth on most devices after you enable Airplane mode. You can use this feature to bypass your phone's cellular connection, saving you money when traveling outside your cellular network provider area or while visiting a foreign country (see http://52tiger.net/enable-iphone-airplane-mode-keep-wifi-while-traveling/).

Switching Connection Types Manually

When you use a mobile device with both Wi-Fi and cellular data services, keep in mind that you can use only one service at a time. Typical device configuration has Wi-Fi running all the time with automatic connection when you revisit a hotspot you've already configured (such as at home or the office).

However, you might run into a situation in which your device is connected to a weak Wi-Fi signal that's not good enough to use or has no Internet connection, although you have a 3G or 4G signal that's strong enough but ignored by your device. In those cases, follow this procedure:

1. Go into your device's Settings menu and turn off Wi-Fi.
2. Your device should connect automatically to your cellular network.
3. When you go back to an area that has a higher-quality Wi-Fi signal with Internet access, enable Wi-Fi again.

Mobile Hotspots and Connection Security

Although signs offering "Free Wi-Fi" are showing up almost everywhere, from hotel lobbies and convention centers to restaurants and coffee shops, you might not want to use those services. If you use them, you are connecting to an unsecure network. With no encryption, email, e-banking, online shopping, and other transactions can be exposed to hackers. Free connections are great for casual Internet use, but if you're trying to work or sign in to bank accounts or use e-commerce, a free connection is not the way to go.

Tip

If you have a secure remote connection service running on your office or home computer, such as Go To My PC, you can connect to that service and use your remote connection to check email or use e-commerce websites. Just use the web browser on the remote computer for your transactions.

Using a Cellular-Enabled Device as a Hotspot

If you have a smartphone, tablet, or laptop that can share its cellular data connection, you have a secure connection for your laptop or tablet. You can share your connection with a single device by using USB tethering, or you can share the connection with multiple devices by using the Wi-Fi hotspot feature.

Using USB Tethering

If you want to use USB tethering, follow these steps:

1. Connect a USB cable from your computer to the data port on your device.
2. Select the USB tethering option on your device (see Figure 3.19).
3. If you are connecting a Windows computer, select the network type (Home) when prompted.
4. Use your computer's web browser and other network features normally.
5. When you're finished, disable USB tethering.

Note

In Device Manager, you will find the tethered USB connection listed as Remote NDIS based Internet Sharing Device in the Network Adapters category.

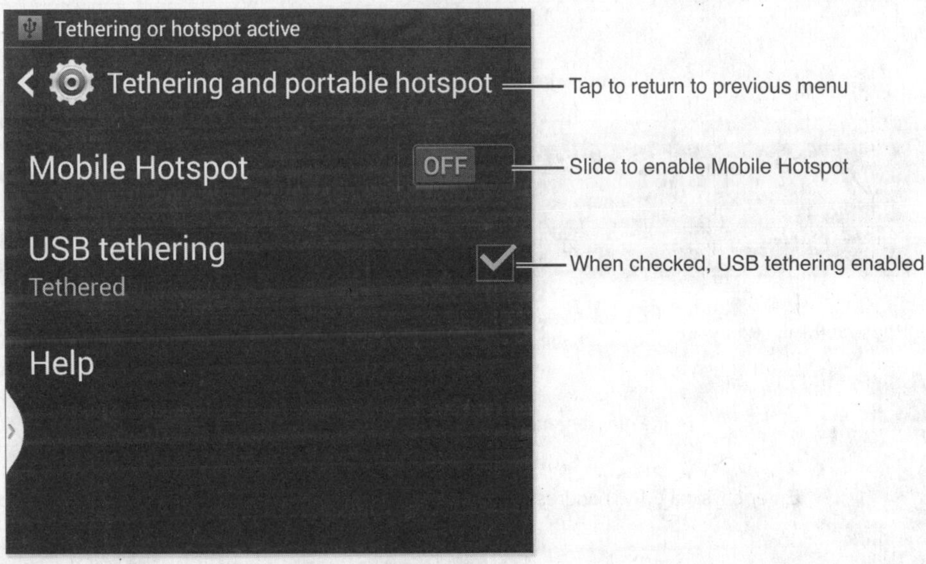

Figure 3.19 Enabling USB tethering mode on a Samsung Android-based smartphone.

Using a Wi-Fi Hotspot

If you decide to use the mobile hotspot feature, follow these steps:

1. Enable the mobile hotspot feature.
2. Select how you want to share your connection wirelessly.

3. If you decide to permit only allowed devices to connect, you must provide a name for each device and its MAC address. The MAC address is listed on a label attached to an external adapter. With either internal or external network adapters, open a command prompt window and use the command `IPConfig/all` to see the MAC (physical) address for the device (see Figure 3.20).
4. Open the Allowed devices menu (refer to Figure 3.21), open Add Device, and enter the address in the display provided (refer to Figure 3.20).

Note

To open a command prompt window in Windows 7, click Start, type `cmd`, and press Enter. To open a command prompt window in Windows 8/8.1, press the Windows Logo+X keys and click Command Prompt. To open a command prompt window from the Windows 8/8.1 desktop, open the Charms menu, click **Search**, type `cmd`, and press Enter. To close the window after you find and write down the MAC address, type `exit` and press Enter.

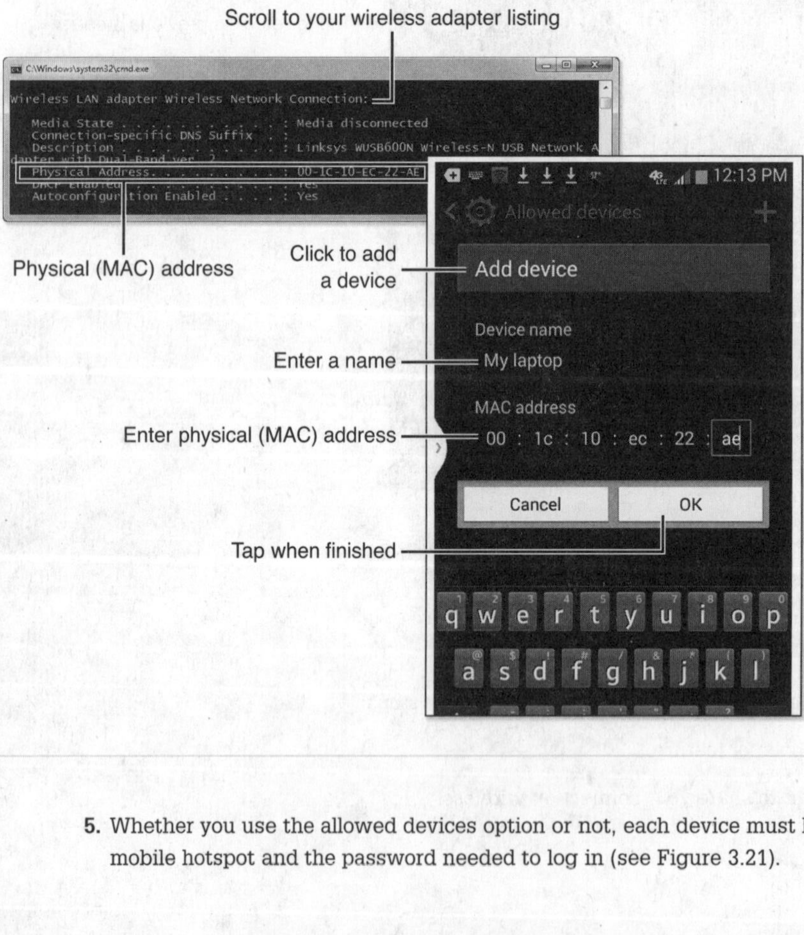

Figure 3.20 Using `IPConfig/all` to display the physical MAC address for your computer and entering it into the Add Device menu on a Samsung Android-based smartphone.

5. Whether you use the allowed devices option or not, each device must be given the SSID for your mobile hotspot and the password needed to log in (see Figure 3.21).

Figure 3.21 Use the SSID (network name) and password listed here to connect to the wireless hotspot.

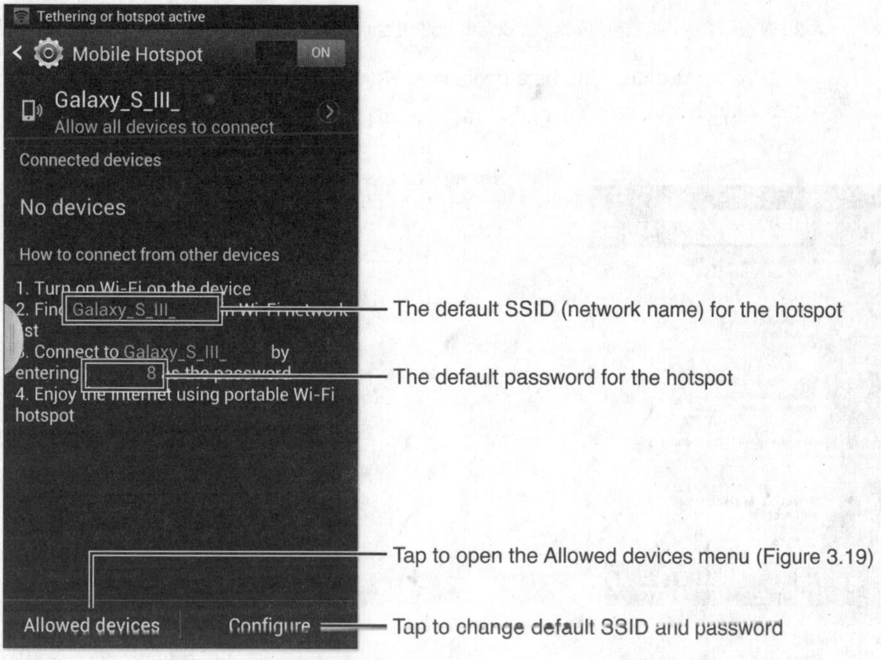

6. Make the connection the same as with any other wireless Internet router or hotspot. Enter the password when prompted.

7. When your devices are finished using the Internet, you should disable the hotspot setting in your device.

Caution

Some cellular providers charge an additional fee if you turn your cellular device into a hotspot. Check with your mobile service provider for details. And keep in mind that the data usage of every device connected to a mobile hotspot is counted toward your total data allocation. If you're not careful, using a mobile hotspot could cost you extra money in overages.

Switching Between Mobile and Desktop Websites

Many websites are designed to support mobile devices with a mobile-optimized version that's easier to read on a small screen. However, if you find that the mobile-optimized version leaves out too much information, there's usually a way to switch to the desktop version:

1. Open the website on your device. If the mobile version is displayed, scroll around until you locate a link to the desktop version (see Figure 3.22).

2. Click the link to open the desktop version.
3. When the desktop version opens, click the Bookmark tool in your browser (see Figure 3.23).
4. Save the desktop URL as a bookmark. Next time you want to go to the desktop version, select the bookmark you created.

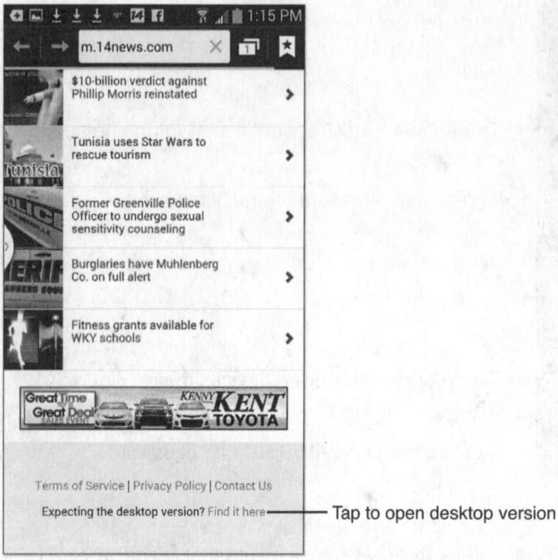

Figure 3.22
Switching to the desktop version of a mobile website.

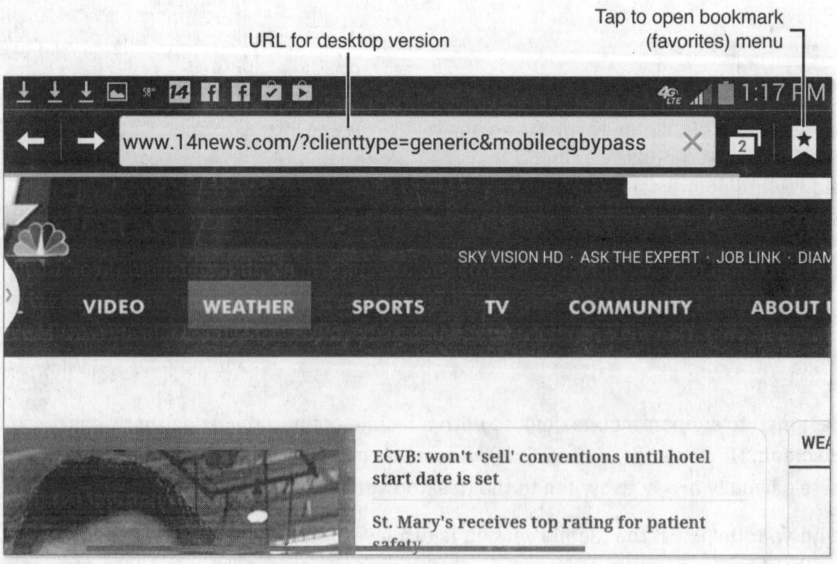

Figure 3.23
Preparing to select the desktop version as a bookmark (favorite).

Router Configuration

To take advantage of the recommendations in this chapter, you might need to adjust the configuration of your wireless router. To get started, follow these steps:

1. Even if you normally connect to your router wirelessly, connect an Ethernet cable to one of the router's switch ports and to the Ethernet port on your computer. Although a few routers can be managed wirelessly, most require you to use a wired connection to view or change settings.
2. Enter the IP address for your router into your web browser. If you don't know the IP address, check your router documentation. You can typically get a PDF or web page version from the router vendor.
3. Provide the username and password when prompted. The default settings are provided in your router documentation. If you change them, be sure to record them for reference.

> **Tip**
> Use `IPConfig/all` from the command prompt to display the IP configuration information for all network adapters in your computer. The Default Gateway listed for your Ethernet port is the IP address of your router.

To change wireless settings such as network name (SSID), security, encryption key (password), channel, and others, go to the Wireless Setup dialog (refer to Figure 3.2).

If you need to use WPS to set up a device, go to the Wi-Fi Protected Setup dialog (see Figure 3.24).

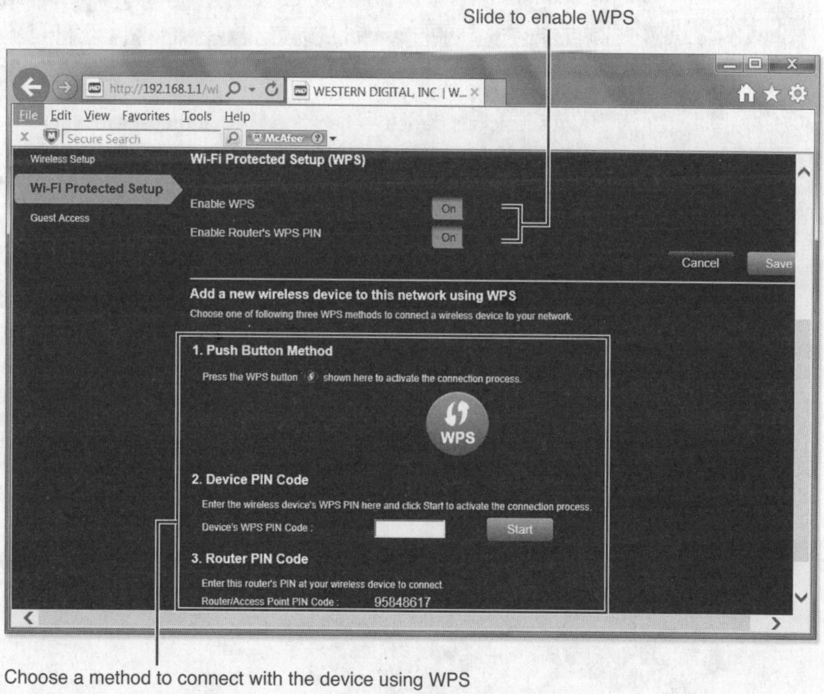

Figure 3.24 This router supports three methods for using WPS.

Use the Device and Client (MAC address, physical address, device listing) table feature to see the names and MAC (physical) addresses of the devices connected to your network (see Figure 3.25).

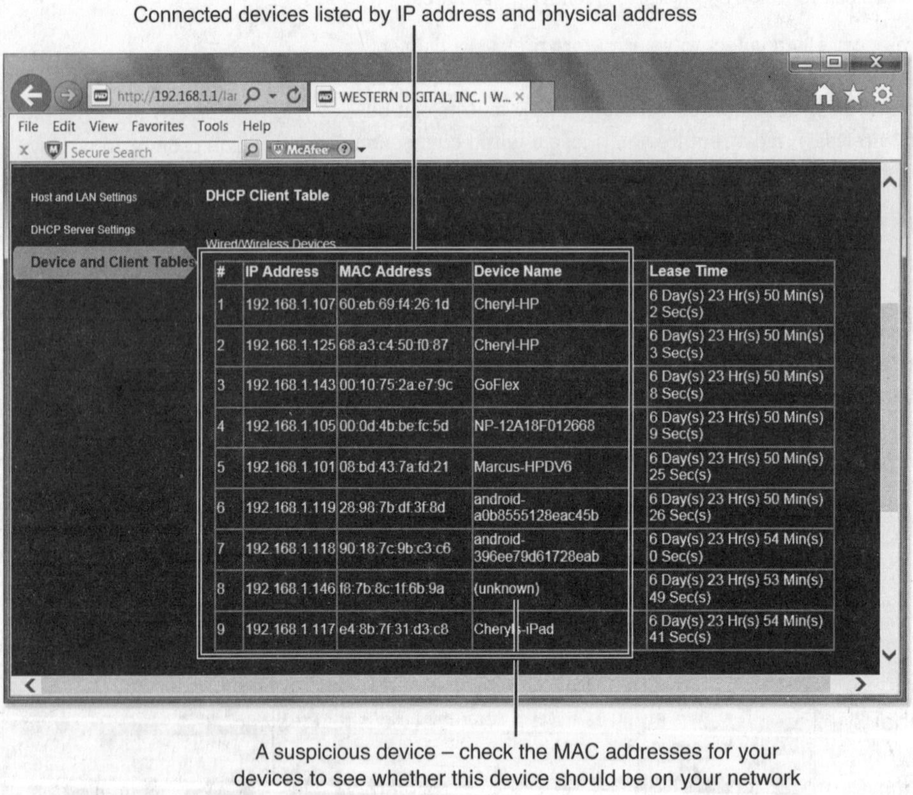

Figure 3.25 Viewing devices connected to the router.

If some game systems are having difficulty connecting to the Internet through the router, you might need to set up port forwarding, or you can set the router to provide direct pass-through of all Internet traffic to and from a particular device on the network (Demilitarized Zone, or DMZ). To make these changes, look for your router's advanced menu.

When you are finished making changes, save your changes (on some routers, there's a Save button at the bottom of each screen) and close the browser. If you normally don't use a wired connection to your router, disconnect the Ethernet cable from your computer. Leave it connected to the router for future use.

Firmware Updates

Firmware, also known as "software on a chip," controls the basic functions of both routers and mobile devices, such as tablets and smartphones. Firmware updates are used to solve problems with a device or to add features.

To obtain a firmware update for a smartphone or tablet, contact the wireless service vendor or the device manufacturer.

Note

For more about the update process, see Chapter 14, "Keeping Your Devices Updated."

Updating Your Router

Firmware updates for your router can come from one of two locations:

- The router manufacturer
- A third-party firmware provider, such as DD-WRT

Vendor-Provided Firmware

To obtain a router update from your vendor:

1. Check the model number and version number of your router. This information is typically provided on a label on the bottom or side of the router. Because different router models might use different chipsets, you must know exactly which router model you are updating.
2. To determine the firmware version that's installed, log in to your router. This information might be located on the initial login page or elsewhere; check your router's documentation for details.
3. To obtain an updated version, go to the router vendor's website and visit the Support or Downloads section of the website. Look up your router and see the firmware revisions available and the problems they fix (see Figure 3.26).
4. If a different firmware revision will solve problems you're having with your router, download the newest firmware revision. The newest version incorporates all previous fixes as well as the specific fixes noted.
5. Before you install the new firmware, be sure to document your router's current settings. You can use screen capture in Windows or a digital camera set for close-ups. This is especially important if you have changed default settings for the router login username and password or have set up port forwarding or other advanced features. Some of these settings could be lost during the update process.
6. Follow the instructions provided in your documentation or on the website for installing the firmware revision. In most cases, you will need to log in to your router with a wired Ethernet connection. If your router has a USB port for use with external storage, you might need to copy the firmware update file to a USB flash drive.

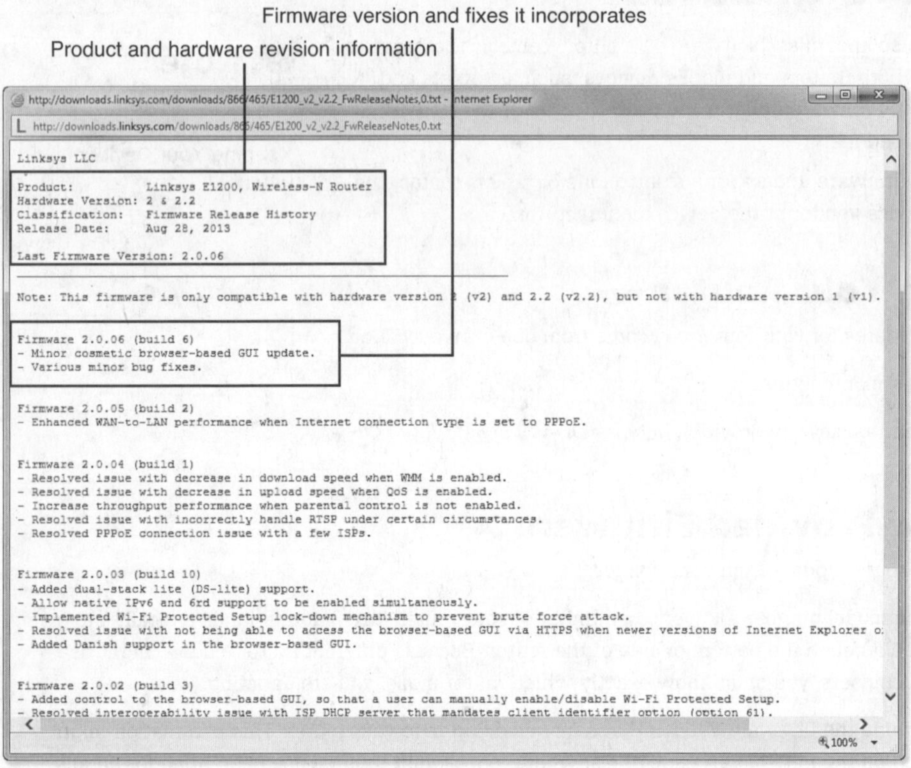


```
Linksys LLC

Product:          Linksys E1200, Wireless-N Router
Hardware Version: 2 & 2.2
Classification:   Firmware Release History
Release Date:     Aug 28, 2013

Last Firmware Version: 2.0.06

Note: This firmware is only compatible with hardware version 2 (v2) and 2.2 (v2.2), but not with hardware version 1 (v1).

Firmware 2.0.06 (build 6)
- Minor cosmetic browser-based GUI update.
- Various minor bug fixes.

Firmware 2.0.05 (build 2)
- Enhanced WAN-to-LAN performance when Internet connection type is set to PPPoE.

Firmware 2.0.04 (build 1)
- Resolved issue with decrease in download speed when WMM is enabled.
- Resolved issue with decrease in upload speed when QoS is enabled.
- Increase throughput performance when parental control is not enabled.
- Resolved issue with incorrectly handle RTSP under certain circumstances.
- Resolved PPPoE connection issue with a few ISPs.

Firmware 2.0.03 (build 10)
- Added dual-stack lite (DS-lite) support.
- Allow native IPv6 and 6rd support to be enabled simultaneously.
- Implemented Wi-Fi Protected Setup lock-down mechanism to prevent brute force attack.
- Resolved issue with not being able to access the browser-based GUI via HTTPS when newer versions of Internet Explorer o:
- Added Danish support in the browser-based GUI.

Firmware 2.0.02 (build 3)
- Added control to the browser-based GUI, so that a user can manually enable/disable Wi-Fi Protected Setup.
- Resolved interoperability issue with ISP DHCP server that mandates client identifier option (option 61).
```

Figure 3.26 A portion of the release notes for a Linksys E1200 router's firmware revisions.

7. After the update is complete, you will need to reset or restart your router.
8. Redo any custom settings that were changed by the update. Use the documentation you created in step 5.

> **Caution**
>
> If you find that revised firmware is causing other problems, you might want to try an earlier revision. We don't recommend upgrading firmware just "because it's there." A firmware update should be done only when it solves a particular problem on your network.

DD-WRT and Other Third-Party Router Firmware

Although updated firmware can correct problems with your router's operation, you might still be disappointed with your router's features. However, your router might have hidden features that can be accessed if your router can use third-party firmware (firmware produced by a vendor other than the router vendor).

Many (but not all) routers support third-party firmware. There are numerous third-party router firmware projects (see http://en.wikipedia.org/wiki/List_of_wireless_router_firmware_projects for a partial list). The best-known of these is DD-WRT.

DD-WRT was originally developed for the Linksys WRT54G series of wireless routers but now supports dozens of models from many vendors. In Figure 3.27, DD-WRT is running on a Netgear WDNR3400. DD-WRT is also being used as the original firmware for a number of current and forthcoming routers from companies such as Buffalo and Linksys.

DD-WRT provides comprehensive, easy-to-view information about your wireless network's configuration and enables many routers to be used as bridges to other networks, as access points, or as repeaters, and to control advanced settings for coexistence with Bluetooth and other wireless networks.

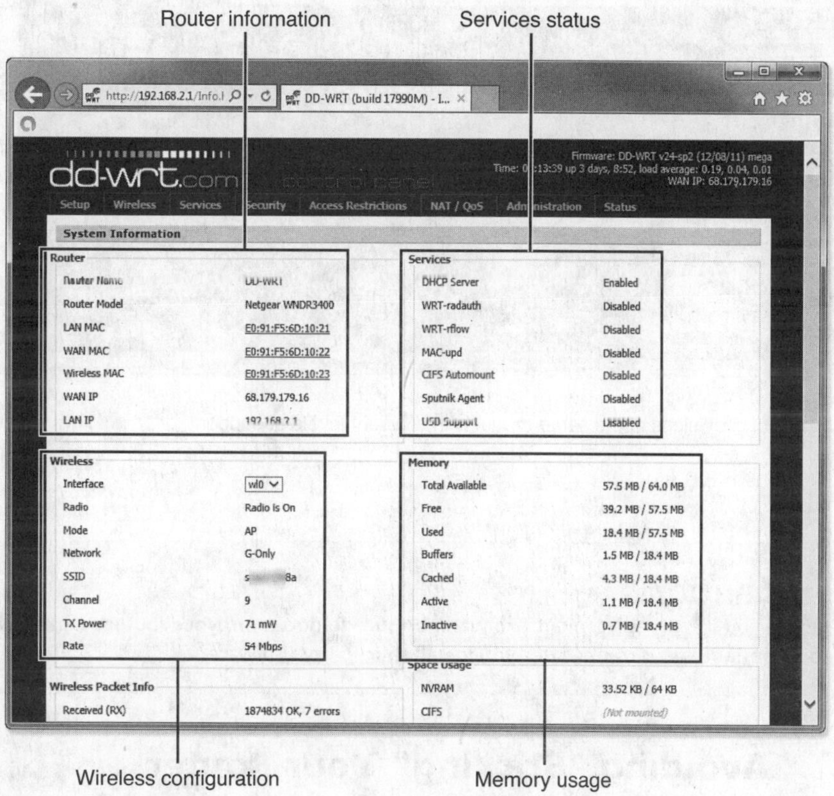

Figure 3.27
A portion of the System Information dialog for a Netgear router running DD-WRT firmware.

To determine whether your router model and revision is supported by DD-WRT, go to the DD-WRT website (www.dd-wrt.com) and use the Router Database to look up your router manufacturer. As you can see from Figure 3.28, it's essential to know the revision as well as the model number of your router because some revisions of a particular router are not supported.

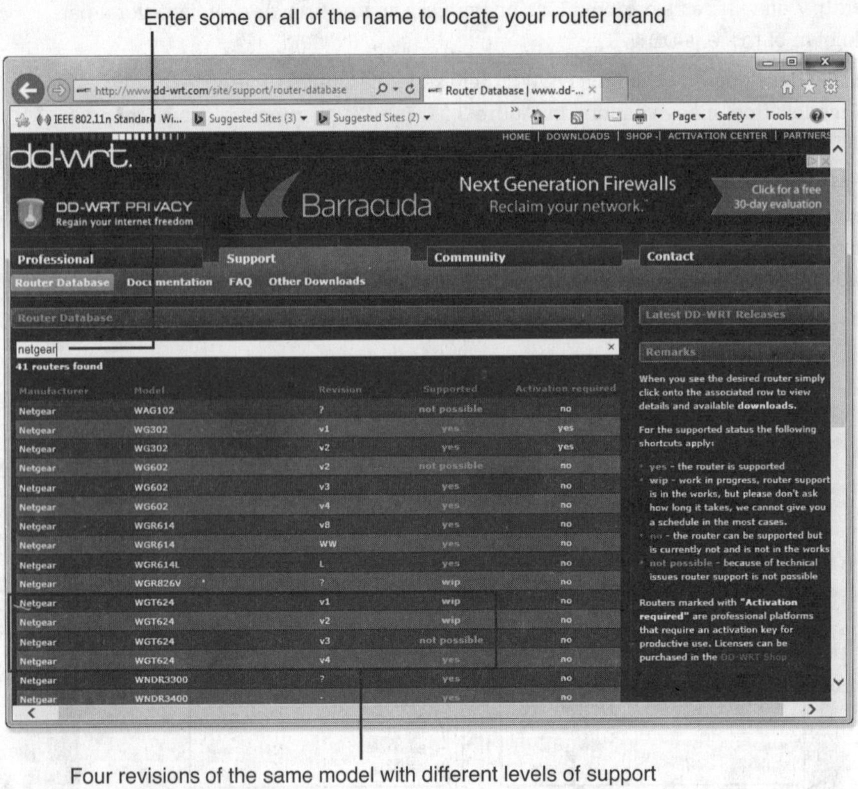

Figure 3.28 A portion of the DD-WRT Router Database listing.

Caution

Before you install replacement firmware, be sure to document your router's current settings. You will need to reconfigure your router after you install third-party firmware.

Avoiding "Bricking" Your Router

The term "bricking" is slang for rendering your device useless through a bad firmware update. To avoid this problem, follow these guidelines:

- If you are installing a firmware update from a PC (desktop or laptop), use a wired Ethernet connection.
- If you are using a laptop, make sure it's plugged into a working AC outlet.

- Do not start the update process if power might be interrupted. If the power goes out during an update, your update fails, and your router will need to be serviced.
- Be sure to download the firmware made for your router number *and* revision. Router manufacturers are notorious for changing the components used in different revisions of a particular model while leaving the exterior trim the same.
- Follow the firmware vendor's directions exactly.

After you complete the process, your router will list the revised firmware version after you log in to it. Depending upon the revision (and particularly if you have installed third-party firmware), you might need to reconfigure some or all of your settings. Use the screen captures or photos you took earlier to help you use the correct settings.

4

CURING MALWARE AND STOPPING SCAMS

Fast Track to Solutions

Table 4.1 Symptom Table

Symptom	Flowchart or Book Section	Page #
I have received a call from Microsoft offering me help with errors on my computer.	Malware Attacks via Phone Calls from Alleged Helplines	114
My web browser is claiming I have viruses on my computer.	Malware Attacks via Your Browser	111
I have received a scary email message from my bank.	Malware Attacks via Email	113
How can I figure out which messages from a company are legitimate?	Avoiding Online and Email Scams	115
How can I tell that a web site is legitimate?	Avoiding Online and Email Scams	115
How can I make sure that Internet Explorer is protecting me?	Microsoft Internet Explorer	118
How can I make sure that Mozilla Firefox is protecting me?	Mozilla Firefox	120
How can I see where a website link goes to?	Check Before You Click	117

Got Malware? What It Is and What It Does

Are you seeing unending pop-up ads on your screen? Has your browser forgotten your home page? Is your formerly fast computer just crawling along? Maybe your browser can't connect to the Internet anymore? These and similar problems might have a single cause: malware.

Malware (short for malicious software) is a general term for software that can slow down your computer, steal information without your knowledge or consent, and threaten your access to your information and to the Internet.

The most common categories of malware include the following:

- **Virus**—A malware program that spreads to other programs when you run it.
- **Trojan horse**—Malware that pretends to help the user (video player, antivirus, and so on). This type of malware often uses names and screen displays that are similar to legitimate programs and apps.
- **Worm**—A malware program that spreads itself automatically over a computer network.
- **Fake security software**—Malware that pretends to find viruses and malware on your system and asks you to pay a fee for removal of the (alleged) malware.
- **Ransomware**—Malware that encrypts (scrambles) your computer's information and issues a demand onscreen for payment so that the process can be reversed. Typically, it includes a time period in which payment must be made to avoid permanent loss of your information.
- **Rootkit**—Malware that hides itself inside the operating system to prevent detection by normal means, such as displaying running programs or processes.
- **Keylogger**—Malware that records each keystroke made on your system, enabling the developer to determine your passwords to various websites, banking information, and other confidential information.
- **Spyware**—Malware that collects information from your computer and transmits it to remote websites.
- **Adware**—Malware that displays pop-up ads, which can slow down your computer.
- **Unwanted browser helper objects (BHOs)**—Malware that changes how your browser works. BHOs can add toolbars to your browser window, redirect searches away from your normal search provider, and change your browser's default home page.

Some legitimate programs might perform some of these tasks. For example, when you install some free programs, you might be asked if you want to install a toolbar or install a new browser as your default. The difference between legitimate programs and malware is that malware makes changes to your computer or web browser without telling you about the changes. Malware works in the shadows. To help you keep your computer running properly and your personal and business information safe, we're going to shine some light on malware and tell you how to deal with it.

Malware Attacks via Your Browser

If you're like most computer or mobile device users, you're probably visiting websites every day, and your web browser can be used as a way to try to deliver malware as well as information. Here are a couple of examples:

A website offers to upgrade your video player (see Figures 4.1 and 4.2).

A website appears to scan your system for viruses and in just a few seconds, displays its results and offers to fix the problem (see Figure 4.3). This fake antivirus program mimics Microsoft Security Essentials, a popular free anti-malware program from Microsoft.

Accept any of these "helpful" offers, and you'll actually install malware on your system.

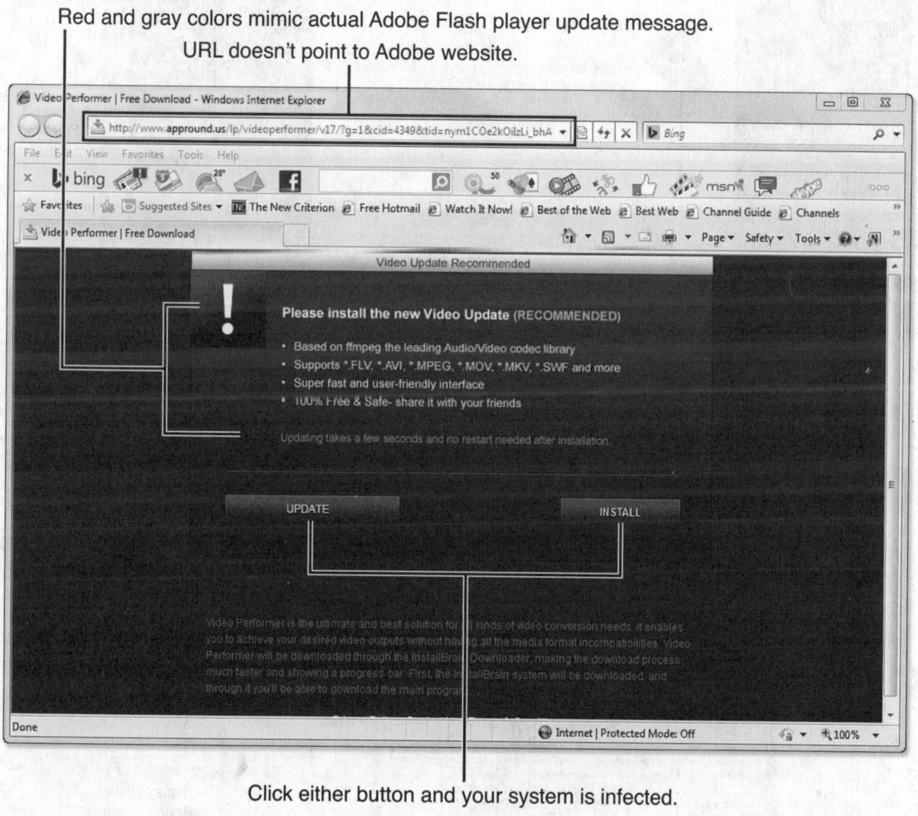

Figure 4.1 A fake video player update that resembles an Adobe Flash player update message.

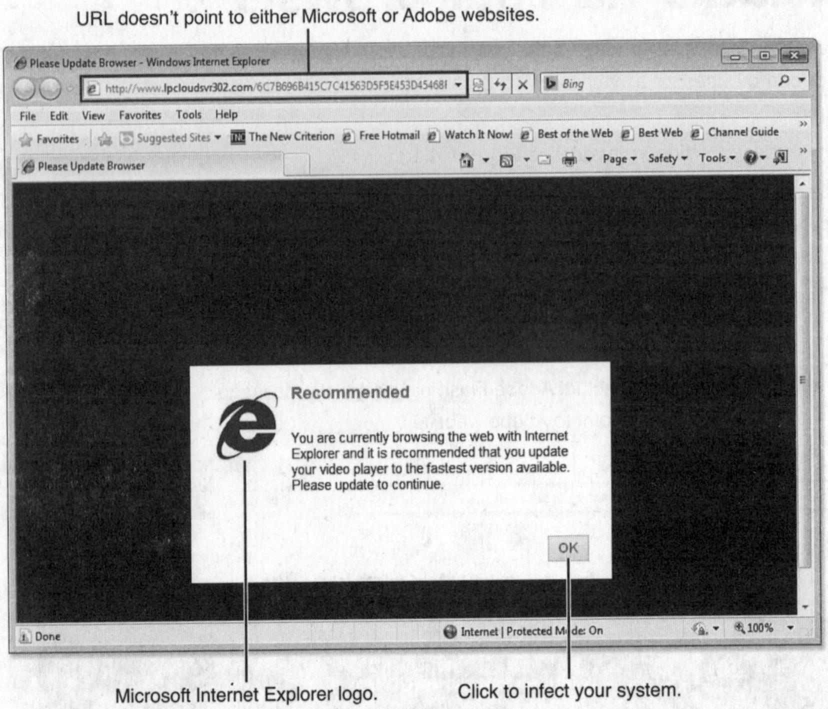

Figure 4.2 A fake video player that resembles an actual Microsoft web page.

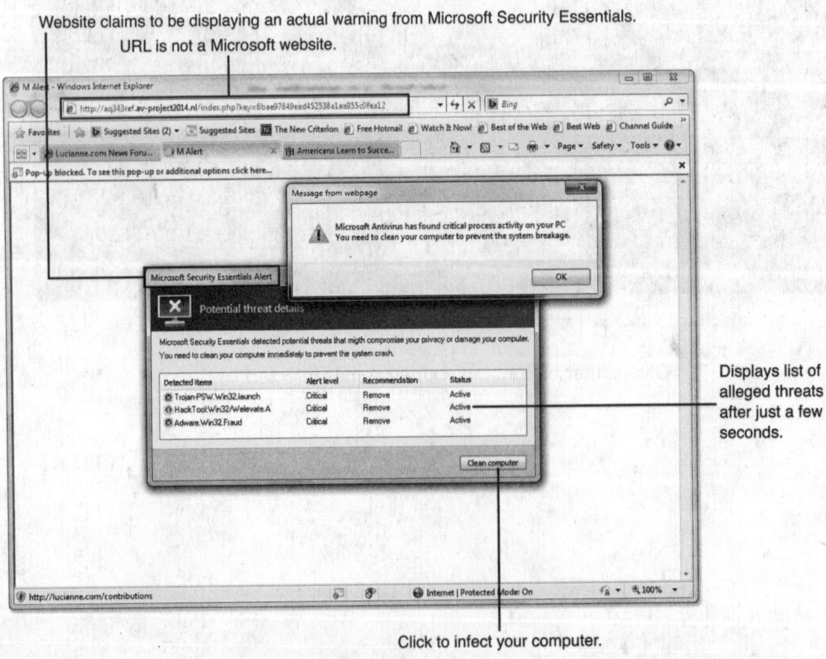

Figure 4.3 A fake antivirus webpage that mimics Microsoft Security Essentials.

Malware Attacks via Email

Emails that purport to be from banks, shippers, or other institutions that you might use are also popular methods of distributing malware. The content of messages (see Figure 4.4 and 4.5) vary, but the objective is to get you to click a link to a file containing malware (Figure 4.4) or a fraudulent website link (Figure 4.5). This type of an attack is also known as "phishing."

Figure 4.4
An email message with malware contained in a compressed (.zip) file that purports to be an invoice.

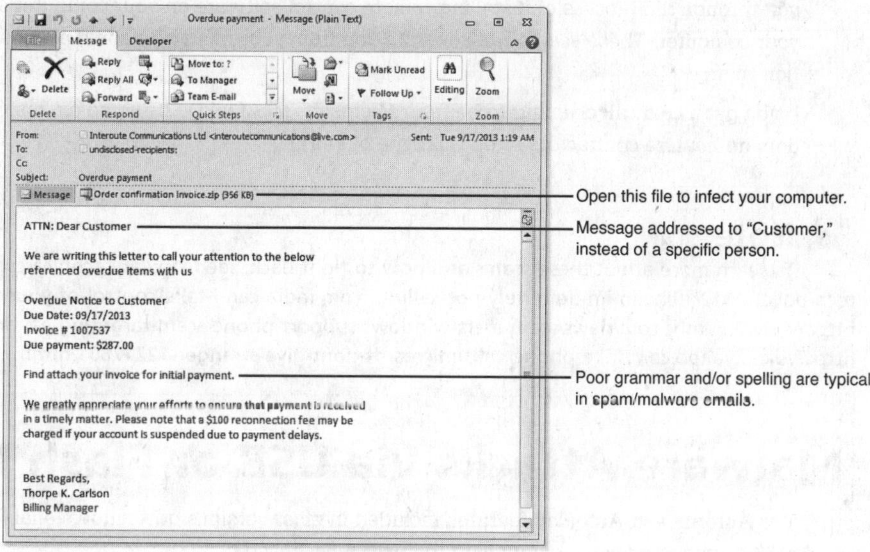

Figure 4.5
An email message with a link purporting to help you reset a bank password.

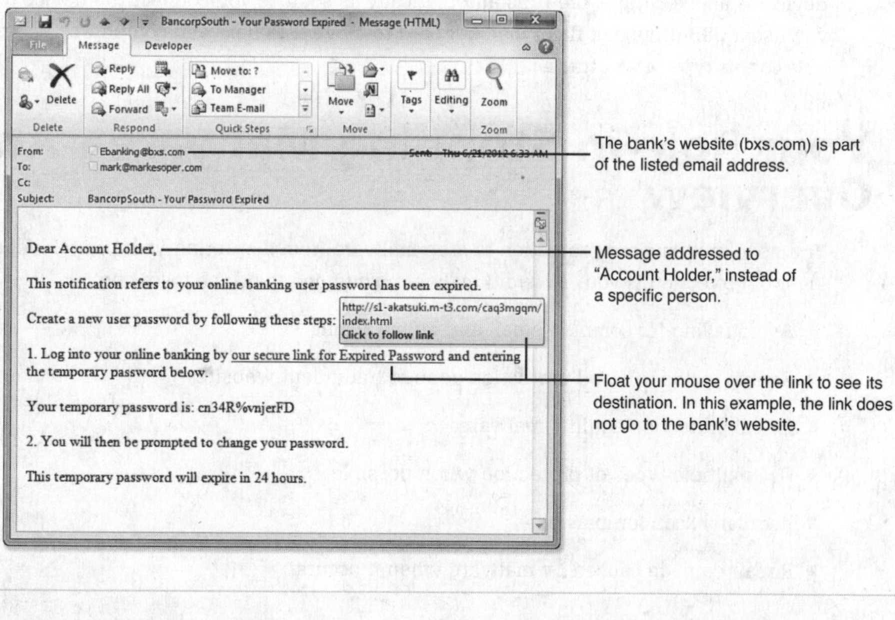

Malware Attacks via Phone Calls from Alleged Helplines

The latest method for convincing you to install malware on your systems is an unsolicited phone call ("cold call") from a person purporting to be a contractor for Microsoft. The caller claims that there are errors on your system, typically by asking you to view the errors listed in Windows Event Viewer. After a misleading pitch about the meaning and severity of these errors, the caller guides you through the process of installing remote control software on your computer and offering to "fix" your computer. These scams can separate you from your money, or could also be used for information theft.

If you get a cold call claiming to be from Microsoft, McAfee, Dell, and so on, just hang up (these vendors do *not* hire contractors to do this type of work).

> **Note**
>
> To learn more about these scams and how to fight back, see http://arstechnica.com/tech-policy/2012/10/hello-im-definitely-not-calling-from-india-can-i-take-control-of-your-pc/, http://www.ketknbc.com/news/scam-alert-windows-support-phone-scam-targeting-ea, and http://voices.yahoo.com/fake-phone-calls-microsoft-dont-give-stranger-12277601.html.

Malware Attacks via USB or Flash Memory

The Autorun and AutoPlay features included in most versions of Windows enable malware infecting a USB drive or a flash memory card to infect a host system.

If your system is configured to automatically start an executable file, any malware stored on your device as an executable file runs automatically as soon as you connect the device to your system. If you use a USB drive or a flash memory card to move files between computers, you might be vulnerable to this type of an attack.

Your Role in Stopping Malware—An Overview

You need multilayered protection to stop malware from disrupting your digital life, and the first layer of protection is you. To avoid malware, you need to do the following:

- Avoid falling for common email and online scams.
- Enable browser-based protection against fraudulent websites.
- Install protection against malware.
- Use multiple types of protection when possible.
- Regularly scan for malware.
- Repair damage caused by malware when it occurs.

Avoiding Online and Email Scams

Scam, *con game*, and *confidence game* are three terms for a series of events that purport to provide you with benefits such as more security, updated information, or more money, but are actually designed to separate you from your money, information, or identity. Many of the threats described earlier in this chapter can be classified as scams or con games.

How can you avoid being scammed? Think carefully about the information or links being provided and avoid suspicious ones. Here are some examples:

- Recognize the differences between legitimate and fraudulent websites.
- Check email links before you click them.
- Beware of Zip-format file attachments.
- Log in to your financial or e-commerce websites with your browser rather than with a link in an email.
- Call your bank or financial institution to determine if an email purporting to come from them was one they actually sent.
- Use browsers designed to warn you of possibly fraudulent websites.

Signs of Fraudulent Websites

One popular method used in creating fraudulent websites is to mimic the legitimate website's "trade dress"—its colors, fonts, and graphic design. For example, compare the fake video player update dialog in Figure 4.1 with this actual Adobe Flash update dialog (see Figure 4.6).

Figure 4.6 An actual Adobe Flash player download page.

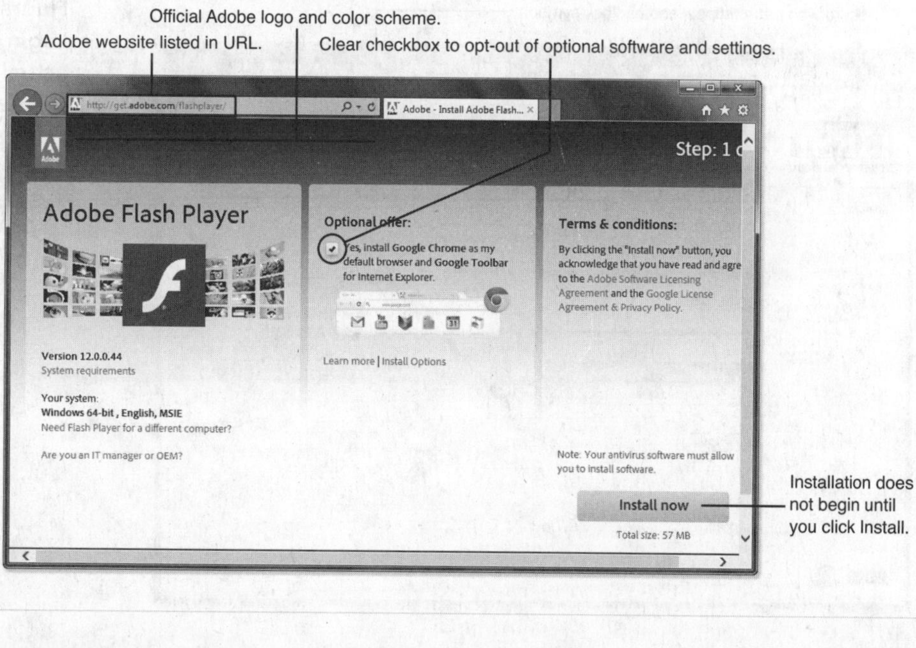

A second tip-off that's especially useful for spotting fraudulent e-commerce and banking sites is the lack of security on the login page. Figure 4.7 shows the login page for a fake bank website, and Figure 4.8 shows the login page for the actual bank website.

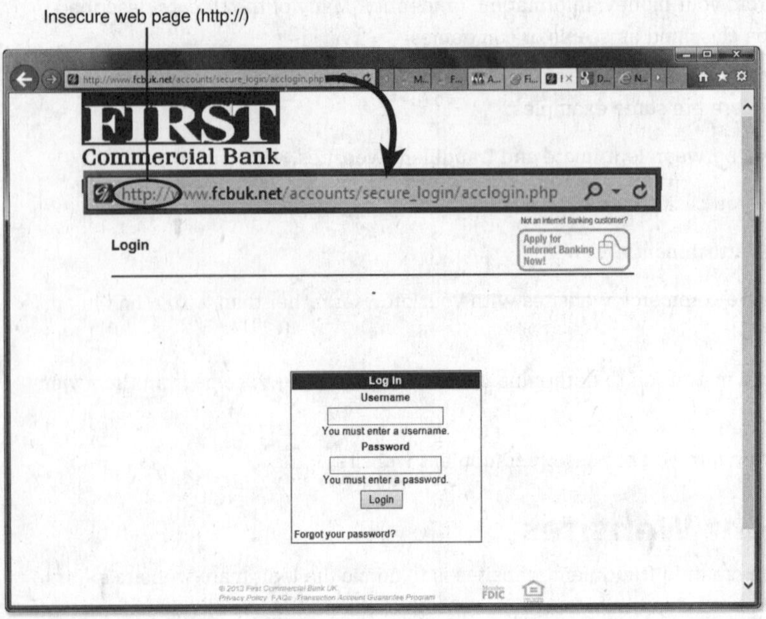

Figure 4.7
Login page for a fraudulent bank website.

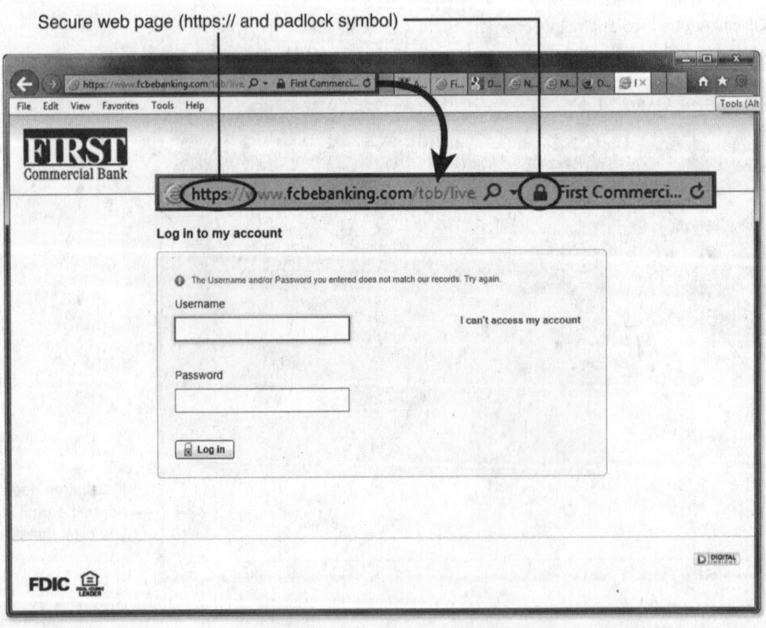

Figure 4.8
Login page for the actual bank website.

Check Before You Click

By floating your mouse over a link in an email or webpage, you can determine the actual destination of that link. Figure 4.5 showed how to use this method to determine that an email was fraudulent. Figure 4.9 shows an example of a legitimate email for comparison.

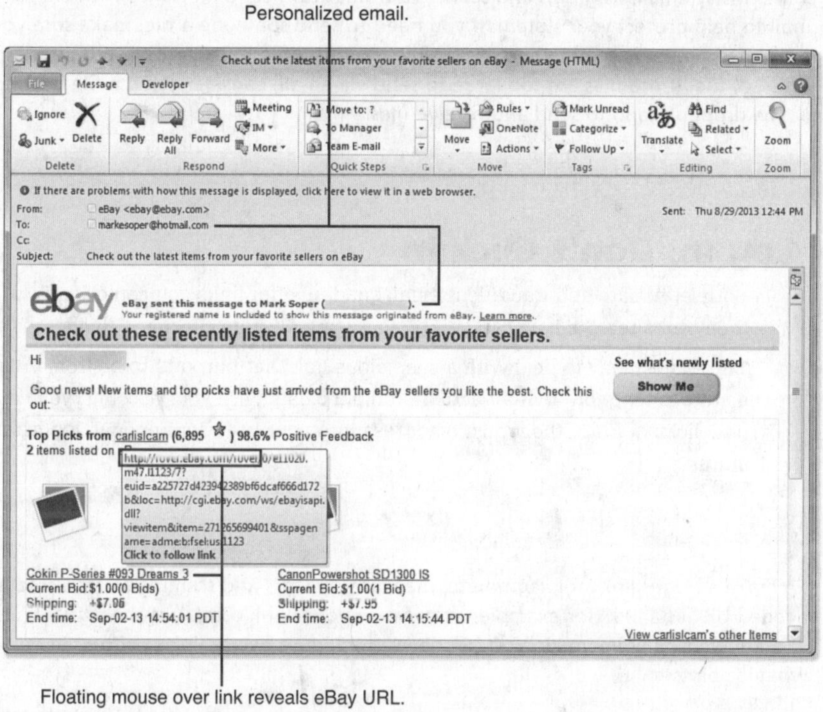

Figure 4.9
Checking links in a legitimate email message from eBay.

Caution

Although the eBay email shown in Figure 4.9 includes an eBay logo, the presence of the company's logo in an email message or on a webpage is not a guarantee that the email or webpage is legitimate. It's easy for malware creators to copy these graphical elements from a legitimate site and reuse them.

Don't Click the Zip

The Zip archive format is very useful for reducing the size of large files for emailing and for gathering two or more files into a single file that you can email, save to disc, or upload. However, Zip files are also one of the favorite ways for malware authors to infect your system because you can't see the contents of the file unless you click it, and that's all it takes to infect your system (refer to Figure 4.4).

There is no need for legitimate vendors to use attachments in email for invoices, messages, or reminders. So, if you receive a message with an attachment that you didn't request or one from an unknown sender, ignore it.

Note

Many email programs and services automatically send messages with Zip-format attachments to junk mail to help protect your system. If you need to send someone a file, make sure you let the recipient know a file attachment is coming and, if possible, send the file in its normal state, not as a Zip archive (compressed) file. If the files are too large to send via email, consider using a file hosting service such as Dropbox (www.dropbox.com) to send and receive files.

Log In, Don't Click In

Both legitimate and fraudulent email senders offer links you can click if you need to interact with their websites. So, how can you protect yourself from clicking a dangerous link?

The easiest way to deal with a suspicious link that purports to be from eBay, PayPal, your bank, or a store is to ignore it. If an actual problem exists with your account, you can find out what it is without clicking. Enter the website address into your browser window, log in, and check your account status.

Tip

To make a bogus link look legitimate, malware creators and scammers often create a link that displays the alleged URL as a link (for example, http://www.your bank.com), but the actual link points to the malware or scam website. Remember, you can hover the mouse over a link in either an email or a web page to see what it points to.

Let Your Browser Protect You

Recent versions of Internet Explorer and some third-party browsers contain a variety of features to help protect you from suspicious websites. Depending on the browser, you might need to use optional add-ons to help protect yourself.

Microsoft Internet Explorer

Internet Explorer versions 9 and later include built-in SmartScreen technology to help protect you while you're browsing. SmartScreen checks for phishing attempts, provides warnings for unknown files, and blocks malware. In Figure 4.10, Internet Explorer 11 blocks a website from downloading a file containing malware.

SmartScreen also blocks access to unsafe websites (see Figure 4.11).

To make sure your SmartScreen filter is turned on, open the Settings (gearbox) menu, click or tap Safety, and review the settings. If SmartScreen filter is turned off, you should turn it on.

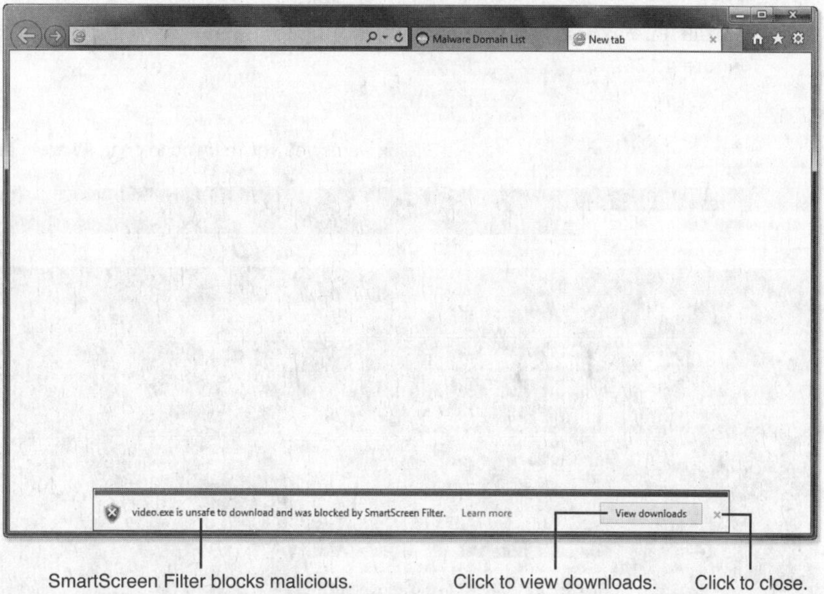

Figure 4.10 SmartScreen Filter notifies you when a website tries to put a malware file on your system.

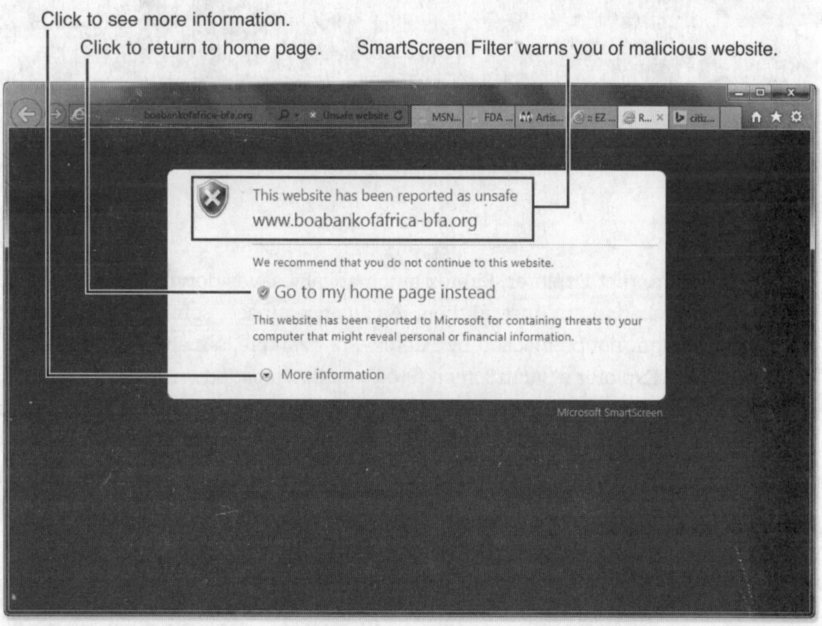

Figure 4.11 SmartScreen filter dialog when you try to open a malicious website.

Mozilla Firefox

Mozilla Firefox also includes built-in blocking for fraudulent websites and known attack pages (see Figure 4.12).

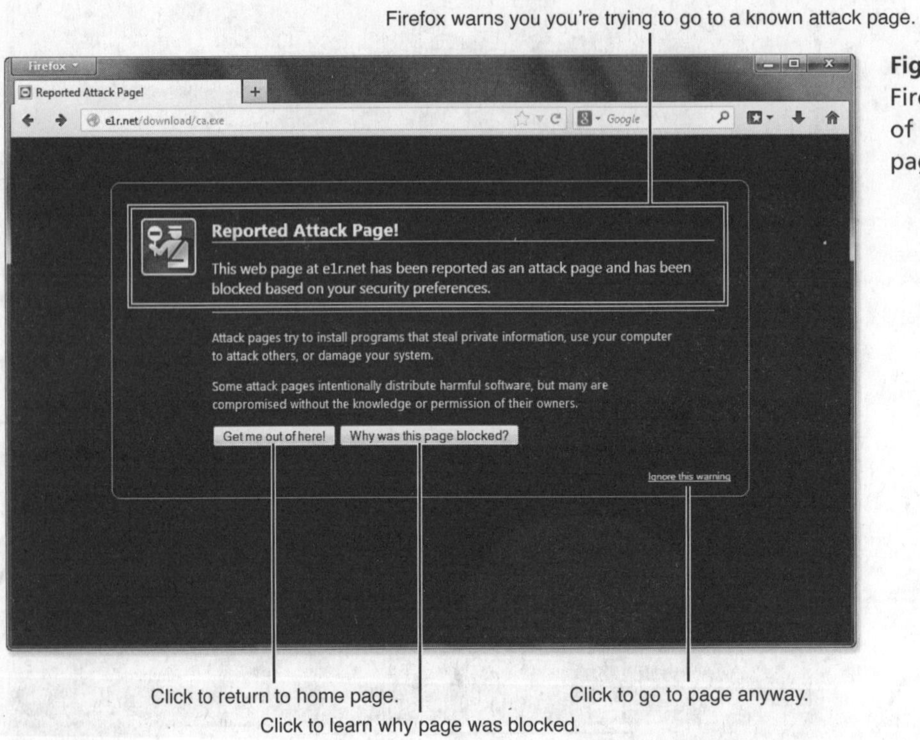

Figure 4.12 Firefox warns you of known attack pages.

Unlike Internet Explorer, Firefox automatically saves downloaded files and leaves it up to you to decide when to run (install) them. As a consequence, some malware that Internet Explorer would block might not be blocked by Firefox. For example, a malware program that was blocked by Internet Explorer's SmartScreen filter was downloaded without a warning by Firefox. However, the real-time protection provided by my system's anti-malware app stopped my system from being infected (see Figure 4.13).

To help improve Firefox's anti-malware protection, I recommend installing the following add-ons:

- **NoScript**—Permits or blocks active scripting on websites as you direct
- **Web of Trust**—Rates websites on their trustworthiness

These are available from the Get Add-ons menu on the Firefox Settings menu. Web of Trust also supports other browsers (see www.mywot.com for details).

Figure 4.14 illustrates how NoScript blocks a script from running and permits you to specify script settings for a particular website.

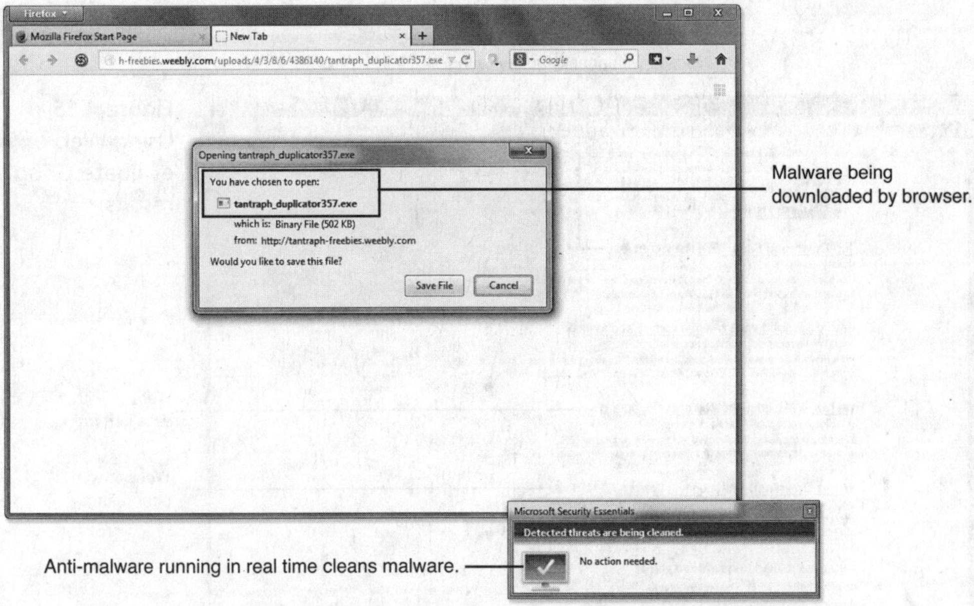

Figure 4.13 Why you need anti-malware: even if the browser lets the file through, your anti-malware can stop the infection.

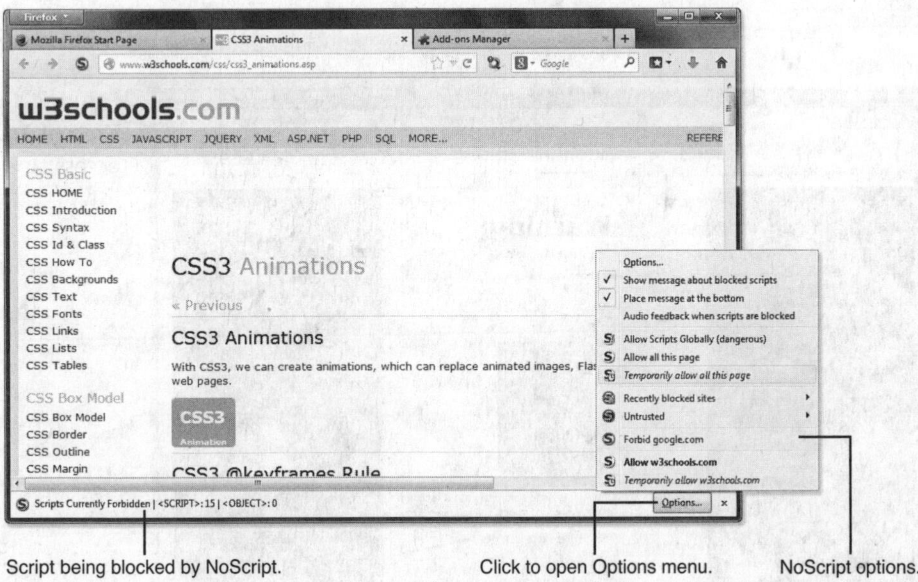

Figure 4.14 Using NoScript to determine whether to run a script on a webpage.

Figure 4.15 illustrates how Web of Trust rates links in a web search. Green rings equal good to excellent reputation; yellow indicates unsatisfactory; red rings indicate poor to very poor reputation (see https://www.mywot.com/en/support/tour for details).

Web of Trust also blocks access to known-dangerous websites (see Figure 4.16).

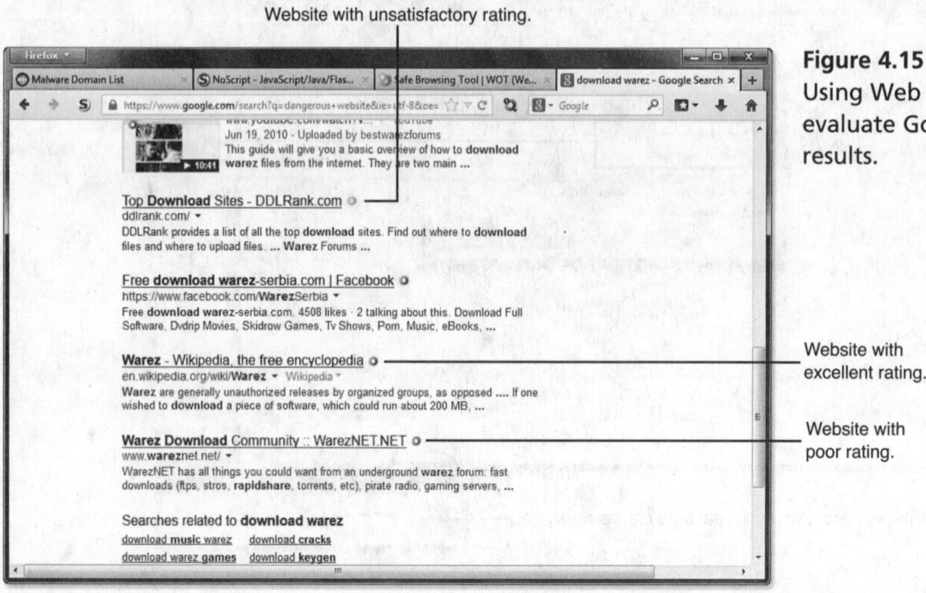

Figure 4.15
Using Web of Trust to evaluate Google search results.

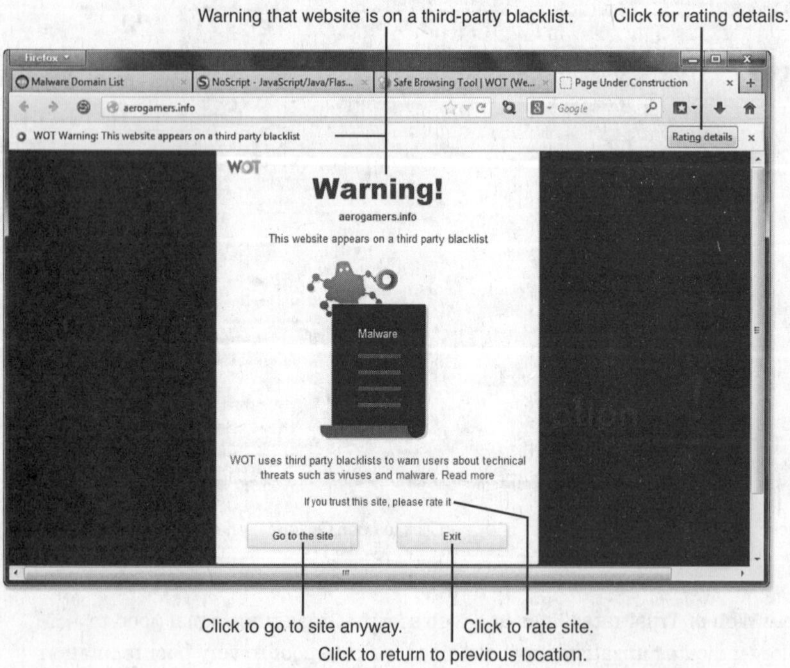

Figure 4.16
Web of Trust blocking access to a site on a blacklist.

Google Chrome

Similar to Internet Explorer, Google Chrome provides built-in protection against malware downloads (see Figure 4.17).

Figure 4.17 Google Chrome checks for malware and blocks it.

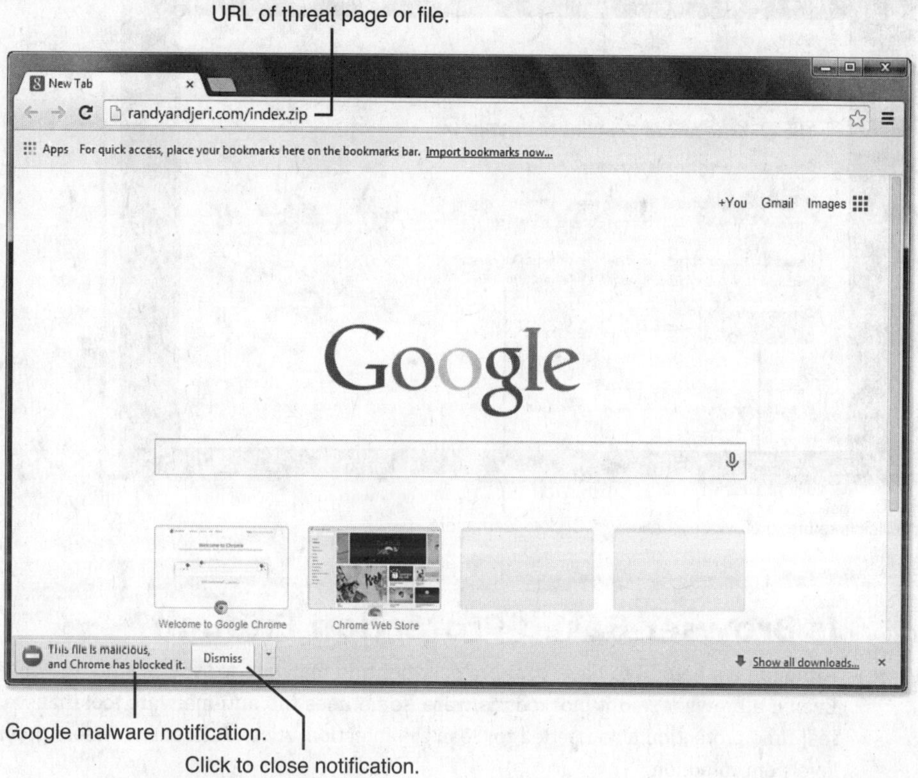

Google provides analysis of websites that show up in Google searches and uses that information to provide advisories like the one shown in Figure 4.18. Click the Advanced button to see full details.

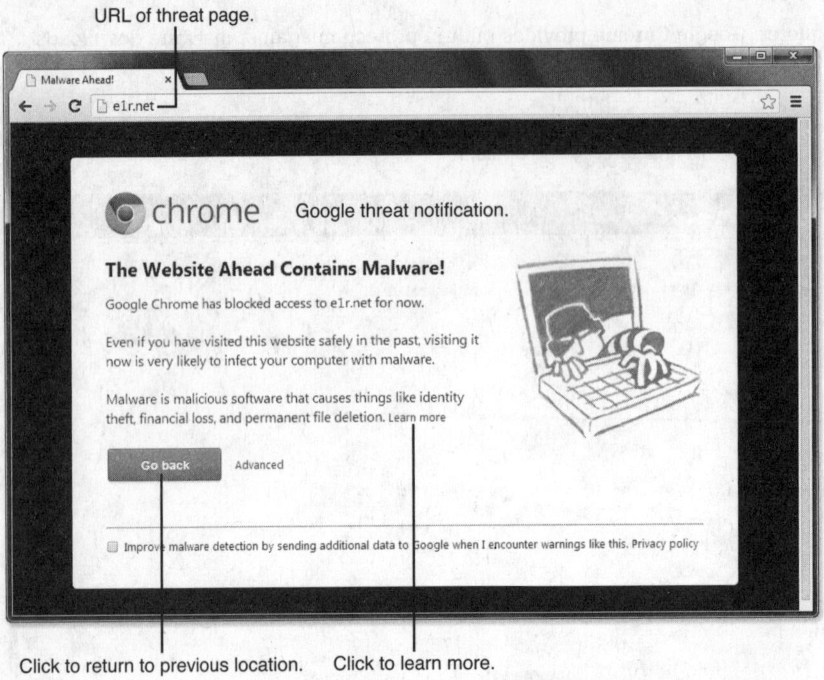

Figure 4.18 Google Analytics is used by Chrome to find dangerous websites and block access to them.

Is Browser-Based Protection Enough?

Although it's helpful to have your browser fighting malware for you, it's not the only tool you need. Even if a browser said it blocked malware, sometimes the anti-malware tool that was running with real-time protection also needed to clean the infection. Also, different browsers provided different levels of protection.

Don't depend on your browser as your only protection, especially if you use Windows or Android devices. The following sections help you understand how to build multilevel protection against malware.

Preventing and Removing Malware on Windows Devices

As you learned in the previous section, modern web browsers provide some tools for battling malware. However, you need additional protection against the following threats:

- Real-time protection against malware accessed via the Web, email, or removable drives
- Malware scanning to remove infections that get past real-time protection
- Spyware scanning to locate and remove privacy threats, such as tracking cookies and apps

Start with a full-featured anti-malware program that provides real-time protection and also periodically scans your drives for malware. Windows 8/8.1 includes Windows Defender, which provides real-time and scan-based anti-malware protection. If you prefer to use third-party anti-malware programs with Windows 8/8.1 or Windows RT, use the Windows Compatibility website to search for compatible products: http://www.microsoft.com/en-us/windows/compatibility/CompatCenter/Home.

For links to commercial products (some of which offer free versions) for older versions of Windows, go to: http://windows.microsoft.com/en-US/windows/antivirus-partners (select Windows 7, Windows Vista, or Windows XP).

Figure 4.19 shows malware detected by Microsoft Security Essentials (a free product available from the Microsoft Antivirus Partners website).

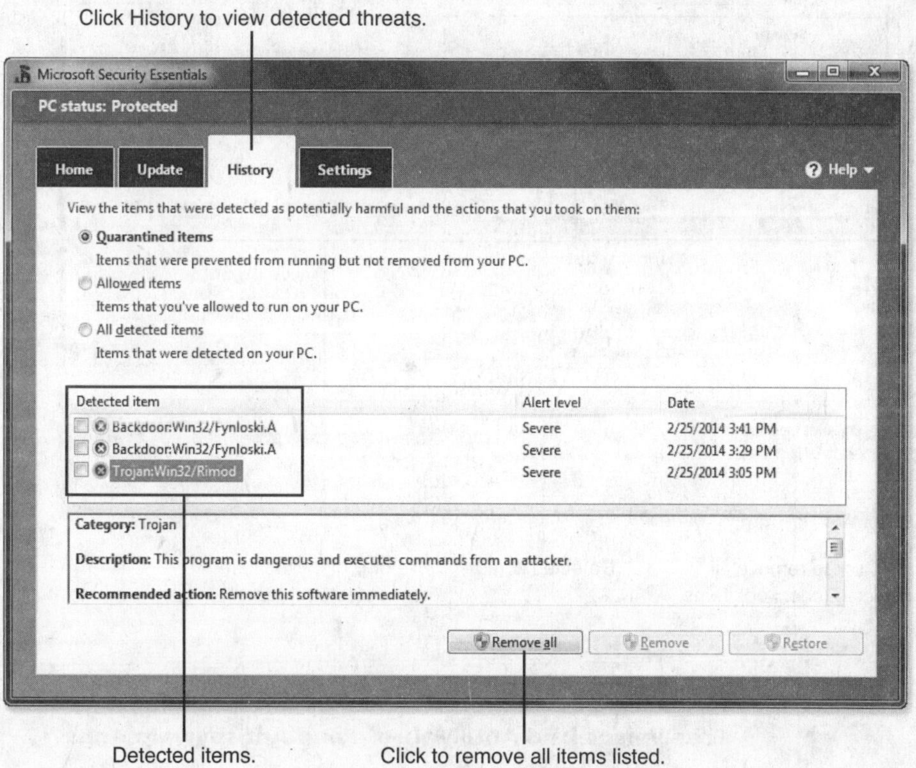

Figure 4.19 Checking for detected threats with Microsoft Security Essentials.

To supplement real-time protection, you should also install an anti-malware scanner that can coexist with real-time protection. Malwarebytes (www.malwarebytes.com) is free, fast, and easy to set up, and it is highly regarded by the industry. Figure 4.20 reveals the results of a scan for malware after browsers and anti-malware apps claimed to stop infections of my system. As you can see, there were still several problems to remove.

To help remove spyware such as tracking cookies or apps, you should also install an antispyware app that can coexist with real-time protection. SUPERAntiSpyware (www.superantispyware.com) is available in a free version and is also well-reviewed by the industry. Figure 4.21 shows the results of a scan, revealing 95 tracking cookies on the system.

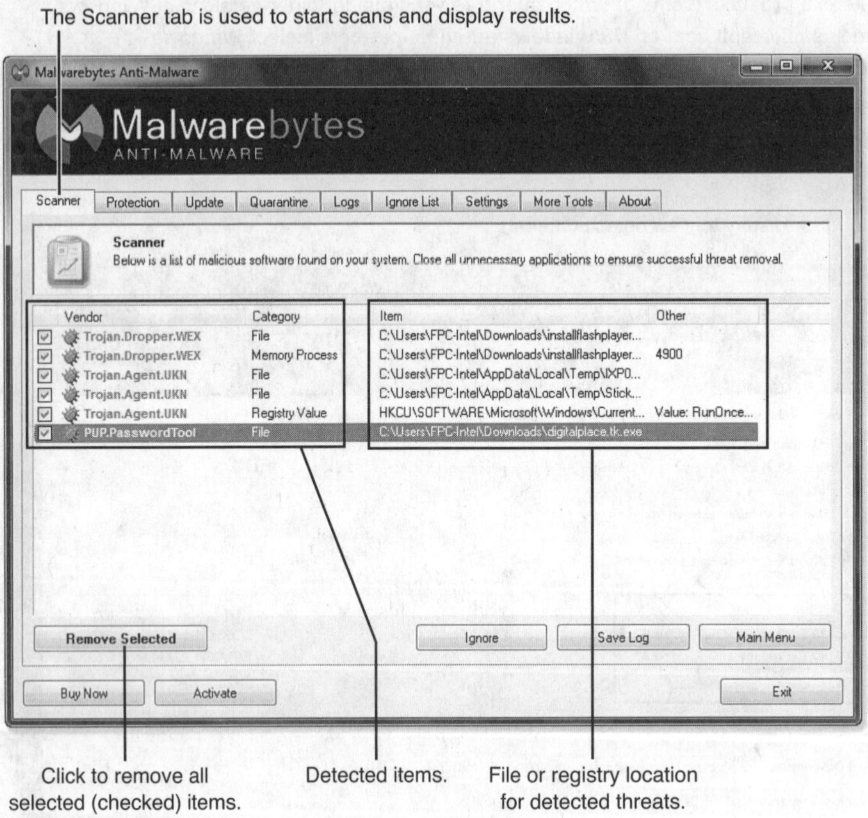

Figure 4.20 Using Malwarebytes to remove threats from a system.

> **Free Versus Paid Anti-Malware and Antispyware Apps**
>
> With a number of highly regarded anti-malware and antispyware apps available free, why pay for protection? A paid version of free apps typically adds features such as telephone or priority product support, automatic updates, real-time protection, or automatic and scheduled scans (see product descriptions for details). If you use free apps, it's up to you to keep them updated and scan your system regularly.

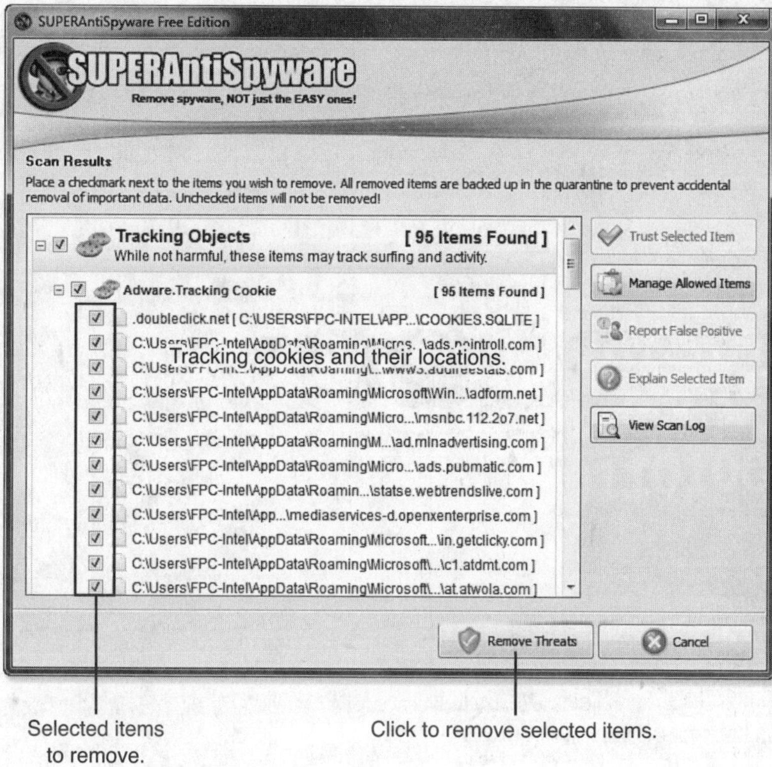

Figure 4.21
Using SUPERAntiSpyware to locate and remove tracking cookies.

Preventing and Removing Malware on iOS Devices

Even though Apple iOS devices are not vulnerable to malware attacks designed to target Windows-based systems, you should still protect your devices against common threats. Because iOS devices exchange information with Windows and MacOS devices, an unprotected iOS device can be used as an attack gateway.

IOS-based anti-malware products provide features such as on-demand email attachment scanning (VirusBarrier iOS), protection against websites that track your activities or contain malware (AVG Safe Browser), and automatic contact backup and discovery of a lost device (Lookout). These and other anti-malware products are available through the iOS App Store.

Figure 4.22 illustrates how VirusBarrier iOS can be used to scan an email attachment.

Figure 4.23 illustrates how AVG Safe Browser checks a website for trackers.

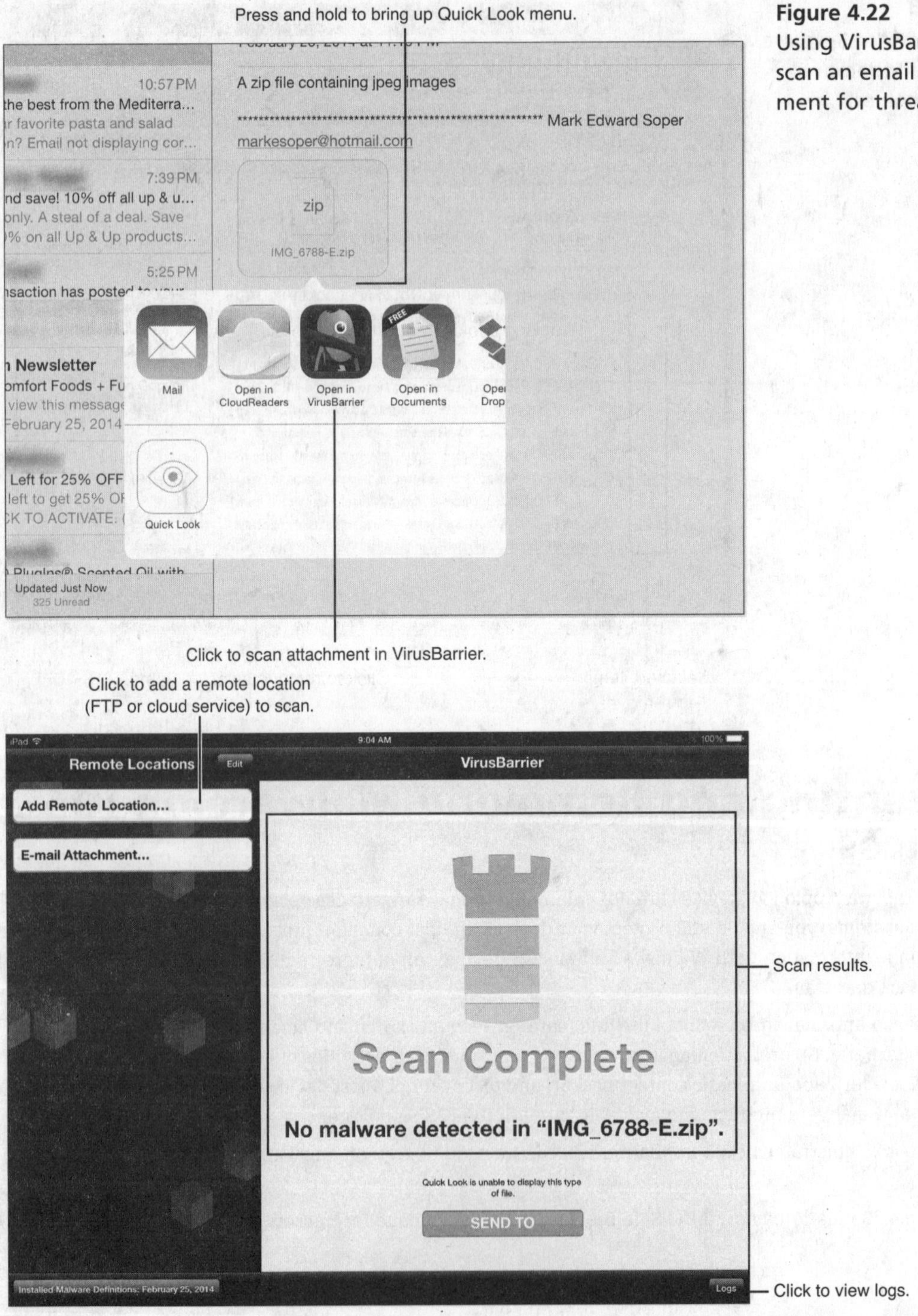

Figure 4.22 Using VirusBarrier to scan an email attachment for threats.

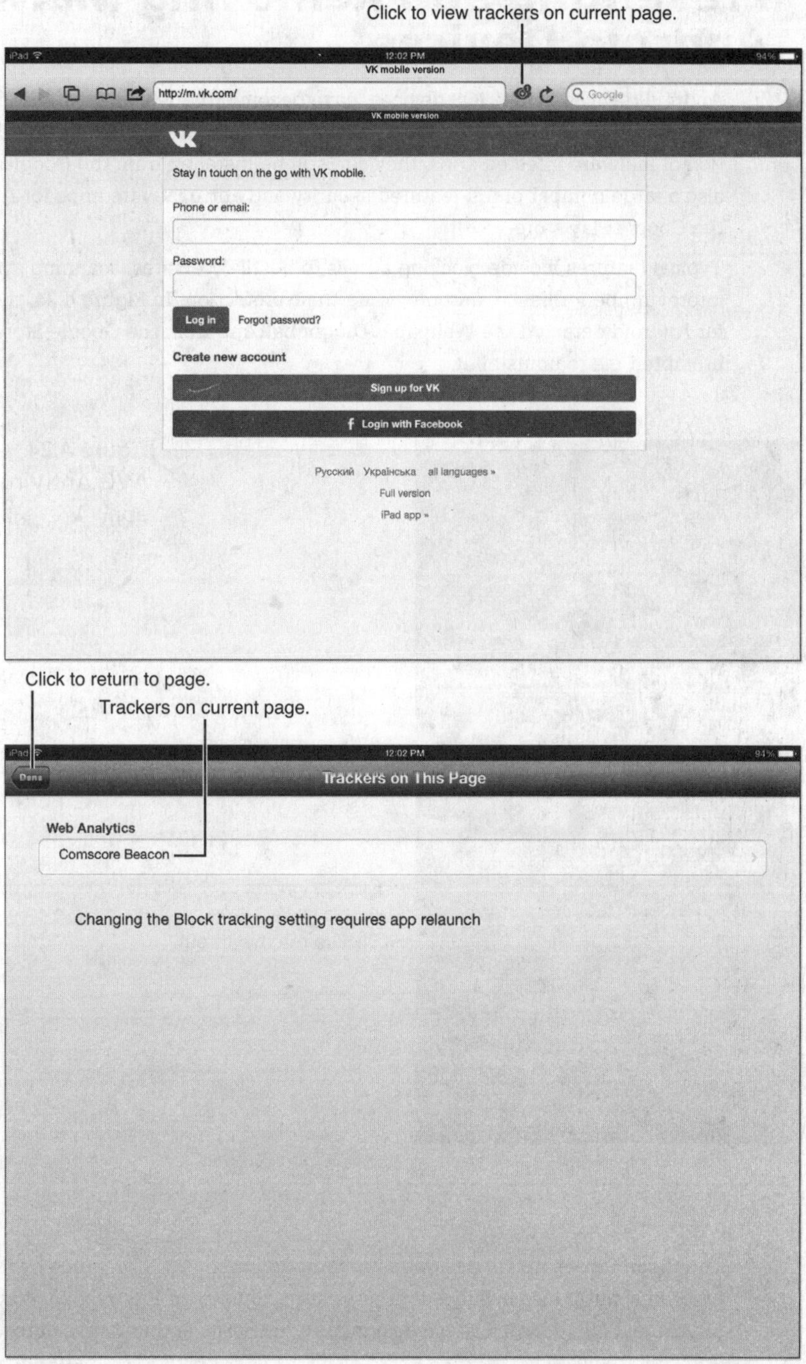

Figure 4.23
AVG Safe Browser checks websites for tracking features that can spy on your browsing habits.

Preventing and Removing Malware on Android Devices

Android devices, unlike iOS devices, have become frequent malware targets. Unfortunately, many apps in the Google Play store are infected with malware. Although Google has improved its detection of malware-infected apps, they can still be installed from the Google Store. Thankfully, there are also a large number of full-featured security and anti-malware apps for Android available through the Google Play store.

Typical features include blocking access to hostile websites, scanning system contents for malware, improving performance, and providing theft protection. In Figure 4.24, the AVG AntiVirus FREE app for Android detected the Wallpaper Dragonball app from the Google Store as intrusive Adware and prompted me to uninstall it.

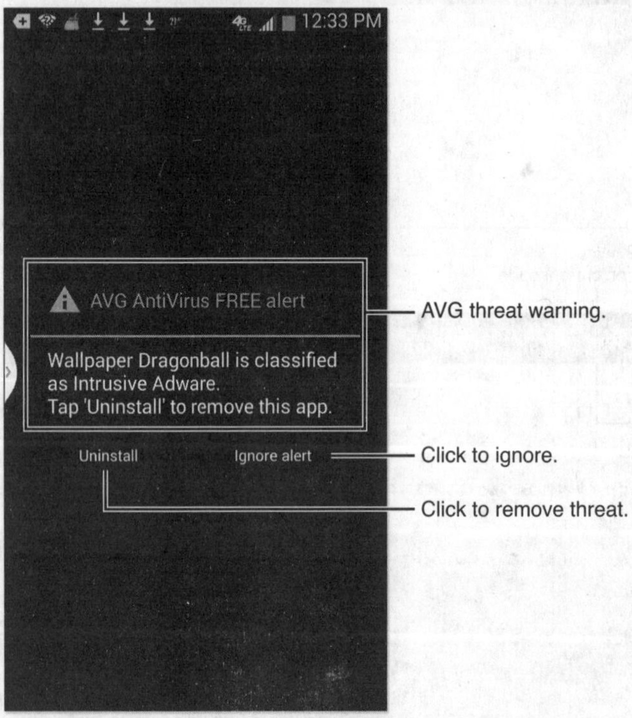

Figure 4.24
AVG AntiVirus FREE catches an adware app.

The Clean Sweep app is designed primarily to improve performance by removing junk files and idle programs, but it also includes anti-malware scanning. In Figure 4.25, it automatically detected the EICAR test file (a harmless file designed to test virus and malware detection) and prompted me to uninstall (remove) it.

Figure 4.25
Clean Sweep detects the EICAR test "virus" file.

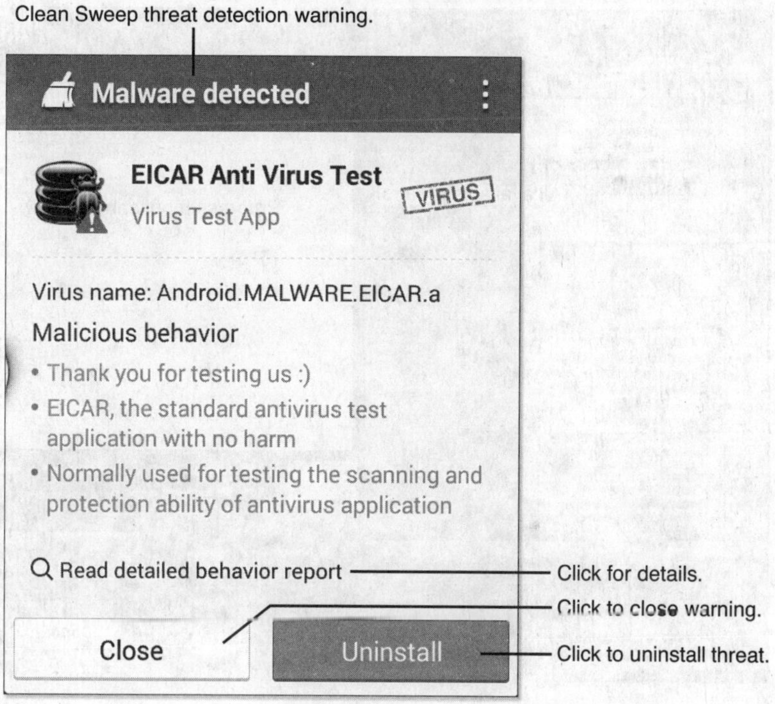

Repairing Malware Damage on Windows Devices

If a Windows-based device is infected with malware, removing the malware itself can sometimes require scanning with more than one program. Sometimes Windows settings are damaged to the point that the system suffers multiple malfunctions.

The Windows Repair tool from the Tweaking.com website provides an easy way to repair Windows problems caused by malware or other problems. Before performing repairs, it prompts you to select options, including running Malware Bytes to check for malware, running Chkdsk to check for disk errors, creating a system restore point, and using System File Checker to replace incorrect versions of system files. Figure 4.26 illustrates a typical run.

If you prefer to make repairs manually, see www.techradar.com/news/computing/pc/how-to-repair-a-malware-damaged-pc-1032838.

What if your system is so badly infected that it won't start even in Safe Mode? Antivirus vendors including AVG, Kapersky, and many others offer downloadable files that you can use to create a bootable CD or USB drive that scans your system for malware and removes it.

The AVG Rescue CD is available at www.avg.com/us-en/avg-rescue-cd. Kapersky Rescue Disk 10 is available at http://support.kaspersky.com/viruses/rescuedisk.

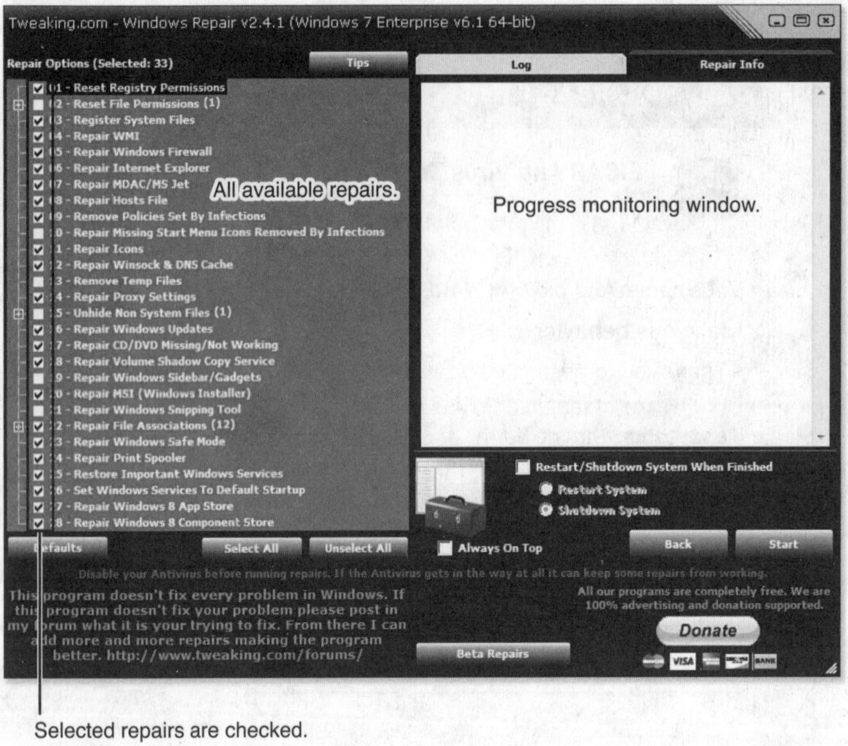

Figure 4.26 Preparing to fix a Windows 7 installation with Tweaking.com's Windows Repair tool.

Links to many other products are available at http://www.malwarehelp.org/anti-malware-bootable-rescue-cd-dvd-download.html.

After products of this type remove serious infections, restart your system and use a utility such as the Windows Repair tool to restore your system to normal operation.

Repairing Malware Damage on iOS or Android Devices

To repair any damage caused by malware on these operating systems, reset the device to its factory settings. Because this step causes your apps and data to be lost, be sure to back up this information first.

Note

To learn how to back up your iOS data, apps, and settings, see "Backing Up Your iOS Device," in Chapter 21, "iOS Troubleshooting."

To learn how to back up your Android data, apps, and settings, see "Performing a Factory Reset/Restore," in Chapter 22, "Android Troubleshooting."

5

SOLVING PROBLEMS WITH VIEWING YOUR PHOTOS AND VIDEOS

Fast Track to Solutions

Table 5.1 Symptom Table

Symptom	Flowchart or Book Section	Page #
RAW files show as icons in Windows.	Can't View RAW Files on Your PC	134
I can't "see" RAW files I copied to my Android device.	Finding and Using RAW Apps for Android	139
I can't "see" RAW files copied to my iOS device.	Can't View RAW Files on Your iOS Device	141
My version of Windows does not include Windows Media Player.	See Note: "The K and KN editions of Windows don't include Windows Media Player."	144
My Android browser won't play Flash videos.	Playing Adobe Flash Video on Android	148

Can't View RAW Files on Your PC

If your digital photos are always shot using the JPEG setting on your camera, your PC has no problem displaying them. However, if you start shooting RAW files, preferred by serious photographers for their improved sharpness, greater ability to fix exposure and color problems, and support for advanced features such as high dynamic range (HDR) imaging, your computer probably won't be able to view or edit the results without some help from software—and you.

Check out Figures 5.1 and 5.2, which illustrate a folder that contains both RAW and JPEG photographs. As you can see, the JPEG files are displayed as thumbnails, but the RAW files are shown as icons. If you're trying to enjoy your photo collection, being stuck in Icon City is not what you have in mind.

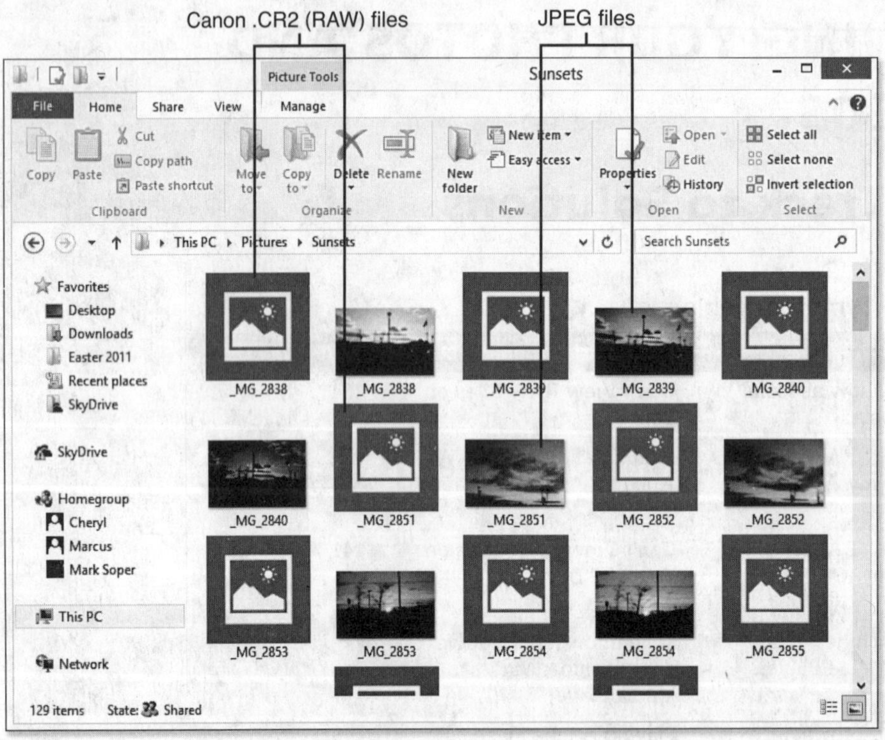

Figure 5.1 Windows Explorer in Windows 7 or File Explorer in Windows 8.x (shown) can display JPEG files without additional software, but RAW files (.CR2 files from a Canon camera) are displayed as icons until appropriate software is installed.

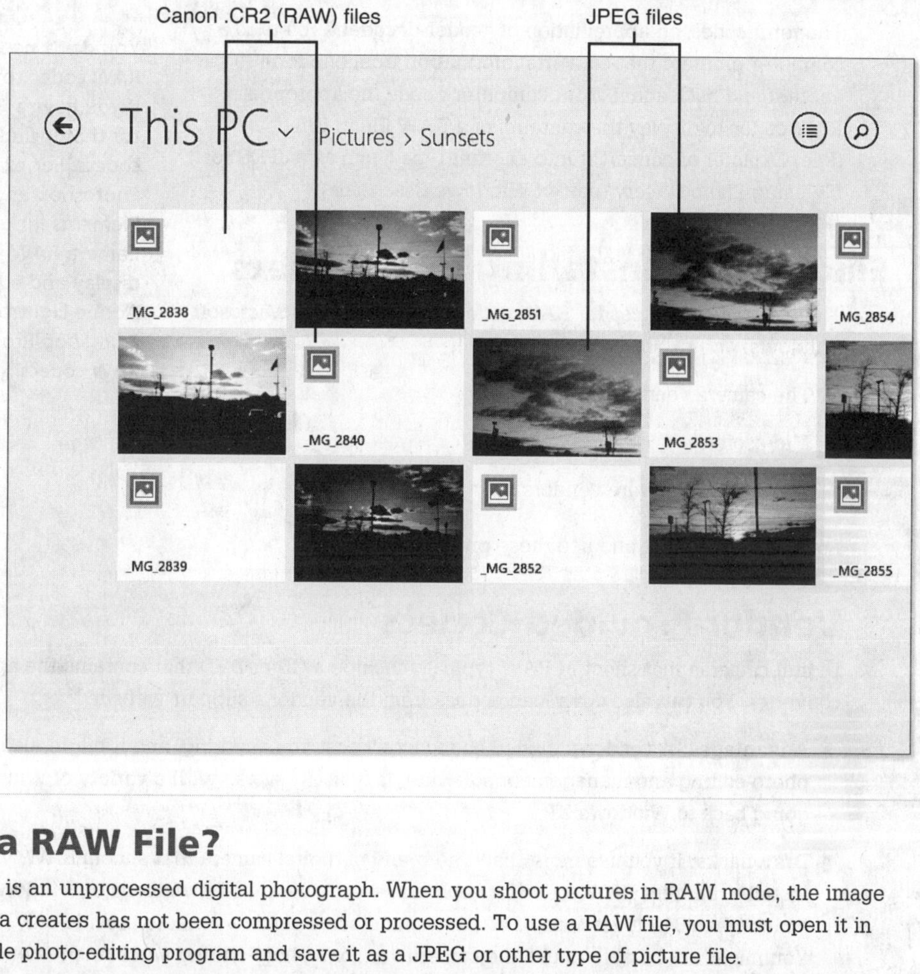

Figure 5.2 The Windows 8.1 Start menu's This PC view of the same folder in Windows 8.1.

What Is a RAW File?

A RAW file is an unprocessed digital photograph. When you shoot pictures in RAW mode, the image your camera creates has not been compressed or processed. To use a RAW file, you must open it in a compatible photo-editing program and save it as a JPEG or other type of picture file.

RAW files are proprietary to individual digital camera and device makers. For example, recent and current Canon-brand cameras that shoot RAW files store them as .CR2 files, whereas Nikon uses the extension .NEF for its RAW files. The RAW files shown in Figures 5.1 and 5.2 were shot with a Canon digital SLR (DSLR) camera.

RAW Versus JPEG Files

Whereas a RAW file must be processed with a program before you can view or use the photo, a JPEG file is processed by the digital camera, camcorder, smartphone, or tablet you use to create it. Settings for image quality, white balance, color settings, and more are applied when the file is created.

Some digital cameras can shoot both RAW and JPEG files at the same time.

What Is a Codec?

The term *codec*, an abbreviation of "coder-decoder," refers to a computer program that converts information from one form to another and back again. Your computer needs the appropriate RAW codec to display the contents of a RAW file in Windows (File) Explorer or convert it into another type (such as a JPEG) of file using Photo Gallery (part of Windows Essentials).

Note

You don't need a separate RAW codec to edit RAW files if you have a RAW photo editor that includes its own RAW codecs. For example, Adobe Photoshop and Photoshop Elements include Adobe Camera RAW so they can display and edit RAW files. Adobe Lightroom and Corel PaintShop Pro have built-in RAW codecs.

Finding and Installing RAW Codecs

There are three sources for RAW codecs that work with Microsoft Windows:

- The camera vendor
- Microsoft
- Third-party software vendors

Let's see how to get and use these products.

Vendor-Provided Codecs

Digital cameras that shoot in RAW typically include a CD or DVD that contains the appropriate RAW converter. You can also download codecs from the vendor's support website.

- **Advantages:** A vendor-provided codec won't cost you anything, and it might also come with photo-editing and management software. It typically works with a variety of Windows versions going back to Windows XP.
- **Drawbacks:** If you use more than one brand of digital camera that shoots RAW, you will need to install a different RAW codec for each brand of camera. 32-bit versions of Windows use different codecs than 64-bit versions of Windows, and some camera vendors provide only 32-bit versions. You might not be able to use the camera vendor's photo-editing and management software with RAW photos from other brands of cameras.

Microsoft-Provided Codecs

Microsoft offers a free downloadable codec for digital cameras that shoot RAW files: the Microsoft Camera Codec Pack. Download it from the Microsoft Download Center at www.microsoft.com/downloads.

- **Advantages:** A single download works with almost all cameras that shoot RAW files, from Canon to Sony (see the download page for details). It also enables Windows Live Photo Gallery (part of Windows Essentials) to display and convert RAW files for editing.
- **Drawbacks:** You will need to choose either the 32-bit (x86) or 64-bit (x64 or AMD64) version, depending on the version of Windows you have. Separate versions are available for Windows Vista SP2/Windows 7, Windows 8, and Windows 8.1.

Note

Follow these links for more information and to download the correct version for your operating system:

- **Windows Vista SP2 and Windows 7**—http://www.microsoft.com/en-pk/download/details.aspx?id=26829
- **Windows 8 and Windows RT 8**—http://support.microsoft.com/kb/2712101
- **Windows 8.1 and Windows RT 8.1**—http://support.microsoft.com/kb/2859675

Windows 8/8.1 typically provides the correct version of the codec pack via Windows Update. However, you can download it manually, and you can check the preceding links to determine the camera models supported.

Third-Party Codecs

Even though Microsoft provides a RAW codec for almost all digital cameras, you might prefer to try a third-party codec to get better performance or more features. Major vendors include the following:

- **Ardfry Imaging, LLC**—www.ardfry.com. Ardfry provides separate codecs for Canon RAW (.CR2), Adobe Digital Negative (.DNG, the Adobe RAW format that can be used with Photoshop, Lightroom, and other Adobe products), and Nikon RAW (.NEF). Ardfry also makes an Adobe Photoshop codec that enables you to view Photoshop (PSD, AI, and EPS) files in Windows Explorer and other apps. Free trials are available.
- **Axel Rietschin Software Developments**—www.fastpictureviewer.com. The FastPictureViewer Codec pack provides single-file support for almost all digital cameras that shoot RAW files and is highly customizable for better performance in viewing both JPEG and RAW files. Free trials are available.

Note

RAW codecs provided by vendors other than the camera manufacturer can provide more viewing and customization options, and some vendors provide a single codec that can work with several types of RAW codecs from different camera brands.

The major advantage of a RAW codec provided by the camera manufacturer is that it will work with the latest models. Sometimes it takes a few months before Microsoft or third-party codecs support new models.

After a suitable RAW codec is installed, you can view RAW and JPEG files on your system in Windows Explorer or File Explorer, as shown in Figures 5.3 and 5.4.

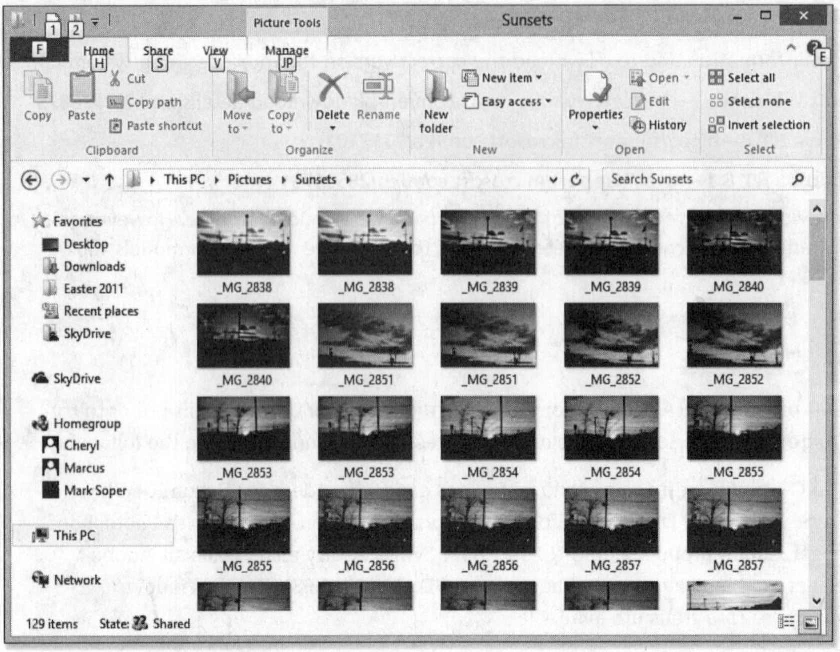

Figure 5.3 After a RAW codec for Canon .CR2 (RAW) files is installed, both RAW and JPEG files display thumbnails in Windows Explorer or File Explorer.

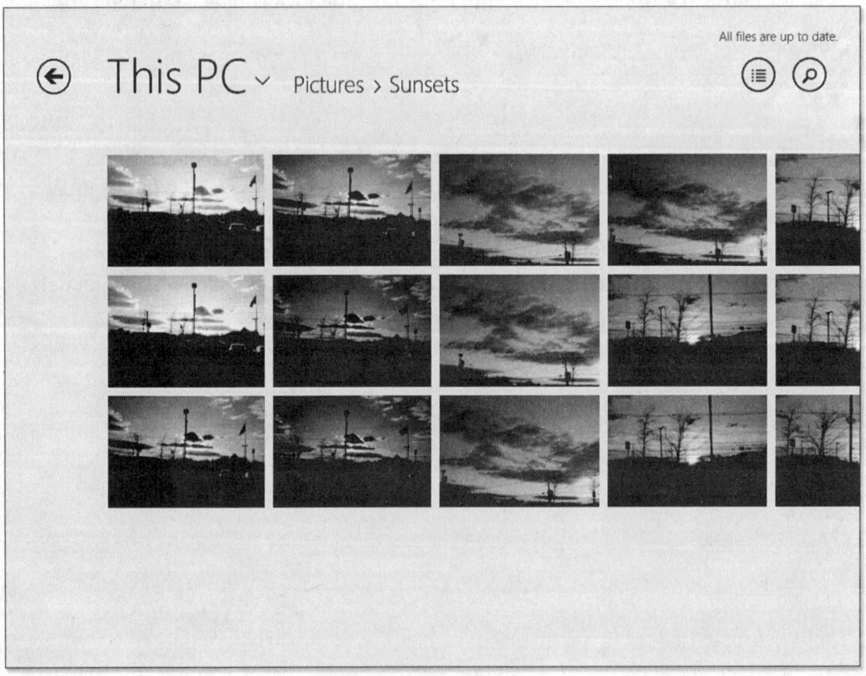

Figure 5.4 After a RAW codec for Canon .CR2 (RAW) files is installed, both RAW and JPEG files display thumbnails in This PC or Pictures on Windows 8.1.

Can't View RAW Files on Your Android Device

If you want to take your favorite photos with you on your Android tablet or smartphone, it's easy to view them if you shot them in JPEG mode. Android's built-in Gallery app has no problem displaying photos you shot with your device's built-in camera (they're stored as JPEG files) or JPEG photos you've downloaded from the Cloud or wireless network or accessed from a flash memory card.

However, if you'd prefer to view, manage, or edit RAW photos on your Android device, you need third-party software. Without RAW software, folders that contain RAW files appear to contain no files (see Figure 5.5).

Figure 5.5
This folder contains Canon .CR2 (RAW) image files, but they're "invisible" to Android's built-in file manager.

In this section, we'll show you where to find RAW apps and how to use them.

Finding and Using RAW Apps for Android

RAW apps for Android devices are available from Google Play, the app store for Android devices. Use searches such as "RAW file viewer," "RAW decoder," and "RAW photo app" to find suitable programs.

After you install a RAW app, use it to view the contents of a location that contains RAW files. RAW apps vary a great deal in features, so take advantage of free trials to see which ones work for you. Depending on the app you select and whether you opt for a free or paid app, you might get the following features:

- Viewing and conversion to JPEG or TIFF (see Figure 5.6)
- Display of exposure metadata (aperture, shutter speed, camera, lens, and so on) (see Figure 5.7)
- RGB exposure histograms (see Figure 5.7)
- RAW image editing
- Batch file rename, export, and import
- Image rating

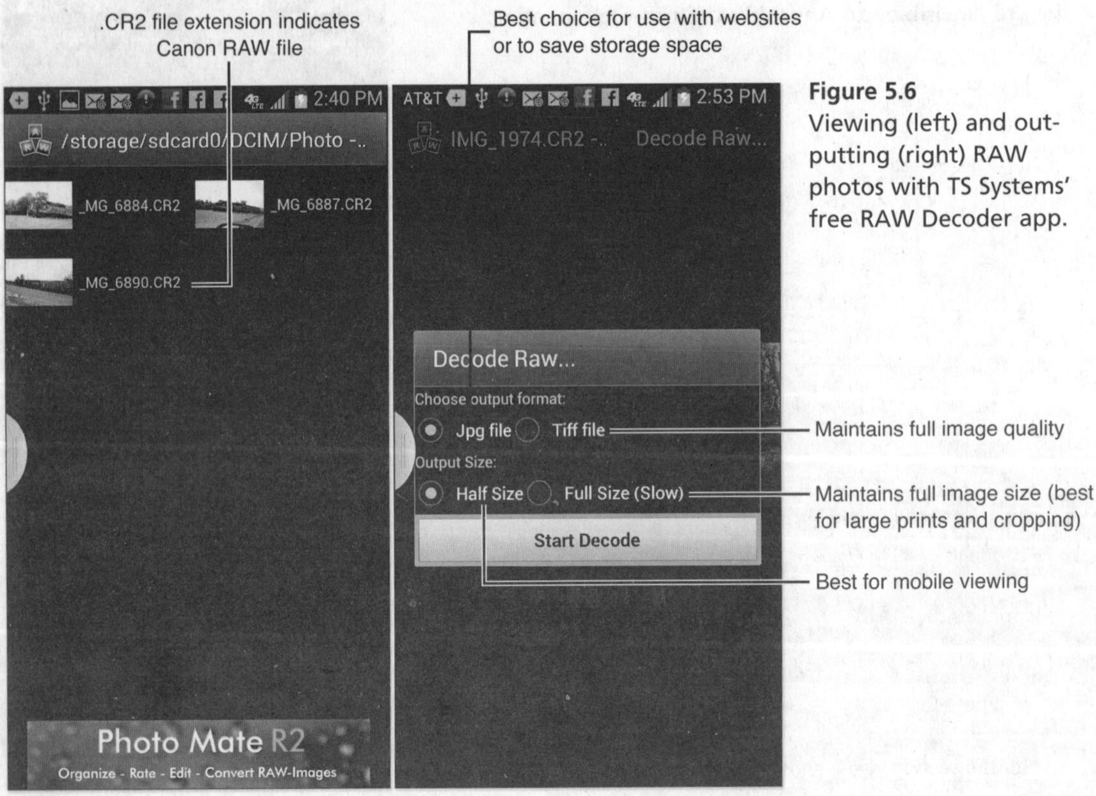

Figure 5.6
Viewing (left) and outputting (right) RAW photos with TS Systems' free RAW Decoder app.

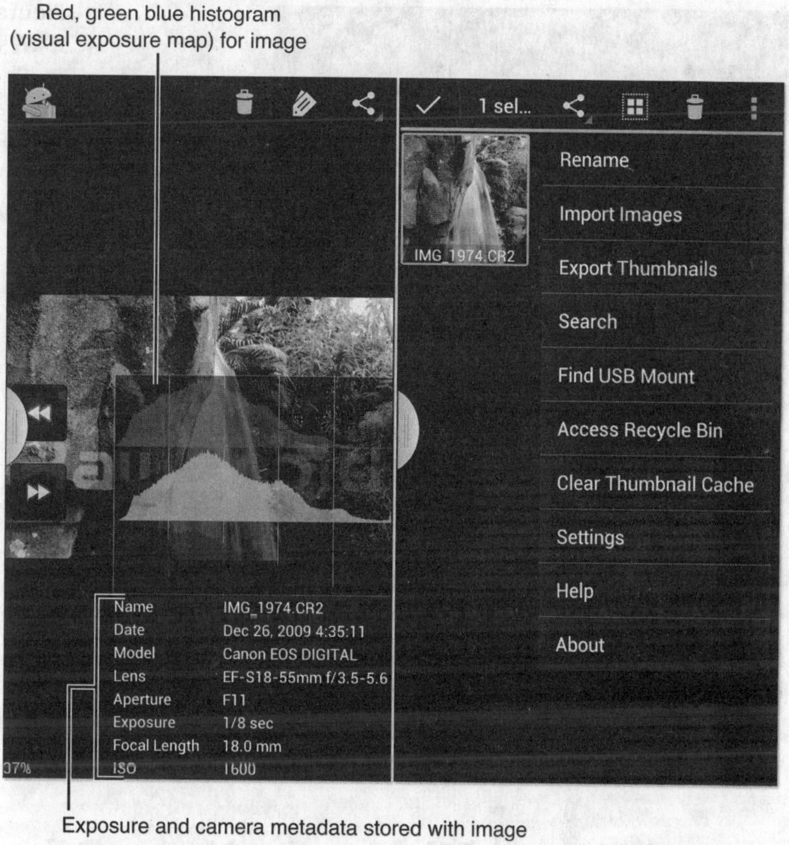

Figure 5.7 Viewing exposure and camera metadata (left) and viewing options (right) with the demo version of Rocketscientist's RAWDroid.

Can't View RAW Files on Your iOS Device

Although there are plenty of RAW viewing and editing apps for Android devices, a recent search of the iOS App Store found only a couple. There's a simple reason why: iPhoto for iOS.

Whether you want to view or edit JPEG or RAW photos, buy a copy of iPhoto for iOS and you have the tools you need. Figure 5.8 shows how you can adjust exposure and add special effects to a RAW file.

> **Note**
> Learn more about iPhoto for iOS at http://www.apple.com/ios/iphoto/.

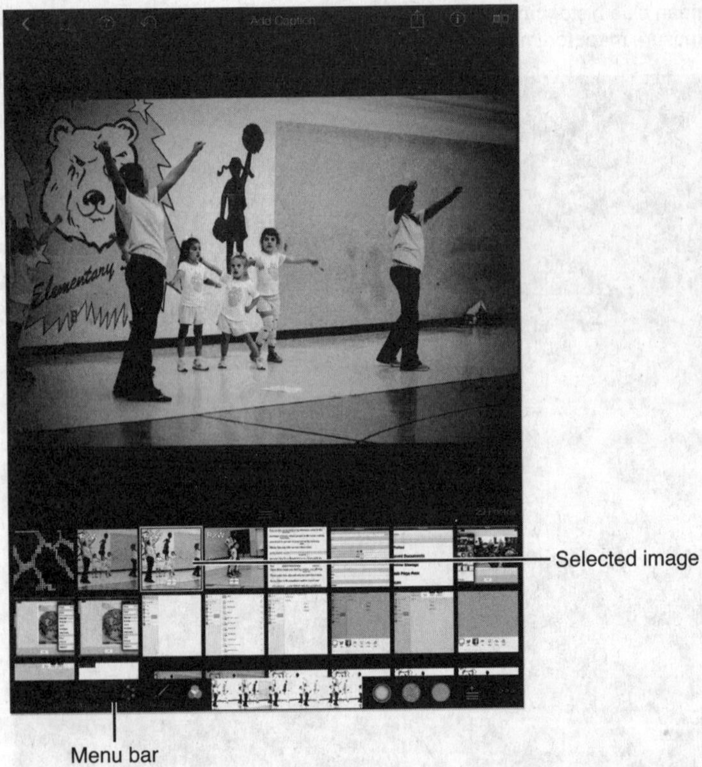

Figure 5.8
RAW and JPEG files are visible in iPhoto for iOS. The selected file has been lightened and had a duotone effect applied.

Can't View Video on Your PC

Whether it's a home movie, a fan-made trailer, or a commercial trailer and movie, the process of making video so it can be played on your computer involves two functions:

- Choosing a method for encoding the audio and video tracks
- Selecting a file format for the resulting video

You can have a playback program that supports the file format of a particular video, but if it doesn't have the necessary audio and video codecs installed, it won't be able to play the video.

There are three ways to help your computer play the video content you want to enjoy:

- Keep Adobe Flash updated.
- Install the audio and video codecs needed for a particular video.
- Install a third-party video player that includes support for playing back a variety of content.

Let's look at each of these in turn.

Updating Adobe Flash

The Adobe Flash player has become the de facto player of choice for online video content. Frequent updates are necessary because of changes needed in player support and to enhance security.

How can you tell when you need to update Adobe Flash (or if you don't have it installed)? You will see a prompt similar to the following when your web browser tries to play a Flash-based video (see Figure 5.9):

Figure 5.9 Websites prompt you to install Adobe Flash if your version is outdated or if Flash is not installed.

Prompt to download Adobe Flash

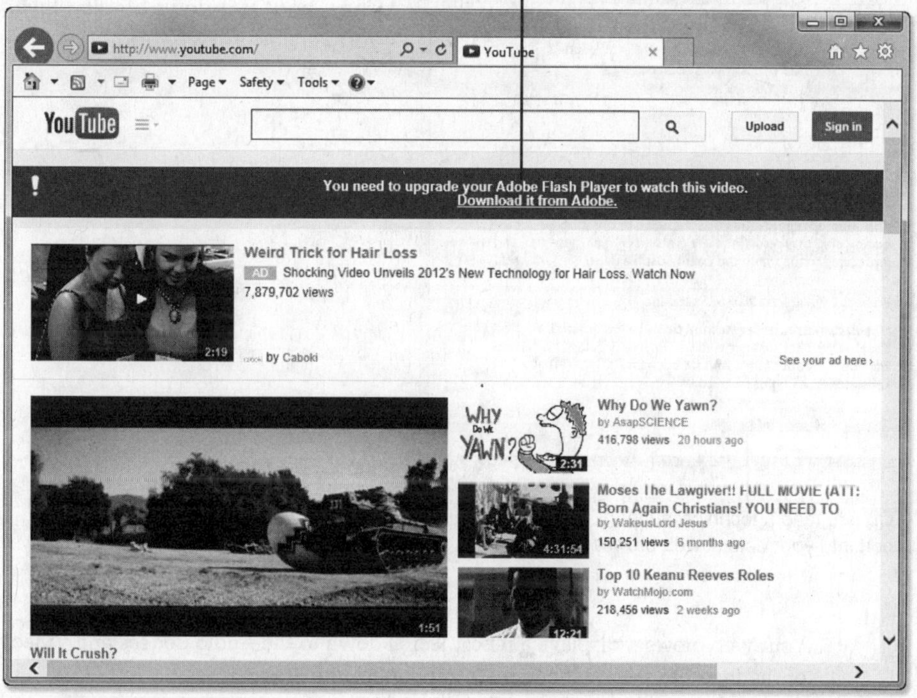

Click the link, verify that you're on the actual Adobe website (refer to Figure 4.6), and follow the prompts to complete installation.

Determining Codecs Used by Windows Media Player

Windows Media Player (WMP) is the standard media playback program included in (or available free for) Windows 7 and Windows 8.x. Windows Media Player includes codecs for playing back many types of video content, but it might not include the codecs you need.

To determine what codecs are installed on your system, follow these steps:

1. Open WMP.

2. If the menu bar is not visible, click **Organize, Layout, Show Menu Bar.**

3. Click **Help**, **About Windows Media Player**.

4. Click the Technical Support Information link (see Figure 5.10).

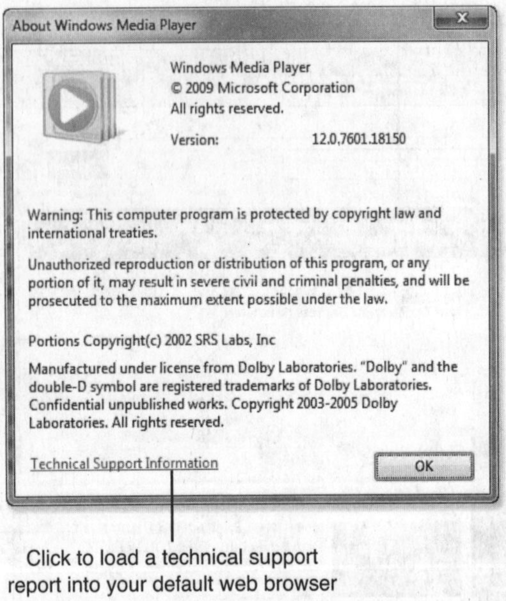

Figure 5.10
The About Windows Media Player dialog shows you version information.

5. Your web browser displays a report. Scroll down to the Audio Codecs and Video Codecs section of the report to review the formats supported (see Figure 5.11).

6. Close the browser tab or window.

Note

The K and KN editions of Windows don't include Windows Media Player. To get it for your version of Windows, follow the appropriate link:

- Get the Media Features Pack (includes WMP) for Windows 8/8.1— http://go.microsoft.com/fwlink/?LinkId=260410
- Get the Media Features Pack (includes WMP) for Windows 7— http://go.microsoft.com/fwlink/?LinkID=178358
- Get Windows Media Player 11 for Windows XP and Windows Vista— http://go.microsoft.com/fwlink/?LinkId=158425

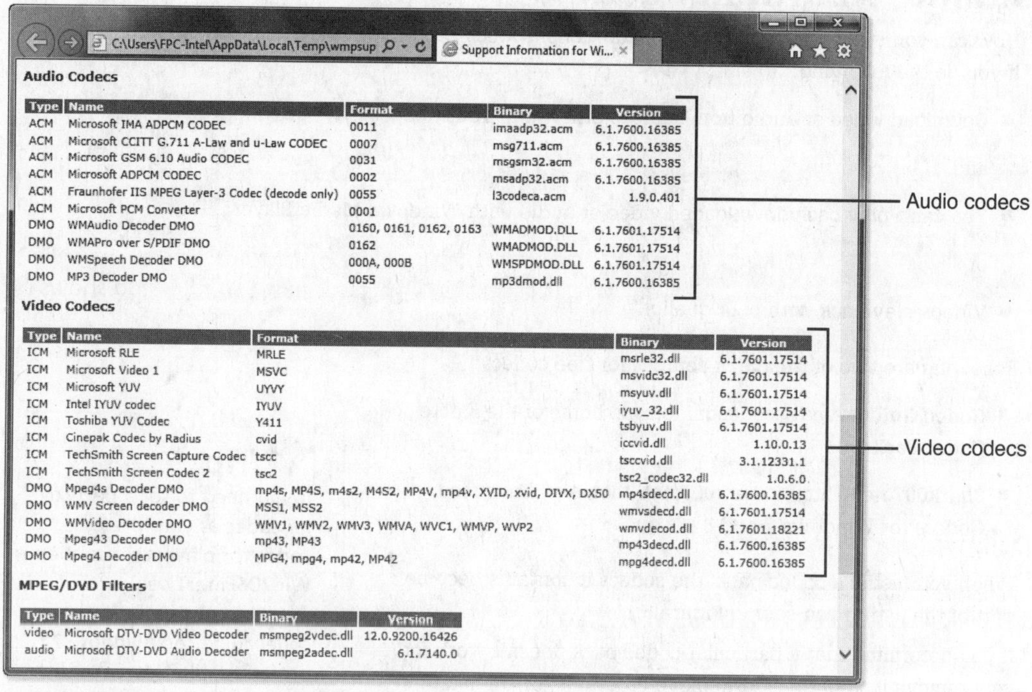

Audio Codecs

Type	Name	Format	Binary	Version
ACM	Microsoft IMA ADPCM CODEC	0011	imaadp32.acm	6.1.7600.16385
ACM	Microsoft CCITT G.711 A-Law and u-Law CODEC	0007	msg711.acm	6.1.7600.16385
ACM	Microsoft GSM 6.10 Audio CODEC	0031	msgsm32.acm	6.1.7600.16385
ACM	Microsoft ADPCM CODEC	0002	msadp32.acm	6.1.7600.16385
ACM	Fraunhofer IIS MPEG Layer-3 Codec (decode only)	0055	l3codeca.acm	1.9.0.401
ACM	Microsoft PCM Converter	0001		
DMO	WMAudio Decoder DMO	0160, 0161, 0162, 0163	WMADMOD.DLL	6.1.7601.17514
DMO	WMAPro over S/PDIF DMO	0162	WMADMOD.DLL	6.1.7601.17514
DMO	WMSpeech Decoder DMO	000A, 000B	WMSPDMOD.DLL	6.1.7601.17514
DMO	MP3 Decoder DMO	0055	mp3dmod.dll	6.1.7600.16385

Video Codecs

Type	Name	Format	Binary	Version
ICM	Microsoft RLE	MRLE	msrle32.dll	6.1.7601.17514
ICM	Microsoft Video 1	MSVC	msvidc32.dll	6.1.7601.17514
ICM	Microsoft YUV	UYVY	msyuv.dll	6.1.7601.17514
ICM	Intel IYUV codec	IYUV	iyuv_32.dll	6.1.7601.17514
ICM	Toshiba YUV Codec	Y411	tsbyuv.dll	6.1.7601.17514
ICM	Cinepak Codec by Radius	cvid	iccvid.dll	1.10.0.13
ICM	TechSmith Screen Capture Codec	tscc	tsccvid.dll	3.1.12331.1
ICM	TechSmith Screen Codec 2	tsc2	tsc2_codec32.dll	1.0.6.0
DMO	Mpeg4s Decoder DMO	mp4s, MP4S, m4s2, M4S2, MP4V, mp4v, XVID, xvid, DIVX, DX50	mp4sdecd.dll	6.1.7600.16385
DMO	WMV Screen decoder DMO	MSS1, MSS2	wmvsdecd.dll	6.1.7601.17514
DMO	WMVideo Decoder DMO	WMV1, WMV2, WMV3, WMVA, WVC1, WMVP, WVP2	wmvdecod.dll	6.1.7601.18221
DMO	Mpeg43 Decoder DMO	mp43, MP43	mp43decd.dll	6.1.7600.16385
DMO	Mpeg4 Decoder DMO	MPG4, mpg4, mp42, MP42	mpg4decd.dll	6.1.7600.16385

MPEG/DVD Filters

Type	Name	Binary	Version
video	Microsoft DTV-DVD Video Decoder	msmpeg2vdec.dll	12.0.9200.16426
audio	Microsoft DTV-DVD Audio Decoder	msmpeg2adec.dll	6.1.7140.0

Figure 5.11
Check the name and format information for your codecs to see if they support the content you want to play back.

If you can't play a video or audio file with WMP, you have two options:

- Install the codecs you need.
- Switch to a third-party media player.

Tip

In Windows 8/8.1, Microsoft no longer provides the codecs necessary for DVD playback and has never included support for Blu-ray (BD) playback. If your computer doesn't include a DVD player program, you can purchase the Media Center Pack with Add Features to Windows 8/8.1 (use Search to locate it).

If you have a Blu-ray (BD) drive and didn't get player software with it, try Corel's WinDVD Pro (www.corel.com) or Cyberlink's PowerDVD 13 Ultra Pro, or Power DVD Live (www.cyberlink.com).

Installing Additional Codecs

How can you tell if you need to install additional codecs? You might need to install additional codecs if you do the following:

- Download video or audio from sources other than YouTube

  and

- You can't play back downloaded video or audio with Windows Media Player

  or

- Videos play back with poor quality.

Following are two of the major sources for free codecs:

- **Codec Guide**—www.codecguide.com, home of the K-Lite Codec Pack
- **Shark007.net**—http://shark007.net/, home of Advanced Codecs for Windows 7 and 8

When you install a codec pack, the codecs it contains become part of the listing you saw in Figure 5.11.

If you determine that a particular codec pack doesn't work for you, remove it through Add/Remove Programs (or Uninstall) in Control Panel.

> **Tip**
>
> If you need to set a particular codec as your preferred codec for playback, use the Win7DSFilterTweaker tool, available from http://www.codecguide.com/windows7_preferred_filter_tweaker.htm.

Alternatives to Windows Media Player

If you decide you'd rather try a different media player for Windows, the most common recommendation is the free, open-source VLC Media Player, available from www.videolan.org. In addition to playing typical media types, it can also play Flash, Video CD, DVB TV files, raw audio and DV, MIDI, supported formats stored in ISO image files, and many other formats.

Can't View Video on Your Android Device

If you can't play a particular video with the video player installed on your Android device, it's time to get a new player. Some leading titles available from Google Play include the following:

- **MX Player**—Special features include hardware acceleration, support for multicore processors, and the capability to install additional codecs when needed to play some files. Figure 5.12 shows a sample of its playback interface.
- **BSPlayer**—Special features include the capability to use software decoding to handle file formats not supported on your smartphone, pop-up video playback over other apps (see Figure 5.13), and add-on packages that tailor the app to particular ARM-based processors.

Figure 5.12 Watching a classic horror movie (*The House on Haunted Hill*) with MX Player.

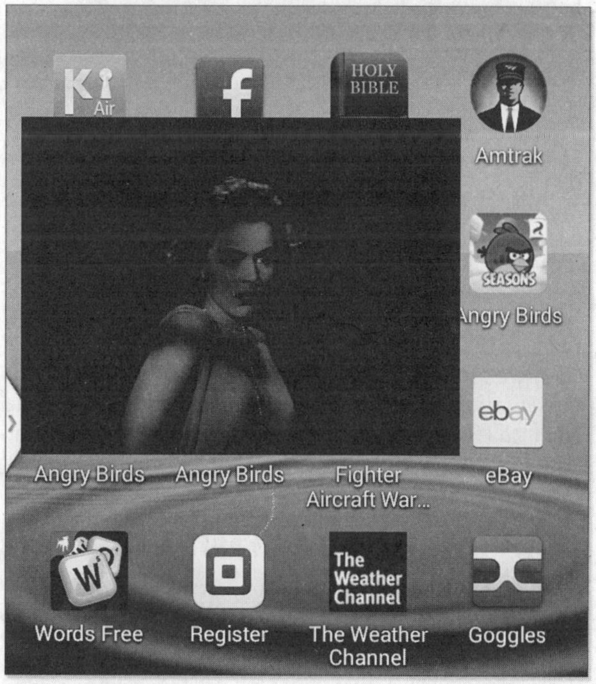

Figure 5.13 BSPlayer's pop-up window lets you watch video while performing other tasks with your Android device.

- **DicePlayer**—Special features include streaming from media servers via Samba or FTP and a pop-up player.
- **MoboPlayer**—Special features include the capability to copy video from your PC to your device, software decoding, and scanning your device for media files (see Figure 5.14).

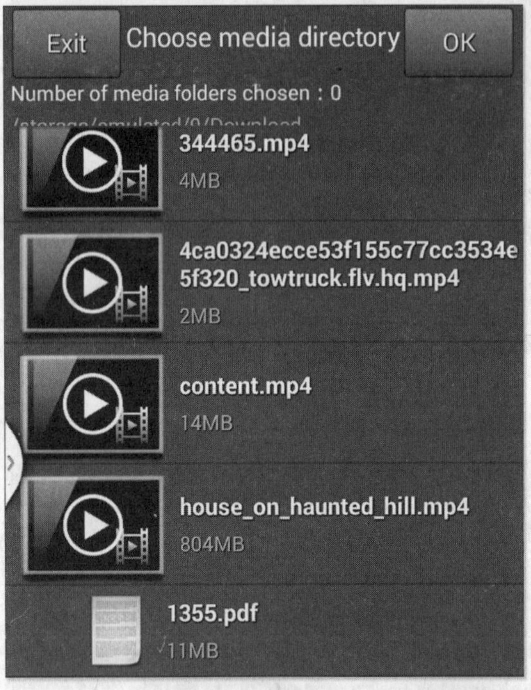

Figure 5.14
MoboPlayer is scanning this device for media files.

Note

For more suggestions, see http://lifehacker.com/5823465/the-best-video-player-for-android, http://www.talkandroid.com/guides/beginner/best-android-video-player-applications-november-2013/, and http://www.tomsguide.com/us/pictures-story/629-7-best-android-video-players.html.

Playing Adobe Flash Video on Android

If you need Adobe Flash support for your Android device, you'll need to try a different browser that has integrated Flash support, because you can no longer get current versions of Adobe Flash for Android. Use "browser flash player" on Google Play to find products with integrated Adobe Flash support.

For the following comparison, we used the Adobe Flash help web page at http://helpx.adobe.com/flash-player.html as viewed with the standard Android browser (see Figure 5.15) and the Flash-enabled FlashFox (Firefox-based) browser available on Google Play (see Figure 5.16).

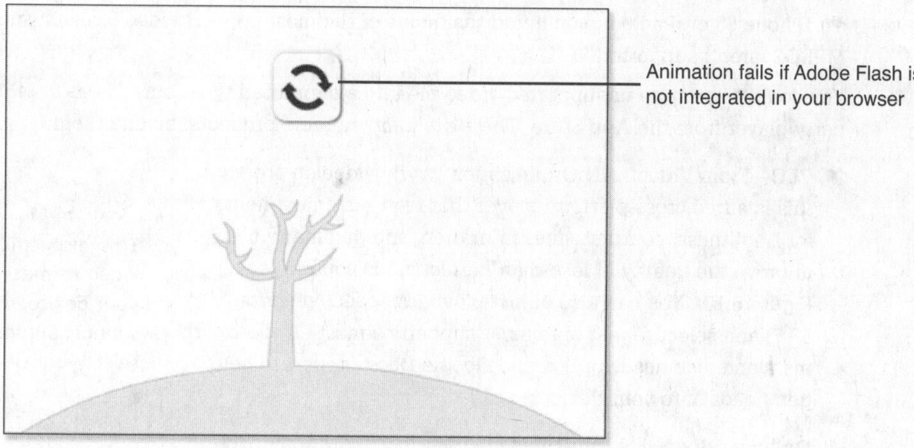

Figure 5.15 The standard Android browser cannot display a Flash animation.

Figure 5.16 An Android browser with integrated Adobe Flash (FlashFox in this example) can display the animation.

Caution

The Adobe Flash help web page has a button you can click to determine if you have Flash installed. Even if you try it with a Flash-enabled browser, it will tell you that you can't get Flash from Google Play anymore. Rely on the Flash animation playback on the same screen (see Figure 5.16) to tell you if your browser's Flash support is working.

Can't Play Video on Your iOS Device

The built-in video player included with iPhone, iPod Touch, and iPad supports a limited number of video formats that vary by model. However, whether you have an old iPhone 4 or iPad2 or the latest iPhone 5S or iPad Air, you'll find that some of the most popular video formats, such as DiVX and MPEG2, aren't supported.

You could convert an unsupported video file into a supported type, but it's easier to choose a third-party player from the App Store. There are many notable products, among them:

- **VLC**—From Video LAN Organization (www.videolan.org/vlc/), this is a free cross-platform player that features adjustments for brightness, contrast, hue, saturation, and gamma to help improve the quality of less-than-perfect video content (see Figure 5.18). You can also adjust playback speed (see Figure 5.17) and select repeat options. It supports almost all video formats and includes DropBox and Google Docs support to help get videos onto your device.
- **Oplayer**—Special features include built-in Wi-Fi transfer settings (see Figure 5.19), the capability to play back incomplete or damaged AVI files, and extensive audio playback options (see Figure 5.20). The free version is ad-supported.

> **Tip**
> To see specific audio and video formats supported by your device, visit http://support.apple.com/specs/ and select your device.

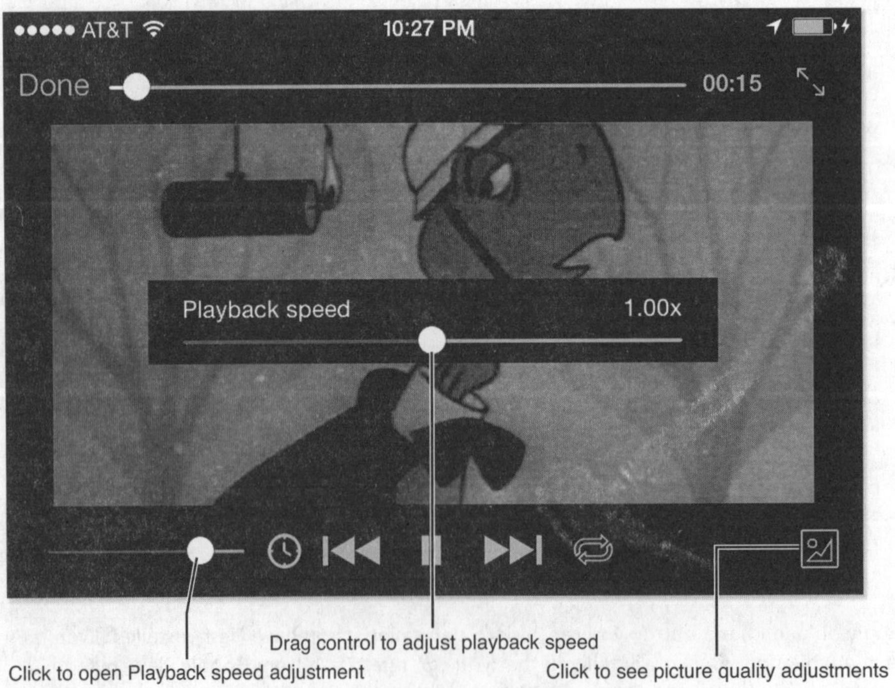

Figure 5.17 Adjusting playback speed with VLC.

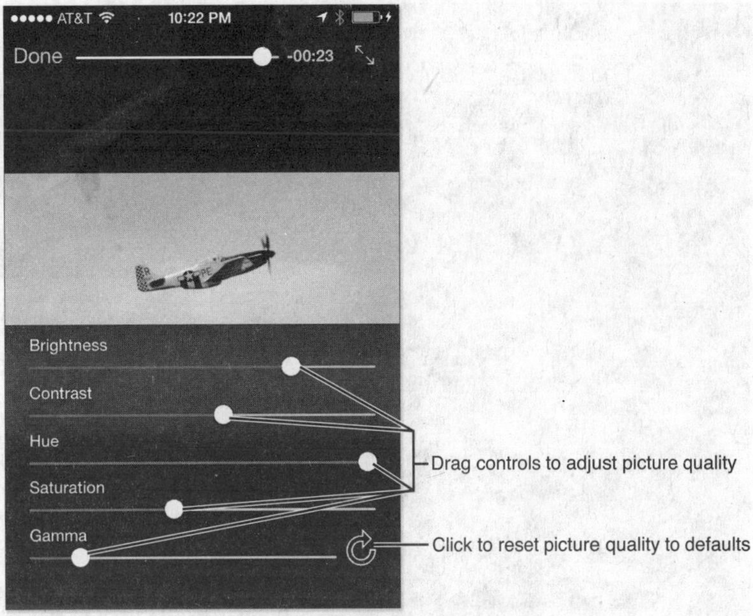

Figure 5.18
Tweaking video playback quality with VLC.

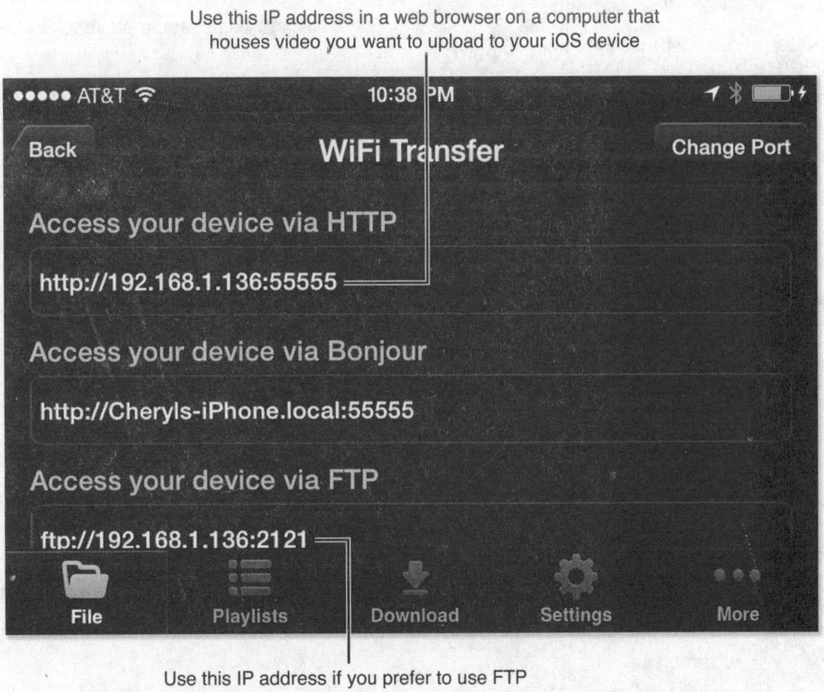

Figure 5.19
Wi-Fi transfer options in Oplayer help you connect to your iOS device from another device for easy media file uploads.

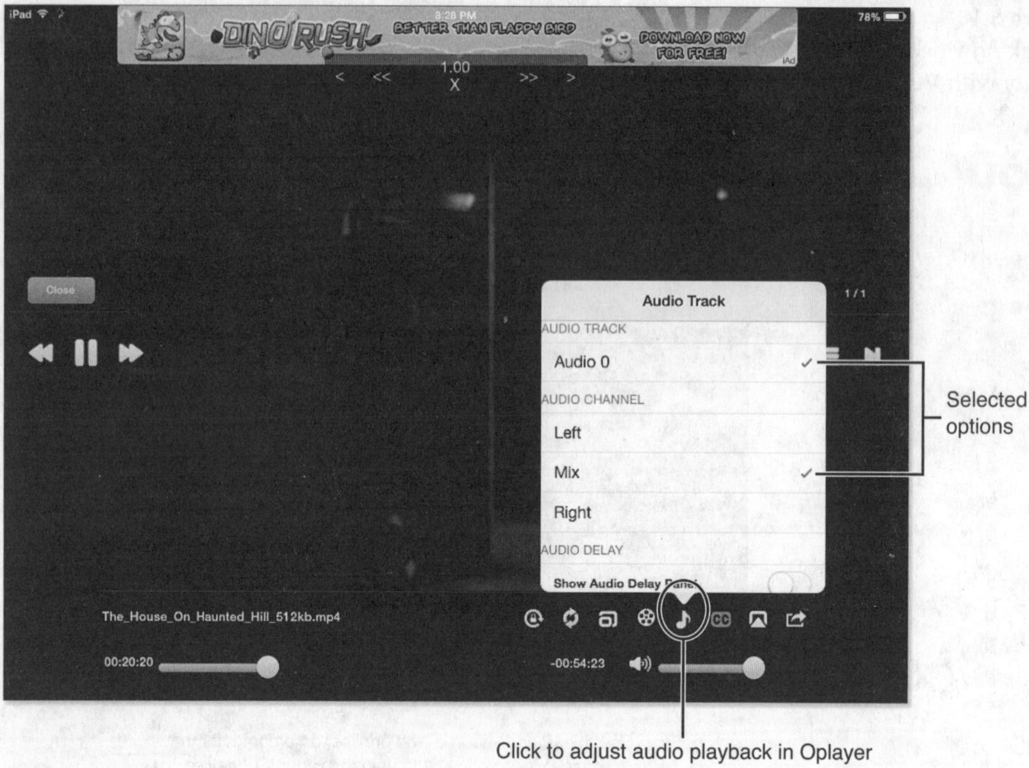

Figure 5.20
Audio playback adjustments in Oplayer.

> **Note**
> For additional player recommendations and reviews, see www.addictivetips.com/ios/the-best-video-players-for-iphone-ipad-ipod-touch/ for details.

Choosing a Video Player for Your PC or Device

Whether you need to play a wider range of videos on a Windows PC, Android device, or iOS device, there are plenty of choices. Consider these key factors:

- Determine support for the file and encoding type(s) used by the videos you want to play.
- For a player used on a tablet or smartphone, determine whether gesture controls are used, and how.

- If you want Dolby audio support, look for it (many players don't include it).
- Most (but not all) "free" players are typically ad supported. It may be worth a few bucks to add features and dump the ads after you find a player (or players) you like.

Troubleshooting Codecs

Even after you install software so you can view RAW files or play more video files, you might still have problems. Check this list of problems and solutions for help:

- **Can't view RAW files after installing RAW codec**—Try rebooting your system.
- **RAW files show up in My Computer/This PC (Windows 8) but not in Pictures**—Right-click or press and hold a RAW file and change the Open With setting from Picture Viewer to Photos. Your RAW files should now be visible in Photos.
- **RAW files from your old digital camera can be displayed, but RAW files from your new camera show up as thumbnails**—You need to update your RAW codec. Check with your RAW codec provider for an update for your camera.
- **You decide to change from the Microsoft Digital Camera Codec pack to a third-party codec in Windows 8/8.1 but can't remove it with Add/Remove Programs (Uninstall)**—To remove the Microsoft Digital Camera Codec pack in Windows 8/8.1, open View Installed Updates in Control Panel, select it from the list, and click or tap Uninstall.

6

KEEPING DEVICES POWERED UP

Fast Track to Solutions

Table 6.1 Symptom Table

Symptom	Flowchart or Book Section	Page #
I don't know whether I can charge my mobile device from my computer's USB port.	Smartphone Versus Tablet—Charging Requirements	155
I want to use my computer's USB ports for charging my devices without leaving the computer on.	Setting Up Your PC's USB Ports for Full-Time Charging Support	157
My computer doesn't have designated USB charging ports. Is there a way to make my USB ports work better for charging my devices?	Software Drivers for Faster Charging	158

Smartphone Versus Tablet—Charging Requirements

Third-party chargers for tablets and chargers abound, but if you choose the wrong charger for your device (or use a USB port instead of a charger), you're looking at slow charging times. So, what are the recommended matchups for charging these devices? Check out Table 6.2 for details.

Table 6.2 Recommended Charger Amperage by Device Type

Device	Use with 1.0Amp Charger	Use with 2.1Amp Charger	Charge with Standard USB Port
iPod Touch	Recommended	OK	Yes*
iPhone	Recommended	Acceptable	Yes*
iPad	Acceptable*	Recommended	No
Android smartphone	Recommended	OK	Yes*
Android tablet	Acceptable*	Recommended	No

*Charging will take longer with these combinations

If you plug a device designed for a 1.0Amp charger into a 2.1Amp charger, the device draws only 1.0Amp. The device won't be damaged.

To determine what amperage a charger supports, check the charger for information. Figure 6.1 shows the markings on a typical 2.1Amp charger for tablets and smartphones.

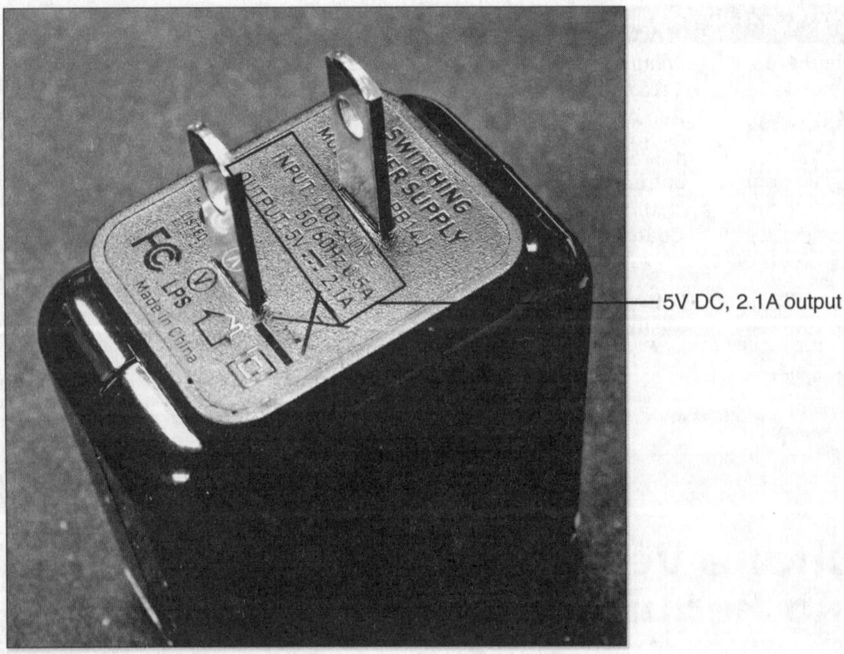

Figure 6.1
This Monoprice charger provides up to 2.1Amp output, making it suitable for tablets and smartphones.

Tip

Use a charger like the one shown in Figure 6.1 with your choice of devices that include a USB charging cable.

Dual USB Port Charging Pitfalls

An increasing number of surge suppressors and third-party chargers include a pair of USB charging ports for use with smartphones and tablets. Unless marked otherwise, these devices typically provide a total of 2.1Amp. What does this mean for you? You can charge a pair of smartphones (either iPhone/iPod Touch, Android, or both) or a single tablet.

A few chargers are designed to support a smartphone and a tablet at the same time. These units have clearly marked 1Amp and 2.1Amp ports. These devices sometimes are marked as providing a total of 3.1 Amp.

Setting Up Your PC's USB Ports for Full-Time Charging Support

As you learned in Table 6.2, you can use your computer's USB ports to charge smartphones. However, you can charge your smartphone with your computer's USB port only if the port doesn't go into sleep mode.

If you don't want to keep your computer on all the time to keep your smartphone charged up, but don't want to use a separate charger, look for laptop or desktop computers that include USB charging support.

Depending on the device in question, this might be implemented as a specially marked USB port and might also require that the feature be enabled in the system BIOS or power management dialog, or that a special driver is installed.

Table 6.3 provides you with a quick reference to this technology as implemented by leading motherboard and system vendors.

Table 6.3 USB Charging Support

Vendor	Term	Supported on Laptops	Supported on Desktops
ASUS	USB Charger Plus	Yes	No
Dell	USB PowerShare	Yes	No
Gigabyte	On/Off Charge	No	Yes
HP	USB Boost	Yes	Yes*
Lenovo	Always On USB	Yes	Yes**
MSI	Super-Charger	No	Yes
Toshiba	USB Sleep-and-Charge	Yes	N/A

*All-in-one models

**All-in-one and desktop models

Note: Check specifications for a particular model from these vendors to determine whether the feature is included.

Note

On a Lenovo computer that supports Always On USB, the Always On USB port is yellow. Some Dell and HP computers use a lightning bolt marking to indicate the USB port with charging features. Check your system documentation to determine if this feature is supported, which port(s) support USB charging, and whether sufficient amperage is provided to charge tablets.

If your device does not start charging, disconnect and reconnect it to the supported port.

Software Drivers for Faster Charging

If your Windows laptop or desktop doesn't include dedicated USB charging ports, you can improve smartphone charging performance and even add tablet charging support with most computers' USB 2.0 or USB 3.0 ports by installing the free ASUS AI Charger utility. It's available from many popular download sites. AI Charger works by increasing charging amperage in USB ports to 1.2AMP.

Tip

To learn which of your USB ports puts out the most power for charging USB devices, get a Practical Meter (www.practicalmeter.com). It's a USB dongle with charge indicator lights and a three-headed charging cable (mini-USB, micro-USB, and iPhone).

Troubleshooting a Device or Battery That's Not Charging

If you can't charge a laptop, tablet, or smartphone, or charge a rechargeable battery, you need to determine which of the following is the problem:

- Not enough wattage or amperage from the charger
- Defective cable
- Defective charger
- Defective battery

In this section, we'll help you figure out the solution that applies to your problem.

Wattage and Amperage

If you're charging a smartphone or tablet, amperage (Amp) is the measure to look for. As you learned from Table 6.2, you should use a charger that matches or exceeds the amperage rating of the device you want to charge.

If you need to replace a laptop AC adapter, the measurement is in watts, but the principle is the same: buy an AC adapter with the same or higher wattage rating that will work with your laptop.

Caution

AC adapters made for netbooks might plug into your laptop, but they probably won't provide enough power.

You don't need to buy an adapter from your laptop vendor, by the way. If you're not sure what brand your next laptop will be, or if you're looking for more "bang for the buck," choose a third-party model with interchangeable tips. Some laptop AC adapters now also include USB charging ports.

Troubleshooting Laptop Power Issues

If you don't have a multimeter available, you can perform a rough "go-no go" test of your laptop's AC adapter by disconnecting it from AC power and removing the battery from your laptop (see Figure 6.2).

Figure 6.2 Slide the release switch for your laptop's battery and remove it before testing the AC adapter.

Reconnect the AC adapter and turn on the laptop. If the laptop turns on, the AC adapter is OK.

In addition to finding out what wattage rating your laptop AC adapter has, the second reason to look at the label on the AC adapter is to determine its output voltage and polarity. You need this information if you want to test your AC adapter or to buy a third-party replacement. In Figure 6.3, the laptop AC adapter is designed to output 19V DC. The positive connection is in the middle of the plug, and the negative connection is the outside of the plug.

If the laptop cannot run without the battery while plugged into an AC outlet, check the following:

- Make sure the laptop is plugged into a working AC outlet. Use a lamp or clock radio to determine if the AC outlet is working. You can also use a portable outlet tester, a voltmeter or a multimeter set to AC voltage to determine if the output is within acceptable limits.
- Make sure the AC power cord running from the AC outlet to the external AC adapter "power brick" is plugged completely into the outlet and the adapter. If the power cord or plug is damaged, replace the cord.

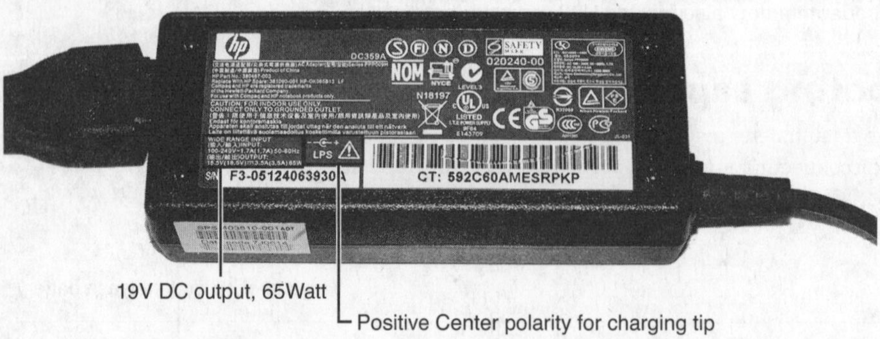

Figure 6.3 The DC voltage rating and polarity for a typical laptop AC adapter.

- To determine whether the adapter is outputting the correct DC voltage, use a voltmeter or multimeter set to DC voltage to test the voltage coming from the adapter and compare it to the nominal output values marked on the adapter. As Figure 6.4 illustrates, it might be necessary to use a bent paper clip to enable an accurate voltage reading. A value of +/–5% is acceptable.

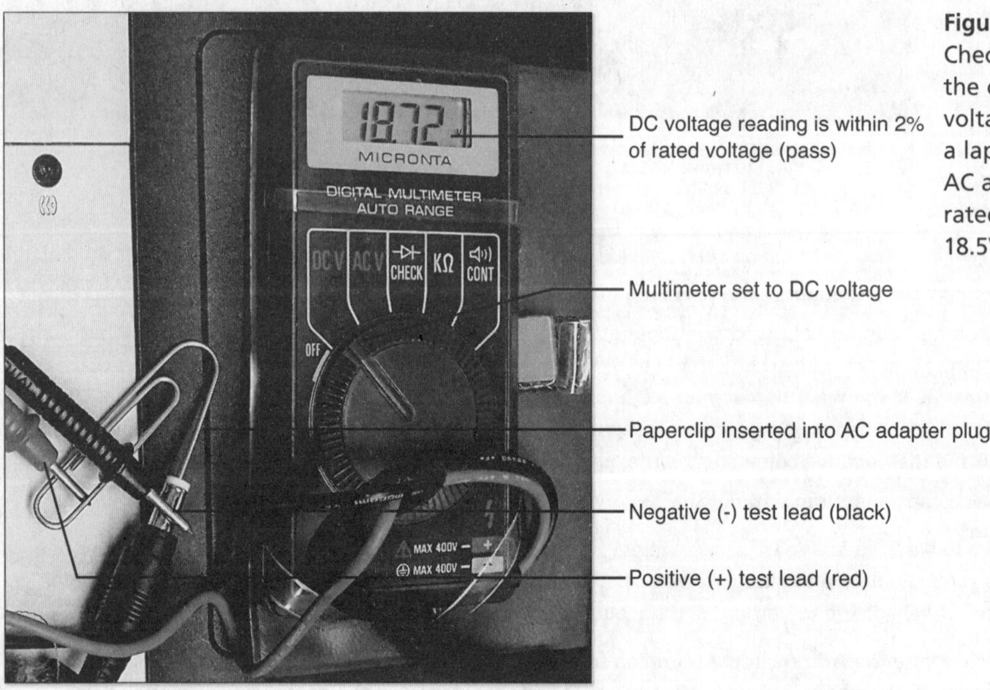

Figure 6.4 Checking the output voltage from a laptop's AC adapter rated at 18.5V.

Smartphone or Tablet Cable or Charger?

If you can't charge your smartphone or tablet with the recommended charger, the problem could be the charger or the cable. Because these types of chargers are difficult to test, follow this procedure:

1. Make sure the charger is plugged into a working AC wall outlet or a surge suppressor that is turned on.
2. Swap the original cable for another cable (preferably a known-working cable, or a brand-new cable if a known-working replacement is not available). If the device now charges, recycle the old cable and use the replacement cable. If the device still won't charge, proceed to step 3.
3. Swap the original charger for another charger (preferably known-working, or a new one if a known-working charger is not available) and use the original cable. If the device now charges, recycle the old charger and use the replacement charger. If the device still won't charge, proceed to step 4.
4. If the battery in the smartphone or tablet can be removed, remove it, wipe off the contacts, and replace it. Retry the charging process. If the device still won't charge, replace the battery or have the unit serviced.

Battery Testing

You can use any of the following methods to test a battery. Choose the best method for your situation:

- Use a multimeter set to the battery's voltage (DC current). Check the battery's markings to determine positive (+) and negative (–) terminals. The red lead from the multimeter goes to the positive terminal; the black to the negative terminal.
- Use a self-contained battery tester set to the battery's voltage. See Figure 6.5.
- Use the battery in a compatible device.

For the first test, a battery fails if it doesn't provide output at the rated voltage. For the second test (see Figure 6.5), a battery fails if it doesn't move the needle into the Good zone. For the third test, a battery fails if the device won't turn on.

If a rechargeable battery fails, recharge it. If it won't take a charge or runs out of power after just a few minutes or a few photos, recycle it. If a throwaway battery (alkaline or lithium) fails, replace it. Dispose of it according to local regulations.

Note

Check the battery's markings to determine positive (+) and negative (–) terminals. The red lead from the multimeter or battery tester goes to the positive terminal; the black to the negative terminal.

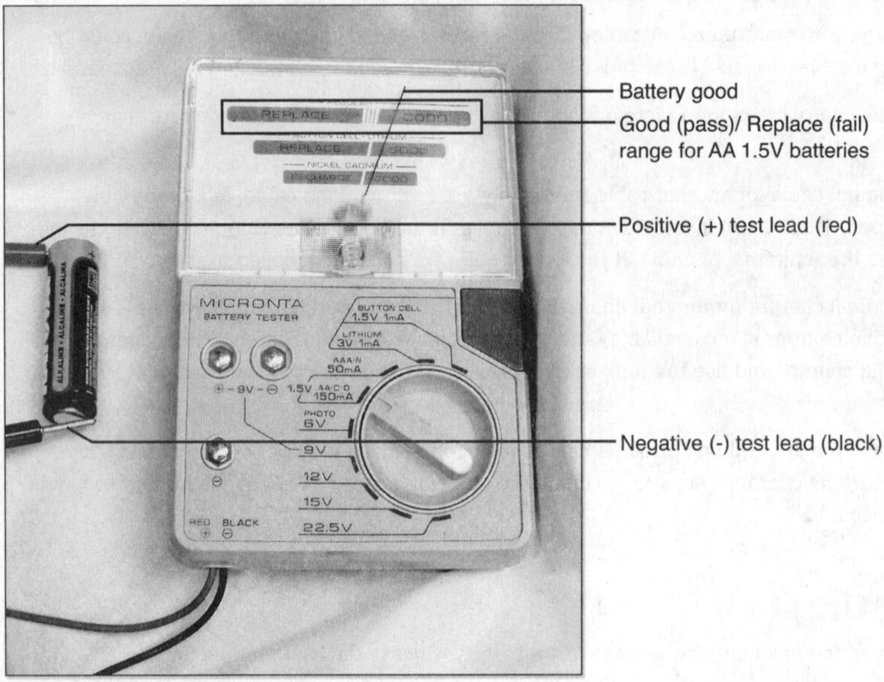

Figure 6.5 Testing an AA alkaline battery with a battery tester.

Battery Not Charging or Not Holding a Charge

If a device works when plugged into AC power, but not on battery power, check the following:

- Make sure that the battery is installed properly.
- Wipe off any corrosion or dirt on the battery and battery contacts.
- Determine whether the battery can hold a charge. Make sure the battery is properly installed and the AC adapter has proper DC voltage output levels. Leave the device plugged in for the recommended amount of time needed to charge the battery, and then try to run the device on battery power. If the battery cannot run the system at all, or if the device runs out of battery power very quickly, replace the battery (if it is user replaceable). If replacing the battery does not solve the problem, or if the battery is built in to the device, the device needs to be serviced or replaced.
- If the battery is hot after being charged or has a warped exterior, it might have an internal short. Replace it.

Replacing Your Device's Battery

Whether you're shopping for a cordless or cell phone battery, a battery for your digital camera, or a set of AAs for a remote control or electronic flash, the sheer number of options can make buying mistakes easy to commit. To help your device work as well (or better) than it did before, follow these suggestions.

Rechargeable AA/AAA/C/D Batteries

If you're tired of shelling out for AA, AAA, C, or D batteries for your electronic devices, the first question to ask is "rechargeable or disposable?" Here's why that question isn't as easy to answer as you might think:

Although rechargeable batteries can be recharged hundreds of times, you can't always replace alkaline or lithium batteries with rechargeables. The number one reason is voltage output: a single AA, AAA, C, or D-cell alkaline or lithium battery provides 1.5V DC power, whereas a single rechargeable NiMh battery provides 1.2–1.25V DC power. If a device isn't designed to use the lower voltage provided by rechargeable batteries, it might not work at all, or it might work erratically.

Before you decide to try rechargeable batteries, check the device's instruction manual. Buy just one set of rechargeable batteries and a charger, charge the batteries, and use them in the device. If the results are satisfactory, buy a second set. If not, the device is not compatible with rechargeable batteries.

When you select rechargeable batteries, look carefully at the mAh rating: the higher the rating, the longer your batteries will last per charge. mAh ratings can vary a great deal between batteries, as shown in Figure 6.6.

Figure 6.6
Choose batteries with a larger mAh rating for longer runtime.

Alkaline Versus Lithium Batteries

Even if you decide that rechargeable batteries are the way to go, it still makes sense to have a set of throwaway batteries in reserve in case you forget to recharge your batteries. What should you buy to keep your electronics happy?

Rule number 1: If it isn't an alkaline or lithium battery, forget it. It might be tempting to pick up a package of "heavy duty" or "super heavy duty" batteries because they're cheap. However, alkaline and lithium batteries last much longer in service.

Rule number 2: Any alkaline battery will do in low-drain applications, such as remote controls or flashlights in storage. However, when used in electronic flash units, digital cameras, or similar high-drain applications, you're better off with high-end alkaline or, better still, lithium batteries.

Rule number 3: For longest use time with high-drain digital devices, use lithium batteries.

Rule number 4: If your device recommends different types of batteries for different conditions (such as an outdoor weather sensor), be sure to use the battery type(s) recommended for the conditions in which you use the device.

Note

Examples of low-end alkaline batteries include most private-label alkaline batteries, Varta Energy, Varta Longlife, Kodak Xtralife, and Eveready Gold (made by Energizer). Mid-range alkaline batteries include Duracell Coppertop, RayOVac Ready Power, Energizer Max, Kodak MAX, CVS MAX, and Varta High Energy. High-end alkaline batteries include Duracell Quantum, Kodak Ultra, RayOVac Advanced High Energy, Varta MaxTech, and Varta Professional Alkaline.

Proprietary Laptop, Digital Camera, or Camcorder Batteries

If you've been accustomed to buying off-the-shelf AA batteries for a low-cost digital camera or camcorder, be prepared for sticker shock when you price proprietary rechargeable batteries for laptops, cameras, and camcorders. If you buy from the camera vendor, you might pay $50–$60 or more for a single battery. An OEM laptop battery can cost $30–$40.

However, you don't need to pay that much. Many third-party vendors produce plug-compatible rechargeable batteries that sell for considerably less. In some cases, you can buy replacement batteries with a higher mAh rating, resulting in more shots per charge (see Figure 6.7).

Note

The greater the number of cells in a laptop or netbook battery, the longer the run time per charge—and the greater the cost. Typical laptop batteries contain six cells, while so-called "long-life" or "extended-life" batteries typically feature nine cells. Once again, you can achieve significant savings by buying third-party replacements.

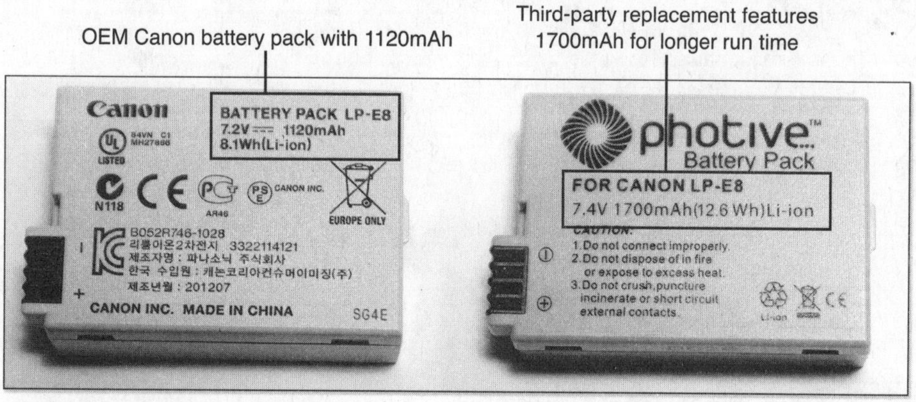

Figure 6.7 Choose batteries with a larger mAh rating for longer runtime.

Built-in Batteries

If your device uses a built-in battery, such as an Apple portable device, you will need to have the unit serviced if the battery fails. If you are considering buying a refurbished iPod, iPad, or iPhone, keep in mind that Apple's refurbishing process includes replacing the battery. Third-party refurbishing typically does not.

Extending Battery Life

To extend battery life in any device, follow these suggestions:

- Use the lowest level of screen brightness that works for you.
- If you can adjust the amount of time your device's LCD displays stays on, reduce it if it stays on when you're not using it.
- Close your laptop to put it into sleep mode.
- Close apps you're not using them.
- Keep your device away from extremely hot or extremely cold environments; batteries, like devices, work best at room temperature.

7

DESKTOP POWER SUPPLY TROUBLESHOOTING

Fast Track to Solutions

Table 7.1 Symptom Table

Symptom	Flowchart or Book Section	Page #
The power supply is very warm to the touch.	Troubleshooting Overheating and Airflow Problems	172
My computer restarts itself, even though I didn't do anything.	System Reboots Itself	175
My computer works well in one room, but if I move it to another room, it crashes frequently.	Checking Wall Outlets	190
When I plug in a bus-powered USB device, the computer doesn't always recognize it.	Determining Whether a Power Supply Should Be Replaced (flowchart)	607
When I plug in an additional drive or add-on card, either the computer can't start or it crashes, but the same device works correctly in another PC.	Determining Whether a Power Supply Should Be Replaced (flowchart)	607

Symptom	Flowchart or Book Section	Page #
My computer locks up frequently.	Random System Crashes or Lockups	172
I'm not sure if my power supply is putting out the right voltage levels.	Random System Crashes or Lockups	172
I have a Dell computer that needs a new power supply. How can I tell if it needs a standard or a special Dell model?	Upgrading Power Supplies in Dell Computers	186
How can I avoid buying a power supply that's too small?	Selecting the Right-Sized Power Supply	185
How can I make sure I'm getting a big enough battery backup unit (UPS)?	Choosing a Battery Backup Device	193
My system won't start.	Troubleshooting a System That Won't Start (flowchart)	Chapter 24
I'm not sure if I need to replace my power supply.	Determining Whether a Power Supply Should Be Replaced (flowchart)	Chapter 24

What Bad Power Does to Your System

If you're planning a system upgrade, it's likely that your power supply is not on the list. After all, it doesn't *appear* to affect a system's performance or features. But appearances can be deceiving. Bad power supplies can cause a lot of grief. A lot of the problems PC users experience that get blamed on memory, Windows, and so on can all be traced to a faulty or poor-quality power supply. Sadly, the power supply is often the first component most PC vendors attempt to skimp on.

What can a bad power supply do to your system? It prevents your computer from running reliably, can cause bus-powered USB and IEEE-1394 devices to be unreliable, and can even cause the computer to reboot spontaneously or fail to boot at all. The trouble is, a bad power supply isn't the only PC component that can cause these kinds of problems: bad device drivers, overclocking your system past its limits, and Windows errors can also cause these symptoms.

In this chapter, we'll put on our deerstalker caps, grab our magnifying glasses, and turn amateur detectives to determine if you have a defective power supply. You'll learn how to protect your power supply and how to replace your power supply with the right model for your needs.

Keep in mind that a "power supply" doesn't contain a small atomic reactor or any other true source of power. Instead, power supplies convert potentially deadly high-voltage AC wall current into safe low-voltage DC power. A byproduct of the transforming process is heat; hence, a desktop PC's power supply contains a built-in fan, which pulls air through the power supply to dissipate heat and help cool the system. Laptop computers work a little differently—they typically use an external "briquette" transformer to turn AC into DC power. Consequently, the laptop's power supply is responsible for fiddling the DC power coming into the unit into the various voltage levels needed for drive motors, cooling fans, and chips.

Now that you understand what a power supply is—and what it does—it's time to find out what makes one conk out.

Determining Whether Your Power Supply Is Overloaded or Failing

A power supply that can't provide the power needed by your computer is often called an *overloaded* power supply. What does that mean?

The motherboard, memory modules, CPU, fans, USB ports, and IEEE-1394 ports built in to your system all require power. Power supplies are rated in terms of output voltage, amps, and wattage. So, what happens if your power supply doesn't provide enough power to drive your devices?

If your power supply doesn't have a high enough wattage rating (larger is better) to handle the power needs of your computer and the components plugged into it, the power supply will wear out prematurely. (Remember, any time you add to the components in your PC, you increase the load on your power supply.) Here are some of the symptoms to look for.

Overheating

As you learned in Chapter 1, "PC, Tablet, Mobile Device, Home Theater, Digital Camera, and Camcorder Anatomy 101," the power supply on a desktop computer is located at the rear of the case. When the system is running, the power supply is normally warm to the touch. However, if it is too hot to touch, the power supply may be overloaded (too high a wattage drain) or the power supply or system fans may have failed.

Bus-Powered USB Devices Are Failing

USB devices are powered in one of two ways:

- **Self-powered**—The device has its own power supply.
- **Bus-powered**—The device draws power from the port.

Self-powered devices use only a small fraction of the power available from a port, whereas bus-powered devices can use most or all of the power available from a port. USB 1.1/2.0 root hubs (ports built into a computer) provide 500mA of power per port, and USB 3.0 root hubs provide 900mA of power per port. Figure 7.1 illustrates typical current draws for a range of USB devices.

What types of devices are bus-powered? Keyboards, mice, and other types of pointing devices are bus-powered, but these devices typically use 100mA or less. However, bus-powered flash memory drives and hard disk drives can use up to 500mA.

If you need to plug and unplug a USB device two or more times before it is detected by the system, especially if it is bus-powered, this can be a sign of an overloaded power supply.

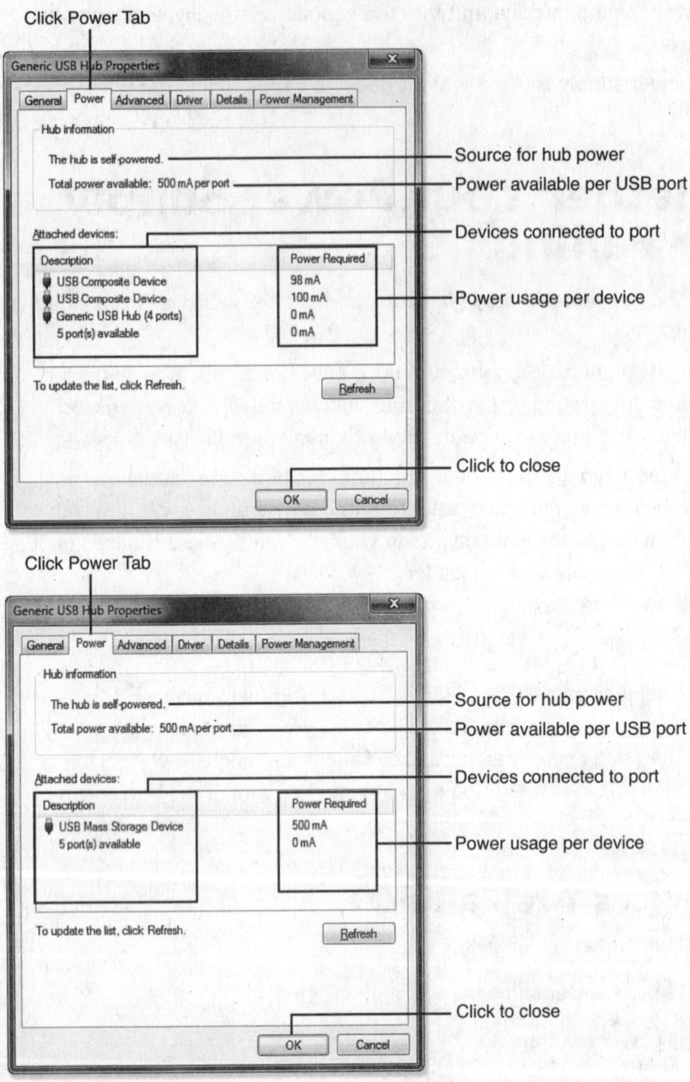

Figure 7.1 USB device power requirements.

Not Enough 12V Power

Until a few years ago, power supplies provided similar levels of +5V and +12V DC power. Originally, +12V DC power was used to power fans and drive motors. However, in recent years +12V DC power has also been used to provide power for processors and for PCIe video cards. As a result, a power supply that appears to have sufficient power in terms of its wattage rating might not have enough +12V DC power for current systems. Figure 7.2 compares the labels for two power supplies of similar wattage.

Figure 7.2 More watts doesn't always mean more +12V DC power.

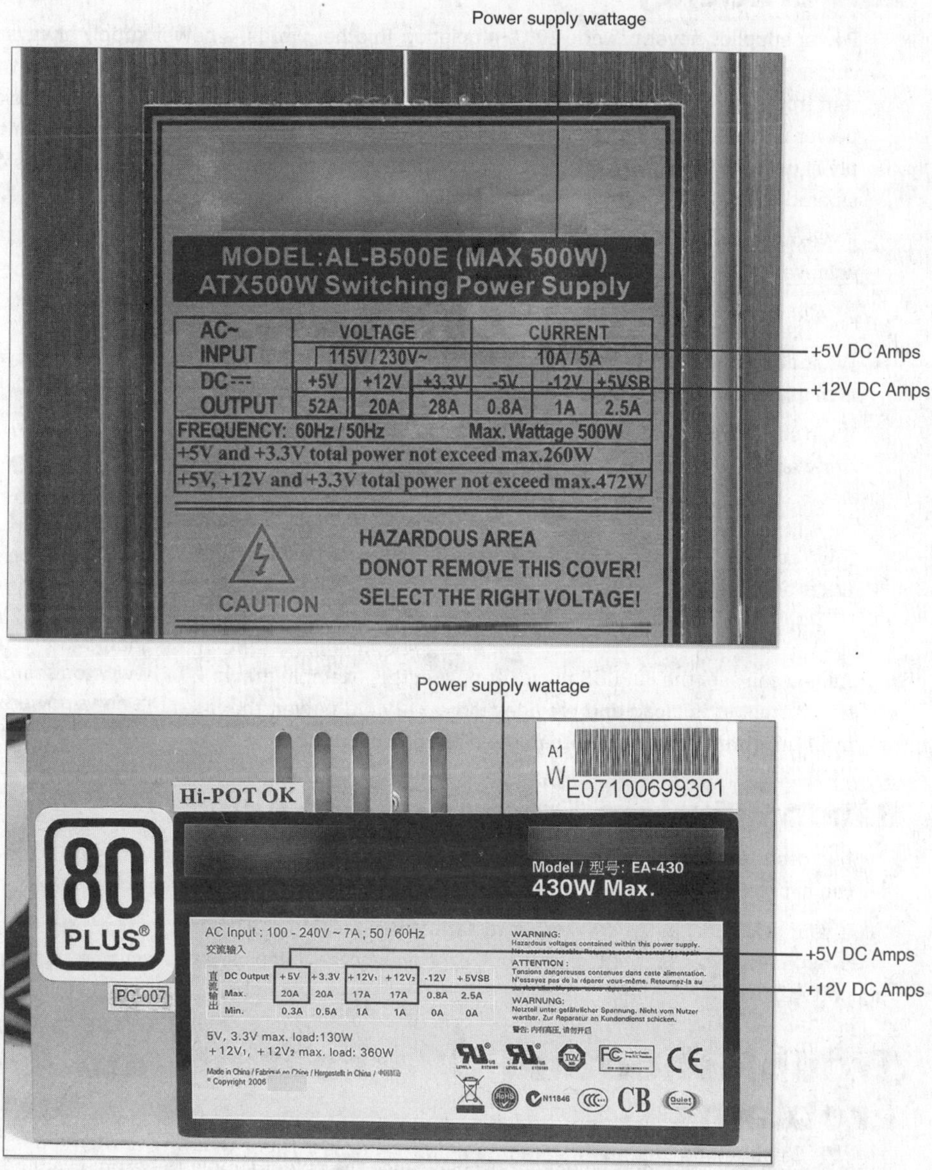

As you can see, the power supply with the lower wattage rating (430) actually has much more +12V DC power (34 Amps versus 20 Amps). Thus, it provides more of the power needed by modern systems. If you use a power supply with an inadequate amount of +12V DC power, adding additional hard disks, SSDs, optical drives, fans, a faster processor, or a PCIe video card that requires a +12V DC power connector could overload the +12V DC line and cause your system to lock up or crash.

Low Efficiency

Power supplies never provide 100% efficiency. In other words, a power supply always draws more current than it provides. For a power supply to provide its rated wattage, it must draw enough current from the AC wall outlet to provide that power. The higher the efficiency, the less additional power is needed. However, the excess power used is minimized when a more efficient power supply is used. Using a more efficient power supply helps minimize heat buildup (excess current is dissipated as heat) and also helps reduce utility costs.

For example, the 430-watt power supply shown in Figure 7.2b has an 80% efficiency rating. To achieve 430-watt output (in other words, a 100% load), it needs to draw 537.5 watts:

430 watts / 0.80 = 537.5

What about the power supply shown in Figure 7.2a? It lacks an efficiency rating, but a general rule is to assume a rating of between 63% and 70% for typical unrated power supplies.

If we assume 63% efficiency, our 500 watt power supply needs to draw about 794 watts at full load:

500 watts / 0.63 = 793.65

If we assume 70% efficiency, the current draw would be 714 watts at full load:

500 watts / 0.7 = 714.28

As you can see, the 80PLUS power supply in this example draws less current at full load and provides more +12V DC power, the most important power level, than the older power supply.

> **Note**
> To learn much more about power supplies than we have space for, see the article "Picking the Right Power Supply: What You Should Know" at http://www.tomshardware.com/reviews/power-supply-psu-review,2916.html.

Random System Crashes or Lockups

Microsoft Windows is very sensitive to power problems. An overloaded or overheated power supply can cause Windows STOP errors (also known as the Blue Screen of Death) at random intervals.

If your system locks up, freezes, or restarts when playing a 3D game, your power supply may be overloaded on its +12V DC power rail, especially if the video card you're using requires its own power cable.

Troubleshooting Overheating and Airflow Problems

Although an overloaded power supply can cause the power supply to become very hot, other problems inside the case can cause overheating issues as well. Before assuming you need a new power supply, check these issues first:

- Make sure the air intakes on the computer case, the air intakes into the power supply, the power supply fan, and the exhaust are clean and free of obstructions.
- Make sure the power supply fan is turning at full speed; if the power supply has a fan facing inside the system, make sure it is turning as well. If the power supply fan has failed, replace the

power supply. If the power supply has a monitoring lead that connects to the motherboard, you can check the system BIOS's hardware monitor or run software supplied by the motherboard or system maker to see if the fan is running at the proper speed.

- If your system uses ribbon cables (used for floppy drives or PATA drives), fold or cable-tie drive ribbon cables inside the case to prevent them from blocking airflow. You can also replace flat cables with pre-rounded cables available from many vendors. Another option is to purchase split-loom or braided-cable sleeving and then fit your PATA and floppy cables into them, securing them with cable ties. This will both increase airflow inside the case and give your case a custom look. Various kinds of cable sleeves can be purchased at computer mod websites or at automotive websites.
- If case fans are not turning, make sure they are properly plugged into the motherboard or a four-pin (Molex) power connector. If the fan can't be turned by hand, it has failed and should be replaced.
- If the fans are turning, make sure they are properly installed. Fans at the front or sides of the case should be installed to pull air into the case, while fans at the back of the case should be installed to push air out of the case.

Has Your Power Supply Failed?

There are several indications that your power supply has failed, but some of them can also be caused by other problems. In other words, don't assume you need a new power supply until you check the other causes.

System Won't Turn On

If you can't get your computer to start up, don't panic! Before you assume that your power supply is pushing up daisies, check the following:

- The computer might not be plugged in.
- The surge suppressor the computer is plugged into might be turned off.
- The power switch on the rear of some power supplies might be turned off (not all power supplies have this switch). Refer to Figure 1.5 (Chapter 1) or 7.15.
- You might have the wrong input voltage selected on the rear of the power supply. Refer to Figure 1.5 (Chapter 1).
- The wiring from the case's on/off switch might not be properly connected to the correct jumpers on the motherboard. Refer to Figure 1.15 (Chapter 1).
- The power connectors to the motherboard might not be properly connected. Some motherboards require you to connect the ATX12V connectors as well as the primary connector to the motherboard for adequate power.
- You might have an internal short that shuts down the power supply as soon as you start the system.
- The motherboard has a "Guardian" function that prevents you from starting the computer unless a working processor fan is plugged into a particular jack.

You're probably using a surge suppressor between your computer and the wall outlet, so don't ignore the possibility that the surge suppressor is turned off or has failed. If the computer runs when you plug it into a wall outlet but won't work when you plug it into a surge suppressor that's turned on, look for a reset button on the surge suppressor and press it. If the surge suppressor doesn't have a reset button, or it still doesn't work after you try it, the suppressor is dead and needs to be replaced.

Power Supply Comes On for a Moment, Then Stops

Your system probably has an internal short if it turns on for a couple of seconds and then stops. Internal shorts can be caused by any of the following:

- Loose screws inside the computer case
- Defective components in the power supply
- Bare wires on the power supply cables or splitter/extensions (which extend or split one 4-pin drive connector to service two devices)
- Damaged add-on cards
- Damaged components plugged into the power supply, such as drives, video cards, or fans

Figure 7.3 illustrates some of these potential problems.

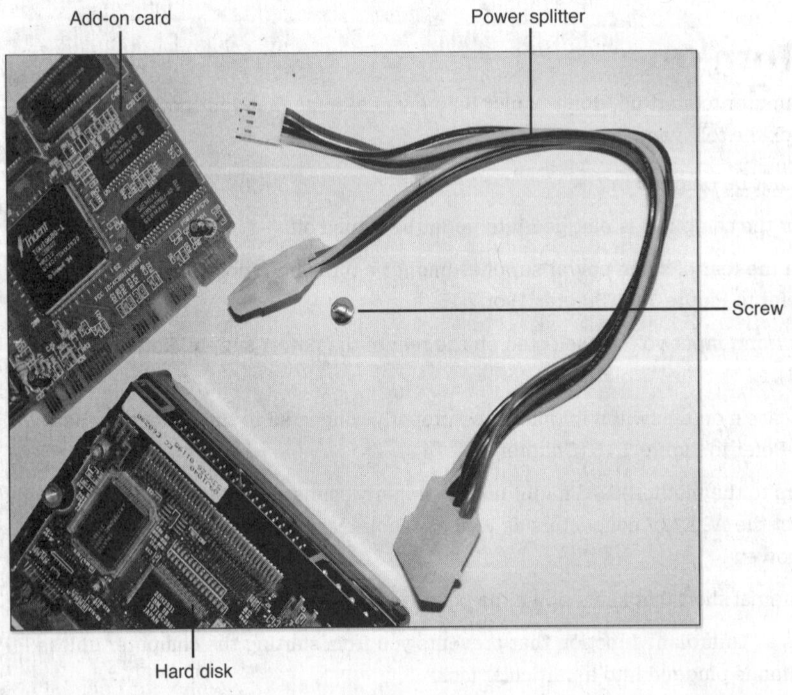

Figure 7.3
Loose screws as well as damaged add-on cards, drives, and power splitter cables can cause shorts in a desktop computer.

To check for loose screws, use this procedure:

1. Shut down the system and turn off the power supply if it has an external switch (refer to Figure 1.5 or 7.15).
2. Unplug the AC power cord.
3. Open the system.
4. Pick up and shake the system gently while you listen for loose screws.
5. Remove any loose screws.
6. Plug the AC power cord back in.
7. Turn the power supply on.
8. Try to restart your computer.

If it restarts, hooray! Turn it off, close it up, and get back to business.

To check for shorts caused by bare wires or bad power splitters, follow a similar procedure, but at step 4, look for bare wires or poorly constructed Y-splitters (used to split one power source into two). Disconnect any of these you find in step 5, and proceed. *Don't disconnect a power splitter that runs your CPU fan—you can (depending on the kind of CPU) fry your CPU in seconds if it's not cooled!*

If disconnecting a Y-splitter or device with a bare wire solves the problem, replace the splitter or device. If a replacement is not available, use electrical tape to cover the bare wire and see if the computer will start. Get a replacement as soon as you can.

To check for shorts caused by bad drives, select a drive that is not using a Y-splitter in step 4 and disconnect it from the power supply in step 5 (you can leave the drive connected to its data cable). If the drive uses a Y-splitter, connect it directly to the power supply. If the system works when you bypass the Y-splitter, replace the Y-splitter. If the system will not start with a particular drive connected to the power, replace the drive.

One hidden benefit of upgrading to a large-wattage power supply is the greater number of drive connectors built in to the new power supply.

To check for shorts caused by bad add-on cards, remove all add-on cards in step 4 and jump to step 6. If the system starts, replace one card at a time until the system stops working. Replace the card that caused the system to fail.

System Reboots Itself

If your system reboots itself, there are two possible causes:

- A STOP error in Windows if the system is configured to restart automatically. To learn how to keep a STOP error on-screen, see "Preparing a Windows-based Computer or Tablet for Easier Troubleshooting," in Chapter 1. To learn more about STOP errors, see "STOP (BlueScreen) Errors at Startup," in Chapter 8, "Fixing Windows Devices that Can't Start."
- A problem with the Power Good line in the main power cable running from the power supply to the motherboard. To determine if your power supply's Power Good line is providing correct voltage, use a power tester that checks the Power Good line, or use a multimeter. A multimeter is a multifunction electrical device tester. To learn more about how to use a multimeter, see "Using a Multimeter," in this chapter.

Note

The "Power Good" line is monitored by the motherboard. If the power level on this line goes below 3V DC or above 6V DC, the motherboard restarts the computer.

Power Supply Fan Fails

Most power supplies have a fan that pulls air through the power supply to help keep it cool, while some also have a fan that faces into the computer's interior. If either fan fails, replace the power supply.

Caution

Even if you think you can replace the power supply's fan yourself, don't risk it. Capacitors inside power supplies retain potentially lethal levels of electricity for considerable amounts of time after a power supply is disconnected from a power source.

Power Supply Smells

When you smell a burnt or acrid smell coming from your computer, it's never good news. These smells indicate a component failure. And, if it's your power supply that smells, its failure could destroy your motherboard and other components connected to it (I lost a hard disk and a USB keyboard when my power supply failed).

A simple rule is this: a smelly power supply means it's time to shop for a new one.

Testing Your Power Supply

Because a defective motherboard or other component can cause your power supply to appear to be defective, it's a really good idea to test the power supply in isolation from the motherboard, fans, and drives. Here's how.

Using a Digital Power Supply Tester

A digital power supply tester enables you to test your system's power supply for basic operation and to determine proper voltage levels. In this example, we'll use the Dr. Power II tester from Thermaltake, but similar testers are available from many vendors.

Here's how to use the tester to test an installed power supply:

1. Turn off the power supply.
2. Unplug the power supply from AC power.
3. Open the computer case.
4. Disconnect the power supply from the motherboard, drives, and fans.

5. Connect the motherboard power connector from the power supply to the tester.
6. Plug the power supply into AC power.
7. Turn on the power supply.
8. Turn on the tester. If the power supply starts and indicates the power supply works, the power supply is okay (see Figure 7.4). If the power supply doesn't start, replace it. If the power supply starts but the indicator displays a problem, replace the power supply (see Figure 7.5).

This particular power supply tester checks voltage levels as well as basic power functionality. Some power supply testers, such as the one shown in Figure 7.6, check on/off functionality only.

If your tester doesn't check voltage, you can use these methods to make sure your power supply is putting out the correct power levels:

- Using the PC Health or Hardware Monitor feature in the system BIOS
- Using a multimeter

Both of these methods are covered in detail later in this chapter.

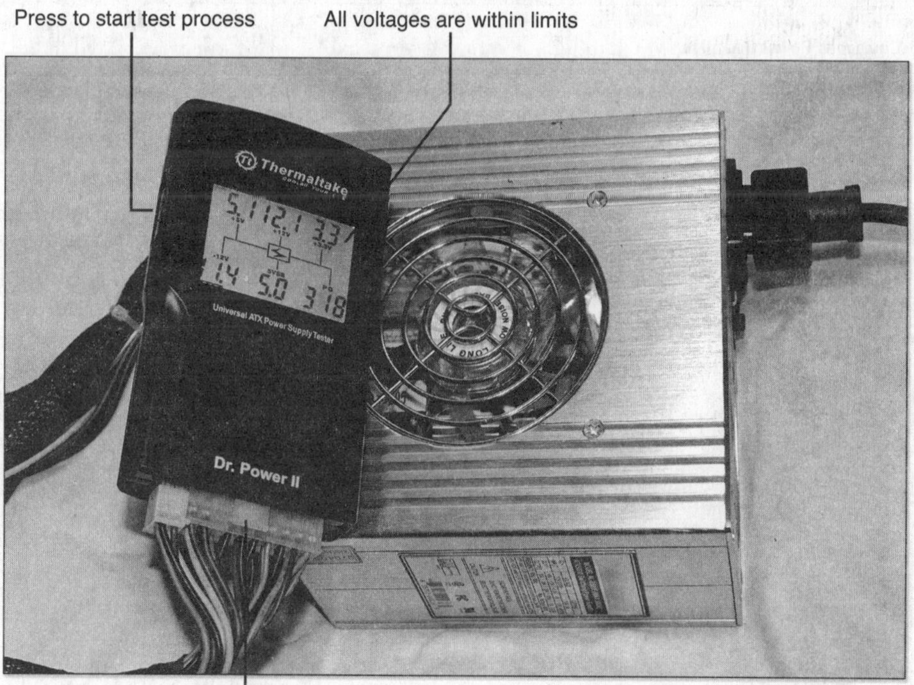

Figure 7.4 This power supply works and provides correct voltage levels.

Figure 7.5
The same power supply fails after the Power Good line was cut.

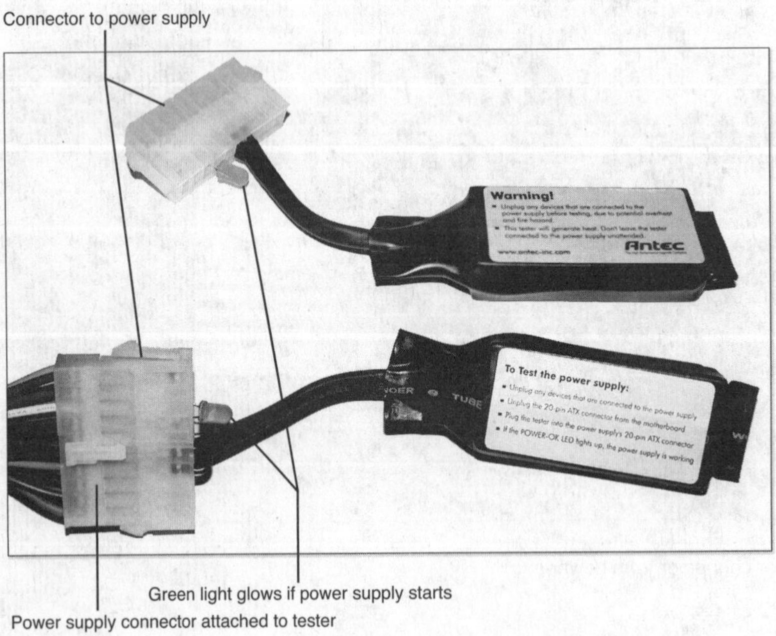

Figure 7.6
This power supply tester is designed for the older 20-pin ATX connector but can also be used with 24-pin power supplies.

Ideal and Acceptable Voltage Levels

As you can see from the voltage levels shown on the power supply labels in Figure 7.2, your computer uses four DC voltage lines: +5, +12, –5, and –12. A fifth line, Power Good, provides a signal that is used to determine that the power supply is working.

Whether you use a self-contained power tester, the PC Health or System Monitor feature in the system BIOS or as displayed by a utility provided by your motherboard vendor, or a multimeter, the voltages your system needs for reliable power are those shown in Table 7.2. If your power supply doesn't provide power within these limits, replace it.

Table 7.2 Acceptable Voltage Ranges

Rated Voltage	Minimum	Maximum
+5V	+4.8V	+5.2V
–5V	–4.5V	–5.4V
+12V	+11.5V	+12.6V
–12V	–10.8V	–12.9V
Power Good	+2.4V	+6.0V

Note that Power Good (which reboots your system if it is not within the specified values) is not displayed by BIOS or software-based system monitors.

Checking Voltage Levels with PC Health/Hardware Monitor

If you're uncomfortable with opening up your system to check the power supply and your system starts, you can use the PC Health or Hardware Monitor feature built in to the system BIOS in your computer. When you start your computer, press the appropriate key to start the System BIOS program. Depending on the system, this information might be displayed as soon as you start the BIOS program (see Figure 7.7), or you might need to navigate to a System Monitor or PC Health dialog (see Figure 7.8).

Using a Multimeter

If you already have a digital multimeter, you can use it to test voltage levels and Power Good. A digital multimeter can also be used to test AC wall outlet voltage, check cable continuity, and check resistance; expect to pay at least $20 for a typical unit, such as the autoranging model shown in Figure 7.10.

So, what are you checking?

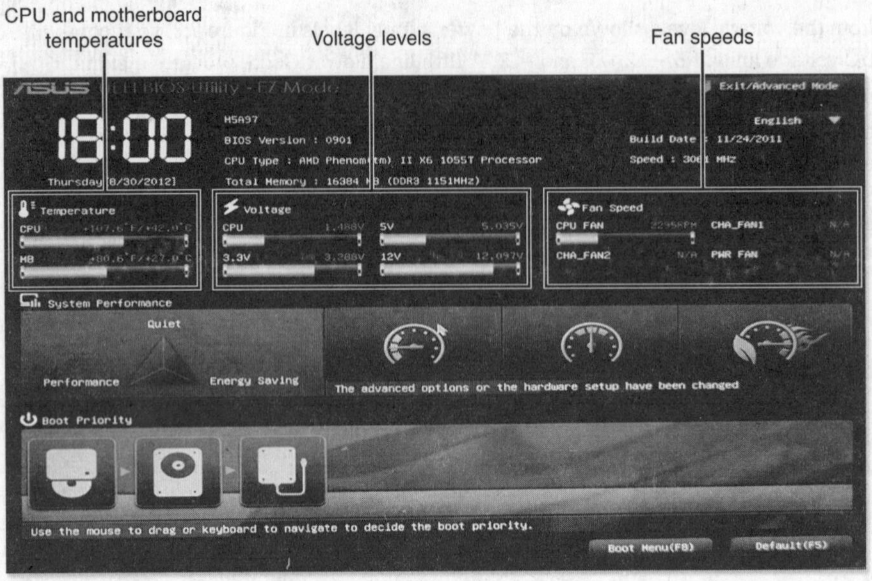

Figure 7.7 A system that displays the system monitor as soon as you start the UEFI BIOS setup program.

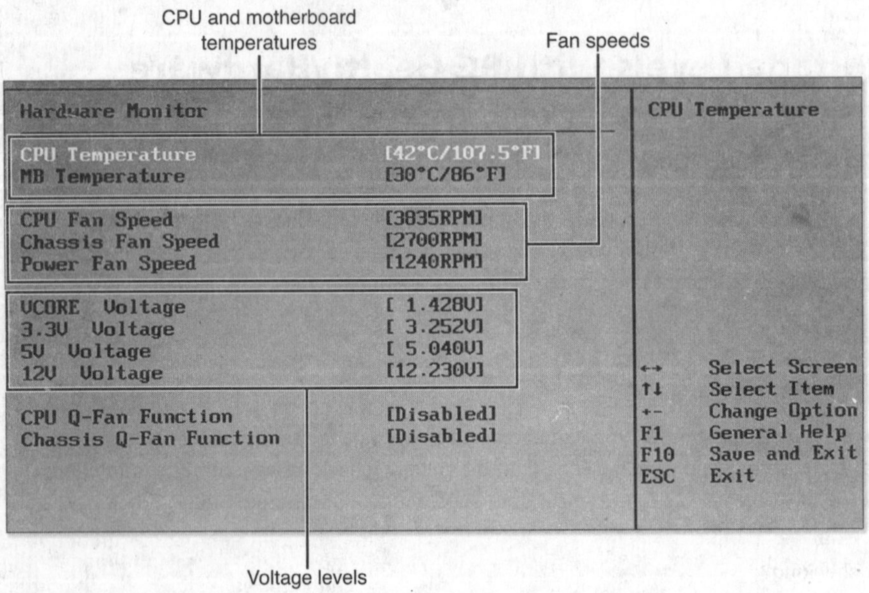

Figure 7.8 A system that has the Hardware Monitor in a submenu of the system BIOS.

Figure 7.9 shows the pinouts used by the 20-pin and 24-pin ATX power supply connectors. The 24-pin ATX power supply pinout is also used by the power supplies used by small-form factor and thin PCs.

Figure 7.9
The 24-pin ATX12V v2.x power supply pinout (bottom) is based on the 20-pin ATX power supply pinout (top). This pinout shows the top view of the connectors as they attach to the motherboard.

ATX 20-pin power connector (top view)

Pin	Signal	Color	Color	Signal	Pin
11	+3.3v	Orange	Orange	+3.3v	1
12	-12v	Blue	Orange	+3.3v	2
13	Ground	Black	Black	Ground	3
14	PS-On	Green	Red	+5v	4
15	Ground	Black	Black	Ground	5
16	Ground	Black	Red	+5v	6
17	Ground	Black	Black	Ground	7
18	-5v	White	Gray	Power Good	8
19	+5v	Red	Purple	+5v Standby	9
20	+5v	Red	Yellow	+12v	10

ATX 12V version 2.x 24-pin power connector (top view)

Pin	Signal	Color	Color	Signal	Pin
13	+3.3v	Orange	Orange	+3.3v	1
14	-12v	Blue	Orange	+3.3v	2
15	Ground	Black	Black	Ground	3
16	PS-On	Green	Red	+5v	4
17	Ground	Black	Black	Ground	5
18	Ground	Black	Red	+5v	6
19	Ground	Black	Black	Ground	7
20	NC	White	Gray	Power Good	8
21	+5v	Red	Purple	+5v Standby	9
22	+5v	Red	Yellow	+12v	10
23	+5v	Red	Yellow	+12v	11
24	Ground	Black	Orange	+3.3v	12

Caution

Some Dell desktop computers use proprietary versions of the ATX power supply. These power supplies route 3.3V DC lines to an additional connector. If you are checking a Dell computer and the power supply line colors and pattern do not resemble those shown in Figure 7.9, your system has a proprietary power supply. You will need to look up the service manual for that model and use the listed pinouts to check voltages. If the power supply is defective, you will need to order one from Dell or buy a third-party model that uses the Dell proprietary pinout. For some examples, see http://www.smps.us/dell_pinout.png.

If you mix Dell proprietary and standard ATX motherboards and power supplies, you get smoke, possibly fire, and a ruined system for sure. See "Upgrading Power Supplies in Dell Computers," p.186, this chapter for help in replacing a proprietary Dell power supply.

How can you test your power supply while the system is running? Follow this procedure:

1. Shut down the computer and unplug AC power from the power supply.
2. Open the computer case and locate the power connector.

3. Turn on your multimeter and set it for DC power.
4. Plug in the power supply computer.
5. Turn on the power supply.
6. Turn on the computer.
7. Check Power Good, +5V, –5V, +12V, and –12V voltage levels by back probing: insert the red lead into the top of the power connector to touch the metal connector inside, and touch the black lead to a ground such as the case frame or power supply case (see Figure 7.10).
8. Check the readings against those shown in Table 7.2. If you see a rating that falls outside the range listed, the power supply is defective and should be replaced.

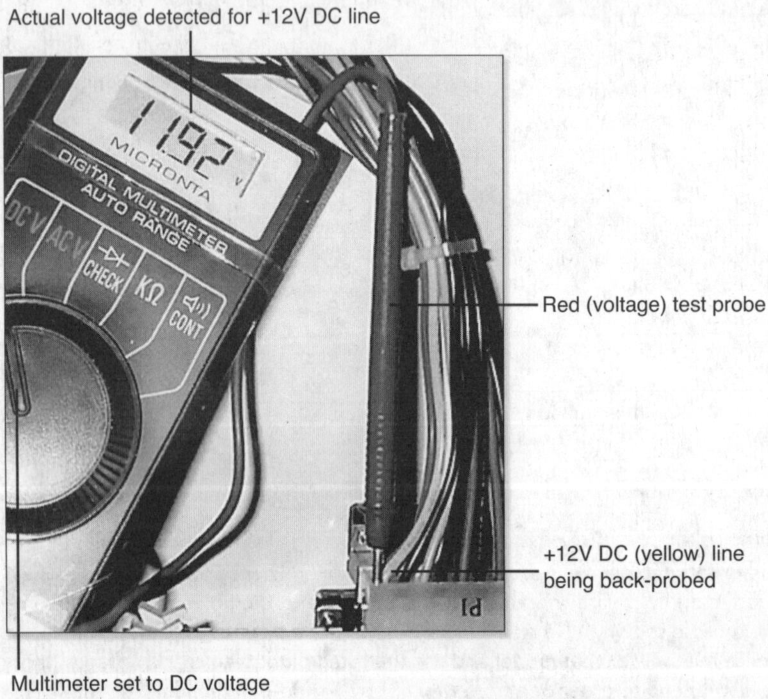

Figure 7.10
Testing a +12V line on a standard ATX motherboard. The actual voltage (+11.92V) is well within specifications.

Replacing the Power Supply

The power supply you're replacing might have been adequate for your needs when you bought (or built) your computer, but it's likely that your next power supply needs to be better than your original. Here's what to look for.

Essential and Desirable Features

Your power supply needs these features:

- Safety rating for your country or region
- Power connectors for your internal devices
- Adequate wattage for your devices

These features aren't essential, but provide additional performance and flexibility:

- Modular power cables
- 80PLUS efficiency ratings

Safety Ratings

Although you can buy very low-cost power supplies that lack UL or other safety ratings, these power supplies can ruin your system. You should never use a power supply that doesn't have safety ratings from an authority such as CSA (Canada), UL (USA), TÜV (Germany), or CE (European Union).

Note

On a UL-listed power supply, the UL marking is a backwards UR (the UL marking for components).

Enough Power Connectors for Your Devices

Your new power supply should feature the power connectors needed by your current hardware and any upgrades you're planning. If your current power supply needs splitters to provide power for devices such as PCIe x16 video cards or SATA drives, make sure your new power supply includes these connectors in sufficient quantity for your hardware. Figure 7.11 illustrates typical connectors on high-quality new power supplies.

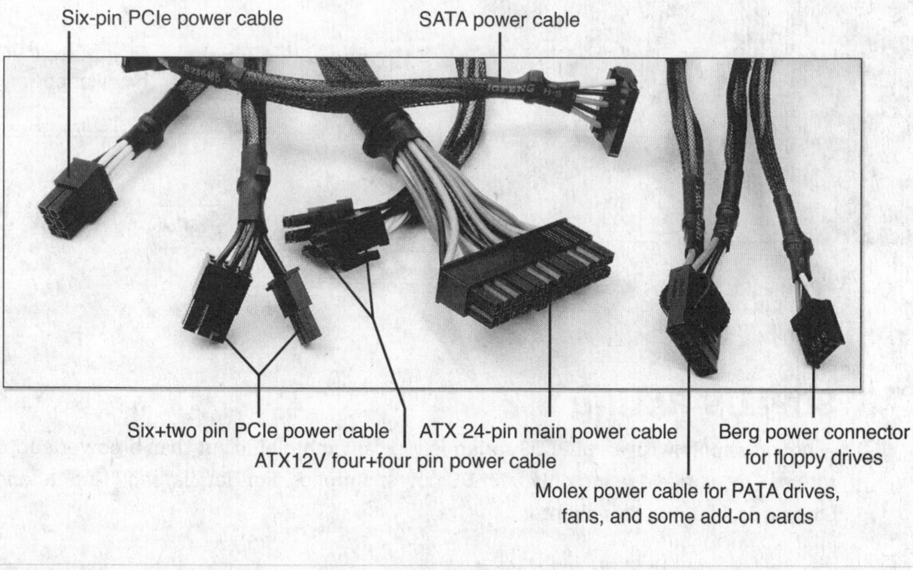

Figure 7.11 Power connectors on a typical power supply.

Adequate Wattage

Your new power supply should include a higher wattage rating than the existing one. You can calculate the power supply needed by using the estimators available at many power supply vendors' websites. For details, see "Selecting the Right-Sized Power Supply," later in this chapter.

Modular Power Cables

Traditional PC power supplies include a tangled nest of cables for drives, additional 12V power, and PCIe video cards. To help make cable management easier, many power supplies now feature modular designs. With a modular power supply such as the one in Figure 7.12, you can plug in only the cables you need for the devices included in your system.

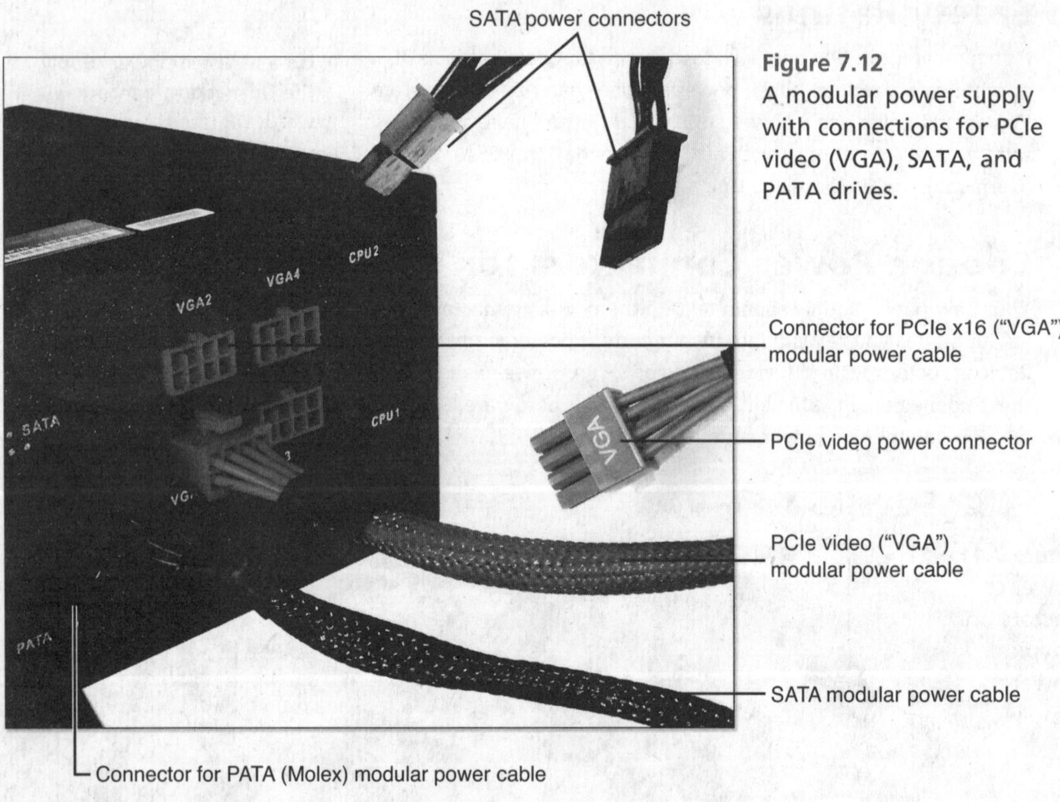

Figure 7.12 A modular power supply with connections for PCIe video (VGA), SATA, and PATA drives.

80PLUS Rating

A power supply with an 80PLUS rating is typically more efficient than a power supply that lacks this rating. I recommend using only 80PLUS power supplies. For details, see "Understanding 80PLUS Standards," later in this chapter.

Selecting the Right-Sized Power Supply

Whether you're replacing your system's power supply because it's overloaded or to provide support for newer technologies (such as PCIe x16 video cards and SATA drives), you should make sure your power supply can handle the devices it's supposed to power.

Some manufacturers provide a quick-reference guide to typical system configurations and the power supply size recommended. For example, PC Power and Cooling's Power Supply Selector is available at http://www.pcpower.com/Power_Supply_Selector.html.

However, if you want a tool that helps you find the specifications you can use to shop for power supplies from any vendor, I recommend the Extreme Outer Vision eXtreme Power Supply Calculator available at http://extreme.outervision.com/psucalculator.jsp. The Lite version is free, and the Pro version, which includes amperage values, is just $7.99 for lifetime (up to 200 years) access. I recommend this version for overclocked systems, systems that include two or more high-performance video cards, or systems that use third-party air cooling or water cooling.

With either version, select the CPU (brand, type, speed), video cards, number of drives, number of memory modules, and other components, and click Calculate for a wattage calculation and power supply recommendation. Figure 7.13 shows a calculation made for a system with a high-performance Intel processor, two NVIDIA graphics cards, and other advanced features. The recommended power supply size is at least 687 watts, and the calculator suggests 750 watt (or larger) power supplies for this configuration.

Figure 7.13
Want to power this high-end system? Get a power supply with at least 687 watts output!

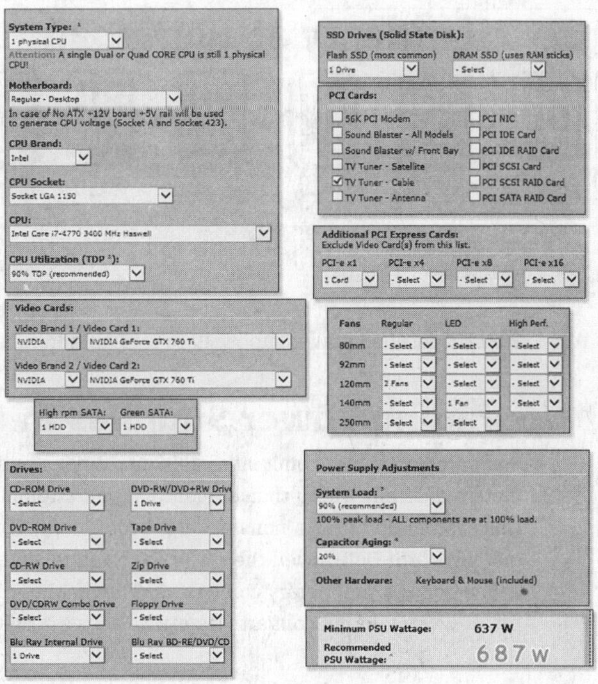

Tip

To determine the processor brand, model, speed, video card type, and other information about your system, you can use the Windows MSInfo32.exe utility. The System Summary page lists the processor brand, model number, and speed, as well as physical memory installed. The video card information is viewed by clicking Components, Display.

For more detailed information about your system, download and run the free SiSoftware SANDRA Lite utility available at www.sisoftware.net.

Understanding 80PLUS Standards

80PLUS power supplies are more expensive than nonrated power supplies, so you might be wondering if the extra cost is worth it. Here's why they're better:

- Any 80PLUS-certified power supply provides at least 80% efficiency at 100% load. There are several levels of 80PLUS ratings. Figure 7.14 gives you the efficiency ratings for the entire family when 115V AC current is used (230V AC efficiencies are a bit higher).
- All 80PLUS-certified power supplies feature active power factor correction (Active PFC) for better efficiency. Active PFC improves the quality of power by putting voltage and current in phase with each other.

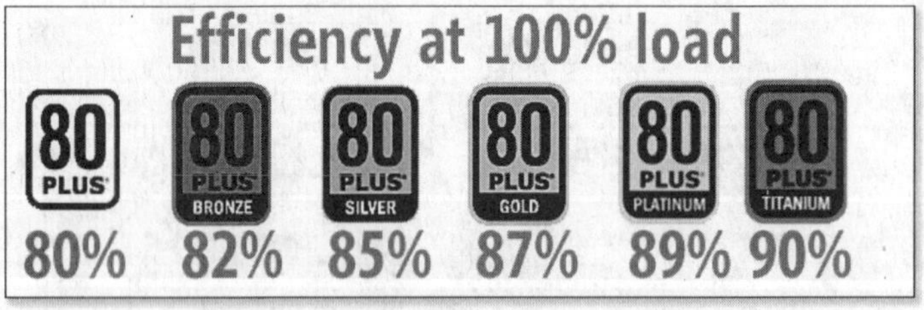

Figure 7.14 80PLUS family power supplies provide 80%–90% efficiency at 100% load.

80PLUS-certified power supplies are available from a variety of retail and online vendors.

Upgrading Power Supplies in Dell Computers

Some Dell computers built since 1998 use a nonstandard version of the ATX connector with completely different wiring than standard. If you attempt to install a standard ATX power supply into a Dell system that uses a nonstandard (proprietary) power supply, you could fry the power supply or motherboard! Dell moved the +3.3V DC (orange) connectors out of the 20/24 pin ATX power connector to a proprietary connectors. The pinouts differ in voltage and pin assignments. See http://www.informit.com/articles/article.aspx?p=339053 for details.

Your options? Some vendors sell adapters that convert a standard 24-pin ATX power supply to the wiring standard used by some Dell models. See http://www.atxpowersupplies.com/Dell-24-to-24-16-adapter.php for such an adapter and a partial list of supported models.

Alternatively, you can buy a Dell-specific power supply from either Dell's parts department or a third-party equivalent from some vendors. For example, see http://www.amazon.com/StarTech-PW400DELL-Replacement-Computer-Supply/dp/B000LRL1QO/ref=pd_sxp_grid_pt_0_0. This page also includes a list of compatible Dell computer models.

Removing the Old Power Supply

After you have purchased your replacement power supply, it's time to remove the old one. Follow this procedure:

1. Shut down your computer.
2. Turn off the old power supply.
3. Disconnect AC power from the old power supply.
4. Remove the side of the case to get access to the power supply. To figure out which side to remove, take a look at the port cluster on the rear of the system. Remove the side away from the port cluster (typically the right side as viewed from the rear; the left side as viewed from the front).
5. Carefully remove all power cables from the cards, drives, and motherboard. SATA, Molex, and floppy cables are not locked in place. However, PCIe, ATX main, and ATX12V cables are locked in place: push the locking tab to remove them (refer to Figure 7.11).
6. Remove the screws (typically four) that hold the power supply in place (see Figure 7.15). If the power supply is on the top of the system, hold it in place as you remove the screws.
7. Slide the power supply out of the system.

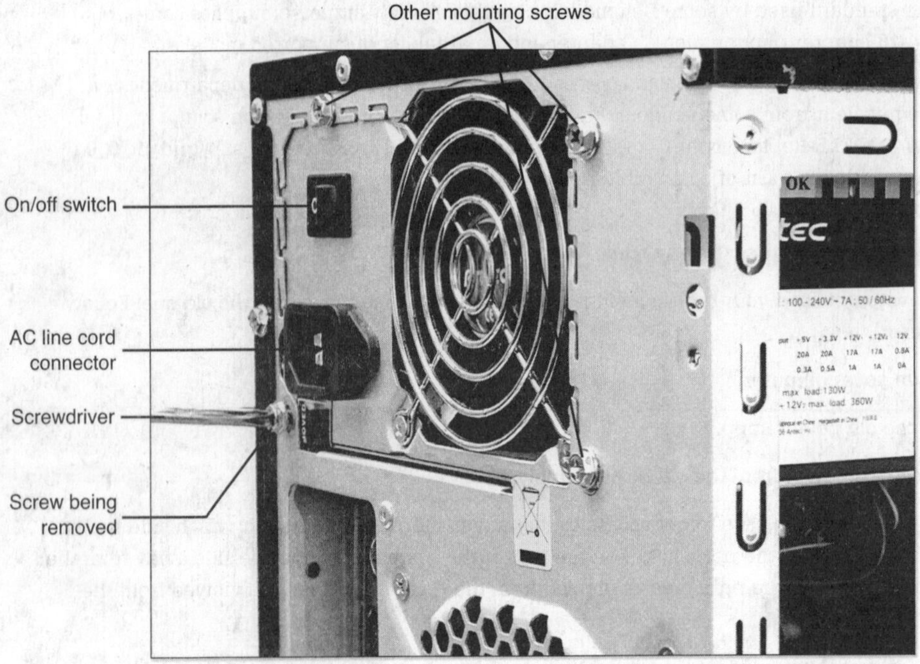

Figure 7.15 Removing a power supply mounting screw.

Installing the New Power Supply

To install your new power supply, follow this procedure:

1. Turn off the power supply before installation.
2. If the new power supply has a voltage selector switch, set it to the correct voltage.
3. Slide the new power supply into the system. If it has a fan that faces into the computer, make sure the fan faces the interior (see Figure 7.16).
4. Fasten the power supply in place with the retaining screws provided (or reuse the screws from the old power supply). If the power supply is top mounted, hold it in place until all screws are secure.
5. If the power supply is modular, connect the cables needed for your devices (refer to Figure 7.12).
6. Connect power leads from the power supply to the motherboard, drives, fans, and cards.
7. Plug the AC power cord into the power supply.
8. Turn on the power supply.
9. Restart the computer.

Figure 7.16
Installing a bottom-mounted power supply with an inward-facing fan.

If the system starts properly, shut down the computer, turn off and unplug the power supply, close up the system, and repeat steps 7–9. You're finished!

If the system doesn't start, check the connections to the motherboard and drives.

Choosing Power Protection Devices

You probably don't connect your computer, monitor, printers, scanners, and external drives directly to your AC wall outlets—and that's good! Most homes and offices don't have nearly enough electrical outlets for the increasing number of PC-related hardware connected to modern systems. You probably use a multiple-outlet device called a *surge suppressor* or *surge protector*. When was the last time you changed it, or even thought about it?

Some so-called surge suppressors aren't very good, and most of the models you can buy at retail stores can wear out over time. If you depend on a worn-out surge suppressor to protect your computer, you might get an unpleasant surprise the next time a power surge happens.

Your computer needs reliable, high-quality power. To make sure you achieve that goal, a complete powerline-protection strategy should include the following:

- Checking wall outlets for proper wiring
- Using surge suppressors with filtering, wiring-fault warning, and high levels of protection against surges and spikes for all AC-connected equipment
- Isolating electrically noisy devices such as laser printers from computers or other devices by using surge suppressors with separate filter banks or separate surge suppressors for the printer and other devices
- Using a battery backup system for your computer and monitor if your area is subject to frequent electrical blackouts (complete loss of power) or brownouts (voltage sags below 100V AC).

Now that you have an overview, let's cover the details.

Checking Wall Outlets

The polarized and grounded design used by wall outlets today is intended to provide high-quality power to your computer and peripherals and other devices in your home or office. However, all too often, incorrect wiring is present, regardless of whether the wiring was performed by professional or do-it-yourself electricians. If you don't determine that the wiring is correct, you could damage your computer or, at least, decrease its reliability by plugging it into an improperly wired outlet. Although some surge suppressors feature a single signal light to indicate if your wiring has a fault or is correct, such units don't provide enough information to help you fix the problem.

Fortunately, it's not difficult or expensive to test your electrical outlets for such problems as incorrect grounding and reversed hot/neutral polarity. You can purchase an outlet tester similar to the one shown in Figure 7.17 from many electronics and home-improvement stores for less than $10. The signal lights on the tester indicate whether the outlet is wired properly, or if it's wired incorrectly, what type of wiring fault is present. Testers include a chart (often attached to the unit, as shown in Figure 7.17) indicating the meaning of the signal lights.

If you live or work in an older building without three-wire grounded electrical outlets, you're asking for trouble with your computer. Using three-prong to two-prong adapters is definitely not recommended, even if you attach a ground wire to a good earth ground (such as a metal water pipe). Have your home office rewired with modern electrical cable attached to ground and put in three-prong outlets.

Figure 7.17
A typical receptacle/outlet tester in use; the signal lights indicate the outlet is correctly wired.

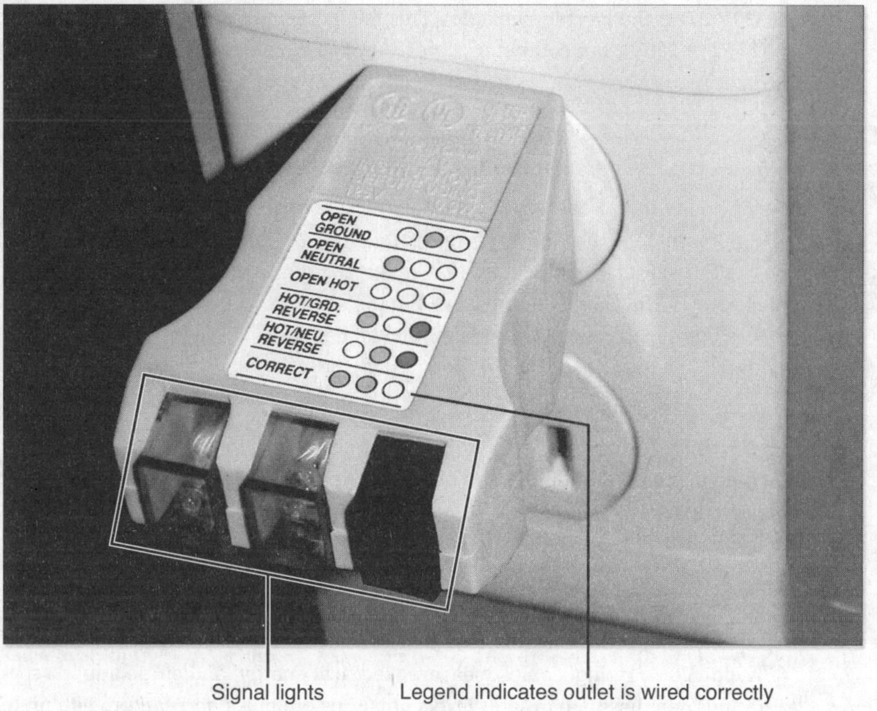

Choosing a Surge Suppression Device

The two types of power problems a properly designed surge suppressor can handle are spikes and surges.

Both spikes and surges are overvoltage events: voltage levels higher than the normal voltage levels that come out of the wall socket. Spikes are momentary overvoltages, whereas surges last longer. Both can damage or destroy equipment.

Surge suppressors seem to multiply like rabbits; every store that carries computer equipment offers a huge number of models from different vendors. It's tempting either to go with the cheapest model to save a few bucks or buy the most expensive model—after all, don't you get what you pay for? However, getting the right surge suppressor isn't that easy.

You can make sure you get the right surge suppressor by looking for the following features:

- Make sure you're looking at a true surge suppressor, which has a UL-1449 rating, and not a multiple-outlet strip (UL-1363 transient voltage tap rating). Some stores and product vendors don't adequately mark their products, so it can be easy to mix up these different types of devices. If you can't find this information on the unit or its packaging, look at the unit's instruction manual. The Technical Information section typically lists this information.

- The surge suppressor should have a low UL-1449 let-through voltage level (400V AC or less; 330V AC is the lowest available). This might seem high compared to the standard line voltages (115V or 230V), but computer power supplies have been tested to handle up to 500V AC without damage.

UL-1449 Third Edition Changes

In 2009, Underwriter's Laboratory made significant revisions to its UL-1449 certification tests for surge suppressors. In addition to more rigorous tests, UL-1449 Third Edition now refers to these devices as Surge Protection Devices (SPDs) instead of the older term Transient Voltage Surge Suppression (TVSS). Surge suppressors manufactured before 2009 are designed to meet the older, less rigorous UL-1449 Second Edition standards.

The improvements in protection, as well as the fact that surge protection devices wear out over time, are good reasons to replace older units with those that meet UL-1449 Third Edition standards.

Contact the manufacturer before you buy to make sure you're getting a model that has passed the revised tests.

- A fast response (under 1 nanosecond) to surges helps prevent damage to equipment.
- A high Joule rating. Joules measure electrical energy, and surge suppressors with higher Joule ratings can dissipate greater levels of surges or spikes and can provide protection longer than suppressors with lower ratings.
- A covered-equipment warranty that includes lightning strikes (one of the biggest causes of surges and spikes).
- A fuse or failsafe feature that prevents fatal surges from getting through and shuts down the unit permanently when the unit can no longer provide protection.
- Telephone, fax, and modem protection if your system has a modem or is connected to a telephone or fax. Many users forget that their telephone lines can act as a "back door" to fatal surges, wiping out their modem and sometimes the entire computer.
- Coaxial cable protection if your system is attached to a cable modem or cable TV. Just as telephone lines can carry damaging surges, so can coaxial cable lines.
- RJ-45/Ethernet cable protection if your system is attached to a network. Network cables can also carry damaging surges.
- EMI/RFI noise filtration (a form of line conditioning). This helps prevent electrically "noisy" equipment such as printers from interfering with computers, but it's best to plug laser printers and copiers into a separate outlet (or separate circuit) from your computer if possible.
- Site fault wiring indicator (no ground, reversed polarity warnings). This can prevent you from using a bad electrical outlet, but it's not a substitute for a true outlet tester.

- Most low-cost (under $50) surge suppressors are based on MOV (metal-oxide varistor) technology; MOVs wear out over time and self-destruct when exposed to a very high surge. A surge suppressor that uses MOVs should be replaced every two years. MOVs also present a potential fire hazard because they have been known to catch fire when exposed to a high-voltage surge. Better-quality surge suppressors supplement MOVs with other components, but the best (and most expensive) models use non-MOV series designs.
- Metal cases are recommended because the metal case helps minimize the risk of fire if the unit fails, and it also helps minimize the odds of electrical interference with other devices.
- If you use devices powered by AC/DC converter "bricks," be sure to use surge suppressors with extra-wide spacing between the plugs to provide adequate clearance.

Power-Protection Vendors Online

- **American Power Conversion by Schneider Electric**—www.apc.com
- **Belkin**—www.belkin.com
- **Panamax**—www.panamax.com
- **Tripp-Lite**—www.tripplite.com

The following vendors sell the more-expensive series-type surge suppressors:

- **Zero Surge, Inc.**—www.zerosurge.com
- **Price Wheeler Corp.**—brickwall.com
- **SurgeX**—www.surgex.com

If you use surge suppressors with these features and attach your system to a properly wired outlet, you will minimize system problems caused by power issues.

Note

For a very helpful review of surge protection products and technologies, see http://thewirecutter.com/reviews/best-surge-protector/.

Choosing a Battery Backup Device

Although high-quality surge suppressors stop damaging overvoltages, undervoltages and electrical blackouts can also damage your system, and they pose even greater risks to your data. If you live or work in an area that is subject to frequent brownouts (voltage under 100V AC compared to normal 115V AC) or blackouts (complete power failure), or if you just don't like surprise power failures, you need to add a battery backup system (also called a *uninterruptible power supply* or *UPS*) to your power protection lineup.

Most so-called UPS systems actually provide battery power only when AC power fails and should be called *standby power supplies (SPS)*. However, the term UPS is used for both SPS-type and so-called "true UPS" systems, which power the computer from a battery at all times.

Most UPS systems contain integrated surge suppression technology but vary greatly in how long they'll run your computer. Because a UPS is designed to run your computer only long enough to shut it down without data loss, a runtime of 10–15 minutes is long enough to provide adequate protection.

Right-Sizing Your Battery Backup System the Easy Way

If you know the wattage or amp requirements of your computer, its peripherals, and your monitor, you can manually calculate the appropriate VA (volt-amp) rating to look for in a battery backup system:

- Multiply the total amps by voltage (115 in North America, 230 in Europe and Asia).
- Multiply the total wattage by 1.4.

However, because it can be difficult to calculate the actual power consumption of your computer and its peripherals, the most convenient (and often more accurate) way to determine the battery backup size you need is to use the vendors' interactive selection tools, available on most UPS vendor websites.

The essential features of a battery backup system include the following:

- **High-quality integrated surge suppression**—In most cases, you should not use a separate surge suppressor with a battery backup unit.
- **Appropriate sizing for your system and runtime**—The price of a battery backup system goes up significantly as the volt-amp (VA) rating climbs. Buying more than 10 minutes of runtime is usually not necessary unless you frequently run programs you can't shut down until the current process is complete.
- **Automatic system shutdown after a power failure has been detected**—This requires that your UPS supports the version of Windows you're using and that you connect the battery backup system to your computer with a compatible USB cable. Although Windows 7 and 8.x have limited support for battery backup units, you will get more information about your battery backup device and have better control of its features by using manufacturer-supplied utilities.
- **Fast battery recharge, particularly if your area suffers frequent blackouts**—Look for systems that recharge in less than 12 hours if you rarely have blackouts, and expect to pay more for recharge times of 6 hours or less.

UPS Vendors

Major vendors of battery backup systems include the following:

- **American Power Conversion (APC) by Schneider Electric**—www.apc.com
- **Tripp-Lite**—www.tripplite.com
- **Eaton**—http://powerquality.eaton.com
- **Liebert**—www.emersonnetworkpower.com

Basic or Enhanced Protection? Your Choice, Your Money

All battery backup (UPS) systems will power your system for several minutes during a blackout. Most will also protect you against power surges, and many will also shut down your system. However, some are designed to protect you against additional power problems, including the following:

- Undervoltage (brownout)
- EMI/RFI interference (line noise)
- Other power quality distortions

More expensive battery backup systems typically provide these types of power-conditioning features as well as basic power-outage protection, but you should carefully review the vendors' datasheets to see the differences in features between battery backup systems with similar VA ratings but wide differences in price.

8

FIXING WINDOWS DEVICES THAT CAN'T START

Fast Track to Solutions

Table 8.1 Symptom Table

Symptom	Flowchart or Book Section	Page #
My computer displays an error message when it starts	Troubleshooting a System That Displays Errors at Startup (flowchart)	Chapter 24
My computer won't start if I have a USB flash drive plugged into it	Disconnecting USB Drives	200
I see a STOP (blue screen) error when I try to start the computer or after I use it for awhile	STOP (Blue Screen) Errors at Startup	203
I just installed an SSD in place of a hard disk, but my computer isn't any faster	Switching to AHCI Mode in Windows 7 and Windows 8.x	205
I'm not sure the power and data cables to my hard disk are plugged in correctly	Loose Drive Data and Power Cables	208
I think my hard disk has failed. How can I find out for sure?	Drive Failure	212
Windows 7 won't start. What do I do next?	Windows 7 Error Recovery and Advanced Boot Options	213
Windows 8/8.1 won't start. What do I do next?	Windows 8 Error Recovery and Advanced Boot Options	222
How can I find out what System Restore will change before I use it?	Using System Restore, Figures 8.22 and 8.23	218-219
How can I prevent unwanted programs from running when I start my computer?	Using MSConfig	220
I just ran Refresh Your PC in Windows 8/8.1 and some of my programs were removed. How do I find out what's missing?	Figure 8.30	227

Troubleshooting a Windows Tablet or Computer That Can't Start

If you turn on a Windows tablet, laptop, desktop, or all-in-one computer and it powers up, but it won't start Windows, there are two possibilities to check:

- Problems with boot configuration in the system BIOS
- Problems with Windows

In this section, you'll learn the clues for each type of problem and the tools and techniques you need to get your balky system running again.

BIOS Configuration Settings

All recent laptop and desktop computers use either hard disks or solid-state drives (SSDs) that connect via SATA ports to the motherboard. SATA drives can be configured in the system BIOS in three ways:

- IDE
- AHCI
- RAID

Here are a couple of examples. In Figure 8.1, the SATA hard disk drives in this system are set to use AHCI. In Figure 8.2, the SATA drives use the older IDE mode setting.

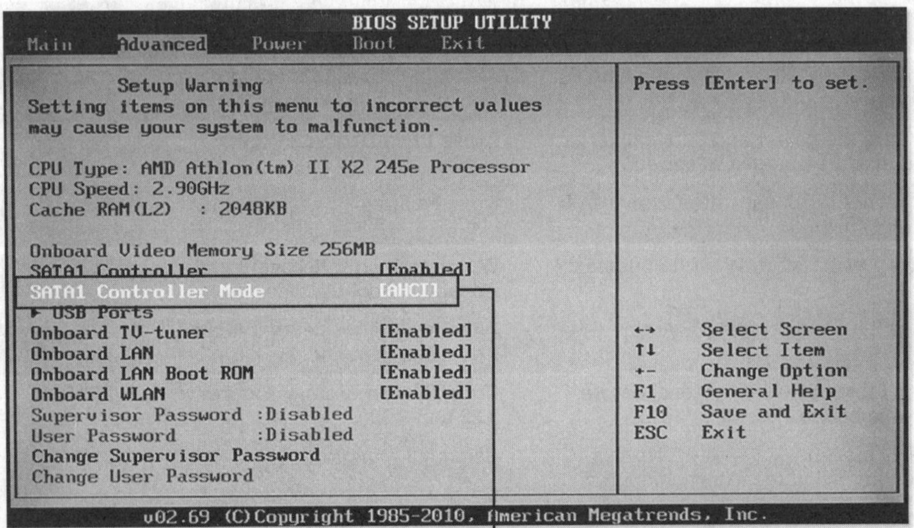

AHCI mode supports full-speed SATA hard disk and SSD devices

Figure 8.1 SATA drives on this system use AHCI settings.

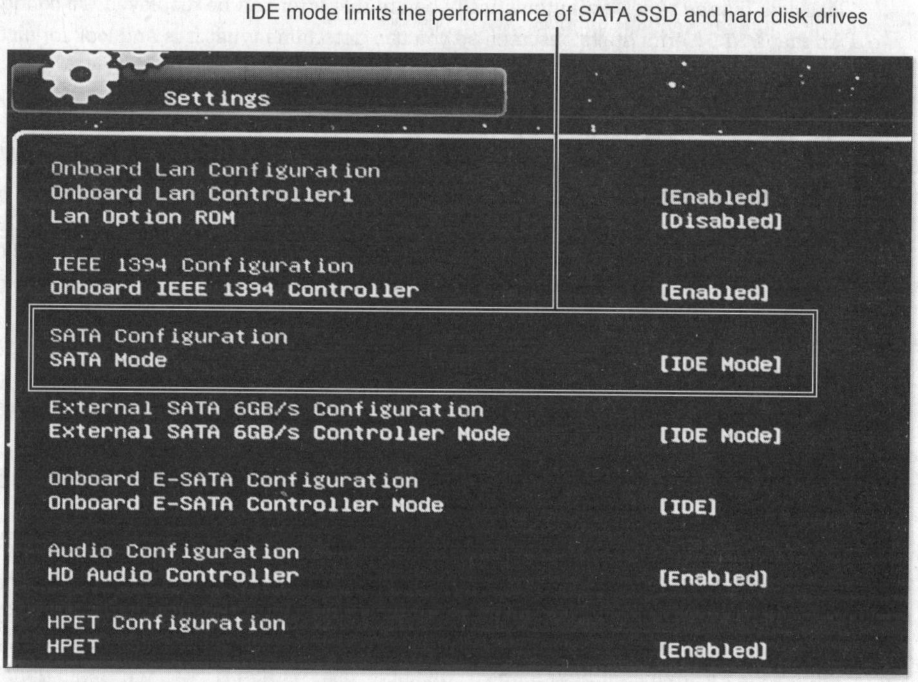

Figure 8.2 SATA drives on this system use IDE settings.

So, what do these settings mean?

- **IDE**—This setting makes the SATA drive act like PATA (IDE) hard disk drives that were once common in Windows-based systems. When this setting is used, the SATA drive can't use advanced features, such as native command queuing and hot-plugging, and SATA 3Gbps and 6Gbps drives run at only 1.5Gbps.
- **AHCI**—This setting supports the SATA drives' advanced functions.
- **RAID**—This setting is used on systems that use two or more drives as a logical unit (RAID 0, RAID 1, RAID 10, and so on).

When Windows is installed on an SATA hard disk, the configuration used in the BIOS or UEFI firmware is recorded in the Windows Registry. Windows checks the Registry at startup to determine how to access the drive. If the drive configuration has changed, Windows crashes.

> **Note**
> To know how your system is configured before you have problems, see "Preparing a Windows-based Computer or Tablet for Easier Troubleshooting," Chapter 1, p.37.

Windows Configuration Issues

In addition to incorrect SATA drive configurations, other Windows configuration issues that can prevent Windows from starting include problems with recently installed hardware or apps, corrupt or missing startup files, and corrupt or missing Windows system files.

These errors can cause Windows to display a STOP (blue screen) error. However, Windows is typically configured to restart automatically before this error can be displayed. To configure Windows so that a STOP error stays onscreen so you can determine what it is and look for solutions, see "Configuring Windows to Keep STOP (Blue Screen) Errors Displayed," Chapter 1, p.41.

BIOS Startup Error Messages and Solutions

When a system has problems starting, it might display error messages at startup. These messages might come from the system BIOS (ROM BIOS or UEFI firmware) or might be generated by Windows. Typical error messages displayed by the BIOS include the following:

- Invalid system disk
- Boot failure
- Hard disk error
- NT boot loader missing
- Missing operating system

These and similar messages indicate that the BIOS or UEFI firmware chip on the motherboard cannot locate startup files for your operating system. Possible reasons can include the following:

- A nonbootable drive containing media is listed first in the boot order (BIOS/UEFI).
- The computer's system drive is not properly identified (BIOS/UEFI).
- Data or power cables from the internal hard disk to the motherboard are loose or have failed (hardware).
- The drive has failed (hardware).

These are listed in order of likelihood. As always, start with the simplest possibility: You've left a USB thumb drive plugged into your computer.

Disconnecting USB Drives

If your system is configured to use USB drives as the first bootable device and you leave a nonbootable USB flash drive plugged into your system (either directly or into a USB hub connected to your system), your system won't boot. Solution? Unplug the drive and restart your system.

If your system restarts correctly, you have a couple of choices:

- Don't leave USB flash drives plugged into your system when you shut down the computer.
- Change your BIOS or UEFI firmware settings to skip USB drives as bootable devices.

Checking and Changing Drive Boot Order

Should you change the boot order? It depends. More and more diagnostic programs can be run from bootable USB flash drives, and you can also install new operating systems from bootable USB flash drives. However, you can also use your system's DVD or BD (Blu-ray) drive for these tasks. So, it's up to you.

We recommend changing the boot order on Windows 7 computers if

- You use USB flash drives to speed up your system using the Windows ReadyBoost feature.
- You frequently use USB flash drives to shuttle information between computers.
- You frequently use USB flash drives for other reasons.

However, you should leave USB flash drives at the top of the boot order if

- You frequently run diagnostic programs from a bootable USB flash drive.
- You install operating systems from a bootable USB flash drive.
- You seldom or never use USB flash drives for data transfer.

> **Tip**
> If you change the boot order to remove USB flash drives or put them after the system hard disk, you can always change the boot order in the future to place USB drives first if you need to run diagnostic programs or install a new operating system.

Here's how to change the boot order in Windows 7:

1. Click **Start**.
2. Click the right arrow next to the **Shut Down** button.
3. Select **Restart**.
4. After your system restarts, press the key that starts the BIOS or UEFI firmware setup program (see Figure 8.3).
5. Navigate to the dialog used to set the drive boot order (see Figure 8.4).
6. Change the boot order to place the optical drive first, followed by the hard disk.
7. Save your changes and restart your computer.

Windows 8.1 (unlike Windows 8) does not support the creation of a CD or DVD repair disc, although you can use your Windows 8.1 distribution media as a repair disc. With Windows 8.1, if your system supports booting from a USB drive, you should create a USB recovery drive instead.

To learn more, see http://windows.microsoft.com/en-US/windows-8/create-usb-recovery-drive.

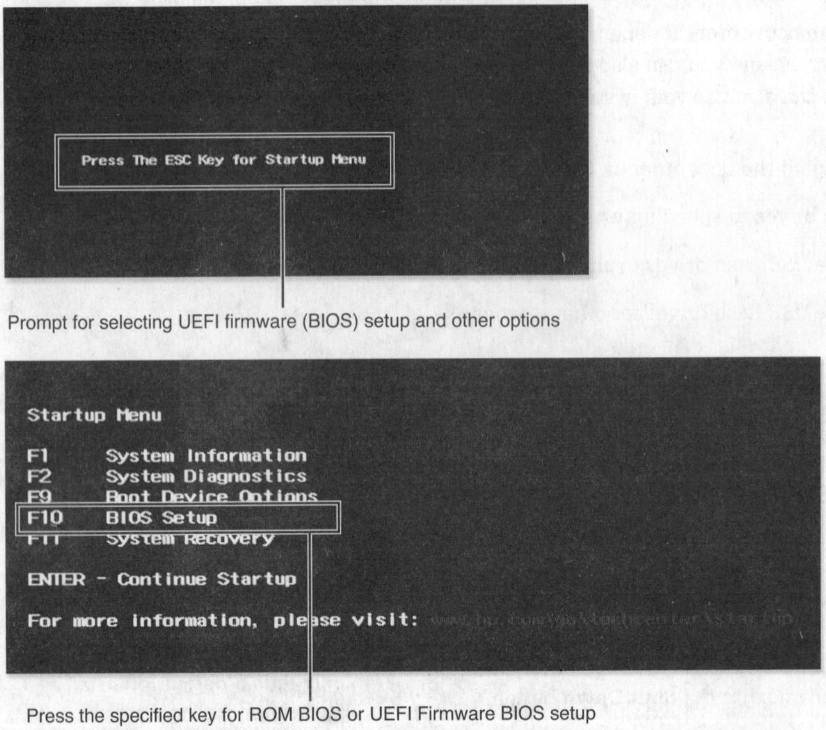

Figure 8.3 On some systems, such as this HP Pavilion DV6 laptop, you might need to press a key (ESC) to see startup options including BIOS setup (F10).

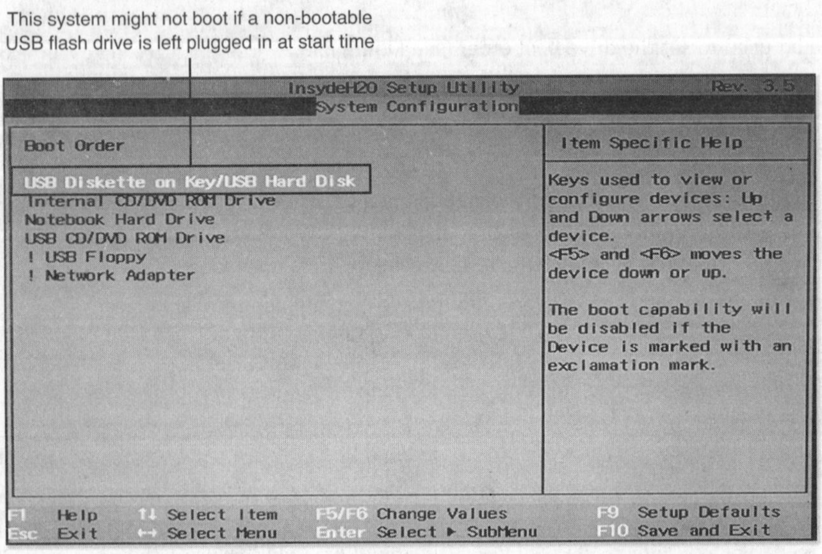

Figure 8.4 This system looks for USB thumb drives as the first bootable devices.

STOP (Blue Screen) Errors at Startup

If you turn on your Windows computer and, instead of seeing the Windows login screen or desktop, you see a screen similar to the one shown in Figure 8.5, you have a STOP error, also known as a "Blue Screen" or BSOD ("blue screen of death) error. What happened?

Figure 8.5
A 0x7B STOP error in Windows 7 caused by changing the SATA interface setting in the system BIOS (a). Windows 8 displays a different STOP error (b).

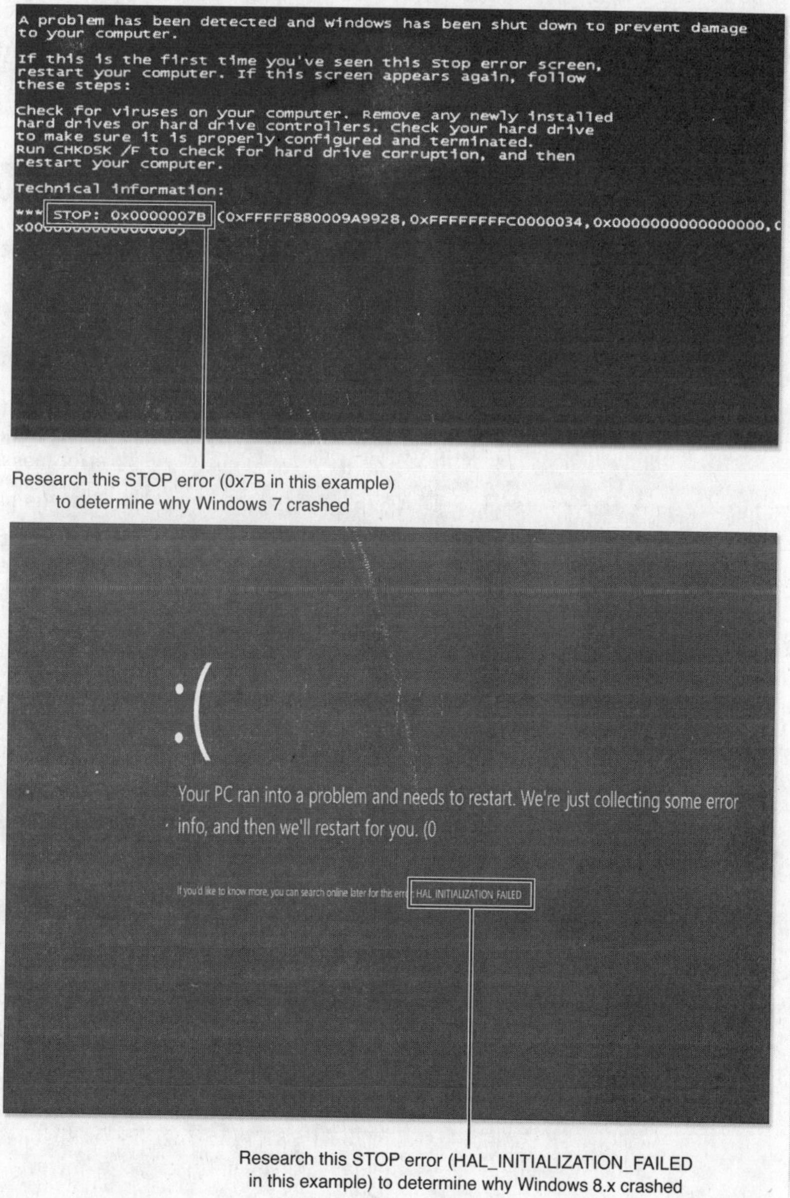

Blue-screen errors can be caused by many problems. At startup, they're typically caused by problems with hard disk device drivers. If a blue screen error appears after you have booted to the Windows desktop, it could be caused by corrupt apps, corrupt device drivers, or memory problems. When you see a BSOD error, be sure to record the numbers listed after the STOP message, such as STOP: 0x0000001E, or 0x1E for short. If the name of the error is displayed, such as KMODE_EXCEPTION_NOT_HANDLED, record it as well. You can then look up the error number and name on the Microsoft Support Site (http://support.microsoft.com) to find Microsoft's suggested solutions.

Table 8.2 lists some of the most common STOP errors and possible solutions.

Table 8.2 Common Windows STOP Errors and Solutions

STOP Error Number	STOP Error Name	Suggested Solutions
0xA	IRQL_NOT_LESS_OR_EQUAL	Check device drivers or services used by backup or antivirus utilities.
0xD1	DRIVER_IRQL_NOT_LESS_OR_EQUAL	Check device drivers or services used by backup or antivirus utilities.
0x1E	KMODE_EXCEPTION_NOT_HANDLED	Illegal or unknown instruction; check the driver referenced in the error message.
0x24	NTFS_FILE SYSTEM	Test the hard disk for errors.
0x2E	DATA_BUS ERROR	Test memory modules; disable memory caching in system BIOS; check hardware configuration.
0x50	PAGE_FAULT_IN_NONPAGED AREA	Check printer drivers.
0x7B	INACCESSIBLE_BOOT_DEVICE	Incorrect or missing hard disk device driver; see "Fixing 0x7B Errors," this chapter, for details.
0x7F	UNEXPECTED_KERNEL_MODE_TRAP	Test hardware and RAM; check SCSI configuration if in use; make sure CPU is not overclocked.
0x9F	DRIVER_POWER_STATE_FAILURE	Check power management and CD-writing software; disable power management temporarily; reinstall or upgrade CD-writing software.
0xC21A	STATUS_SYSTEM_PROCESS_TERMINATED	Reinstall third-party programs; use System File Checker with the Scannow option (SFC/Scannow) to check system files.

Unfortunately, Windows is typically configured to restart the system immediately when a STOP error is displayed, so you can't read it. To configure Windows so that a STOP error stays onscreen so you can determine what it is and look for solutions, see "Preparing a Windows-Based Computer or Tablet for Easier Troubleshooting," Chapter 1, p.37.

Tip

You can also disable rebooting in case of a STOP error with the startup option to Disable Automatic Restart After Failure or Disable Automatic Restart on System Failure. See "Disable Automatic Restart on System Failure," this chapter, p.222.

Fixing 0x7B Errors at Startup

If you are building a computer, have just upgraded to a new hard disk, or have just replaced the motherboard battery that maintains system settings, it's possible that your computer has "forgotten" the correct hard disk configuration settings.

Almost all hard disks are configured using Auto as the hard disk type. Thus, if the setup information is lost, the default (normal) setting is Auto and the drive will be properly detected.

However, the setting for the SATA interface used by your hard disk can be a problem. There are several possible settings for the SATA interface (IDE, AHCI, and RAID), and if your system is configured using one setting, but a different setting is used in the system BIOS or UEFI firmware, your computer won't start, displaying a 0x7B STOP error (refer to Figure 8.5).

If you know the correct setting, follow these steps:

1. Shut down the computer and restart it.
2. Start the BIOS or UEFI firmware setup program.
3. Change the SATA setting to the correct value.
4. Save settings and restart the computer.
5. Select Start Windows Normally if prompted.

Tip

If you don't know the correct setting to use in step 3, choose IDE (also known as ATA or Compatible) if the system is set to AHCI, or AHCI if the system is set to IDE, ATA, or Compatible.

Switching to AHCI Mode in Windows 7 and Windows 8.x

If your SATA drives are currently set to run in IDE mode, but you are planning to install an SSD, keep in mind that an SSD cannot provide you with faster performance unless you use AHCI mode. If the system crashes when you change SATA modes, how can you safely change from IDE to AHCI mode?

Note

AHCI mode is also recommended for full performance with SATA 3Gbps and 6Gbps hard disk drives.

Before you make the switch, you need to enable Windows to use AHCI drivers when necessary. The easiest way for Windows Vista and Windows 7 is to use the Fix-It wizard available from http://support.microsoft.com/kb/922976. This page also details manual Registry changes that make the same changes as the Fix-It Wizard.

After you run the Fix-It Wizard or make the needed changes manually, you can safely enable AHCI mode in the system BIOS or UEFI firmware setup dialog (refer to Figure 8.8), and your system will install the appropriate drivers and run properly.

To switch from IDE mode to AHCI mode in Windows 8.x, follow this procedure (adapted from http://superuser.com/questions/471102/change-from-ide-to-ahci-after-installing-windows-8):

1. Search for and run **msconfig.exe**.
2. Click the **Boot** tab.
3. Click the empty **Safe Boot** box (see Figure 8.6).

Figure 8.6
Make sure Safe Boot is checked before you click OK.

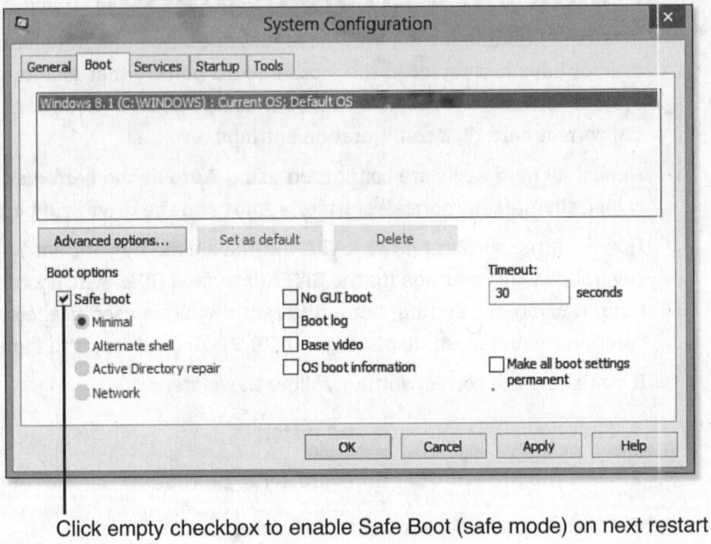

4. Click **OK**.
5. Swipe from the right or move your mouse to the lower-right corner of the screen and click or tap **Settings**.
6. Click or tap **Change PC Settings**.
7. Click or tap **Update and Recovery**.
8. Click or tap **Recovery**.
9. Click or tap **Restart Now** (see Figure 8.7).
10. Press the key or keys needed to enter the UEFI firmware setup program.
11. Change the SATA mode to AHCI (see Figure 8.8).
12. Select the option to save changes and restart your computer.
13. Search for and run **msconfig.exe**.
14. Click or tap the **Boot** tab.
15. Clear the **Safe Boot** check box.

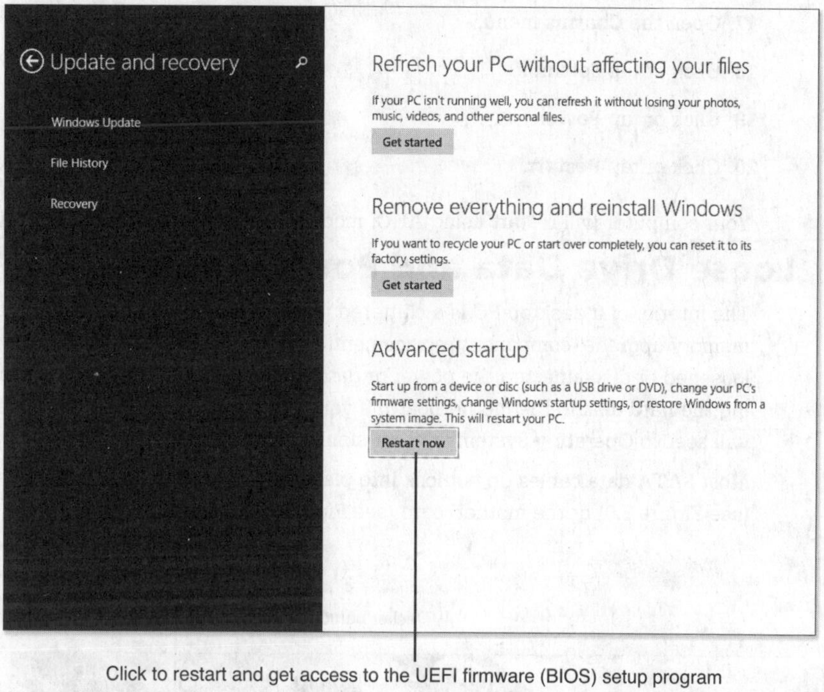

Figure 8.7 Restart Now enables you to change firmware (BIOS/UEFI) settings.

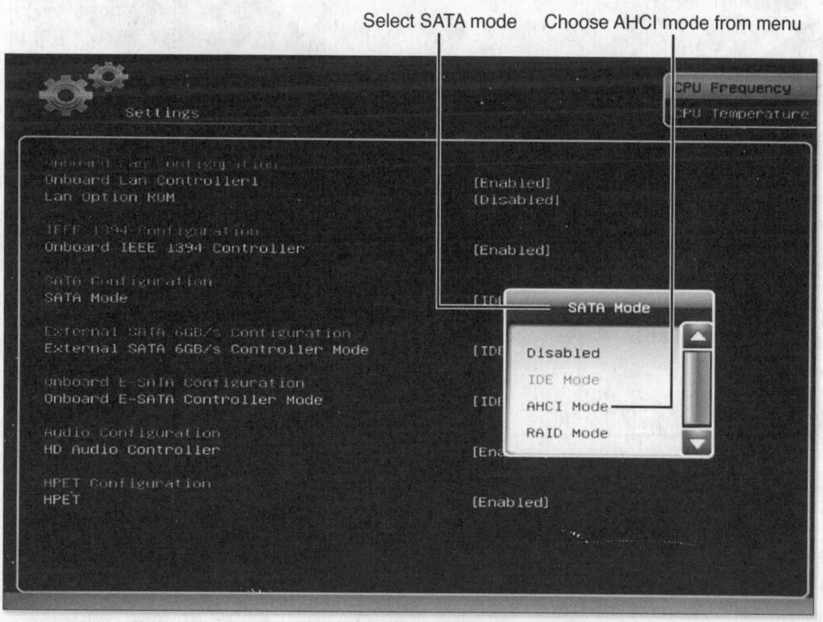

Figure 8.8 Preparing to change a system configured for IDE mode to AHCI mode.

16. Click or tap **OK**.
17. Open the **Charms** menu.
18. Click or tap **Settings**.
19. Click or tap **Power**.
20. Click or tap **Restart**.

Your computer will restart using AHCI mode for full performance of your SATA devices.

Loose Drive Data and Power Cables

The interior of a desktop PC is a cluttered place. Whether you had your system opened up for a memory upgrade, component replacement, or just to see what's "under the hood," you might have loosened or disconnected the power or data cables going to the hard disk or the data cable connecting the hard disk to the motherboard. If your system (C:) drive has disconnected or loose cables, you will see No Operating System or other similar error messages.

Most SATA data cables do not lock into place, so it's easy to have a loose cable on either a drive (see Figure 8.9) or the motherboard (see Figures 8.10 and 8.11).

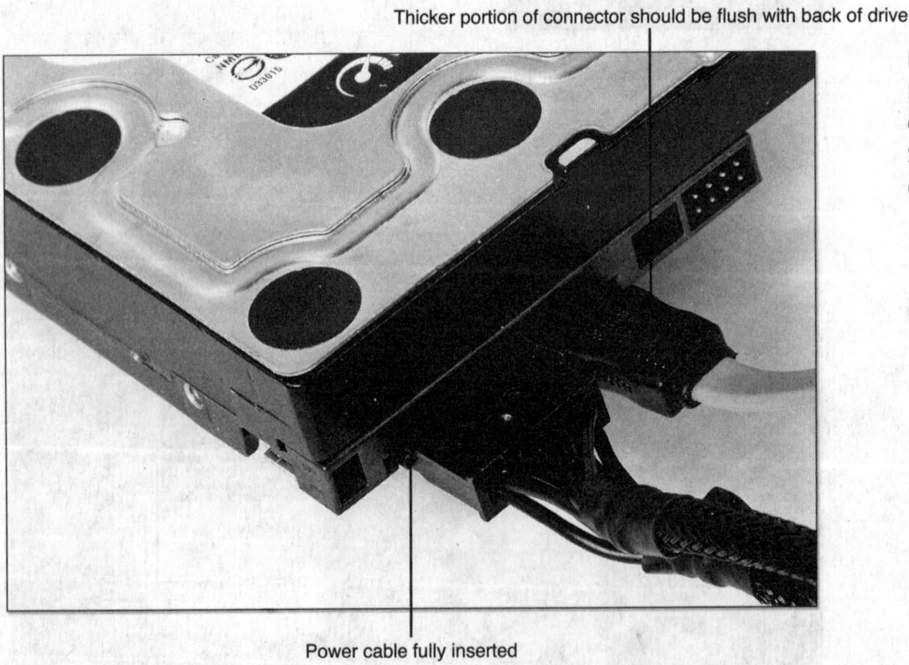

Figure 8.9 Loose data cable on an SATA hard disk.

Figure 8.10 An SATA motherboard host adapter with a loose data cable.

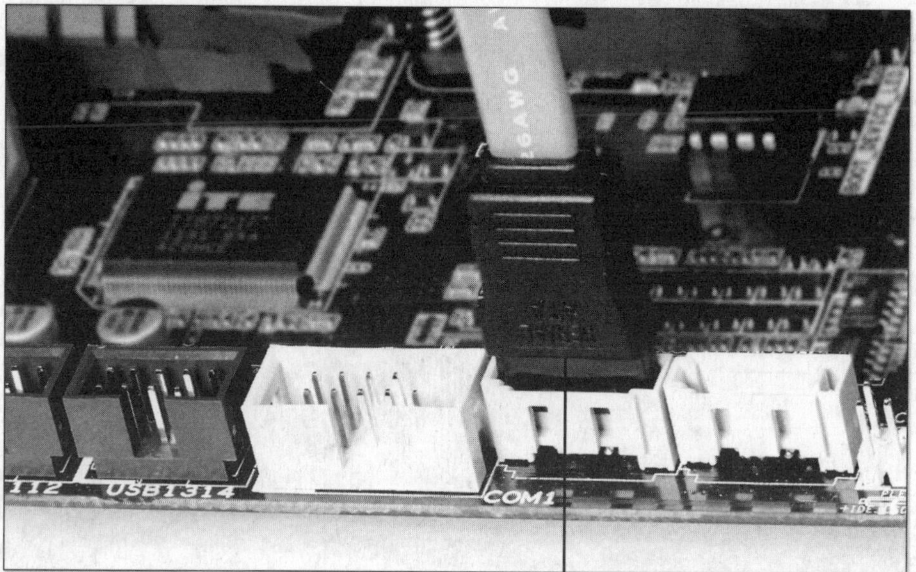

Push cable all the way into SATA port

Figure 8.11 Some motherboards use front-mounted SATA ports, like this one, which also features a loose data cable.

Push cable all the way into port

Similarly, SATA power cables can come loose from drives (see Figure 8.12).

Figure 8.12 The power cable on this SATA drive is not connected tightly.

To solve problems with loose or disconnected cables:

1. Shut down the computer.
2. Disconnect the power supply from AC power.
3. Open the system.
4. Check the hard disk or SSD for loose or disconnected cable(s).
5. Check the motherboard for loose or disconnected SATA data cables.
6. Securely plug the cable(s) into place (see Figures 8.13, 8.14, and 8.15).
7. Close the system.
8. Reconnect the power supply to AC power.
9. Restart the computer.

Figure 8.13 An SATA hard disk with properly connected power and data cables.

Figure 8.14 A correctly installed SATA data cable plugged into a top-facing motherboard port.

Fully-inserted SATA data cable

Figure 8.15 A correctly installed SATA data cable plugged into a front-facing motherboard port.

Drive Failure

If your hard disk is making a loud or rattling noise when it's running, it has probably failed. If the hard disk was dropped or smacked hard, a failure is very likely.

However, a hard disk might have failed if it is absolutely silent even when you place your ear next to it or does not get warm after the system has been on for several minutes.

Before assuming a hard disk has failed, perform this isolation test to determine whether the problem is the hard disk, its power cable, or its data cable:

1. Shut down the computer.
2. Disconnect the power supply from AC power.
3. Open the system.
4. Locate the power cable running between the hard disk and the power supply.
5. Disconnect the power cable from the power supply.
6. If the power cable used a splitter or converter to provide power to the drive, plug the drive directly into the power supply (if possible). If that is not possible, replace the splitter or converter and make sure it is securely plugged into the power supply lead and the drive.
7. Reconnect the power supply to AC power.

8. Restart the computer.
9. If the drive is still not working, repeat steps 1 and 2.
10. Reconnect the drive to the original power cable (and splitter or converter).
11. Remove the data cable from the hard disk drive and the computer.
12. Install a known-working replacement cable.
13. Plug it into the SATA port on the motherboard and drive.
14. Repeat steps 7 and 8.
15. If the drive is still not working, the drive has failed. Replace it.

Note

If you have backed up your information, you can replace your hard disk and restore your system from a backup. However, if you have no backup and the information is vital, you can use a data recovery company to recover your data. These companies have clean rooms that enable safe replacement of failed components and advanced data-extraction techniques. Expect to pay hundreds of dollars for recovery – if the drive's condition permits it.

Windows 7 Error Recovery and Advanced Boot Options

If Windows 7 is unable to start normally, Windows will display the Windows Error Recovery dialog. On a system that does not have Startup Repair files installed, the Windows Error Recovery dialog looks like the one in Figure 8.16. You can use a Windows installation disc or a Windows repair disc to repair your computer.

Tip

To learn how to create a Windows 7 repair disc, see "Preparing a Windows-Based Computer or Tablet for Easier Troubleshooting," Chapter 1, p.37.

On a system that has Startup Repair files installed, the Windows Error Recovery dialog provides the options shown in Figure 8.17 when your system can't start.

On a system that didn't shut down properly the last time it was used (for example, if you used the power button because the system locked up), Windows Error Recovery offers Safe Mode options, Last Known Good Configuration (advanced), or Start Windows Normally.

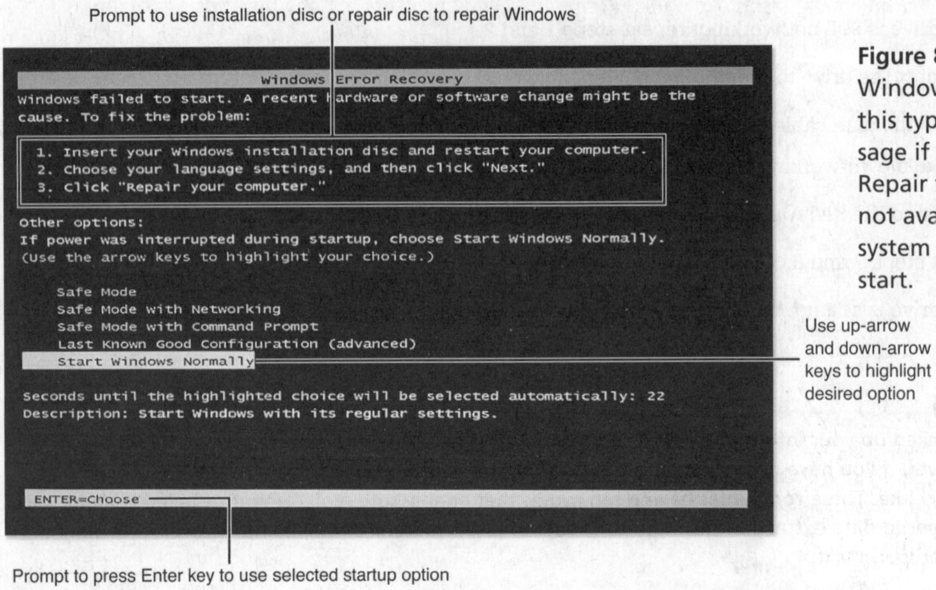

Figure 8.16 Windows 7 displays this type of message if Startup Repair files are not available on a system that can't start.

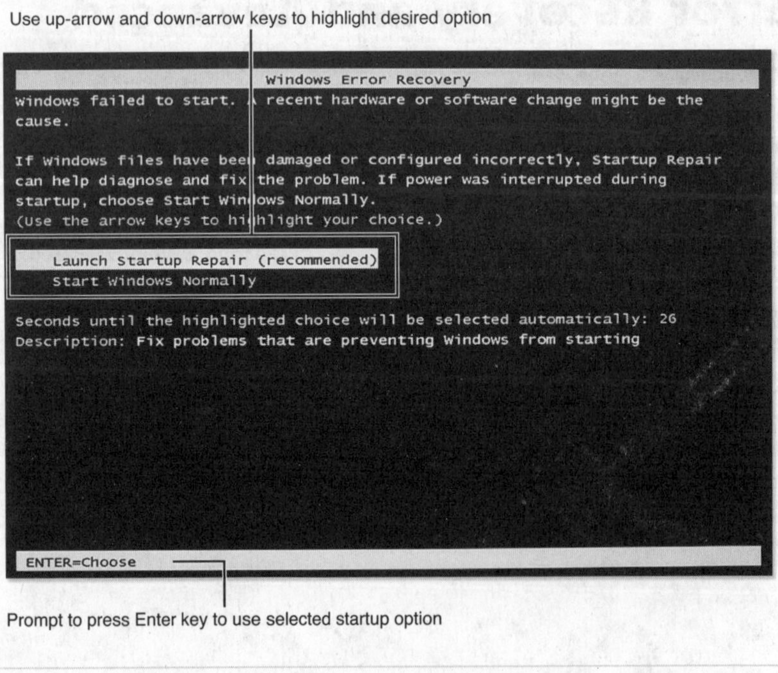

Figure 8.17 Windows 7 displays this type of message if Startup Repair files are available on a system that can't start.

If you suspect that Windows is not working as well as it could, but Windows 7 does not launch Windows Error Recovery, you can still choose from these and other options by pressing F8 repeatedly on startup until the Advanced Boot Options menu shown in Figure 8.18 appears.

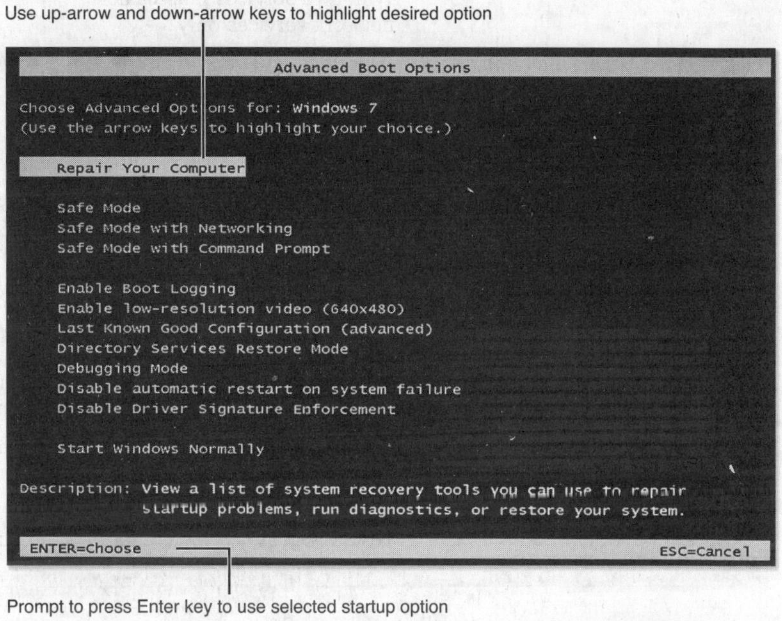

Figure 8.18 Windows 7's Advanced Boot Options menu.

Using Windows 7 Repair Tools

Windows 7's repair tools can be accessed in a variety of ways. Table 8.3 provides a quick reference to these tools and how to access them.

Table 8.3 System Repair Tools for Windows 7

Repair Tool	How Used	How to Use
Automatic System Repair (Startup Repair)	Repairs system and startup files	Runs automatically as needed or can be launched from Recovery Environment (repair disc)
System Restore	Resets Windows hardware and software settings back to a specified date	Recovery Environment
Command Prompt	Uses commands to copy or delete files, changes Windows settings, and other command-line functions	Recovery Environment

Repair Tool	How Used	How to Use
Safe Mode	Loads essential Windows drivers and services only	Advanced Boot Options or Windows Error Recovery
Safe Mode with Networking	Loads essential drivers and Windows services plus basic network services only	Advanced Boot Options
Safe Mode with Command Prompt	Loads essential drivers and Windows services but boots to command prompt	Advanced Boot Options
Last Known Good Configuration	Loads Windows with the last known good configuration	Advanced Boot Options
Enable Boot Logging	Creates text log of all startup processes	Advanced Boot Options
Enable Low-Resolution Video	Starts Windows with basic VGA driver	Advanced Boot Options
Disable Automatic Restart After Failure	Keeps STOP (blue screen) error on-screen until you restart system manually	Advanced Boot Options
System Image Recovery	Restores a system image backup to the system drive (or an empty hard disk)	Recovery Environment
Windows Memory Diagnostic	Tests RAM memory modules for errors	Recovery Environment

Using Automatic Startup Repair

If Windows is unable to start because of damaged or missing system files, you should run Automatic Startup Repair. Automatic Startup Repair scans your system drive for problems and attempts to repair them.

If Startup Repair is successful, you have the option of seeing a report dialog (see Figure 8.19). A typical report dialog is shown in Figure 8.20.

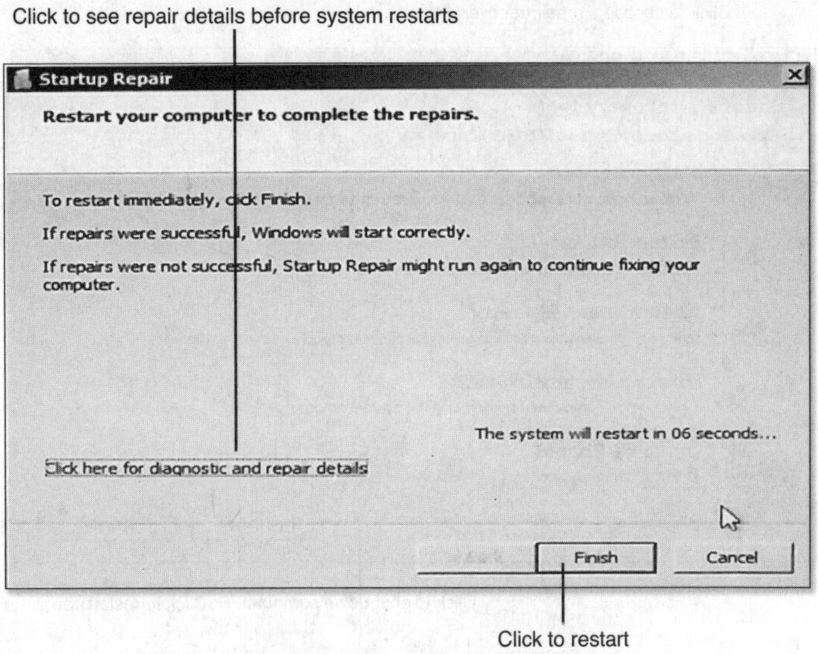

Figure 8.19
Click the link to see the repairs performed on this system.

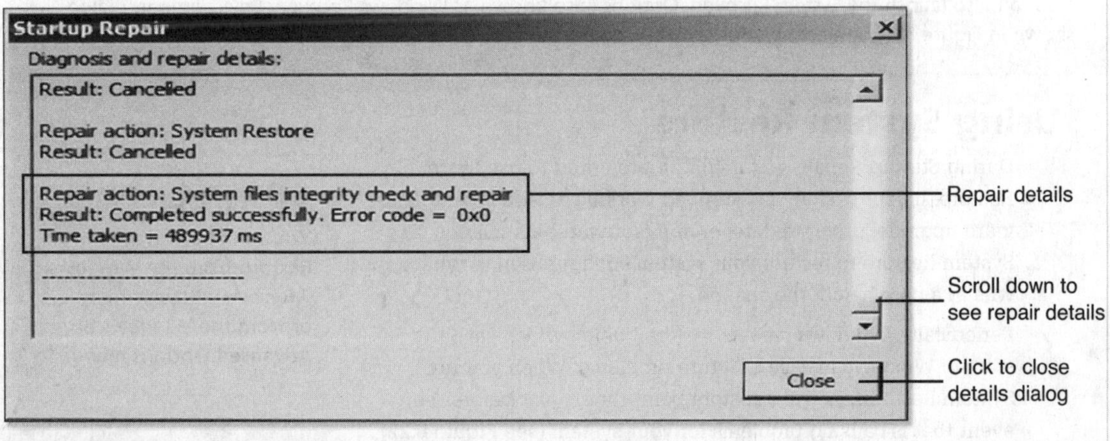

Figure 8.20
Scroll down through the report to see the tests performed and their results.

If repairs were not successful, you can choose from other repair tools (see Figure 8.21).

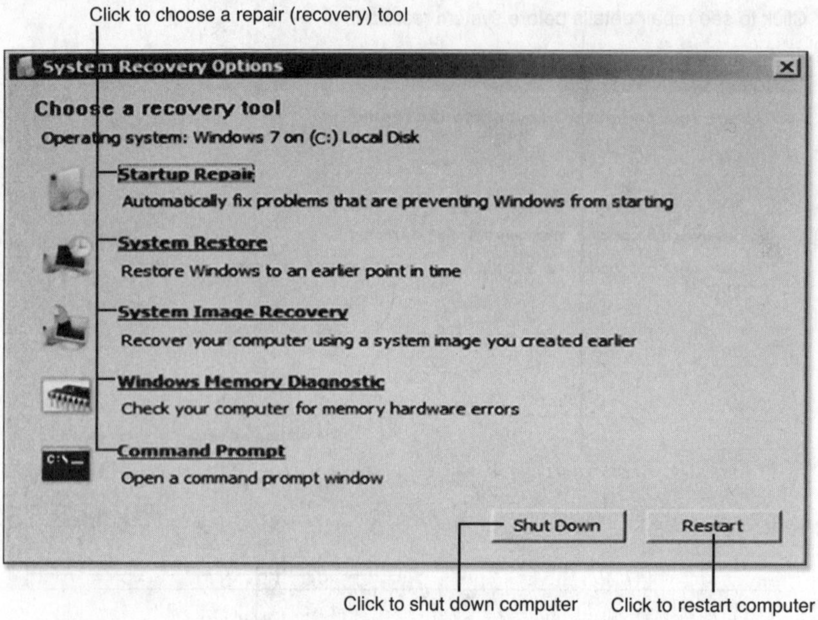

Figure 8.21 System Recovery Options in Windows 7's Windows Recovery Environment.

> **Note**
> You can also launch the System Recovery Options (also known as Windows Recovery Environment) dialog shown in Figure 8.21 by starting your system with the Windows 7 installation disc or a Windows 7 repair disc.

Using System Restore

During Startup Repair, you might be prompted to use System Restore. If your system has stopped working after a recent hardware upgrade, driver update, or app (software) installation, use System Restore to restore your system configuration to what it was at a date before the change.

> **Note**
> You can also run System Restore from the Windows 7 Recovery Environment or from the Windows 8.x Advanced Options menu.

Periodically, Windows creates restore points, which save the state of Windows in case of future problems. When you run System Restore, choose a restore point that is just before the event that is causing problems for your system (see Figure 8.22).

To see which programs or drivers will be affected, click the Scan for Affected Programs link. Programs and drivers that will be removed are listed on top, followed by programs and drivers that will be restored (see Figure 8.23).

> **Caution**
> Programs and drivers that will be restored might not work properly. Plan to reinstall any programs or drivers listed.

After you confirm the restore point to restore, Windows restores the settings as they were and restarts your computer.

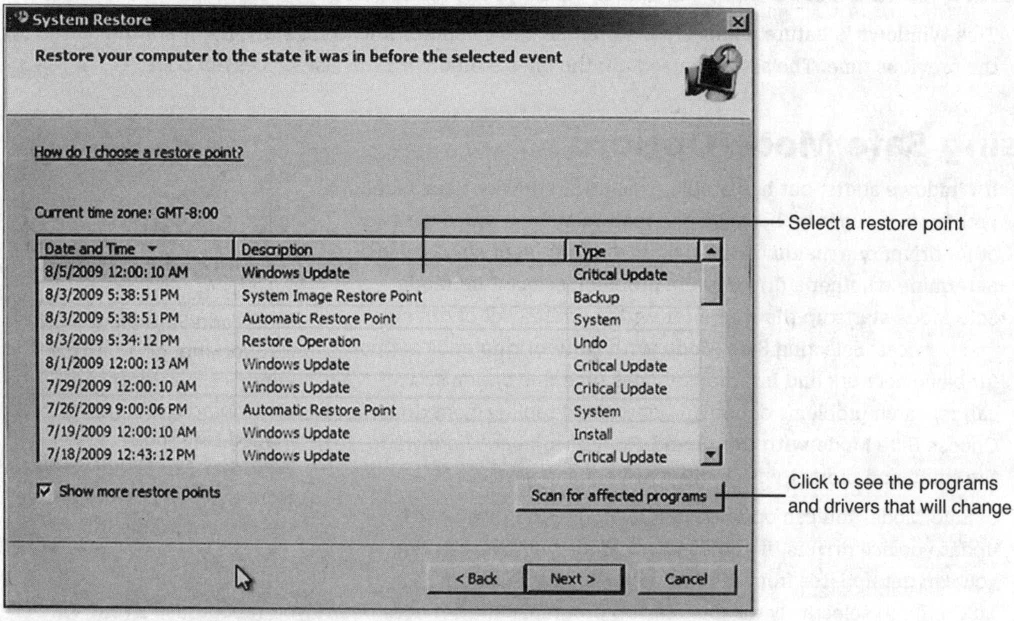

Figure 8.22
Selecting a date with System Restore.

Figure 8.23
When System Restore runs on this computer, two programs will be deleted, and one will be restored.

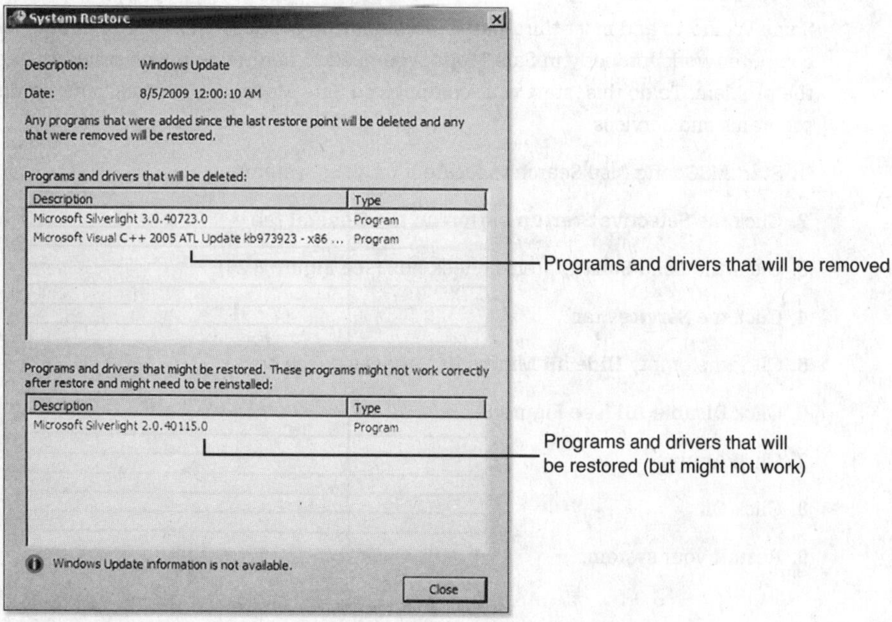

Using Last Known Good Configuration

This Windows 7 feature enables you to restart the computer if it won't start, but it started correctly the previous time. The settings used are the ones stored with the last successful boot.

Using Safe Mode Options

If Windows starts, but has problems shutting down or has video problems, it might be because of a malfunctioning video card or other driver or a malfunctioning startup program or service. To determine whether a driver is the problem, select **Safe Mode**. Safe Mode starts up the computer with a limited set of drivers and services. Selecting **Safe Mode with Networking** adds support for basic network and Internet services (use this option so you can research problems online and download replacement drivers). Choose **Safe Mode with Command Prompt** to boot Windows to the command prompt with limited drivers and services.

> **Note**
> For a list of the drivers and services launched in Safe Mode and Safe Mode with Networking, go to http://windows.microsoft.com/en-us/windows/which-drivers-loaded-safe-mode. Select Windows 7 or Windows Vista from the pull-down menu to see the applicable list.

In Safe Mode, you can open Device Manager and disable or update device drivers (if you use Safe Mode with Networking, you can get updates from the Internet). You can also run MSConfig to selectively disable startup programs and services before you reboot, use Event Viewer to see problems with your computer, and use the Registry Editor to make manual changes to how Windows runs.

Using MSConfig

Some Windows and most third-party programs and services will not run in Safe Mode. Thus, if your computer works properly in Safe Mode, you need to determine which program or service is causing the problem. To do this, start your computer in Safe Mode and run MSConfig to disable all startup programs and services:

1. Start MSConfig (use Search to locate it on your system).
2. Click the **Selective Startup** button on the **General** tab.
3. Clear the **Load Startup** Items check box (see Figure 8.24).
4. Click the **Services** tab.
5. Click the empty **Hide all Microsoft Services** check box.
6. Click **Disable All** (see Figure 8.25).
7. Click **Apply**.
8. Click **OK**.
9. Restart your system.

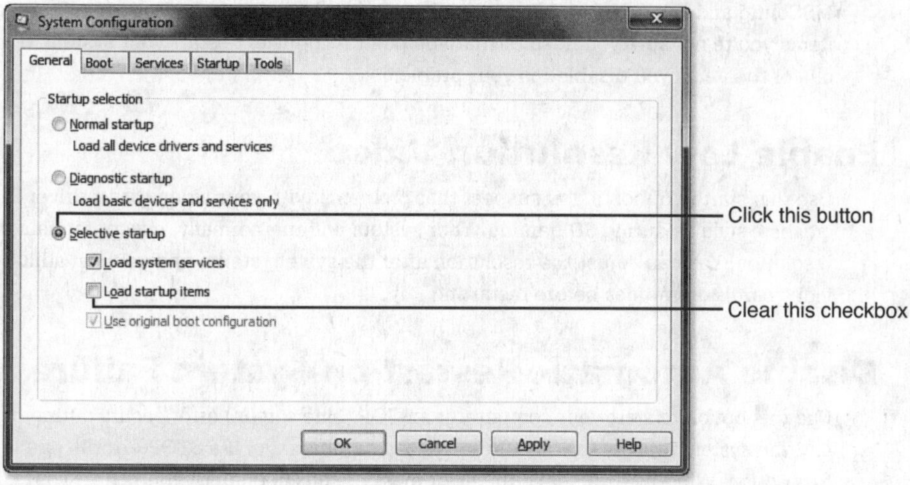

Figure 8.24 Disabling the Load Startup Items option with Microsoft System Configuration (MSConfig).

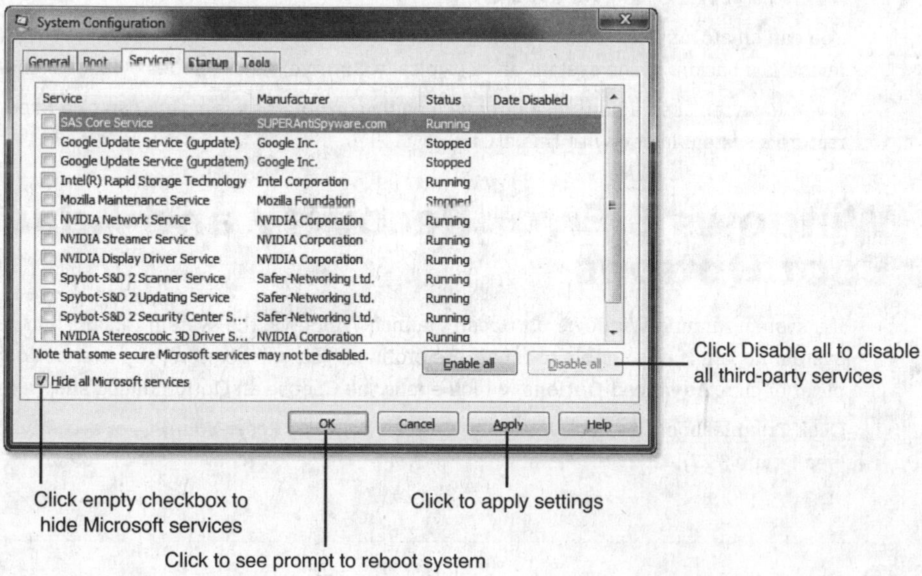

Figure 8.25 The Services tab after hiding Microsoft services and disabling third-party services.

What's next? If your system starts normally, either a startup item or a non-Microsoft service is causing problems. To find out, enable one non-Microsoft service at a time until the system won't start normally. Uninstall the app or program that uses the service.

If you are able to enable all non-Microsoft services and your system boots normally, restart MSConfig and select **Normal Startup** on the General tab. Click the **Startup** tab and disable startup items you're not sure you need or that you don't recognize. Restart your system. If it starts normally, one of the items you disabled is your problem.

Enable Low-Resolution Video

Use this startup option if you suspect that problems with your video card's driver is causing system crashes, such as during 3D gaming. Your system will run normally, except for using a low screen resolution. You can adjust the resolution after the system starts, and you can adjust or replace your video card's driver files before restarting.

Disable Automatic Restart on System Failure

Use this option to start your computer if a STOP (blue screen) error occurs during or after startup and the system reboots too quickly to see the full message. If a STOP error happens after you use this option, Windows will leave the error message onscreen until you restart your computer.

System Image Recovery

You can create a system image backup with the Backup and Restore utility in Windows 7. A system image is a backup of the system drive (typically C: drive) that includes Windows and system files.

If you have replaced a hard disk or have a badly corrupted system that can't be fixed, you can restore a system image with this utility.

Windows 8 Error Recovery and Advanced Boot Options

If a system running Windows 8.x doesn't launch Windows, the system reboots and runs Automatic System Repair. If it is unable to repair the problem, you will be prompted to shut down your computer or click **Advanced Options**, which opens the Choose an Option dialog shown in Figure 8.26.

Click **Troubleshoot** to select options to Refresh Your PC, Reset Your PC, or see Advanced Options (see Figure 8.27).

> **Note**
>
> If you want to restore a complete backup (system image) made with a third-party backup program that uses a bootable USB or optical disc, insert that drive or disc, then choose **Use a Device**, and choose the drive to reboot from.

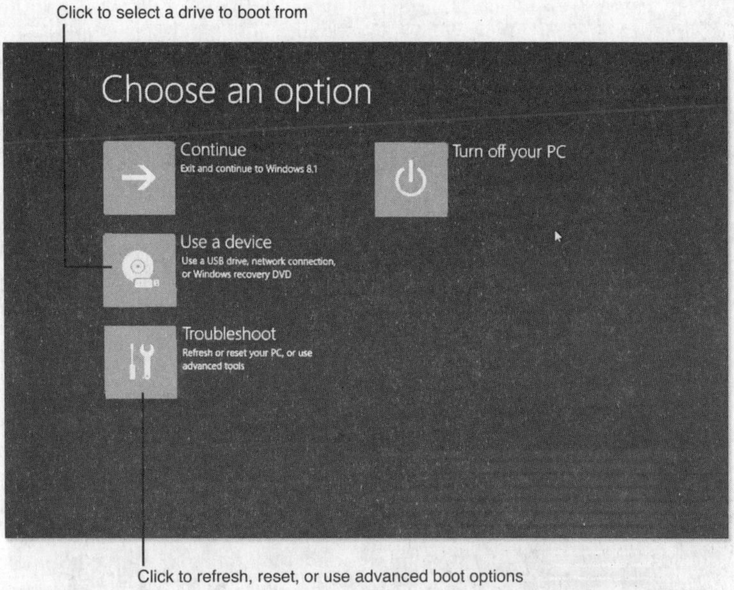

Figure 8.26
You can boot from a Windows USB drive or disc, choose from troubleshooting tools, turn off your computer, or try to restart Windows 8.1 from the Choose an option menu.

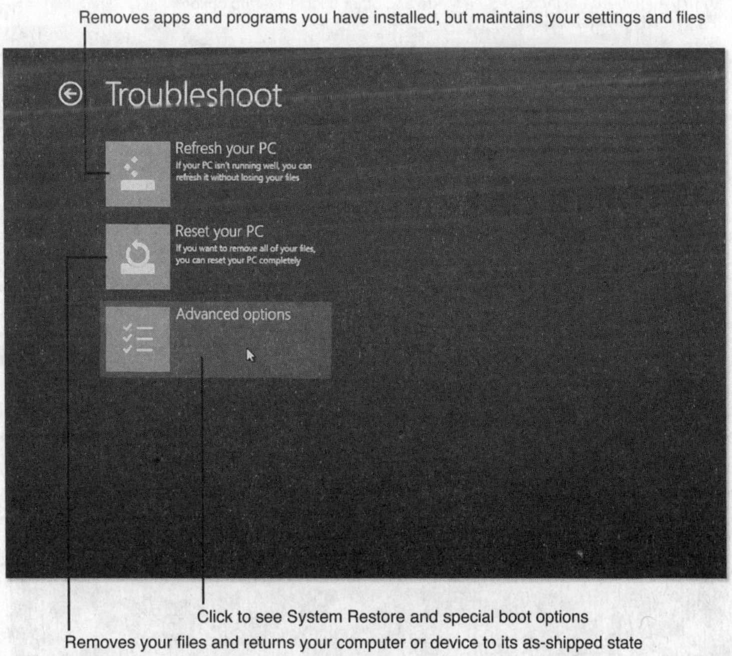

Figure 8.27
The Troubleshoot dialog lets you refresh or reset your PC.

The Advanced options dialog (see Figure 8.28) provides options for accessing your system via the command prompt, for changing your computer's UEFI firmware settings, and more.

If you select **Startup Settings** from the Advanced menu, you will see the options shown in Figure 8.29.

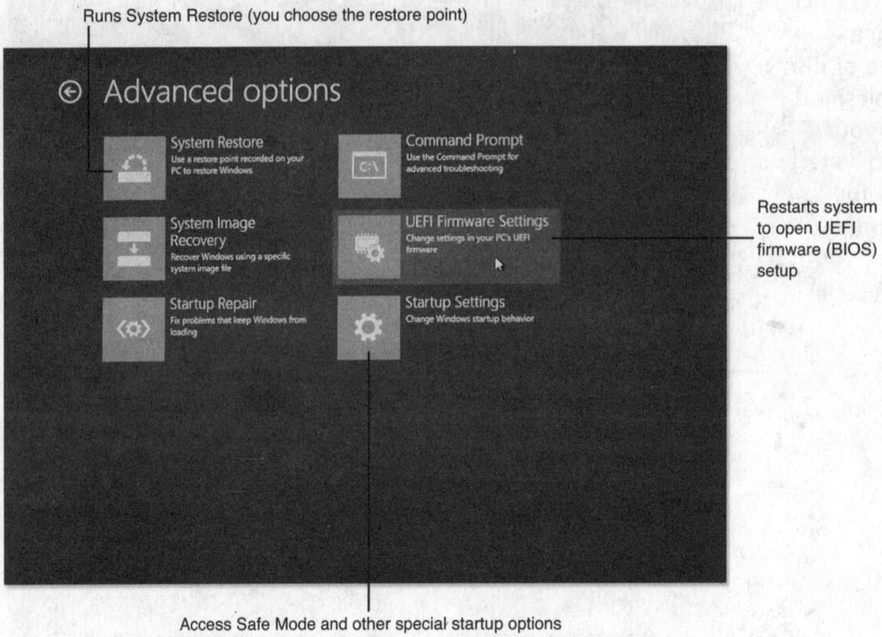

Figure 8.28 Use the Advanced Options menu to run System Restore, repair startup files, use Startup settings such as Safe Mode, or change UEFI firmware settings.

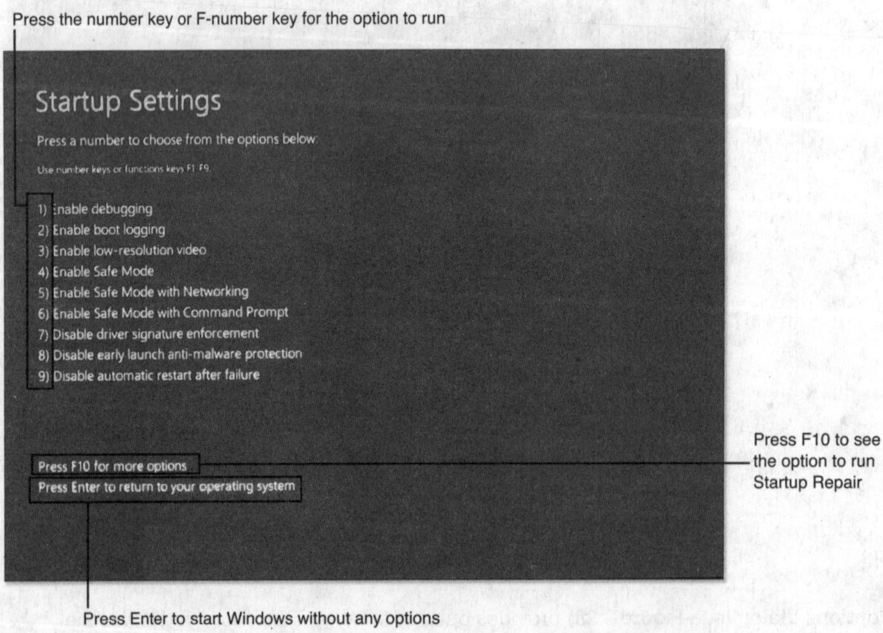

Figure 8.29 Choose an option to restart your system.

Using Windows 8/8.1 Repair Tools

Windows 8/8.1's repair tools can be accessed in a variety of ways. Table 8.4 provides a quick reference to these tools and how to access them.

Table 8.4 System Repair Tools for Windows 8/8.1

Repair Tool	How Used	How to Use
Automatic System Repair (Startup Repair)	Repairs system and startup files	Runs automatically as needed or can be launched from Recovery Environment (repair disc)
Refresh Your PC	Removes non-Windows Store apps and returns Windows to proper operation without removing user files	Launches from Troubleshoot dialog
Reset Your PC	Returns Windows to its as-shipped configuration (removes user files)	Launches from Troubleshoot dialog
System Restore	Resets Windows hardware and software settings back to a specified date	May be offered during Startup Repair or launched from Advanced Options dialog
Command Prompt	Uses commands to copy or delete files, change Windows settings, and other command-line functions	Launches from Advanced Options
Safe Mode	Loads essential Windows drivers and services only	Launches from Startup Settings
Safe Mode with Networking	Loads essential drivers and Windows services plus basic network services only	Launches from Startup Settings
Safe Mode with Command Prompt	Loads essential drivers and Windows services but boots to command prompt	Launches from Startup Settings
Use a Device	Selects a drive (SSD, hard disk, USB, or optical) to boot from	Launches from Troubleshoot dialog
System Image Recovery*	Refreshes Windows from a specific image backup file so you can keep your desktop (non-Windows Store) apps	Launches from Advanced Settings
UEFI Firmware Settings	Starts the UEFI firmware (BIOS) setup program	Launches from Advanced Settings
Enable Boot Logging	Creates text log of all startup processes	Launches from Startup Settings
Enable Low-Resolution Video	Starts Windows with basic VGA driver	Launches from Startup Settings

Repair Tool	How Used	How to Use
Disable Automatic Restart After Failure	Keeps STOP (blue screen) error onscreen until you restart system manually	Launches from Startup Settings

**You can create a custom recovery image using the command-line recimg.exe program.*

Note

To learn more about using recimg.exe to create a custom image backup with Windows 8/8.1, see http://blogs.msdn.com/b/b8/archive/2012/01/04/refresh-and-reset-your-pc.aspx and http://support.microsoft.com/kb/2748351

Many of these options work the same way as in Windows 7, but two options in this list are unique to Windows 8/8.1: Refresh Your PC and Reset Your PC. They're covered in the following sections.

Refresh Your PC

Windows 8 introduced Refresh Your PC as a way to solve major problems with your computer without wiping out your information. Windows 8.1 also includes Refresh Your PC.

If you are unable to start your computer or have other major problems with it, choose **Refresh Your PC** from the Troubleshoot menu shown in Figure 8.27. Refresh Your PC removes programs you installed but does not disturb your personal files. After you run it, your system reboots. At that point, you will need to reinstall apps and software you have downloaded from sources other than the Windows Store or installed from optical or USB media (apps you installed from the Windows Store or that were bundled with your computer are not affected). If you want to keep these apps, create a custom refresh image using recimg.exe and start the refresh process with System Image Recovery (refer to Figure 8.28).

Windows displays a list of removed apps on the Windows Desktop after your system restarts. Figure 8.30 shows an example of the Apps Removed report after running refresh on a system running Windows 8.

Caution

If your system was originally set up with Windows 8 and you have updated it to Windows 8.1, keep in mind that using Refresh Your PC resets your computer to Windows 8. You will also need to reinstall Windows 8.1 from the Windows Store.

Figure 8.30 Windows 8.x stores removed apps as an HTML file on the Windows Desktop after you refresh your system.

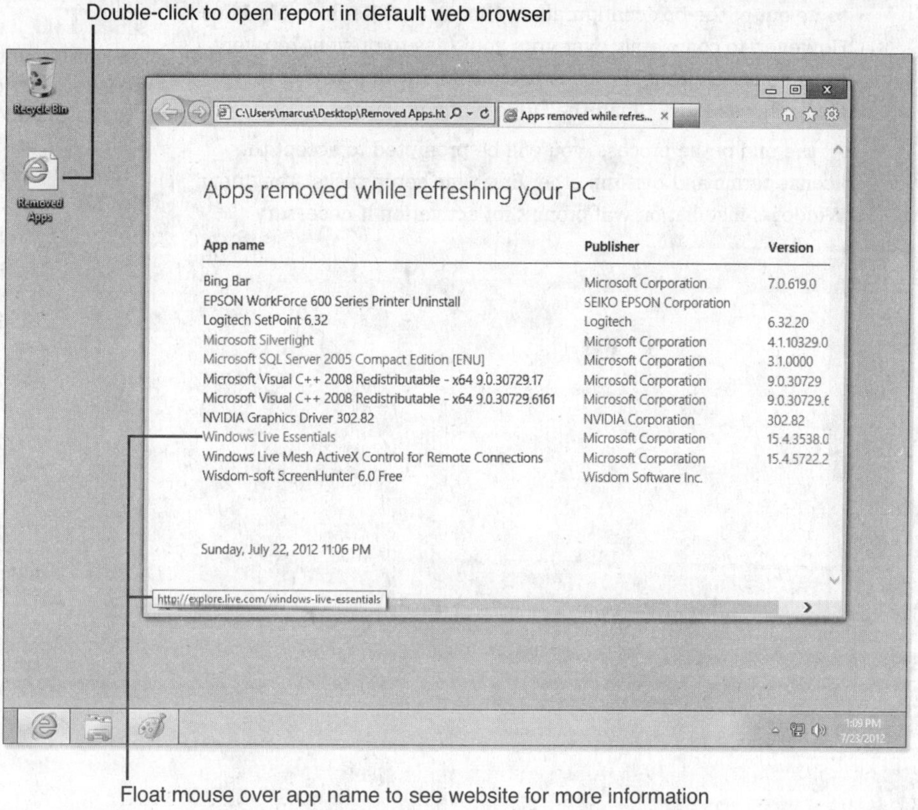

Reset Your PC

If it's time to give your PC to another user, or to sell it or recycle it, the one thing you don't want left on it is any personal information. Use **Reset Your PC** to set your Windows 8.x system back to its original out-of-the-box condition.

Before you reset your PC, be sure to do the following:

- Disconnect all external drives connected to your computer.
- Back up any of your personal files on internal drives.

> **Tip**
> To learn how to back up your files, see "Preparing a Windows-Based Computer or Tablet for Easier Troubleshooting," Chapter 1, p.37.

To use Reset Your PC, you will need a Windows 8.x installation disc or a USB Recovery drive.

During the process, you are prompted to delete your files from all drives or from the Windows drive only. Choose **All Drives** to remove your files from all internal drives.

If you are planning to keep the computer and just need to reset it to its out-of-the-box configuration, choose **Just Remove My Files**. However, to completely overwrite your files to prevent recovery (recommended if the device is being sold, given away, or recycled), choose **Fully Clean the Drive** when prompted.

At the end of the process, you will be prompted to accept the license terms and perform other first-time setup tasks. The "new" Windows installation will prompt for activation if necessary.

Tip

To learn how to make a USB Recovery drive, see "Preparing a Windows-Based Computer or Tablet for Easier Troubleshooting," Chapter 1 p.37.

9

SOLVING FILE SHARING PROBLEMS

Fast Track to Solutions

Table 9.1 Symptom Table

Symptom	Flowchart or Book Section	Page #
I don't see the option to join a homegroup in Windows 7.	Choosing Home as the Network Type in Windows 7	234
I don't see the option to join a homegroup in Windows 8/8.1.	Choosing a Private Network in Windows 8/8.1	235
I can't connect to a home-group.	Can't Join an Existing Homegroup	241
Help me through the steps to get connected to a home-group.	Can't Join or Create a HomeGroup (flowchart)	Chapter 24
I need to fix my homegroup.	Using the HomeGroup Troubleshooter	243
I need to change files on another user's computer.	Enabling Read/Write Access to a Folder	255
I need to share files with Windows XP or Windows Vista computers.	Sharing Files Without Usernames or Passwords	256
I want to limit the media that other users can stream.	Streaming Media	260
I want to view media from my mobile device without copying files to it.	File Sharing with Portable Devices	261

Troubleshooting HomeGroup Settings

If you use Windows 7 or Windows 8/8.1 at home or in a small office, HomeGroup network technology is an easy way to share folders and printers. Because it's password protected, HomeGroup protects your information. But because only a single password is needed and setup uses a simple check box method, HomeGroup is also easy to manage. However, like any other network technology, HomeGroup might stop working. In this section, we'll help you get your HomeGroup working again.

> **Note**
> Homegroups are not supported in older versions of Windows (Vista, XP, and so on). To learn how to share folders with these versions of Windows, see "Sharing Files Without Usernames or Passwords," p.256, this chapter.

Creating a Homegroup—and What to Do if You Can't

A HomeGroup is a secure network feature included in Windows 7, 8, and 8.1. Any computer on the network can create a homegroup, and then others can join it—with one big exception: computers connected to a domain-based network can't be part of a homegroup.

Here's how to get started in Windows 7 or from the desktop in Windows 8/8.1:

1. Open Control Panel.
2. Click or tap **Network and Internet**.
3. Click or tap **Network and Sharing Center**.
4. If you see the **Ready to Create** link next to HomeGroup, click the link to set up a homegroup (see Figure 9.1).
5. Click **Create a Homegroup**.
6. Select the items to share. By default, the music, videos, and pictures libraries are shared, as are the printers installed on your system. To share documents, click the empty check box next to Documents. If you don't want to share a library, clear the check box for that library (see Figure 9.2). Click **Next** to continue.
7. After shared items are selected, the homegroup password is displayed (see Figure 9.3). Write down or print the password, because it must be used by other Windows 7, Windows 8, or Windows 8.1 computers or tablets that want to join the homegroup. Click **Finish**.

> **Note**
> If HomeGroup status is Joined, the computer is already part of a homegroup. If HomeGroup status is Available to Join, click the link to join an existing homegroup.

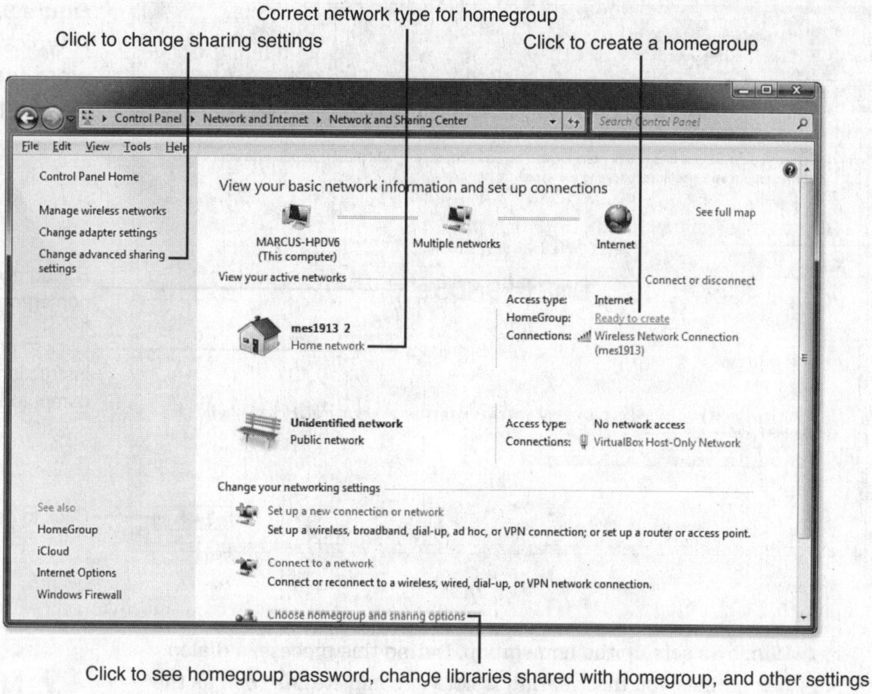

Figure 9.1 Preparing to create a homegroup in Windows 7.

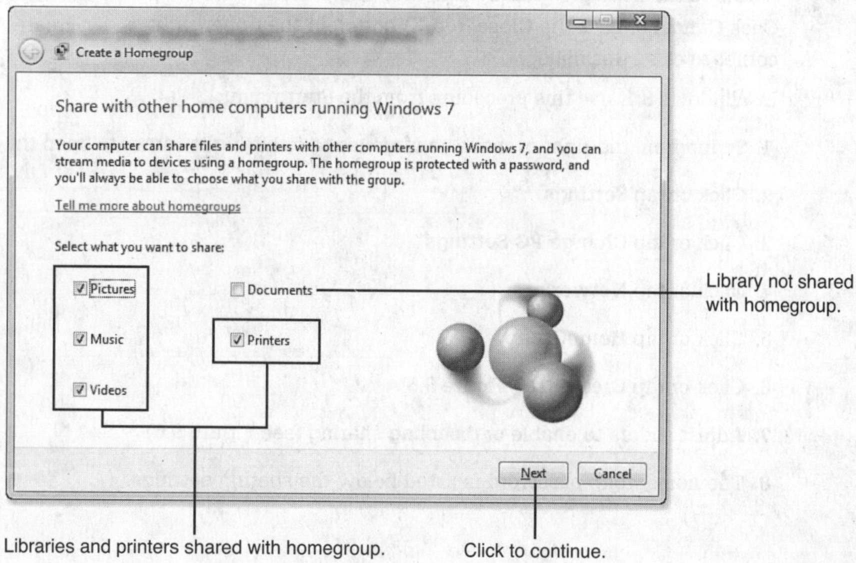

Figure 9.2 Selecting items to share in a homegroup (Windows 7).

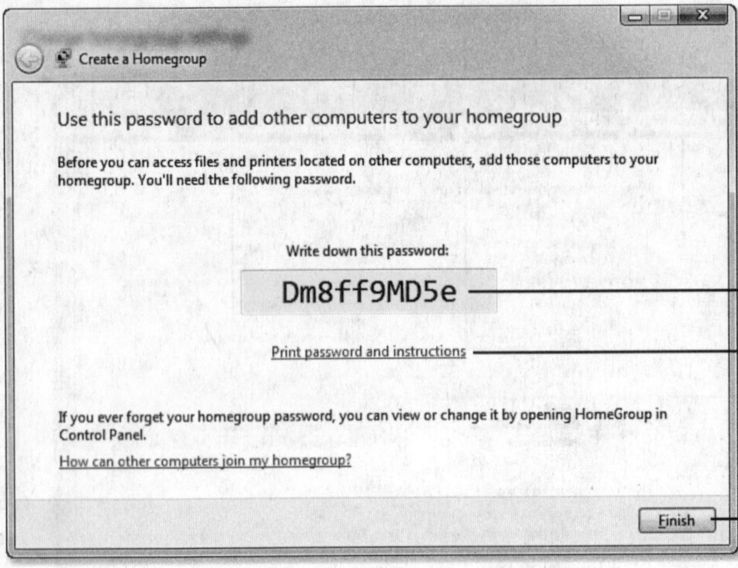

Figure 9.3
A typical homegroup password (generated randomly by Windows).

Windows sets up the homegroup. During this process, a dialog box notifies you that sharing is not yet complete. As soon as the process is complete, you will see the Change Homegroup Settings dialog shown in Figure 9.4. At this point, you can add other computers to the homegroup and share files and printers with them. Click **Cancel** or click the **Close** (red X) button in the upper-right corner to close this dialog.

> **Note**
> It can take a half-hour or longer to complete homegroup setup on the computer that creates the homegroup.

In Windows 8.1, use this procedure from the Start menu:

1. Swipe from the right or move your mouse to either right corner to open the Charms menu.
2. Click or tap **Settings**.
3. Click or tap **Change PC Settings**.
4. Click or tap **Network**.
5. Click or tap **HomeGroup**.
6. Click or tap **Create** (see Figure 9.5).
7. Adjust sliders to enable or disabling sharing (see Figure 9.6).
8. The homegroup password is listed below the sharing settings.

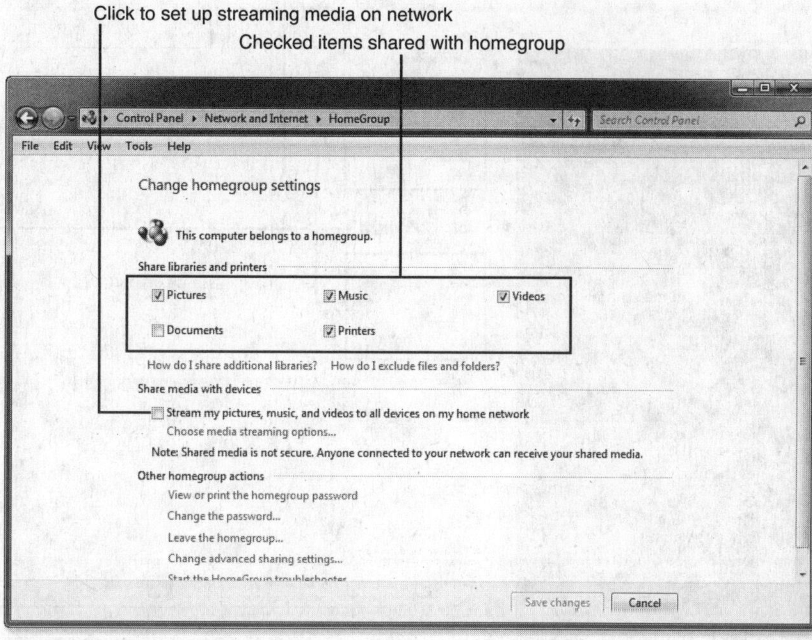

Figure 9.4
Your homegroup is ready.

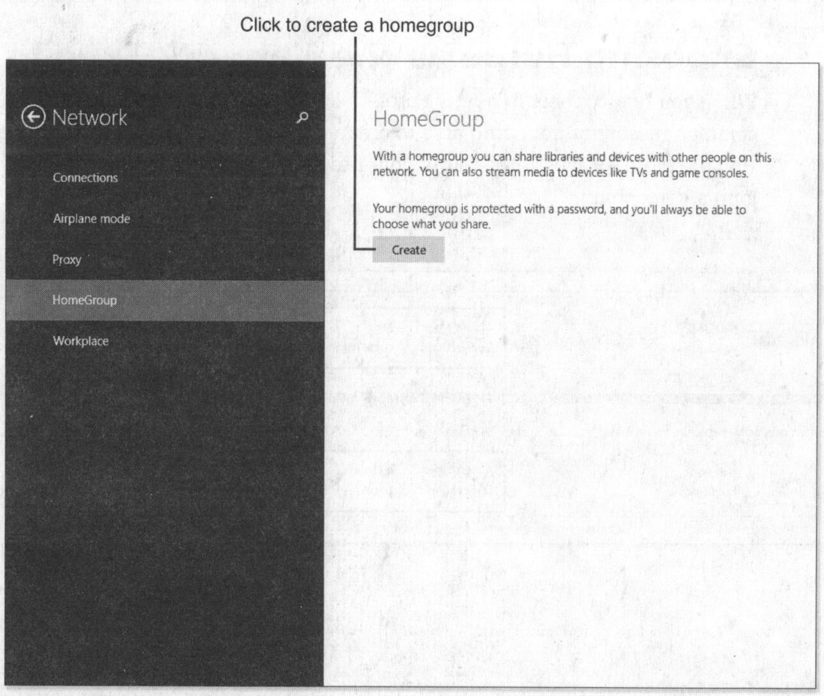

Figure 9.5
Preparing to create a homegroup from the Windows 8.1 Start menu.

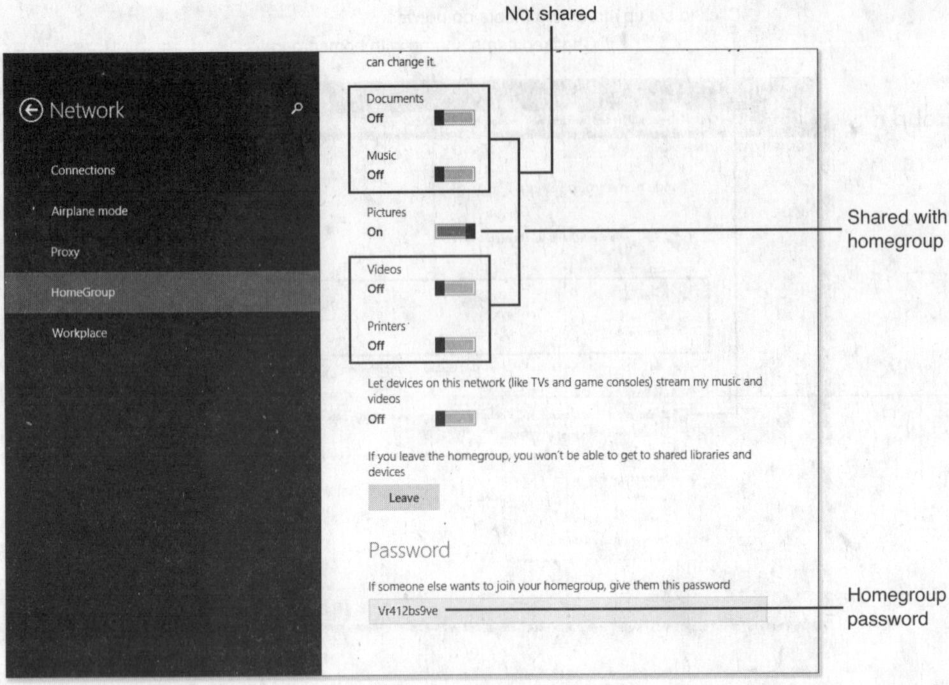

Figure 9.6 Selecting libraries to share and viewing the homegroup password with Windows 8.1.

Choosing Home as the Network Type in Windows 7

When you first connect to a new wireless or wired network, you select the network type. The most common reason for not being able to create (or join) a homegroup is if the network type is not set to Home. Figure 9.7 illustrates that if your network type is set to Work or Public, you can't create (or join) a homegroup.

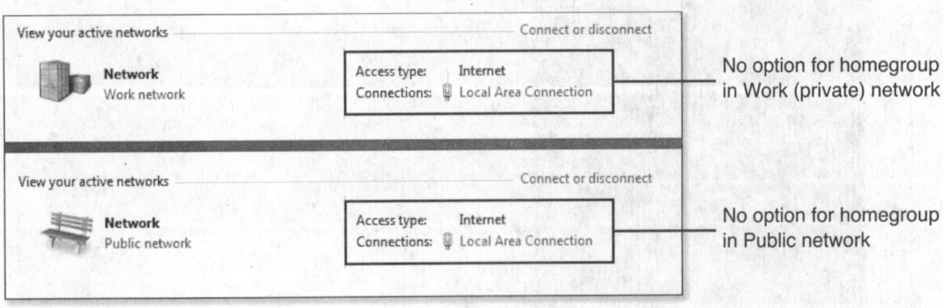

Figure 9.7 Work or Public network types (shown in Network and Sharing Center) don't support homegroups.

To change the network type, click it. From the Set Network Location dialog, click Home as the network type (see Figure 9.8). After you make this change, the Network and Sharing Center displays Home as the network type and prompts you to create or join a homegroup.

Figure 9.8
Click Home as the network type if you want to use homegroups with this computer.

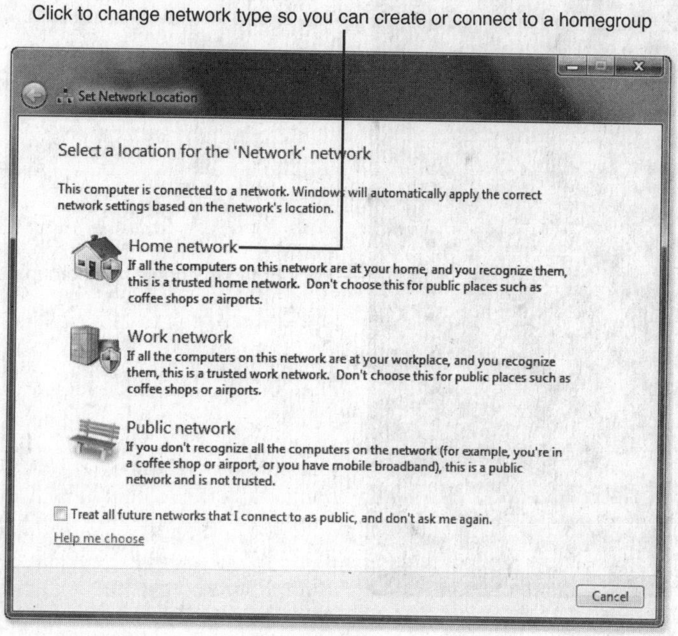

Caution

If you click the Treat All Future Networks That I Connect to as Public, and Don't Ask Me Again check box shown in Figure 9.8, you won't be prompted to select a network type when you connect to a new network.

This is convenient when you frequently use nonsecure networks (such as those in restaurants, hotels, and other public places), but it will require you to manually select Home as the network type when you want to connect to a new network with a homegroup.

Choosing a Private Network in Windows 8/8.1

Windows 8/8.1 have only two network types: public and private. When you first connect to a wireless network with Windows 8/8.1, you are prompted to click or tap Yes if you want to find PCs, devices, and content on this network (see Figure 9.9). When you select this option, you are connecting to a private network, and you can create a homegroup (if none exists on the network) or join one.

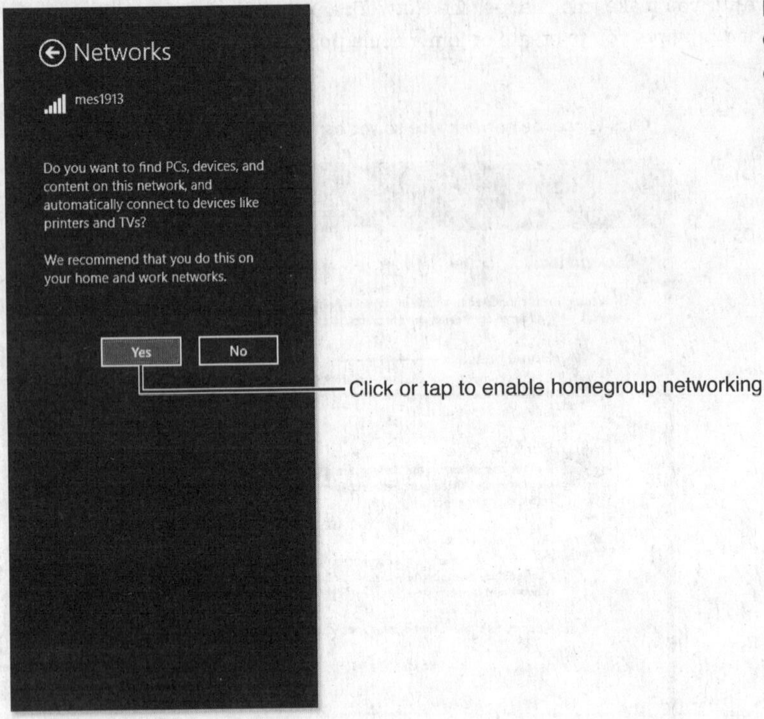

Figure 9.9
Clicking or tapping Yes enables you to create a homegroup or connect to one.

Click or tap No for a public network, such as those used in restaurants, hotels, and other public places. You cannot create or connect to a homegroup in Windows 8/8.1 if you select No.

How can you change the network type if you made the wrong choice at connection time? As you can see from Figure 9.10, you cannot change the network type from the Network and Sharing Center dialog directly.

To solve this problem, you need to enable your network to look for other computers and devices. Here's one method:

1. Swipe from the right or move your mouse to either right corner to open the Charms menu.
2. Click or tap **Settings**.
3. Click or tap **Change PC Settings**.
4. Click or tap **Network**. The Connections menu opens.
5. Click or tap your current connection.

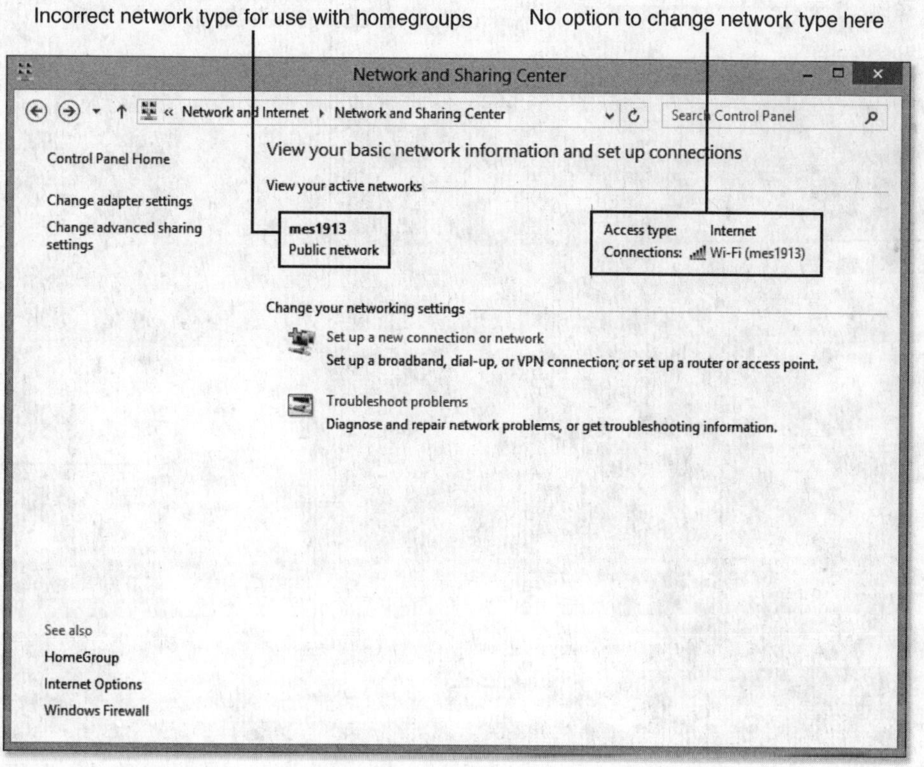

Figure 9.10 The Network and Sharing Center in Windows 8/8.1 displays your network type, but does not allow you to change it.

6. Click or tap and drag the **Find Devices and Content** slider to **On** (see Figure 9.11).
7. Click the back arrow.
8. From the Networks menu, click or tap **HomeGroup**. You can now create or join a homegroup.

> **Tip**
> You can also change the network type by clicking the **HomeGroup** link shown in Figure 9.10 and selecting **Change Network Type**. Refer to Figure 9.8.

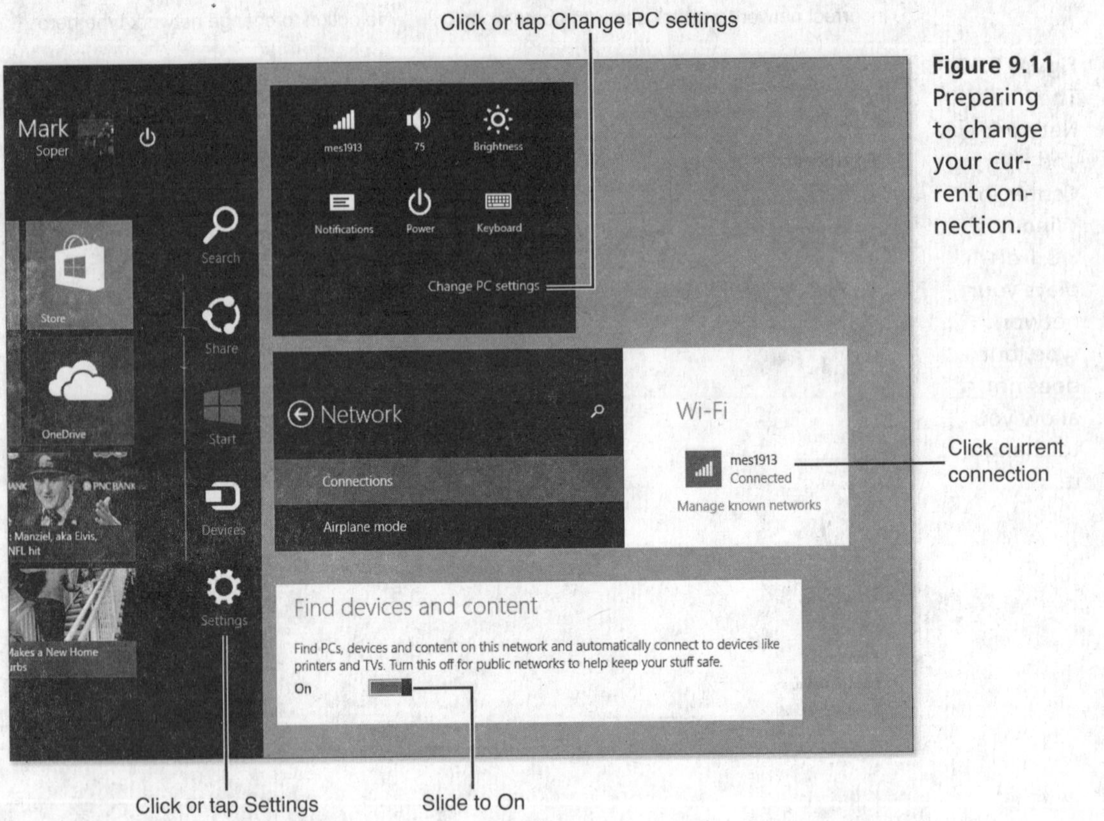

Figure 9.11 Preparing to change your current connection.

Joining an Existing Homegroup

After you create a homegroup on your home network, other Windows 7/8/8.1 computers or tablets can join it. Here are the requirements to join a homegroup:

- The network type must be set as Home (Windows 7) or private (Windows 8/8.1).
- The homegroup password must be entered correctly.
- The computer or tablet must be connected to the same physical network as the computer that created the homegroup.

> **Note**
> You can have a mixture of wired and wireless computers on the same homegroup as long as they connect through the same router or a repeater that repeats signals from the router.

Joining a Homegroup in Windows 7

The process for joining a homegroup is similar to the process for creating a homegroup:

1. Open **Control Panel**.
2. Click **Network and Internet**.
3. Click **Network and Sharing Center**.
4. Click the **Available to Join** link next to HomeGroup.
5. Click **Join Now** (see Figure 9.12).

Figure 9.12 Preparing to join a homegroup in Windows 7.

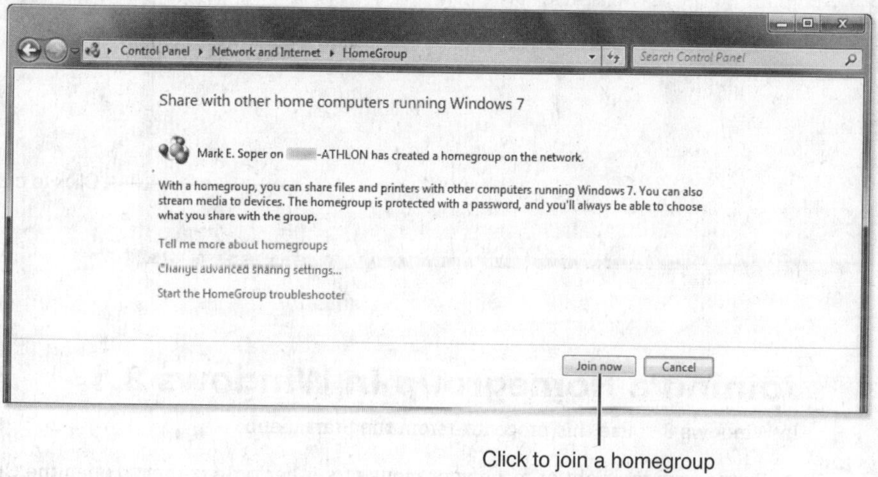

6. Select the items to share. Click **Next** to continue.
7. Enter the homegroup password when prompted (see Figure 9.13).
8. Click **Next**, then **Finish**.

Windows adds the computer to the homegroup. During this process, a dialog box notifies you that sharing is not yet complete. As soon as the process is complete, you will see the Change Homegroup Settings dialog (refer to Figure 9.4). At this point, you can connect computers to the homegroup and share files with them. Click Cancel or click the Close (red X) button in the upper-right corner to close this dialog.

> **Note**
> This procedure also works in Windows 8/8.1, if you prefer to work from the Windows desktop.

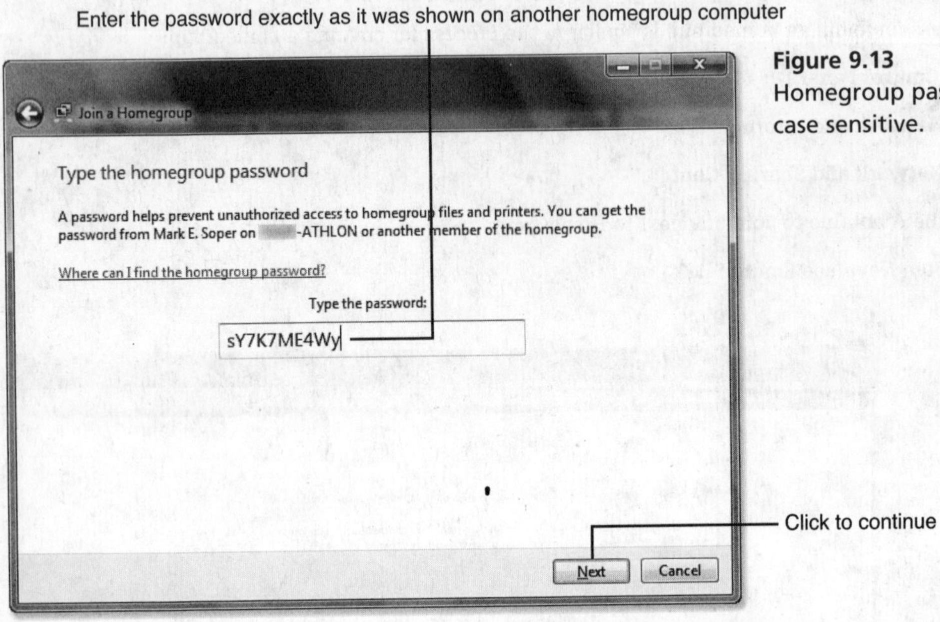

Figure 9.13
Homegroup passwords are case sensitive.

Joining a Homegroup in Windows 8.1

In Windows 8.1, use this procedure from the Start menu:

1. Swipe from the right or move your mouse to either right corner to open the Charms menu.
2. Click or tap **Settings**.
3. Click or tap **Change PC settings**.
4. Click or tap **Network**.
5. Click or tap **HomeGroup**.
6. Enter the homegroup password and click **Join** (see Figure 9.14).
7. Adjust sliders to enable or disable sharing of content folders (refer to Figure 9.6). You can now access folders and printers shared with the homegroup.

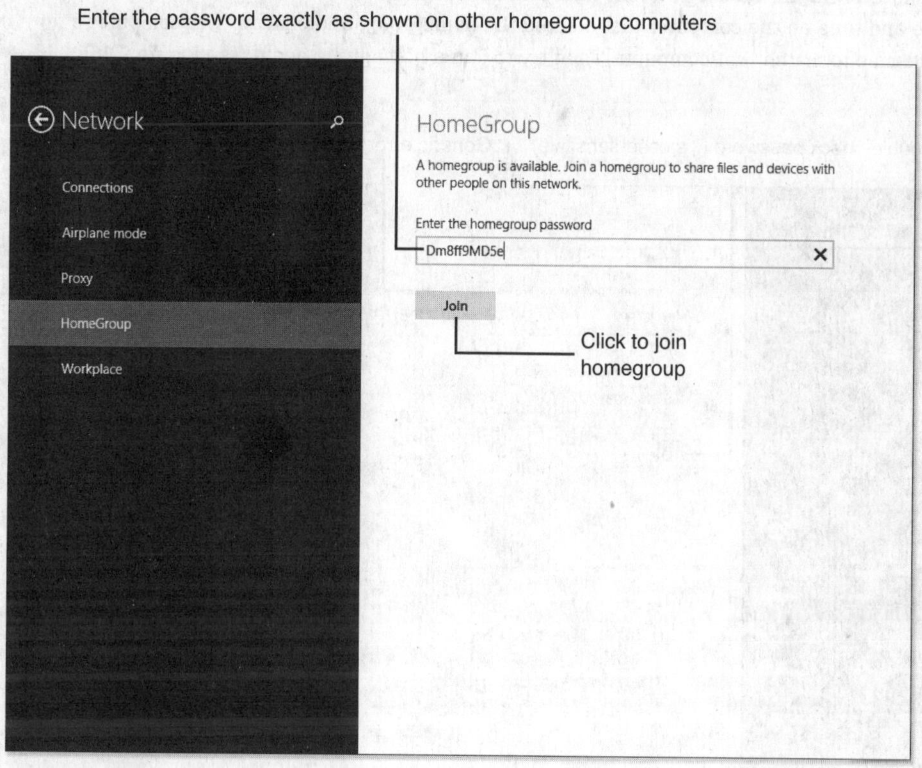

Figure 9.14
Joining a homegroup with Windows 8.1.

Can't Join an Existing Homegroup

If you attempt to join an existing homegroup, you might see an error message when you enter the homegroup password (see Figure 9.15). Because homegroup passwords are case sensitive, the problem might be that you misspelled the password. However, if you spelled the password correctly, this message indicates that a problem exists with your system that is preventing it from joining the homegroup.

If you can't join an existing homegroup, there are several possible reasons:

- **The network type you selected is Public**—See "Choosing a Private Network in Windows 8/8.1," p.235, this chapter, or "Choosing Home as the Network Type in Windows 7," p.234, this chapter, for the solution.
- **Your computer has Windows updates pending**—To solve this problem, finish installing updates and restart the system if prompted. After restarting your computer, attempt to join a homegroup again.

- **Your computer might have a different date and time than the rest of the homegroup**—Check the date and time on the computer that created the homegroup, and change your computer's date and time to match that computer. Then try to join a homegroup again (see Figure 9.16).

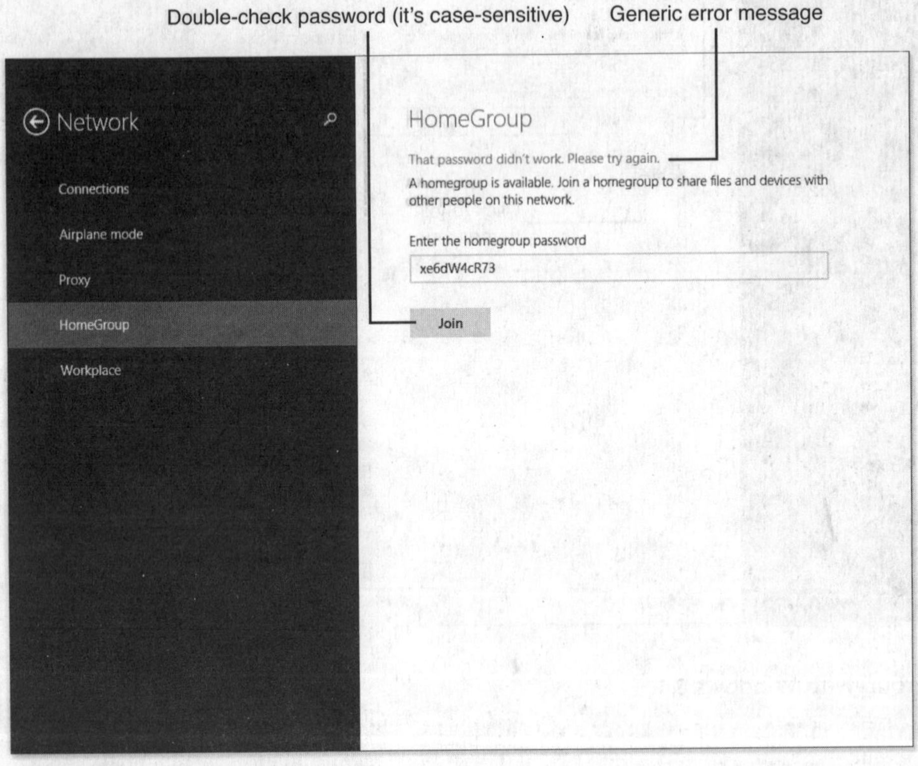

Figure 9.15 It's not necessarily a wrong password, but something is preventing you from joining the homegroup.

Note

You can also change the date and time in Windows 8.1 from the Windows taskbar as you would with Windows 7 and earlier versions. To change the date and time as shown in Figure 9.16:

1. Open the Charms menu.
2. Click or tap **Settings**
3. Click or tab **PC settings**.
4. Click or tap **Time and Language**.
5. Click or tap **Date and Time**.
6. Slide the **Set Time Automatically** slider to Off.
7. Click the **Change** button.
8. Set the date, time, and time zone as needed and click **Change**.

- **Check network settings**—If your network settings are incorrect, you can't connect to a homegroup. The easiest way to check network settings and to troubleshoot other typical causes of homegroup problems is to run the HomeGroup troubleshooter.

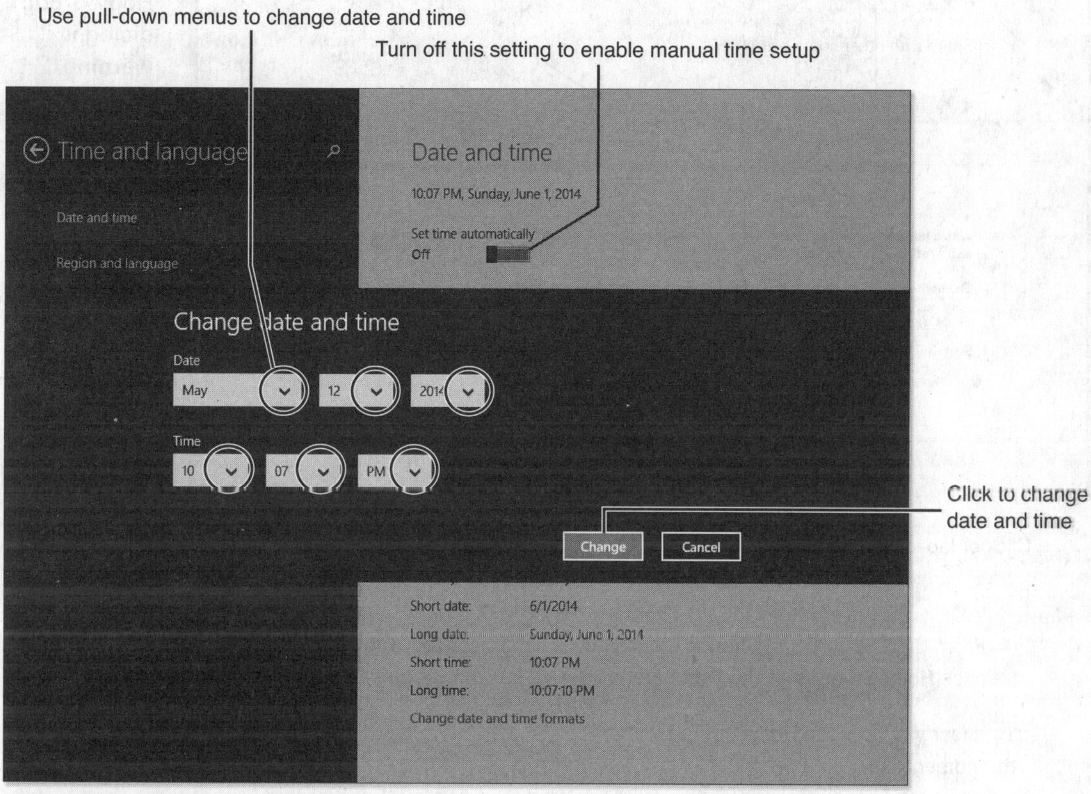

Figure 9.16
Changing the date and time in Windows 8.1.

Using the HomeGroup Troubleshooter

Use the HomeGroup troubleshooter if you are having problems setting up a homegroup, joining a homegroup, or using homegroup shared folders and printers.

You can start the HomeGroup troubleshooter from two locations in Control Panel in Windows 7, 8, and 8.1:

- Launch the troubleshooter from the HomeGroup dialog, which is part of Network and Internet (see Figure 9.17).

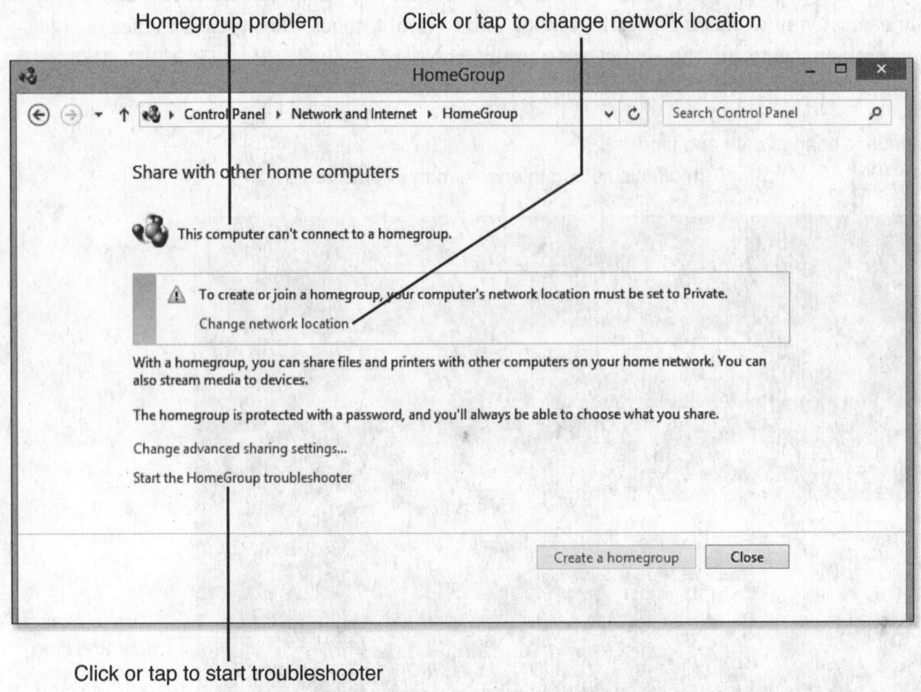

Figure 9.17 This HomeGroup dialog is warning of a problem with network type, but also offers a troubleshooter to solve other problems.

- From the Network and Sharing Center, click Troubleshoot Problems (refer to Figure 9.10), then click HomeGroup from the list of Network and Internet troubleshooters (see Figure 9.18).

To show you how the HomeGroup troubleshooter works, we made two changes to a computer on the homegroup:

- We changed the date so it didn't match the rest of the homegroup, and then restarted the computer.
- We disconnected it from the wireless network.

Follow this procedure to use the troubleshooter:

1. The first screen in the HomeGroup troubleshooter briefly explains how it works. Click **Next** to continue.
2. Click **Troubleshoot Network Problems** when prompted. Don't skip this option unless you are sure your computer's network connection is running properly.
3. If the troubleshooter detects any network problems, it displays a diagnosis and, if possible, offers to automatically fix the problem. In Figure 9.19, my computer was not connected automatically to the preferred wireless network.

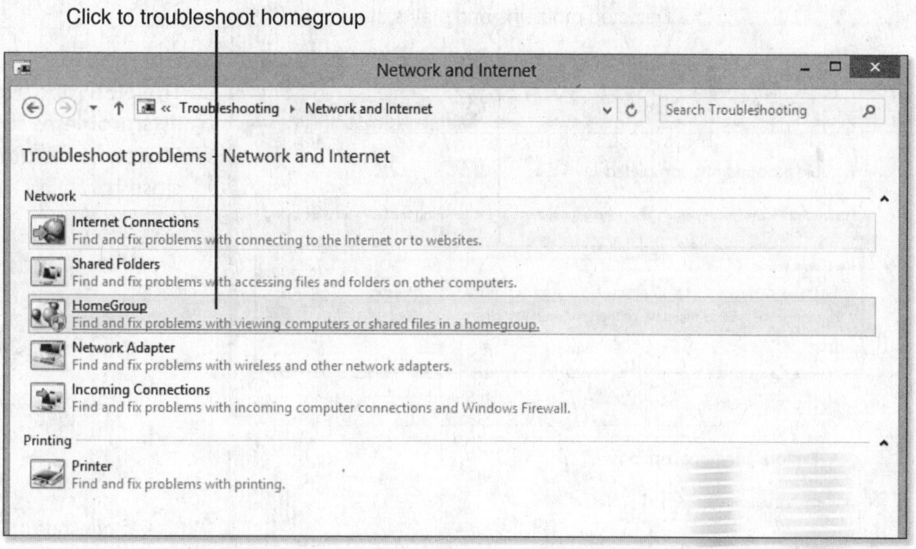

Figure 9.18 Windows offers a HomeGroup troubleshooter as part of its collection of Network and Internet troubleshooters.

4. As needed, click **Apply This Fix** or follow instructions to solve other problems (such as reconnecting a network cable or turning on your wireless adapter).
5. Review the network problems detected and fixed, and click **Close** or **Close the Troubleshooter** to continue with HomeGroup troubleshooting (see Figure 9.20).

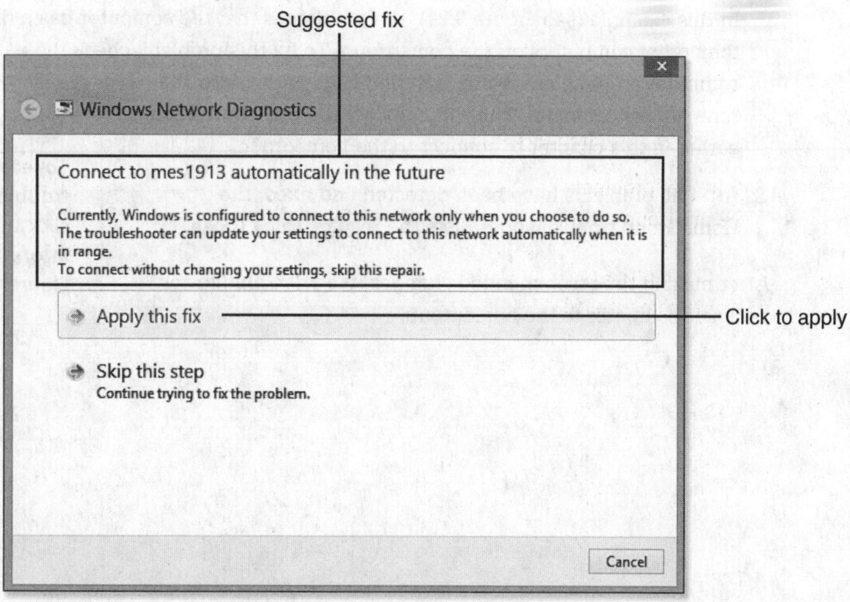

Figure 9.19 The Network troubleshooter has detected a problem with wireless network settings on this computer and can fix it.

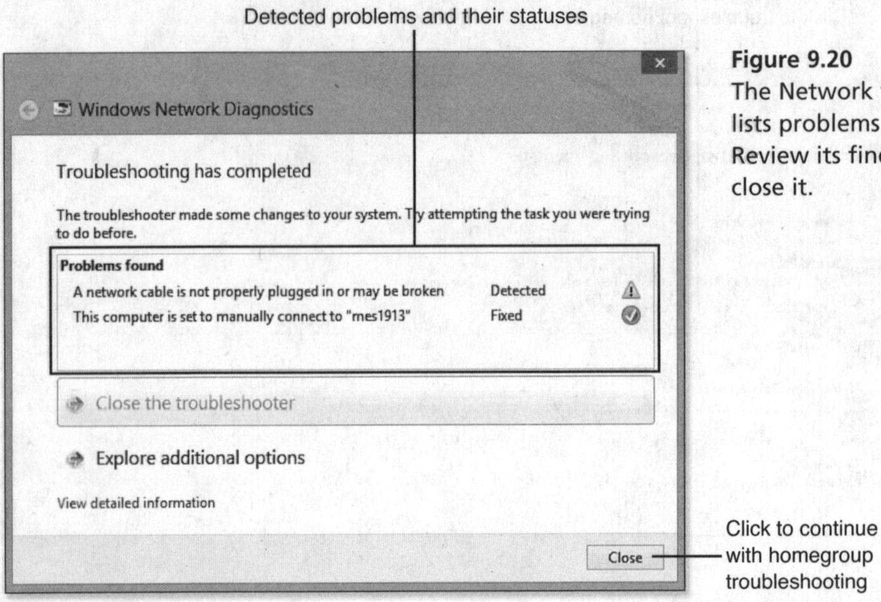

Figure 9.20
The Network troubleshooter lists problems found and fixed. Review its findings before you close it.

6. The HomeGroup troubleshooter can be used on a computer that's trying to set up a homegroup or on a computer that's trying to join a homegroup. When prompted, select **I'm Trying to Join a Homegroup** if you are using the troubleshooter to help you join an existing homegroup.

7. When the troubleshooter finds problems, it might be able to fix them, or it tells you what to do. In this example (see Figure 9.21), the problem is that the computer has a different date and time than other computers on the homegroup. To fix this problem, check the date and time on another computer on the homegroup and then change the date and time on this computer. After this, follow the procedures listed earlier in this chapter to connect to the homegroup.

8. After all problems have been detected and fixed, the HomeGroup troubleshooter lists the results. Click **Close**.

After making the recommended changes, we were able to connect this computer to the homegroup.

Note

To learn more about what a troubleshooter has detected, click the View Detailed Information link shown in Figure 9.20.

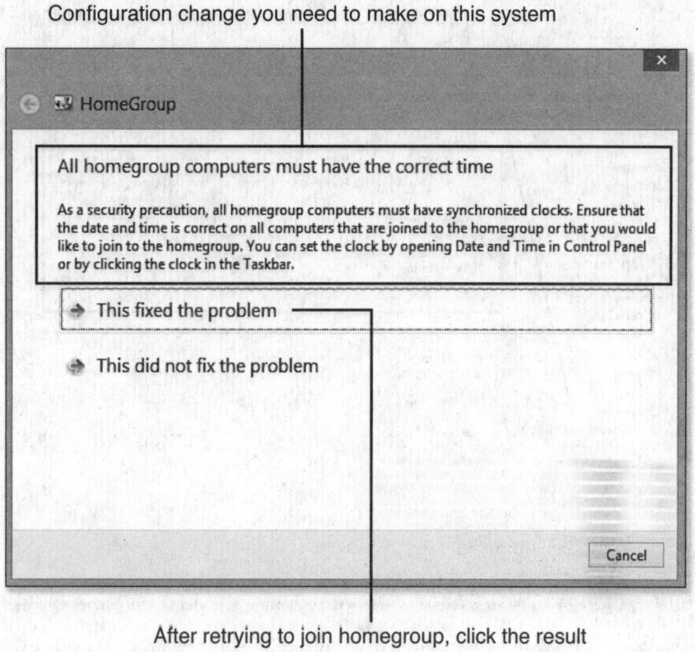

Figure 9.21
After making the changes requested by the troubleshooter, click or tap the appropriate response.

Opening Homegroup Folders

To open a homegroup folder and the folders inside it, open Computer or Windows Explorer(Windows 7), File Explorer (Windows 8/8.1 Desktop), or This PC (Windows 8/8.1 Start menu).

From Computer, Windows Explorer, or File Explorer, follow these steps:

1. Click or tap **Homegroup**.
2. Click or tap a computer in the homegroup to see the folders it is sharing (see Figure 9.22).
3. Click or tap a library or folder to see its contents.
4. Click or tap a file to open it.

When you view homegroup shares from a computer running Windows 7, they'll look like the ones shown in Figure 9.22.

When you view homegroup shares from a computer running Windows 8/8.1 using File Explorer, they'll look like the ones shown in Figure 9.23.

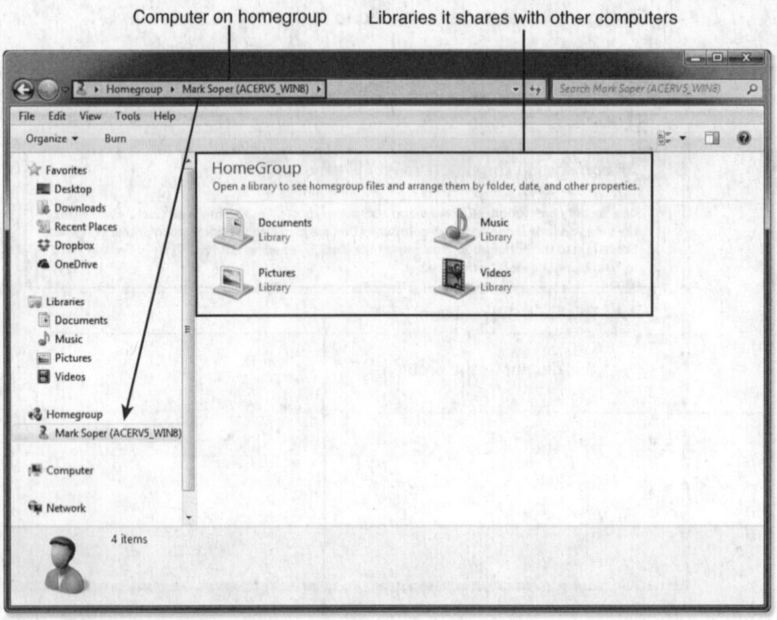

Figure 9.22 Typical homegroup shares as viewed from Windows 7's Windows Explorer.

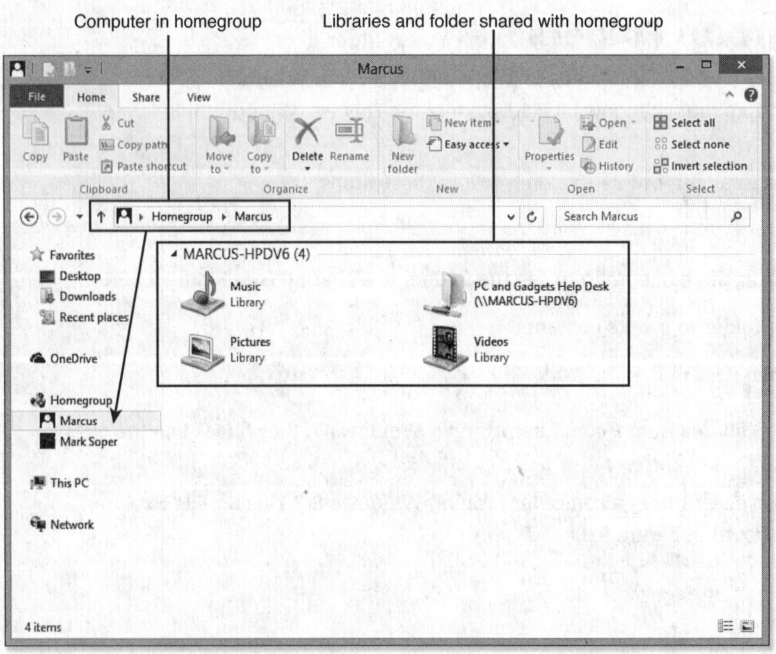

Figure 9.23 Typical homegroup shares as viewed from Windows 8.8.1's File Explorer.

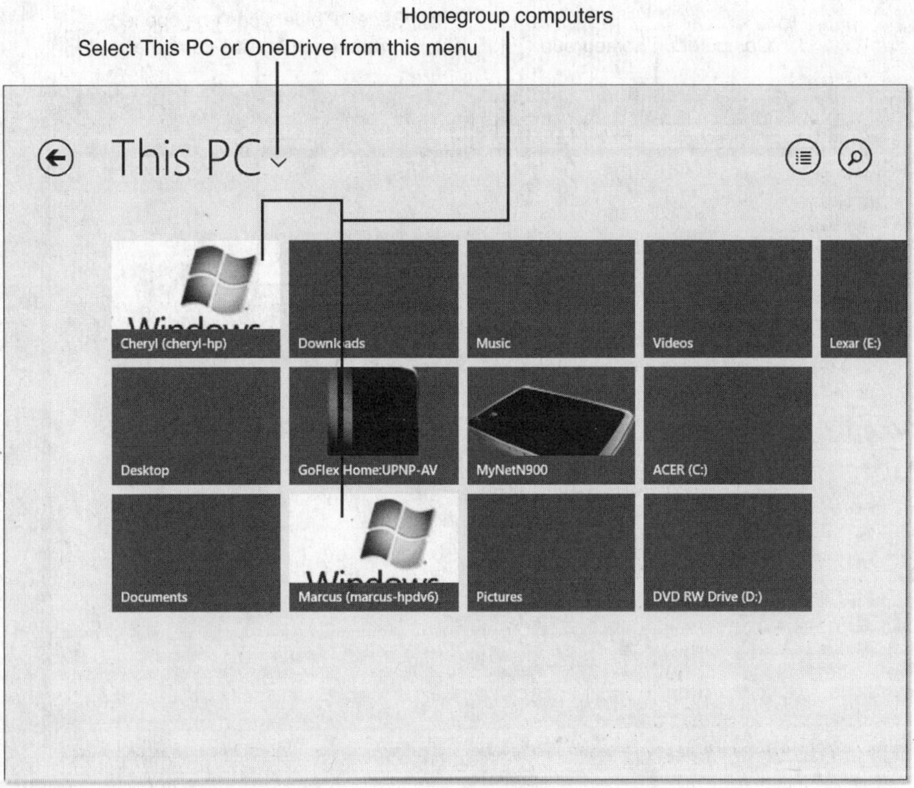

Figure 9.24 Typical homegroup shares as viewed from Windows 8.8.1's File Explorer.

Homegroup computers, local drives, and folders as viewed from This PC in Windows 8/8.1 look like the ones shown in Figure 9.24.

> **Tip**
> To open This PC from the Windows 8/8.1 Start menu, tap or click OneDrive (formerly SkyDrive) and select This PC from the pull-down menu.

Homegroup Manual Repairs

If you have problems with setting up, joining, or using a homegroup, we recommend using the HomeGroup troubleshooter first. However, if the HomeGroup troubleshooter doesn't find any problems, or its recommended solutions or automatic fixes don't work, your homegroup might have more serious problems that require several steps to repair.

Generic Icons

If you see generic icons when you open a homegroup icon on your computer, the homegroup features on your computers are not working (see Figure 9.25). You will not be able to open a homegroup share or its contents.

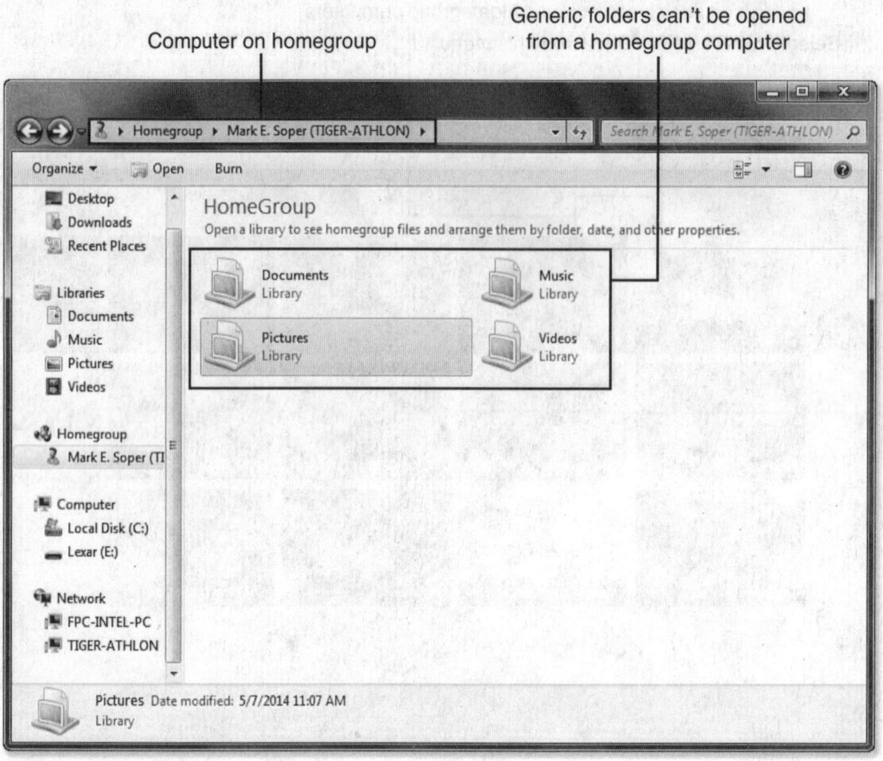

Figure 9.25 Generic folders indicate your homegroup is broken.

Unfortunately, the HomeGroup troubleshooter does not seem to be able to fix this problem. In our experience, the best way to solve this problem is to follow this procedure on each computer in the homegroup:

1. Close Windows Explorer or File Explorer.
2. Start Control Panel.
3. Click or tap **Network and Internet**.
4. Click or tap **Choose Homegroup and Sharing Options** (see Figure 9.26).
5. From the Change Homegroup Settings menu (refer to Figure 9.4), click or tap **Leave the homegroup**.
6. Click **Leave the Homegroup** on the next dialog.

After completing these steps on each computer, follow this procedure:

1. Connect a computer that has not previously connected to the homegroup (I used one running Windows 8.1) to the same network that the homegroup used.

2. Create a new homegroup on that computer.
3. Join each of the other computers to the new homegroup.
4. If the computers on the homegroup now display normal icons as in Figures 9.23 or 9.24, you have repaired the problem.

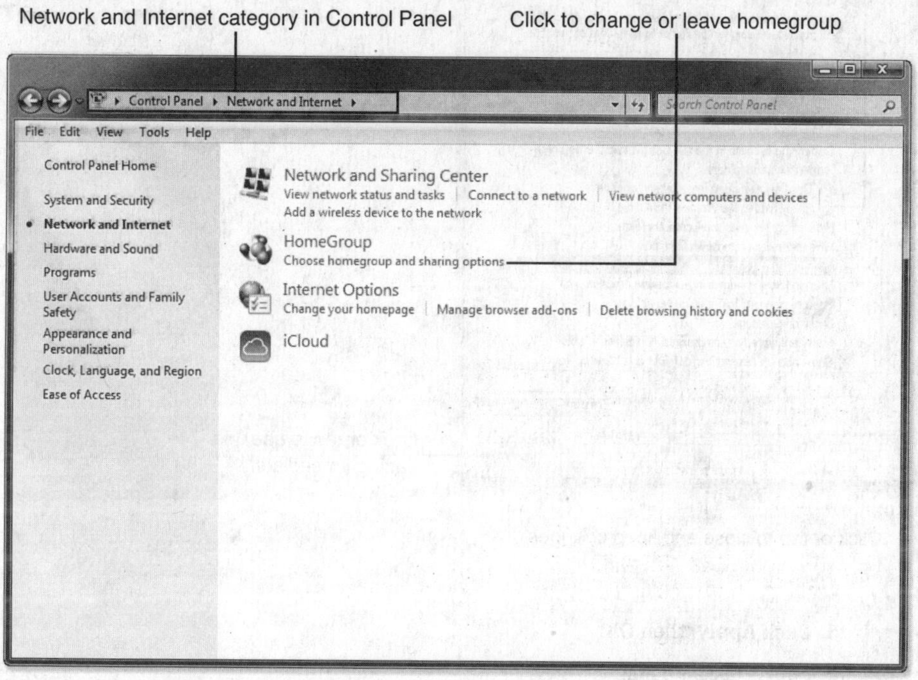

Figure 9.26 Preparing to change network settings.

Cleaning Out Old Homegroup Files

If you cannot create, join, or leave a homegroup, or if the generic icons repair procedure doesn't work, the problem might be related to leftover homegroup files on your system. Here's how to make these files visible and remove them (as suggested by www.eightforums.com/network-sharing/24281-homegroup-sharing-problems-win7-8-a.html):

1. Open **Control Panel**.
2. Click or tap **Appearance and Personalization** (change view to **View by: Category** if necessary first).
3. Click **Show Hidden Files and Folders** in the Folder Options section.
4. Click the **Show Hidden Files and Folders** button in the View (Advanced Settings tab) box (see Figure 9.27). This setting enables the normally hidden AppData folder (see step 8) to be visible.

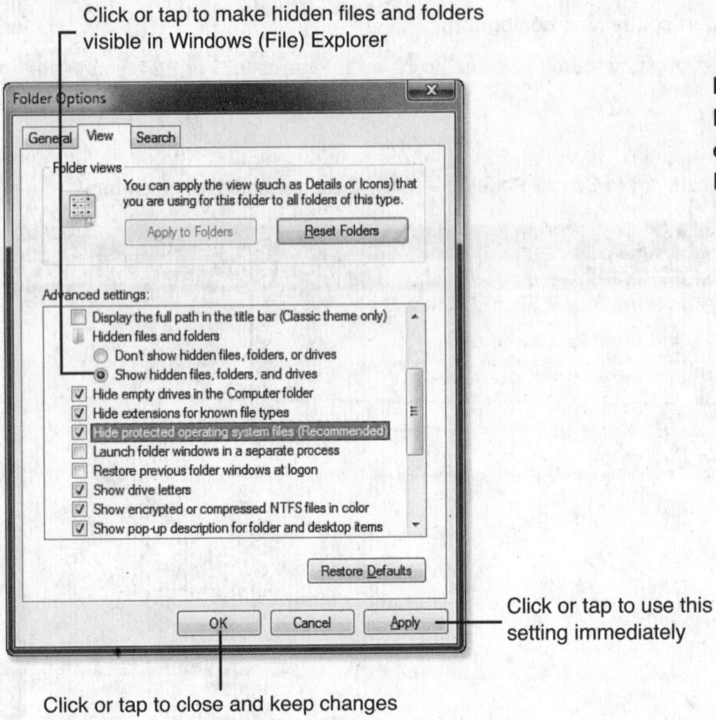

Figure 9.27
Making hidden files and folders visible in Windows (File) Explorer.

5. Click **Apply**, then **OK**.
6. Close Control Panel.
7. Open Windows Explorer (Windows 7) or File Explorer (Windows 8/8.1).
8. Navigate to C:\windows>serviceProfiles\LocalService\AppData\Roaming\PeerNetworking.
9. Highlight all files and folders in the PeerNetworking folder.
10. Press the Delete key, or right-click the highlighted files and folders and select **Delete.**
11. Click **Yes** (see Figure 9.28).

After deleting these files, retry the homegroup operation you tried previously.

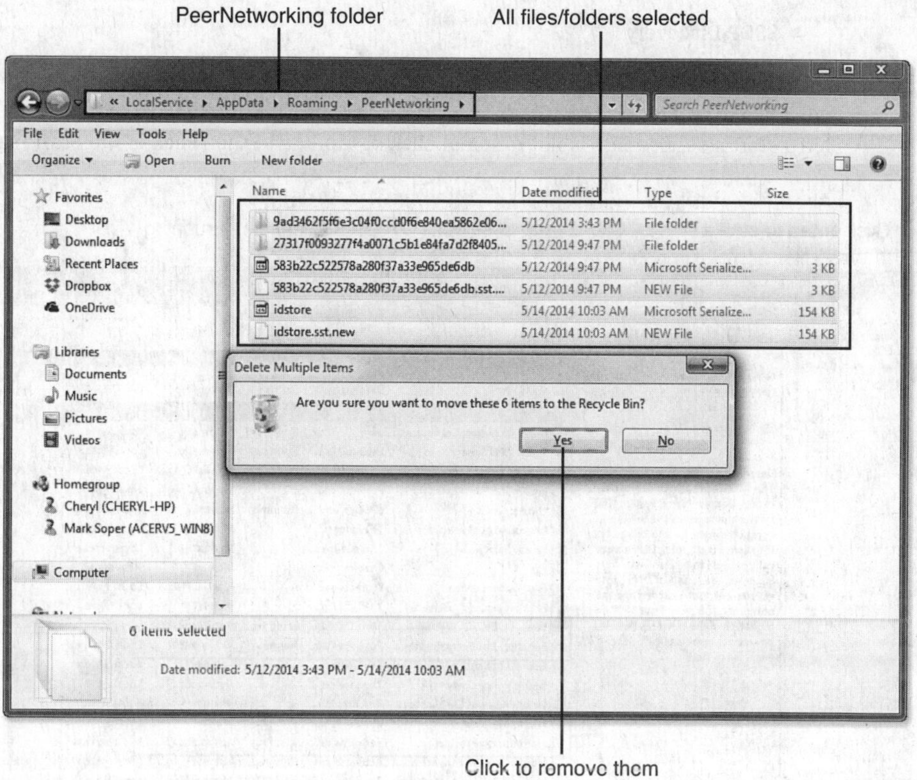

Figure 9.28 Cleaning out old homegroup files.

Restarting HomeGroup Services

If you are unable to create or connect to a homegroup, some or all of the services Windows needs to run might not be started. Follow this procedure to start them:

1. With Windows 7: Click **Start** and type `services.msc`. Press the **Enter** key. With Windows 8/8.1: Open the Charms menu, click or tap **Search**, and type **`services`**. Click or tap **View Local Services**.
2. From the Services (Local) menu, scroll to each of these services and make sure they're running:
   - DNS Client
   - Function Discovery Provider Host
   - Function Discovery Resource Publication
   - HomeGroup Provider
   - HomeGroup Listener

- Peer Networking Grouping
- SSDP Discovery
- UPnP Device Host

3. To start a service that is not running, click or tap it, and then click or tap **Start** (see Figure 9.29).

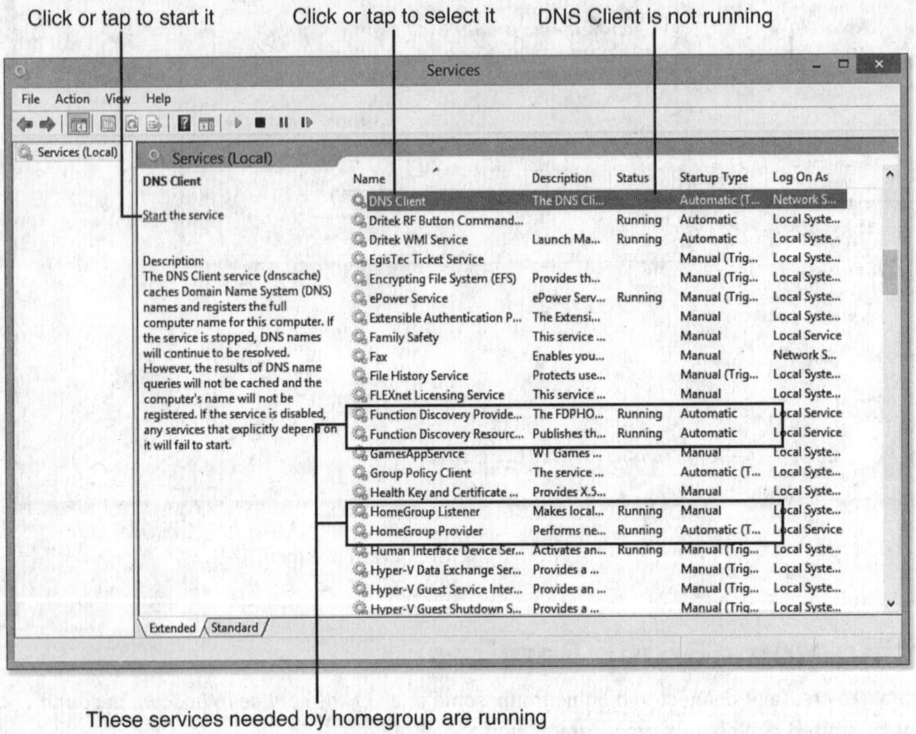

Figure 9.29 Preparing to start the DNS Client service, one of many services needed by HomeGroup.

After you verify that all services needed by HomeGroup are running, retry the homegroup operation you tried previously.

Custom Sharing Settings

You can make additional changes to sharing files, depending on your needs. These include enabling read/write access to a folder, sharing a specific folder, or sharing a specific folder with specified users rather than using homegroup networking.

Enabling Read/Write Access to a Folder

HomeGroup shares files on a read-only basis. In other words, computer A shares a file, and computer B can open (read) it, but can't change or delete the file on computer A. The standard homegroup sharing settings work well if you only want to open files, but if you need to make changes to those files and keep those changes on the original computer, you need to change how HomeGroup shares those files. Here's how:

1. Right-click or press and hold a library or folder in Windows Explorer or File Explorer.
2. Select **Share With**.
3. Click or tap Homegroup (Read/Write).

See Figure 9.30.

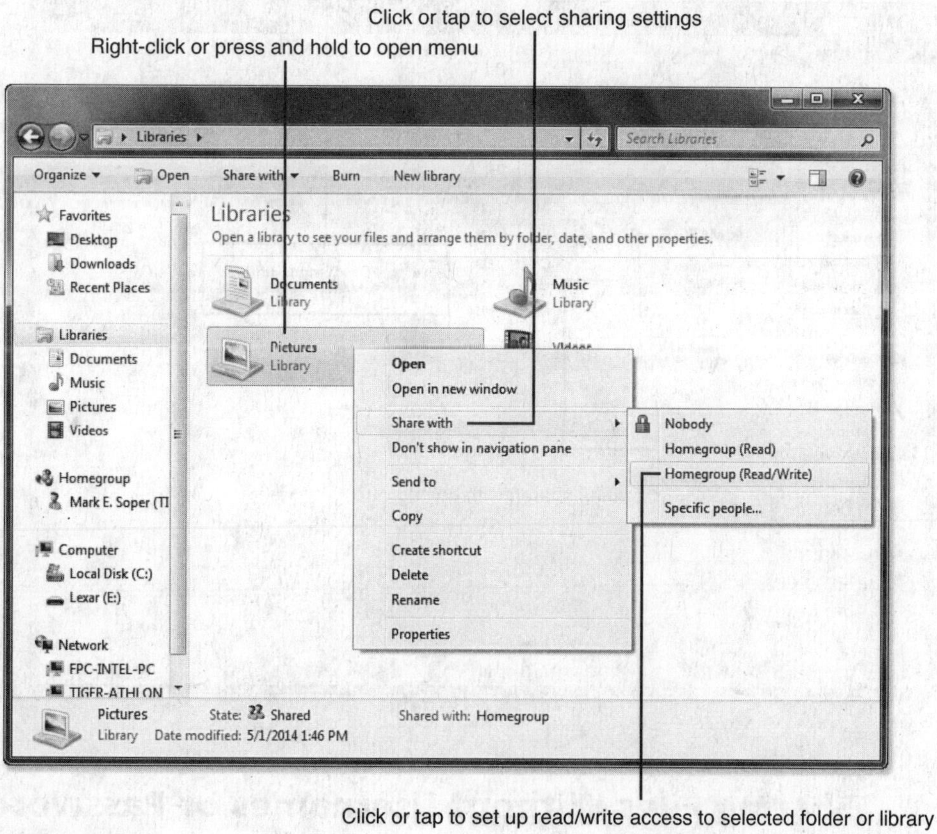

Figure 9.30 Setting a folder for read/write access by homegroup users.

Depending on the number of files and folders in the library or folder, it may take some time to change sharing settings. After the process is complete, all homegroup users can add, change, or delete files in the library or folder, just as if they were sitting in front of that computer.

Sharing or Turning Off Sharing for a Specific Folder

The normal setup for a homegroup encourages you to share your documents, videos, music, and pictures folders with other users. However, you can share just a few folders if that's what works for you at home or in the office. You can also prevent sharing of specific folders.

Follow the same procedure as in the previous section, but in step 3, select the level of sharing. In Figure 9.31, homegroup is being used to share a folder on an external drive.

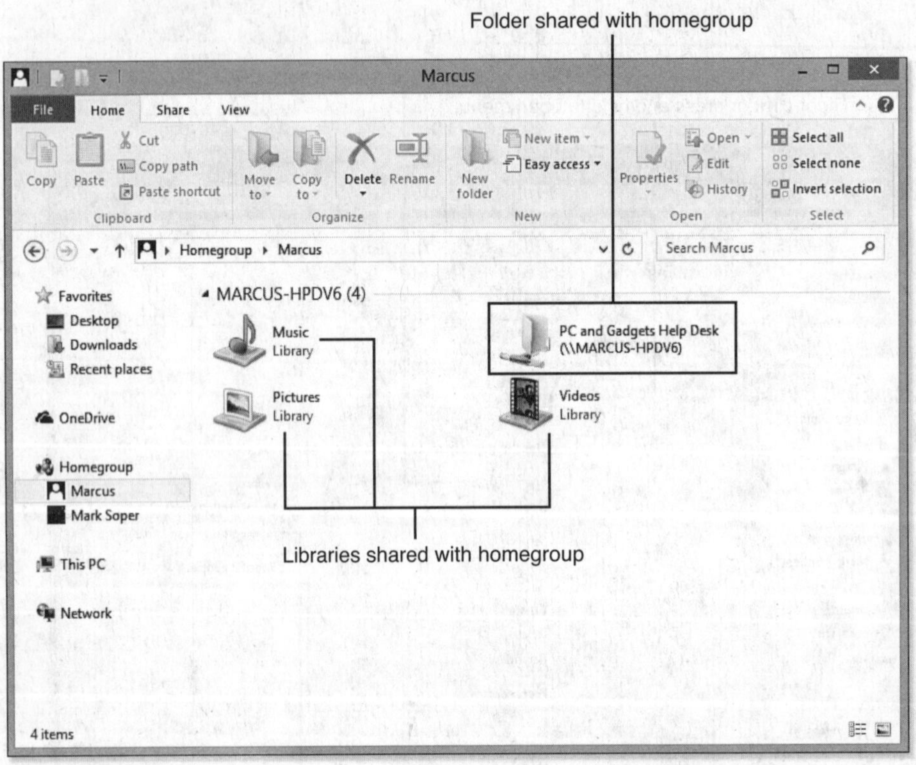

Figure 9.31 The Homegroup view of the author's computer shows a folder on an external drive.

Sharing Files Without Usernames or Passwords

If you have a mixture of Windows XP and/or Windows Vista computers on your network along with Windows 7 and/or Windows 8/8.1 computers, you can't use homegroup to share folders with everyone. However, there are two ways that you can share folders:

- You can turn off password-protected sharing.
- You can set up user accounts on each computer that needs to share information with other users and then select those users.

Turning off password-protected sharing should be used only if you have an encrypted wireless network or if your wired network can be physically secured against unauthorized users. Windows XP refers to this type of sharing as Simple File Sharing, and it is enabled on most Windows XP systems at home or in small offices.

Note

To share folders without using HomeGroup, make sure the workgroup name for all computers is set to the same name. Windows Vista, 7, and 8/8.1 use the default name WORKGROUP, as does Windows XP Professional. However, Windows XP Home uses MSHOME. The workgroup name is changed through the System properties sheet for each computer.

To turn off password-protected sharing in Windows Vista, open the Network and Sharing Center and set Password protected sharing to Off.

To turn off password-protected sharing in Windows 7 or Windows 8/8.1, follow these steps:

1. Open the Network and Sharing Center.
2. Click or tap **Change Advanced Sharing Settings**.
3. Select the Home/Work profile (Windows 7) or Private profile (Windows 8/8.1)and click the option for **File and Printer Sharing;** then click the option to turn off **Password Protected Sharing** (see Figure 9.32).
4. Close the Network and Sharing Center.

Note

If you need to change Simple File Sharing settings, see http://support.microsoft.com/kb/304040.

Note

For more information, see http://technet.microsoft.com/en-us/library/bb727037.aspx.

To complete this task, you need to make the folders you want to share shared with Everyone. See the following section for details.

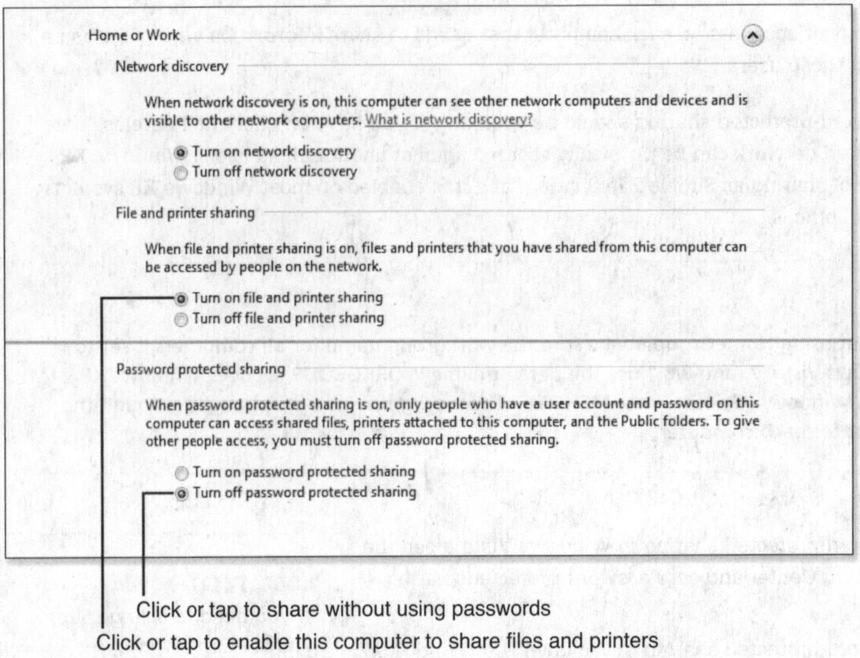

Figure 9.32 Selecting options to share without using passwords.

Sharing Files with Everyone

You can share folders with specific users or with Everyone (all users). Here's how.

To share a folder with Everyone after turning off password-protected file sharing, follow these steps:

1. Open Windows Explorer or File Explorer.
2. Right-click or press and hold the folder you want to share, and select **Share With**.
3. Select **Specific People** (see Figure 9.33).
4. Select **Everyone** from the pull-down menu.
5. Click or tap **Add**.
6. Under Permission Level select **Read** (other users can't change your files) or **Read/Write** (other users can change your files).
7. Click or tap **Share** (see Figure 9.34).

Follow steps 2–7 for each folder you want to share with everyone else on the network.

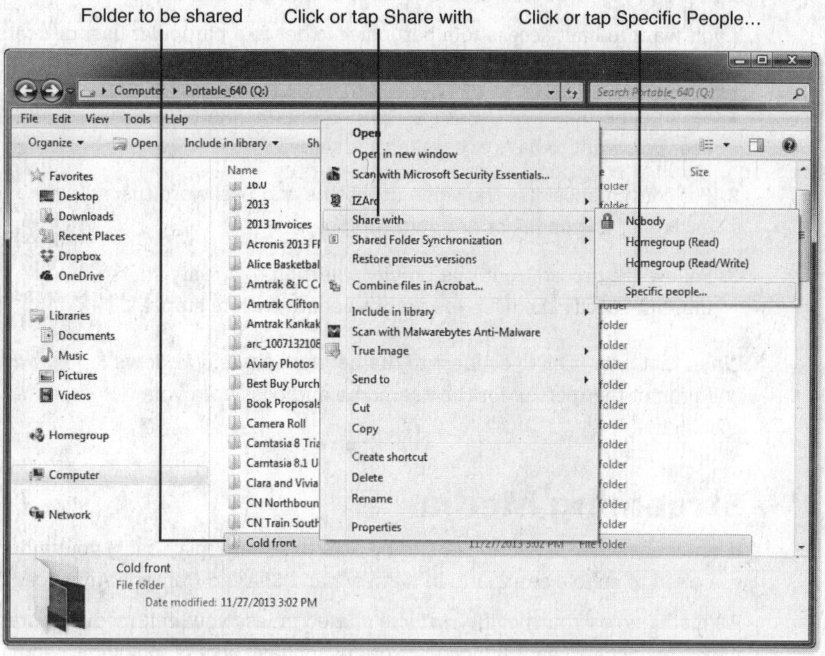

Figure 9.33
Selecting the option to share a folder with specific people.

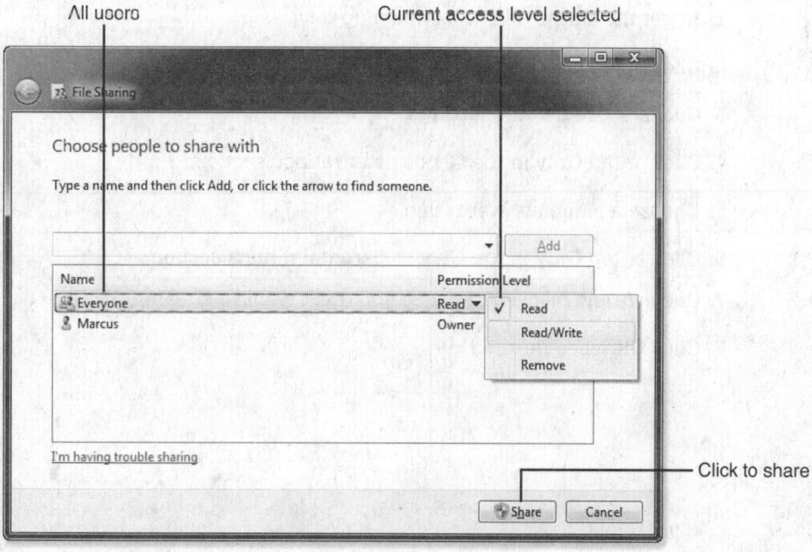

Figure 9.34
Sharing a folder with Everyone.

Sharing Files with Specific Users

If you want to limit access to a particular folder to a particular user or users, leave password-protected sharing enabled. You also need to do the following:

1. Set up an account on the computer hosting the share for each user you want to have access to that share.
2. For convenience, use the same username and password that each user has on his or her own computer.
3. Follow the procedure in the previous section to specify sharing, but specify the user you want to share with in step 4.

When that user tries to connect to the network share, Windows will prompt that person for the username and password you specified.

> **Caution**
>
> If you are sharing with specific users who are running Windows XP, you will need to change the encryption method from 128-bit to 40-bit or 56-bit in Network and Sharing Center's Advanced sharing settings dialog.

Streaming Media

If you want other network users to be able to stream (play back) your videos, music, and pictures, you need to enable streaming in Network and Sharing Center's Advanced Sharing menu.

All media types you specified will be shared unless you limit media by star rating or parental ratings. You can also limit which network users have access to your streaming media (see Figure 9.35). Streaming media is played back using Windows Media Center.

To limit streamed media by star or parental ratings:

1. Hover the mouse over the streaming device.
2. Click or tap **Customize**.
3. Uncheck **Use default settings**.
4. Click or tap **Only** in the Choose star ratings section.
5. Choose a minimum star rating.
6. Click or tap **Only** in the Choose parental ratings section.
7. Uncheck any media categories you don't want to stream.
8. Click **OK** when finished.

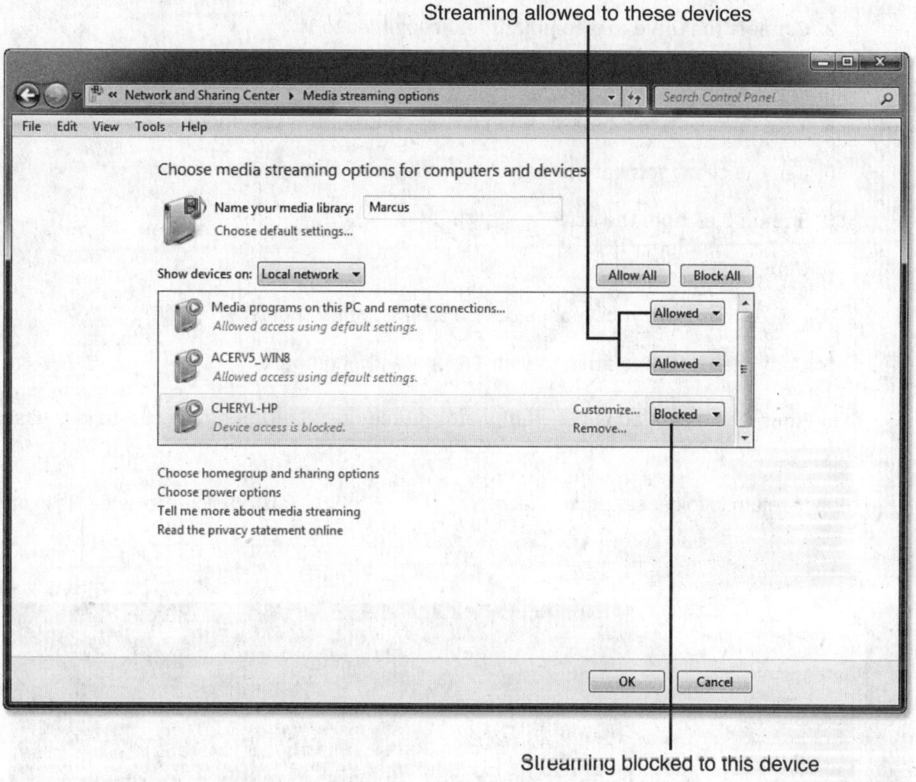

Figure 9.35 Customizing streaming settings.

File Sharing with Portable Devices

Portable devices (those that run iOS or Android) can share files with your Windows PCs in a variety of ways. As discussed in Chapter 18, you can use programs such as Dropbox or Google Drive to copy files between devices. However, the problem with this approach is that mobile devices have limited storage capacity and little or no expandability. Cloud-based services provide large amounts of storage, but can't be used in locations where Internet access is not available.

If you want access to files on mobile devices even when an Internet connection is not available, you can combine wireless drives made for file sharing and streaming with special client software that can run on mobile devices so they can stream media content and upload (or download) files between devices. This method also eliminates the need to install additional network software on your Windows PCs (such as Samba, used for networking with MacOS computers).

Wireless drives such as the SanDisk Connect Wireless Flash Drive and Seagate's Wireless Plus hard disk are compatible with PCs, MacOS, iOS, and Android devices. Here are the general steps involved in using these drives:

1. Charge the drive.
2. Connect the drive to a computer and copy files to it.
3. Install the client software on your mobile device.
4. Turn on the drive's built-in Wi-Fi (wireless Ethernet) networking.
5. Use the client software to detect the drive and configure it.
6. Stream files from the drive.
7. Copy files to the drive.
8. Delete files from your mobile device after copying them.
9. Copy files from the drive to your PC or MacOS computer.

In Figure 9.36, an iPad is viewing photos stored on a SanDisk Connect wireless flash drive.

Figure 9.36
Using a SanDisk Connect wireless flash drive with an Apple iPad.

In Figure 9.37, the Seagate Media app is being used to select storage for viewing.

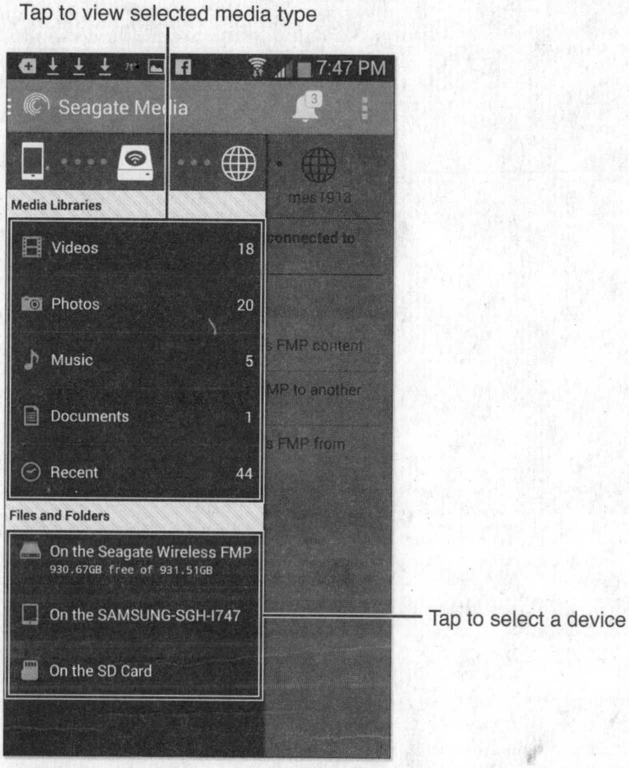

Figure 9.37
Using Seagate Media with a Samsung smartphone equipped with MicroSD storage.

Troubleshooting File Sharing with Portable Devices

If you have problems with your wireless drive, check the following:

- **Can't connect to drive**—Make sure the drive is turned on and has a full charge. Make sure the drive is on the same network as your mobile devices. If the drive is plugged into a computer, the wireless radio might shut off automatically; disconnect the drive from the computer.
- **Can't view contents of drive**—Make sure you select the wireless drive in your client software. Because you can upload and download files between devices, your wireless drive client software can view the contents of your mobile device and the wireless drive.
- **Can't locate files you uploaded to drive**—Depending on the drive's software, the file from your mobile device might be stored in one or more folders named after your mobile device. If you have more than one folder named after your device on the drive, open all of them to locate your files.

10

TROUBLESHOOTING DEVICE SHARING

Fast Track to Solutions

Table 10.1 Symptom Table

Symptom	Flowchart or Book Section	Page #
Printer or multifunction device is not visible on wireless network.	Connecting a Device to a Wireless Network	268
Printer or multifunction device is visible to some computers, but not to others.	Installing a Network Multifunction or Printer Driver	270
I don't know what settings I need for a wireless printer.	Figure 10.2	269
I can see a network-attached drive on the network, but I can't use it.	Installing a Network-Attached Drive	272

Setting Up a Printer or Multifunction Device on the Network

There are three ways to add a printer or multifunction (print/scan/copy or print/scan/copy/fax) device to your network:

- Connect it to a local computer and share it.
- Connect it directly to a wired network.
- Connect it directly to a wireless network.

Using the first method is easy, especially if you use the Windows 7/8/8.1 workgroup sharing method:

1. Install the normal printer driver on the computer that will host the device.
2. Connect the device when prompted.
3. After the installation is complete, check your workgroup or network share settings to make sure the device is being shared.
4. The first time that another computer on the network wants to use the device, it needs to have appropriate drivers installed. (These might be provided over the network or from drivers installed on the remote computer.)

> **Note**
> To learn more about setting up and using a Windows homegroup, see "Troubleshooting HomeGroup Settings," p.230, in Chapter 9, "Solving File Sharing Problems."

If sharing a printer or multifunction device is so easy when you use a homegroup, why use the other methods? There are two important reasons:

- If the computer hosting the device is shut down or fails, nobody on the network can print.
- Network printer sharing supports printing only. The other functions the device can perform won't work if you use homegroup or other network sharing.

To enable all computers on a network to use all the functions available in a multifunction device or printer, the device needs to be connected directly to the network, and the computers that connect to it need to use network drivers for the device or printer.

Connecting to a Wired Network

To connect a multifunction device or printer directly to a wired network, plug a suitable Ethernet cable from the switch or router to the Ethernet (RJ-45) port on the printer and configure the printer to connect via the network.

> **Caution**
> Some multifunction devices and printers use different drivers for local printing, for a first-time install to a network, and for additional computers on a network. Be sure to install the correct driver.

Depending on the printer and the driver, you might configure the device via its driver installation and setup program or through an LCD menu on the device.

Tip

If you're not sure if the device or printer has been configured for network connection, use the Confirm Network Settings or equivalent menu selection on your device to see its current settings.

To connect to a wired network, configure the following:

- **Device name**—If you have more than one multifunction device or printer, consider changing the device name to a name that specifies its location, such as DEN or OFFICE.
- **Automatic or manual IP address (TCP/IP setting)**—Usually, you should choose the option to get an IP address from the router (Auto/DHCP server). If you choose Manual, you must enter an IP address in the same range as other devices on your network but one that does not duplicate any other device's IP address.

After you complete these steps, print the settings or view them on your device or printer's LCD display (see Figure 10.1).

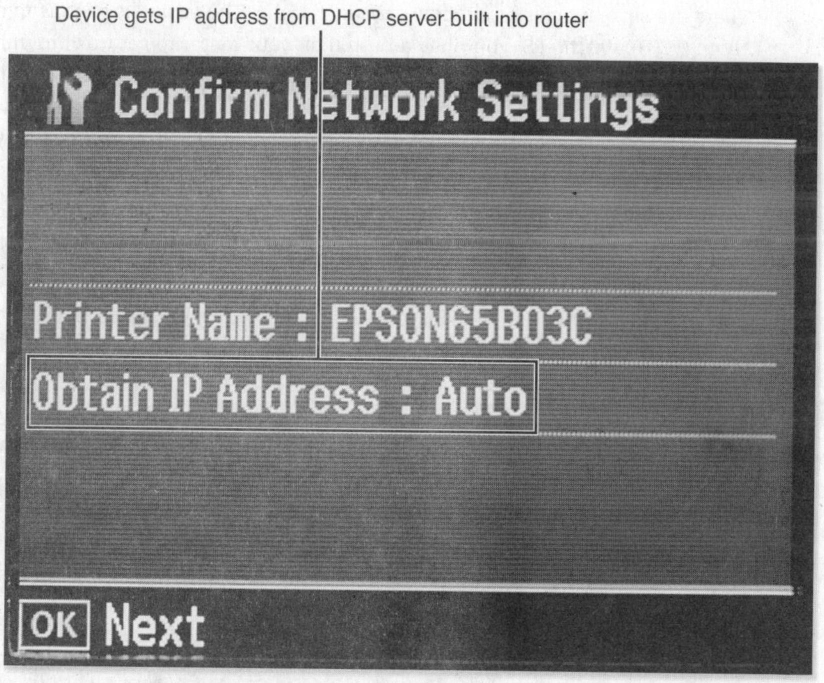

Figure 10.1 Viewing wired network settings on an Epson WorkForce 600 multifunction device.

After the device or printer is configured, a network-compatible driver must be installed on each computer or mobile device that will use the device on the network. See "Installing a Network Multifunction Device or Printer Driver," p.270, this chapter, for details.

Connecting a Device to a Wireless Network

To connect a multifunction device or printer directly to a wireless network, you must configure the device or printer to use the wireless network and its security settings.

With some multifunction devices or printers, you might need to set up the same configuration options discussed in the previous section before setting up wireless options. See your device's documentation for details.

To connect to a wireless network with your multifunction device or printer, you typically need to do the following:

- Enable wireless networking on the device
- Select an SSID (wireless network) to use
- Select a connection type
- Select an encryption type
- Enter the encryption key

There are several ways to configure these options. The easiest option is to use Wi-Fi protected setup (WPS). With WPS, you push a button on your router to set up your wireless network. With SecureEasySetup (SES), you must have SES-compatible wireless hardware (typically used in corporate networks). With WCN (Windows Connect Now), you plug a USB drive with the WCN information from another computer on the network into your device. With Manual, you select the SSID, encryption, and other options needed. Note that not all network multifunction devices or printers offer all these options.

If you use a wireless router on your network (required for Internet access), choose Infrastructure mode if prompted.

The strongest encryption mode is WPA2, also known as WPA-PSK (AES). However, you need to use the same encryption mode and encryption key on all devices on your network.

If you don't know what the correct encryption mode and key are, you can get this information from a Windows 7/8/8.1 computer connected to the network:

1. Open **Control Panel**.
2. Open **Network and Internet**.
3. Open **Network and Sharing Center**.
4. Open **Change Adapter Settings**.
5. Open the wireless network adapter you're using to see the SSID (see Figure 10.2).
6. Click **Wireless Properties** and click the **Security** tab. The security type and encryption type are displayed.
7. To see the network security (encryption) key, click the empty **Show Characters** check box (refer to Figure 10.2).

After you complete these steps, print the settings or view them on your device or printer's LCD display. Figure 10.3 shows typical settings for a wireless network on a multifunction device's LCD display.

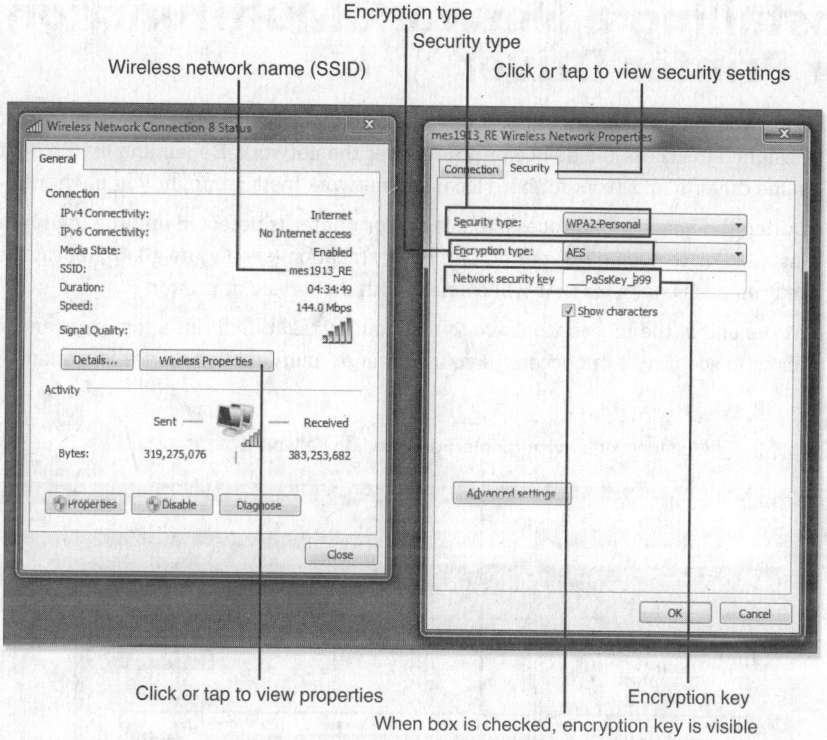

Figure 10.2 Viewing wireless network settings with Windows 7.

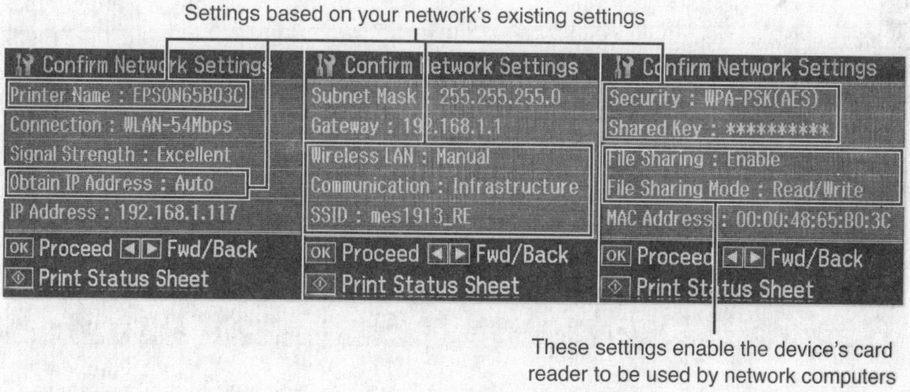

Figure 10.3 Wireless configuration settings on an Epson WorkForce 600 multifunction device.

After the device or printer is configured, a network-compatible driver must be installed on each computer or mobile device that will use the device on the network.

See "Installing a Network Multifunction Device or Printer Driver," p.270, this chapter, for details.

Installing a Network Multifunction Device or Printer Driver

After you set up network support on a multifunction device or printer, you must install drivers designed to access the device or printer over the network. Depending on the device or printer, the same driver might work for both local and network installation, or you might use different drivers.

During the installation process, the device or printer is detected and the appropriate programs are installed on the computer performing the installation (see Figure 10.4). Repeat the installation process on each computer that will connect with the device or printer.

At the end of the process, be sure to test your installation. Print a test page and scan a document or photo to see if network access to your printer or multifunction device is working.

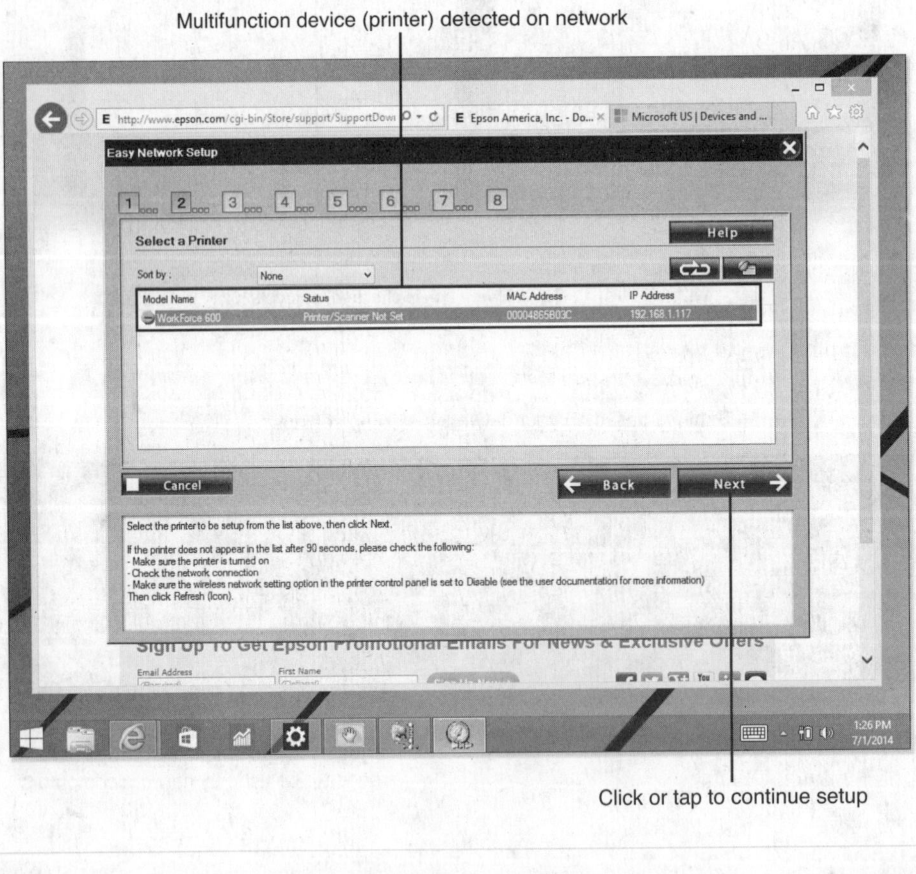

Figure 10.4 Installing network printing support for an Epson WorkForce 600 printer.

Troubleshooting a Network Multifunction Device or Printer

If you are unable to scan, print, or perform other tasks with your networked device or printer, check the following:

- Open Devices and Printers from the Control Panel and make sure the device or printer is listed as available (see Figure 10.5).
- Right-click the device or printer and select **Troubleshoot** to detect problems.
- If you are unable to see any network devices or access the Internet, run a network troubleshooter to find the problem.
- If the network is working and the printer you want to use is offline (ghosted out), make sure the device or printer is turned on and is not displaying an error.
- Make sure the device or printer is turned on. If it is not displaying an error, check the network configuration. Reconfigure the device or printer and try printing again.

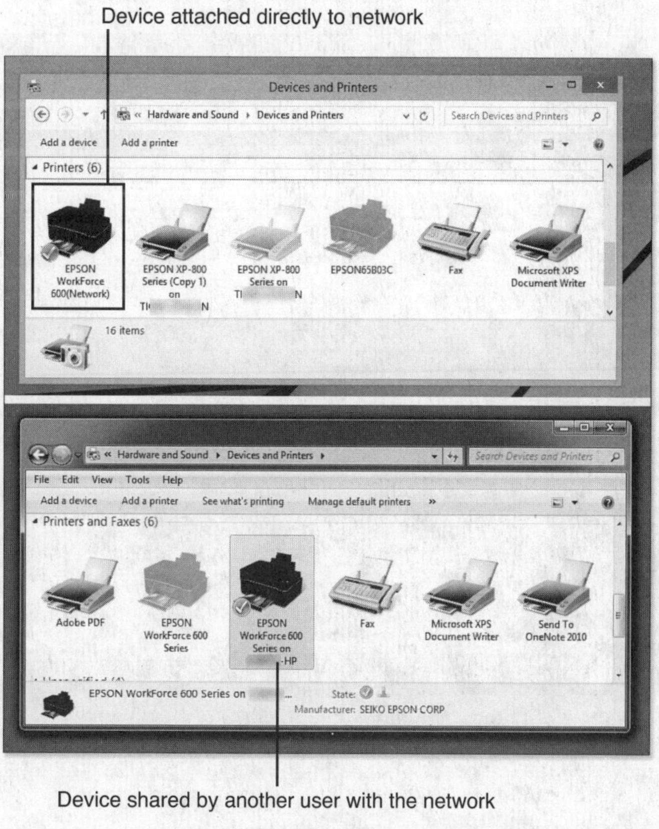

Figure 10.5
A printer share and a network-attached printer as displayed in Devices and Printers.

Note

You can launch network troubleshooters from the Network and Sharing Center. To learn more, see "Using the HomeGroup Troubleshooter," p.243, in Chapter 9, "Solving File Sharing Problems."

Installing a Network-Attached Drive

The process of installing a network-attached drive includes the following:

- Connecting the drive to your network
- Installing drive access software on all computers and devices that will use the drive

Network-attached drives typically connect to the network via Ethernet: plug an Ethernet cable into the drive and a router. The router provides wired or wireless access to the drive after the drive is configured by the setup software provided by the drive vendor. Figure 10.6 shows the Seagate Dashboard app used to manage a Seagate GoFlex Home network-attached drive.

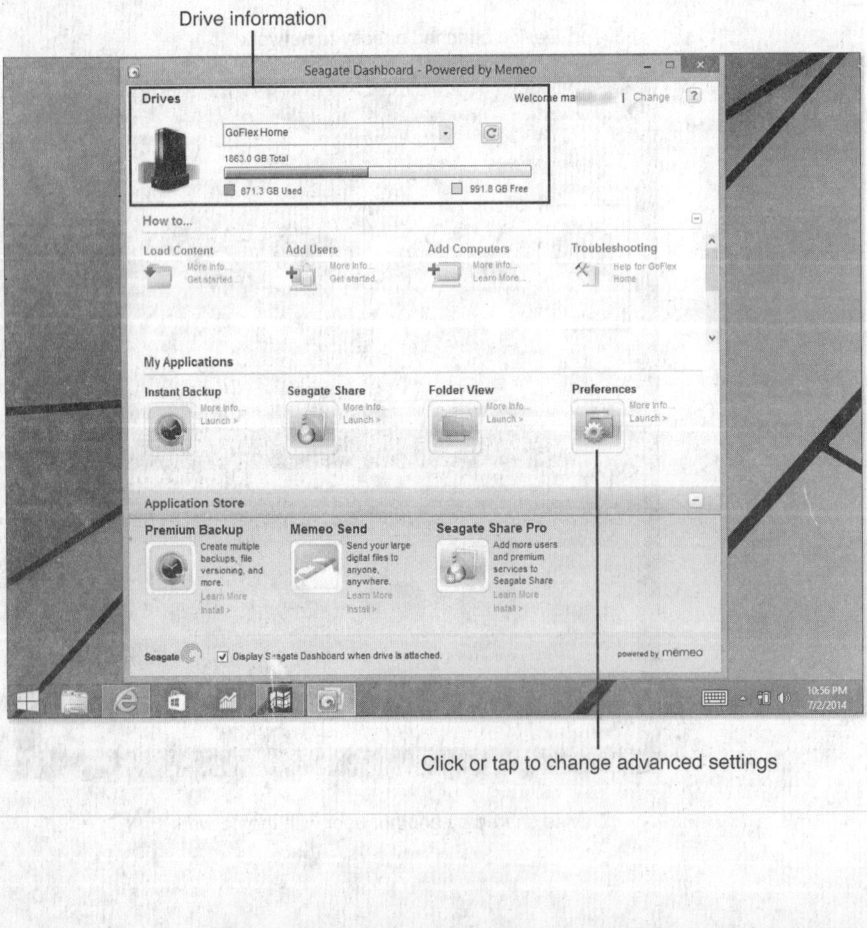

Figure 10.6 A Seagate network-attached drive as viewed in Seagate Dashboard.

After the setup software is installed, the drive will be visible in Windows Explorer (Windows 7), File Explorer (Windows 8/8.1 desktop), and This PC (Windows 8/8.1 Start screen). Figure 10.7 compares the File Explorer (This PC) view of the author's laptop before and after installing software for a Seagate GoFlex Home network-attached drive.

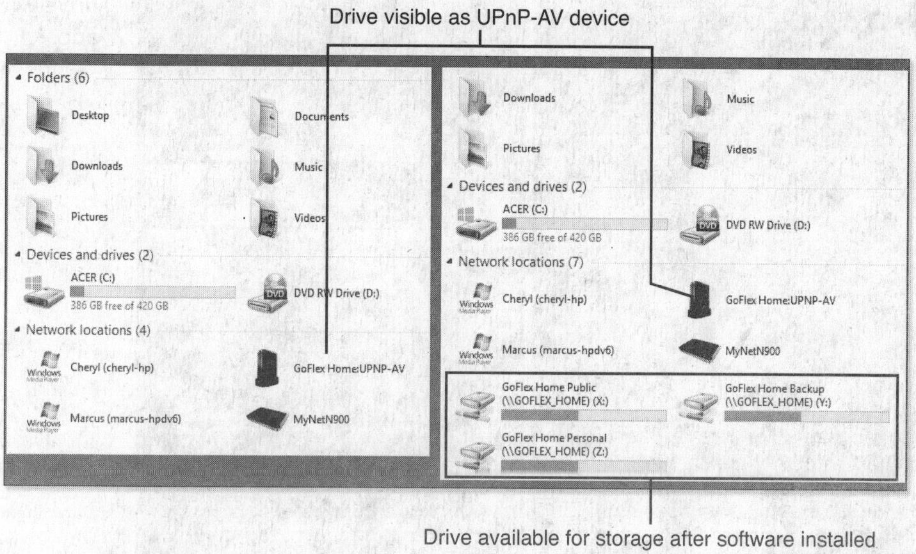

Figure 10.7 The drive is visible on the network before installing software, but after installing software, it can be used for data storage.

To access the drive from mobile devices, install the vendor's mobile app from the App Store (Apple) or Google Play (Android) stores. Figure 10.8 shows access to the GoFlex Home drive with Seagate GoFlex Access for Android.

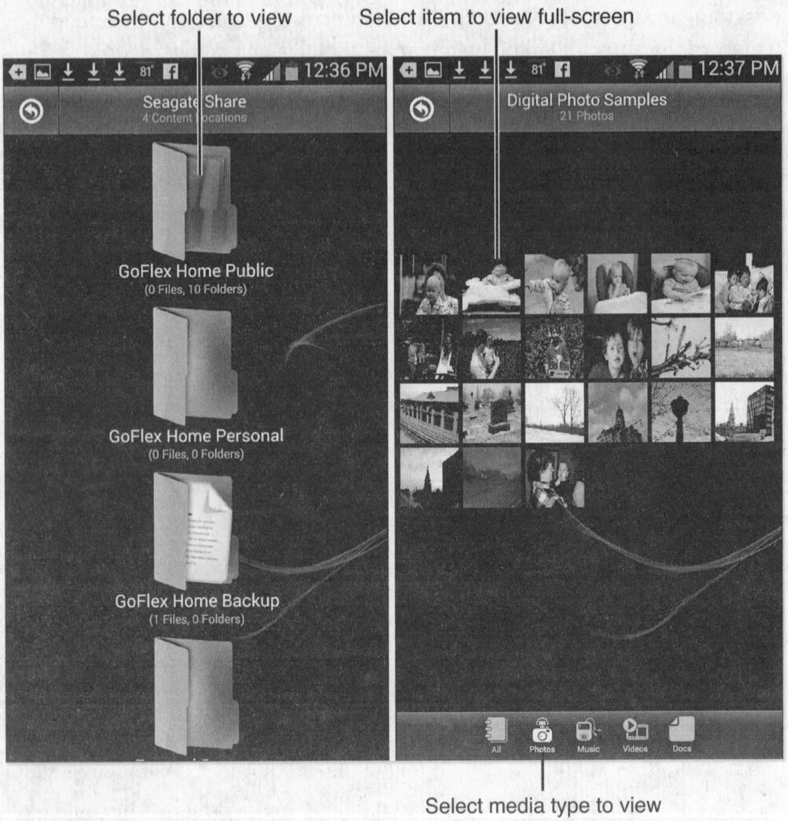

Figure 10.8
Viewing content on a network-attached drive with a mobile app.

Troubleshooting a Network-Attached Drive

Problems with a network-attached drive can be caused by the following:

- Network connection issues
- Router issues
- Software issues
- Drive issues

If no other network resources or Internet connections are available, troubleshoot your network connection. Troubleshooters are available from the Network and Sharing Center. These troubleshooters test your network adapter, connectivity with the network and the Internet, and provide solutions for you.

To solve router issues, shut off your router for about a minute and turn it on again. Wait a couple of minutes, and you should be able to connect to your network-attached drive and other network resources.

If other network resources are working, but your drive is not visible, check the drive for problems. Disconnect and reconnect the power and network cables, and look for problems indicated by signal lights on the unit. If the unit appears to be working correctly, reinstall the software.

If the drive is visible from some computers or mobile devices, but not others, make sure those computers and devices are using the latest version of the drive's software and that those computers and devices are authorized to use the drive.

11

TROUBLESHOOTING PRINTING

Fast Track to Solutions

Table 11.1 Symptom Table

Symptom	Flowchart or Book Section	Page #
I need a new printer driver, but I'm not sure what edition of Windows I'm using.	32-bit Versus 64-bit Windows and Printer Drivers	278
Oops! I installed the wrong printer driver and need to remove it.	Removing an Incorrect Printer Driver	282
My inkjet printouts have gaps and missing lines.	Cleaning Print Heads	289
Vertical lines are not straight in my inkjet printouts.	Aligning Print Heads	292
My prints on plain paper look OK, but when I try to print on glossy photo paper, I'm unhappy with the results.	Selecting the Correct Paper Type and Print Quality Settings	293
I have a printer I like, but I'm having problems finding a Windows 7 or 8/8.1 driver for it.	No Driver for Your Version of Windows? Workarounds and Fixes for You	284
I'm unhappy with my inkjet printer's print quality, but I'm not sure what to do.	Troubleshooting Inkjet Print Quality (flowchart)	Chapter 24

Symptom	Flowchart or Book Section	Page #
My printer doesn't recognize my digital SLR's memory card, although I know it contains hundreds of RAW files.	Troubleshooting Printing from Memory Cards	295
My laser printer has smudges on all printouts.	Troubleshooting Marks and Smudges on the Printout	301
I can't print a large graphic with my laser printer.	Can't Print a Full Page	302
How can I print from my mobile device to my inkjet printer?	Troubleshooting iOS and Android Printer Support	306

Troubleshooting Printer Driver Issues

Everyone keeps talking about a "paperless" office, but printers, especially multifunction or all-in-one units that also scan, copy, and fax, continue to be big sellers to home, small-office/home-office (SOHO), and corporate users. In this chapter, we'll help you get your printer to give you the print quality you deserve and help your mobile devices use your printer, too.

So, what's the first problem to tackle? Making sure your printer/all-in-one unit works with your version of Windows.

Note

In this chapter, I'll use the term "printer" for both single-function and multifunction devices. I'm not being lazy: it's just that there's no difference between the way each type of device prints.

32-Bit Versus 64-Bit Windows and Printer Drivers

Most laptop and desktop computers that run Windows use a 64-bit version of Windows, and most tablets and almost all netbooks use a 32-bit version of Windows. They look alike, but they don't act alike. What's the big difference? 64-bit processors are designed to work with much larger amounts of RAM than once-common 32-bit processors (which are limited to 4GB of RAM and frequently have 2GB or less). 64-bit versions of Windows fully support 64-bit processors. Most of the current systems that use 32-bit processors (and therefore use 32-bit versions of Windows) are netbooks or tablets. These computers are designed for long battery life, not high performance.

Although 32-bit apps work fine on 64-bit Windows, device drivers (the instructions that make hardware and Windows talk to each other) must be designed for 32-bit or 64-bit devices. In other words, drivers for 32-bit versions of Windows won't work with 64-bit Windows.

If you have a recent printer or all-in-one unit, this isn't a big problem, because these devices are typically supported by both 64-bit and 32-bit drivers. However, if you have an older printer or device that still works, you could be a Windows upgrade away from not being able to use it anymore.

How do you find out which type of Windows you have? With Windows XP through Windows 7, follow these instructions:

1. From the Windows Start menu right-click **My Computer (Computer)**.
2. Select **Properties**.
3. The edition of Windows is displayed along with the type (32-bit or 64-bit). See Figure 11.1.

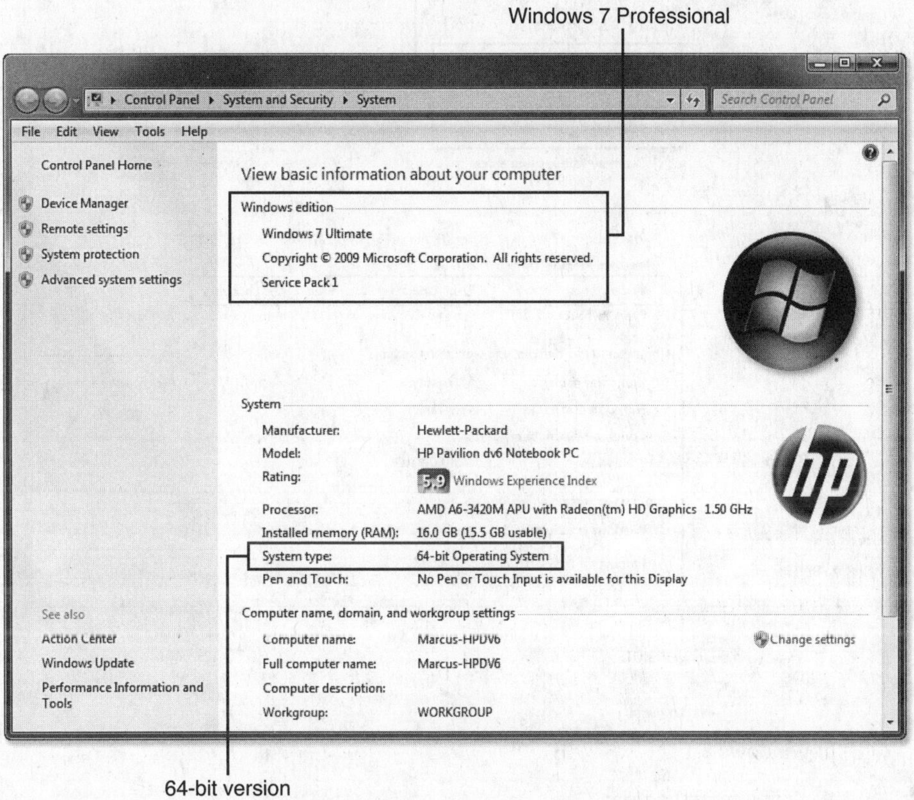

Figure 11.1 This system is running a 64-bit edition of Windows 7 Ultimate.

Here is another way to see this information in Windows 7, as well as in Windows 8/8.1:

1. Press the Windows key plus the Pause key on your keyboard.
2. The edition of Windows is displayed along with the type (32-bit or 64-bit). See Figure 11.2.

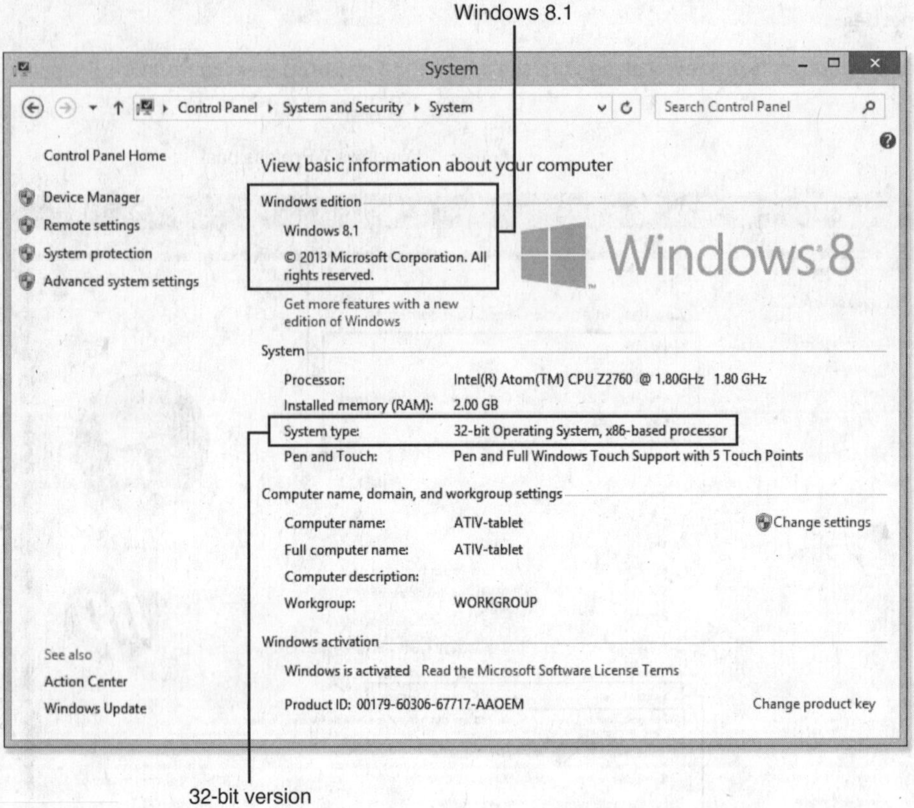

Figure 11.2 This system is running a 32-bit edition of Windows 8.1.

In Windows 8.1:

1. Swipe from the right.
2. Select **Settings**.
3. Click Change **PC Settings**.
4. Click **PC and Devices**.
5. Click **PC Info** (see Figure 11.3).

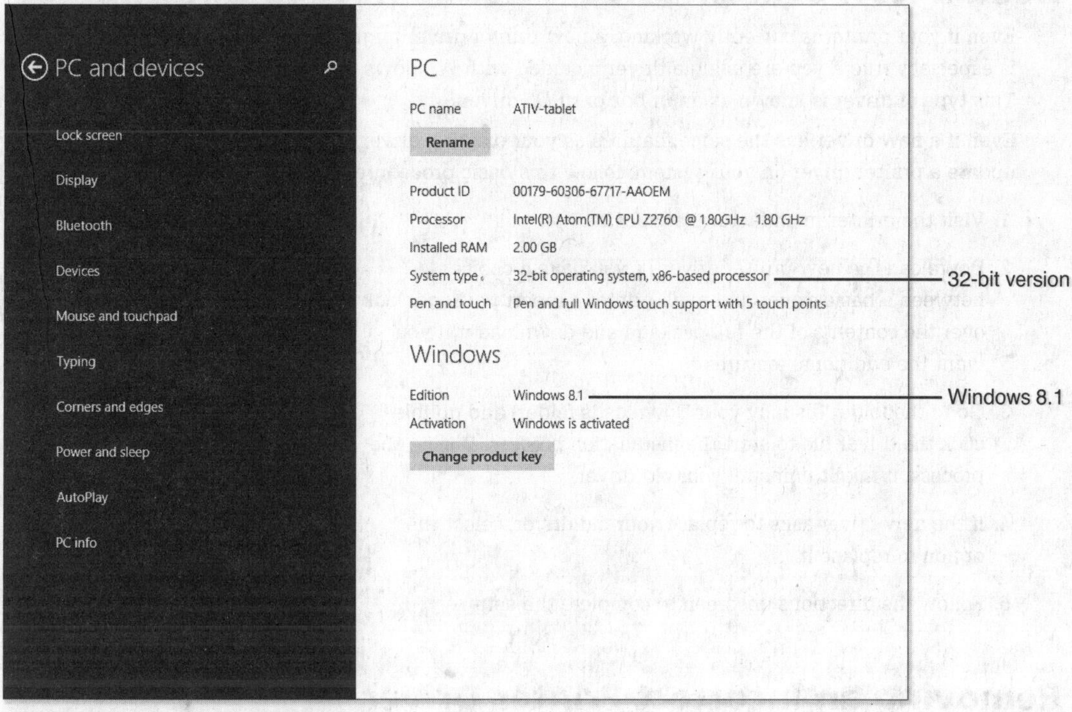

Figure 11.3
This system is running a 32-bit edition of Windows 8.1.

Get All the Printer Features You Paid For

It's a myth that all the software included with a printer can be downloaded if you lose your disc. Although you can get replacement (or updated) drivers for printing and scanning/faxing/copying, additional items such as page recognition software and photo-editing software (for all-in-one units) and print head maintenance utilities might not be downloadable.

To get all the software you paid for, use the installation disc included with your printer. If the installation disc doesn't include support for your version of Windows, download an updated driver and install it, then run the installation disc installer again and see if you can select only the bonus programs or utilities.

> **Tip**
> If you have lost the installation disc, contact the printer vendor for a replacement. There is typically a charge for a replacement disc. Be sure to ask if the disc contains the bonus apps.

Need a New Printer Driver? Here's How to Get One

Even if your printer is currently working, a new printer driver might add additional features. This is especially true if you are using a driver included with Windows or with a Windows service pack. This type of driver is known as an *in-box* or *in-OS* driver.

Even if a new driver has the same features as your existing driver, it can be more reliable. To update a printer driver on your system, follow this basic procedure:

1. Visit the printer manufacturer's website.
2. Download the new printer driver; if you have a choice between a basic driver and a full printer support package, look over the contents of the full package and download it if you want the additional features.
3. Go to the folder (usually your Downloads folder) and double-click the driver file to start the installation process. During the process, it might uninstall your old driver.
4. If the new driver asks to replace your old driver, select the option to replace it.
5. Follow the directions onscreen to complete the setup.

> **Tip**
>
> If you're not sure which driver you need, see if the vendor offers automatic driver detection on its website. This feature can analyze your system to determine what printer you have and whether you need a new driver. You will need to give permission for the detection program to run.

Removing an Incorrect Printer Driver

Although most printer drivers check to see that you're using the correct driver for your version of Windows, it's up to you to select a driver that works with your printer. If you choose a driver that doesn't work or a driver that doesn't match your printer, take the following steps to remove it from your system in Windows 7 or 8/8.1:

1. Open the Devices and Printers folder in Control Panel.
2. Right-click the printer you want to remove.
3. Select **Remove Device** (see Figure 11.4).
4. Click **Yes** to remove the device.

Depending on the printer, you might also need to remove the printer driver and support files with Control Panel's Uninstall a Program:

1. Open **Uninstall a Program**.
2. Click the program to remove.
3. Click **Uninstall**.
4. Click **Yes** to confirm removal.

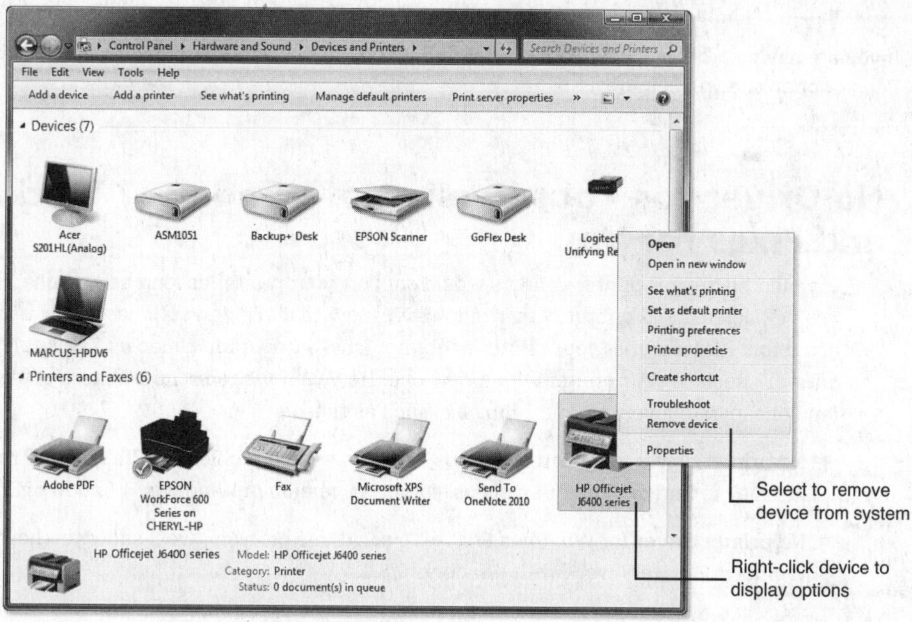

Figure 11.4 Removing an all-in-one device from Windows 7's Devices and Printers folder.

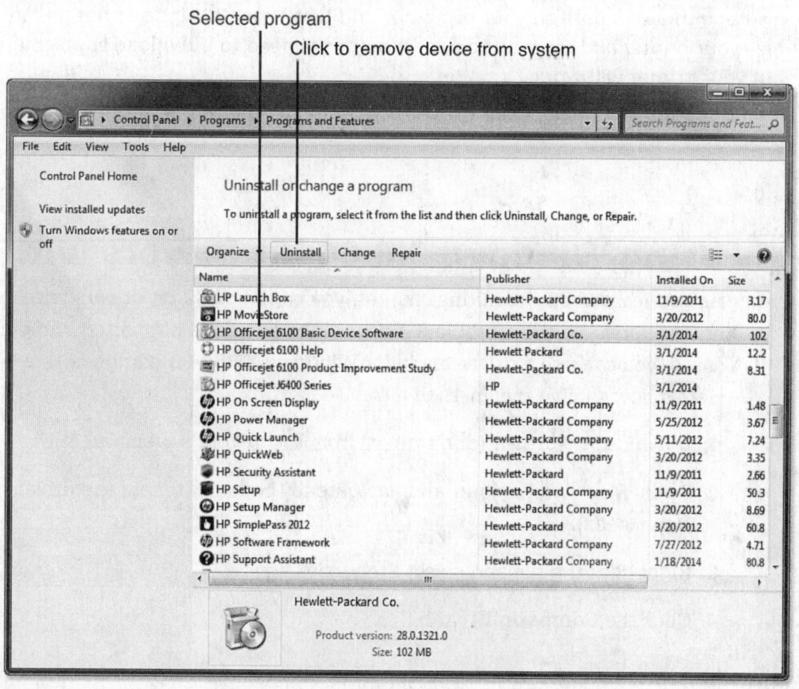

Figure 11.5 Removing printer files with Control Panel's Uninstall a Program.

Tip

If you are having problems with your printer and you don't want to download an updated driver, try the Repair option shown in Figure 11.5.

No Driver for Your Version of Windows? Workarounds and Fixes for You

It would be great if printer vendors would support your printer as long as it works. However, if you've been using a printer with Windows XP, now that Windows XP has finally been retired, you might discover that your printer might not have a driver for Windows 7 or 8/8.1. The obvious answer? Replace your printer with a new one. However, we're in the business of giving you better (and cheaper) answers to your problems, such as these:

- **No printer driver for 64-bit Windows 7**—To solve this problem, we're going to reach "back, back in time" to find drivers for an almost-forgotten version of Windows: Windows XP 64-bit edition.
- **No printer driver for Windows 8/8.1**—To solve this problem, we'll show you how to make Windows 7 drivers work with Windows 8/8.1.

Tip

Before you decide that your new edition of Windows doesn't include a driver for your printer, plug the printer into a USB port on your computer and turn it on. If Windows has an "in-box" driver, it will recognize your printer and set it up for you. You might need to download supplemental apps for your printer, but your printer will work.

If your printer isn't recognized, turn it off and follow the tips in the next section.

Using Windows XP 64-bit Drivers with Windows 7

As you learned earlier in this chapter, you can't use 32-bit drivers with a 64-bit version of Windows, or vice versa. This is a problem if your old printer isn't supported on 64-bit Windows 7. In some cases, you can use a driver made for Windows XP 64-bit edition with a 64-bit edition of Windows 7. Here's how to give this method a try:

1. Download the driver (don't run it) from the vendor's website.
2. Open Windows Explorer and navigate to the folder where the driver was downloaded (usually Downloads).
3. Right-click the file and select **Properties**.
4. Click the **Compatibility** tab.

5. Click the check box for **Run This Program in Compatibility Mode For**.
6. Select **Windows XP (Service Pack 2)**.
7. Click the check box for **Run This Program as an Administrator**.
8. Click **Apply** and then **OK** (refer to Figure 11.6).
9. Double-click the installer file in Windows Explorer to start the install process.
10. Follow the prompts to install the driver file.
11. If you get a security prompt indicating that Windows can't verify the publisher, click **Install This Driver Software Anyway**.
12. Depending on additional programs the installer might try to install, it might stop at some point. To determine whether your printer has been installed, open the Devices and Printers folder. If the printer is listed, it has installed successfully. You can then cancel the remainder of the install.
13. Try to use your printer. If it doesn't work, remove the driver. See "Using Compatibility Settings with Extracted Files" for other steps you can try.

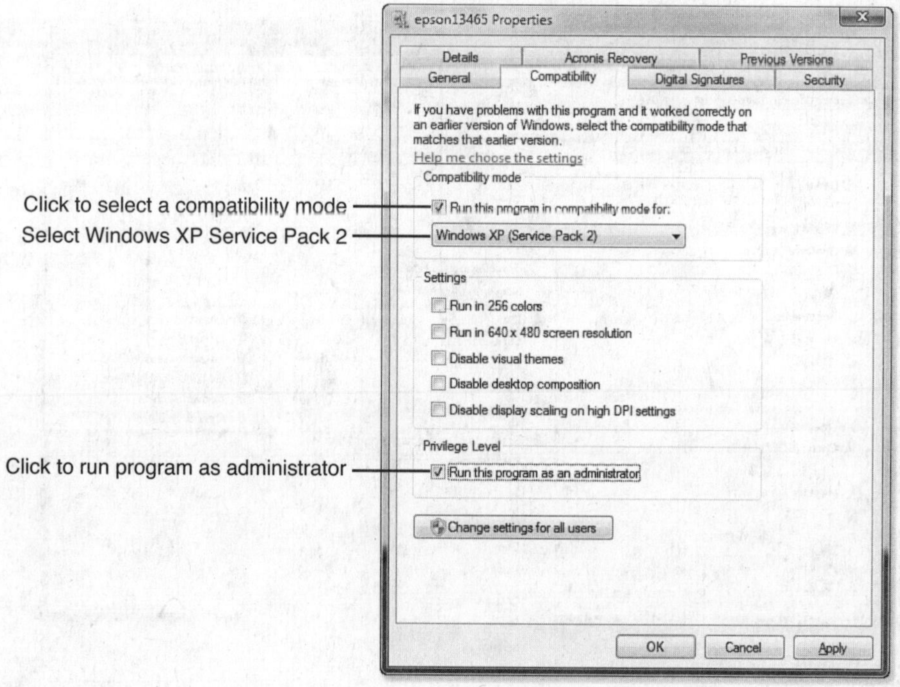

Figure 11.6 Selecting recommended compatibility mode settings for a 64-bit Windows XP printer installer file.

Using Compatibility Settings with Extracted Files

If a driver install program uses a self-extracting archive (see Figure 11.6), you can use a third-party unzipping utility to open the archive file without running it and apply compatibility settings to the setup programs inside the archive file.

1. Download a third-party unzipping utility such as WinZip (www.winzip.com) or IZArc (www.izarc.org).
2. Install the utility.
3. Right-click the installer file and select the option to extract the file to the current folder (see Figure 11.7).
4. Locate the .EXE files in the extracted folder and select **Windows XP SP2** and **Run as Administrator** options (select **Windows Vista** if Windows XP SP2 is not available).
5. Double-click the installer in the top-level folder and let it install the rest of the files and apps.

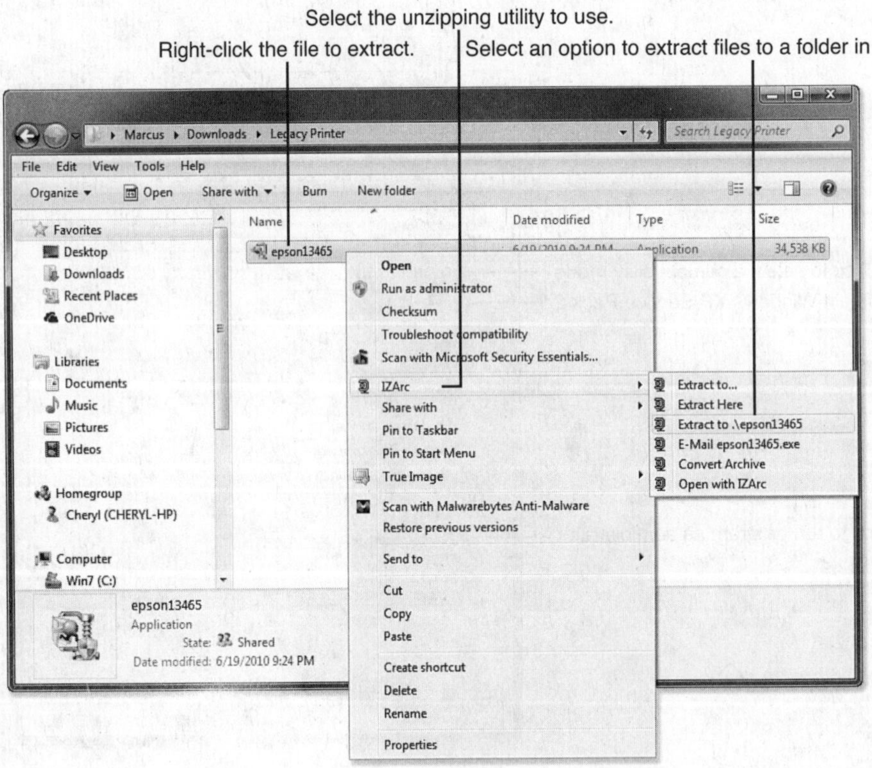

Figure 11.7 Extracting the contents of a legacy printer self-extracting archive (.EXE) file.

Using Windows 7 Drivers with Windows 8/8.1

You can often use Windows 7 printer drivers with Windows 8/8.1 by using a variation on the Compatibility tab method shown earlier in Figure 11.6. Instead of selecting Windows XP Service Pack 2 as the operating system to emulate, select Windows 7 and choose the **Run as Administrator** option.

Troubleshooting Inkjet Printers

Inkjet printers are the most popular type of printer in homes, small office/home office, and office environments. They can print labels, photos, and documents with stunning color, crisp text, and at high speeds. Unfortunately, the fact that they use hundreds of tiny nozzles to produce documents and photos means that ink quality, paper quality settings, and nozzle clogging all threaten to diminish print quality. With printer ink being one of the most expensive liquids in the world, you want to get top-quality printing every time you click Print. This section helps you achieve that goal.

Testing Print Quality

The more often you use your printer, the less likely it is that your printer's print nozzles will become clogged. Typically, I recommend that you save money and wear and tear on your printer by ordering prints of your favorite photos from a photo print kiosk at a local store or online. However, if you use your printer for photo prints, business cards, or other projects where print quality is paramount, it pays to check print quality before you use your printer. Here's how.

Creating Test Prints

The quickest way to see if your inkjet printer is working correctly is to create a test print. You can create a test print from the Printer Properties menu:

1. In the Control Panel open **Devices and Printers**.
2. Right-click the printer you want to test.
3. Make sure plain paper is loaded.
4. Select **Printer Properties** (see Figure 11.8).
5. Click **Print Test Page** (see Figure 11.9).
6. Click **Close** on the confirming dialog.
7. Click **OK** to close the printer properties sheet.

A good test print resembles the results in Figure 11.10. However, if you see streaks, blotches, or blank areas in either the text or the Windows graphic in the test page, you should consider cleaning the print heads before printing anything else.

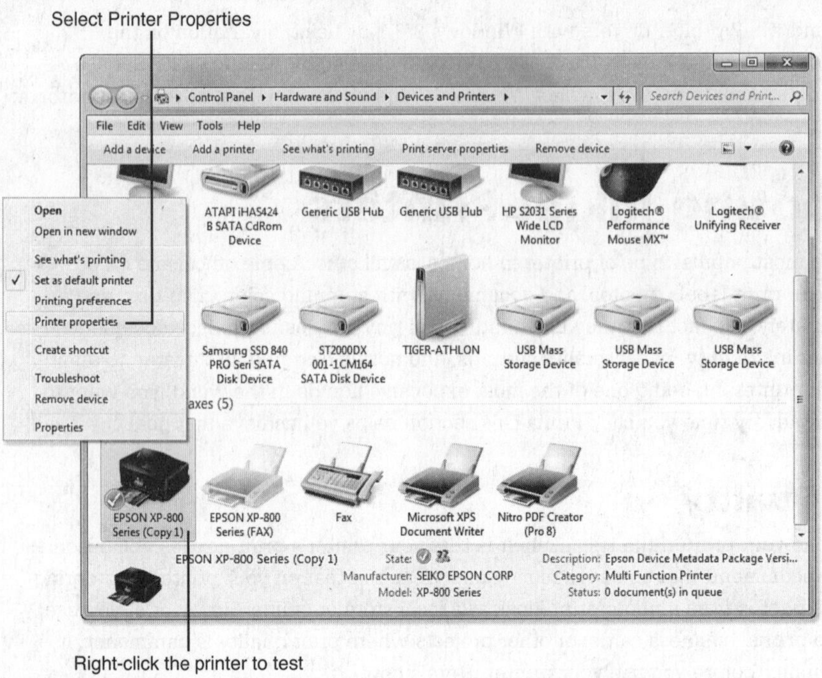

Figure 11.8 Opening the Printer properties sheet.

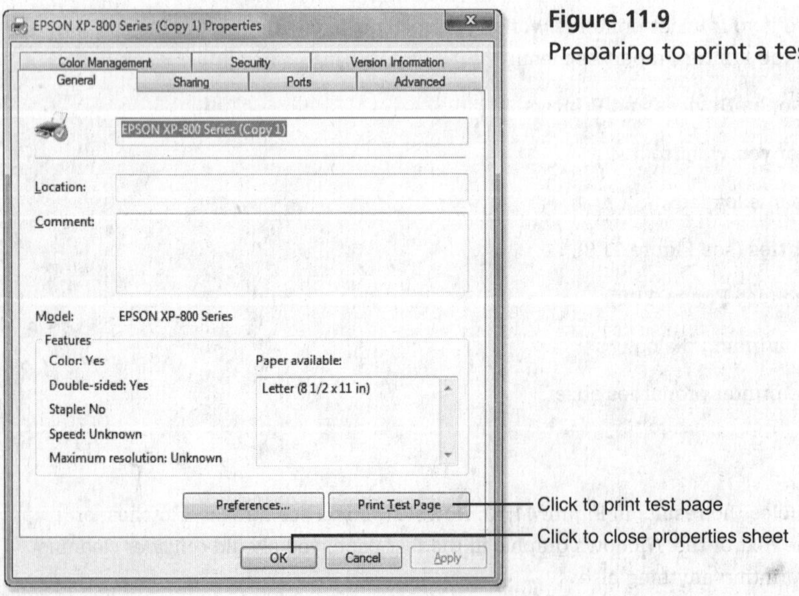

Figure 11.9 Preparing to print a test page.

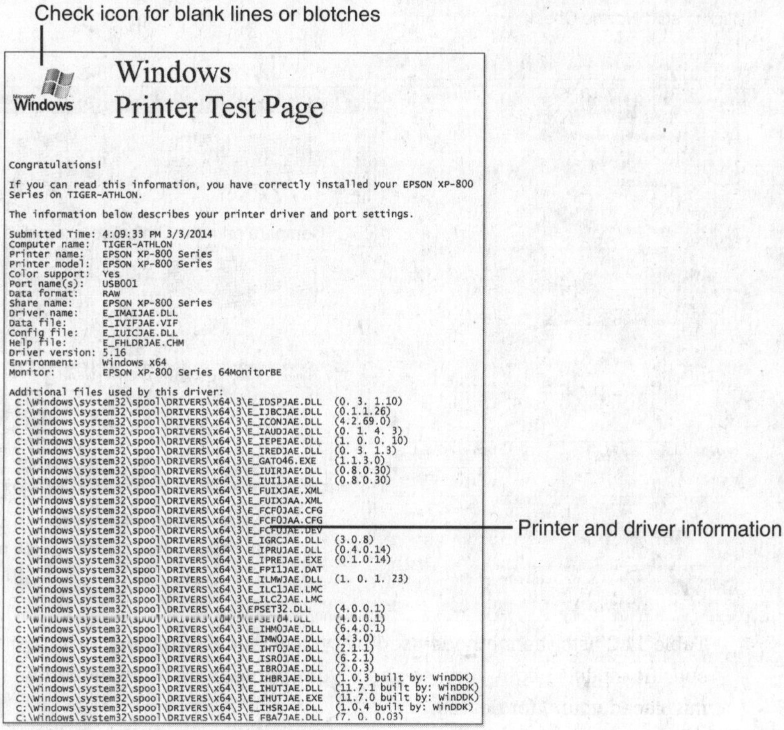


```
Windows
Printer Test Page

Congratulations!

If you can read this information, you have correctly installed your EPSON XP-800
Series on TIGER-ATHLON.

The information below describes your printer driver and port settings.

Submitted Time: 4:09:33 PM 3/3/2014
Computer name:  TIGER-ATHLON
Printer name:   EPSON XP-800 Series
Printer model:  EPSON XP-800 Series
Color support:  Yes
Port name(s):   USB001
Data format:    RAW
Share name:     EPSON XP-800 Series
Driver name:    E_IMAIJAE.DLL
Data file:      E_IVIFJAE.VIF
Config file:    E_IUICJAE.DLL
Help file:      E_FHLDRJAE.CHM
Driver version: 5.16
Environment:    Windows x64
Monitor:        EPSON XP-800 Series 64MonitorBE

Additional files used by this driver:
 C:\Windows\system32\spool\DRIVERS\x64\3\E_IDSPJAE.DLL  (0. 3. 1.10)
 C:\Windows\system32\spool\DRIVERS\x64\3\E_IJBCJAE.DLL  (0.1.1.26)
 C:\Windows\system32\spool\DRIVERS\x64\3\E_ICONJAE.DLL  (4.2.69.0)
 C:\Windows\system32\spool\DRIVERS\x64\3\E_IAUDJAE.DLL  (0. 1. 4. 3)
 C:\Windows\system32\spool\DRIVERS\x64\3\E_IEPEJAE.DLL  (1. 0. 0. 10)
 C:\Windows\system32\spool\DRIVERS\x64\3\E_IREDJAE.DLL  (0. 3. 1.3)
 C:\Windows\system32\spool\DRIVERS\x64\3\E_GATO46.EXE   (1.1.3.0)
 C:\Windows\system32\spool\DRIVERS\x64\3\E_IUIRJAE.DLL  (0.8.0.30)
 C:\Windows\system32\spool\DRIVERS\x64\3\E_IUI1JAE.DLL  (0.8.0.30)
 C:\Windows\system32\spool\DRIVERS\x64\3\E_FUIXJAE.XML
 C:\Windows\system32\spool\DRIVERS\x64\3\E_FUIXJAA.XML
 C:\Windows\system32\spool\DRIVERS\x64\3\E_FCF0JAE.CFG
 C:\Windows\system32\spool\DRIVERS\x64\3\E_FCF0JAA.CFG
 C:\Windows\system32\spool\DRIVERS\x64\3\E_FCF0JAE.DEV
 C:\Windows\system32\spool\DRIVERS\x64\3\E_IGRCJAE.DLL  (3.0.8)
 C:\Windows\system32\spool\DRIVERS\x64\3\E_IPRUJAE.DLL  (0.4.0.14)
 C:\Windows\system32\spool\DRIVERS\x64\3\E_IPREJAE.EXE  (0.1.0.14)
 C:\Windows\system32\spool\DRIVERS\x64\3\E_FPI1JAE.DAT
 C:\Windows\system32\spool\DRIVERS\x64\3\E_ILMWJAE.DLL  (1. 0. 1. 23)
 C:\Windows\system32\spool\DRIVERS\x64\3\E_ILC1JAE.LMC
 C:\Windows\system32\spool\DRIVERS\x64\3\E_ILC2JAE.LMC
 C:\Windows\system32\spool\DRIVERS\x64\3\EPSET32.DLL    (4.0.0.1)
 C:\Windows\system32\spool\DRIVERS\x64\3\EPSET64.DLL    (4.0.0.1)
 C:\Windows\system32\spool\DRIVERS\x64\3\E_IHM0JAE.DLL  (6.4.0.1)
 C:\Windows\system32\spool\DRIVERS\x64\3\E_IMW0JAE.DLL  (4.3.0)
 C:\Windows\system32\spool\DRIVERS\x64\3\E_IHT0JAE.DLL  (2.1.1)
 C:\Windows\system32\spool\DRIVERS\x64\3\E_ISR0JAE.DLL  (6.2.1)
 C:\Windows\system32\spool\DRIVERS\x64\3\E_IBR0JAE.DLL  (2.0.3)
 C:\Windows\system32\spool\DRIVERS\x64\3\E_IHBRJAE.DLL  (1.0.3 built by: WinDDK)
 C:\Windows\system32\spool\DRIVERS\x64\3\E_IHUTJAE.DLL  (11.7.1 built by: WinDDK)
 C:\Windows\system32\spool\DRIVERS\x64\3\E_IHUTJAE.EXE  (11.7.0 built by: WinDDK)
 C:\Windows\system32\spool\DRIVERS\x64\3\E_IHSRJAE.DLL  (1.0.4 built by: WinDDK)
 C:\Windows\system32\spool\DRIVERS\x64\3\E_FBA7JAE.DLL  (7. 0. 0.03)
```

Figure 11.10
A printer test page from a color inkjet printer that is working properly.

Cleaning Print Heads

Print heads can become clogged for a variety of reasons (dried ink, paper debris, unplugging the printer rather than turning it off, and so on), but whatever the reason, clogged print heads will ruin your prints. To help prevent this, most inkjet printers provide some method for cleaning the print heads.

Cleaning the print heads uses ink, so you don't want to perform it any more often than necessary. Some printer vendors provide a feature typically known as Nozzle Check to help you determine whether print head cleaning is needed.

To perform a nozzle check:

1. Load plain paper into the printer.
2. Select **Nozzle Check** (see Table 11.2 for details).
3. After the Nozzle Check process is over, compare the actual printout with the sample provided onscreen. Figure 11.11 shows an example from an Epson XP-800 multifunction device.

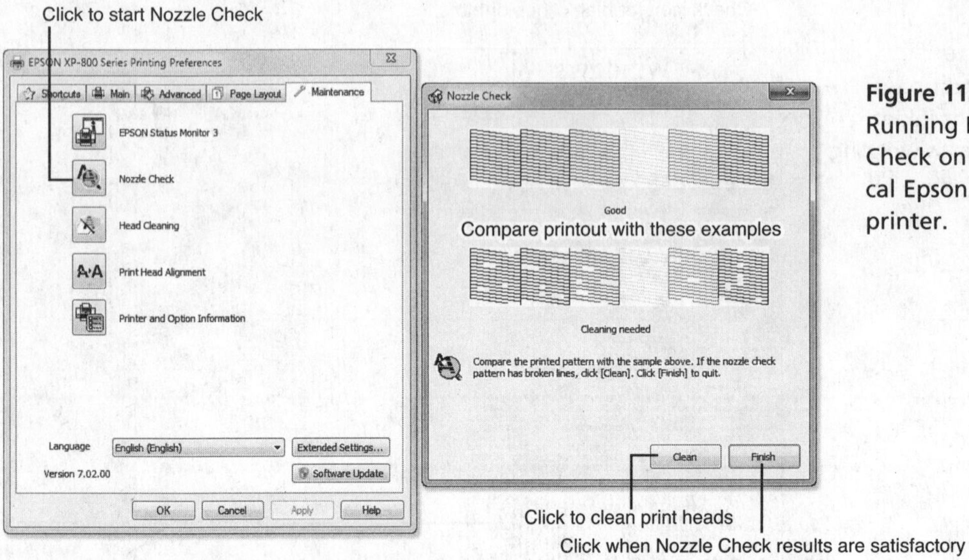

Figure 11.11 Running Nozzle Check on a typical Epson inkjet printer.

Table 11.2 lists the methods used by typical models from major printer vendors. Keep in mind that specific models might vary, so check your printer's instruction manual (available online if you've misplaced yours) for details.

Table 11.2 Typical Inkjet Print Head Check and Clean Features

Printer Brand	Menu	Nozzle Check	Clean Options	Figure
Canon	Properties, Maintenance tab	Yes	Cleaning, Deep Cleaning	Figure 11.12
Epson	Preferences, Maintenance tab	Yes	Head Cleaning	Figure 11.11
HP*	Preferences, Features tab, click Printer Services**	Yes***	Clean the Print heads	Figure 11.13
Lexmark/Dell	Front-panel controls	No	Head Cleaning	—

*Some printers use front-panel controls for maintenance (see instruction manual for details).

**Install HP Toolbox utility if Services tab is not visible; available from HP website (use Windows Vista version for Windows 7).

***Click the Print a PQ (Print Quality) Diagnostic Page button for this feature

Note
HP printers and multifunction devices can also use the HP Print and Scan Doctor for device diagnostics. See the HP website for details.

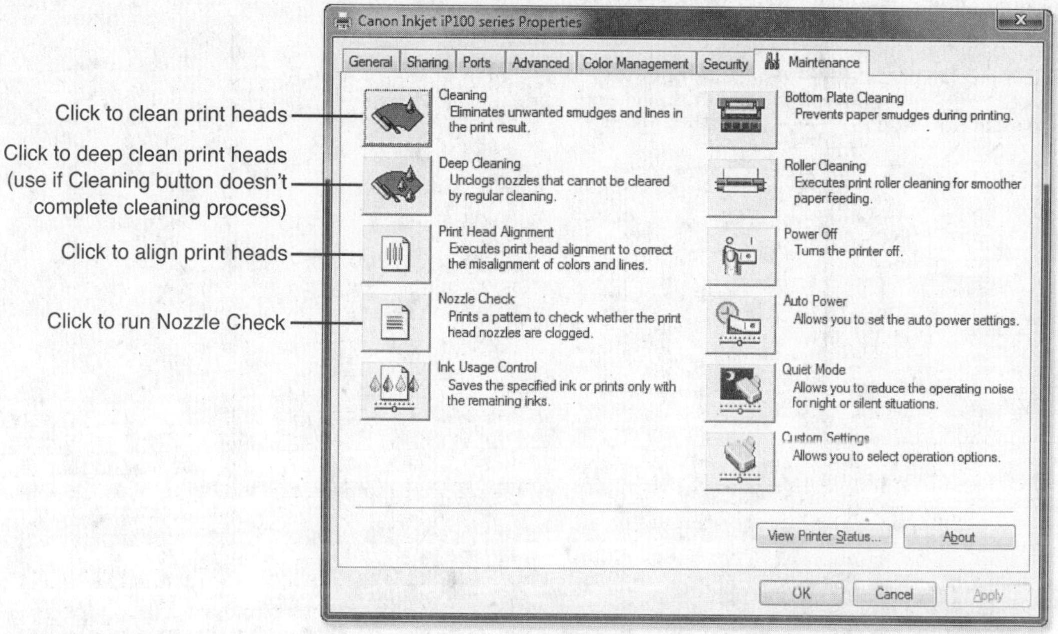

Figure 11.12
Maintenance options on a typical Canon inkjet printer.

With all printers, use the Nozzle Check or Print Quality Diagnostics feature (when available), followed by the cleaning routine. Rerun Nozzle Check after cleaning to see if additional cleaning is necessary.

On Canon models, use the Cleaning button for the first cleaning. If the printer needs additional cleaning, use the Deep Cleaning button. With HP, Epson, and Lexmark (Dell) printers, you should not exceed three cleaning cycles at a time to avoid cartridge damage.

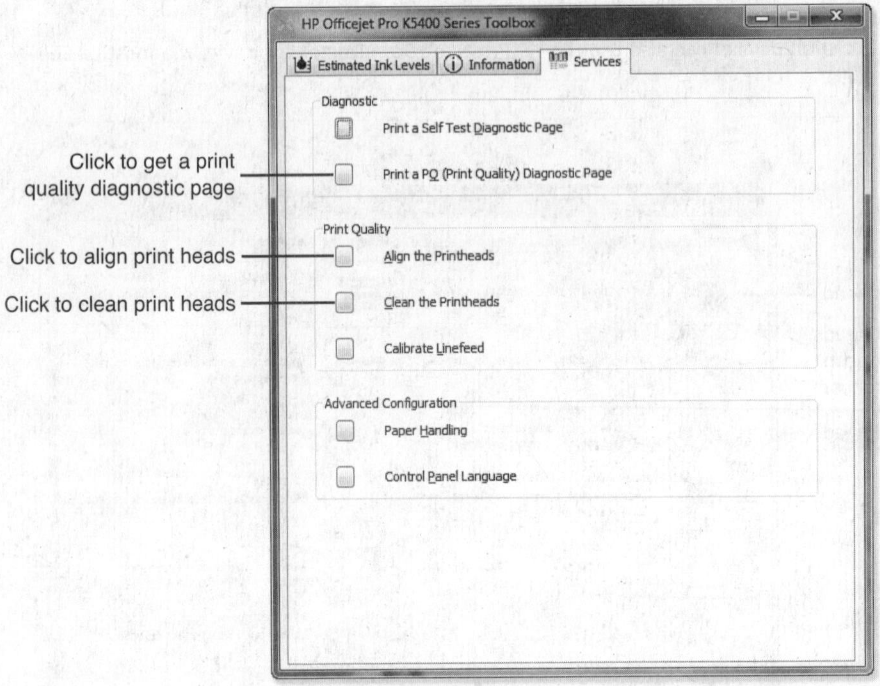

Figure 11.13 Service options on a typical HP inkjet printer.

Aligning Print Heads

Did you ever wonder how inkjet printers create large fonts and graphics with a tiny print head? The printer prints the document in horizontal strips, and the strips must align correctly. A misaligned black print head can produce an effect similar to Figure 11.14, whereas misaligned color print heads produce grainy output.

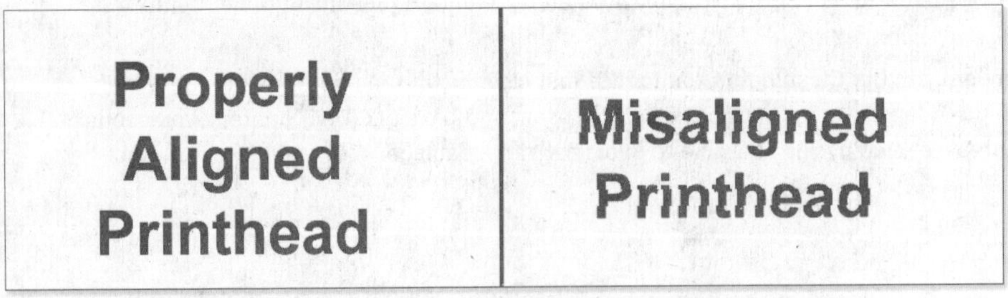

Figure 11.14 A simulation of proper print head alignment (left) and misalignment (right).

To solve this problem, use the print head alignment feature in your printer driver. Figure 11.15 shows the Epson XP-800 menu and one of the dialogs in the print head alignment process.

During the process, you will be asked to choose the best-aligned output from your printer for both black and colored inks. Most printers will remember this setting and use it from that point on. However, some printers require you to realign the print heads after you change ink cartridges, and others perform this task automatically for you. See your printer manual for details.

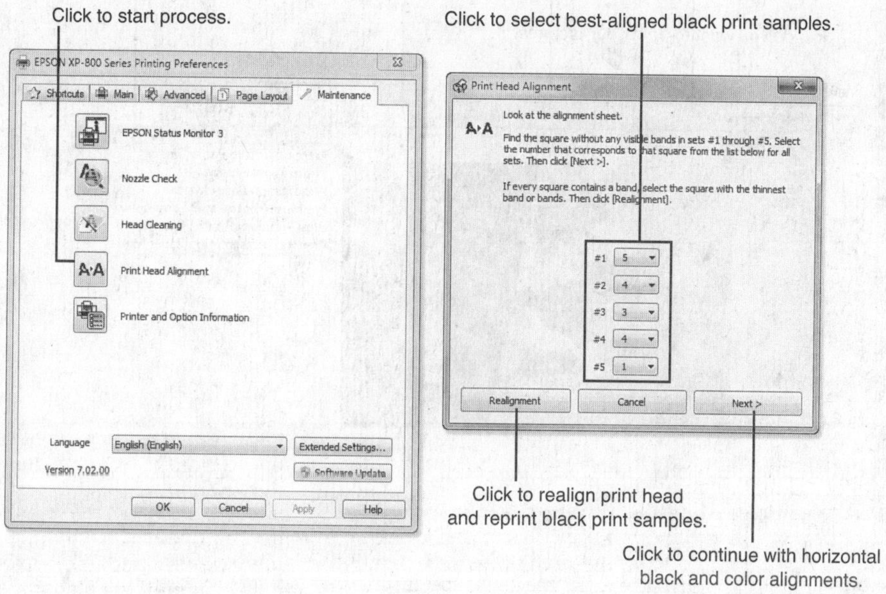

Figure 11.15 Using the Print Head Alignment feature in the Epson XP-800 multifunction device.

Selecting the Correct Paper Type and Print Quality Settings

If you mismatch photo quality and paper type settings, you'll have problems getting good prints, whether you use the built-in Windows Photo Printer (Figure 11.16) or an app's own photo printing features.

Figure 11.17 compares the results when printing a photo on premium glossy paper with the Best Photo setting using the built-in Windows Photo Printer app, printing the same photo on premium glossy paper using the plain paper setting from a third-party app, and printing the same photo on the wrong side of the paper using the Best Photo setting.

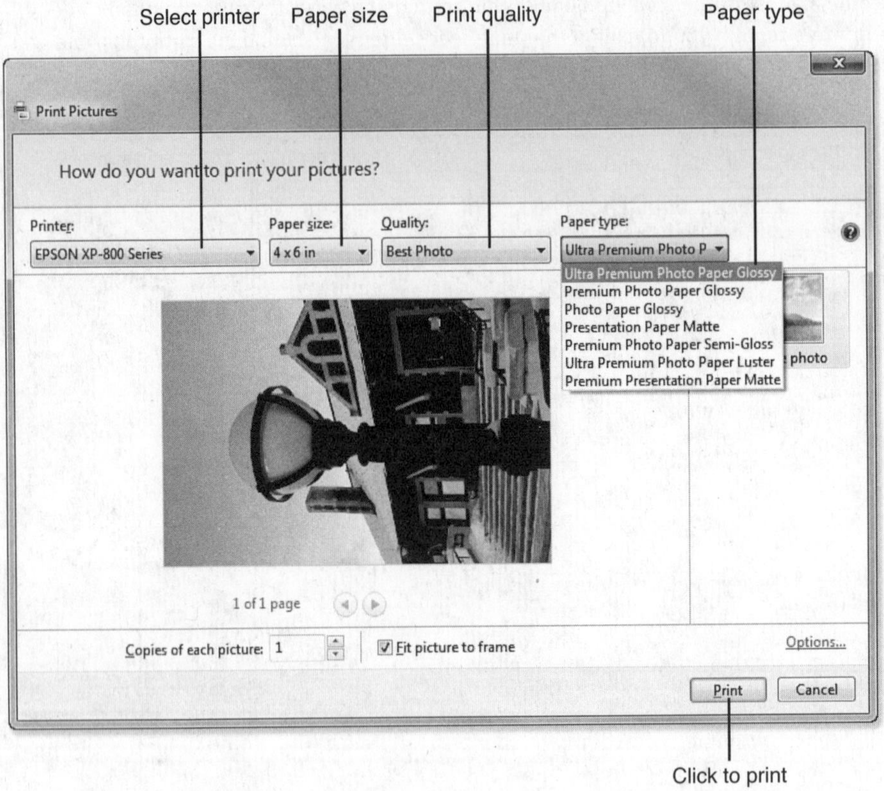

Figure 11.16 Using Windows Photo Printer to print a photo in Best Quality.

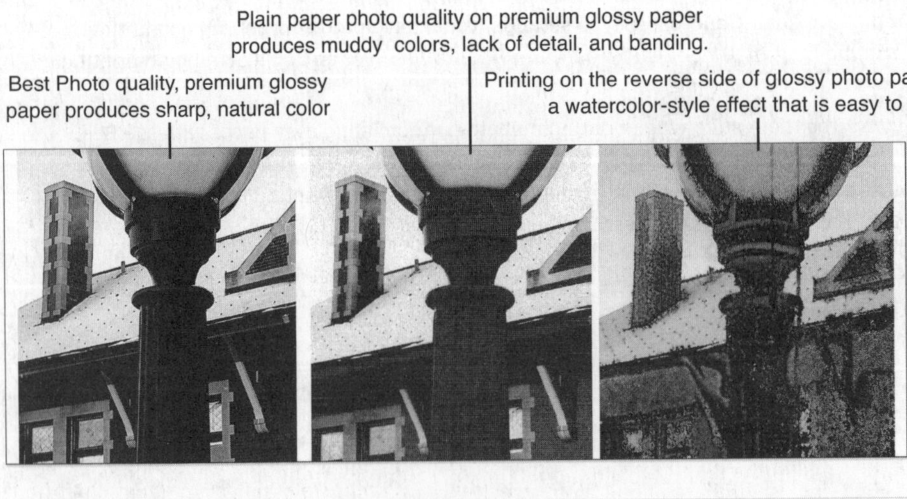

Figure 11.17 Comparing the same photo printed with correct (left) and incorrect (middle, right) paper type and print quality settings.

Third-Party Versus OEM Inks

It has frequently been said that original equipment manufacturer (OEM) inkjet printer inks are the most expensive liquids in the world on an ounce-for-ounce basis. It's not surprising that many users have turned to third-party inks. They're certainly less expensive, but lower cost isn't the only factor to consider.

Reviews over the past decade from many sources suggest that third-party inks typically produce less-durable prints and are more prone to cartridge malfunctions. For these reasons, I don't recommend third-party inks. There are other ways to save money without risking image loss or damage to your printer.

High-Capacity Inks and Ink Cartridge Recycling

To save money on OEM ink, I recommend the following methods:

- **Buy high-capacity ink cartridges**—Most printer manufacturers offer at least two capacities of ink for their late-model printers (and some offer as many as three capacities). For example, the Epson 97 ink cartridge for some WorkForce series printers provides the same page capacity as two Epson 68 cartridges for $10 less (Office Depot, March 2014) and prints 50% more pages than two Epson 69 cartridges for $3.50 less. Check your favorite stores and ink types for details.
- **Buy multipacks**—For example, you can buy a two-pack of Epson 97 cartridges for about $8 less than buying two single cartridges.
- **Don't overbuy**—Inkjet printers eventually fail, and with today's rapid turnover of models, the odds are slim that ink cartridges for your current printer would fit a new model. Have one spare for each color and one to two spares for black.
- **Know the rules for ink cartridge recycling and save money**—Be sure to join the store loyalty program so you get credit for ink purchases and cartridge recycling and be sure to spend the credits you get. Some stores give you credit for recycled cartridges only if you buy ink at the same time you return cartridges, so coordinate your recycling of ink cartridges and ink purchasing (recycle and buy on the same trip), and don't recycle more than the limit per month.

Troubleshooting Printing from Memory Cards

Although it's a lot cheaper to get prints of your digital photos from a store's quick-print kiosk or online service, sometimes there's no substitute for the immediate gratification of printing directly from a memory card using your own printer (Figure 11.18). Keep these tips in mind for trouble-free printing.

- **Insert the memory card all the way into the printer**—As Figure 11.19 reveals, a card inserted only partway isn't inserted at all as far as the printer is concerned. Push the card into place until you see a blinking light, which indicates the printer is reading the card's contents.

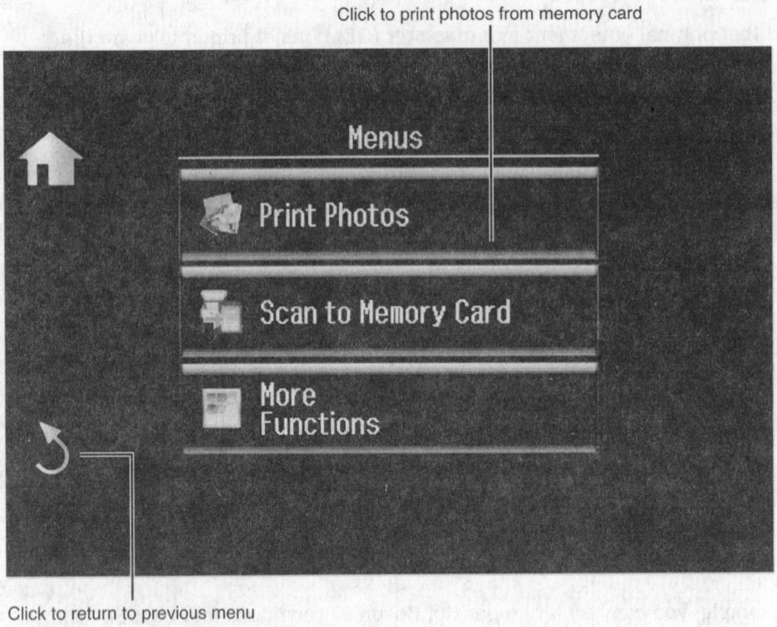

Figure 11.18 Selecting the view and print from memory card option on a typical inkjet printer (Epson XP-800).

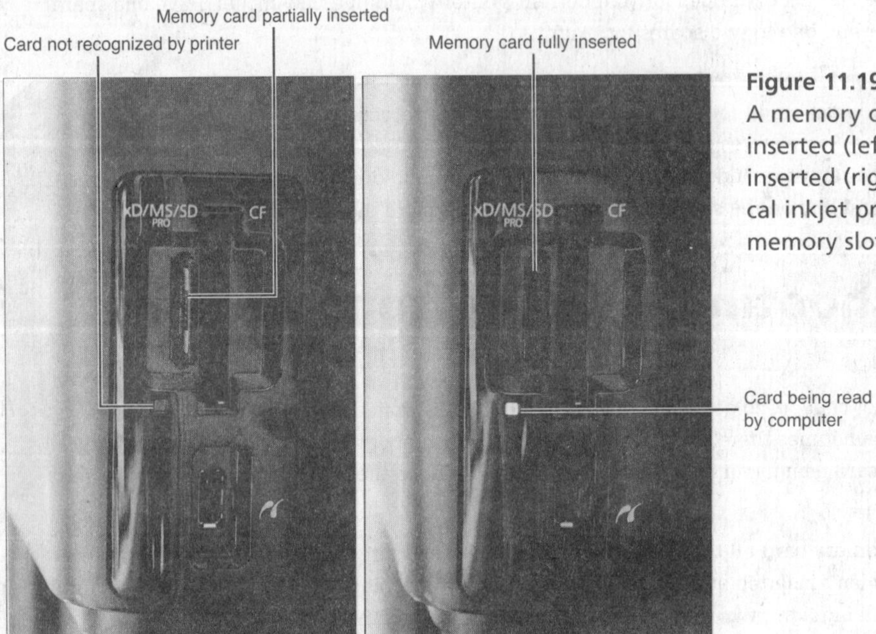

Figure 11.19 A memory card partially inserted (left) and fully inserted (right) into a typical inkjet printer's SD flash memory slot.

- **Printers want JPEG files**—RAW files need not apply. Although RAW files are better for extensive editing, they must be converted into JPEG images before you can print. In other words, if your memory card has nothing but RAW images on it, your printer will read your memory card's contents as "0 prints." If you want to have RAW files for editing and JPEG files for quick prints, set your digital camera for RAW+JPEG.
- **Choose the files you want to print**—Use the preview feature to select the best photos from your card. Your memory card can hold hundreds or even thousands of photos; you probably don't want prints of all of them (see Figure 11.20).

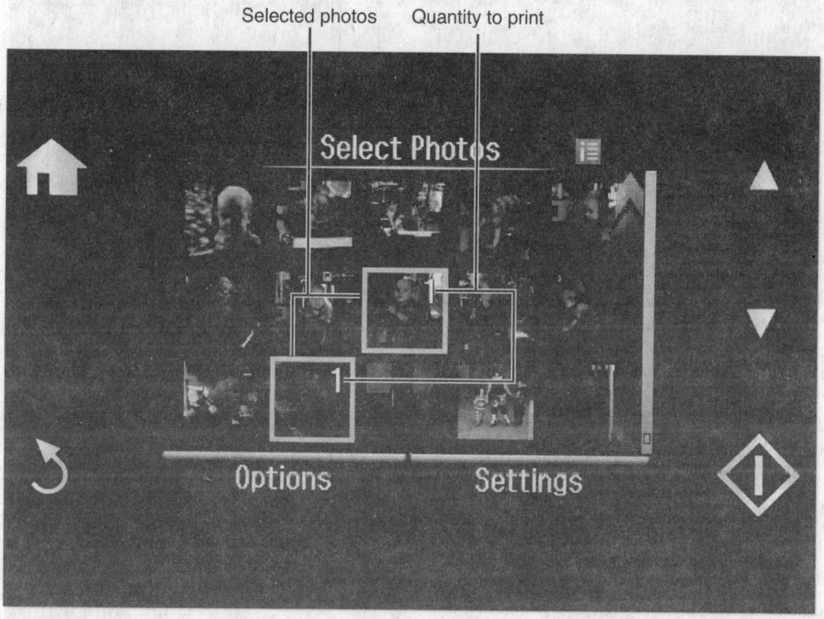

Figure 11.20
Selecting pictures and quantities to print on an Epson WorkForce 600.

- **Check your paper tray**—Make sure you have enough paper loaded for prints and that you have it inserted the right way. If your printer has more than one paper tray (or cassette), be sure you're using the correct one for photo paper.
- **Crop it yourself the way you want it**—It's a long-time problem in both traditional and digital photography that most print sizes don't match the dimensions of negatives or image sensors. Your printer will turn your photos into 4×6-inch prints, even though the proportions produced by most digital cameras are different. Use the Crop feature in your printer to crop images to print size. You'll do a better job than the printer will (see Figure 11.21).
- **Select paper size, print style, and print quality before you print**—In addition to cropping, you can select borders or borderless, whether to perform photo improvements, and other options (see Figure 11.22).

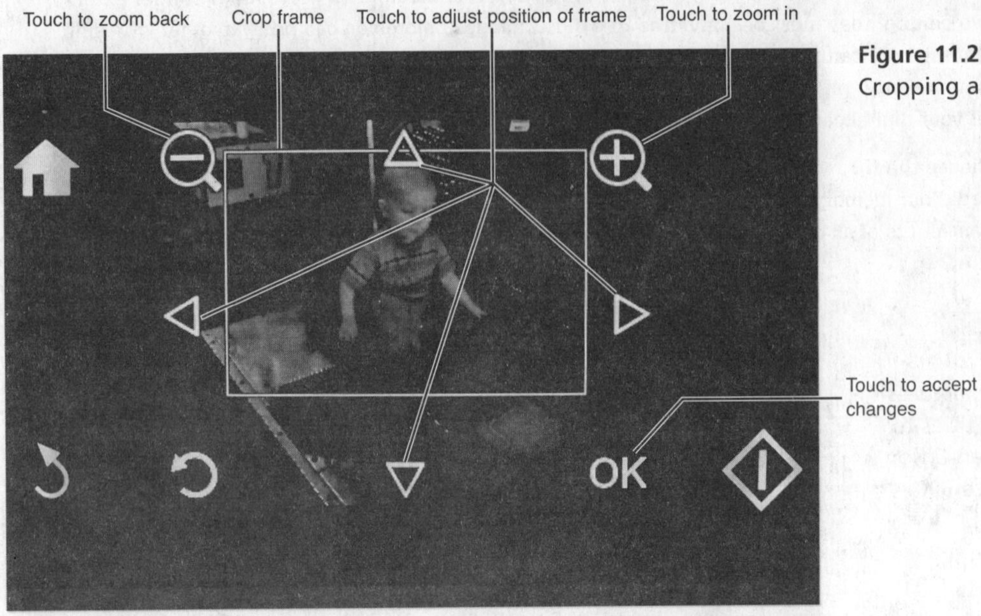

Figure 11.21 Cropping a photo.

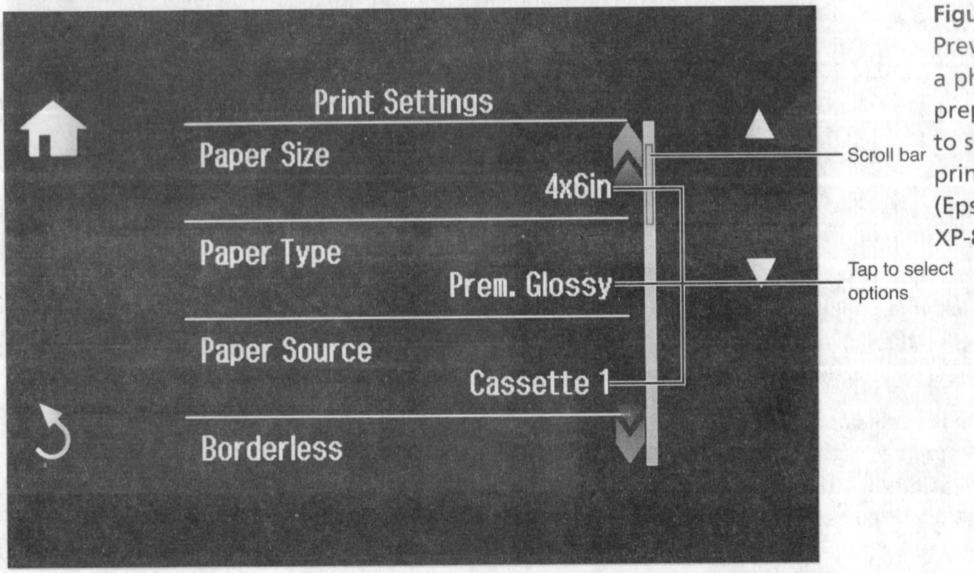

Figure 11.22 Previewing a photo and preparing to select print options (Epson XP-800).

Troubleshooting Laser Printers

Many home and small-business users who don't need color have found that laser printers and all-in-one units provide faster printing and save big money over color inkjet printers (color inkjets are cheaper in use than color laser printers, however). Laser printers work differently and have different print quality problems than inkjet printers do.

Unlike inkjet printers, in which most moving parts are readily visible to the naked eye, a laser or LED printer's mechanism is concealed within the printer cover. In fact, much of the imaging process is performed within the printer's toner cartridge. Figure 11.23 diagrams a typical laser printer's internal components. The numbers refer to the steps performed in printing a page: 1 (processing), 2 (charging), 3 (exposing), 4 (developing), 5 (transferring), 6 (fusing), and 7 (cleaning).

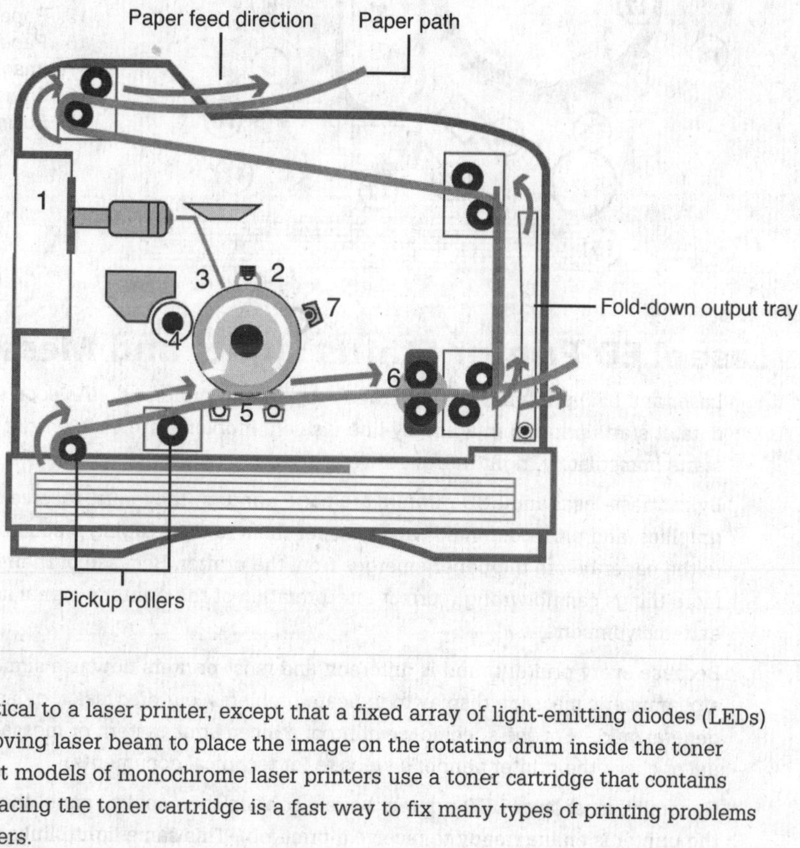

Figure 11.23 The components of a typical laser printer. Some laser printers use a separate toner supply and imaging drum design, but most models use a design similar to the one shown in this figure.

An LED printer is identical to a laser printer, except that a fixed array of light-emitting diodes (LEDs) is used in place of a moving laser beam to place the image on the rotating drum inside the toner cartridge. Because most models of monochrome laser printers use a toner cartridge that contains the imaging drum, replacing the toner cartridge is a fast way to fix many types of printing problems with laser or LED printers.

Color laser printers are becoming increasingly common as prices drop. Most recent models use four separate toner cartridges to enable faster single-pass printing (Figure 11.24). As with monochrome laser printers, many image-quality problems with color laser printers can be solved by replacing the toner cartridge(s).

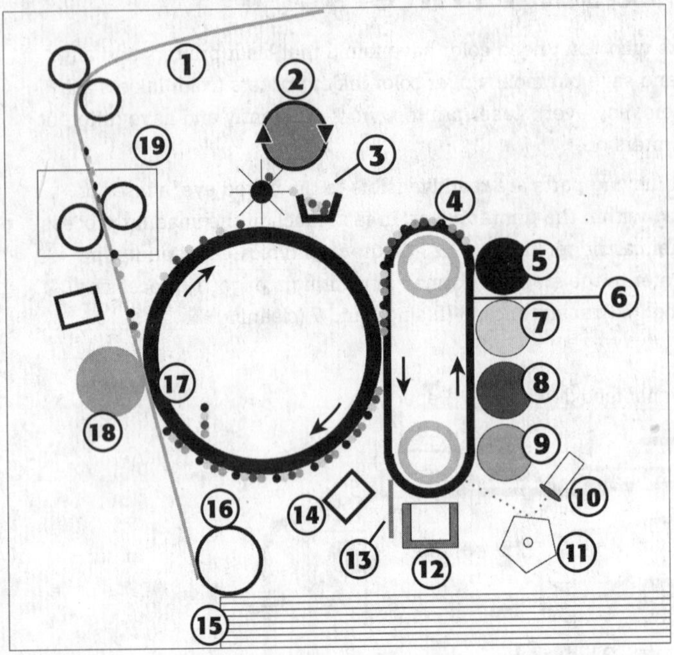

1. Paper path
2. Cleaning unit
3. Waste toner
4. Toner particles
5. Black toner
6. OPC belt
7. Yellow toner
8. Magenta toner
9. Cyan toner
10. Laser
11. Laser mirror
12. Charger
13. Cleaning blade
14. Erase lamp
15. Paper in paper tray
16. Paper pickup
17. Imaging drum
18. Transfer roller
19. Fusing rollers

Figure 11.24 The components of a typical color laser printer that uses a toner belt to transfer the image.

Laser/LED Printer Status Lights and Messages

Laser and LED printers work differently than inkjet printers do. As soon as an inkjet printer receives data, it starts printing in a line-by-line fashion. Problems are visible right away because the printout starts immediately, right in front of your eyes.

By contrast, laser and LED printers are page printers; they must receive an entire page of text, graphics, and print commands and transfer them to the imaging mechanism, which transfers them to the paper before the paper emerges from the printer. Because of their more complex operation, more things can go wrong; correct interpretation of the printer's signal lights or status messages is extremely important.

Because every printer brand is different, and most printers now use signal lights instead of an alphanumeric message display to indicate problems, our discussion of laser printer problems is a general guide. For the specific meaning of a given light pattern or message, see your printer's manual or check the printer vendor's website for technical documents.

Generally, most laser/LED printers have a light on their control panel that glows steadily to indicate the printer is online (ready to receive a print job). This same light blinks when the printer is receiving a print job.

Most printers have two or more other lights that will shine or blink in various patterns to indicate problems such as the following:

- Out of memory (The contents of the page are larger than the printer's available memory.)
- Paper jam
- Paper out
- Toner cartridge problems
- Imaging drum problems

Although a few printers might use an alphanumeric display panel to provide the error message, you will normally need to look up the light pattern for your printer to determine the problem and its solution.

The bottom line is, learn the difference between normal and abnormal light displays on your printer.

Common Laser/LED Problems and Solutions

Typical problems with laser and LED printers include the following:

- Poor print quality
- Incomplete page printouts of graphics-heavy pages
- Slow printing of graphics-heavy pages
- Pages printed in reverse order when using the manual feed tray
- Trying to print an image that's too low quality for satisfactory reproduction
- Running out of paper

Use the following sections to solve the most common problems you are likely to encounter with your laser printer.

Troubleshooting Marks and Smudges on the Printout

Because of the different sizes used by the rollers, which are part of a laser or LED printer's paper path, you can often determine the exact cause of repeating or continuous extraneous markings on your printer's output by examining the distance between repeated markings on the output.

For example, with the HP LaserJet M1530 series all-in-one unit, repetitive print defects every 27mm, 29mm, or 75mm typically indicate a damaged printer cartridge. Other marks indicate dirt or damage to other parts of the unit. See the instruction manual for your printer to learn which marks are caused by problems with which part of the unit and how to clean it.

If the damaged or dirty rollers are within the toner cartridge, you might need to replace the toner cartridge. A continuous vertical black streak along all pages of the printout usually indicates a damaged toner cartridge that must be replaced. Be sure to turn off and unplug the printer before changing toner cartridges or cleaning the printer.

Can't Print a Full Page

Even the lowest-cost laser printers should be able to print a page of text or a page with small graphics. However, if you try to print a page composed mostly of graphics, a page that has several fonts, or a page with visible gridlines (such as a spreadsheet), you may run out of laser printer memory, causing an out-of-memory error. Because the printer could not finish printing the page, the page will remain in the printer until you eject it. When you eject it, only the part of the page that would fit in the printer's memory will be printed.

Here's how to cure problems with partial page printouts.

- **Error recovery**—To recover from this error, eject the current page (see your printer's manual); note that the page will not be completely printed but will appear to be cut off at the point where the page contents exceeded the laser printer's memory.
- **Workaround**—If the page uses only one or two fonts but has a lot of graphics, the easiest way to print the page is to decrease the graphics resolution of the printer in the printer's properties sheet. For example, reducing a 1,200 dpi (dots per inch) laser printer's graphics resolution to 600 dpi reduces the amount of required printer memory by a factor of 4 (see Figure 11.25). Although graphics won't be as finely detailed, text quality is unaffected. If the printer uses PostScript, reduce the number of fonts in the document.

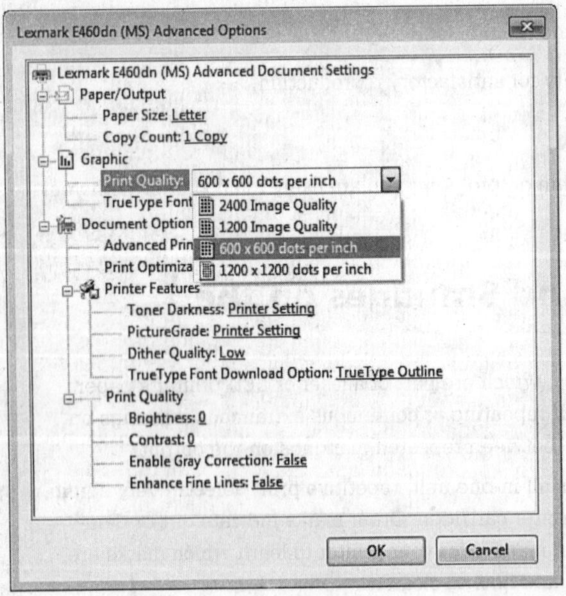

Figure 11.25
Reducing the graphics resolution on a Lexmark laser printer with the Layout, Advanced, Graphics, Print Quality menu (Windows 7).

- **Solution**—Install more memory in the laser printer. The amount of RAM required to print a page varies with the printer's resolution, the size of the graphics, the number of fonts on the page, the size of the page (letter or legal size paper), and the printer's ability to compress graphic data. For a 600 dpi laser printer, your memory upgrade should add at least twice the amount of memory originally installed in the printer. For example, if your printer has 2MB of onboard memory and prints at 600 dpi, you should add at least 4MB (for a total of 6MB of RAM). If you are upgrading a 1,200 dpi laser printer, add at least four times the amount of memory originally found in the printer. This will enable you to print complex pages at their highest resolution and print two or more pages on a single sheet of paper. It may also speed up printing because the printer doesn't need to spend as much time compressing data.

See your printer's instruction manual for the type of memory module or card needed to upgrade the printer's memory. You can get some types of laser printer memory from memory specialist vendors such as www.Crucial.com.

Paper Jam

Paper jams can be caused by incorrect paper loading, wrinkled or damaged paper, or damp paper. Here's how to deal with a paper jam, and how to prevent it.

- **Error recovery**—Shut down and unplug the printer and open it to locate the paper jam. You might need to remove the toner cartridge on some models to find the paper jam. Remove the misfed sheet(s) and be sure to remove any torn paper or loose labels. Resend the print job after you turn on the printer. If the paper jam is located near the end of the paper path, beware of the hot fusing assembly when you remove the paper jam.
- **Solution**—Be sure to load the paper tray properly and insert it completely into the printer. Use only laser-compatible labels; copier labels aren't designed to handle the heat of laser printing and can come off inside the printer, possibly causing damage. If you can switch to a straight-through paper path (usually an optional rear paper tray) for labels and similar heavy stock, do so to minimize the chances of a paper jam (see Figure 11.26). Avoid using paper that is damaged, stuck together, warped, or wrinkled. Don't use media that is thicker or heavier than the printer is rated to accept.

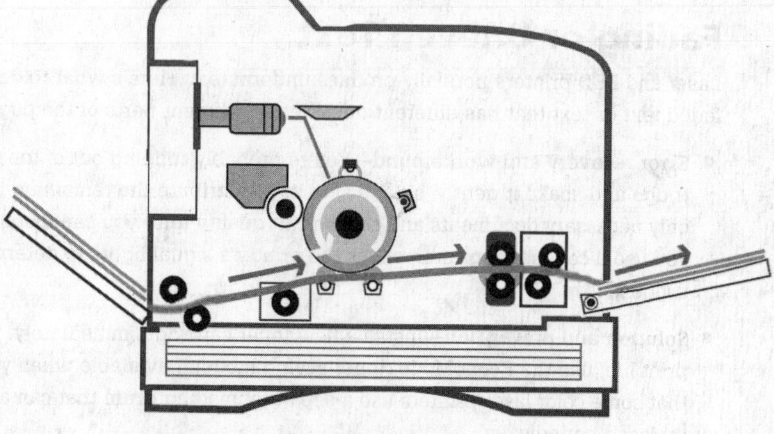

Figure 11.26 Switching to a straight-through paper path (rear feed and front paper tray) helps avoid problems with label or envelope stock.

Paper Out

Running out of paper is a normal part of printing, but you can minimize the interruption to your printing task by filling the paper tray before you start printing a long document. Here's how to avoid paper-out interruptions.

- **Error recovery and solution**—Open the paper tray and properly install new paper. Some printers will print as soon as you close the paper tray, whereas others require you to press the online/paper feed button to continue printing after you insert paper.
- **Workaround**—If the paper tray is defective or if it isn't completely inserted into the printer, you might continue to get a paper-out signal even after you fill the paper tray and reinsert it. In these cases, use the manual paper tray option (if available), use a replacement paper tray, or service the printer if the paper tray isn't a removable item.

Toner Cartridge Problems

A damaged toner cartridge will put extraneous marks or smudges on every page it prints, and an empty toner cartridge can't print anything. Sooner or later, you will need to replace the toner cartridge for one reason or the other. Here's how to make sure whether the toner cartridge is the culprit.

- **Error recovery**—Shut down the printer and remove the toner cartridge (refer to your manual for specifics). Verify that the toner cartridge is properly inserted and contains toner. Watch for print quality problems when the first print jobs emerge after you reinstall an existing toner cartridge or install a new one.
- **Solution**—If the new toner cartridge doesn't improve print quality, recheck the printer for other problems; you may need to have it serviced.

If you use a color laser printer, you need to determine which toner cartridge has run out or is damaged. The colors are the same as those used in four-color inkjet printers: cyan, magenta, yellow, and black. Replace the correct color.

Fading or Uneven Text

Laser and LED printers normally produce uniform text. Here's what to do if your printer is producing faded text or text that has different densities in different parts of the page.

- **Error recovery and workaround**—You're probably running out of toner. Remove the toner cartridge and shake it gently, side to side, to redistribute the remaining toner more evenly. Print only necessary documents and check print quality until you can install a new toner cartridge. If you use a color laser printer, check the printer's signal lights to determine which color toner cartridge is low.
- **Solution and prevention**—Install a new toner cartridge immediately. To maximize toner cartridge print life, use the EconoMode (toner saving mode) if available when you print draft copies. Note that some color laser printers use a separate imaging drum that can also run out and must be replaced periodically.

Print Falls Off the Page

The fuser assembly is designed to "bake" the toner to the page. If the fuser stops working, the toner won't stick to the page.

- **Error recovery and workaround**—Clean the fuser assembly and retry the print job. If the problem persists, replace the fuser.
- **Solution and prevention**—Install a replacement fuser assembly. These are typically included as part of a maintenance kit.

Checking Firmware and Number of Pages Printed

If you print thousands of pages with your printer, you will probably wear out more than your toner cartridge (imaging drum). See your instruction manual to learn how to print a status page that displays the firmware used by the printer, the amount of RAM installed, and the number of pages printed. Some models of laser printers require installation of a maintenance kit after a specified number of pages.

Using Maintenance Kits

Many HP and other laser printers feature components that should be replaced at periodic intervals. These components often include fuser assemblies, air filters, transfer rollers, pickup rollers, other types of rollers, and separation pads. These components wear out over time and can usually be purchased as a maintenance kit as well as separately.

A printer that uses a maintenance kit will display a message or an error code with a meaning such as "Perform printer maintenance" or "Perform user maintenance" when the printer reaches the recommended page count for maintenance kit replacement. Depending on the printer model and whether it is used for color or monochrome printing, the recommended page count could be as few as 50,000 pages or as much as 300,000 pages or more.

> **Note**
> Sources for maintenance kits can also provide useful installation instructions. Sources for HP and Lexmark printers include PrinterTechs.com, Inc. (http://www.printertechs.com/maintenance-kits.php) and Depot International http://www.depot-america.com) among others.

Troubleshooting Scan/Copy/Fax Issues

If you use an all-in-one unit, you've reduced the amount of clutter on your desk, but you now have a device that can cause additional headaches. Here are solutions for the most common ones.

Documents Jamming in Paper Feeder

The paper feeder makes it easy to do double-sided copying, scanning, and faxing, but only if the pages you feed it are in perfect shape:

- Remove staples and paper clips.
- Don't try to feed torn or folded pages.
- Avoid feeding pages with sticky notes.

For pages with these and similar problems, use the flatbed scanner.

What Scan/Copy Settings Should I Use?

If you're scanning or copying a black-and-white document, use the Document setting. Adjust contrast or brightness as needed for the best quality results. Scan at 300 dpi.

To scan a black-and-white or color photo you want to reproduce at the same size or smaller, scan at 300 dpi. Select 8-bit grayscale for black and white photos, and 24-bit color for color photos.

To scan a black-and-white or color photo you want to reproduce at a larger size (or if you plan to crop the image and use only a portion of it), scan at 600 dpi.

The automatic scan or copy features provide little or no control over the image and are recommended for "perfect" pages or photos. To get more control over the final result, select a scan option with more settings.

Can't Use Fax

Be sure to follow the instructions for setting up your fax. If your office uses VoIP (voice over IP) telephones, check with the vendor or your support staff to learn whether you can use a fax and what type of a connection to use.

In many cases, you will need to enter 9 to get an outside line and pause while the system switches to an outside line. If you don't program in the outside line code, you won't be able to send faxes.

Lines, Streaks, or Specks

If you see lines, streaks, or specks in copied or scanned printouts, check the scanner glass or the underside of the scanner lid for dirt. To clean the top of the scanner glass, shut off the scanner, unplug it, and spray glass cleaner on a clean, lint-free cloth. Use the cloth to clean the glass or the underside of the scanner lid.

Troubleshooting iOS and Android Printer Support

If you can put your printer or device on your home or office's wireless network, you can print to it with your iOS or Android tablet or smartphone. Follow these basic steps:

1. Configure your device to connect to the wireless network. If your office doesn't have a wireless network, configure your device to permit ad-hoc connections (typically up to four devices only).
2. Make sure your device is visible on the network. It must have its own IP address.

3. Install the software provided by your printer vendor for Android or iOS printing. The software is typically provided through the App Store (iOS) or Google Play (Android).
4. Turn on the printer's wireless network support.
5. Use the print software on the tablet or smartphone to locate the device.
6. Check ink levels.
7. Select print options.
8. Print document, web page, photo, or other item desired.

Figure 11.27 illustrates how Epson's iPrint for Android works.

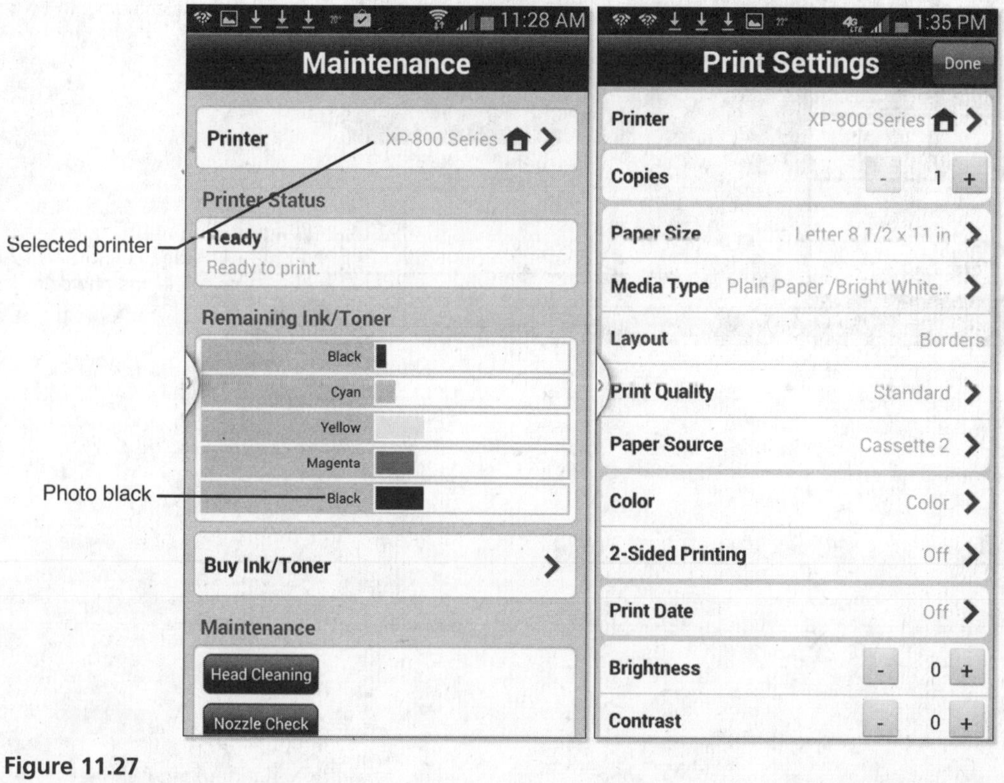

Figure 11.27
Monitoring ink levels (left) and setting print options (right) with Epson iPrint for Android smartphones.

iPrint for iOS offers similar functions. Figure 11.28 illustrates the process of selecting a photo on an iPad running iPrint.

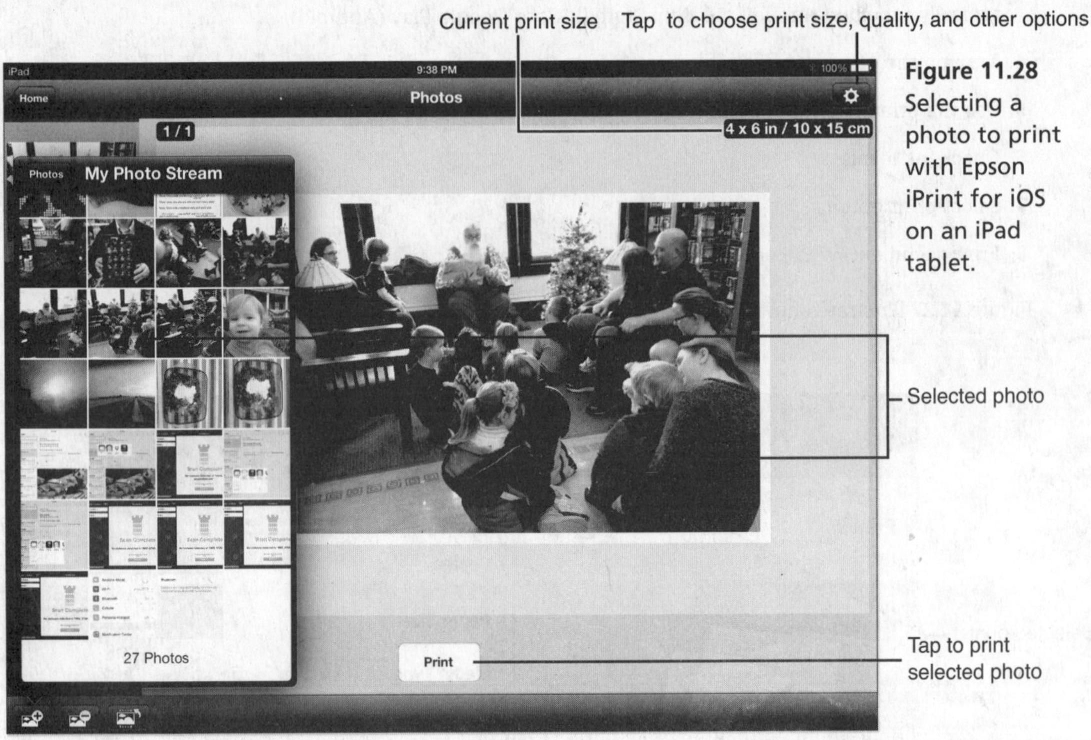

Figure 11.28 Selecting a photo to print with Epson iPrint for iOS on an iPad tablet.

12

TROUBLESHOOTING HOME THEATER, HDTVS, AND PROJECTORS

Fast Track to Solutions

Table 12.1 Symptom Table

Symptom	Flowchart or Book Section	Page #
I can't see anything on my HDTV or projector connected to my Windows PC.	Detecting HDTV, Projector, or Additional Monitor with Windows	314
My HDTV won't display my entire Windows Desktop or Start menu.	Adjusting the HDTV Desktop Size in Windows	317
I'm not sure my rear speakers on my computer are working.	Figure 12.18	325
I can't play anything on my receiver via Bluetooth.	Using Bluetooth on iOS Using Bluetooth on Android	328 332
Most of the music on my Windows PC isn't recognized by iTunes.	Selecting Your Entire Music Library with iTunes	335
My music tracks from ripped CDs must be converted before iTunes can use them. How can I change how I rip them?	Selecting the Correct Settings for Ripping a CD	338
Blu-ray discs won't play in HD resolution.	Troubleshooting Blu-Ray Playback Quality (flowchart)	Chapter 24

I Can't See Computer or Device Display on HDTV, Projector, or Monitor

HDTVs projectors, and most monitors are designed to receive signals from multiple inputs. If you don't select the correct input, or if you don't configure your computer properly, your HDTV, projector, or monitorwon't have anything to display. Use the information in this section to enable your HDTV, projector, or monitor to communicate with your home theater system or computer.

Troubleshooting TV and Video Inputs

To make it easier to select the correct input settings on your HDTV, projector, or monitor, you need to know which types of devices you have connected and where they are connected.

Typical HDTVs and projectors have the following ports:

- **Cable/antenna port**—Connects to cable TV, cable TV boxes, or antennas
- **HDMI port**—Connects to Blu-ray players, DVD players, streaming media players, receivers, and computers
- **VGA port**—Connects to computers
- **Component video port**—Connects to DVD players
- **S-video port**—Connects to VCRs and older DVD players
- **Composite video port**—Connects to VCRs, older DVD players, and streaming media players
- **S/PDIF digital audio port**—Connects to receivers
- **USB port**—Connects to USB flash memory drives and streaming media players

LCD and LED monitors have HDMI, VGA, or DVI ports. These ports (except for USB and DVI ports), are shown in Figure 12.1. Refer to Figure 1.4 (Chapter 1) for DVI and USB ports.

Figure 12.2 illustrates typical video cables used by computers, HDTVs, and projectors.

To display a picture from any video source, you must follow these steps:

1. Connect the video source to the HDTV or projector or to an AV receiver that is connected to an HDTV or projector.
2. Turn on the projector or HDTV.
3. Turn on the video source and AV receiver.
4. Turn on the video source.
5. If necessary, select the correct output from the video source.
6. Select the matching input on the projector, HDTV, or AV receiver.

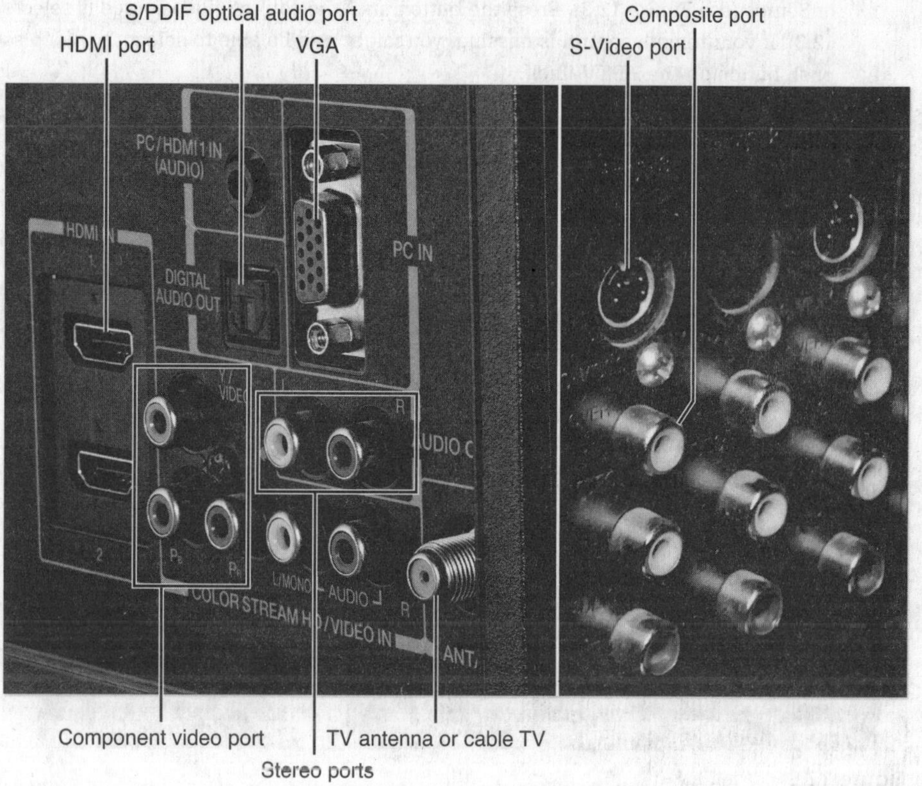

Figure 12.1 Typical video and audio ports on HDTVs.

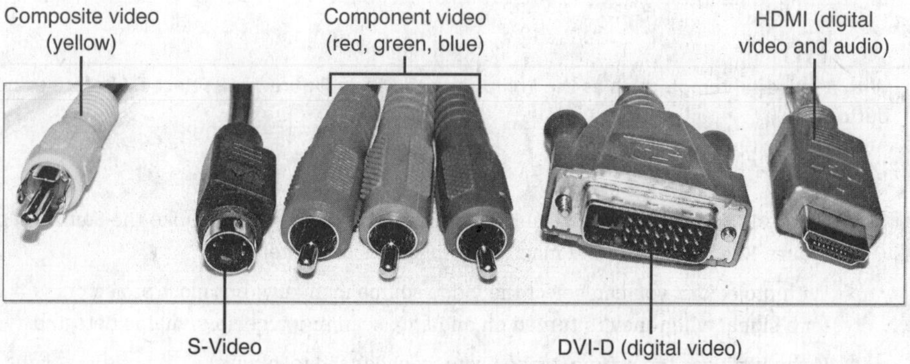

Figure 12.2 Typical video cables.

On HDTVs, the selection process is performed by using a button on the remote control called Input or Source (see Figure 12.3). Press the button until the correct video source is selected (see Figure 12.3). If your remote control is missing, you might also be able to select the video source using a push button on the HDTV itself.

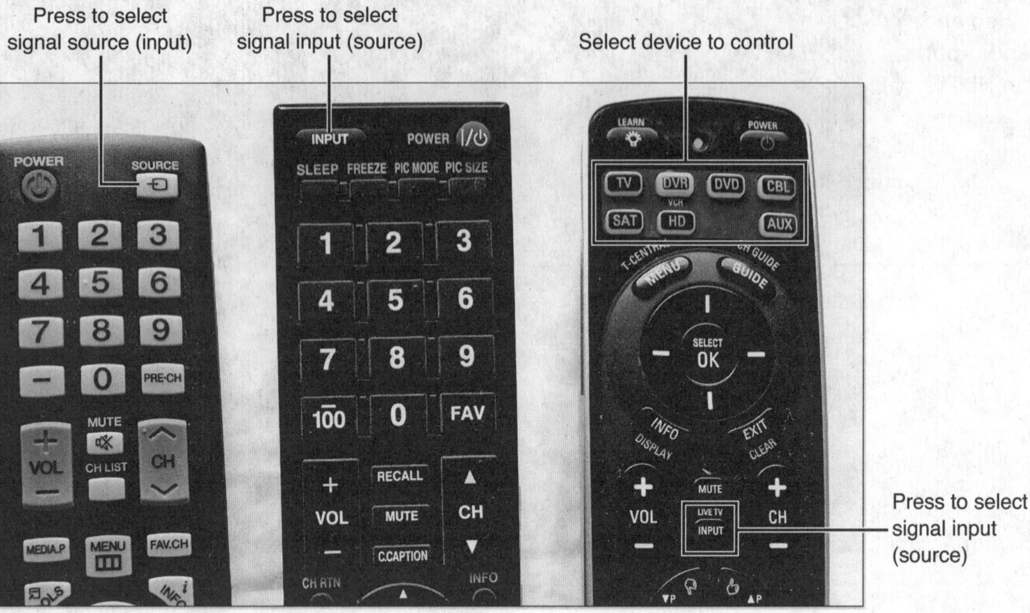

Figure 12.3
Typical HDTV remotes.

> **Tip**
> With a universal remote such as the Philips one shown in Figure 12.3, select TV before using the Input button.

Figure 12.4 illustrates a typical HDTV input menu. Some HDTVs, like the Samsung model shown in Figure 12.4, list in-use and inactive connections separately.

With projectors, you can select the video source manually, but most projectors will scan each port for a signal when they're turned on and stop scanning when a signal is detected.

If you can't see input from a video source, check the following:

- Is the device turned on?
- Is the cable properly attached to the device?

- Is the cable properly attached to the HDTV or projector?
- Have you selected the correct input? Most HDTVs have two or more HDMI connections, and some have multiple component or composite connections. Try another input until you find the correct one.

Figure 12.4
Selecting an input on an HDTV.

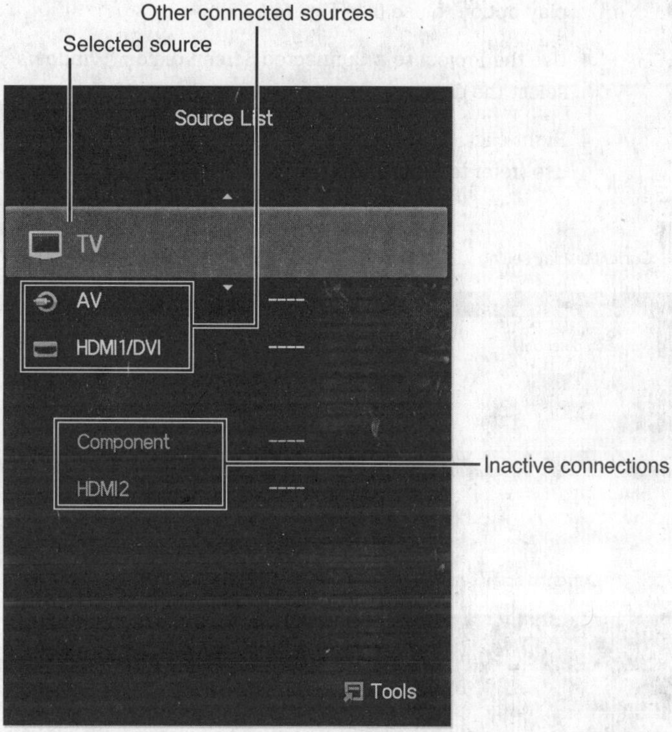

If you are connecting a Windows computer or tablet to your HDTV or projector, you must also configure Windows correctly before you can see the Windows Start screen or Desktop on your HDTV or projector.

Tip

On some HDTVs, only one of the HDMI connections, often port 1, can be used for connection to a computer. If you are unable to see the connection from a computer on your HDTV, make sure you are using the recommended port for your computer. If necessary, move other device cables to different HDMI ports to free up the recommended port.

Detecting HDTV, Projector or Additional Monitor with Windows

With Windows, you can use the following methods to connect to an HDTV, projector, or additional monitor:

- Use the Connect to a Projector dialog (Windows 7). Press the Windows key+P and select the display option to use (see Figure 12.5).
- Use the Project to a Connected Screen dialog (Windows 8/8.1). Press the Windows key+P and select the display option to use (see Figure 12.6).
- Right-click the Windows 7 or 8/8.1 desktop, select **Screen Resolution**, and select the option to use (refer to Figure 12.7).

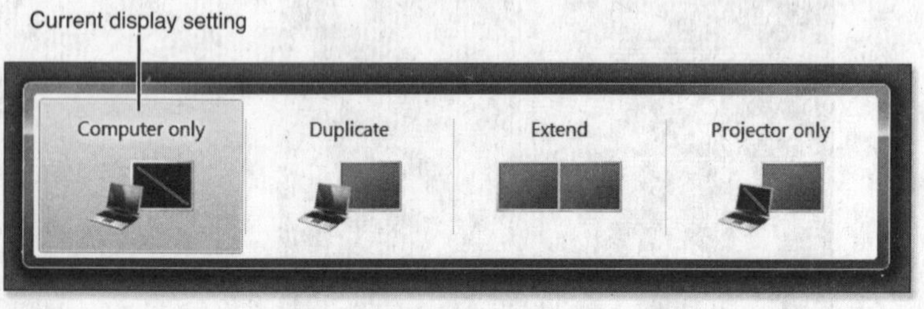

Figure 12.5
Using the Connect to a Projector dialog in Windows 7.

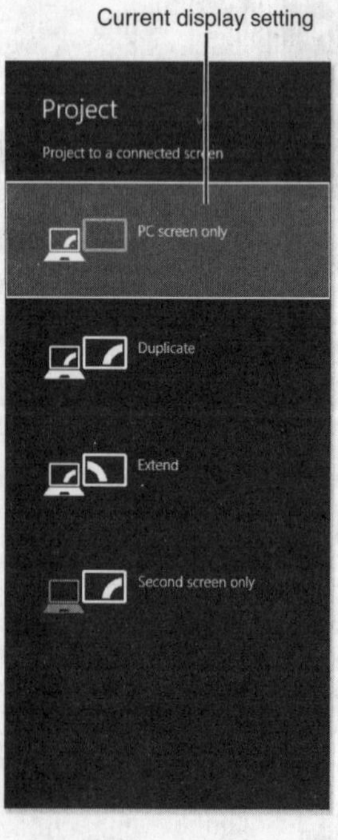

Figure 12.6
Using the Project to a Connected Screen dialog in Windows 8/8.1.

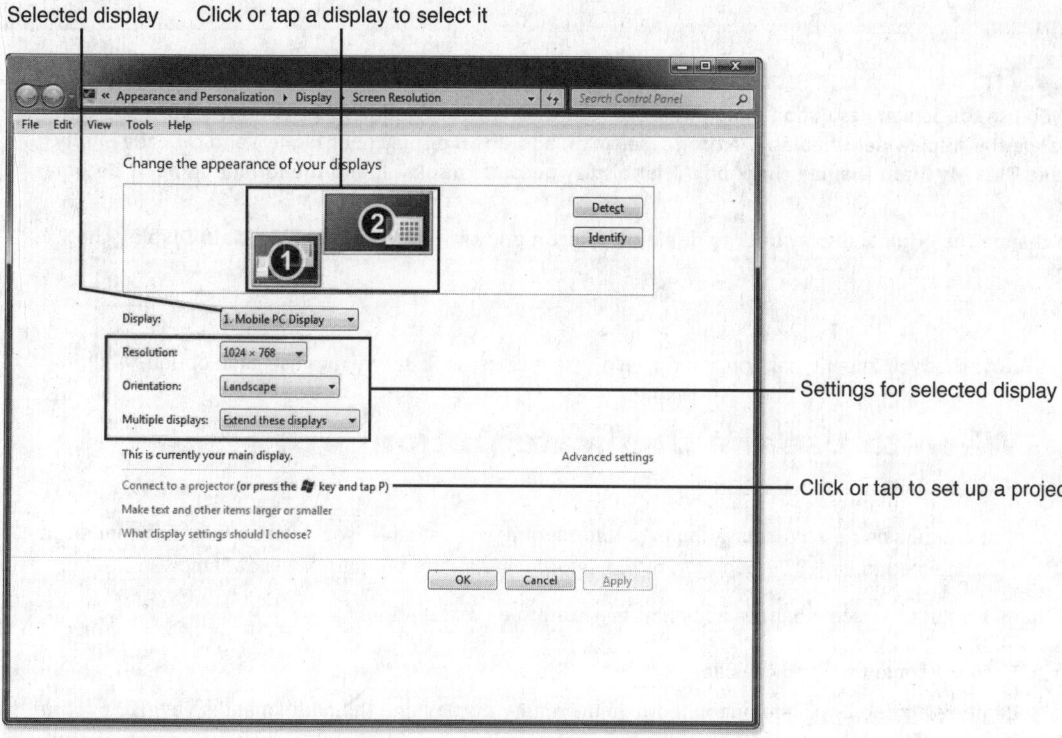

Figure 12.7

Using the Screen Resolution dialog (Windows 7 version shown) to set up an HDTV or projector.

From these dialogs shown, you have the following options:

- **Use the Computer (PC) Screen Only**—Choose this option to turn off output to your HDTV, projector, or additional monitor.
- **Duplicate**—Choose this option to display the same program at the same resolution on the computer screen and HDTV, projector, or additional monitor.
- **Extend**—Choose this option to display separate programs in full screen or in Windows on each screen or projector. The resolution of each display can be different.
- **Projector Only or Second Screen Only**—Choose this option to turn off output to your computer's built-in or primary display.
- **Show Desktop Only on 1**—Choose this option to use only the display identified as 1.

> **Note**
>
> You can also open the Connect to a Projector or Project to a Connected Screen dialogs from the Screen Resolution dialog (refer to Figure 12.7).
>
> These same options work in the same way to set up and configure an additional computer display.

- **Show Desktop Only on 2**—Choose this option to use only the display identified as 2.

> **Tip**
>
> If you use the Screen Resolution dialog (refer to Figure 12.7) with Windows 7 or Windows 8/8.1, you can change the display identified as 1. To do so, select an additional display (2 or higher) and click the empty **Make This My Main Display** check box. That display becomes display 1, and the former display 1 becomes display 2.
>
> To change the original display back to display 1, select it and click its **Make This My Main Display** check box.

Now that you know what you can do, let's take a closer look at when to use each option.

When to Use the Duplicate Option

Use the Duplicate option when

- You are using both displays to share information—for example, you have an informational kiosk connected to an HDTV, monitor, or projector facing a different part of the audience.
- You need to see what the audience sees during a presentation.

Here are some issues to consider:

If you select the Duplicate option, both your primary display and the additional display (HDTV, projector, or monitor) will be set to the same resolution. In Figure 12.8, we compare the resolutions of the laptop display and an additional display before and after duplicating the displays.

If your primary display and HDTV or projector don't use the same recommended resolution (as in Figure 12.8), this can cause problems.

If you are using this setup for a presentation, the resolution selected for the projector might not be the best possible setting. For example, if you are connecting to a projector that has 800x600 recommended resolution, you will need to select 1024x768 for both your display and projector if you want to be able to run Windows and Windows software adequately. The projector will use image compression to display higher-resolution signals, and you might need to increase text size using the Make Text and Other Items Larger or Smaller menu to compensate.

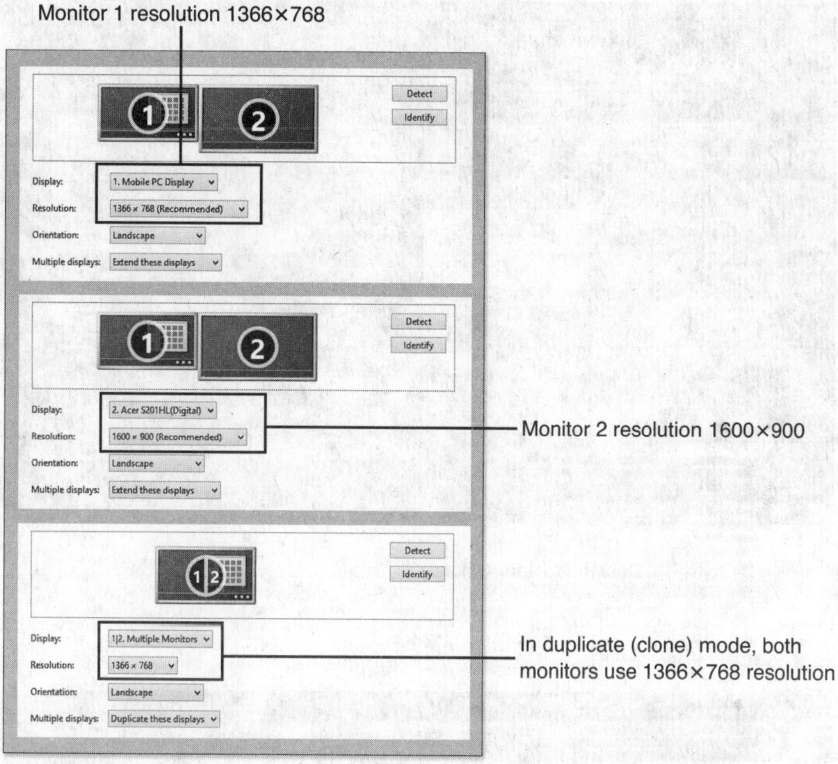

Figure 12.8 When you use Duplicate on displays with different resolutions, the lower resolution is used for both displays.

When to Use the Extend These Displays Option

Use the Extend These Displays option when you

- Need to see speaker notes or other content while displaying a presentation
- Want to use the higher-resolution display at maximum resolution
- Need to run different apps on each display

If you use Extend These Displays with a slide show app and you want to run the slide show on the extended desktop, make sure the app can be set to run on an extended display, or use the option to switch display 1 and display 2, making your projector, HDTV, or monitor your primary display.

Adjusting the HDTV Desktop Size in Windows

HDTVs sometimes don't display the entire desktop or Start menu when used with Windows. This feature is known as Overscan. Compare the appearance of the Windows 8.1 Spring 2014 update Start screen on a laptop's built-in display (see Figure 12.9) with the way it appears on a typical 1080p HDTV (see Figure 12.10).

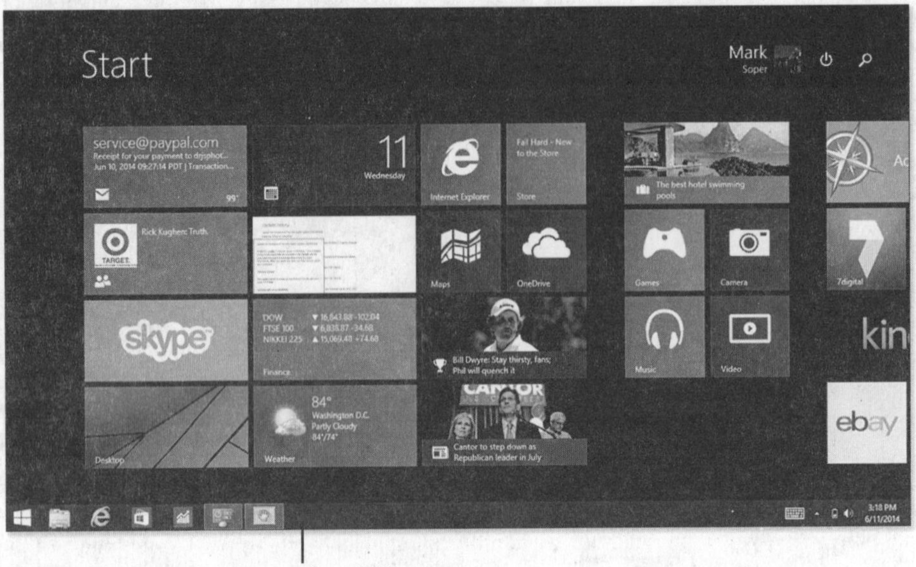

Figure 12.9 The Windows 8.1 Spring 2014 update Start screen on a 1366x768 laptop display.

Figure 12.10 The Windows 8.1 Spring 2014 update Start screen on a 1080 Full HD display.

Although the HDTV shows more icons because of its higher resolution, note that the icons are cut off on the right side and the Windows 8.1 desktop taskbar is missing in Figure 12.10 (compare it to Figure 12.14, this chapter, p.321).

Depending on the graphics card or integrated graphics your computer uses, you might be able to solve this problem. With computers running Intel integrated graphics (see Figure 12.11), you can select a custom scaling setting that will enable the entire Windows Start menu or Desktop to be visible.

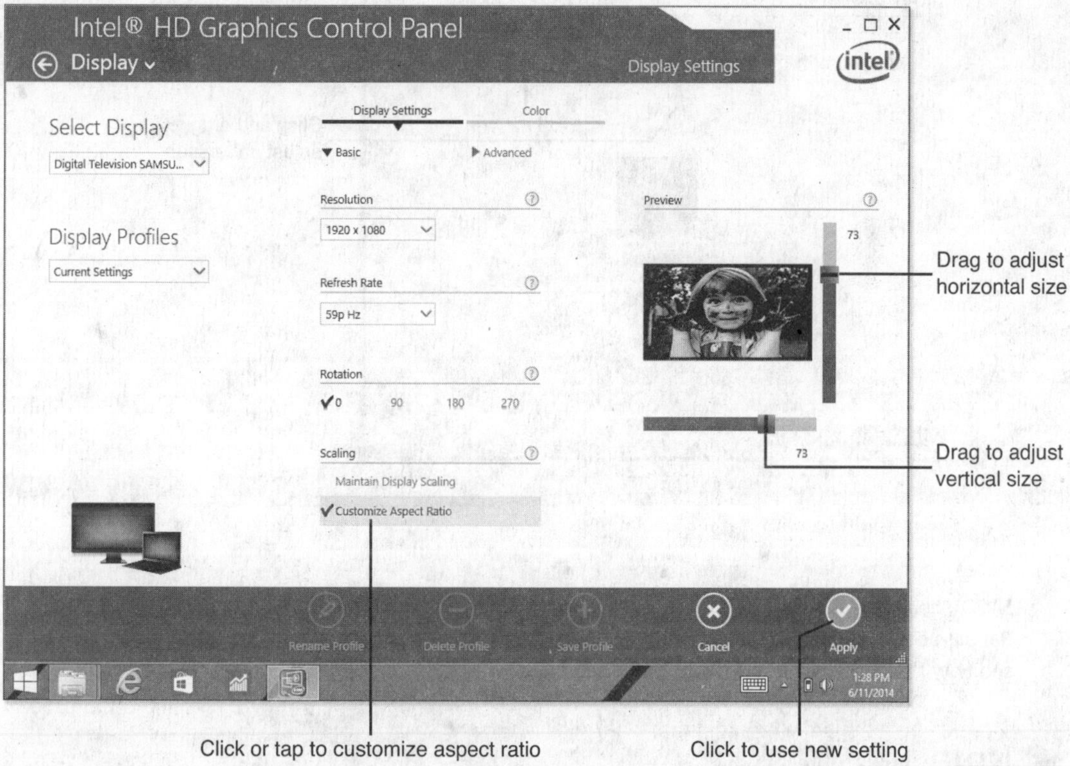

Figure 12.11
Selecting a custom scaling setting for horizontal and vertical resolution on a laptop equipped with Intel graphics.

On a computer using AMD VISION or RADEON graphics, use the AMD graphics configuration program to adjust the underscan of the HDTV (see Figure 12.12). Underscan reduces the size of the onscreen image.

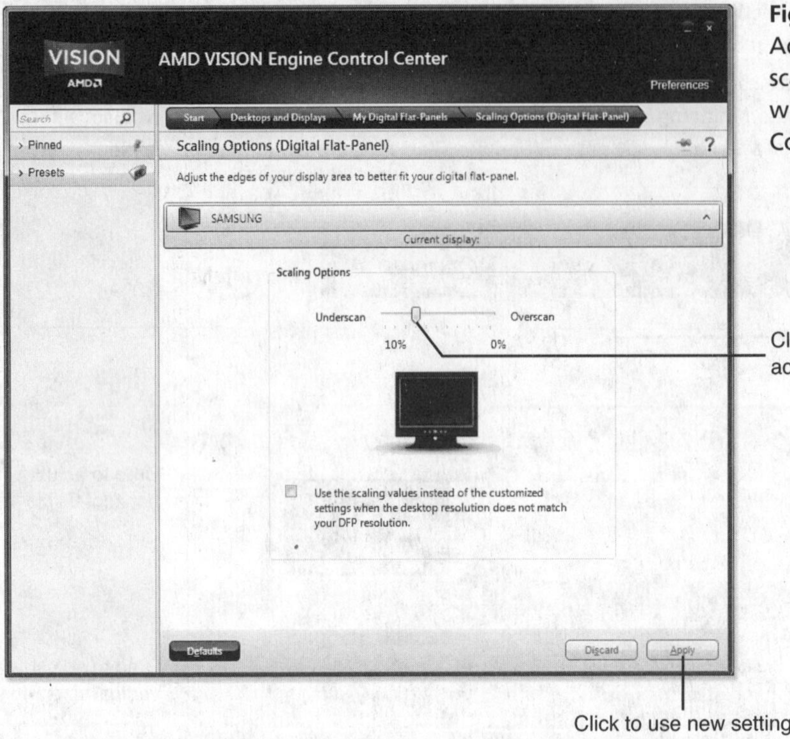

Figure 12.12
Adjusting the underscan setting for an HDTV with AMD VISION Engine Control Center.

NVIDIA-based computers use the Adjust Desktop Size and Position feature in the NVIDIA Control Panel to set up a custom resolution (see Figure 12.13). The green arrows in the corners help the user see how the changes affect the picture size.

Note

You can use the Underscan adjustment shown in Figure 12.12 if the HDTV is supported at its recommended ("native") resolution. If it is not, you can also create a custom resolution setting that will have a similar effect.

After making these changes, apply them and look at the HDTV's display. If you can now see the entire Start screen or Windows Desktop (see Figure 12.14), save your changes and use that setting from now on when you use that HDTV.

Tip

If your video driver lacks these adjustments, see if your HDTV has built-in overscan adjustment. See your HDTV's menus or instruction manual for details.

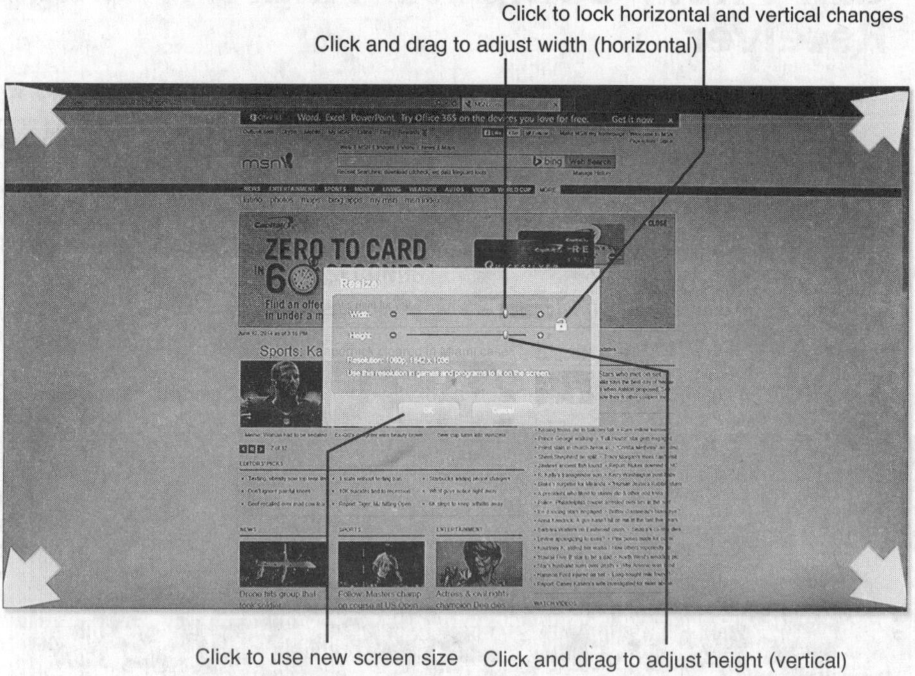

Figure 12.13 Using the NVIDIA Control Panel to create a custom resolution to remove overscan on an HDTV.

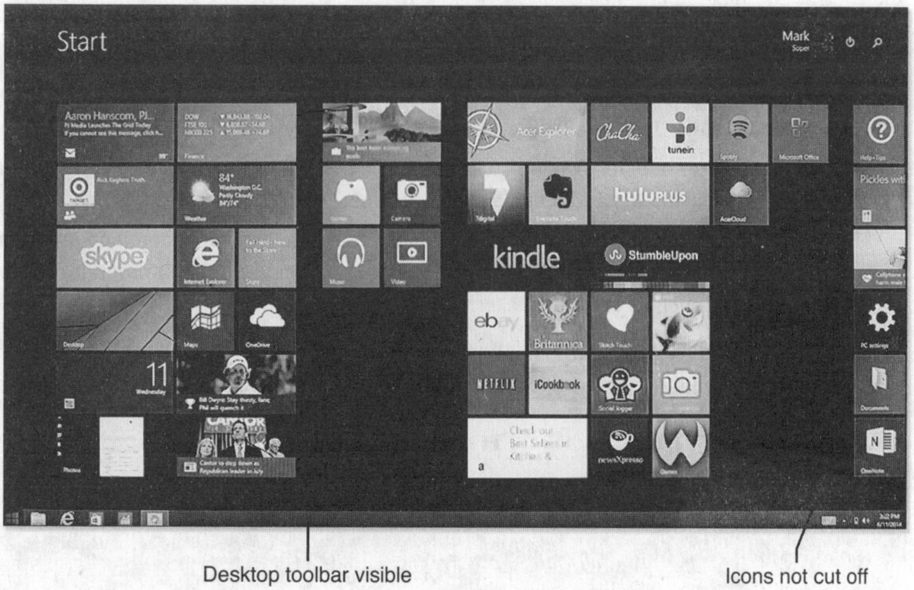

Figure 12.14 This HDTV now displays the full Windows 8.1 Start screen after adjustments to the display driver's HDTV settings.

Can't Hear Computer Audio Through AV Receiver

Whether you have an old receiver designed before the advent of HDMI ports (which carry both audio and video data) or a current model that's loaded with HDMI ports, hearing computer audio through your receiver depends on these factors:

- Correct cabling between your computer and your receiver.
- Correct configuration of Windows sound settings to use your receiver.

Figure 12.15 illustrates S/PDIF and analog audio jacks on a typical desktop computer.

Figure 12.15 Analog and digital audio jacks on a typical desktop computer's rear port cluster.

Connecting Analog Audio Ports to a Receiver

If your computer or your receiver lacks support for HDMI or the older S/PDIF digital audio standards, you need to use analog audio cables between your PC and your receiver.

On a desktop PC, connect the stereo mini-jack port (usually color-coded lime green) mini-jack port on the sound card or integrated audio section of the port cluster to an appropriate set of stereo jacks on your receiver, such as the Aux jacks.

On a laptop or tablet, use the headphone jack if a separate stereo jack is not available.

A mini-jack to RCA stereo cable (see Figure 12.16) is the easiest way to make this connection.

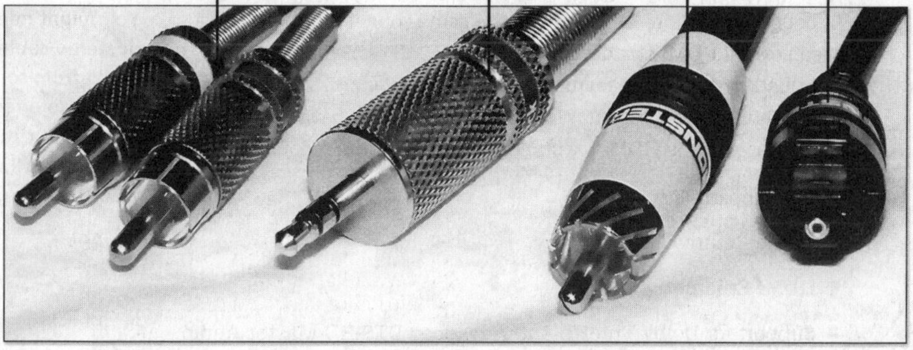

Figure 12.16 Analog and digital audio cables.

Connecting Digital Audio to a Receiver

Many computers also offer one or more ways to output digital audio to a receiver. These include

- HDMI (carries both audio and video signals)
- S/PDIF coaxial
- S/PDIF optical

> **Note**
> The Sony/Philips Digital Interface (S/PDIF or SPDIF) standard supports both coaxial and optical connections. Some sound cards and integrated audio include both types of connectors.

S/PDIF Coaxial

The S/PDIF coaxial cable (refer to Figure 12.16) uses an RCA connector similar to those used by stereo analog audio cables, but the cable is heavier. You push it into place.

S/PDIF Optical

The S/PDIF optical cable (refer to Figure 12.16) is a fiber optic cable. The connectors on each end of the cable are protected with caps that must be removed before the cable can be used. The optical connector on an HDTV or receiver (refer to Figure 12.1) has a hinged door to protect against dust. Push the cable until it snaps into place.

> **Note**
> On a computer, the S/PDIF optical connector is usually covered with a removable cap. Remove the cap to make the connector shown in Figure 12.1 visible.

HDMI

An HDMI cable (refer to Figure 12.2) can carry digital audio and digital video at the same time.

Although all versions of HDMI use the same connector, there have been several HDMI standards over time. HDMI cables are now identified by supported features, rather than by standards, because some features are optional. We recommend cables that meet the key features of the HDMI 1.4 standard, including the following:

- 3D compatibility
- Audio Return Channel
- HDMI Ethernet
- Support for Dolby TrueHD and Advanced DTS-HD Master Audio

> **Note**
> You might need to use S/PDIF or stereo cables to transmit audio from some Blu-ray players to a receiver. To learn more about HDMI standards, see the HDMI website at www.hdmi.org.

Selecting the Correct Audio Output Type on Your PC

Some computers automatically detect the correct audio output to use when you connect to a receiver via HDMI. However, other types of audio output must be selected manually. From the Control Panel in Windows 7 or Windows 8/8.1, follow this procedure:

1. Click or tap **Hardware and Sound**.
2. In the Sound category, click or tap **Manage Audio Devices**.
3. Click or tap a playback device on the Playback tab (see Figure 12.17).
4. To make the selected device your default, click or tap **Set Default**.
5. Click **Apply**, then **OK** to use your new selection.

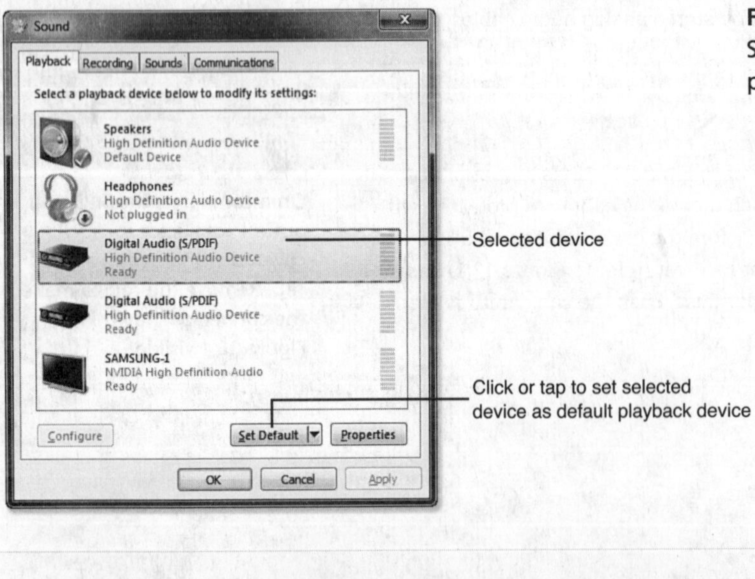

Figure 12.17
Selecting a digital audio output (S/PDIF) on a PC.

Selecting the Correct Speaker Configuration on Your PC

Depending on the audio type you select, you might need to select the correct speaker configuration. S/PDIF devices support stereo speakers. However, other types of audio might support up to seven speakers plus a subwoofer.

To select the correct speaker configuration, click the **Configure** button shown in Figure 12.17 when it's available. Select the number of speakers your audio output is connected to (see Figure 12.18). Use the **Test** button to play a sequence of notes through each speaker. To test a specific speaker, click it.

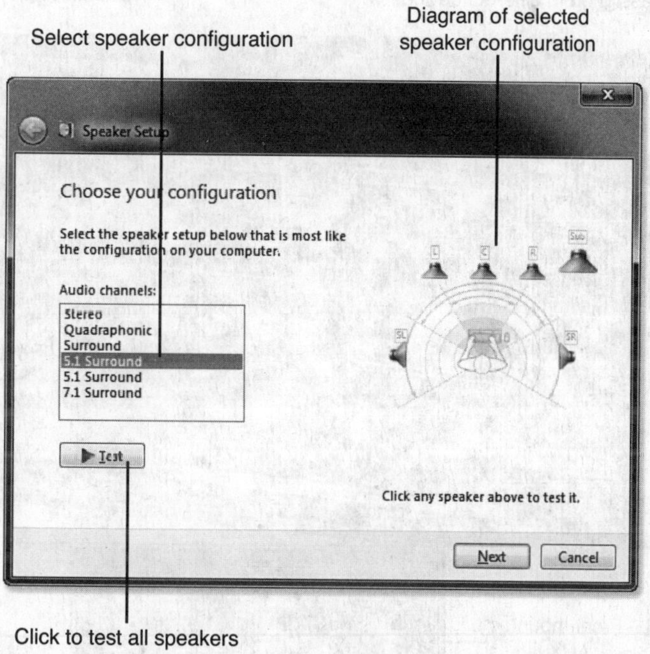

Figure 12.18
Selecting and testing a 5.1 surround audio speaker configuration.

Note

There are two 5.1 surround configurations shown in Figure 12.18; one for side-facing speakers and one for front-facing speakers.

If you use full-range speakers (speakers without a subwoofer), select that option from the next dialog.

Selecting the Correct Input Type on Your Receiver

The previous section's instructions apply whether you are connecting directly to speakers or through a receiver. However, if you are connecting to a receiver, you must also select the correct input type on your receiver.

As Figure 12.19 indicates, a typical receiver has several inputs ready for different types of audio and video connections. Most of them are on the rear, but many receivers also feature front-mounted inputs.

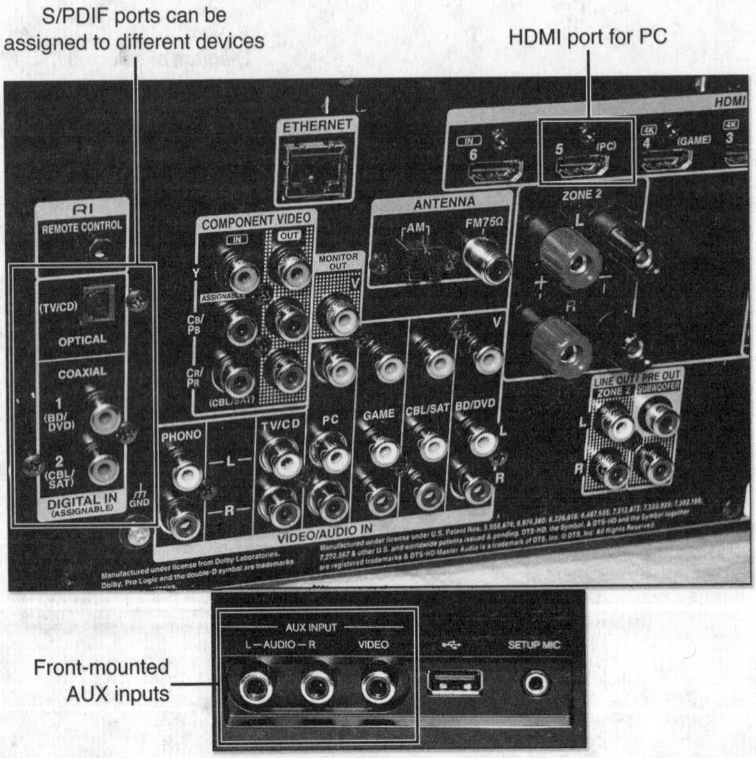

Figure 12.19
Front and rear A/V input/output connections on an Onkyo 7.2 receiver.

Some connections are very simple. For example, if your PC has an HDMI port, connect it to HDMI port #5, labeled (PC) in Figure 12.19. However, if you want to connect the S/PDIF port on your PC or other device to the receiver, connect it to either the Optical or one of the Coaxial ports on the left side of Figure 12.19.

If you use an assignable connection (a connection that can be used by various devices), you must use the receiver's setup program to specify which device uses that connection.

After you connect your device to the appropriate input and assign that input (if necessary), you must select the correct input on the receiver. You can use either the front-panel controls or the receiver's remote control. If you select the wrong input, you will not hear your computer or other device.

Note

For ports labeled as "Assignable," such as S/PDIF ports, you must use the receiver's setup menus to select the input that will be used for the port. See your receiver's instruction manual for details.

I Want to Play Music on My iOS Device Through My Receiver

Your receiver is a great way to enjoy your music. Depending on your receiver, there are many ways to make a connection: audio cable, docking device, Bluetooth, Apple Airplay, or Wi-Fi.

Tip

If you can't hear anything coming from your home theater system after you connect your device and start playing a song, check the volume controls on both your receiver/sound bar and your device.

Using an Audio or USB Cable

The headphone or earbud jack or the USB charging port on your iPhone, iPod, or iPad are the easiest ways to connect to higher-quality sound. Just plug in your device, select the appropriate output on your receiver, and select the music you want to play.

Caution

On some receivers, the USB connection does not work with your tablet or smartphone: it is reserved for USB storage devices. Be sure to check the receiver's specifications to determine what types of devices the USB port supports.

Some receivers don't have a mini-jack port for your tablet or smartphone. If RCA input connections are available, you can use a stereo RCA to mini-jack adapter.

Using a Docking Device

Docking devices for iOS devices are available in many varieties, including those that enable your iOS device to connect to a receiver. If you have an iOS device with a 30-pin connector for the USB charging cable, you have more choices than those with the newer Lightning connector.

As an alternative, most late-model AV receivers now support Bluetooth or Wi-Fi wireless connections. If you have a mixture of 30-pin and Lightning connection iOS devices, using Bluetooth or Wi-Fi avoids connection issues.

Using Bluetooth on iOS

If your receiver has Bluetooth capability, use your device's Bluetooth feature to connect to it and play your audio:

1. Select your music track.
2. Enable Bluetooth on your device.
3. Select **Bluetooth** on your receiver.
4. Pair the devices.
5. Open your device's Control Center (see Figure 12.20).
6. Select **Bluetooth**.
7. Tap **Play** to enjoy your music.

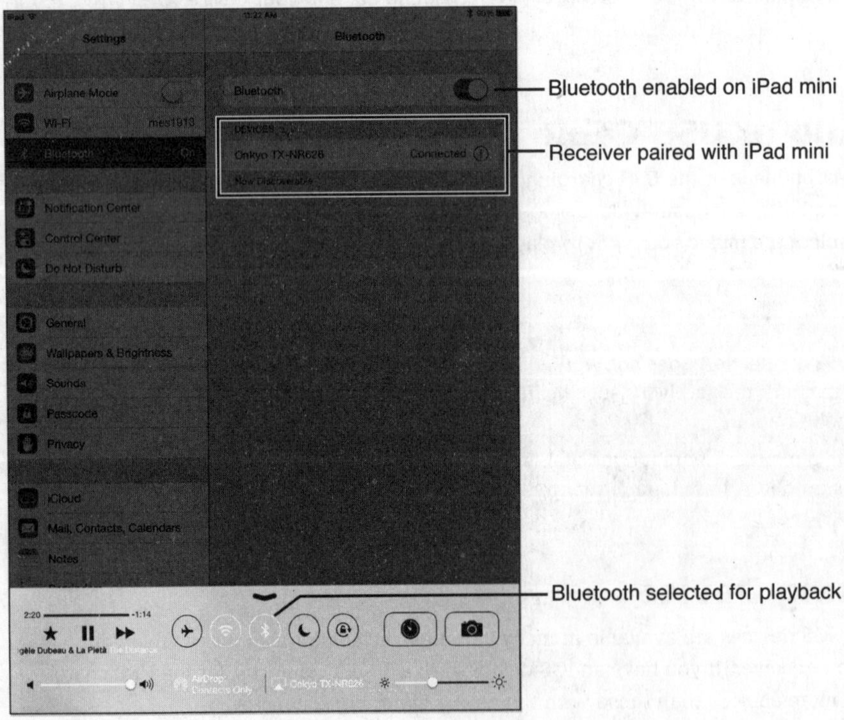

Figure 12.20 Playing music on an iPad Mini using Bluetooth.

Note

The iOS Control Center is opened by swiping up from the bottom of the screen. You can use it to select a connection to other devices and control media playback. To learn more, see http://support.apple.com/kb/HT5858.

Apple AirPlay

Apple's AirPlay technology, originally developed for Apple TV, is supported by many late-model AV receivers for music playback. AirPlay provides better audio quality than Bluetooth and enables playback of music from a greater distance than Bluetooth. Use the Control Center to select a device to stream to (see Figure 12.21).

Using Wi-Fi

If your AV receiver supports Wi-Fi and offers a remote control app for your iOS device, you can use your iPhone, iPad, or iPod Touch to control your receiver. To connect to your receiver with Wi-Fi:

1. Connect your receiver to the same Wi-Fi network used by your device.
2. Turn on your device's Wi-Fi capability.
3. Install the remote control app for your receiver (or a compatible third-party app) from the App Store.
4. Detect your receiver with the app.
5. Use the app to stream music from your iOS device or other supported devices, control your receiver, and play Internet radio.

I Want to Play a Movie on My iOS Device Through a Home Theater System

IOS devices don't have an HDMI port, so to stream movies or other video content from your device to an HDTV, you must connect to your receiver or HDTV via a device that has an HDMI port. Your options include Apple AV cable, Apple TV, third-party docking devices, or third-party software that supports Apple's AirPlay technology. Let's take a look at each of them in turn.

Apple AV Cable and Compatible Cable and Docking Products

The least expensive Apple-branded hardware device you can use to connect your iOS devices to a home theater system or HDTV is the appropriate version of the Apple AV cable:

- **Apple composite AV Cable**—Composite video and stereo audio cables that use RCA jacks (refer to Figures 12.2 and 12.16) for 30-pin iOS devices. This is suitable for use with AV receivers that have an AUX port, SDTVs, or DVD players that have a composite input.

- **Apple 30-pin digital AV adapter**—HDMI A/V port (refer to Figure 12.2) and 30-pin charging port.
- **Apple 30-pin to VGA adapter**—VGA port and 30-pin charging port.
- **Lightning digital AV adapter**—HDMI A/V port and Lightning charging port.
- **Lightning to VGA adapter**—VGA port and Lightning charging port. This is suitable for use with older HDTVs that lack HDMI ports or with computer displays.

> **Note**
> For detailed compatibility information about the different models of Apple AV cables, see http://support.apple.com/kb/ht4108. These devices automatically send video or mirror your display when you connect them to a supported display. Select the appropriate input on your HDTV or AV receiver.

There are many third-party equivalents to the 30-pin digital AV adapter, and some vendors also offer docking products that enable your iOS device to stand upright while being connected and charged.

> **Caution**
> Beware of fake and counterfeit products, particularly 30-pin versions. Also, note that playback of certain types of content, especially protected content, doesn't always work with either Apple or third-party HDMI adapters. Read reviews carefully.

Apple TV

Apple TV offers a number of advantages over HDMI adapters. These include

- Hardware-based HDMI, rather than using DLNA converted to HDMI, for better compatibility with protected content.
- S/PDIF optical connector for digital music for use with home theater systems or TVs that don't support audio through HDMI.
- Wi-Fi or wired Ethernet connections to your home network.
- Support for both 2.4GHz and 5GHz Wireless-N networking, so it's also compatible with all other wireless networks (A, B, G, AC).
- AirPlay support for streaming video and audio from major streaming vendors such as Netflix, Amazon Prime, Hulu, and others.
- Streaming media from Windows PCs and MacOS devices.

You can configure Apple TV with your iPad 3 or later or iPhone 4s or later using Bluetooth (see http://support.apple.com/kb/HT5900 for details) or with the included remote. Using your iOS device via Bluetooth is easier than using the remote, because Apple TV can read your network configuration from your device.

In either case, you will need to have your iTunes Store username and password and the usernames and passwords for any third-party streaming media services you want to set up.

Using AirPlay and Mirroring

After you connect your iOS device via Apple TV, you need to select that device for streaming or mirroring. Here's how to do it with iOS 7 or later:

1. Flick the bottom of the screen upward to open Control Center (refer to Figure 12.20).
2. Open the AirPlay menu.
3. Tap **Apple TV**.
4. After selecting the media you want to play, click **Play** and the media will play through your Apple TV device.
5. To mirror your iOS device screen on the display connected to Apple TV, enable mirroring (see Figure 12.21).

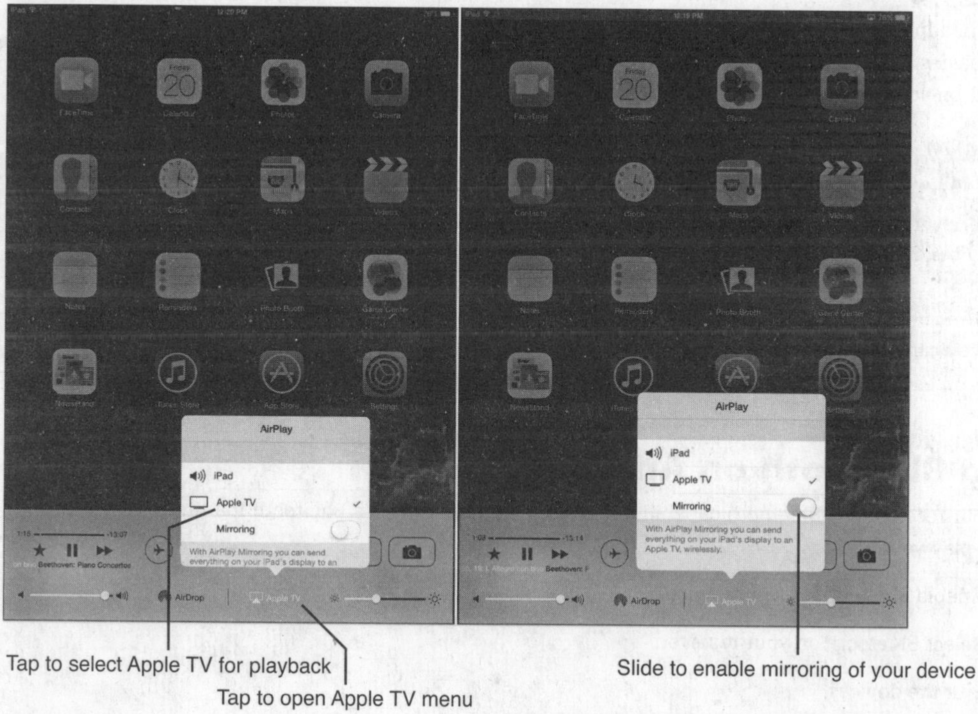

Figure 12.21
Using Apple TV to stream (left) or mirror (right) content to a home theater system.

I Want to Play Music on My Android Device Through a Home Theater System

Android devices, like iOS devices, can connect to your receiver in a variety of ways: audio cable, Bluetooth, or Wi-Fi.

Tip

If you can't hear anything coming from your home theater system after you connect your device and start playing a song, check the volume controls on both your receiver/sound bar and your device.

Using an Audio or USB Cable

The headphone or earbud jack or the USB charging port on your Android smartphone or tablet are the easiest ways to connect to higher-quality sound. Just plug in your device, select the appropriate input on your receiver, and select the music you want to play.

Caution

On some receivers, the USB connection does not work with your tablet or smartphone: it is reserved for USB storage devices. Be sure to check the receiver's specifications to determine what types of devices the USB port supports.

Some receivers don't have a mini-jack port for your tablet or smartphone. If RCA input connections are available, you can use a stereo RCA to miniplug adapter.

Using Bluetooth on Android

If your receiver has Bluetooth capability, use your Android device's Bluetooth feature to connect to it and play your audio:

1. Enable Bluetooth on your device.
2. Select Bluetooth on your receiver.
3. Pair the devices.
4. Enable Media audio for the paired receiver.
5. Select the track to play.
6. Tap **Play** to enjoy your music.

Using Wi-Fi on Android

If your AV receiver supports Wi-Fi and offers a remote control app for your Android device, you can use your Android device to control your receiver. To connect to your receiver with Wi-Fi:

1. Connect your receiver to the same Wi-Fi network used by your device.
2. Turn on your device's Wi-Fi capability.
3. Install the remote control app for your receiver (or a compatible third-party app) from Google Play.
4. Detect your receiver with the app.
5. Use the app to stream music from your Android device or other media servers on your network, control your receiver, and play Internet radio (see Figure 12.22).

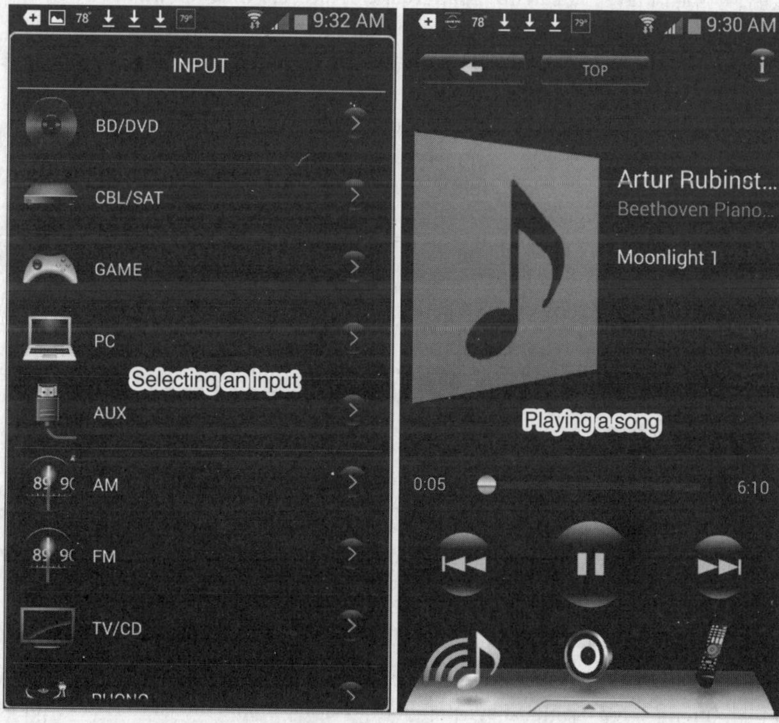

Figure 12.22
Using the Onkyo AV receiver remote app.

I Want to Play a Movie on My Android Device Through a Home Theater System

Android devices offer three ways to play back video stored on the device:

- If you have a tablet with a mini-HDMI (also known as HDMI Type C) connector, you can use a mini-HDMI to HDMI cable to play back content directly from your tablet to most HDTVs or AV receivers.
- If you have a smartphone that supports mobile high-definition link (MHL), you can buy a cable that attaches your smartphone to an AV receiver, HDTV, Blu-ray disc player, or other media device that supports MHL.
- If you have an Apple TV box or other device that supports AirPlay, you can get apps from Google Play that can be used to stream video from your device. For example, the free version of the AppleTVMedia player from Zappotv.com plays videos and photos stored on your device and YouTube videos. Low-cost add-ons provide support for playing media located on Windows streaming media servers on your home network.

Note

MHL-compatible devices might use a proprietary cable, a micro-USB to HDMI cable, or an MHL cable. See your device's documentation or vendor website for details.

The Google Chromecast device, rather than playing back content stored on your Android device, allows you to view Netflix, YouTube, or other supported streaming video services on an HDTV or AV receiver.

Note

Learn more about Google Chromecast at www.google.com/intl/en/chrome/devices/chromecast/

I Can't Sync Music with my iOS or Android Device

You can enjoy music from Internet radio stations with your iOS or Android device, but if you prefer to create your own playlist from your own digital music tracks, you will need to sync your device, using iTunes (iOS) or the sync software provided with your Android device.

Troubleshooting Syncing to an iOS Device

You can use iTunes to sync your existing music tracks to iTunes either via USB or wirelessly. iTunes might have problems syncing your existing music tracks to iTunes for several reasons:

- iTunes doesn't know where your files are located.
- Your music is in an unsupported format.
- You need to enable the sidebar.
- You need to enable Wi-Fi syncing.

Selecting Your Entire Music Library with iTunes

When you install iTunes on a Windows PC, it creates the iTunes\iTunes Music folder in your Music library. To enable the entire Music library to be recognized for syncing, follow these steps:

1. Start iTunes.
2. Select **Music** as the library type.
3. Click or tap **File**.
4. Click or tap **Add Folder to Library**.
5. Navigate to the Libraries view.
6. Select the **Music** library.
7. Click or tap **Select Folder** (see Figure 12.23).
8. iTunes will add the folders in your **Music** library to its library.

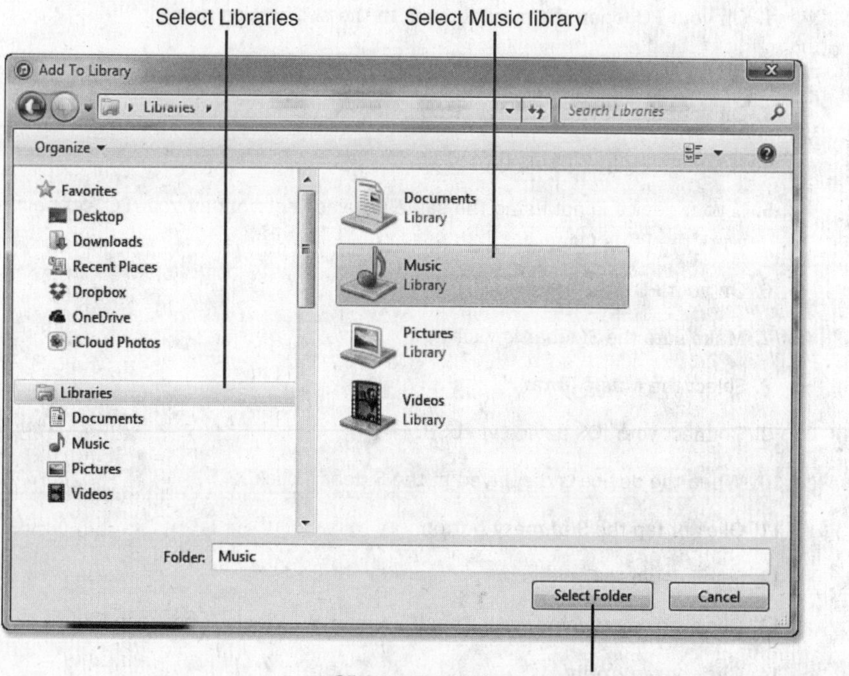

Figure 12.23 Adding the Windows 7 Music library to the iTunes Music library.

All files are copied into the iTunes\iTunes Music folder using the same folder structure as the original files.

Converting Files During Sync

During the sync process, any Windows Media Audio (WMA) files in your folders are converted to Apple's AAC format (.m4a) during the copy process. Your original files are unchanged. MP3 files are copied, but no conversion is necessary.

Displaying the Sidebar

The Sidebar displays playlists and iOS devices. To make the Sidebar visible, do the following:

1. Click or tap **View**.
2. Click or tap **Show Sidebar**.

Syncing via Wi-Fi

Before you can sync via Wi-Fi, you must enable this feature in iTunes and on your iOS device. Here's how:

1. On your PC, open the network icon in the notification area.
2. Note the name of the wireless network the computer is using.
3. On your iOS device, open **Settings**.
4. Make sure that Wi-Fi is turned on.
5. If your device is not using the same wireless network as your PC, connect to the wireless network the PC is using.
6. On your PC, start iTunes.
7. Make sure the Sidebar is visible.
8. Select the **Music library**.
9. Connect your iOS device via USB.
10. When the device is displayed in the Sidebar, click it.
11. Click or tap the **Summary** button.
12. Scroll down to Options.
13. Click the empty **Sync with This iPad over Wi-Fi** check box (see Figure 12.24).
14. Click or tap **Apply**.
15. Disconnect your iOS device from USB. The device should continue to be visible in the Sidebar.
16. When your device is visible in the Sidebar, you can drag items to its libraries.

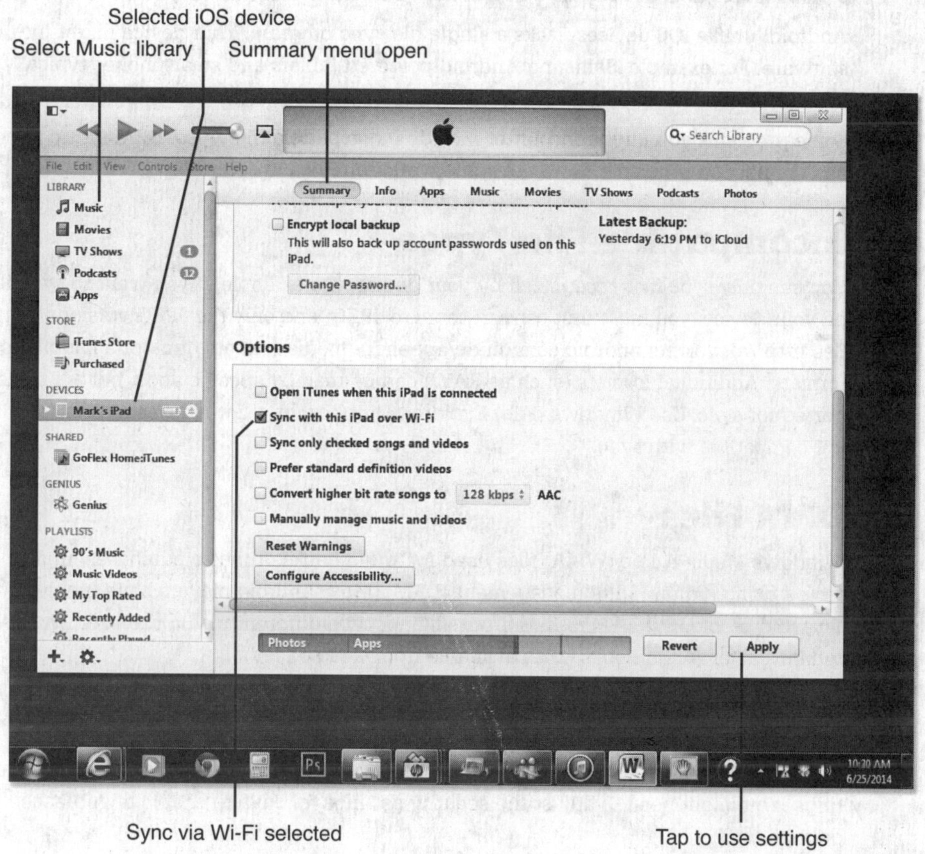

Figure 12.24 Configuring iTunes and an iOS device for sync via Wi-Fi.

Caution

Wi-Fi synchronization doesn't always work. To troubleshoot Wi-Fi syncing, see http://support.apple.com/kb/ts4062. Additional solutions suggested by some users include the following:

- Stop and restart services used by iTunes on a Windows PC: Bonjour and those listed in http://support.apple.com/kb/HT3960.
- Try a different wireless network (note: both your computer and your iOS device must always use the same wireless network).
- Use a different wireless router or get a firmware update for your router.

If you cannot get Wi-Fi synchronization to work reliably, we recommend using USB sync.

Troubleshooting Syncing to an Android Device

Android, unlike iOS devices, lacks a single file sync program. Your device might include file sync software. For example, Samsung Android-powered tablets and smartphones typically include Kies sync software. However, you can get additional sync apps from Google Play.

Some problems you might encounter include incompatible file types, DRM music or audio book files, and connection problems. Here are some workarounds and solutions:

Incompatible File Types

You can only sync files recognized by your device. For example, if you want to sync RAW photo files on your device, you must first convert them to JPEG, and only the JPEG versions can be synced. See http://developer.android.com/guide/appendix/media-formats.html for a list of supported media formats. Additional formats (such as RAW) can be read by specific apps, but are typically not supported for sync. Use Windows (File) Explorer, Dropbox, or other utilities to transfer file types that are not compatible with sync.

DRM Files

Windows Media Audio (WMA) files used for audio books or music purchases might be copy protected using digital rights management (DRM). Most Android players have problems with DRM files. To avoid problems, use MP3 files if possible, or try a different media player, such as VLC for Android or MortPlayer Audio Books (both available from Google Play).

Connection Problems

If you want to use a web-based wireless sync program, you might have problems with Java settings. You might need to adjust the security settings for Java to enable a web-based transfer program to work.

Selecting the Correct Settings for Ripping a CD

If you want to rip your CD collection for playback with a mobile device or desktop media players, you can use Windows Media Player. Before you rip your CDs, configure your rip settings:

1. Start Windows Media Player.
2. Click or tap **Tools**.
3. Click or tap **Options**.
4. Click or tap the **Rip Music** tab.
5. Select **MP3** as the format.
6. Adjust the size/quality slider.
7. If you want to rip each CD as soon as you insert it, click or tap the **Rip CD Automatically** check box.
8. Click **Apply**, and then **OK** (see Figure 12.25).

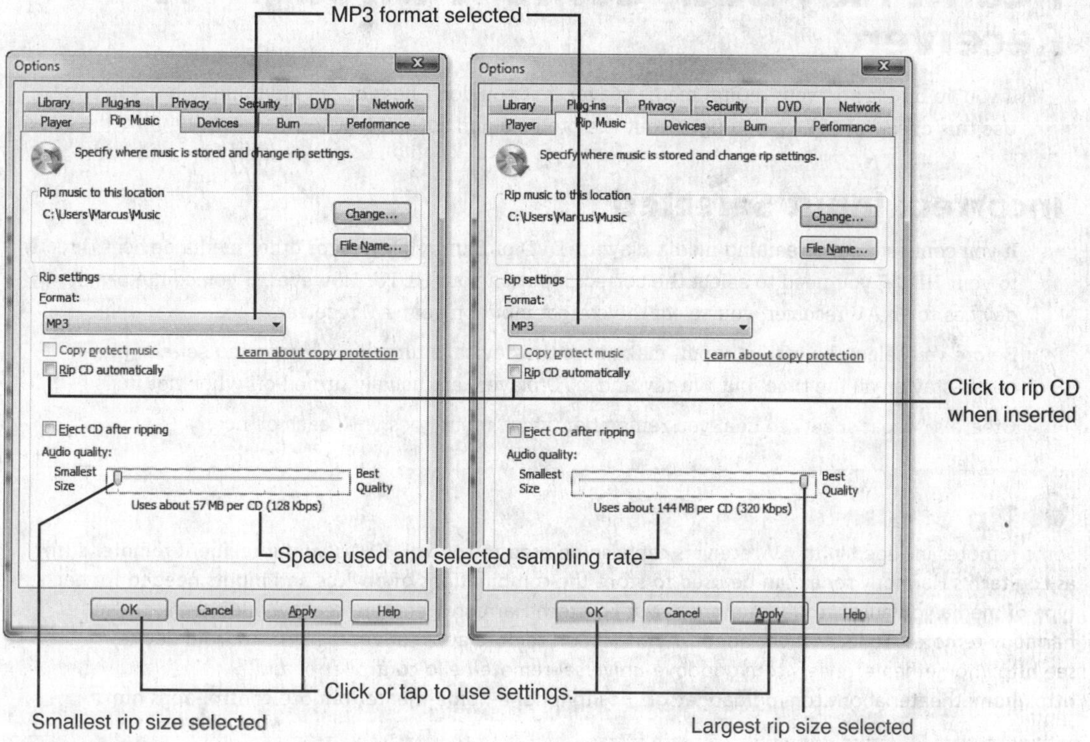

Figure 12.25
MP3 settings for ripping a CD with Windows Media Player.

When you insert your music CD and begin the rip process, these settings will be used for each track ripped from the CD to a digital music file.

Tip

If you plan to play your music through an AV receiver, select better quality (160Kbps or higher). If you plan to play your music using a portable device's own speakers or with earbuds, select smallest size (128Kbps). I typically rip at 320Kbps (best quality, largest file size). Some sync programs, such as iTunes, can reduce the size of music files during the sync process.

You can use iCloud, Google Play, or Wi-Fi–enabled storage devices to store your music in the cloud or off your device so you can use higher quality ripping without using up space on your device. For more about iCloud for iOS devices, see www.apple.com/icloud/features/. For more about Google Play, see https://play.google.com/about/music/allaccess/#/. For more about wireless media storage, see "File Sharing with Portable Devices," in Chapter 9, "Solving File Sharing Problems," p.229.

I Can't Play Back Content Through AV Receiver

If you've hit Play on your digital media player, but you don't hear or see anything, what's wrong? Use this checklist to help you figure out the problem and solve it fast.

Incorrect Input Selected

If you connect your streaming media players, DVD or Blu-ray players, or other media devices directly to your HDTV, you need to select the correct input on your HDTV. However, if you connect your devices to an AV receiver, you select the correct input on your AV receiver.

Before you select the correct input, make sure the device is turned on (streaming set-box player boxes stay on all the time, but Blu-ray and DVD players are usually turned off when not in use).

Create a "cheat sheet" to help you remember which input goes with each device.

> **Tip**
> Some remotes included with AV receivers can also be used to control HDTVs, and intelligent remotes such as Logitech's Harmony series can be used to store the combinations of devices and inputs needed for each type of media you enjoy. To learn more about Logitech Harmony remotes, see www.logitech.com/en-us/harmony-remotes. To learn more about multifunction remote apps for your iOS or Android device, see http://hometheaterreview.com/goodbye-universal-remote-hello-control-app/ and http://hometheater.about.com/od/gadgetsgizmos/tp/iphone-home-theater-remote-control-apps.htm.

Incorrect Cabling Between Devices

If your device uses a single HDMI cable to the AV receiver or HDTV, it's practically foolproof. However, if you are connecting multiple cables, there's a lot that can go wrong.

Take advantage of color-coded RCA connectors for stereo audio (red and white) and component video (red, green, blue). Most cables and device connectors use these standard color codes to make connection easier.

If your HDTV needs to use an S/PDIF return audio cable to the receiver, make sure it's plugged in correctly and that the receiver is properly configured to use it.

Loose Speaker Wires

If you lose one side of your stereo sound or the rear audio disappears after you've been enjoying surround-sound realism, check the speaker and the receiver for loose wires.

> **Tip**
> Be sure to leave some slack when you install or reinstall speaker wires so the receiver and speakers can be moved without putting stress on the wires.

Receiver or Device Muted

Both a receiver and mobile device can be muted, so if you don't hear any audio, make sure your devices are not muted. If none of the devices are muted, be sure to turn up the volume on both devices until you hear a comfortable audio level.

Content Not Supported

If you are unable to play a particular media file, make sure it is supported by the playback app or device. You can get apps for Windows and mobile devices to convert media files into different formats if necessary.

If the content uses DRM, you must play it back on the original device or obtain a license to play it on a different device. See the content vendor's website for details.

I Can't Play Back My Blu-ray Movies

Problems with Blu-ray movie playback can be caused by a variety of issues, such as the following:

- Not all devices used for playback support high-bandwidth digital copy protection (HDCP).
- Incorrect or loose cabling between player and HDTV or AV receiver.
- Outdated firmware.

Here's how to deal with these problems.

Checking Your Device for HDCP Support

If you are unable to play your Blu-ray discs through an AV receiver, but they play correctly when the Blu-ray player is connected directly to an HDTV, the AV receiver lacks HDCP support. Check for a firmware update for the receiver to add HDCP support. If you can't get one, use an S/PDIF cable from the Blu-ray player to carry digital audio, and use the receiver for audio only until you can replace it.

If you prefer to play Blu-ray media directly from your PC, some PC displays and video cards lack HDCP support. Cyberlink offers its BD & 3D Advisor app to check your computer's hardware support. Get it from http://www.cyberlink.com/prog/bd-support/diagnosis.do.

Checking the AV Cable Connections Between Your PC or Player and Your Display or HDTV

If you connect your Blu-ray player to your HDTV or AV receiver via component video rather than HDMI, your playback is limited to 480i (DVD quality) standards. Component video is no longer supported for Blu-ray playback. If you have an early HDTV that lacks HDMI ports, use it with DVD content, and get a newer model for use with your Blu-ray player.

Upgrading Firmware in Your Blu-ray Player

Because Blu-ray players and media use ever-changing versions of HDCP to protect content, a Blu-ray player might not be able to play the latest movies. You can avoid this problem by making sure to connect your Blu-ray player to your network and checking for updates periodically.

For older Blu-ray players that have upgradeable firmware but lack a network connection, check with your vendor for specific firmware upgrade instructions.

Note

The Blu-ray.com website has a listing of older devices and links for firmware updates at www.blu-ray.com/firmware/.

13

FIXING SLOW 3D GAMING

Fast Track to Solutions

Table 13.1 Symptom Table

Symptom	Flowchart or Book Section	Page #
My HDTV is blurry when I watch sports or fast action.	Faster-Response HDTVs	361
I'm thinking about a new video card for faster 3D, but I don't know what's installed right now.	Figure 13.1	344
How can I control the 3D settings for games that have no 3D settings inside the game?	AMD 3D Settings NVIDIA 3D Settings	346 348
I've installed a second NVIDIA card, but my 3D games don't run any better.	Enabling SLI	352
I've installed a second AMD card, but my 3D games don't run any better.	Enabling CrossFireX	354
How can I tell if I've over-clocked my graphics card too much?	Using Overclocking Software	356

Updating Drivers

3D graphics performance depends in large part on three factors:

- The performance of your card's graphics processing unit (GPU) chip, chipset-based integrated graphics, or CPU-integrated graphics
- The amount of RAM on your graphics card or available to integrated graphics
- The drivers used by your card or integrated graphics

Of these, the only one you can improve without replacing your existing graphics card is the third factor: graphics drivers.

Manufacturers update graphics drivers to improve performance for specific games and game engines, fix rendering problems, and improve stability. Here's how to update your drivers on a desktop computer with a separate (discrete) GPU:

1. Determine the manufacturer and model number of your computer's graphics chip (GPU). We recommend using TechPowerUp's GPU-Z available from www.techpowerup.com/downloads/SysInfo/GPU-Z/. Figure 13.1 illustrates GPU-Z's report on two computers, one with an AMD RADEON GPU and the other with an NVIDIA GeForce GTS GPU. On systems with two or more graphics cards installed, GPU-Z has a selection option at the bottom of the dialog so you can choose from the installed cards.

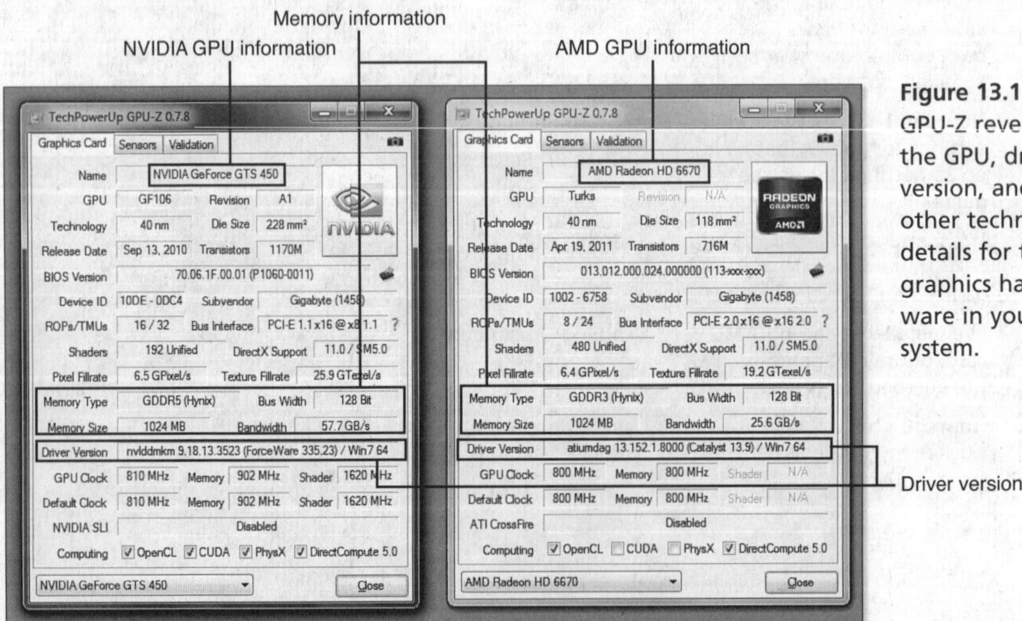

Figure 13.1 GPU-Z reveals the GPU, driver version, and other technical details for the graphics hardware in your system.

2. Download the latest version of the driver for your graphics hardware from the GPU or integrated graphics vendor website.
3. Install the driver. Reboot your system if prompted to complete the process.
4. Review the technical notes for any issues that might affect your software or system.

> **Tip**
> Both AMD and NVIDIA offer automatic detection of your hardware and selection of the best match for your hardware. Visit http://support.amd.com/en-us for AMD RADEON and VISION drivers. Visit www.nvidia.com for NVIDIA drivers. Graphics drivers are very large, so we recommend that you save them to your system before installing them.

If you have a laptop, an all-in-one touchscreen desktop computer, or a desktop computer that uses motherboard or GPU-integrated graphics, driver updates might be provided in two ways:

- By the computer manufacturer's website
- From the graphics hardware manufacturer's website

If you cannot get an update from the computer manufacturer's website, try the graphics hardware vendor's website.

If a graphics driver update fails or causes your system to be unstable, you can revert to your last-installed driver. Here's how:

1. Open Device Manager from the System properties sheet or Control Panel.
2. Expand the **Display adapters** category.
3. Double-click the display adapter to open its properties sheet.
4. Click the **Driver** tab.
5. Click the **Roll Back Driver** button (see Figure 13.2).
6. Click the **Close** (X) button to close each dialog after the rollback is complete.

Figure 13.2
Preparing to roll back a driver in Device Manager.

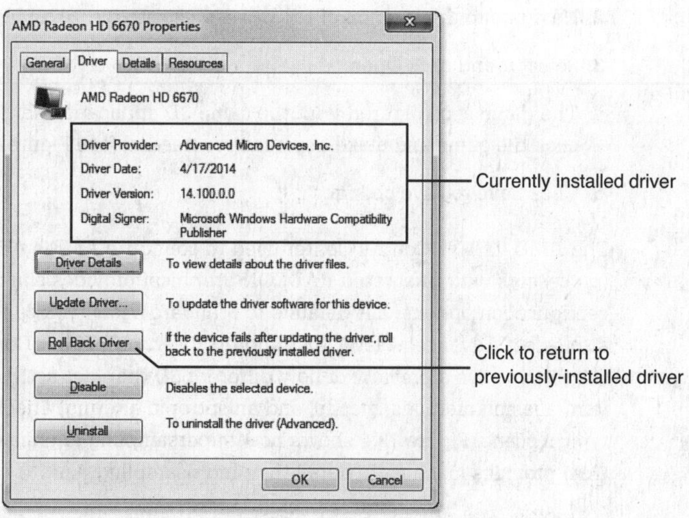

Adjusting 3D Settings

3D settings enable you to control the balance between lifelike objects and fast rendering. The more powerful your graphics hardware, the more likely it is that you can favor realism in rendering over rendering speed. Whatever your preference, here's how to make those adjustments.

> **Tip**
> Use the 3D settings dialog to set the options you plan to use most often. Use game-specific settings for particular games that need different settings than normal for better performance. If a game has settings that do the same job as the 3D graphics driver, let the application make the settings instead of the driver.

AMD 3D Settings

AMD provides two ways to adjust 3D settings:

- Manually through its CATALYST (for systems with AMD GPUs) or VISION (for systems with AMD APUs) control centers for all games.
- Automatically with AMD Gaming Evolved.

Here's how to use CATALYST to tweak overall 3D settings:

1. Right-click an empty portion of the Windows desktop and select **AMD Catalyst Control Center**.
2. Click **Gaming**.
3. Click **3D Application Settings**. The default menu preference is **Advanced View** (refer to Figure 13.3), but you can select **Standard View** (refer to Figure 13.4).
4. Scroll down through the 3D settings. To change a setting, click it and select the option desired.

You can also configure 3D settings for a particular game:

1. After opening the 3D Application Settings dialog, click the **Add** button.
2. Navigate to the location of the game's executable (.exe) file.
3. Select it and click **Open**.
4. The game is configured with the same 3D application settings set up for all games. To change it, click the game and make any changes needed (see Figure 13.3).
5. Click **Save** to save changes.

The AMD VISION Control Center used to configure AMD's APUs (processors with integrated RADEON graphics) provides similar configuration options, but defaults to Standard View (you can also select Advanced View). In Standard View with either Control Center, you see a preview of how different 3D graphics settings (anti-aliasing methods, modes, and anisotropic filtering) affect a typical scene. Figure 13.4 shows how supersampling antialiasing (AA) provides much more detail than multisampling AA.

> **Note**
> To learn more about 3D graphics terms such as anti-aliasing, multisampling, supersampling, anisotropic filtering, and tessellation, see the 3D About.com Glossary at http://3d.about.com/od/3D-Glossary/.

Selected game

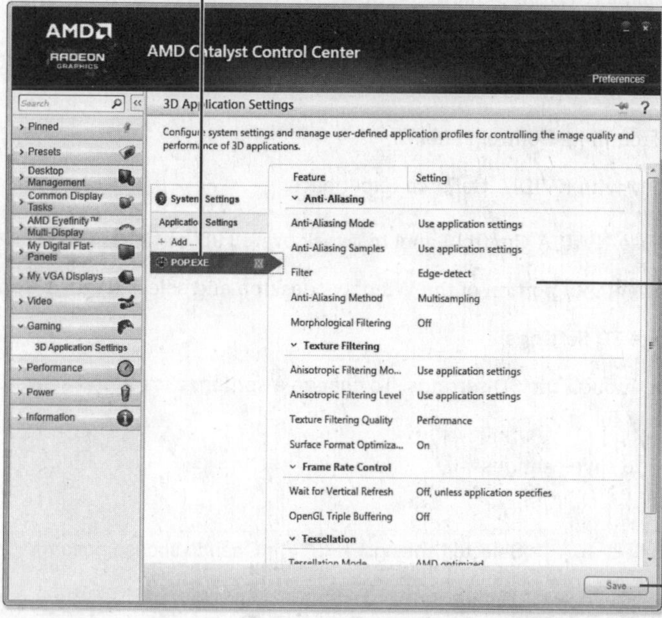

Click a feature to change settings

Click to save settings for selected game

Figure 13.3 Configuring 3D application settings in Catalyst Control Center using Advanced View.

Zoomed preview shows loss of detail

Zoomed preview shows fine detail

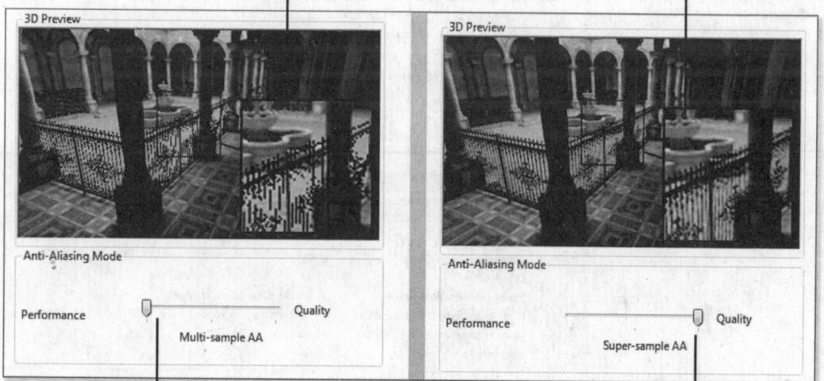

Multi-sampling AA selected for best 3D performance

Supersampling AA selected for best 3D quality

Figure 13.4 Multisampling versus super-sampling AA in AMD VISION Control Center standard view.

The AMD Gaming Evolved utility can be downloaded as part of a 3D graphics update. It enables you to install and play free-to-play games, stay in touch with other gamers, and automatically optimize

3D settings for specific games based on user recommendations. To learn more, see www.amd.com/en-us/markets/game/community.

NVIDIA 3D Settings

NVIDIA provides two ways to adjust 3D settings:

- Manually through its Control Panel.
- Automatically with NVIDIA GeForce Experience.

Here's how to use NVIDIA Control Panel to tweak overall 3D settings:

1. Right-click an empty portion of the Windows desktop and select **NVIDIA Control Panel**.
2. Click **Manage 3D Settings**.
3. Scroll down through the 3D settings. To change a setting, click it and select the option desired (see Figure 13.5).
4. Click **Apply** to save changes.

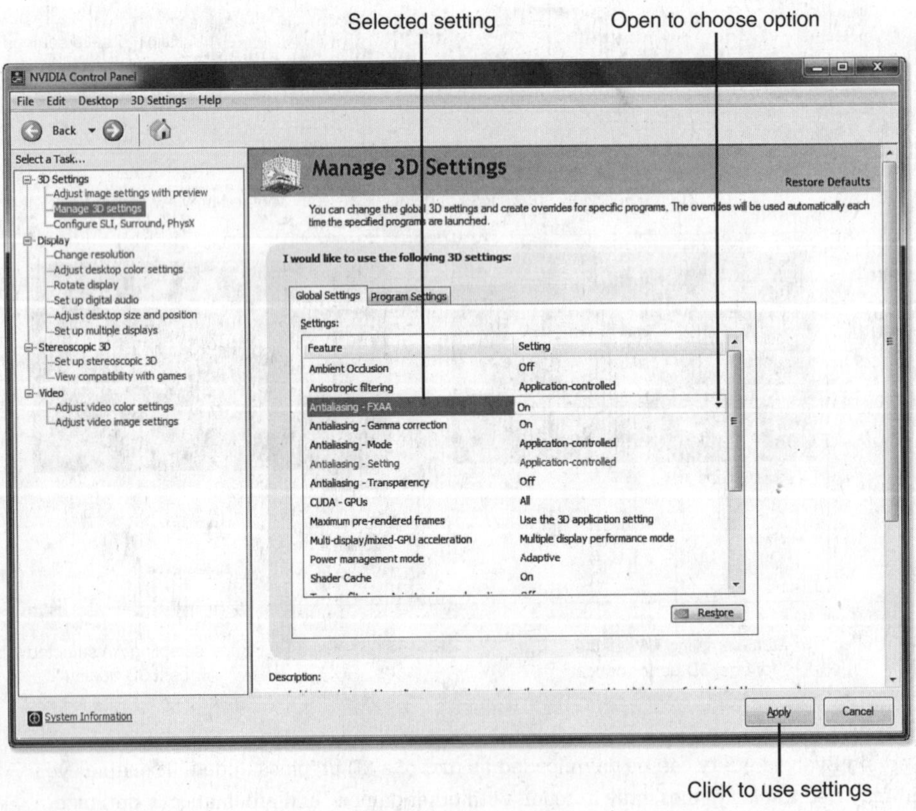

Figure 13.5 Configuring 3D application settings in NVIDIA Control Center.

You can also configure 3D settings for a particular game:

1. After opening the Manage 3D Settings dialog, click the **Program Settings** tab.
2. Select a listed program and change settings as desired.
3. Click **Apply** to save settings.
4. To configure an unlisted game, click **Add** after step 1. Click **Browse** to locate the game's executable file. Click the game you want to add, and then return to step 2.
5. Click **Save** to save changes.

The NVIDIA GeForce Experience utility is downloaded as part of a GeForce driver update. It enables you to view information about your current GPU hardware, stream games to supported mobile devices, capture video of your gameplay, and automatically optimize 3D settings for specific games based on user recommendations. To learn more, see www.geforce.com/geforce-experience.

In-Game Controls

Most 3D games also include in-game controls that can be used to adjust 3D quality. Figure 13.6 compares how low-quality and high-quality settings change the appearance of a tank in a typical 3D game, Desert Thunder.

Figure 13.6 Low-quality (left) versus high-quality (right) 3D rendering.

If your 3D game has options that match those in your 3D graphics card driver, select **Application-Controlled** or **Use Application Settings** if you prefer to set those options in the game. The 3D graphics card settings are used for other settings and for games that lack any 3D settings.

Installing a Second Graphics Card

If you have a single AMD or NVIDIA PCIe graphics card installed, but you have a slot for a second card (Figure 13.7), you can speed up your system's 3D rendering performance by adding an additional card that is compatible with your first card. AMD refers to its multi-GPU technology as CrossFireX; NVIDIA uses the term SLI (Scalable Link Interface). Both technologies enable two or more GPUs to render 3D scenes at rates close to 2 times the single GPU speed.

Figure 13.7
This system is ready for a second PCIe graphics card.

To select and install a second graphics card, follow these steps:

1. Use GPU-Z (refer to Figure 13.1) to determine the current graphics processing unit (GPU) chip used on the card in your system. An additional card must be compatible with this card.
2. Check the NVIDIA or AMD websites to determine which cards are compatible. For AMD, see the chart link at http://support.amd.com/en-us/search/faq/108. For NVIDIA, see the configuration tool at www.geforce.com/hardware/technology/sli/system-requirements.
3. If your cards require an SLI or CrossFire bridge cable, make sure you have one. These cables (see Figures 13.9 and 13.11) might be provided with a compatible card, a compatible motherboard, or can be purchased separately.
4. Before continuing, verify that your motherboard can operate in CrossFireX or SLI mode. Many motherboards are marked to indicate this. Otherwise, check your motherboard documentation.
5. If necessary, update the drivers used by your motherboard to the latest version.
6. Install the latest drivers for your video card.
7. Check your power supply for CrossFire or SLI compatibility. Compatible power supplies have at least two six-pin or six+two-pin (eight-pin) PCIe power connectors. See Figure 7.11 in Chapter 7, "Desktop Power Supply Troubleshooting," p.183, for details.
8. Make sure your power supply has adequate power to run an additional 3D graphics card. See "Selecting the Right-Sized Power Supply," in Chapter 7 for more information.
9. If your power supply isn't powerful enough, replace it before installing an additional card.
10. Turn off the computer and disconnect it from AC power.
11. Remove the case panel that covers the expansion slots.
12. Take precautions to avoid ESD, such as wearing an anti-ESD wrist strap that is clipped to a metal part inside the case.
13. Unscrew and remove the bracket(s) that correspond to the PCIe x16 card slot. Most cards require that two brackets be removed to make room for the card and its cooling shroud.
14. Line up the card (see Figure 13.8) with the expansion slot and push it straight down until it locks into place.
15. Screw the brackets into place using the screws removed in step 13.
16. Connect a six-pin or eight-pin PCIe power lead to the power connector on the card.
17. Attach the appropriate SLI (see Figure 13.9) or CrossFire (see Figure 13.11) bridge cable (if needed) to the card.
18. Close up the computer, reattach AC power, and restart the computer.

To complete the process, you need to enable the multi-GPU feature in the 3D graphics driver.

Figure 13.8 A typical PCIe 3D graphics card that supports multi-GPU operation (SLI).

Enabling SLI

Except for cards based on the NVIDIA GTX 295, GeForce GTX 590, and GeForce GTX 690 GPUs, you need to connect the cards with an SLI bridge cable, such as the one shown in Figure 13.9, before you finish the installation.

After the system restarts, enable SLI in the NVIDIA graphics driver:

1. Open the NVIDIA Control Panel.
2. Open the **3D Settings** menu.
3. Click or tap **Configure SLI, Surround, PhysX**.
4. Click **Maximize 3D performance** (see Figure 13.10).
5. Click **Apply**.
6. Close Control Panel.

After you enable SLI, all 3D programs automatically use it to speed up 3D rendering.

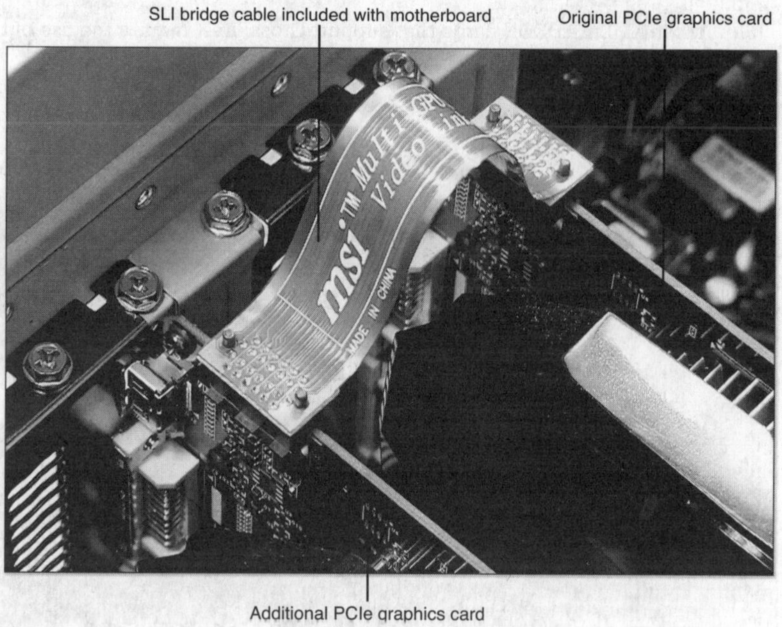

Figure 13.9
The SLI bridge cable is required by most SLI setups.

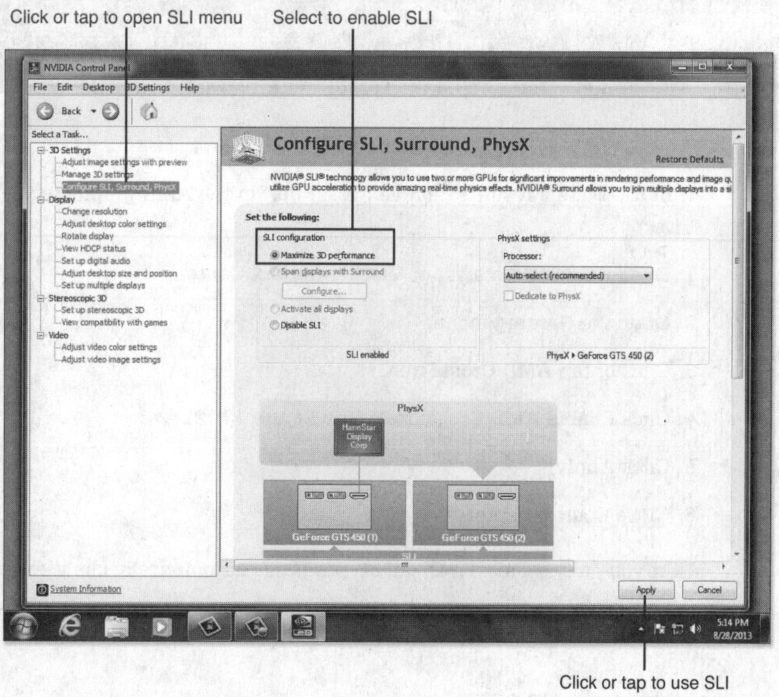

Figure 13.10
Enabling NVIDIA SLI.

Enabling CrossFireX

Most AMD RADEON cards that support CrossFireX require the use of the CrossFireX bridge cable shown in Figure 13.11.

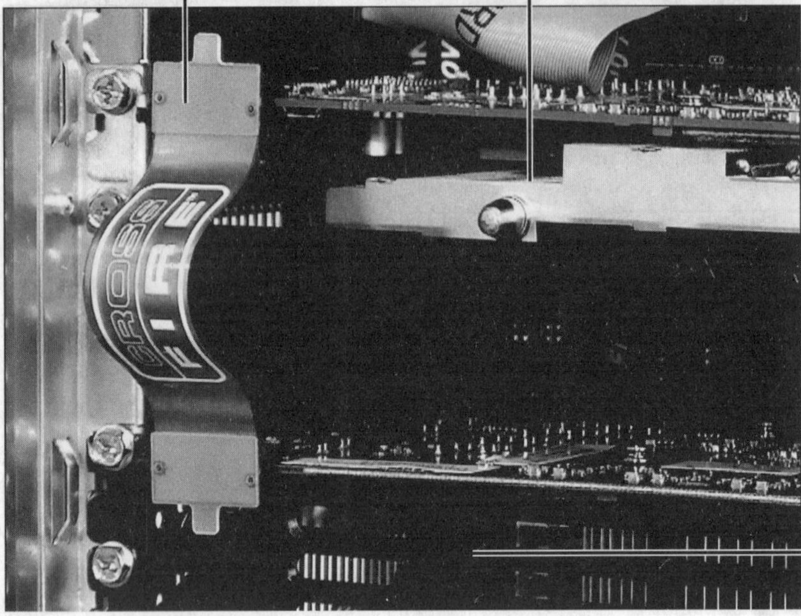

Figure 13.11 The CrossFireX bridge cable is required for most CrossFireX setups.

After the system restarts, enable CrossFireX in the AMD graphics driver:

1. Open the AMD Catalyst or VISION Control Center.
2. Open the **Gaming** menu.
3. Click or tap **AMD CrossFireX**.
4. Click **Enable AMD CrossFireX** (see Figure 13.12).
5. Click **Apply**.
6. Close Control Center.

> **Note**
> Some cards in the new R9 series use XDMA connections in the PCIe bus rather than a CrossFireX bridge cable to run in CrossFireX mode. See the documentation for these cards for details.

After you enable CrossFireX, all 3D programs automatically use it to speed up 3D rendering.

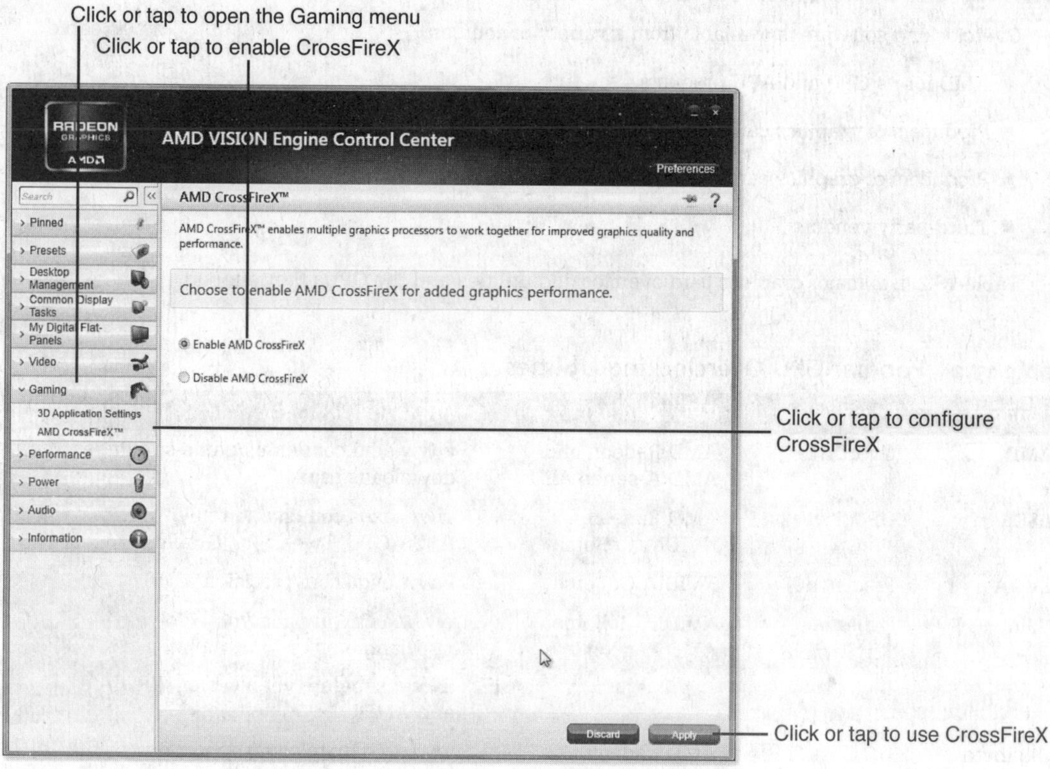

Figure 13.12
Enabling AMD CrossFireX.

Note

If you have a computer that uses an AMD APU (a CPU with built-in RADEON graphics), you can use a single RADEON card along with the APU to improve 3D performance. This feature is known as AMD RADEON Dual Graphics (it was previously known as Hybrid CrossFireX. To learn more, see http://support.amd.com/en-us/search/faq/176.

Overclocking Your Graphics Card

No matter how fast your 3D performance is, you might want even faster frame rates. By running your graphics card at faster-than-normal speeds, a process called *overclocking*, you can achieve faster performance. However, overclocking can lead to system instability. In this section, you'll learn about overclocking utilities and how to troubleshoot their use.

Using Overclocking Software

Overclocking software is available from a variety of sources:

- AMD for its GPU and APU products
- Producers of graphics cards using NVIDIA GPUs
- Producers of graphics cards using AMD GPUs
- Third-party vendors

Table 13.2 lists major graphics card overclocking utilities and the GPUs they support.

Table 13.2 Popular GPU Overclocking Utilities

Vendor	Program	GPU Brand(s)	URL
AMD	OverDrive	AMD Radeon and AMD A-series APUs	www.amd.com/en-us/game-site/Pages/downloads.aspx
ASUS	GPU Tweak	AMD Radeon, NVIDIA GeForce	www.asus.com/supportonly/ASUS_GPU_Tweak_for_Graphics_cards/
EVGA	Precision X	NVIDIA GeForce	www.evga.com/precision/
Gainward	Expertool	NVIDIA GeForce, AMD Radeon	www.gainward.com/main/download.php?lang=en (Note: separate versions for NVIDIA and AMD)
Gigabyte	OC Guru II	AMD Radeon, NVIDIA GeForce	www.gigabyte.com/support-downloads/utility.aspx?cg=3
Guru3D	RivaTuner*	Nvidia TNT-GeForce	www.guru3d.com/content-page/rivatuner.html
MSI	Afterburner	AMD Radeon, NVIDIA GeForce	http://event.msi.com/vga/afterburner/download.htm
Sapphire	TriXX	AMD Radeon	www.sapphireselectclub.com/ssc/TriXX/
Zotac	Firestorm	NVIDIA GeForce	www.zotac.com/z-zone/zotac-firestorm.html

**RivaTuner is designed to support Windows 98 through Windows XP and GPUs of similar vintage.*

Caution

Check the products supported before installation. Some overclock utilities work only with graphics cards from the specific vendor shown. For reviews of many of these utilities, see http://wccftech.com/article/gpu-overclocking-utilities-revisited/.

Depending on the product you use and the features of your GPU and graphics card, you might be able to adjust many features, such as the following:

- GPU speed
- Memory clock speed
- Memory bus speed
- GPU and memory voltage

Figure 13.13 illustrates adjusting GPU performance with the AMD Graphics OverDrive utility from within the Catalyst Control Center.

Figure 13.13 Increasing GPU and memory clock speeds with AMD Catalyst Control Center's Graphics OverDrive.

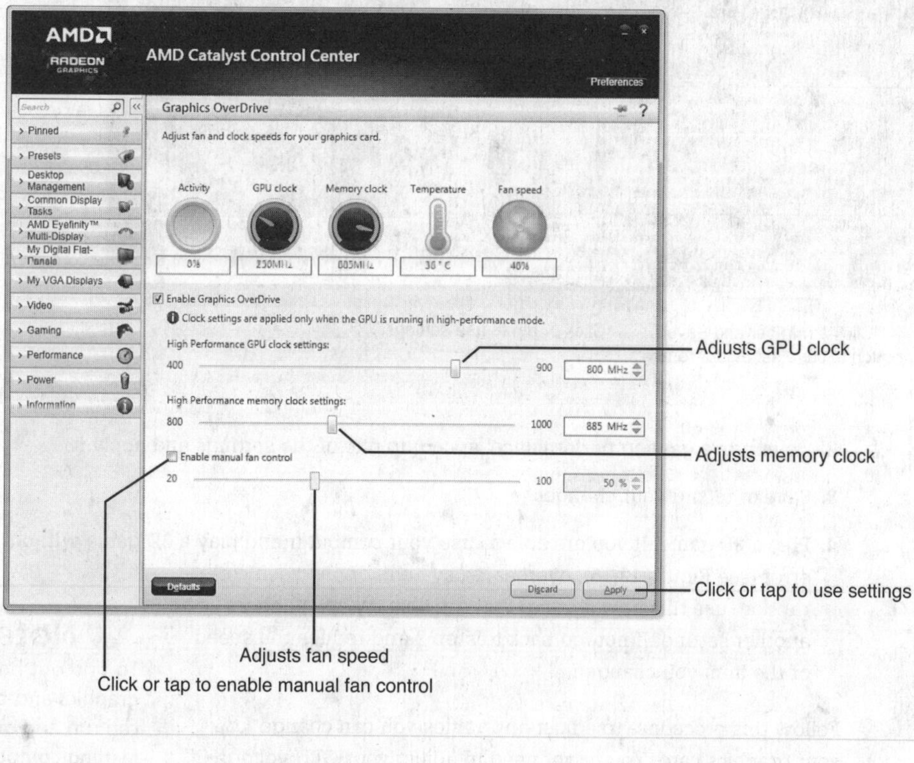

Figure 13.14 illustrates adjusting GPU performance for a system running two NVIDIA cards in SLI mode with MSI Afterburner.

Here's how to use utilities like these to safely improve performance:

1. After you start your favorite utility, note the current GPU performance settings. If your utility has an option to save the current value, use it. Otherwise, you can use screen capture or a digital camera/smartphone to record the current values.

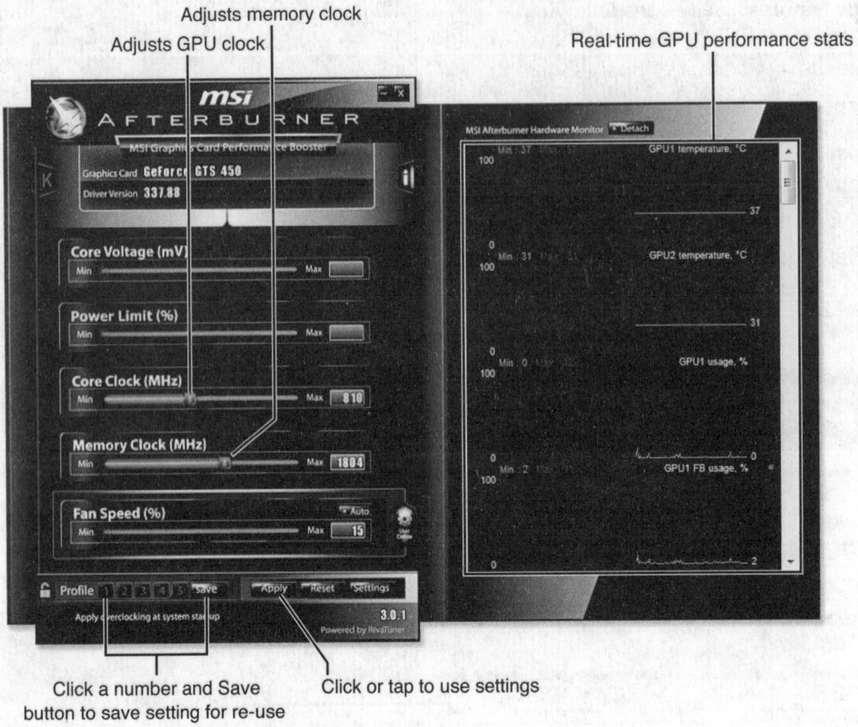

Figure 13.14 Increasing GPU and memory clock speeds with MSI Afterburner.

2. To improve gaming performance, speed up one of the settings and apply it.
3. Save or record your changes.
4. Play a 3D game. If you are able to use your computer and play a 3D game without a video driver error (see Figure 13.15), overheated system, or onscreen corruption, use this new setting. You can also try speeding up another setting. If not, go back to step 2 and reduce the speed of the item you changed.

Follow this procedure to adjust any values you can change for your graphics card. You might need to adjust your GPU voltage (if this option is available in your driver) or improve system cooling to help your system be more stable at higher GPU speeds.

> **Note**
> To find out how fast your graphics and other hardware can run and get insights from leading component vendors, visit hwbot.org.

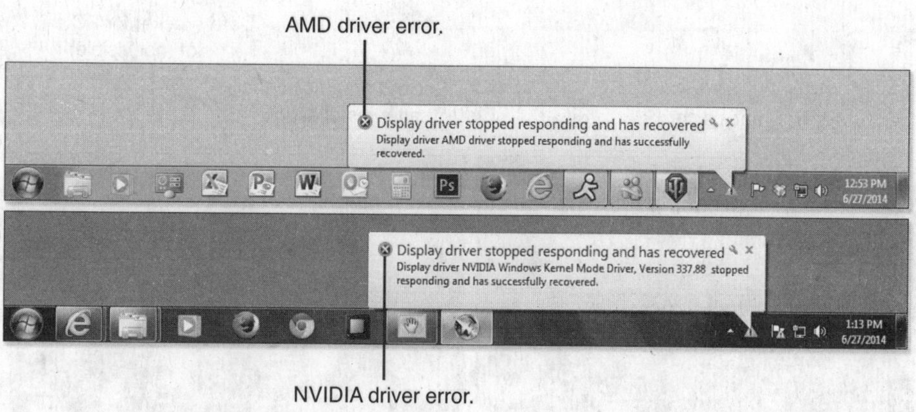

Figure 13.15 Display errors like these can occur if you use too-aggressive settings when over-clocking.

Improving GPU Cooling

The GPU chip is one of the hottest-running components inside your computer. Although overclock-friendly graphics cards are usually fitted with large fans and fan shrouds to help keep the card's memory and GPU cool, overclocking while 3D gaming pushes cards to the limits of stability. Fortunately, there are some low-cost ways to help keep your system running as cool as possible:

- Keep air intakes and exhausts clean of dust, debris, and pet hair.
- Add additional case fans to the front and top of your system if they're not present.
- Keep the slots next to the fan side of each graphics card open to help avoid heat buildups.

> **Note**
> For more about cleaning air intakes, exhausts, and installing fans, see Chapter 16, "Keeping Devices Cool."

If you have already added fans to your system, keep your intakes and exhaust clean, and you're still having problems with GPU overheating, consider keeping the slots next to your graphics cards unused.

Let's take a look at the system shown in Figure 13.16.

If you want to keep the slots next to both cards empty, the only usable expansion slot remaining is the slot to the right of the original graphics card (not visible in these photos). Although most expansion devices today connect via USB, some users might still need to add high-performance sound cards or specialized network adapters via an internal slot.

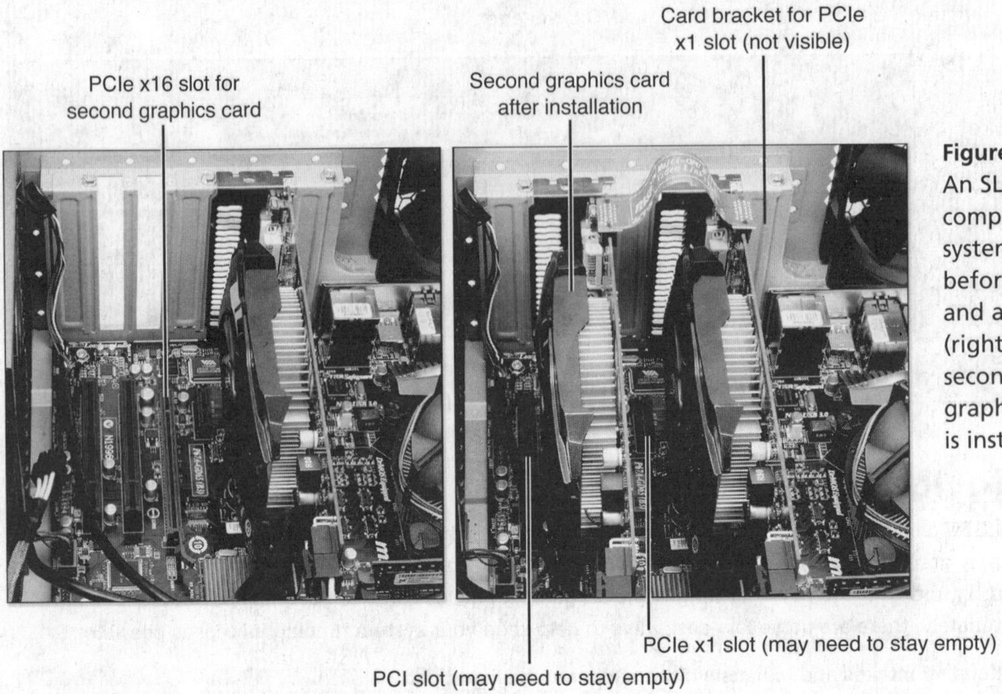

Figure 13.16 An SLI-compatible system before (left) and after (right) the second graphics card is installed.

Improving Your Display

The display you use also has an effect on the quality of your 3D gaming. If you decide that you need to upgrade to a better display, the critical technologies to look for include LED displays with in-plane switching (IPS) and LED HDTVs with refresh rates of 120Hz or faster.

Upgrading to IPS LED Displays

In-plane switching (IPS) enables a much wider viewing angle than previous technologies such as Twisted Nematic (TN): 178 degrees horizontal and vertical, compared to 160 degrees vertical and 170 degrees horizontal.

Higher-quality IPS displays can display more than 1 billion colors, compared to 16.7 million colors with LCD TN and lower-quality LED IPS displays.

Keep in mind that IPS displays vary widely in their connectivity. Low-cost models and almost all LCD TN displays still on the market typically have only DVI-D digital and VGA analog connections. Higher-cost units typically add HDMI and additional connections for more flexibility.

Before purchasing a replacement display, check the following:

- **Screen size**—We recommend 22-inch or larger diagonal measurement unless your space is limited.

- **Viewing angles**—Wider is better.
- **Connection types**—We recommend support for HDMI and VGA, or DVI-D and VGA.
- **Support for HDCP**—This feature helps assure that you can use the display to watch Blu-ray movies.
- **Refresh rate**—Faster is better for gaming.
- **Compliance with VESA wall or table mounts**—By using a VESA wall or table mount, you can put your display in more places.
- **Warranty**—A longer warranty is better, but be sure to look into how warranty claims are handled.
- **User ratings**—User ratings help you cut through manufacturers' hype to see how products really work in the field.

Faster-Response HDTVs

Although you could watch movies and sports on your PC's display, it's more likely that you'll be enjoying video and TV content on your HDTV. To avoid blurring during fast-moving sports or action sequences, look for LED HDTVs with a refresh rate of 120Hz or faster. If you want to enjoy 3D Blu-ray content, look for displays designed specifically for 3D.

Note

3D support also requires a 3D-compatible Blu-ray player, high-speed HDMI cable, and a receiver that has 3D HDMI passthrough.

14

KEEPING YOUR DEVICES UPDATED

Fast Track to Solutions

Table 14.1 Symptom Table

Symptom	Flowchart or Book Section	Page #
I need to keep Windows Update from rebooting my system when I'm not around.	Viewing and Changing Windows Update Settings	365
I just heard about a new Windows security issue and don't want to wait for automatic updates.	Installing Updates Manually	370
I don't know if my system has the service pack for Windows 7.	Getting Service Packs	374
The updated driver I just installed is causing problems.	Rolling Back Bad Driver Updates	378
I can't get updates for my iOS device while I'm using 4G cellular service.	Updating iOS Devices	379
What's the fastest way for me to get updates for my 3D graphics card?	Updating Device Drivers	378

Using Windows Update

Whether you're looking for better security, more stability, or a new feature or two for the version of Windows you run, Windows Update is your friend. However, if your work patterns don't match the way Microsoft thinks you should use it, Windows Update can also drive you crazy. In this section, we'll show you how to make Windows Update work for you.

Normal Settings for Windows Update

Whether you use Windows Vista, Windows 7, or Windows 8/8.1, the normal settings for Windows Update put Microsoft in charge of when you get updates:

- Microsoft posts important updates (formerly known as "critical") monthly on "Patch Tuesday," the second Tuesday of each month; these are downloaded and installed automatically. If there are immediate threats to Windows, Microsoft will post them as needed.
- Recommended updates are also posted at various times as needed; these are also downloaded and installed automatically.
- Microsoft offers optional hardware and Windows updates you can choose from. These are not installed automatically.

Windows Update typically runs in the wee hours of the morning (2:00 a.m.). After updates are downloaded and installed, your system may need to be rebooted. Windows Update takes care of that for you.

Keeping your system updated helps protect your computer from malware and attacks. This is especially the case with Windows 8/8.1, which uses Windows Defender as its built-in anti-malware app. If you didn't use Windows Update, Windows Defender wouldn't be updated either.

So what's the problem? There are a few situations in which Windows Update is doing you no favors with its default settings:

- If you are running backups overnight, Windows Update can interfere with them.
- When your system is rebooted after being updated, any remote-access sessions you are running are dropped.
- If you also run updates to other software overnight, Windows Update might interrupt those processes as well.
- Depending on the updates it installs, Windows Update may need to make lots of changes to your system after you shut it down. If you're turning off your system to make a run for the airport, needing to wait five or ten minutes or even longer for Windows Update to install updates could make you late for your appointment or your flight.

Fortunately, you can tweak Windows Update to keep your system protected without getting in your way. The next sections look at the options for Windows Update and show you your choices.

Viewing and Changing Windows Update Settings

To see your current Windows Update settings in Windows 7 (or Windows 8/8.1 from the Windows desktop):

1. Open Control Panel.
2. Click **System and Security**.
3. Click **Windows Update** to see the current status of Windows Update (see Figure 14.1), including whether Windows is up-to-date, whether you are receiving updates for other Microsoft products, and the last time updates were installed.

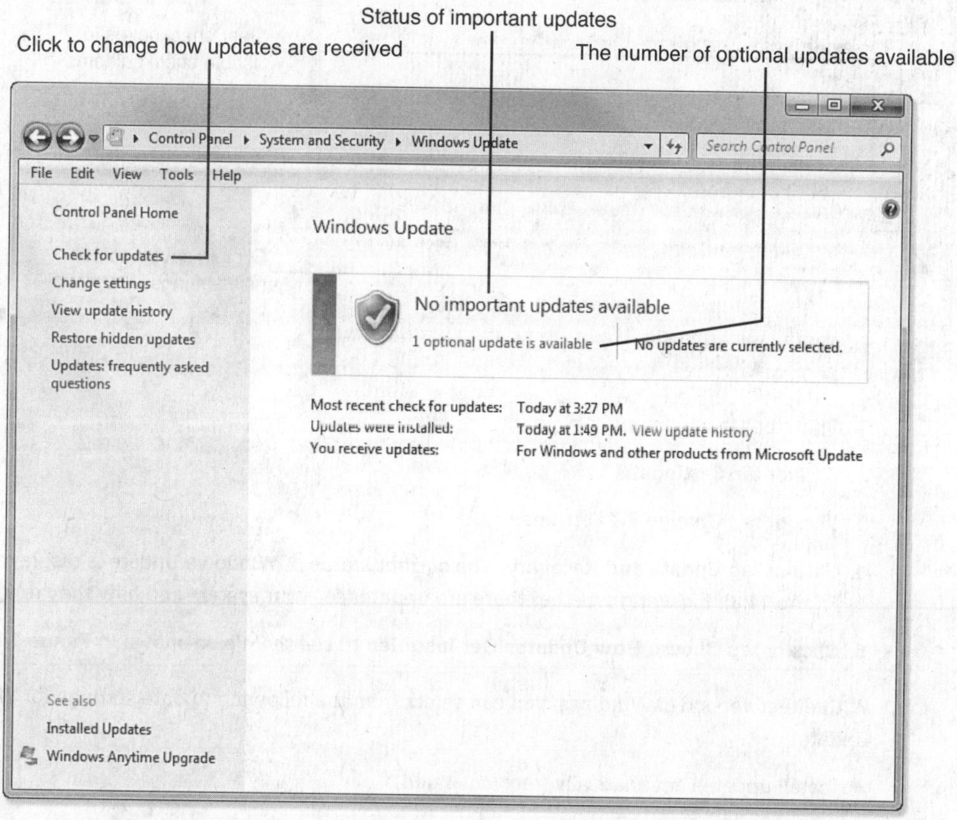

Figure 14.1 Windows Update's main menu (Windows 7).

4. Click the **Change Settings** link in the left pane to see the dialog shown in Figure 14.2.

To see Windows Update settings from the Windows 8/8.1 Start screen:

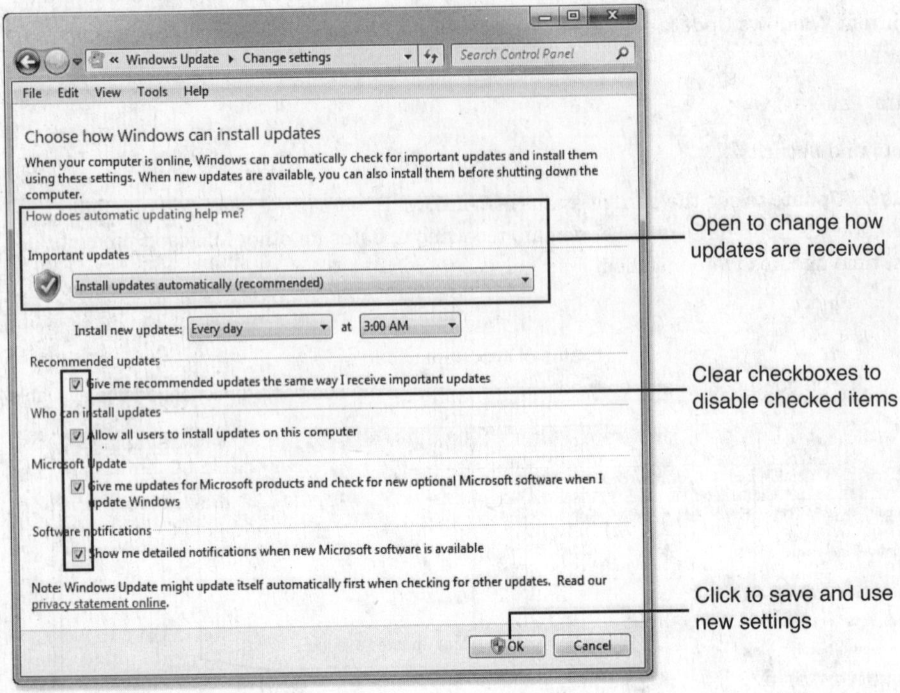

Figure 14.2 Windows Update typical settings (Windows 7).

1. Open the Charms menu.
2. Click or tap **Settings**.
3. Click or tap **Change PC Settings**.
4. Click or tap **Update and Recovery**. The current status of Windows Update is displayed (see Figure 14.3), including whether there are updates for your system and how they're installed.
5. Click or tap **Choose How Updates Get Installed** to see the dialog shown in Figure 14.4.

With either version of Windows, you can select from the following update settings for Windows Update:

- Install updates automatically (recommended)*
- Download updates but let me choose whether to install them
- Check for updates but let me choose whether to download and install them
- Never check for updates (not recommended)

*This is the default (normal) setting.

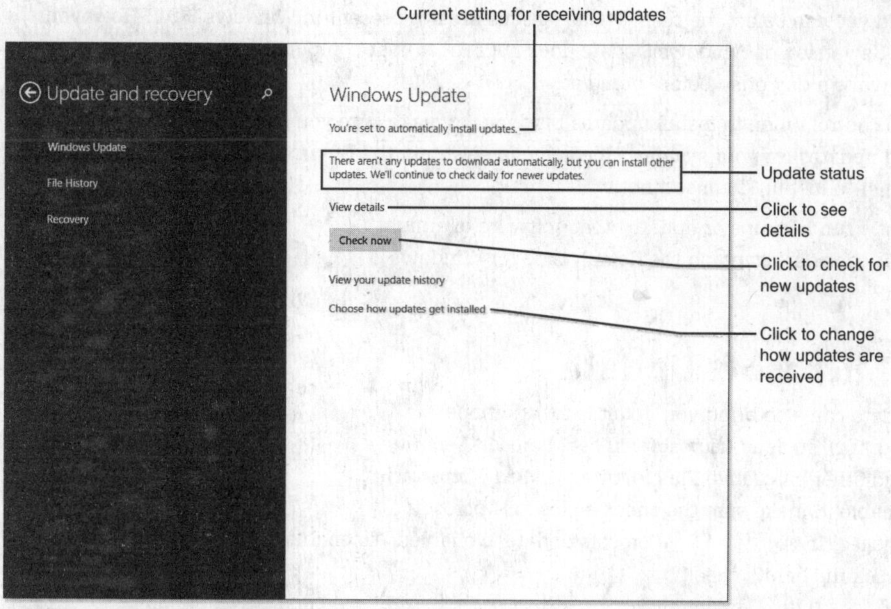

Figure 14.3 Windows Update's main menu (Windows 8.1).

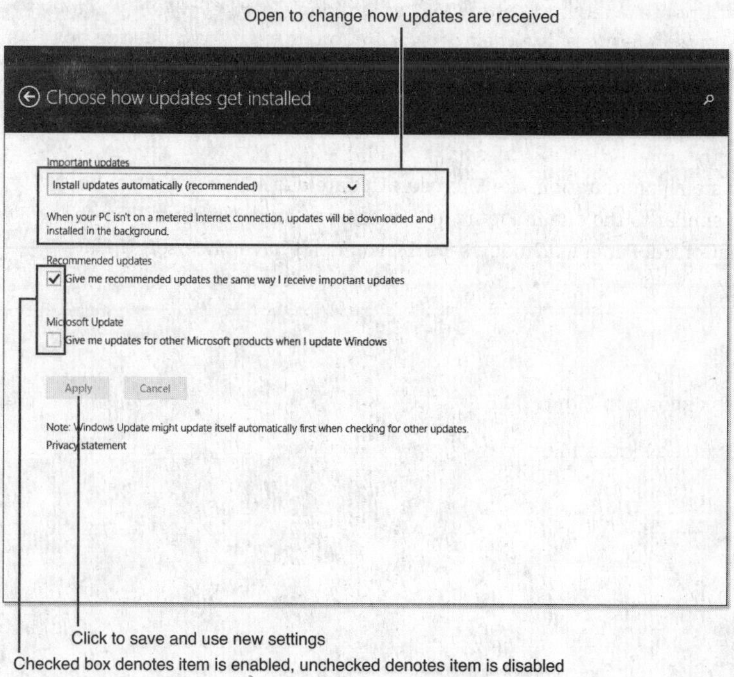

Figure 14.4 Windows Update typical settings (Windows 8.1).

With Windows 7, you can also select when to install new updates—every day, or a selected day of the week—and you can select the time. These options are not present in Windows 8/8.1. However, Windows 8/8.1's version of Windows Update does not reboot your computer as soon as updates are installed, but waits a day or so before doing so.

If you want to control when to install updates but want to make sure you get all the important and recommended updates for your system, I recommend selecting the Download Updates but Let Me Choose Whether to Install Them setting.

If you frequently run backups or update other software overnight on Windows 7, consider changing the default time for Windows Update to run.

> **Note**
> Windows 8/8.1 downloads updates in the background (unless you're on a metered connection) and lets you know when they're ready to install.

Enabling Microsoft Update

Windows Update can also bring you updates for additional Microsoft programs, such as Microsoft Office, Microsoft Security Essentials, and other programs. This feature is called Microsoft Update. To enable it, make sure the check boxes for Microsoft Update are clicked. In Figure 14.2, Microsoft Update is enabled. To enable it on the system shown in Figure 14.4, click the empty check box.

> **Caution**
> If you use Microsoft Security Essentials (MSE), the free anti-malware package for Windows 7 and earlier versions, keep in mind that Microsoft Update labels updates for MSE as Optional. In other words, you must select them manually or wait until Microsoft Security Essentials decides to update itself. If you decide not to use Automatic Updates, I recommend that you check for updates daily and select updates for MSE whenever you see them to keep MSE up-to-date as quickly as possible.

Depending on your current system configuration, the Microsoft Update check box might not be displayed. If you see a dialog similar to the one in Figure 14.5 when you start Windows Update in Windows 7 (or start it from Control Panel in Windows 8/8.1), you don't have Microsoft Update enabled.

To fix the problem:

1. Click the **Find Out More** link shown in Figure 14.5.
2. Click the empty **I Agree** box (see Figure 14.6).
3. Click **Install**.

Figure 14.5 This system is not using Microsoft Update. Click the link to fix the problem.

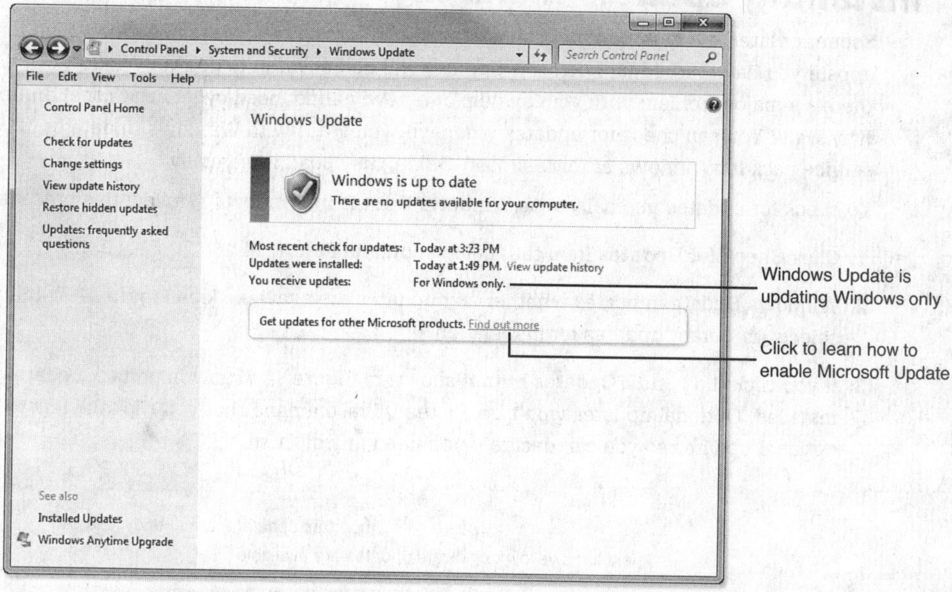

Figure 14.6 Enabling Microsoft Update in Windows 7.

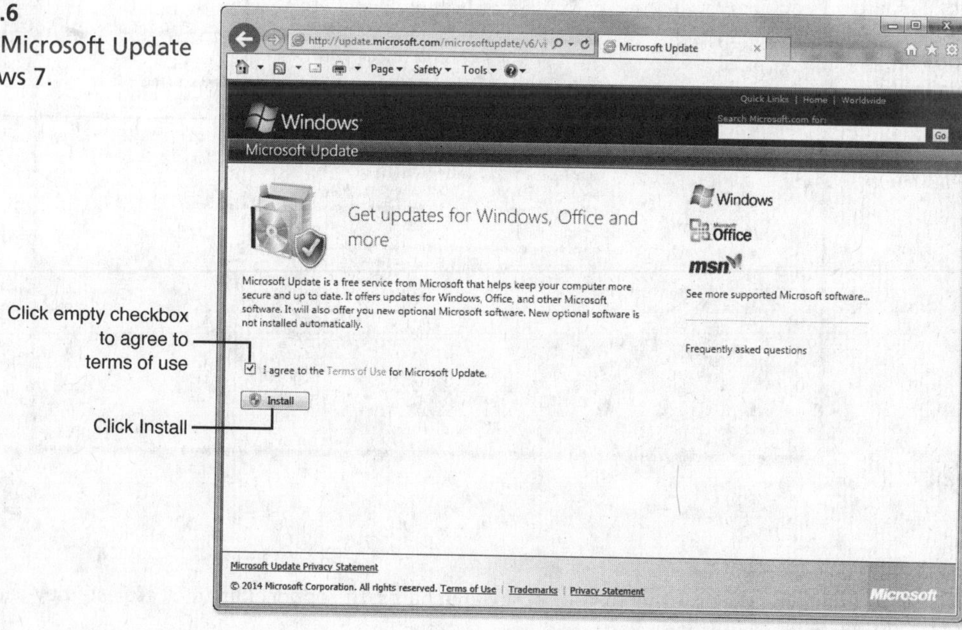

Installing Updates Manually

Sooner or later, every important or recommended Microsoft update for Windows (and for supported apps if you have turned on Microsoft Update) will be delivered to you via Windows Update. But, if there's a major problem with your system or a newly announced cyber attack that an update can fix, why wait? You can check for updates whenever you want with Windows Update or, if you need a service pack for Windows or for Microsoft Office, download it manually.

To check for updates manually with Windows Update in Windows 7, follow this procedure:

1. Click **Check for Updates** from the dialog shown in Figure 14.1.
2. Windows Update indicates whether any updates are available (see Figure 14.7). It automatically selects important updates for installation.
3. If you click the **Install Updates** button shown in Figure 14.7, only important updates will be installed. Optional updates won't be. Instead, I recommend that you click the link to view the optional updates so you can decide if you need any of them.

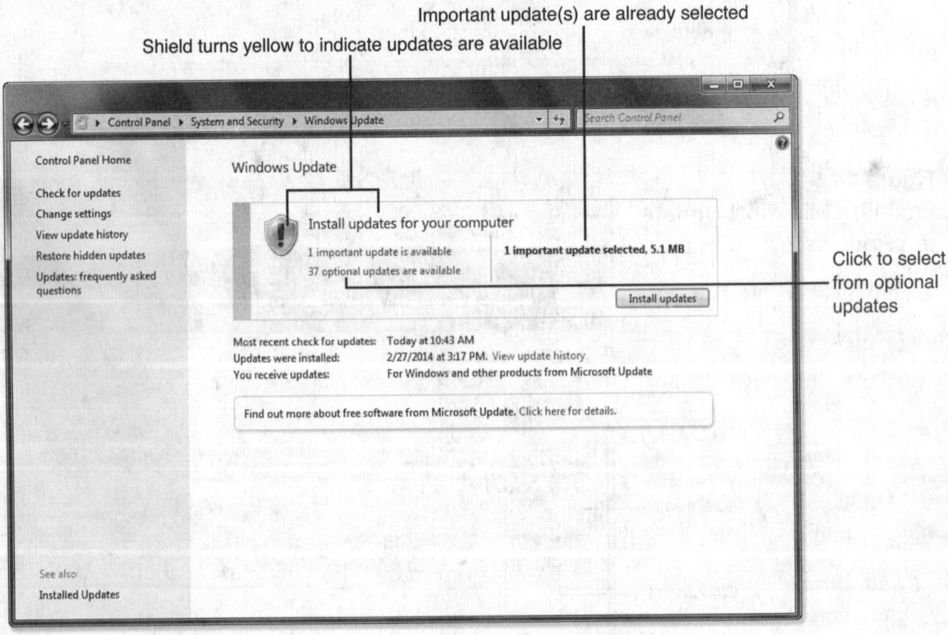

Figure 14.7 Windows Update indicates updates are available.

4. When you click the link to view optional updates, the optional updates are listed by category.
5. Click the empty check boxes next to the updates you want. In Figure 14.8, the update for Microsoft Security Essentials has been selected.

6. If you want to exclude an important update, click the **Important** tab in the left pane and clear the update's check box.
7. Click **OK** to return to the Windows Update opening dialog.

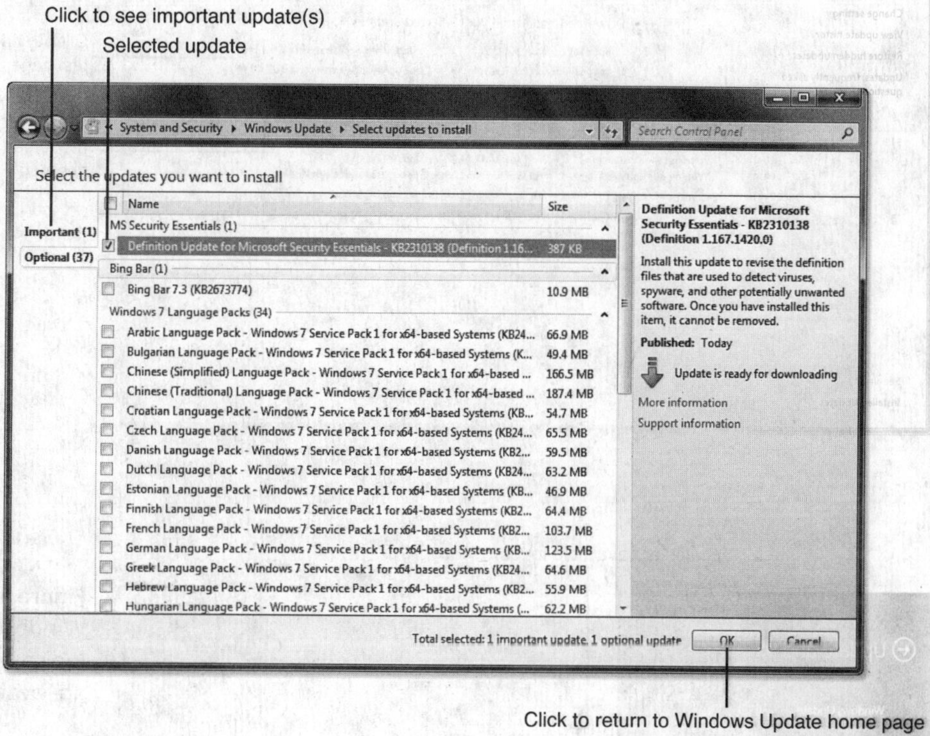

Figure 14.8 Selecting an optional update with Windows Update.

8. Click **Install Update(s)** to install the updates you selected (see Figure 14.9).
9. If you need to restart your system after the updates are installed, make sure you save your work and close your open apps before you restart your system.
10. During the shutdown and restart process, Windows might need to complete installation and configuration processes on some updates. An onscreen message informs you of update progress. Do not turn off (or unplug) your computer during an update.

To check for updates manually with Windows Update from the PC settings menu in Windows 8/8.1, follow this procedure:

1. Click **Check Now** from the Windows Update dialog shown in Figure 14.3.
2. Windows Update indicates whether any updates are available. Important updates will be installed automatically. To install them immediately, or to choose other updates, click **View Details** (see Figure 14.10).

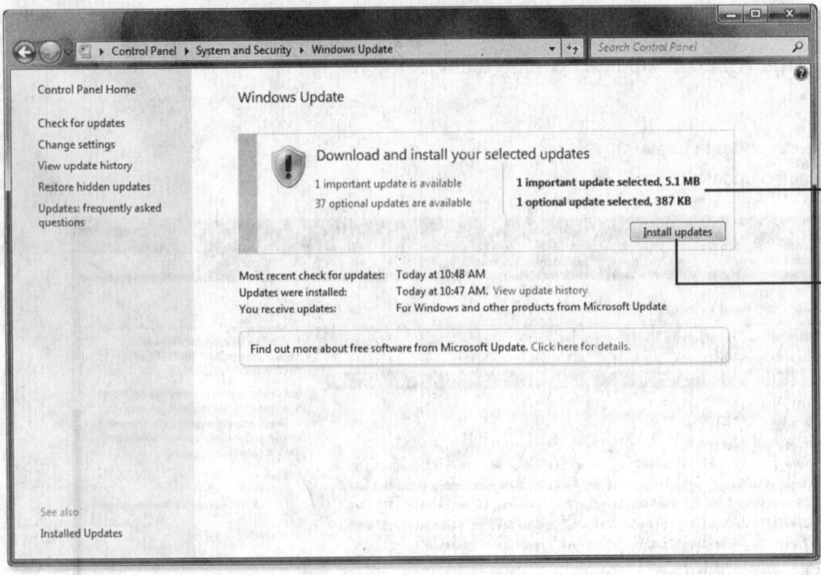

Figure 14.9 Preparing to install updates for Windows 7 with Windows Update.

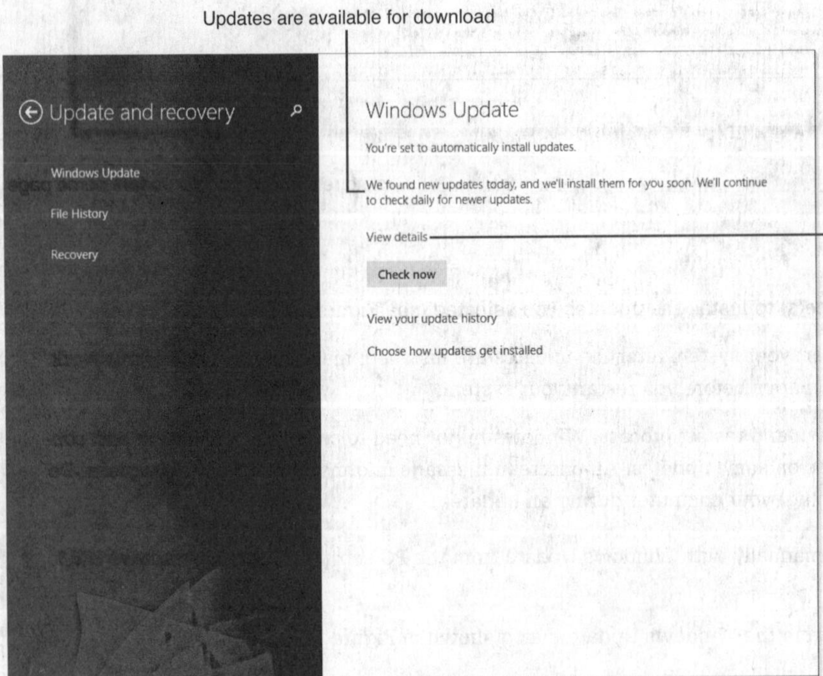

Figure 14.10 Windows Update indicates updates are available.

3. Important updates are listed at the top, with optional updates listed below.
4. Click the empty check boxes next to the updates you want (see Figure 14.11).
5. To learn more about an update, click **Details**.
6. Click **Install** to start the installation process.

Figure 14.11 Preparing to install important and optional updates for Windows 8.1.

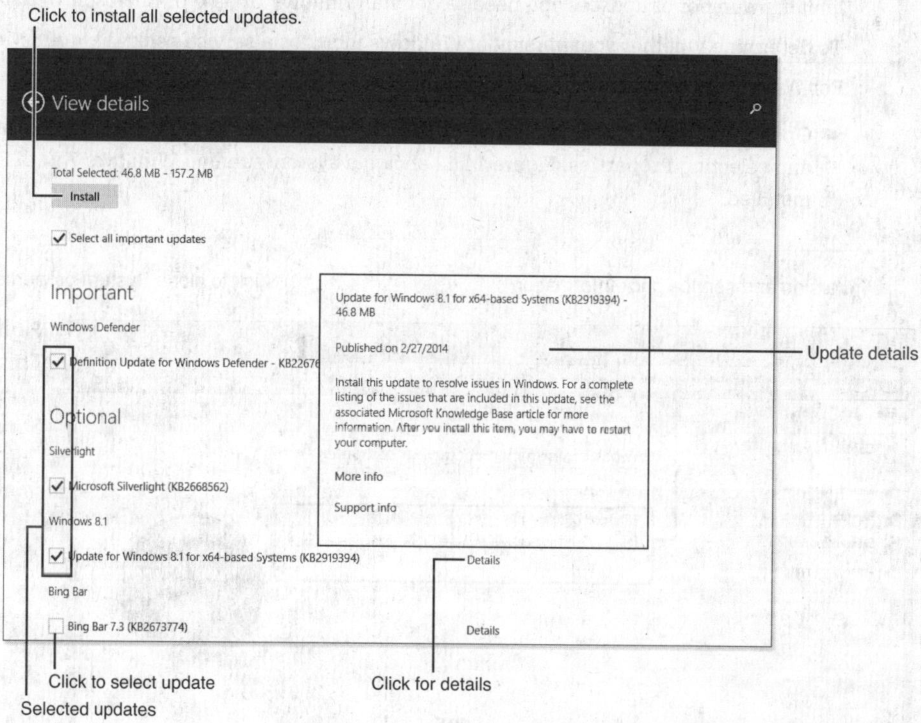

7. If you need to restart your system after the updates are installed, make sure you save your work and close your open apps before you click Restart.
8. During the shutdown and restart process, Windows might need to complete installation and configuration processes on some updates. An onscreen message informs you of update progress. Do not turn off (or unplug) your computer during an update.

Note

If you prefer to run Windows Update from Control Panel in Windows 8/8.1, the update process is similar to the one for Windows 7.

Getting Service Packs

Although both Microsoft Windows and Microsoft Office are frequently updated via Windows Update, it is sometimes better to get most of the updates you need by installing a service pack. A service pack is a large file (typically more than 100MB in size) that contains all the updates for the program or operating system in question. If you install a version of Windows or Office that does not include the latest service pack, download and install the latest service pack right after installation to limit the number of updates you need to get via Windows Update or Microsoft Update.

To determine whether your version of Windows includes a service pack:

For Windows 7 or Windows 8/8.1 desktop:

- Open the System properties sheet via the Control Panel or by right-clicking **Computer (My PC)** and selecting **Properties**. Figure 14.12 shows a system running Windows 7 with Service Pack 1 installed.

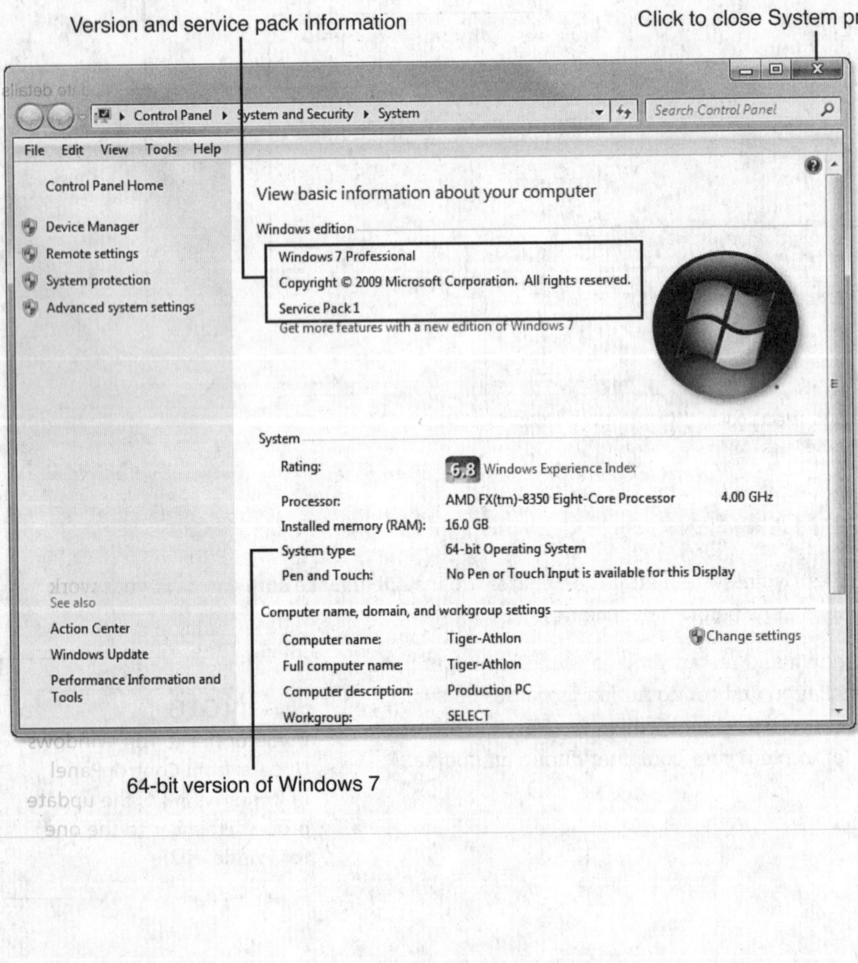

Figure 14.12 This computer has Windows 7 with Service Pack 1.

For Windows 8.1 from the Start screen, if you have a keyboard:

- Press the Windows Logo key+X, and then **System.**

If you are using a tablet (no keyboard):

- Open the **Charms** menu, click **Settings, Change PC Settings, PC and Devices, PC Info**.
- Figure 14.13 shows a system running Windows 8.1 with no service packs.

Figure 14.13 This computer has Windows 8.1.

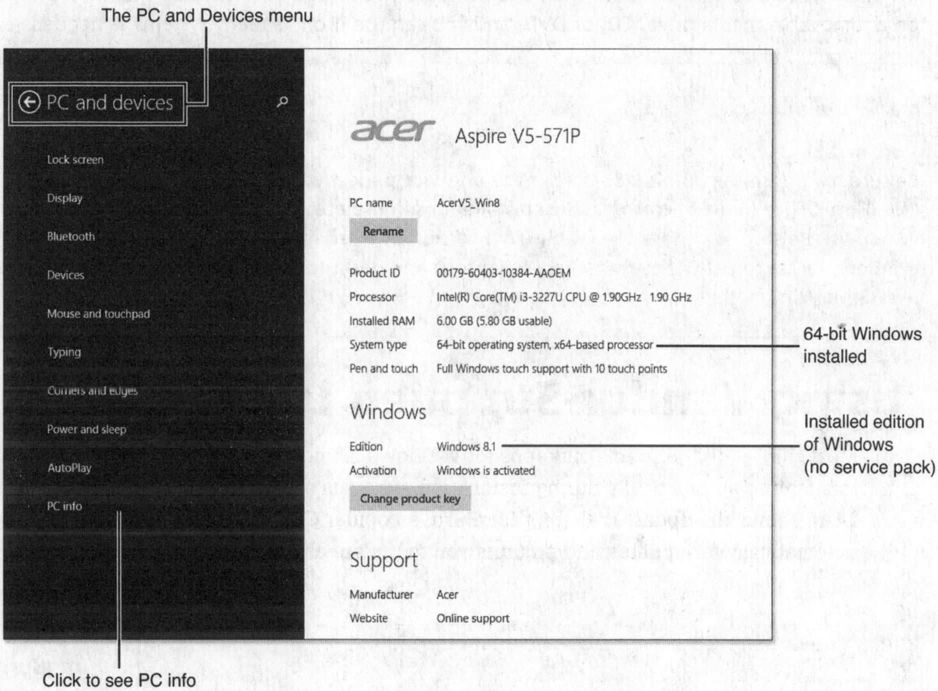

To see whether Microsoft Office has a service pack installed (and which one), see the following links:

- For Office 2013: http://support.microsoft.com/kb/2817457
- For Office 2010: http://support.microsoft.com/kb/2687455
- For Office 2007: http://support.microsoft.com/kb/928116

If your version of Microsoft Office doesn't have the latest service pack included, you need to install only the latest service pack (it includes the contents of previous service packs). Depending on when the latest service pack was created, there probably will be additional updates needed via Windows Update.

To download and install a Microsoft Office service pack, visit http://office.microsoft.com, click Support, and click Downloads and Updates. Use the Search tool to locate a specific service pack.

To download and install a Microsoft Windows service pack, visit www.microsoft.com, open the Support menu, click Windows, and use the Search tool to locate a specific service pack.

Tip

Another benefit of using the download method to get a service pack is that if you need to install an Office or Windows service pack on more than one computer, you need to download the file only once. Put the file on a removable-media drive, CD, or DVD, and you can use it on as many systems as needed.

Caution

Be sure to choose the 32-bit (x86) version of a service pack if you are using a 32-bit version of Windows or Microsoft Office (most Microsoft Office installations in use are 32-bit, even on computers running 64-bit Windows). Be sure to choose the 64-bit (x64) version of a service pack if you are using a 64-bit version of Windows or Microsoft Office (most recent laptops and desktops use 64-bit Windows, whereas many tablets use 32-bit Windows).

Using Vendor-Supplied Update Tools

Most third-party programs and apps for Windows include some type of update process. Some enable this feature automatically during installation, whereas others require you to update manually. Figure 14.14 shows the update dialog for ImgBurn, a popular CD/DVD mastering program. ImgBurn checks automatically for updates and prompts you to update as needed.

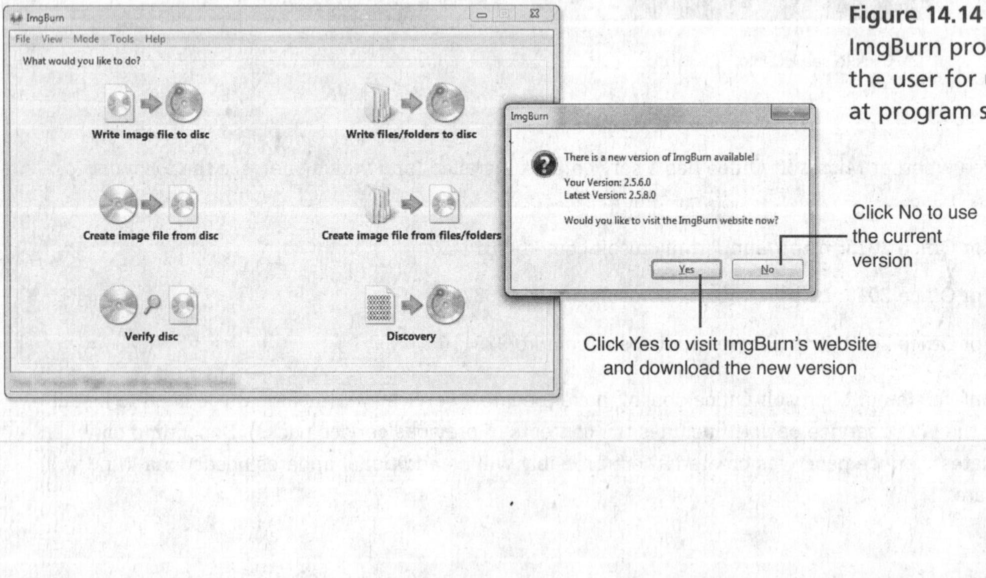

Figure 14.14 ImgBurn prompts the user for updates at program startup.

Note

One typical benefit of using paid instead of free versions of anti-malware and other utilities is better protection through automatic updates. If you're the forgetful type, it might be worthwhile to upgrade to paid versions of your favorite utilities for this feature alone.

If you are not sure how your programs or apps are updated, check the Help dialogs. If you don't see an update option, you can search Help for more information. Figure 14.15 shows the update option in the Help menu for Camtasia Studio, a popular motion-screen capture utility.

You will be prompted if you need to close your application before the update is installed.

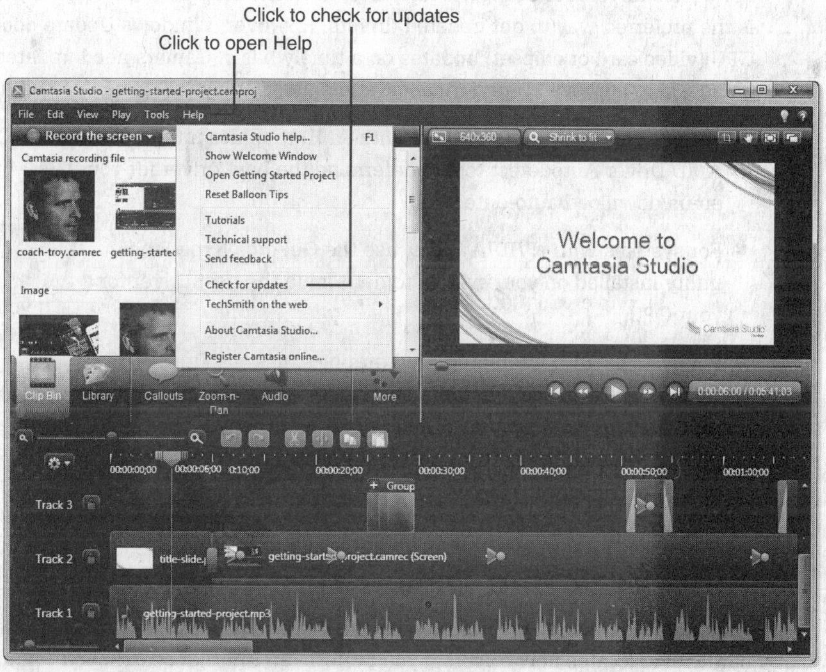

Figure 14.15
Using Camtasia Studio's Help menu to locate updates.

Caution

Is this update necessary? Generally speaking, security updates for Windows or apps (software) should be installed as soon as you can. However, updates for apps or drivers or major updates or service packs for Windows don't need to be updated immediately unless they specifically deal with a problem you're having. By waiting, you can discover if other users are having problems with the update. If the update causes problems, don't install it until the problems are resolved.

To determine whether an update is causing problems, check the support forums for the app or for Windows. Microsoft's support forums are located at http://answers.microsoft.com/en-us.

Updating Device Drivers

Device drivers enable your hardware, from mice and keyboards to multifunction devices and displays, to work with your operating system. If a driver stops working correctly, you can get updated drivers. In recent versions of Windows, there are four ways to get updated device drivers:

- Windows Update
- The Update Driver button in a device's Device Manager properties sheet
- Right-clicking a device in Device Manager and selecting Update driver software
- Downloading it from the vendor's website

For device drivers for USB ports, displays, network adapters, and storage devices, Windows Update is the preferred way to get updated drivers. However, Windows Update doesn't always display GPU (video card or chipset) updates on a timely basis. Gamers need updates to support the newest games, help improve 3D performance, and solve display problems. Instead, use these methods:

- For systems with AMD GPUs or with AMD graphics integrated into the CPU (an APU), use the AMD Driver Autodetect tool to determine the best driver for your GPU: http://support.amd.com/en-us/download/auto-detect-tool.
- For systems with NVIDIA GPUs, use the GeForce Experience utility installed on your system to determine the best driver for your GPU.
- For systems with Intel integrated graphics, use the Driver Update Utility to see whether you can use generic Intel graphics drivers on your system or must get them from your computer vendor: http://www.intel.com/p/en_US/support/detect/graphics.

> **Tip**
> If you're not sure what video card or chipset your system uses, open the System Properties sheet, click Device Manager, and open the Display Adapter section.

Rolling Back Bad Driver Updates

Although the Update Driver button on the Driver tab of a device's Device Manager properties sheet hardly ever locates new drivers if you perform an Internet search, you can use it to install drivers you downloaded manually. And, if you install a new driver that doesn't work properly, use the Roll Back Driver on the same tab to remove it and return to the previous version (see Figure 14.16).

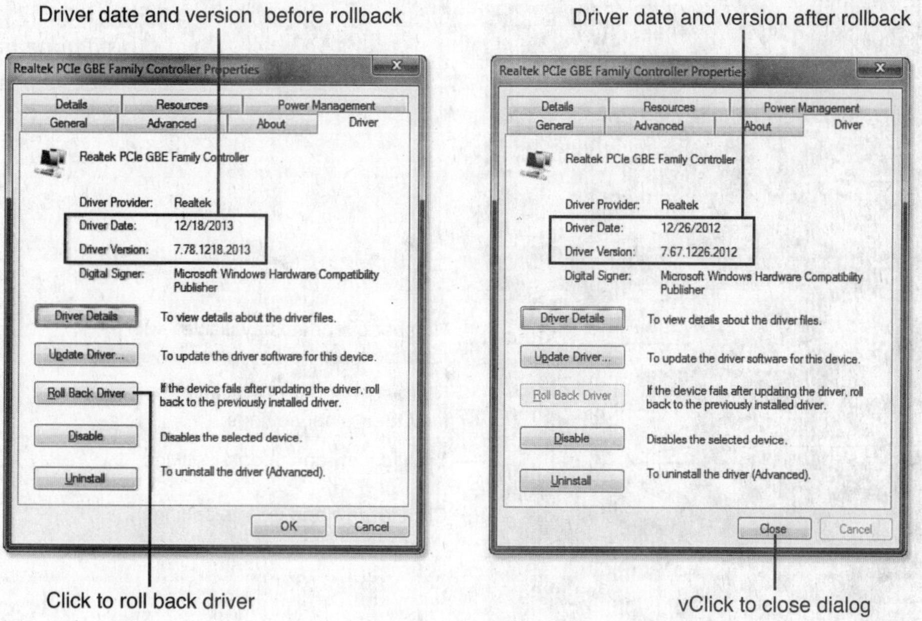

Figure 14.16 Rolling back a driver in Windows 7's Device Manager.

Updating iOS Devices

Updates to your iOS App Store apps or iOS itself can help improve stability and add features. Your iOS device (iPad, iPod Touch, or iPhone) can perform updates in one of two ways:

- Automatically
- Advise you of updates and let you choose when to install them

The latter method is preferred, especially if you don't use Wi-Fi connections very often, because running a lot of automatic updates on a cellular connection could make your device exceed your account's data limits.

To determine whether your device needs updates, check the icons for the App Store and Settings (typically visible as soon as you unlock your device). In Figure 14.17, we can see that 34 updates are available for apps in the App Store, and there's also a system update.

To update App Store apps, follow these steps:

1. Tap the **App Store** icon shown in Figure 14.17.
2. Tap the **Updates** icon when App Store opens.
3. To see what's new (iPhone/iPod Touch only), click the **What's New** arrow to see a brief description of changes. If you are updating an iPad, the description appears automatically.

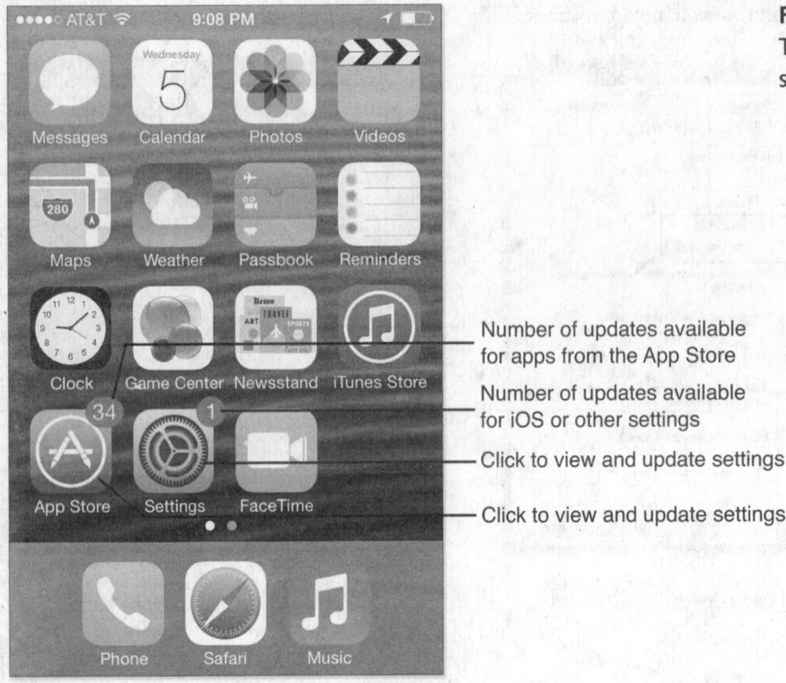

Figure 14.17
This iPhone has app and system updates available.

4. To update an individual app, tap the **Update** button for that app.
5. To update all listed apps, tap **Update All** (see Figure 14.18).

To update the software on your device, follow these steps:

1. Tap the **Settings** icon shown in Figure 14.17.
2. Tap **General**.
3. Tap Software Update.
4. Tap **Install Now**. Be sure to plug in your device if prompted (see Figure 14.19).
5. If prompted, agree to terms and conditions. The update is downloaded and installed.

To change how iTunes and App Store items are updated, follow these steps:

1. Tap **Settings**.
2. Tap **iTunes & App Store**.
3. Use the sliders to select automatic downloads (see Figure 4.20).

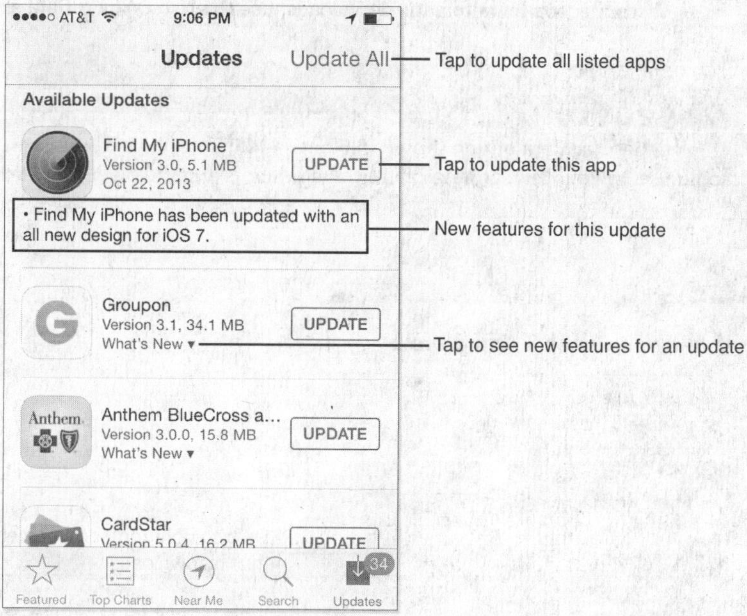

Figure 14.18
Viewing available App Store updates and details.

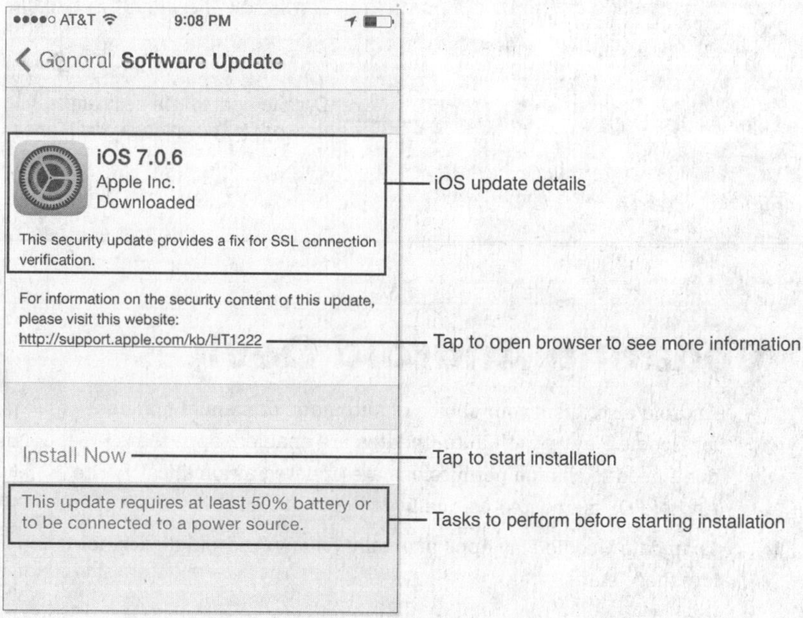

Figure 14.19
Preparing to install an update to iOS.

4. If you are using an iPhone or an iPad with a cellular modem and you want to use your cellular data connection for automatic downloads, use the Use Cellular Data slider also shown in Figure 14.20.

Caution

The Use Cellular Data option shown in Figure 14.20 is normally turned off. If you enable this feature, you could use up your cellular data plan's transfer limits and incur additional charges.

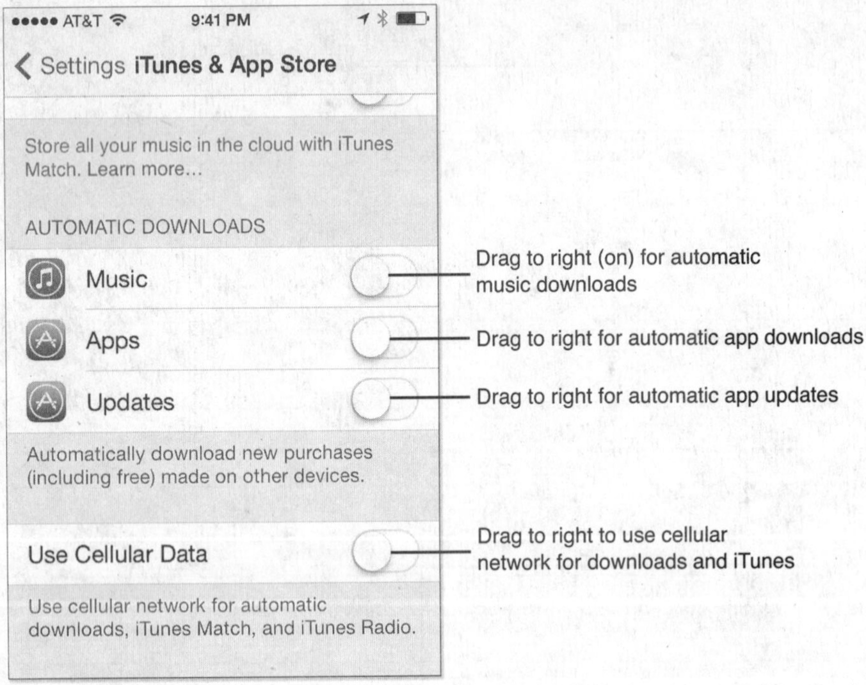

Figure 14.20 You can enable automatic updates for music, apps, and other updates and choose whether to use a cellular data connection with iTunes and App Store content.

Updating Android Devices

Android also offers your choice of automatic or manual updates for Google Play apps. If auto-updates are enabled, apps that don't need to change permissions are updated automatically. The Android OS is updated manually.

To update Google Play apps manually on any Android device, follow these steps:

1. Tap the **Google Play** icon on your Android device.

2. Open the Google Play menu.

Note

If an update needs to change permissions, you must grant approval before the update can run. Permissions include settings such as access to storage, contacts, and your location.

3. Tap **My Apps** (see Figure 14.21).

Figure 14.21
Preparing to view your apps in Google Play.

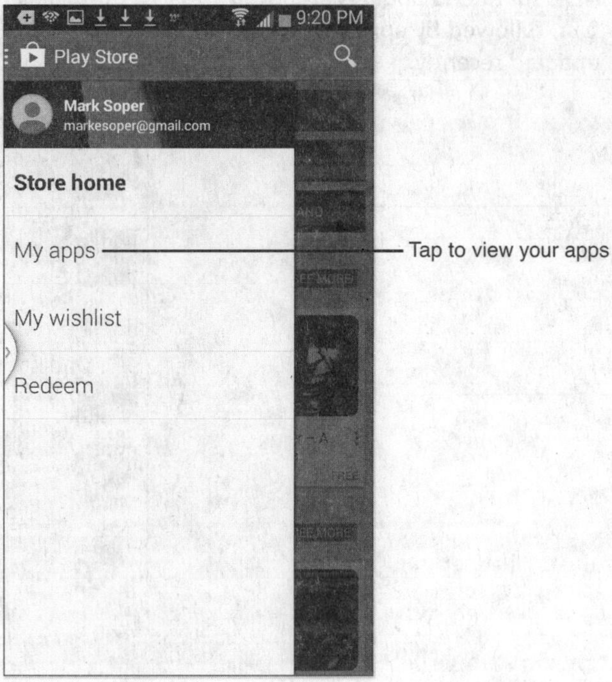

4. To update all apps needing updates, tap **Update All**. To update an individual app, click **Update** in the app's listing (see Figure 14.22).
5. Review the app permissions (new permissions are marked New), and click **Accept** to complete the update process for that app.

After all apps are updated, you might receive a notification listing the updated apps. To change how you receive app updates on a smartphone or a tablet with cellular data, follow these steps:

1. From the My Apps dialog shown in Figure 14.21, open the Settings menu on your device (see your device manual for details).
2. From the Settings menu (see Figure 14.23), tap **Auto-Update Apps**.
3. Click the update option you prefer (see Figure 14.24).

To update your Android OS version on either a smartphone or a tablet, follow these steps:

1. Tap the **Settings** (gear) icon on the home screen.

Figure 14.22
Apps that need updates are listed first, followed by apps that were updated recently.

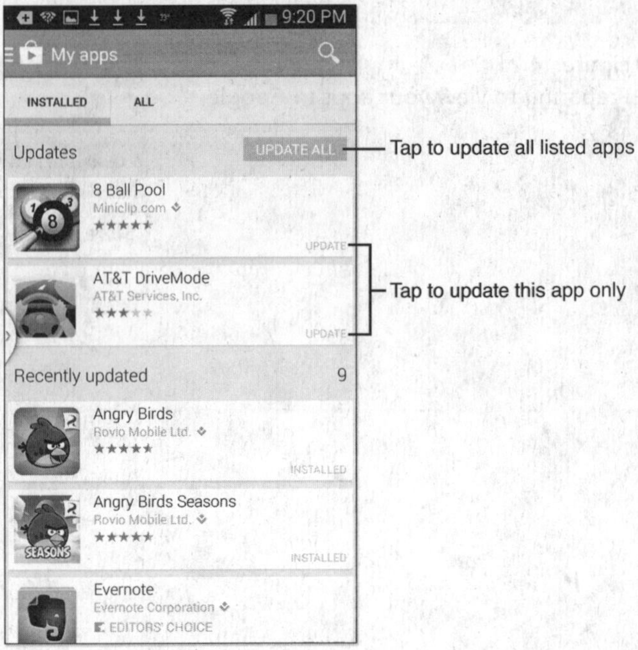

Figure 14.23
The Settings menu for a typical Android smartphone.

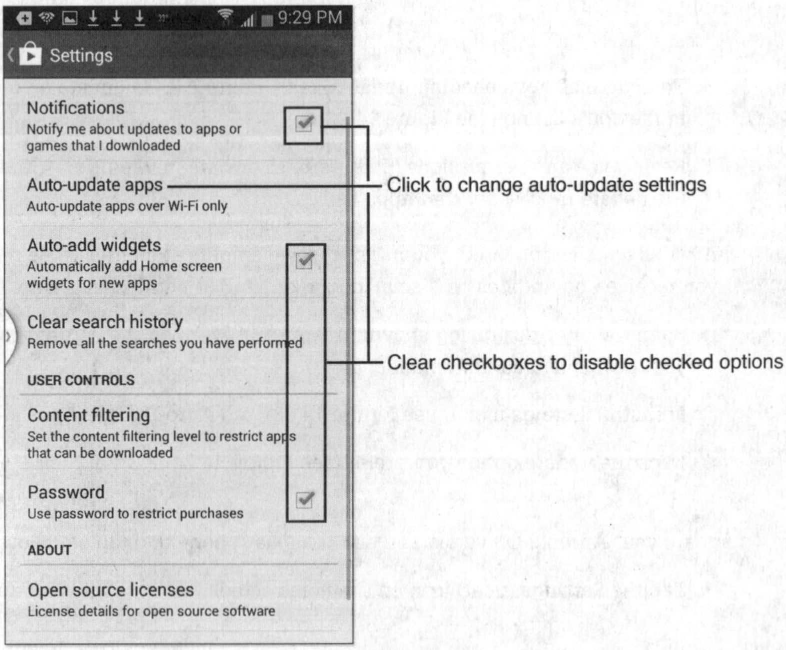

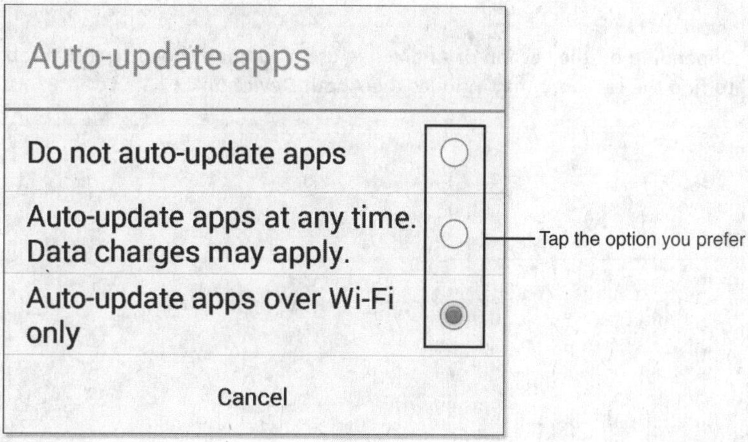

Figure 14.24
Choosing a method for updating apps.

2. Tap the **About Device** icon (see Figure 14.25).
3. Tap **Software Update**.
4. Follow the prompts to check for an update and install it if an update is available. Restart your system as prompted.

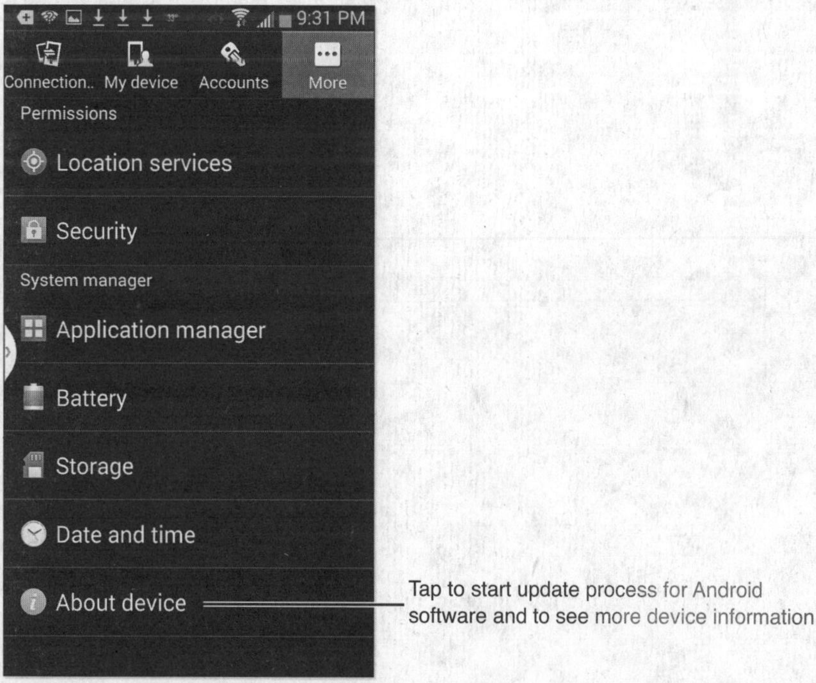

Figure 14.25
Preparing to check for a software update.

Note

Depending on the version of Android in use, you might need to click a tab at the top of the Settings screen to find the category that includes the About Device link.

15

DEALING WITH CONTRARY MEMORY

Fast Track to Solutions

Table 15.1 Memory Problems and Solutions

Symptom	Flowchart or Book Section	Page #
I'm not sure how much RAM my system needs	Table 15.2	390
I have a memory module, but I don't know if it's DDR2 or DDR3	Figure 15.4	392
What's different about high-performance RAM?	Figure 15.7	396
How can I make sure I'm getting the right RAM for my computer?	Choosing a Memory Upgrade	391

Troubleshooting Slow System Performance

Although many components affect system performance, such as the graphics card and hard disk, perhaps the two most important components affecting system performance are the memory and the processor (CPU). Although processor upgrades often require motherboard changes on desktop computers and can't be performed on notebook computers, virtually every computer can benefit from added memory. Adding memory is not only one of the best ways to boost performance, but it is also one of the least expensive. How can you tell if you need to add memory? Here are some signs that your system may have a memory shortage:

- You see the Windows "I'm busy" hula hoop or ball-bearing loop appear frequently when you have multiple program windows open.
- The hard disk activity light is blinking furiously as you work.
- Switching between programs takes measurable time instead of being instantaneous.
- When you open a new folder, Windows takes several seconds to display the icons inside.

Is a lack of RAM (random access memory) really the problem? Use the following methods to determine whether the performance bottleneck is caused by a lack of system memory:

- Determine the amount of memory you currently have installed on your system.
- Determine how many programs you run at the same time (on average).
- Check the performance of your system.

To find out how much physical memory is available to Windows (and how fast your processor is, too), use one of these methods:

For Windows 7 and Windows 8/8.1 (Windows Desktop): right-click **Computer** and select **Properties**. This displays the System Properties dialog, as shown in Figure 15.1.

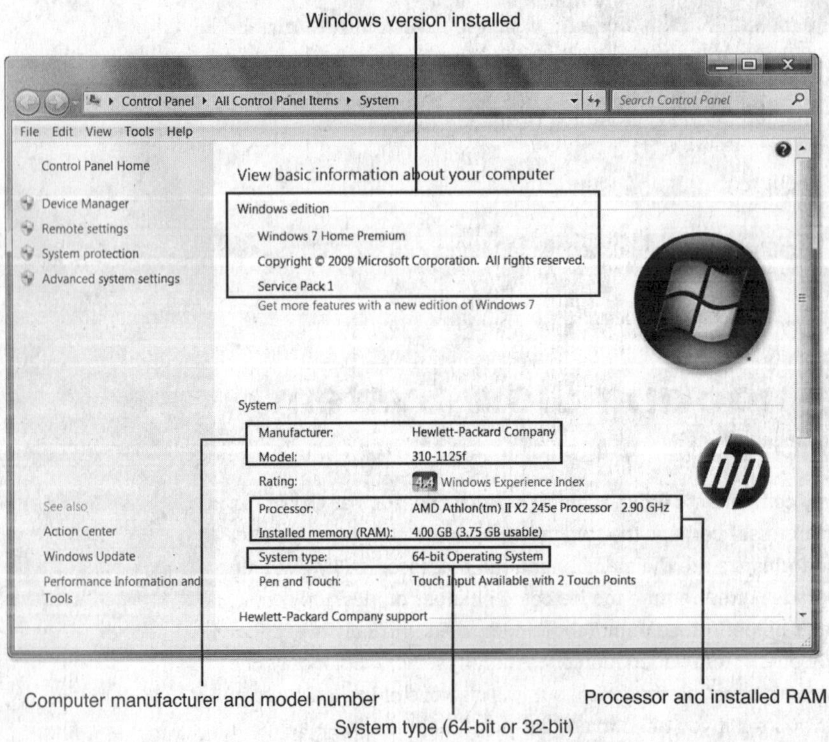

Figure 15.1 The System Properties dialog in Windows 7.

From Windows 8/8.1, you can also press the Windows logo key and the letter X, and then click **System**.

If you prefer to use the touchscreen in Windows 8.1:

1. Open the **Charms** menu.
2. Tap **Settings**.
3. Tap **Change PC Settings**.
4. Tap **PC and Devices**.
5. Tap **PC Info** (see Figure 15.2).

Note
Depending on your computer's specific hardware, System Properties might be able to identify your system's brand and model number (as shown in Figure 15.1).

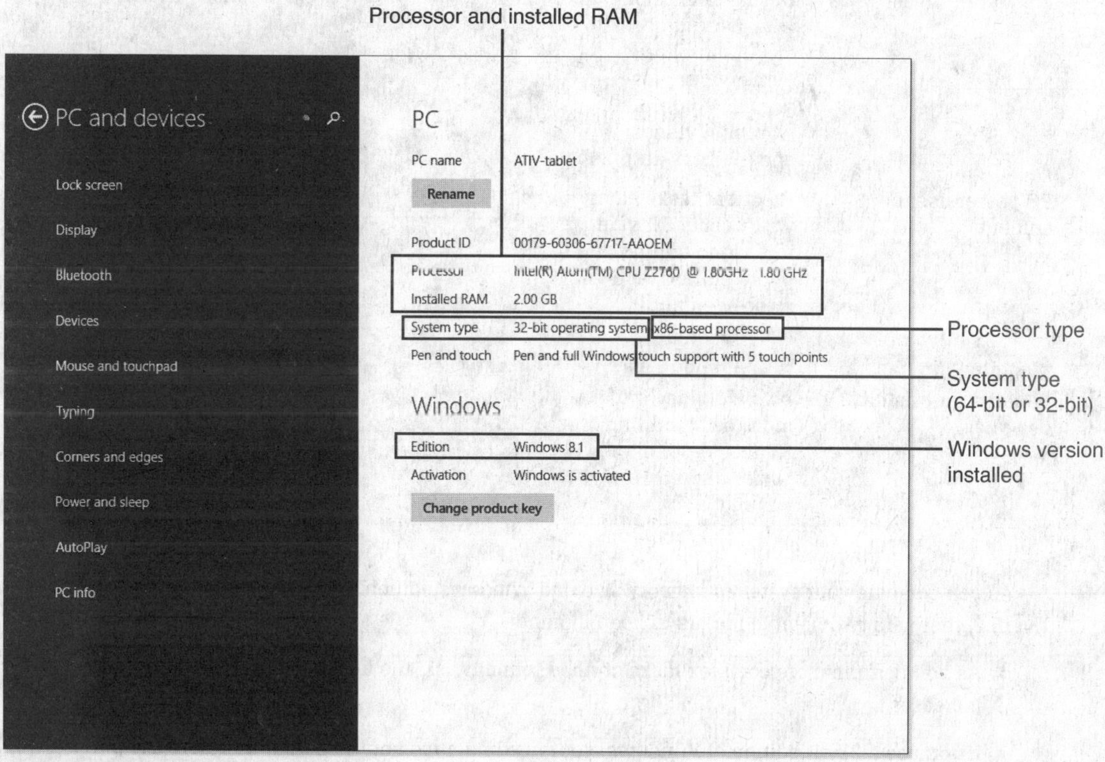

Figure 15.2
The PC info dialog in Windows 8.1.

According to memory vendor Crucial.com, the amount of RAM memory you need in your system varies with the types of tasks you perform. We've adapted their recommendations (see http://www.crucial.com/support/howmuch.aspx) for Table 15.2 to help you plan your upgrades.

Compare the amount of available memory in your system to the figures in Table 15.2 to determine whether adding memory could speed up your system.

Table 15.2 Recommended Memory Sizes by Tasks

User Type	Typical Applications	Recommended Memory Size	Recommended Windows Edition
Casual PC user	Web browsing (Internet Explorer, Firefox, Chrome, etc.), email, and playing digital music	1–2GB	32-bit or 64-bit
Frequent PC user	Casual tasks along with word processing, Flash-based games, entry-level graphics programs, watching videos, and multitasking	2–4GB	32-bit or 64-bit
PC power user or student	Frequent tasks along with casual 3D gaming, video editing, photo editing, and intensive multitasking	4–8GB	64-bit
Professional PC user or gamer or graphics designer	Power user tasks plus HD video and multimedia editing, 3D modeling, high-performance 3D gaming	8–16GB	64-bit

As you compare your system's memory size and Windows edition to the recommendations in Table 15.2, there are two notable factors to keep in mind:

- As you perform more complex tasks or need to multitask, the likelihood of a RAM upgrade increases.
- If you use a 32-bit edition of Windows, your maximum memory size (and therefore the performance of your system) is limited.

Note

32-bit editions of Windows cannot use more than 4GB of RAM. In addition, memory over 3GB can conflict with installed devices that also use memory spaces. If you need 4GB of RAM or more, you need a computer with a 64-bit processor running a 64-bit edition of Windows. System Properties identifies your processor type and Windows edition.

If you purchased a new laptop or desktop in the past three or four years, chances are you're using a 64-bit edition of Windows. In that case, the amount of RAM you can install is dictated by the design of your system's motherboard. However, if you have a Windows tablet, you might have two limitations to deal with: many low-cost Windows tablets use a low-powered 32-bit ATOM processor with nonexpandable memory (usually 2GB). As Table 15.2 suggests, these are great for casual use, but if you're planning to edit photos or videos, you need a system with a faster processor and more RAM.

Keep in mind that if your computer runs out of actual RAM, it will use its *virtual* memory, which is stored in a file called the *page file* (also called the *swapfile*). The page file is an area of free space on your hard disk that the computer treats like additional RAM. Unfortunately, the difference between accessing data from system RAM and your hard drive is like the difference between making photocopies in your office or driving across town to an office supply store for copies. It's a very slow substitute.

> **Tip**
>
> To help prevent your system from running out of physical RAM, close programs you are not using. If your system is short of physical RAM, having fewer programs will help your system switch between programs faster.

Choosing a Memory Upgrade

Although all PCs use RAM, you can't go into a retail store and simply ask for "RAM." Desktop computers use various types of DIMM memory modules, whereas laptops and all-in-one computers use reduced-size versions known as small outline DIMMs (SODIMMs). Both DIMMs and SODIMMs are available in various sizes, speeds, and memory technologies customized for specific computers. Figure 15.3 illustrates typical laptop memory modules, and Figure 15.4 illustrates typical desktop memory modules. Most recent laptop and all-in-one computers use two SODIMM modules, whereas desktop computers can use two, three, or four DIMM modules.

To make sure you get the right memory for your computer, I recommend one of the following methods:

- Use a memory configuration program provided by the memory vendor.
- Look up your computer brand and model on a memory vendor's website.

Although you can purchase memory from your computer manufacturer, I generally recommend using a major memory vendor instead. You can get a wider variety of options at lower prices, and computer manufacturers get their RAM from the same vendors.

Crucial.com offers a memory configuration program that runs from your web browser to detect your specific system, current memory configuration, and suggested upgrades. Crucial also offers a database of systems you can check. Other major memory vendors typically offer only a database of systems you can review to locate recommended memory.

I recommend using a memory configuration program because I have found it can be very difficult to locate the exact model number of your system, and even after you do, many system database listings are incomplete and you might not find your particular model listed. This is a particular problem with laptop computers.

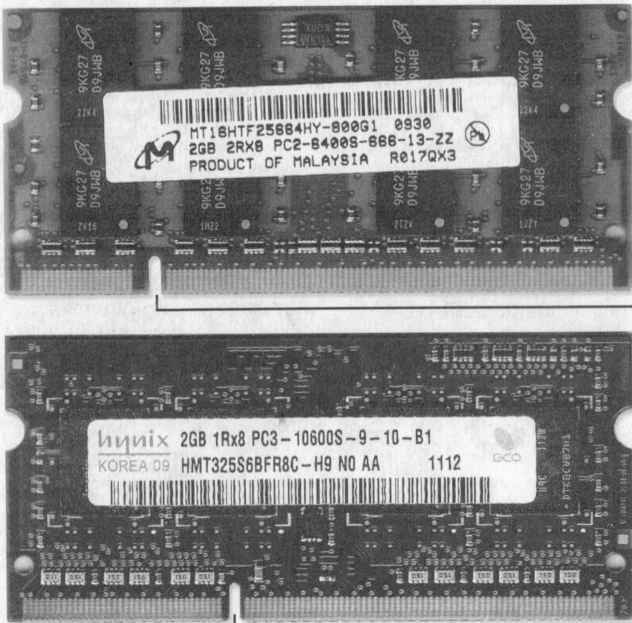

Figure 15.3
Typical DDR2 (top) and DDR3 (bottom) SODIMM modules used in laptops and all-in-one computers.

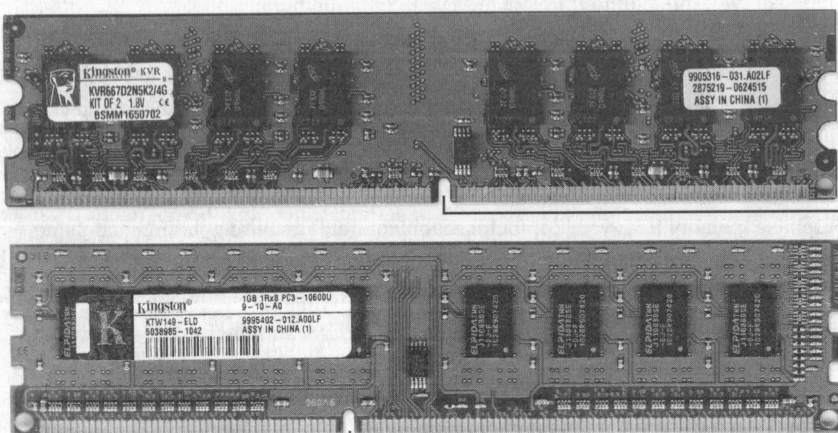

Figure 15.4
Typical DDR2 (top) and DDR3 (bottom) DIMM modules used in desktop computers.

Here's how to use a memory configuration program (in this example, we'll use the Crucial.com version):

1. Go to the memory vendor's website.
2. Click the link to the memory configuration program (Crucial calls theirs "System Scanner").
3. Follow the instructions onscreen to download and run the scanning program.
4. After the program runs, you will see your current configuration and upgrade options.

Figure 15.5 lists the results of a scan of an HP TouchSmart 310-1125f touchscreen computer. It has 4GB currently installed as two 2GB modules. The recommended upgrade is 8GB as two 4GB modules.

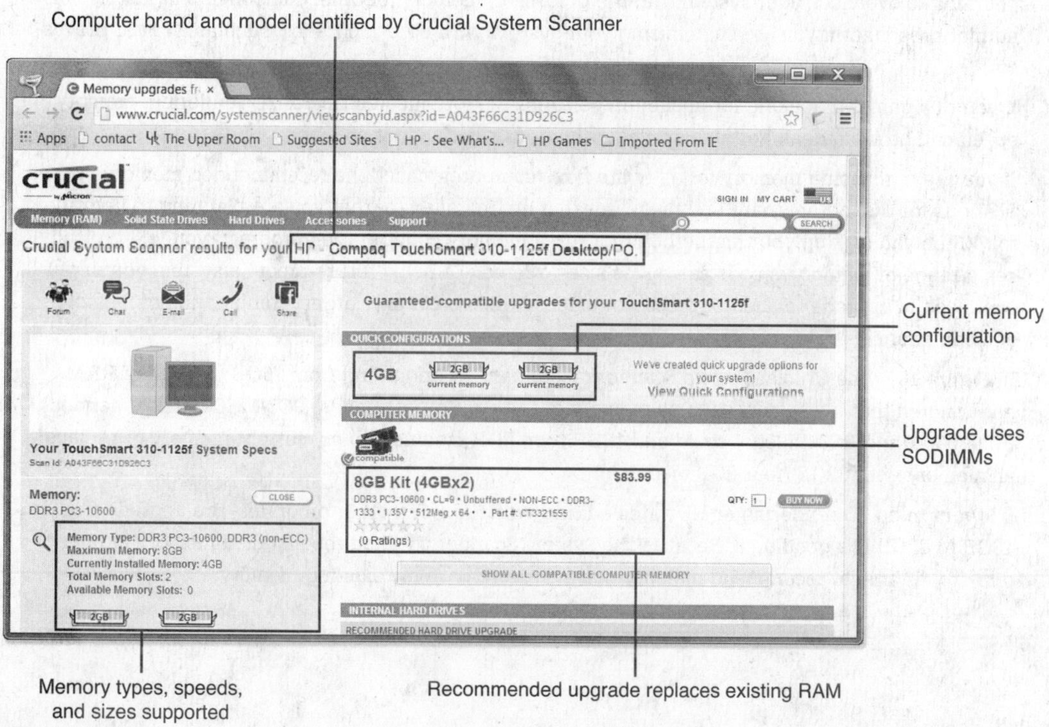

Figure 15.5

The Crucial.com memory scanner recommends an 8GB (2×4GB) memory upgrade for this computer.

If you prefer to purchase memory from another vendor, you can use the technical information shown as part of the memory description to look up comparable modules.

Note

Information such as type (DDR3), speed (PC3-10600 and DDR-1333), timing (CL9), voltage (1.35V DC), and internal design (512Meg × 64) are critical in finding comparable modules. Look up the module part number if you are not sure if the memory is standard-size DIMMs or SODIMMs.

Upgrading to Faster Memory

Memory is rated by speed. Changing to faster memory can improve system performance if you are planning to overclock your system (run the processor, memory, or other components at faster-than-normal speeds) or if you are customizing your system with other upgrades, such as a faster processor.

If you're a gamer or looking for maximum performance for video editing or 3D rendering, memory speed can be a big deal. For web surfing or home budgeting, not so much.

If you are purchasing memory for a "white-box" computer, check the recommended memory specifications for the motherboard and processor that are installed (or that you are planning to upgrade to). When you look up your motherboard or run a memory configuration program, you will typically see a range of memory speeds as well as sizes offered. To help "future-proof" a system you might overclock or upgrade to a faster processor, choose the fastest and largest combination of memory you can afford.

In Figure 15.6, the Crucial System Scanner recommended upgrading from 16GB to 32GB of RAM, and it noted that my system can use memory of three different speeds: PC3-12800 (recommended), PC3-10600, and PC3-14900. I could add 16GB (two 8GB modules) to my current memory or replace all memory with 32GB (four 8GB modules).

If I want to do 3D rendering or HD video editing while running other programs, the upgrade from 16GB to 32GB is a good deal. Because the System Scanner checked the installed memory in my system, it was able to recommend memory that will work with my existing memory.

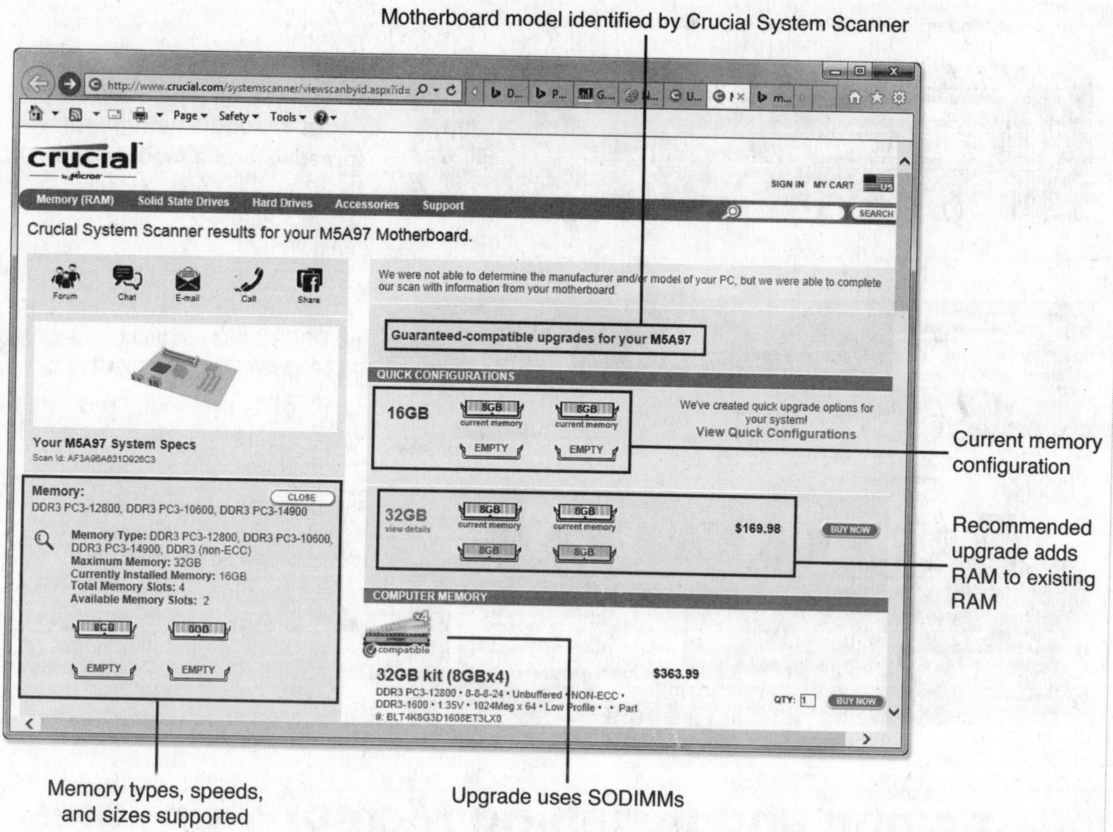

Figure 15.6
Two options for this system: upgrade from 16GB to 32GB or replace all existing memory with 32GB of RAM.

When to Choose High-Performance Memory

Standard memory modules are designed to run at standard speeds. However, if you are planning to overclock your system, consider buying memory that is not only faster, but is designed to help maintain reliable performance when run at faster-than-normal speeds.

Figure 15.7 compares a standard Kingston DDR3 module (top) to two modules made for overclocking: Crucial Ballistix Sport (middle) and G.Skill Ripjaws (bottom). The heat spreaders over the RAM modules on the Crucial module and the finned heat sinks on the G.Skill module dissipate heat to prevent lockups or crashes.

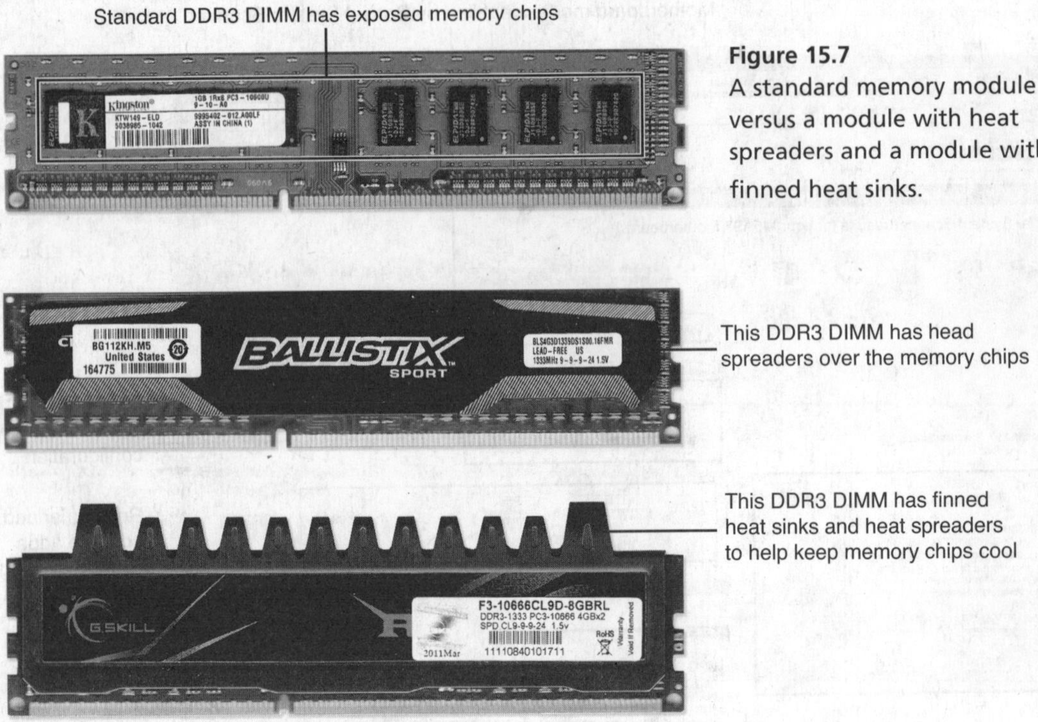

Figure 15.7 A standard memory module versus a module with heat spreaders and a module with finned heat sinks.

Removing and Installing Memory Modules

Before you install a memory module, get ready to do it safely:

1. Disconnect the system from electrical power. If you are installing memory into a laptop, also remove the battery.
2. Remove the system cover (desktop) or memory compartment cover (laptop).
3. Put on an antistatic wrist strap and use the alligator clip to connect to a metal part inside the computer.

Removing and Installing SODIMMs

Because most laptops or all-in-one computers have no more than two SODIMM sockets, it's often necessary to remove one or both SODIMMs before you can install a memory upgrade. To remove an SODIMM module on a laptop or all-in-one computer, follow these steps:

1. Push the securing clips on either side of the module away from the module (see Figure 15.8).
2. Swing the module up (see Figure 15.9).
3. Remove the module (see Figure 15.10).

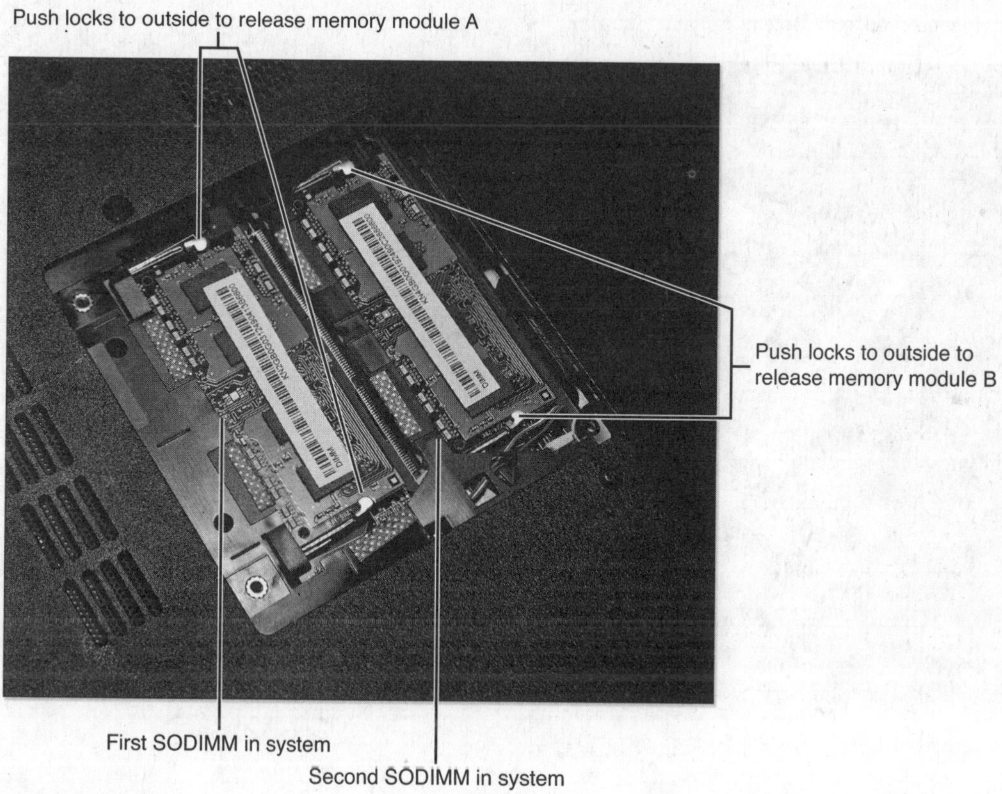

Figure 15.8
DDR3 SODIMM memory modules in a typical laptop computer.

To insert an SODIMM module, follow these steps:

1. Line up the connectors on the module with the socket.
2. Push the module into the connectors (refer to Figure 15.9).
3. Push the module into place until the securing clips lock into position (refer to Figure 15.8).

Caution

Whether you're installing DIMMs or SODIMMs, don't force the module into place. You can break a module if it's not properly aligned with the socket. When you install an SODIMM, it's very important to insert the module completely into the socket before pushing it into place (review Figure 15.10).

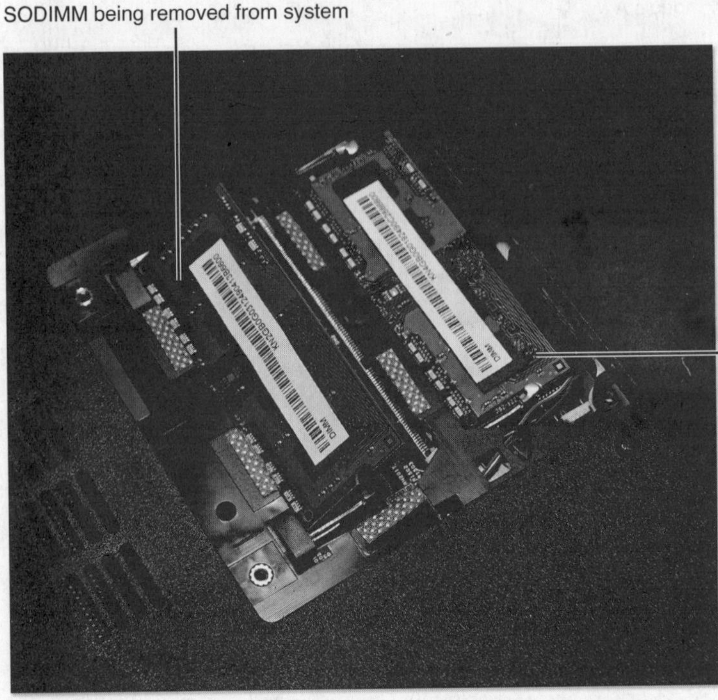

Figure 15.9
Preparing to remove an SODIMM from a laptop.

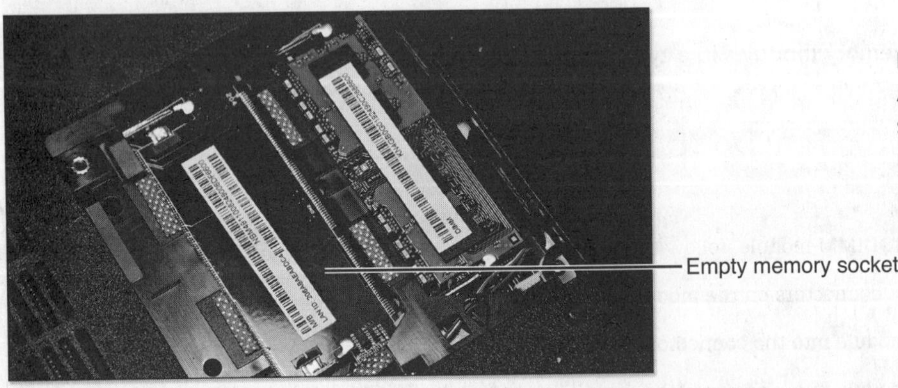

Figure 15.10
An SODIMM socket after the memory module has been removed.

Installing and Removing DIMMs

In some cases, you can install additional DIMMs on a desktop computer without removing any. To insert a DIMM module:

1. Line up the connectors on the module with the socket (see Figure 15.11).
2. Push the module down into place until the securing clips lock into position (see Figure 15.12).

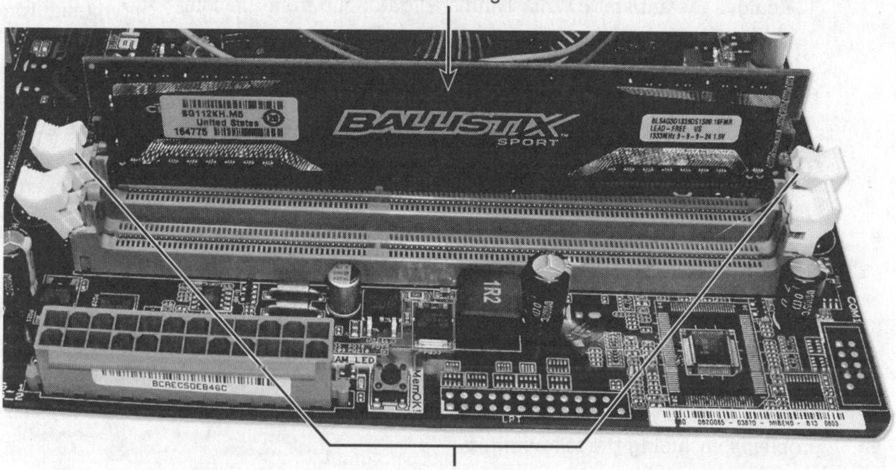

Figure 15.11 Preparing to insert a DIMM into a memory socket on a desktop computer.

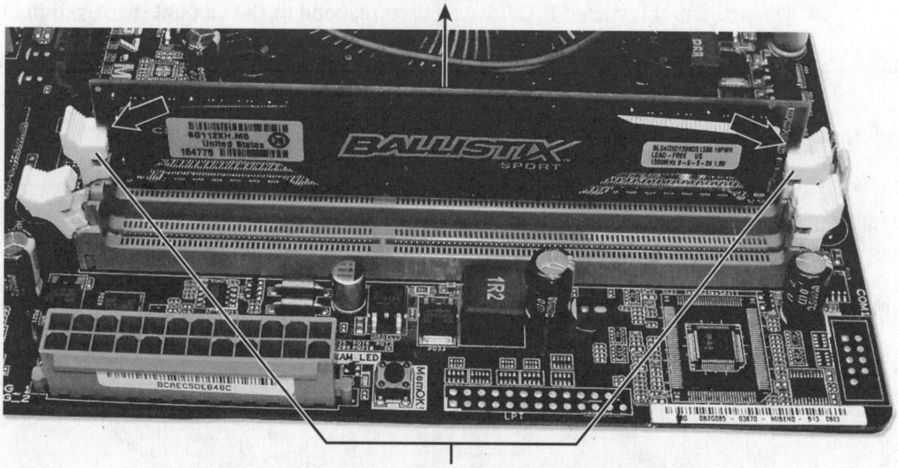

Figure 15.12 Preparing to remove a DIMM module after installation.

To remove a DIMM module, follow these steps:

1. Swing the retaining clips up and out of the way.
2. Pull the DIMM straight up out of the socket.

Completing the Process

After the memory is installed, follow these steps:

1. Remove the antistatic wrist band's alligator clip from the computer.
2. Close up the computer, and fasten the case or memory socket cover into position with the appropriate screws.
3. Restart the computer.

> **Caution**
> With some computers, you will be prompted to rerun BIOS setup if the memory size has changed. As soon as the BIOS setup program displays the main menu, save the new settings and exit. Your system will restart and boot to the operating system.

Signs of Memory Problems

The RAM in your desktop or laptop computer is the workspace used by your operating system and your apps to get work done. Until you save a new document, photo, video, or music clip or save your changes to an existing one, your work resides in memory only. If your system locks up or crashes before you save your work, you've lost it. Memory that's not working correctly can cause a variety of problems, including the following:

- System lockups and crashes, especially after the system has been running for a while.
- The system powers up when you turn it on but won't boot to the operating system.
- The system might beep and not boot to the operating system.
- The amount of installed RAM does not correspond to the amount displayed in System Properties.

When a system locks up during operation, the problem could be memory related, but it could also be attributable to problems with other hardware, with viruses, or with Windows. The contents of memory can be corrupted by excessive heat or by problems with the system power supply.

To learn more about detecting problems with your system's power supply, see "Testing the Power Supply," Chapter 7, p.176.

To learn more about reducing heat buildup inside your system, see "Keeping Your Desktop Computer Cool," Chapter 16, p.406.

To learn about detecting and removing malware, see Chapter 4, "Curing Malware and Stopping Scams," p.109.

Although your computer might perform a quick memory test with its Power-On Self-Test (POST) process when you turn it on, you can test installed memory with a memory-testing program. A memory-testing program does a much more thorough job of looking for memory problems than the BIOS can.

Finding a Defective Memory Module

If you can turn on your computer but it won't start—it won't even display the prompt to open the BIOS setup menu—a bad memory module is very likely the cause.

To determine whether you have a bad memory module installed, follow these steps:

1. Follow the instructions for removing a module from your system.
2. Leave the module that is closest to the processor or the motherboard.
3. Follow the instructions for closing up the system and restarting it.
4. If your system starts, the module you removed is defective. Replace it.
5. If your system does not start, go back to step 1, remove the module you left in the system, and install the module you removed. Follow step 3. If the system starts, the module you just removed is defective.

Testing Memory

If your system boots but you suspect that your computer's RAM is not working correctly (for example, you experience system crashes and lockups), you can use a variety of testing programs to check it. Windows versions 7/8/8.1 include Windows Memory Diagnostic, which can be run from the Administrative Tools folder in System and Security, which is in the Control Panel (see Figure 15.12). You can run the test immediately or the next time you restart the computer.

During the test process (see Figure 15.13), you can change the number of times the tests run (default is twice) and select the testing level by pressing the F1 key, selecting the option(s) desired, and pressing F10 to apply them. After the tests are over, the results are provided when you boot to the Windows desktop.

If you need to test memory on systems that run Linux or MacOS as well as Windows, try Passmark Software's free Memtest86 (www.memtest86.com). Passmark Software is a leading developer of benchmark software for PCs.

If the memory test locates defective memory, follow these instructions to determine which module is defective:

1. Follow the instructions for removing a module from your system.
2. Leave the module that is closest to the processor or the motherboard.
3. Follow the instructions for closing up the system and restarting it.
4. Restart your computer and rerun the memory test.
5. If the memory test shows no errors, the module you removed is defective. Replace it.

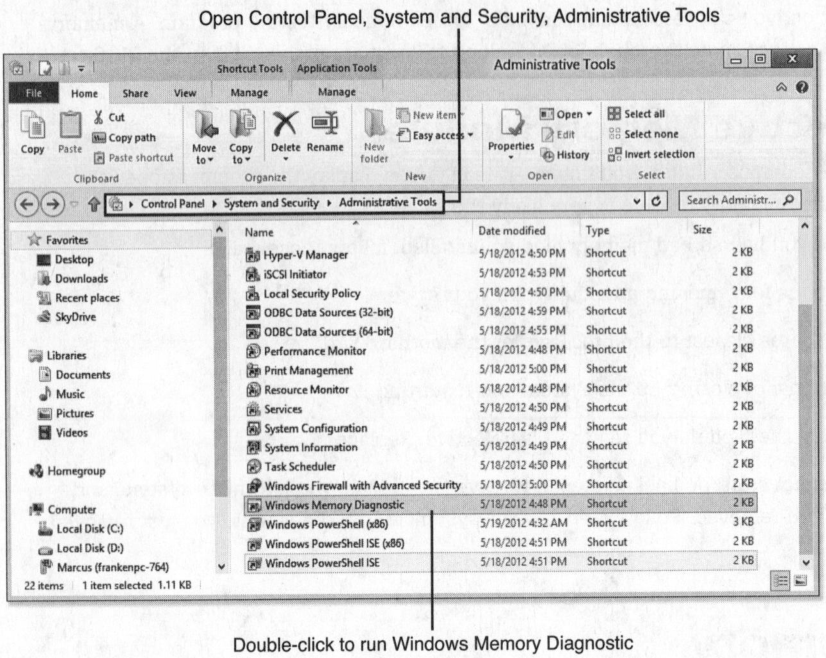

Figure 15.13 Starting the Windows Memory Diagnostic from Control Panel.

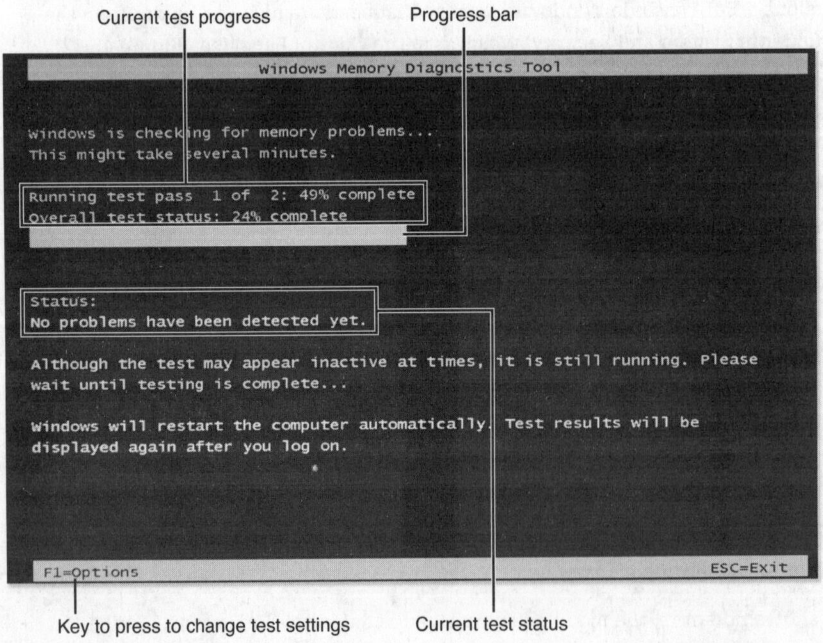

Figure 15.14 The Windows Memory Diagnostic tests runs before Windows boots.

6. If the memory test reports errors and you have only one module left in the computer, the module that is still installed is defective. Remove and replace it.
7. If you have more than one module in the computer, remove one of them and rerun the test. Continue until you determine which module is defective. Remove and replace it.

If you need to replace a memory module, consider upgrading the total amount of RAM in the system. Use the methods discussed earlier in this chapter to decide on the amount of RAM you need.

16

KEEPING DEVICES COOL

Fast Track to Solutions

Table 16.1 Symptom Table

Symptom	Flowchart or Book Section	Page #
High-pitched squealing noise inside computer.	Troubleshooting Noises Inside Computer (flowchart)	Chapter 24
Laptop crashes after being on for a while.	Troubleshooting Laptop Crashes (flowchart)	Chapter 24
Need to see processor temperature while in Windows.	Using Desktop Health Monitoring Software	410
Battery charge runs out quickly on laptop or tablet.	Adjusting Power Settings	418
Computers near pets are overheating.	Preventing Desktop and Laptop Overheating with Preventative Maintenance	421
Fan speeds indicate fan failure.	Adding and Replacing Fans	411
Newly installed case fan not detected by PC Health.	Fan Connections on the Motherboard	408
Processor temperatures increase sharply when system overclocked.	Using Third-Party Active Heat Sinks for Your Processor	415

What Excessive Heat Does to Your Device

Whether you're using a tablet, a smartphone, a laptop, or a desktop PC, heat is not your friend—or your device's friend, either. Excessive heat can cause your device to slow down to cool off, its noise levels (due to fan noise) to increase, its battery life to drop, and its operation to become less stable, which can crash your device, and, in extreme cases, cause it to fail.

So, keeping your device cool during operation is a really good idea. In this chapter, we'll show you how to avoid overheating to keep your devices, your data, and you very happy.

Keeping Your Desktop Computer Cool

From multiple high-performance 3D video cards and multiple memory modules to fast multicore processors and the voltage regulators they use for power, desktop computers have the greatest potential to run hot because of the heat-producing components onboard.

Your desktop computer relies on airflow through the case to keep its components cool. In addition to the fan in the power supply and the fan/heat sink on the processor, most desktop computers have a rear-mounted fan to pull hot air out of the computer, and most have provisions for additional fans. Many video cards also have cooling fans (see Figure 16.1).

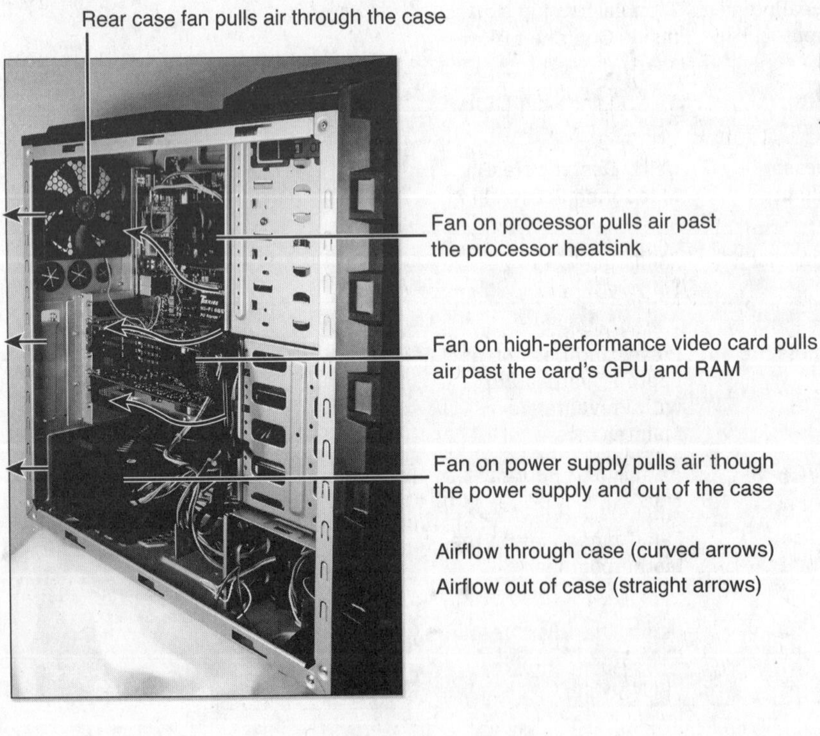

Figure 16.1
Fans in a typical desktop computer.

If any of these fans fail, your system will probably overheat, causing the system to slow down or stop. Thus, keeping an eye on fan speeds and temperature is very important. There are two ways to check this information: system BIOS features and programs that run after Windows starts.

Checking Fan Speeds and System Temperatures with the System BIOS

The system BIOS on most desktop computers includes a feature that displays processor and motherboard temperatures and fan speeds. It's often referred to as System Monitor or PC Health. Figure 16.2 and 16.3 provide two typical examples of this information.

Note that the system shown in Figure 16.2 does not display fan speeds for chassis-mounted fans (SYS FAN1, SYS FAN2). Compare that to the information shown for fan speeds in Figure 16.3.

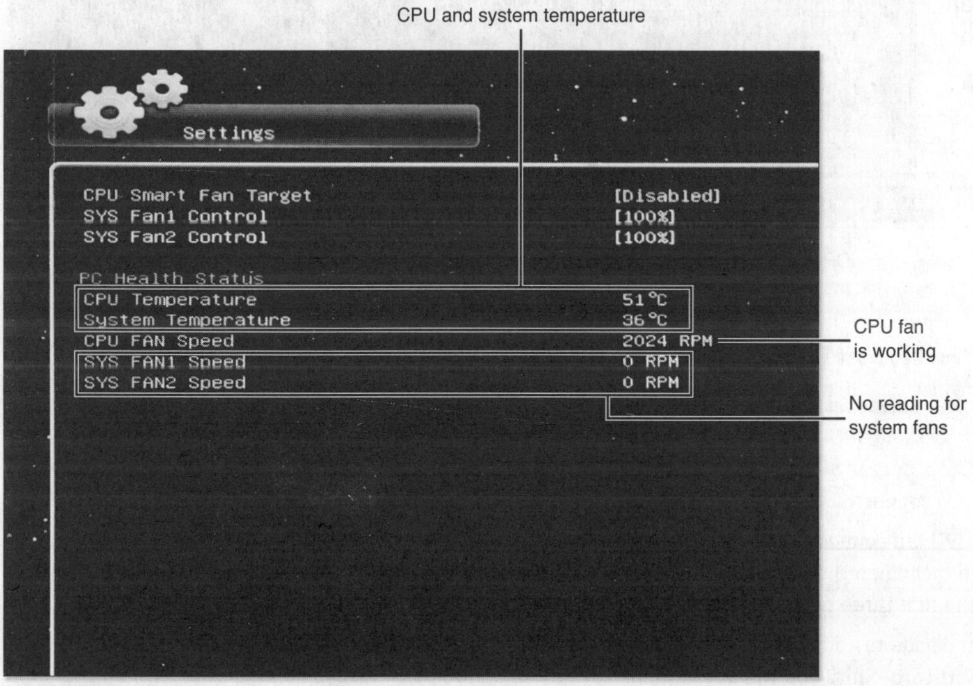

Figure 16.2
A PC Health Status display from a UEFI BIOS shows CPU (processor) and system temperature, CPU fan speed, and system (SYS) fan speeds.

How does the system pictured in Figure 16.3 know that these fans are working? Does the system pictured in Figure 16.2 have defective fans, or no fans? To find out, let's take a closer look at how fans connect to the motherboard.

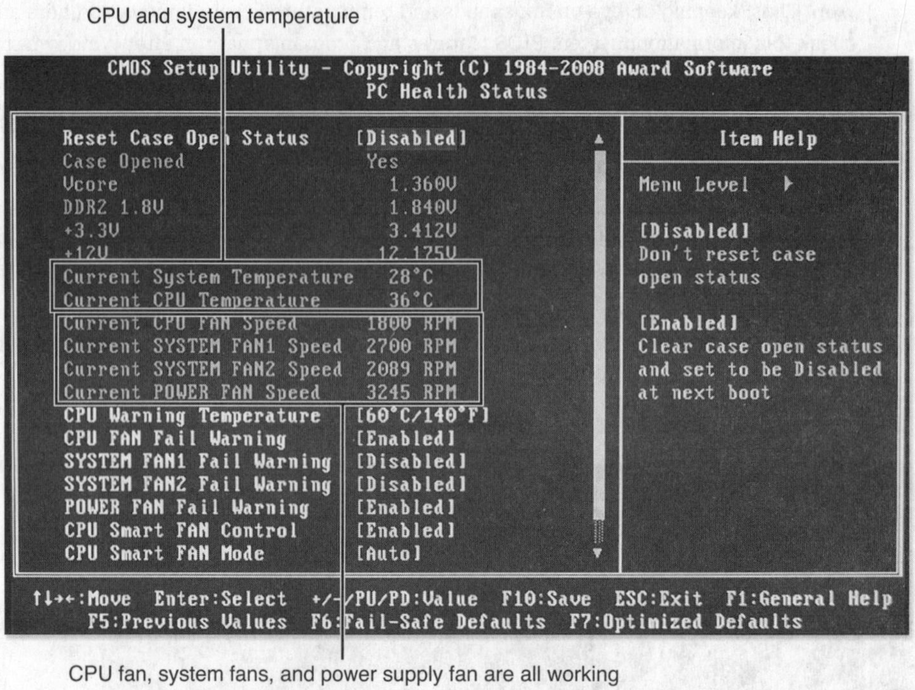

Figure 16.3 A PC Health Status display from a traditional BIOS shows CPU and system temperature as well as fan speeds for four fans.

Fan Connections on the Motherboard

A typical desktop computer's motherboard has two types of fan connectors: a four-pin connector for the processor (CPU) fan and one or more three-pin connectors for system fans (fans mounted on the front, top, or rear of the case). Figure 16.4 illustrates how these connections look before and after fans are connected to them.

The CPU fan connector (front) has a ground wire, a +12V DC power wire, a fan speed (also known as fan tachometer) wire, and a fan control wire (controls fan speed). The system fan connector (rear) has the first three wires but lacks a fan control wire.

If you decide to add fans, you should connect additional fans to the system fan connections to the motherboard—until you run out of them.

Some system fans are not connected to the motherboard. Instead, they get their power from a four-pin Molex power connector (Figure 16.5). Older fans used only the Molex connector, whereas newer fans like the one in Figure 16.5 are designed to use the three-pin motherboard power connector or a Molex connector. When a Molex connector is used, a single-wire connector is provided to connect to the motherboard for fan monitoring.

> **Note**
> Some systems have three or four motherboard connectors for system fans, but the BIOS might display information for only two fans.

If the single-wire connector isn't plugged into a system fan header on the motherboard (for example, if no headers are left or the wire is too short to reach a system fan header), there is no way to monitor the fan's performance. As far as the BIOS is concerned, the fan doesn't exist.

Figure 16.4
CPU and system fan connectors compared.

Figure 16.5
Connection and power options for a case fan.

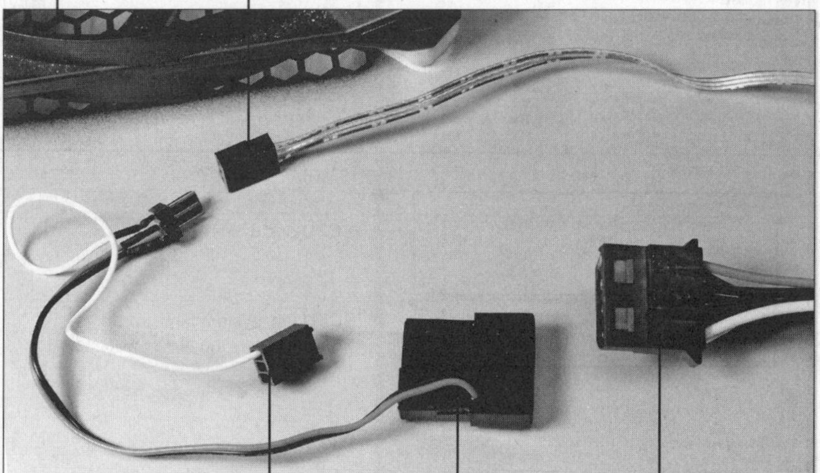

Troubleshooting Fan Failures

If a fan is connected to the motherboard and is monitored by the BIOS, you can use the PC Health Status or Hardware Monitor dialog to determine if the fan has failed. If a case fan starts dropping in speed or if either fan starts turning much more slowly than normal, suspect fan failure.

If there is no RPM readout, shut down the computer, turn off the power supply, and try to hand turn the fan. A working fan turns freely; a defective fan won't turn or turns only with effort. Use this method to diagnose fans that are not monitored by the BIOS.

See the section "Adding Additional Fans," later in this chapter, to learn how to replace case fans. See the section "Using Third-Party Heat Sinks and Fans," in this chapter, to learn how to replace the processor (CPU) fan and heat sink.

Using Desktop Health Monitoring Software

Some retail store computers and motherboards include desktop health monitoring software. These programs display the information gathered by the system BIOS while you run Windows so you don't need to restart your system to see temperature, fan speed, or voltage information. Some programs display additional technical information.

If your system didn't include this type of software, you can download monitoring packages from third-party vendors. You can get a sample of CPUID's HW Monitor Pro at http://www.cpuid.com/softwares/hwmonitor.html. Figure 16.6 illustrates a typical report from the trial version. The licensed version displays information in place of the word TRIAL.

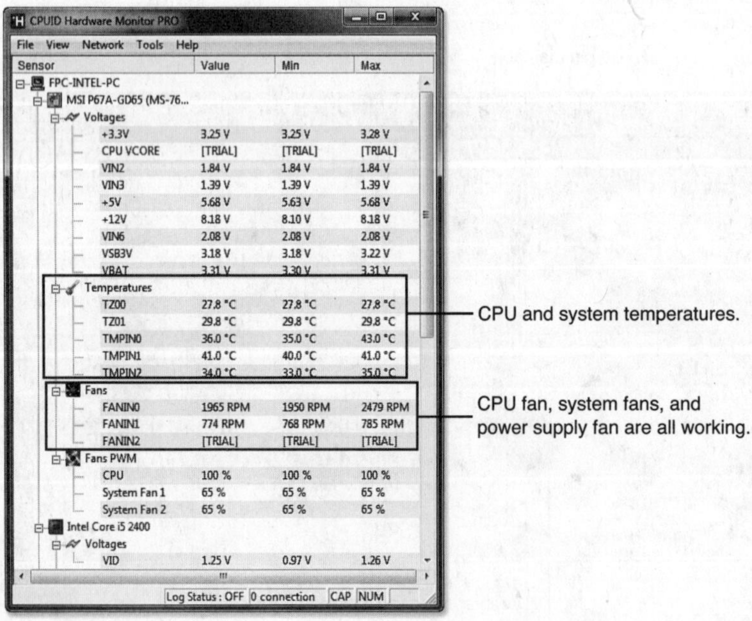

Figure 16.6
Using the trial version of HWMonitorPRO.

If you prefer a free, open source product, the Open Hardware Monitor is available at www.openhardwaremonitor.org (see Figure 16.7). Although it provides somewhat less detail than HWMonitorPRO, it provides the essential information you need about system cooling.

Note

In HWMonitorPRO, the CPU fan is typically identified as FANIN01, SYS Fan 1 as FANIN02, and SYS Fan 2 as FANIN03.

Figure 16.7 Using Open Hardware Monitor on the same system shown in Figure 16.6.

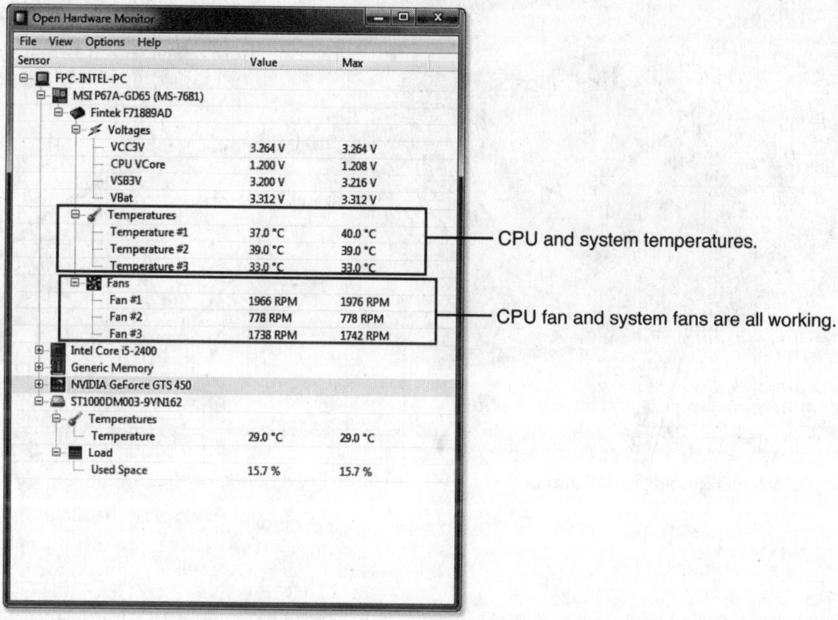

Adding and Replacing Fans

Because fans are called upon to pull air through your system, making your computer into a sort of low-efficiency vacuum cleaner, system fans may fail over time. Fans that use ball bearings last longer than sleeve-bearing fans, but both types may eventually fail.

Selecting a Replacement (or New) Fan

Here's how to select a replacement fan:

1. Determine the size of the fan (in mm). Older systems or those with small cases typically use 80mm or 92mm diameter fans, and late-model mid-size and full-size systems use 120mm, 140mm, or even 200mm fans. Figure 16.8 compares 120mm and 140mm fans. Use a measuring stick or tape to determine the width of one side of the fan (for a square opening) or the short and long

sides of a fan (for a rectangular opening). If there is limited clearance between between the fan opening and components on the inside of the case, be sure to measure the distance between the fan opening and components that might interfere with fan mounting.

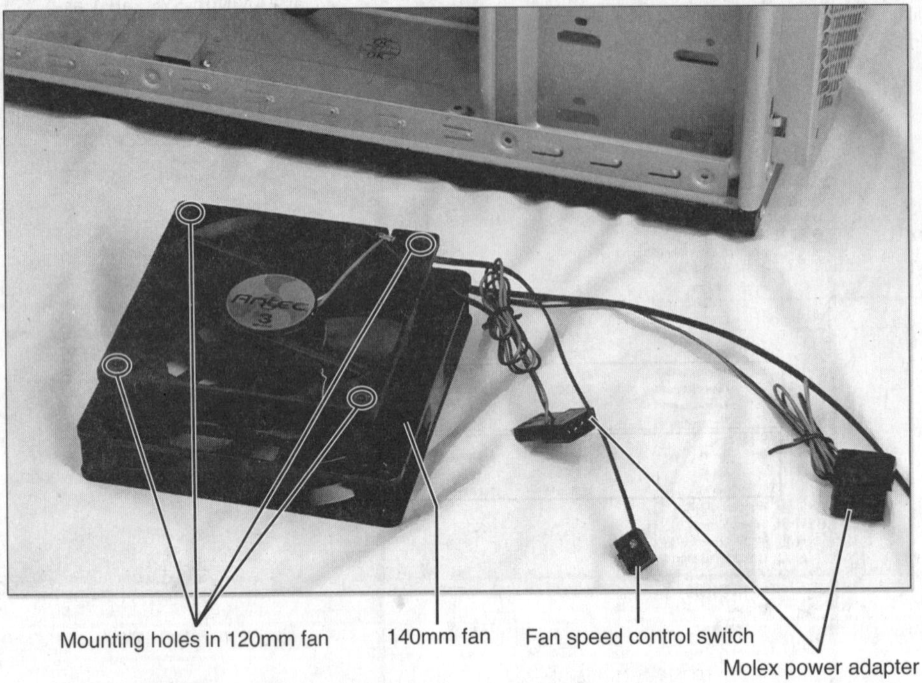

Figure 16.8 120mm fan (top) compared to 140mm fan (bottom). These fans do not feature FAN_TACH (speed monitoring) cables.

2. When you shop for a replacement fan, the noise level (dBA), airflow (CFM), and bearing type (ball bearing preferred) are important considerations. If you overclock your system (run it at faster than normal speeds) or play high-performance 3D games, get fans that have higher CFM (cubic feet per minute) ratings. if you are in an office environment and not overclocking or playing 3D games, look for quiet operation (lower decibel [dBA] values).
3. If you want to use your motherboard to monitor your fan speed, make sure the fan includes either a three-pin fan connector (power plus monitor) or a four-pin Molex drive power connector with a one-pin fan connector (monitor).

If you are buying an additional fan for your system, check the diameter of the fan opening you are planning to use in step 1. Steps 2 and 3 are the same.

Note

Larger fans can spin more slowly to provide comparable or superior airflow. For example, a 92mm Antec case fan spins at 2600 RPM, has a noise level of 33 dBA, and features air flow of 42.4 CFM.

A 120mm Antec TriCool three-speed case fan lets you strike a balance between high-performance cooling and a lower noise level:

- 1200 RPM/25 dBA/39 CFM
- 1600 RPM/28 dBA/56 CFM
- 2000 RPM/30 dBA/79 CFM

Virtually any fan you choose for your system will cost less than $20, a small price to pay for better cooling and longer, more reliable, system life.

Removing and Installing a Case Fan

To remove an old fan, follow this procedure:

1. Shut down the computer and unplug it.
2. Open the case.
3. Note where the fan is connected to the computer (motherboard, four-pin Molex power connector, or both).
4. Carefully disconnect these wires from the motherboard or power cable.
5. Locate the screws that hold the fan in place.
6. Remove these screws: hold the fan so it doesn't fall inside the case and damage other components.
7. Remove the fan from the case.

To install a new or replacement fan, follow this procedure:

1. Shut down the computer and unplug it.
2. Open the case.
3. Locate the screws packaged with the fan. Most cooling fans use a short-barreled screw like the ones shown in Figure 16.9.
4. Hold the fan inside the fan opening in the case with the wiring harness toward the inside.
5. Use the screws to fasten the fan in place: one screw to each corner (Figure 16.10).
6. Connect the fan to the motherboard (preferred) or to a four-pin Molex connector (refer to Figures 16.4 and 16.5). If the old fan was not connected to the motherboard, but there is a monitored fan header available (SYS Fan 1 or SYS Fan 2) and your new fan can use it, connect your fan to that header.
7. Close the case, plug in the power supply, and restart the computer.

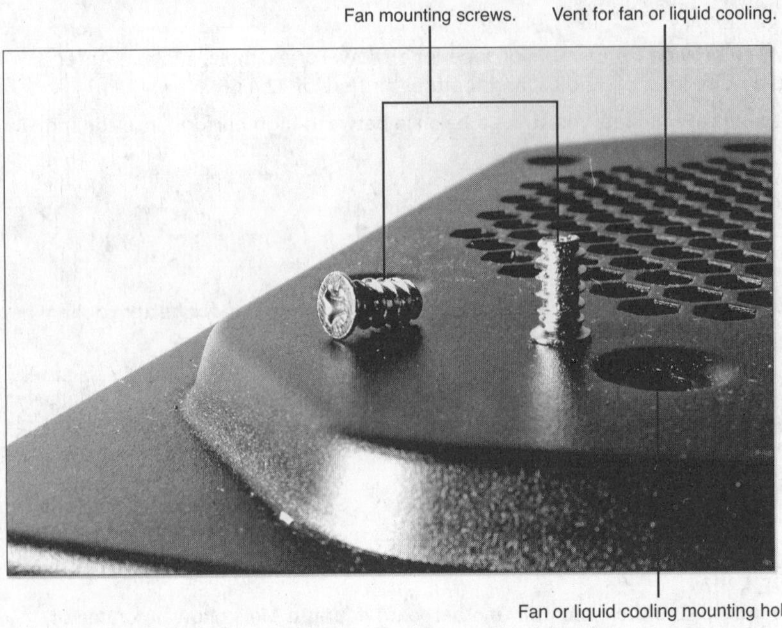

Figure 16.9
Typical fan mounting screws compared to a fan mounting hole.

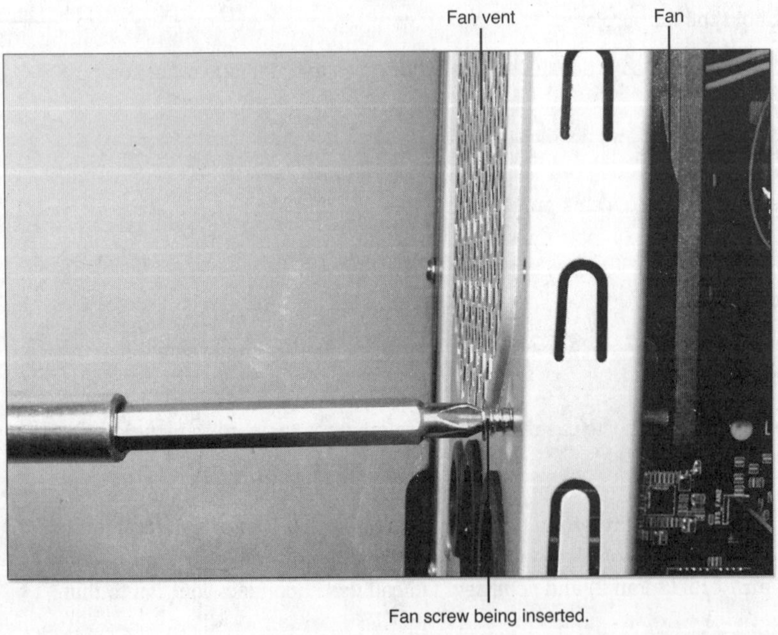

Figure 16.10
Attaching a rear-mounted fan.

Using Third-Party Active Heat Sinks for Your Processor

Almost all computers use a combination of a heat sink (a metal assembly with fins to dissipate heat) and a fan to keep the processor (CPU chip) cool. This type of cooler is called an active heat sink.

> **Note**
> Some video (3D graphics) cards also use active heat sinks for cooling.

You might want a better active heat sink for your processor than the one it was supplied with. Why change?

- You might want better cooling for overclocking.
- Third-party heat sinks are often better looking than the OEM versions (especially important if you use a clear-sided case).

There are no shortages of third-party active heat sinks you can choose. If the fan fails on your current active heat sink, you can get an exact replacement or take the opportunity to move up to a replacement.

Before you make the change, keep these factors in mind:

- Make sure the replacement works with your processor.
- If you're interested in overclocking, try to find reviews of the active heat sink in use to determine how it does with an overclocked system.
- Check the free space around the processor socket. Third-party active heat sinks are typically taller and wider than OEM versions.
- You will need to remove the old active heat sink and remove the thermal grease or phase-change material from the top of the processor. Use 91% alcohol or pure alcohol to remove this residue.
- Find out whether the new active heat sink comes with thermal grease. If not, you can purchase this separately. You will need to use thermal grease between the top of the processor and the bottom of the heat sink to enable the heat sink to work properly. Follow the heat sink or processor vendor's instructions for details.
- Many replacement heat sinks require you to remove the motherboard to install special hardware to hold the new heat sink in place.

> **Caution**
> When I installed the third-party active heat sink featured in this section, the fan prevented a memory module from properly locking into place on my motherboard. I had to move the fan to the other side of the heat sink fins and reverse-mount it so it would pull air through the heat sink. It works, but I could have avoided some trouble if I'd measured first and selected a smaller model.

Figure 16.11 compares an OEM Intel heat sink for a Core i5 processor with a Cooler Master Hyper 212 (the current model, the Hyper 212 Plus, looks similar but includes support for additional Intel processors and improved heat pipes). The Cooler Master model is much taller, features many more fins, and has a removable fan for easy modification.

The Intel active heat sink has expandable pegs that fit into holes on the motherboard. The Cooler Master active heat sink uses a separate X-shaped clip (Figure 16.12) and a back plate that fits on the bottom of the motherboard. You'll need to remove the motherboard to install it (Figure 16.13).

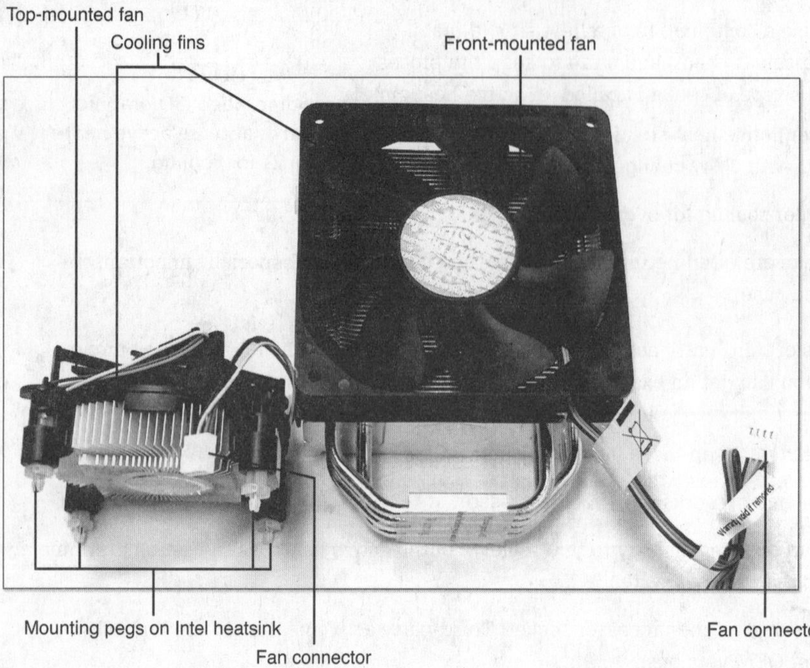

Figure 16.11
OEM Intel active heat sink (left) versus a typical third-party active heat sink (right).

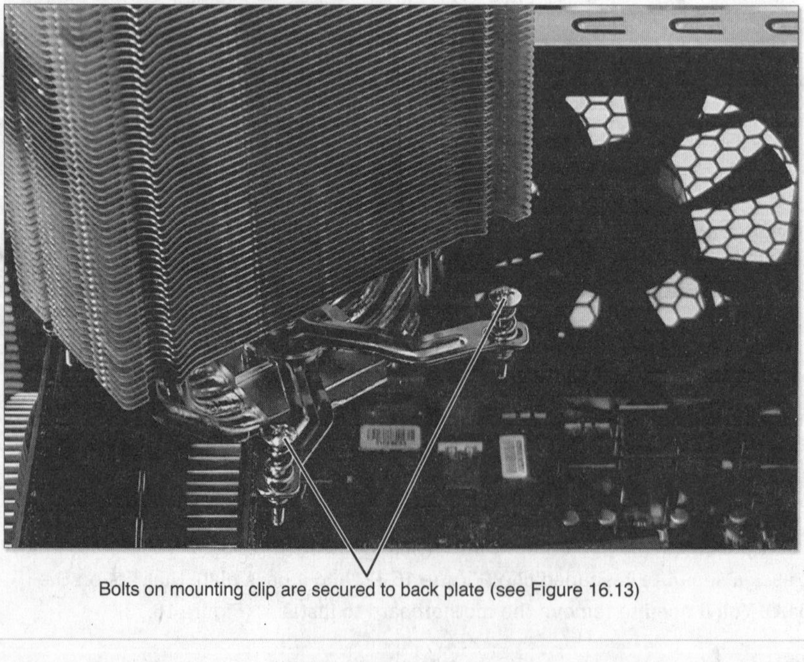

Figure 16.12
A Cooler Master heat sink (without fan) and its mounting clip.

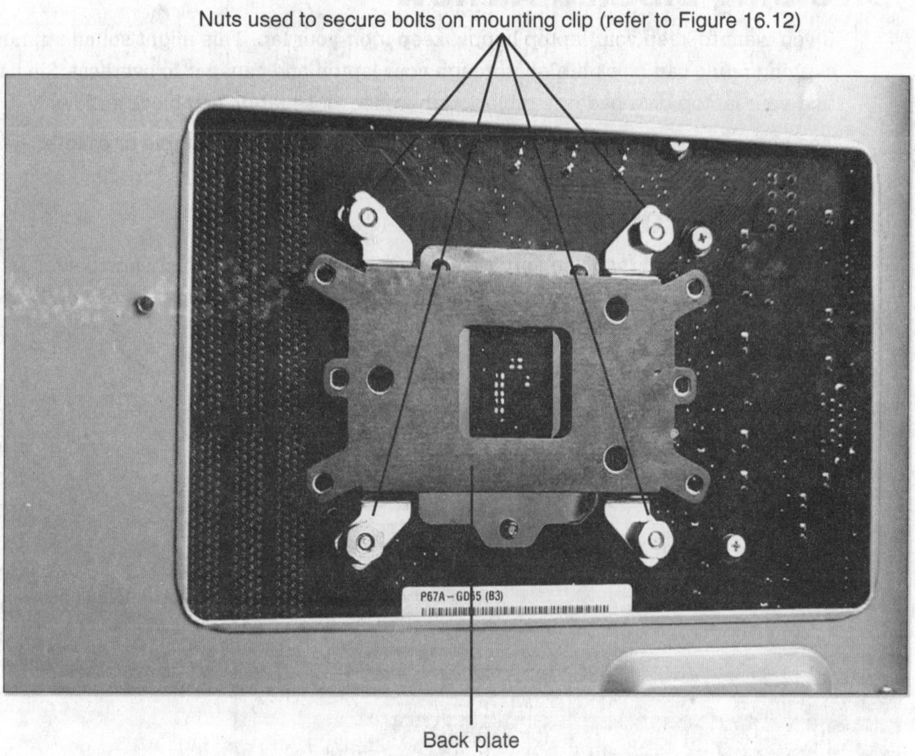

Figure 16.13 The mounting plate used by the Cooler Master active heat sink shown in Figure 16.11.

Keeping Your Laptop Cool

Laptops, unlike desktops, don't offer internal options for better cooling or a lot of details in their system BIOSes to tell you how hot things are getting "under the hood." To prevent your laptop from overheating, there are three methods you can use:

- Avoid blocked airflow
- Adjust power settings
- Use a cooling pad

Tip

Before you buy a replacement heat sink, check the dimensions and installation instructions; they're typically available at the manufacturer's website.

Avoiding Blocked Airflow

If you want to keep your laptop happy, keep it off your lap. This might sound strange, but loose clothing fabric can block airflow through your laptop and cause it to overheat. Similarly, avoid putting your laptop on a bed or a tablecloth because loose fabric can block airflow.

The best place to put your laptop is on a hard surface, such as a table or counter.

Adjusting Power Settings

The second method is to use appropriate power settings. You can change power settings from the notification area in Windows or by going to the Control Panel. Click the power icon in the notification area to get started (Figure 16.14).

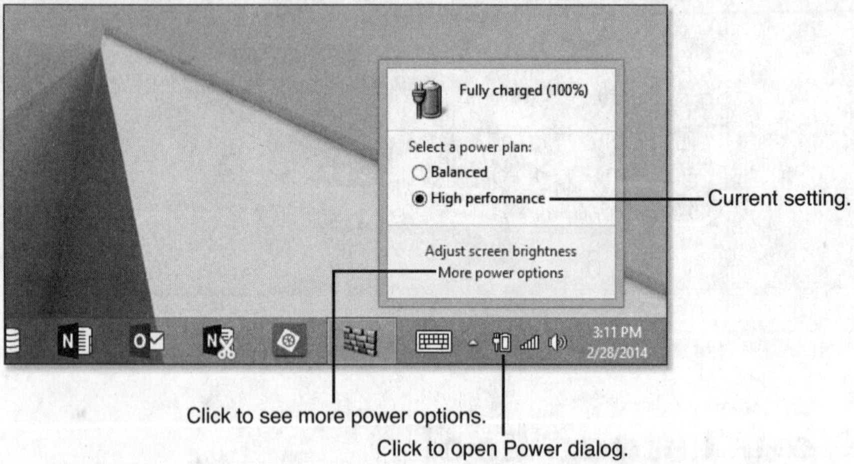

Figure 16.14 Click the power icon in the notification area of the Windows desktop to see your current power setting.

The default Balanced power setting (Figure 16.15) is designed to slow down the processor when the system is idle to extend battery life. If you keep your system plugged in all the time, High Performance might be more your speed. However, if you're trying to stretch battery life and keep the interior cool, use the Power Saver setting. Your system will run slower and the screen will be dimmer, but your battery will last longer per charge and the system will run a bit cooler.

Tip

Do you run your laptop mainly on AC power? To keep your battery in top shape so it has the best possible run time when you do use it on battery power, remove it from your laptop when you don't need it. Charge it when you need to run on battery power. If you leave it plugged in all the time, the battery tends to lose its ability to get a full charge, reducing run time.

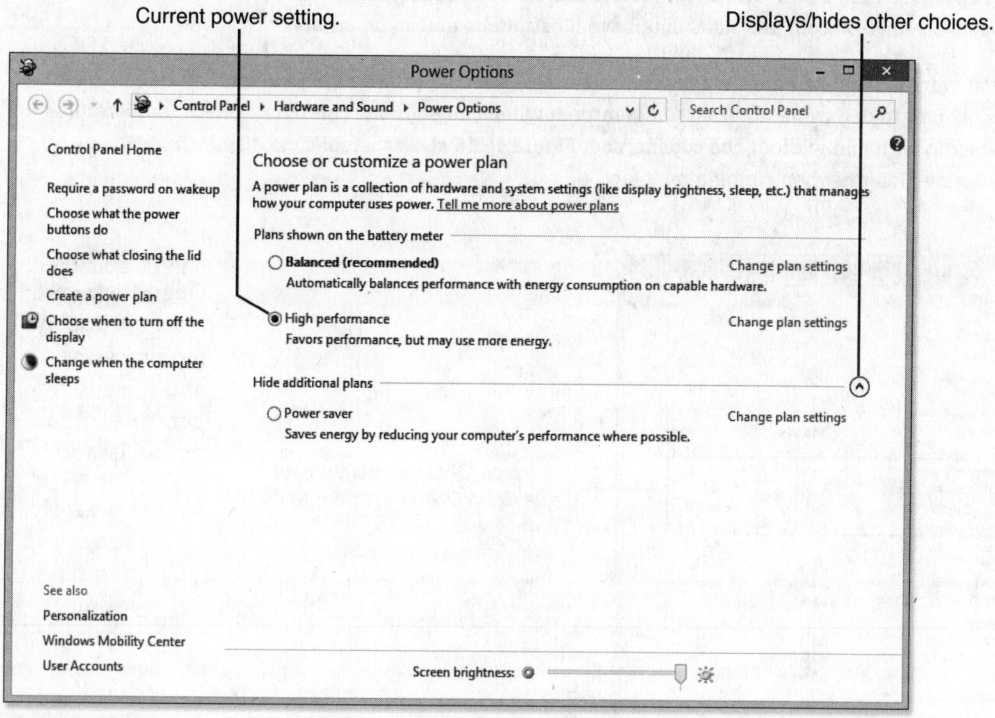

Figure 16.15
Choose a power plan that matches how you use your laptop.

Note

Windows tablets and netbooks have similar power plan options. You can also adjust power settings on desktops, but desktops only list AC power options

Cooling Pads for Laptops

Although you can't plug extra fans into your laptop, you can do the next best thing by buying a cooling pad for your laptop. Put the cooling pad on a counter or table (or your lap), put the laptop on the cooling pad, and if you've selected a good unit, your laptop will stay cooler.

Although a few of these use passive cooling, most have one or more fans that are run from a spare USB port or with an AC adapter. Typically, two or more fans work better than one fan, and metal cooling pads are more durable than plastic ones.

If you're not sure which models are worth a closer look, check out these review sources:

- **Top Ten Reviews http://laptop-coolers-review.toptenreviews.com/**—Evaluates cooling, noise levels, and construction quality of products reviewed

- **Laptop Cooling Pad World http://www.laptopcoolingpadworld.com/**—Lists high-rated products on Amazon.com and adds extensive illustrations and commentary

If you want to conduct your own tests, you can use the Open Hardware Monitor discussed earlier in this chapter to determine internal temperatures when you start the computer. Check temperatures at startup with and without the cooling pad. Figure 16.16 shows a real-time display from Open Hardware Monitor when running on a laptop.

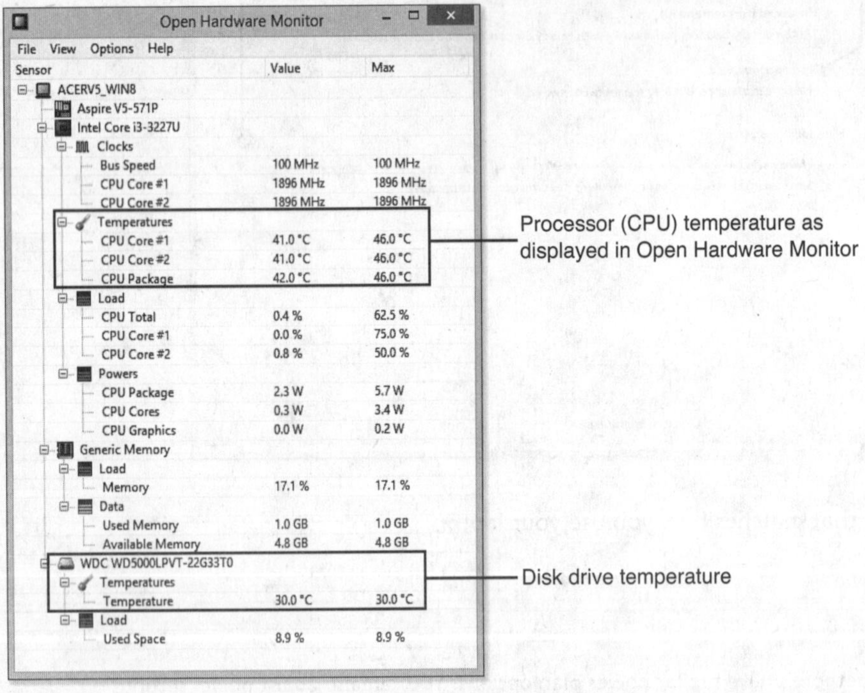

Figure 16.16 Open Hardware Monitor displaying processor and drive temperatures on a typical laptop.

To determine how well the cooling pad works, download a copy of the latest edition of PCMark Basic Edition, a free benchmarking tool from Futuremark (www.futuremark.com). Use it to stress the system with and without the cooling pad. If the cooling pad is effective, you should see lower temperatures while running PCMark with the pad in use.

Note

See http://www.megatechnews.com/megatech-reviews-cooler-master-notepal-lapair-notebook-cooling-pad/ for an example of this type of test.

Preventing Desktop and Laptop Overheating with Preventative Maintenance

If you have dogs, cats, or other household pets that shed, your computer is going to have a harder time keeping cool if you don't actively work to keep it clean. I have seen computers fatally overheat because their cooling vents and fans were completely clogged with pet hair. Even ordinary dust and dirt causes problems over time, such as fan slowdowns and failures.

How can you avoid problems?

- Keep your desktop computer off the floor—As you learned earlier in this chapter, desktop computers use fans that pull air through the system to cool internal parts. If pet hair is blocking the front and side vents or internal fans, overheating is inevitable.
- Use a computer-grade vacuum cleaner to remove hair and dust from your computer. If you have pets, check your systems every six months or so if the computer is on a table or desk. If it's on the floor, check it more often, especially during shedding season.
- Use compressed air if you can't use a vacuum cleaner to remove hair and dust. Try to blow the hair and dust out of the computer, and put old newspapers or a drop cloth around the computer to catch dislodged dust and hair.
- Use the monitoring programs discussed earlier in this chapter to see warning signs of fan failure or overheating.
- Keep your computer away from windows which receive direct sunlight, especially if the windows are not designed to reduce heat from direct sunlight.
- If you hear screeching or tapping noises coming from inside your computer, check inside for a failed fan or a loose wire blocking a fan. Use nylon cable ties to gather up excess wire, and replace dying or dead fans immediately.

Troubleshooting iOS and Android Device Overheating

Tablets and smartphones based on iOS and Android typically don't have problems with overheating, but if you watch hours and hours of video content on them, you could have problems. To prevent these devices from overheating (and to get longer battery life per charge), follow these recommendations:

- Turn off features you're not using. For example, if you don't use a Bluetooth headset, turn off Bluetooth (Figure 16.17).

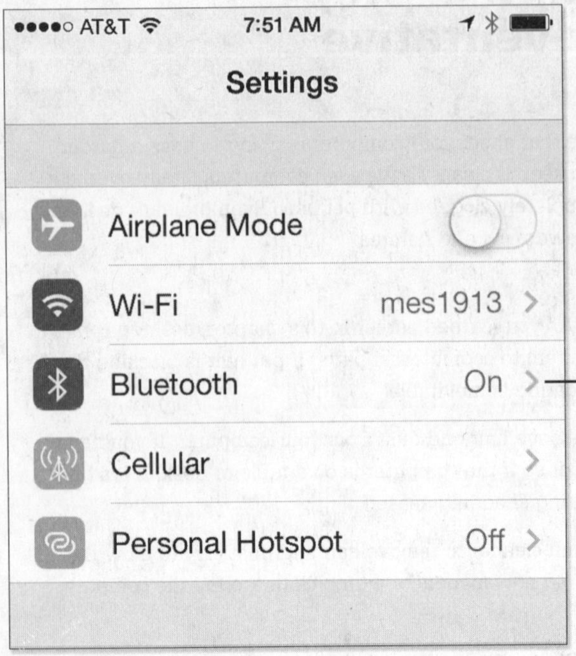

Figure 16.17
Preparing to turn off Bluetooth on an iPhone that isn't using the feature.

- If you can't shut down your device while you charge it, be sure to close any apps you're not using.
- Check for app and OS updates frequently, as some of these can help fix problems with overheating caused by app or OS buds.
- If your device is overheating, take it out of its case.

17

TROUBLESHOOTING TOUCHSCREENS, KEYBOARDS, AND MICE

Fast Track to Solutions

Table 17.1 Symptom Table

Symptom	Flowchart or Book Section	Page #
I can't use my wireless keyboard.	Troubleshooting Wireless Keyboards (flowchart)	Chapter 24
I can't use my wireless mouse.	Troubleshooting Wireless Mice (flowchart)	Chapter 24
I need a bigger mouse pointer.	Table 17.2, Figure 17.5	430
My infrared (IrDA) keyboard won't work.	Troubleshooting IR Keyboards	444

Cleaning Mobile and PC Touchscreens

A dirty touchscreen will cause your device to be difficult to use, but thankfully there's an easy fix. You can use premoistened wipes, an antistatic spray on a microfiber cloth, or special touchscreen cloths to clean up finger smudges, dust, dirt, and grease.

If your touchscreen is unresponsive or seems to be sluggish in scrolling or opening links, try cleaning the touchscreen before you do anything else.

Caution

Never, never spray your device's touchscreen with a liquid cleaner. You could damage your device. Instead, dampen a microfiber or lint-free cloth. Whatever type of cleaning cloth you use, use a gentle circular motion and be sure to remove surface grit before you put pressure on your screen.

Calibrating and Testing Touchscreens

If your touchscreen isn't registering your touches or selects the wrong option, it might need to be recalibrated. Unfortunately, not all touchscreens can be calibrated by the user,, in which case you will need to contact the vendor.

Calibration in Windows 7/8/8.1

To recalibrate a touchscreen with Windows 7 and 8/8.1, follow these steps:

1. Open Search and type **Calibrate**.
2. The Tablet PC Settings dialog appears (see Figure 17.1). Click or tap **Calibrate**.

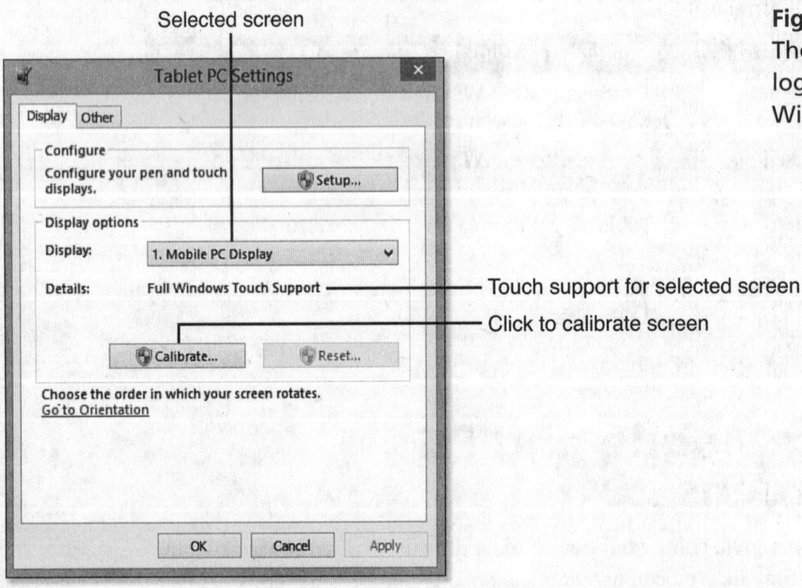

Figure 17.1
The Tablet PC Settings dialog is used to calibrate a Windows touchscreen.

3. Tap the crosshair when it appears on each intersection on the grid (see Figure 17.2).

4. Click **Save Calibration Data** when you are finished.
5. Close the Tablet PC Settings dialog.

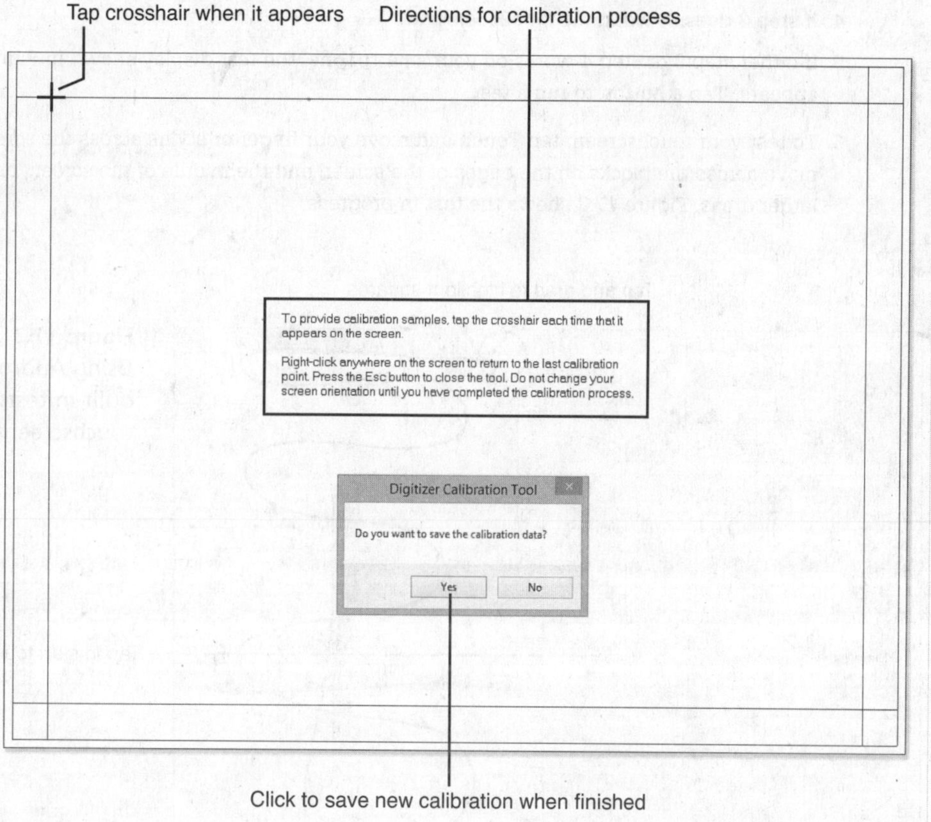

Figure 17.2 Calibrating a Windows touchscreen.

Test the touchscreen. If your touchscreen is working better, success! If the touchscreen is still not responding properly, repeat step 1. At step 2, click **Reset** to reset the screen calibration to its original settings. If the touchscreen still doesn't respond properly, contact the vendor for help.

Testing and Calibration in Android

Some Android devices include support for calibration, whereas others do not. If your device includes calibration support, you can find it in the **Settings** menu. The calibration option prompts you to enter text using your device's onscreen keyboard.

To help determine whether your smartphone's touchscreen is working properly, you might be able to run a touchscreen test utility. To use it, do the following:

1. Tap **Phone**.
2. Tap **Keypad**.
3. Tap ***#0*#**.
4. If step 3 doesn't work, tap ***#*#2664#*#***.
5. If either step 3 or step 4 works on your smartphone, the test display shown in Figure 17.3 appears. Tap a button to run a test.
6. To test your touchscreen, tap **Touch** and move your finger or stylus across the screen. Be sure to move across the blocks on the edges of the screen and the middle of the screen, as well as the larger areas. Figure 17.3 shows the test in progress.

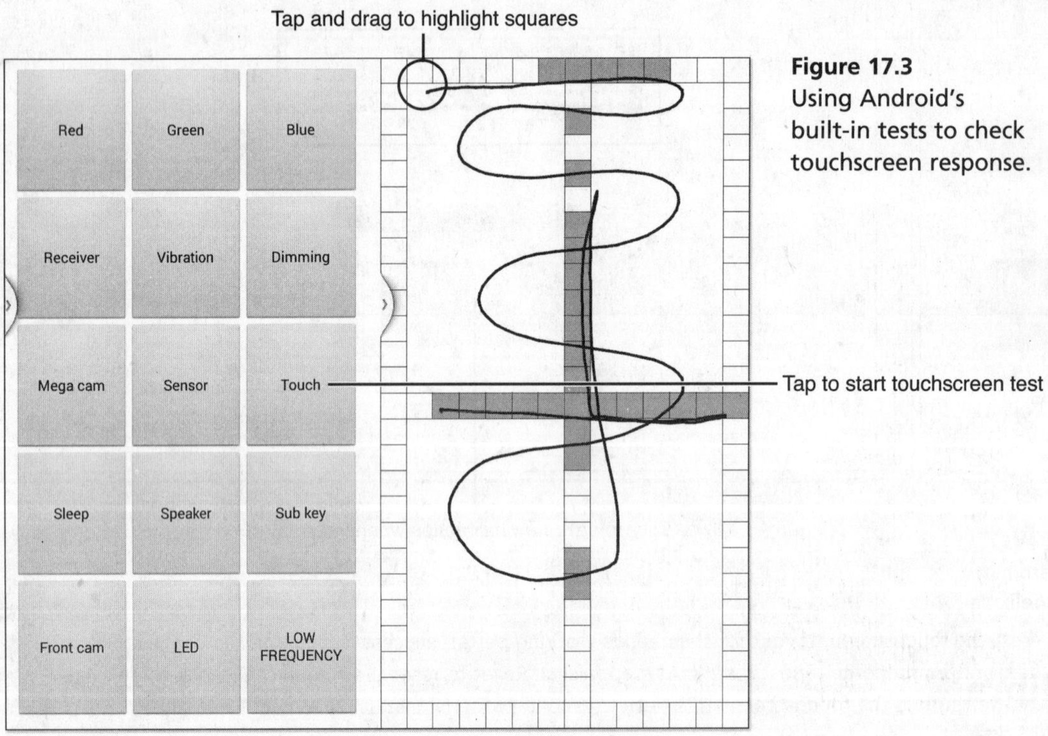

Figure 17.3
Using Android's built-in tests to check touchscreen response.

7. Use the Back key on your device to leave the program.

If your Android smartphone doesn't include the self-test shown in Figure 17.3, or if you need to test your tablet, visit Google Play (also known as Play Store) to find test programs. The Test Your Android utility shown in Figure 17.4 includes a multitouch test as well as many other tests.

If your touchscreen does not respond properly to the tests you run, contact your vendor for help.

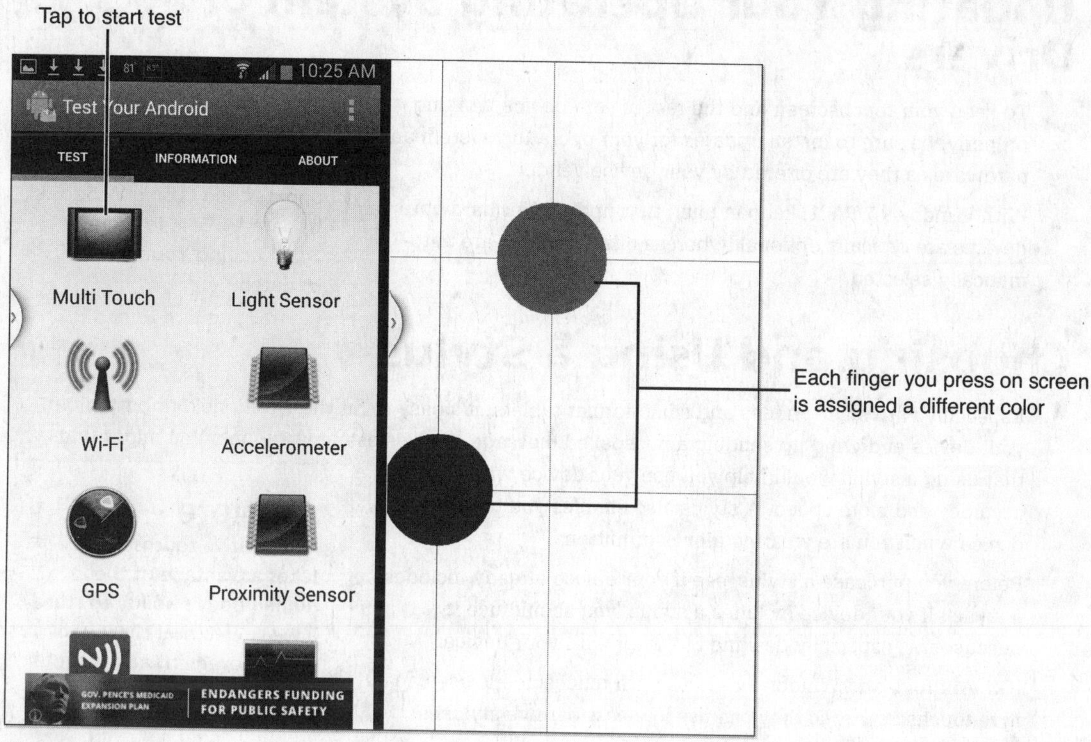

Figure 17.4
Using Test Your Android to test multitouch capability.

> **Note**
> To learn more about the keyboard calibration feature available on some Android devices, see http://felixidea.com/how-to-calibrate-the-touch-screen-on-android/.

Calibration on iOS

IOS does not include a manual configuration utility, but you can sometimes correct calibration issues by rebooting your device. Shut it down, wait for a few moments, and restart it.

If the screen is still not responding properly to taps, you can use Reset or Restore to reset your iOS hardware. Keep in mind that you need to make backups before you try either of these options. We recommend contacting Apple support if you have calibration problems with your iOS device.

> **Note**
> To learn more about using Reset or Restore, see "Troubleshooting an iOS Device That Stops Responding," in Chapter 22, "iOS Troubleshooting."

Updating Your Operating System or Drivers

To keep your touchscreen and the rest of your device working properly, be sure to install updates for your operating system and hardware as they are offered by your device vendor.

With Windows 7/8/8.1, keep in mind that updates for hardware devices are typically optional, whereas other updates are automatically selected.

Note

To learn more about driver updates, see "Using Windows Update," p.364, in Chapter 14, "Keeping Your Devices Updated."

Choosing and Using a Stylus

Especially with smartphones and small-format tablets, it's easy to hit the wrong field or button on your device and wind up sending a misspelled message or a useless browser link. You might find that using a stylus would help you use your device with greater accuracy and more speed. A stylus also enables you to use your device when you are wearing gloves or mittens.

Before you purchase a stylus, see if your device already includes a stylus. If your device includes a stylus, you should use it, because it is especially designed to work with your device.

IOS, Android, and Windows devices with touchscreens use capacitive touchscreens, so they can use low-cost passive styluses available at many retailers.

Choose larger tips for use with tablets and smaller tips for use with smartphones. Check reviews for specific models to evaluate feel, line width, and durability. Note that low-cost styluses often have very soft tips that can wear out quickly.

A few manufacturers make active styluses that connect via Bluetooth. These are designed especially for use with graphics arts programs. See www.wired.com/2013/11/meet-pencil-the-best-ipad-stylus-yet-from-the-makers-of-paper/.

Note

A capacitive touchscreen takes advantage of the human body's ability to store a weak electrical charge to sense movement across the touchscreen's surface.

Note

For a useful review of different stylus designs, see http://tabtimes.com/review/ittech-accessories/2012/05/18/roundup-best-stylus-ipad-or-android-tablets.

Troubleshooting Wired Mice and Keyboards

There are four possible sources of trouble with wired keyboards, mice, and similar pointing devices:

- The port the device is plugged into
- The device itself
- The device driver
- The device configuration in Control Panel

If a USB port is not working, nothing plugged into the port is working. If an input device is not working, it will fail no matter what port you plug it into.

If the input device is not using the correct driver, you might not be able to use the device's advanced features (most input devices can operate with basic functions by using Windows native keyboard and mouse drivers).

USB keyboards and pointing devices are referred to as *Human Interface Devices (HIDs)*, and each HID-compliant device has at least two listings in Device Manager. One listing is for the device, and all other listings are for the HID functions of that device.

HID allows an input device to support additional buttons or features, such as the multimedia or web browser control buttons common on most keyboards. If the keyboard has a scroll wheel, that feature will be listed separately as another HID-compliant mouse.

Tip

Although installing drivers for standard mice isn't always necessary to use them, it's vital when you use a gaming mouse. Most gaming mice include programmable buttons to make playing games easier, and some also include calibration features. Be sure to visit the mouse vendor's website for the latest drivers for your gaming mouse.

A Fast Introduction to USB Terminology

No matter how much you know about other types of PC hardware, your first view of the Universal Serial Bus controller category in Device Manager is likely to be confusing. Here are some quick definitions of typical terms:

Universal Host Controller—Controls USB 1.1 ports.

Enhanced Host Controller—Provides USB 2.0 support.

USB 3.0 Host Controller—Provides USB 3.0 support.

Root hub—Each root hub corresponds to two (or sometimes more) USB ports.

Generic USB hub—A hub connected to a root hub. A generic hub can be a standalone unit or might be built in to a keyboard or monitor base.

Composite device—A USB device that has two or more interfaces in different categories. For example, a USB receiver for a wireless mouse and keyboard is a composite device.

Troubleshooting Pointing Device Problems with Control Panel

If your mouse or other pointing device works, but you are not satisfied with its performance, compatibility, appearance, or movements, use the Mouse Properties sheet in the Windows Control Panel to adjust these settings. Figure 17.5 shows the properties sheet tabs for a standard wheel mouse using standard Windows drivers. If you use a mouse with vendor-specific drivers or additional hardware features, you might see additional options.

Table 17.2 shows you how to use the Mouse Properties sheet for Windows to solve common pointing device problems. The numbers in parentheses in Table 17.2 correspond to the callouts in Figure 17.5.

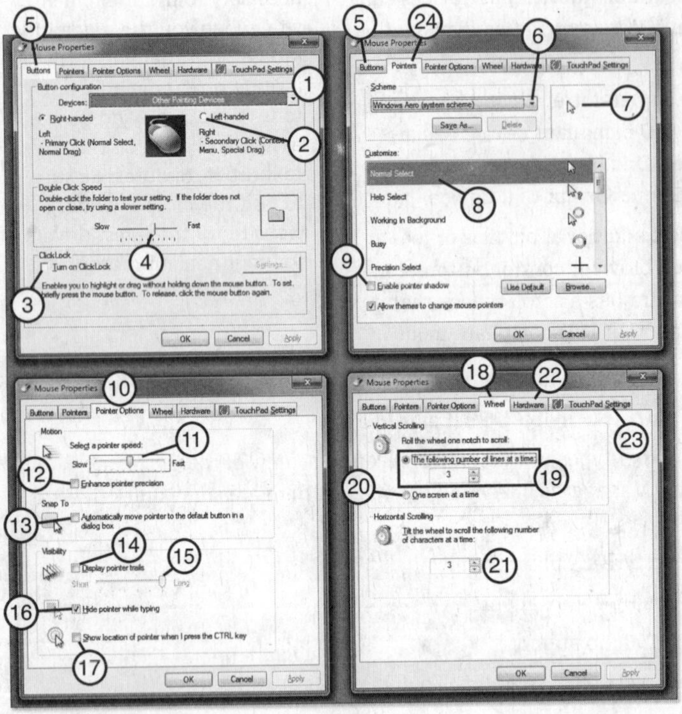

Figure 17.5
The Mouse Properties sheet in Control Panel for a Windows 7 system.

Table 17.2 Using the Pointing Device Properties Sheet

Problem	Properties Sheet Tab to Use	Solution
I need to set up the mouse for a left-handed user.	Buttons (5)	Click the **Left-handed** option button (2).
Double-click doesn't work consistently.	Buttons	Use the **Double Click Speed** slider and test box to adjust the speed (4).
Items are dragged around the screen after I click them, even if I don't hold down the primary mouse button.	Buttons	Clear the **ClickLock** option box (3); if the ClickLock option isn't selected, the primary mouse button is probably broken and the mouse should be replaced.

Problem	Properties Sheet Tab to Use	Solution
I need different (larger, animated, high-contrast) mouse pointers.	Pointers (24)	Select the desired mouse scheme (8) from the menu (6); note the preview (7).
The pointer moves too fast or too slow.	Pointer Options (10)	Adjust the **Motion** (pointer speed) slider (11) to the desired speed.
The pointer is hard to move over short distances or hard to stop.	Pointer Options	Enable the **Enhance Pointer Precision** (12) option.
I'm tired of moving the pointer to a dialog to click OK.	Pointer Options	Enable the **Snap To** (13) option.
The pointer disappears when it's moved quickly.	Pointer Options	Enable the **Pointer Trails** (14) option and select the desired trail length (15).
The pointer covers up typed text.	Pointer Options	Enable the **Hide Pointer While Typing** (16) option.
The pointer is hard to find on a cluttered screen.	Pointer Options	Enable the **Show Location When I Press the CTRL Key** (17) option.
The vertical scroll wheel's motion is too fast or too slow.	Wheel (18)	Select the number of lines to scroll with each click of the wheel (19), or select one screen at a time (20).
The horizontal scroll wheel's motion is too fast or too slow.	Wheel	Select the number of characters to scroll as the wheel is tilted (21).
I'm not sure which pointing devices are active.	Hardware (22)	This properties sheet displays the current device(s) and provides shortcuts to the hardware properties sheets also visible from Device Manager.
I need to adjust the settings for my touchpad.	TouchPad Settings (23)	Click this to open a special properties sheet (Figure 17.6) with touchpad settings.
I need to adjust another pointing device.	Device menu (1)	Open this menu and select the device you want to configure.

Figure 17.6 illustrates the properties sheet for the Synaptics Touch Pad, a popular touchpad used on many laptop models. Click the **TouchPad Settings** button on the Mouse properties sheet to open the Properties sheet shown at right. You can use the properties sheet to disable the touch pad when a USB mouse is plugged in, enable multifinger motions, and tweak pointing motions.

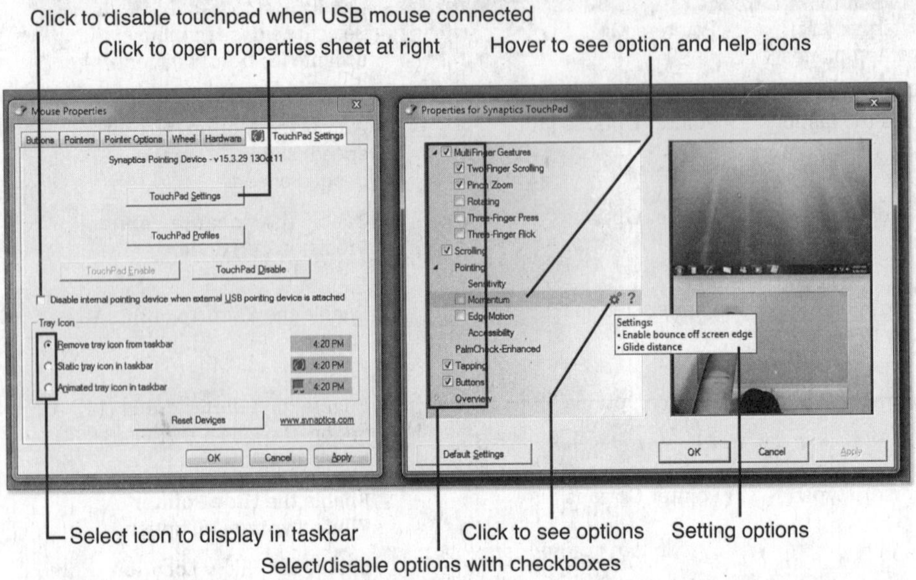

Figure 17.6 The Synaptics TouchPad properties sheets.

Troubleshooting Wireless Mice and Keyboards

Wireless mice and keyboards that have stopped working present a special troubleshooting challenge. The problem could be with any of the following:

- Their transceivers (which plug into the same connectors as normal input devices) can cause the devices to fail.
- The devices' transmission and reception of signals from the transceivers can also cause device failure.
- Problems with battery life will cause temporary device failure when the batteries are exhausted.

Most wireless input devices use radio signals, but a few devices use infrared (IR) signals instead.

Using Device Manager to Troubleshoot Wireless Mice and Keyboards

One major weakness of the Windows Device Manager is that it detects problems with the transceiver, not the device connected to the transceiver. For example, if the batteries in your wireless mouse or keyboard fail, the Device Manager will still report that the device works correctly. You can use the Device Manager to detect problems with how the transceiver is connected to your system.

To troubleshoot wireless-specific problems, see the next section, "Troubleshooting Problems with Wireless Input Devices."

Troubleshooting Problems with Wireless Input Devices

Even if the transceiver used by a wireless input device is working properly, the device itself might fail to work for one of the following reasons:

- An inability to exchange radio signals with the input device.
- The transceiver is not configured to work with additional input devices.
- A power failure occurred because of dead batteries or dirty/corroded battery terminals.

Connecting to a Wireless Receiver

Most wireless input devices use the 2.4GHz range also used by most Wi-Fi networks. To connect your input device to its receiver, press the **Connect** button on the receiver and the input device. Some receivers don't use a pushbutton and are automatically detected when you press the **Connect** button on the device.

> **Tip**
> If you have a mouse and keyboard sold as a matched set, check the documentation or device labeling to see if you need to connect them in any particular order.

Adding Support for Additional Input Devices

Logitech and HP now offer wireless input device receivers capable of working with multiple input devices:

- Logitech's Unifying Receiver (http://www.logitech.com/en-us/support/unifying) supports up to six devices.
- HP's Link-5 receiver (www.hp.com, search for Link-5) supports up to five devices.

The Logitech Unifying Receiver is paired with the device it was shipped with. To pair it with other devices, you must download the Logitech Unifying Software program from the Unifying Receiver website and run it (see Figure 17.7).

To unpair a device, right-click it and click **Un-pair**.

> **Note**
> Some low-cost Logitech input devices are shipped with a Nano receiver, which is the same size as the Unifying receiver, but supports only the device it was shipped with. Some of these devices can also be paired with a Unifying receiver. Look for the stylized asterisk symbol shown in Figure 17.7 on the packaging or the device to determine which Logitech input devices are compatible with the Unifying Receiver.

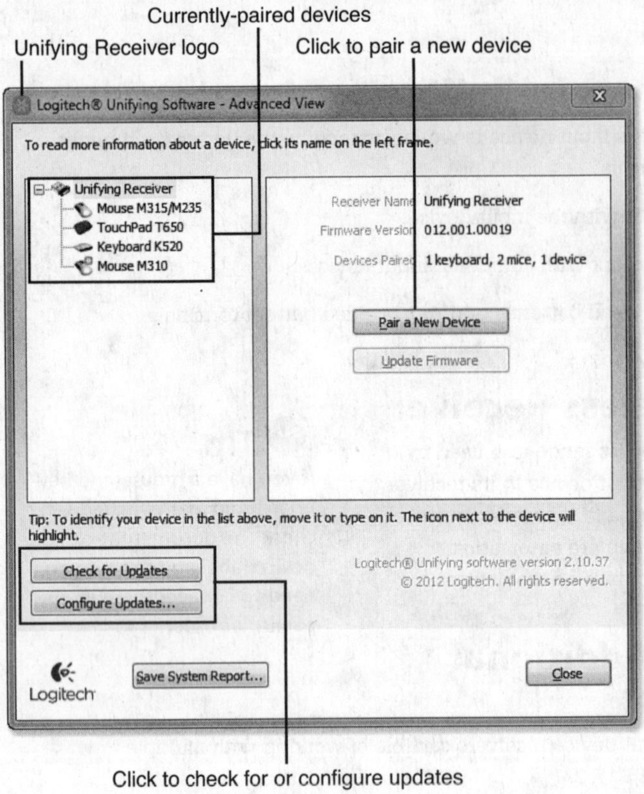

Figure 17.7
Viewing paired devices with Logitech Unifying Software's Advanced view.

To connect other devices to the HP Link-5 receiver, move the device within one foot of the computer with the Link-5 receiver, press a button on the device, and press a button or key on the device to pair it with the receiver.

Can't Pair Device with Receiver

If you can't pair your device with a receiver, check the following:

- **Mismatch of receiver and device**—You can't mix brands of receivers and input devices. You must use a receiver made for the particular device or device family. For example, you can't use a Logitech Nano receiver with a Microsoft or HP input device.
- **Incorrect pairing method**—Be sure to follow the directions for the device to pair it with the receiver.
- **Device is out of range**—Although some devices can work up to 20 feet away from the receiver, you need to have the device next to the receiver for pairing. Move the device within one foot of the receiver and try re-pairing the device and receiver.

- **Pairing software not configured**—If you use Logitech Unifying Receiver-compatible devices, be sure the device is listed as paired in the Advanced view shown in Figure 17.7. From this view, you can also discontinue device pairing and retry pairing. If the device is not listed, follow the directions to pair the device and receiver.
- **Device turned off**—You can't pair or use a wireless input device if it's turned off. Wait a few seconds for the device to respond before attempting to pair it or use it.
- **Battery failure**—Weak or dead batteries prevent your device from pairing or working. If your device uses removable batteries, replace your device's batteries with fresh alkaline batteries (most won't work with rechargeable NiMH batteries because they produce lower voltage). If your mouse uses rechargeable batteries, plug it into its charger. If the batteries have leaked, clean the battery contacts on the unit and look for signs of corrosion. To see the battery status of a device connected using Logitech Unifying software, open the software and click the device.

Troubleshooting Bluetooth Mice and Keyboards

The Bluetooth radio built in to mobile devices and some laptops can be used for many devices, including headsets, printers, and input devices such as mice and keyboards. Before a Bluetooth device can work with your computer or mobile device, it must be paired with the device.

Pairing a Bluetooth Mouse

The process of pairing a Bluetooth mouse requires you to do the following:

- Make sure your computer or mobile device's Bluetooth radio is on and set as discoverable.
- Select the mouse after it is recognized for pairing.

Let's look at the details.

Bluetooth Mouse (Windows 7 and Windows 8/8.1 Desktop)

To pair a Bluetooth mouse with a Windows 7 computer or with a Windows 8/8.1 computer from the desktop:

1. Click the Bluetooth icon in the taskbar.
2. Click **Open Settings**.
3. Enable **Discovery**.
4. Enable **Allow Bluetooth Devices to Connect to This Computer** (see Figure 17.8).

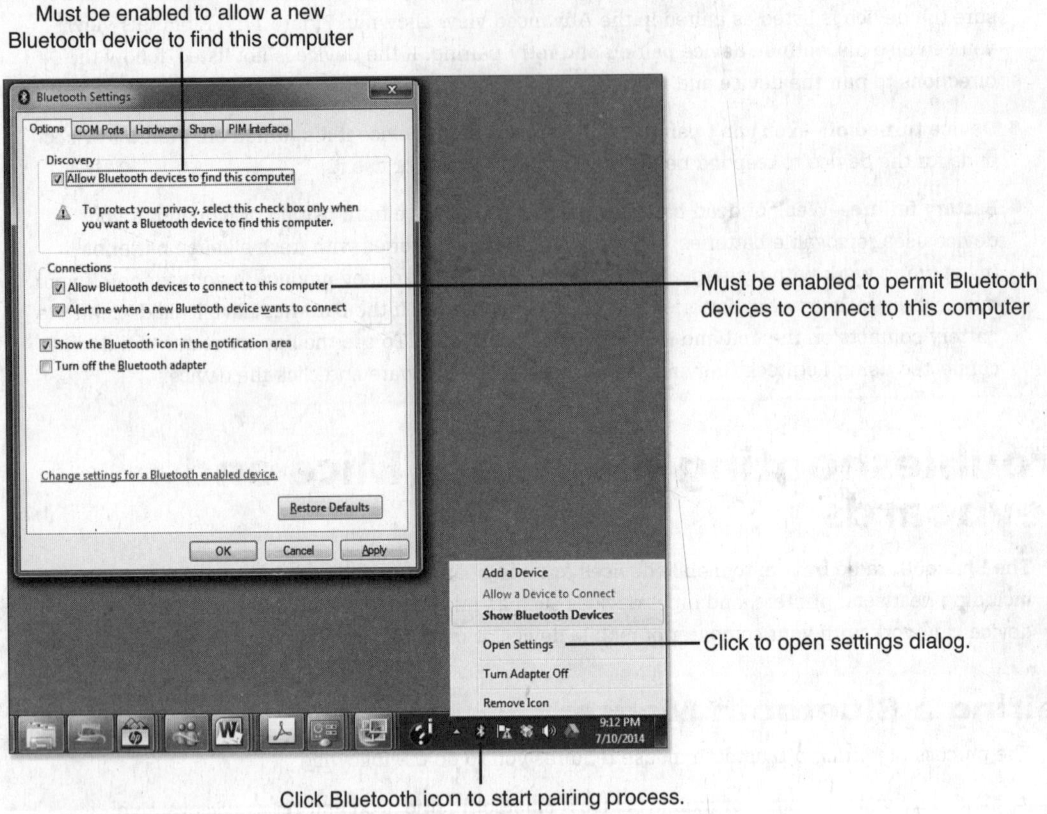

Figure 17.8
Enabling discovery and connections to Bluetooth devices.

5. Open the Bluetooth icon in the Taskbar and click or tap **Add a Device**.
6. Press the **Connect** button on the mouse.
7. Select the mouse from the list of Bluetooth devices and click **Next** (see Figure 17.9).
8. After the mouse is detected and the drivers have been installed, click **Close**.
9. To prevent connections from unauthorized Bluetooth devices, disable discovery until the next time you want to add a Bluetooth device.

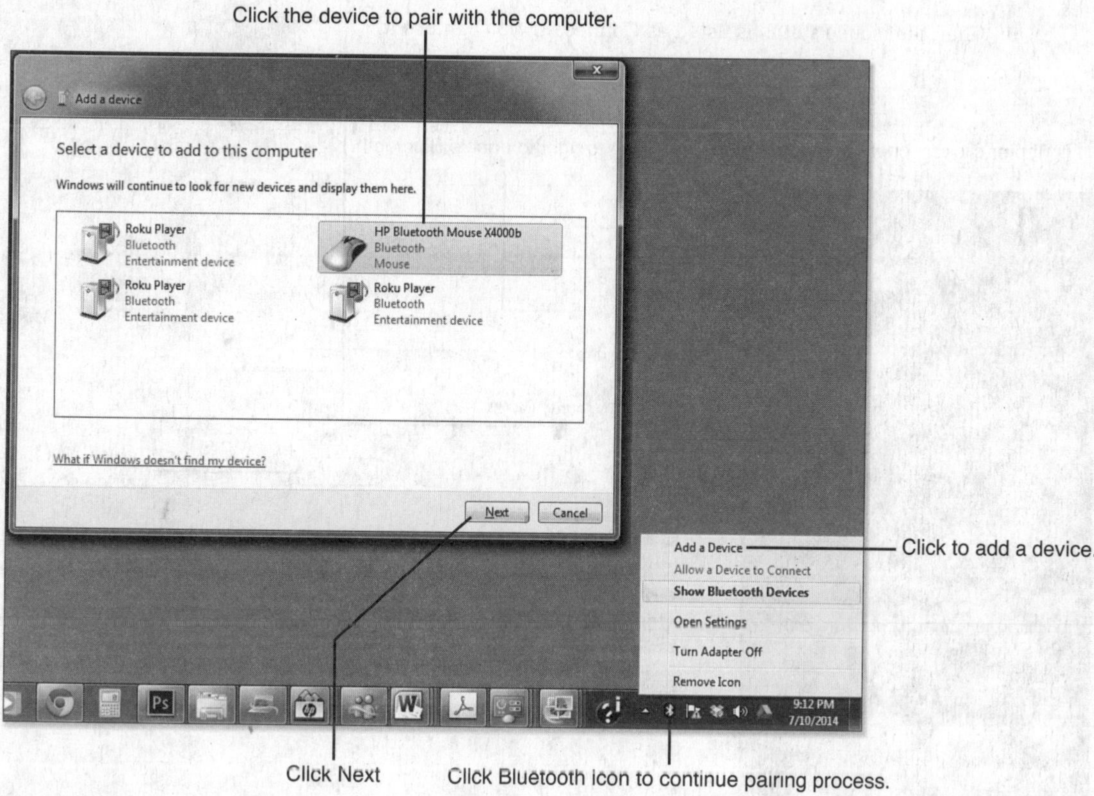

Figure 17.9
Enabling discovery and connections to Bluetooth devices.

Bluetooth Mouse (Windows 8/8.1 Start Screen)

To pair a Bluetooth mouse with a Windows 8/8.1 computer from the Start screen, follow these steps:

1. Open the Charms menu and click or tap **Settings**.
2. Click or tap Change PC Settings.
3. Click or tap **PC and Devices**.
4. Click or tap **Bluetooth**.
5. Turn on Bluetooth if it is turned off.
6. Turn on the mouse.
7. Press the **Connect** button on the mouse.

8. Click or tap **Pair** (see Figure 17.10).
9. When the mouse status is listed as Connected, you can use it.

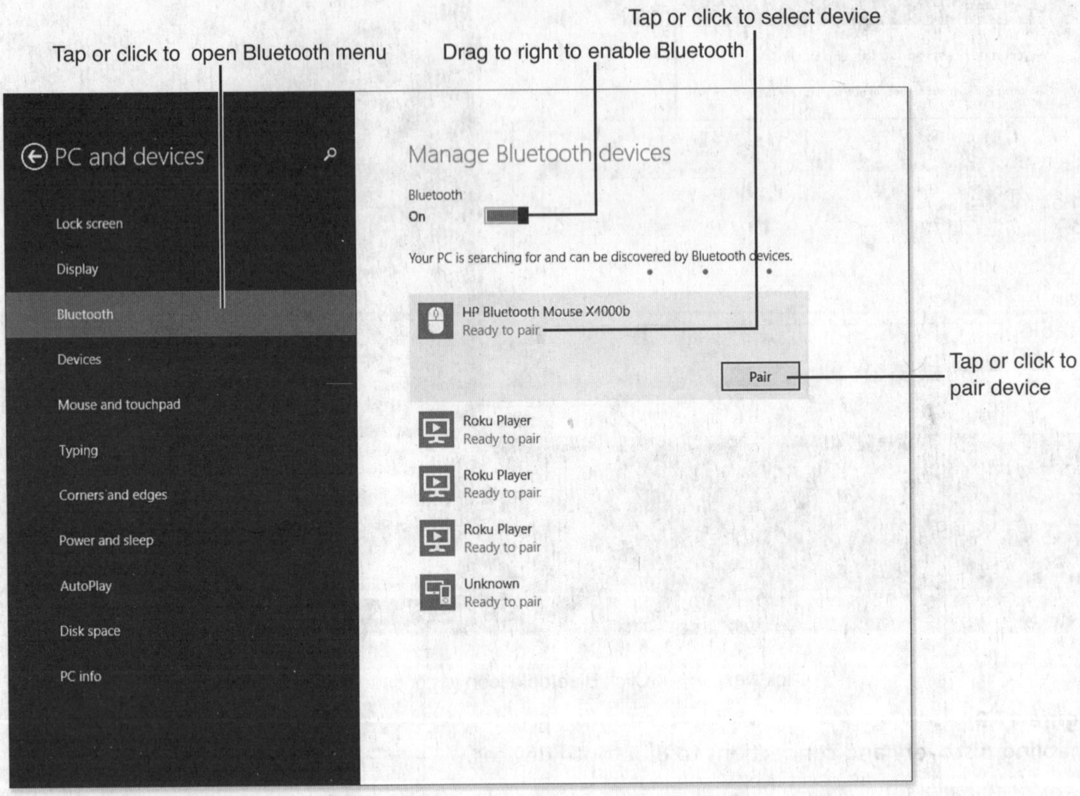

Figure 17.10
Connecting to a Bluetooth mouse.

Bluetooth Mouse (Android)

To pair a Bluetooth mouse with an Android device:

1. Tap **Settings**.
2. Turn on Bluetooth if it is turned off.
3. Tap **Bluetooth**.
4. Make sure the Visible to All (discovery) check box is checked.
5. Turn on the mouse.

6. Press the **Connect** button on the mouse.
7. Tap the mouse listing (see Figure 17.11).
8. When the mouse is listed in the Paired devices category and shows as an input device, you can use it.

Figure 17.11 Pairing a Bluetooth mouse with an Android tablet.

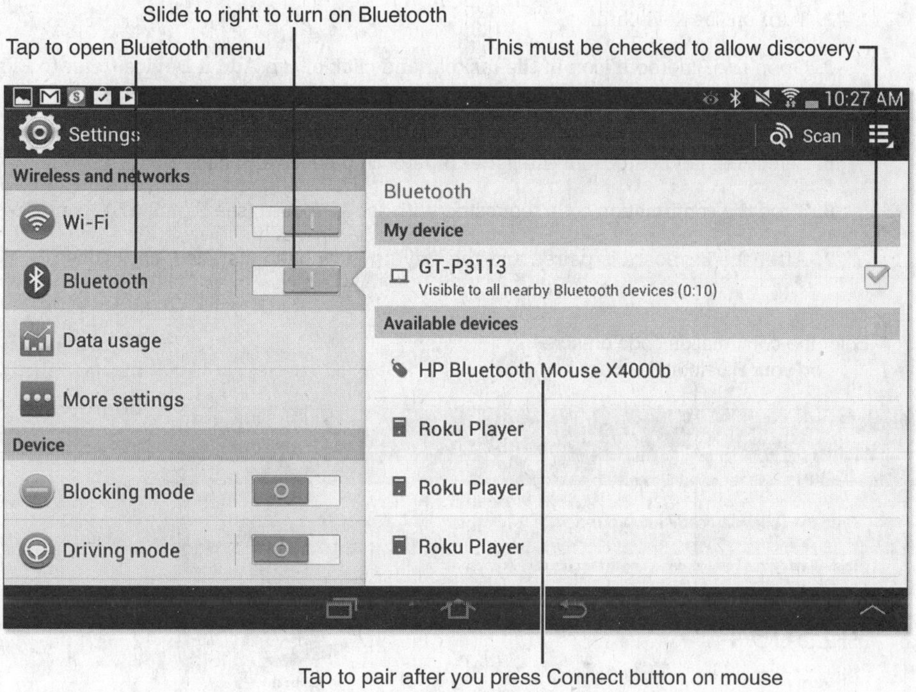

Pairing a Bluetooth Keyboard

The process of pairing a Bluetooth keyboard requires you to

- Make sure your computer or mobile device's Bluetooth radio is on and set as discoverable.
- Enter a confirmation code after the keyboard is recognized.

Let's look at the details.

Bluetooth Keyboard (Windows 7 and Windows 8/8.1 Desktop)

To pair a Bluetooth keyboard with a Windows 7 computer or with a Windows 8/8.1 computer from the desktop, follow these steps:

1. Make sure Bluetooth is turned on and set as discoverable (refer to Figure 17.8).
2. Turn on the keyboard.
3. Open the Bluetooth icon in the taskbar and click or tap **Add a Device** (refer to Figure 17.9).
4. Press the **Connect** button on the keyboard.
5. Select the keyboard from the list of Bluetooth devices and click **Next**.
6. Type the confirmation code requested with the keyboard (see Figure 17.12) and press the **Enter** key.
7. After the keyboard is paired and the drivers have been installed, click **Close**.

Enter the confirmation code on-screen on your Bluetooth keyboard

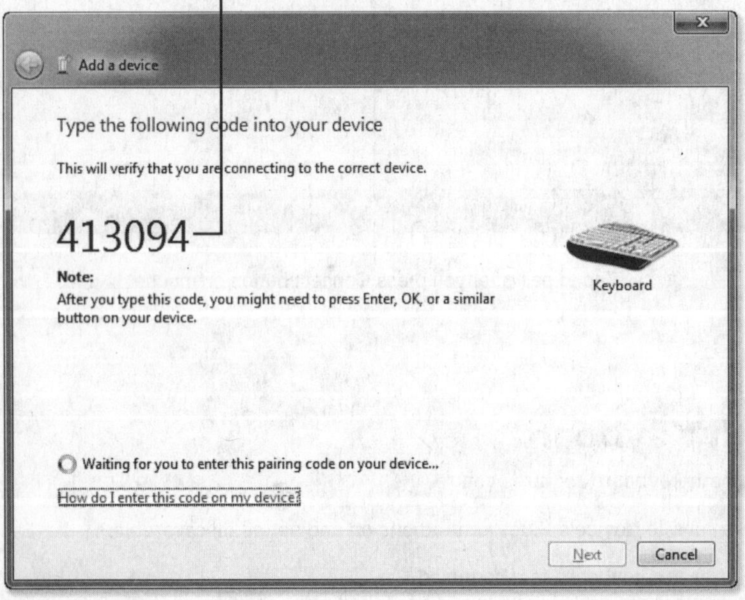

Figure 17.12
Pairing a Bluetooth keyboard with Windows 7.

Bluetooth Keyboard (Windows 8/8.1 Start Screen)

To pair a Bluetooth keyboard with a Windows 8/8.1 computer from the Start screen, follow these steps:

1. Open the Charms menu and click or tap **Settings**.
2. Click or tap **Change PC Settings**.
3. Click or tap **PC and Devices**.
4. Click or tap **Bluetooth**.
5. Turn on Bluetooth if it is turned off.
6. Turn on the keyboard.
7. Press the **Connect** button on the keyboard.
8. Click or tap **Pair**.
9. Type the confirmation code requested with the keyboard and press the **Enter** key.
10. When the keyboard status is listed as Connected, you can use it.

Bluetooth Keyboard (Android)

To pair a Bluetooth keyboard with an Android device, follow these steps:

1. Tap **Settings**.
2. Turn on Bluetooth if it is turned off.
3. Tap **Bluetooth**.
4. Check the **Visible to All** (discovery) check box.
5. Turn on the keyboard.
6. Press the **Connect** button on the keyboard.
7. Enter the confirmation code displayed on your mobile device and press the **Enter** key.
8. When the keyboard is listed in the Paired Devices category and shows as an input device, you can use it.

Bluetooth Keyboard (iOS)

To pair a Bluetooth keyboard with an iOS device, follow these steps:

1. Tap **Settings**.
2. Turn on Bluetooth if it is turned off.
3. Tap **Bluetooth**.
4. Turn on the keyboard.
5. Press the **Connect** button on the keyboard.
6. When the keyboard is listed as Connected, you can use it (see Figure 17.13).

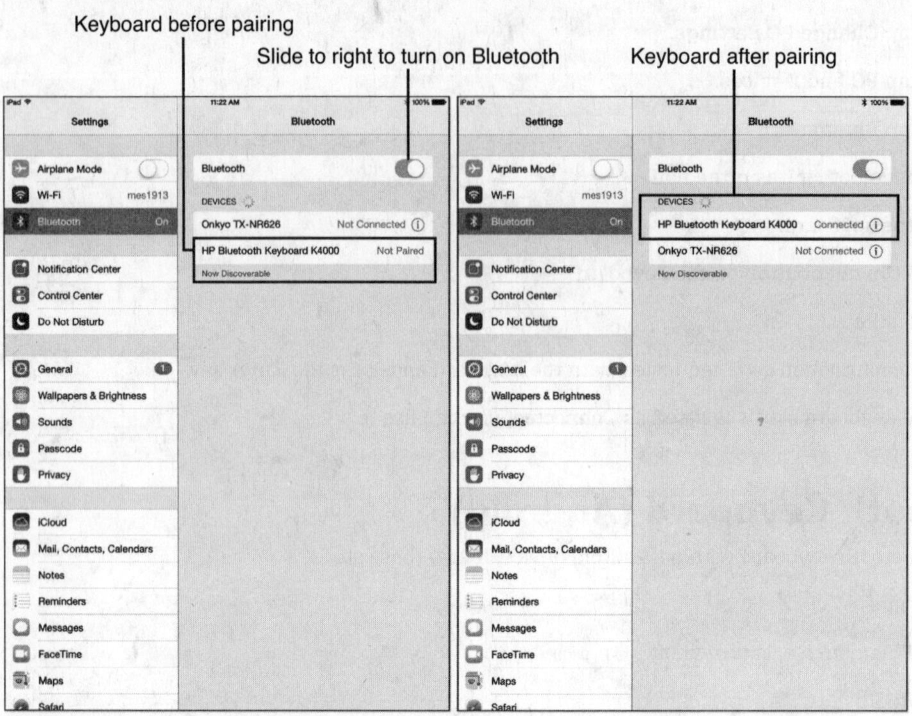

Figure 17.13 Pairing a Bluetooth keyboard with iOS 7.x.

Troubleshooting Problems with Bluetooth Devices

Some of the problems you can have with Bluetooth devices include the following:

- Device compatibility issues
- Pairing issues
- Range issues
- Battery issues
- Bluetooth disabled issues

The following sections provide solutions to these problems.

Device Compatibility Issues

Some mobile devices don't support as many types of Bluetooth devices as others. For example, both iOS and Android support Bluetooth keyboards, but iOS does not support Bluetooth mice, whereas Android does.

Some Bluetooth devices won't work with certain operating systems. However, the compatibility listing on a Bluetooth device might not be complete. So, if you have a Bluetooth device and you're not sure it will work with your mobile device or computer, try it anyway.

Pairing Issues

If you are unable to pair a Bluetooth device with your mobile device or laptop, check the following:

- Make sure your computer or mobile device is set as discoverable. When you turn on Bluetooth using Windows 8/8.1 from the Start screen or iOS, your device is automatically discoverable. However, Android and Windows 7 (and Windows 8/8.1 from the Windows desktop) require you to make the device discoverable after your turn on Bluetooth.
- Make sure you press the Connect button on the Bluetooth device right away. When you enable discovery on Android or Windows 7/8/8.1, you have a limited time to connect with your device.
- If your device is not detected by the pairing utility, it might not be supported. The device might also be too far out of range.

Range Issues

Bluetooth devices have a much longer range after being paired than normal wireless mice and keyboards. However, you could still be too far away from the host computer for the device to be paired or to work.

Try moving the Bluetooth device closer to your computer or mobile device and try re-pairing or connecting again. If you have 2.4GHz-band mobile phones or microwave ovens in use near your Bluetooth device, it might have problems with reliable operation.

Battery Issues

Your computer or mobile device's battery will run down faster when Bluetooth is enabled. If your mobile device is very low on power, you might not be able to pair with a Bluetooth device or stay connected until you recharge your mobile device's battery.

Your Bluetooth device will also stop working reliably when low on battery power, and it won't work at all when the battery is completely run down. Use high-quality batteries (usually alkaline) in your Bluetooth devices, and be sure to remove them if you plan to store them for more than six months.

Bluetooth Disabled Issues

Even if Bluetooth is turned on, other changes you make to your computer or mobile device's configuration can turn off Bluetooth. Mobile devices with onboard Wi-Fi and Bluetooth typically have an Airplane mode option (also available in Windows 8/8.1). When this option is enabled, all onboard radios (including Wi-Fi and Bluetooth) are disabled.

If you turn off wireless support with a function-key combination or a special push button on a Windows 7 laptop, you will turn off both Wi-Fi and Bluetooth.

Troubleshooting IR Keyboards

Infrared (also known as IrDA) keyboards (sometimes including an integrated pointing device mouse equivalent) are available for use with PCs and some types of mobile devices.

IR-based input devices need a clear line-of-sight established between the transceiver and the input device. This is relatively simple to do with an input device placed on the desktop, but it can be a lot harder if you use a wireless keyboard or keyboard/ mouse combo on your lap.

The greater the distance between the IR receiver built in to or attached to your computer or mobile device and the keyboard, the more likely it is that an obstacle will block the IR signal.

> **Note**
>
> Fentek Industries (www. fentek-ind.com) is a useful source for unusual keyboards, mice, and other input devices, including IR and left-hand-optimized keyboards, vertical mice, trackballs, and foot pedals. They offer products for PCs, Android, and iOS devices.

18

UPGRADING AND TROUBLESHOOTING STORAGE DEVICES

Fast Track to Solutions

Table 18.1 Symptom Table

Symptom	Flowchart or Book Section	Page #
I'm seeing a SMART error message on my computer. What does it mean?	Using SMART Drive Monitoring	446
How do I run CHKDSK to check my drive for errors?	Checking Your Windows Drives for Errors	449
When I connect a USB drive to my Windows 8.1 computer, I see a message telling me it might have errors.	Checking USB and Flash Memory Devices for Errors	451
I need to reformat a drive that's causing problems. How should I do this?	Using Format to Solve Disk Errors	452
I just erased a file I need. Can I get it back?	Restoring Files from the Recycle Bin	457
I just erased a file in Windows 8/8.1 but it didn't go to the Recycle Bin. Can I get it back?	Restoring a Previous Version or Deleted File in Windows 8/8.1	462

Symptom	Flowchart or Book Section	Page #
I just erased a file in Windows 7 after I ran a backup. Can I get it back?	Retrieving Files from a Backup (Windows 7)	466
I just erased a file, have no backup, and no File History. Can I get it back?	Retrieving Deleted Files That Bypassed the Recovery Bin	469
My Windows tablet or Ultrabook is short of space.	Using Disk Cleanup	476
What cloud storage programs work with Windows and my mobile devices?	Using Cloud Storage	481

Signs of Drive Problems

Storage devices such as hard disk drives, SSDs (solid-state drives), flash memory, and optical media are used to store your favorite photos and music, important household and business documents, and your computer or device's operating system.

When you experience one or more of the following problems, problems with your storage device should be at the top of your list of usual suspects:

- Files that formerly opened quickly take a long time to open.
- "Disk read error" messages.
- Grinding noises from your drive.
- Windows requests permission to run a disk check.
- A drive can't be recognized by Windows or by a mobile device.
- A file you opened can't be played or viewed.

> **Note**
> An SSD is a drive based on fast flash memory. Unlike USB flash drives or flash memory cards, an SSD looks like a hard disk to your computer and performs much faster than a hard disk. However, an SSD is much more expensive per GB than a hard disk.

In this chapter, you'll learn how to help prevent problems with your media, how to recover "lost" information, and how to retrieve information from a backup. Whether you're concerned about storage on a Windows computer, a tablet, a media player, a smartphone, or an e-reader, this chapter can help.

Using SMART Drive Monitoring

Almost all PCs use Serial ATA (SATA) hard disks for mass storage, and some older models use Parallel ATA (PATA or ATA/IDE) hard disks. Both of these drive types support a detect-warning feature known as Self-Monitoring, Analysis, and Reporting Technology, or SMART (also referred to as S.M.A.R.T.).

Most computers are designed to monitor the condition of SMART-compatible hard disks so you can be warned of impending failures. However, in practice, warnings generated by the system BIOS about SMART failures often occur just before complete disk drive failure, leaving no time for backups.

> **Note**
>
> SMART is also supported by most external hard disk drives connected to USB or FireWire ports.

How can you make sure that SMART monitoring is working to keep you alerted of hard disk problems? First, if your system BIOS has an option to enable SMART capability, enable it unless you use a SMART monitoring program that can't coexist with SMART monitoring. In Figure 18.1, we see an advanced BIOS dialog in which SMART monitoring is disabled.

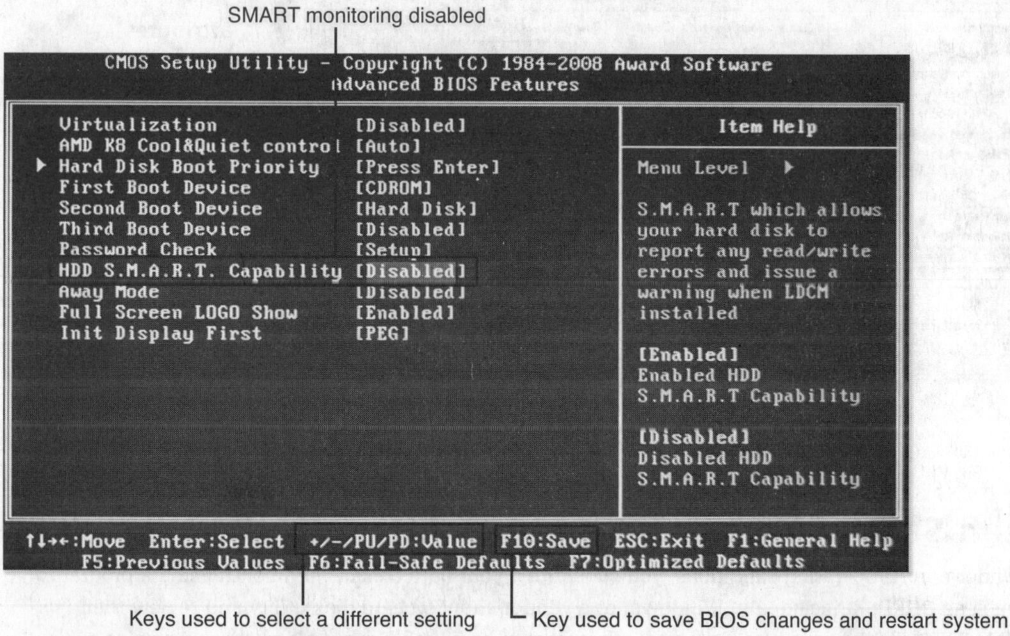

Figure 18.1
To enable SMART hard disk monitoring on this system, press the +,-, PgUp, or PgDn keys to select Enabled, and then press F10 to save changes and exit.

Second, use hard disk testing software from your drive vendor to help determine if a drive is in danger of failing. For details, see "Using Drive Vendors' Disk Testing Software," p.454, this chapter.

If you cannot determine if your hard disk drive is supported by a vendor-supplied hard disk testing program, download and run a disk-testing program that works with virtually all drives, such as PassMark's DiskCheckup (see Figure 18.2). DiskCheckup is free for personal use and is available from www.passmark.com/products/diskcheckup.htm. It displays SMART attributes, rates your drive's condition, and can be used with internal and external hard disks.

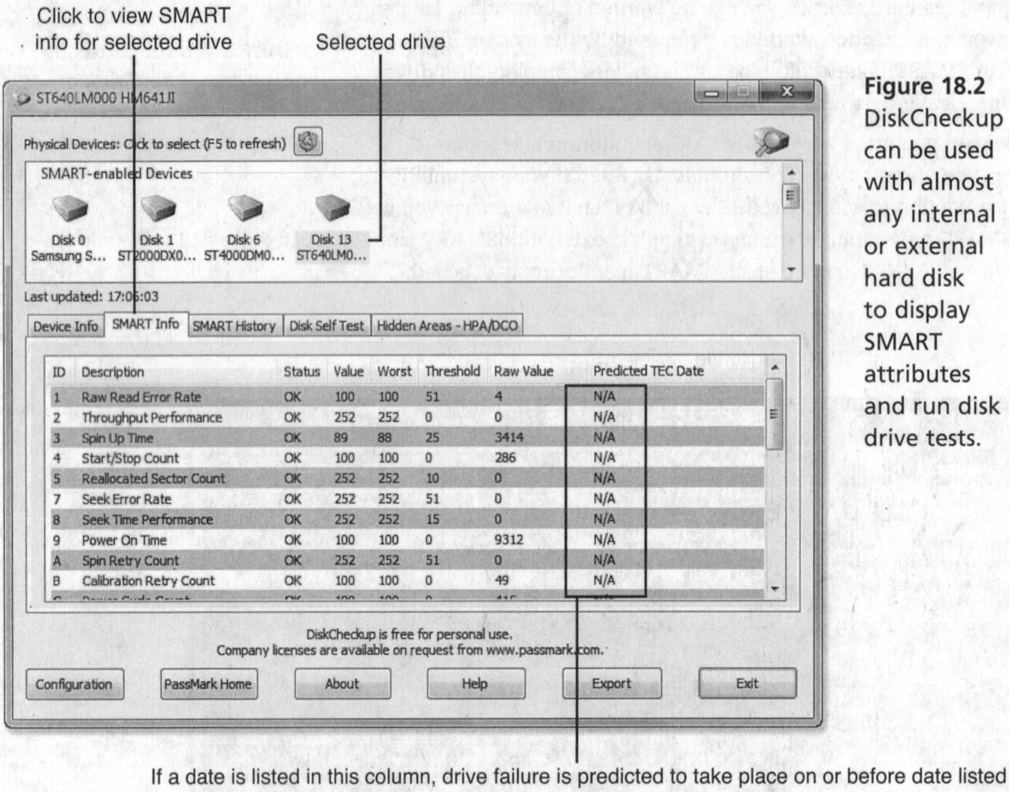

ID	Description	Status	Value	Worst	Threshold	Raw Value	Predicted TEC Date
1	Raw Read Error Rate	OK	100	100	51	4	N/A
2	Throughput Performance	OK	252	252	0	0	N/A
3	Spin Up Time	OK	89	88	25	3414	N/A
4	Start/Stop Count	OK	100	100	0	286	N/A
5	Reallocated Sector Count	OK	252	252	10	0	N/A
7	Seek Error Rate	OK	252	252	51	0	N/A
8	Seek Time Performance	OK	252	252	15	0	N/A
9	Power On Time	OK	100	100	0	9312	N/A
A	Spin Retry Count	OK	252	252	51	0	N/A
B	Calibration Retry Count	OK	100	100	0	49	N/A

Figure 18.2 DiskCheckup can be used with almost any internal or external hard disk to display SMART attributes and run disk drive tests.

When Should You Check SMART Attributes?

Under normal operating conditions, you should test your hard disks every month using a program such as CHKDSK (included in Windows) or a vendor-supplied hard disk utility and review their SMART attributes for errors. On a portable or laptop hard disk, I recommend checking twice a month, because these drives are in greater danger of being physically damaged or overheating.

If a drive displays even a single SMART problem area (in other words, a SMART attribute is listed as FAIL or a failure date is listed), it's time to back it up and replace it before it fails and takes your information with it.

Note

To learn more about SMART attributes, including which ones are most likely to indicate drive failure, see the well-documented S.M.A.R.T. article at Wikipedia: http://en.wikipedia.org/wiki/S.M.A.R.T.

Checking Your Windows Drives for Errors

Although Microsoft Windows 7 and 8/8.1 have automated disk defragmentation to help improve performance, you need to test your drives for errors periodically. Use the Windows Error-Checking program (CHKDSK.EXE) to make sure your drive's file structure is working properly. Here's how to use to check your system (C:) drive:

1. Open Windows Explorer (Windows 7) or File Explorer (Windows 8/8.1).
2. Right-click C: drive and select **Properties**.
3. Click the **Tools** tab.
4. Click **Check (Windows 8/8.1) or Check Now** (Windows 7).
5. Click **Start**.
6. Click **Schedule Disk Check** (see Figure 18.3). Windows will run CHKDSK.EXE the next time you start your computer and display the results when Windows starts.

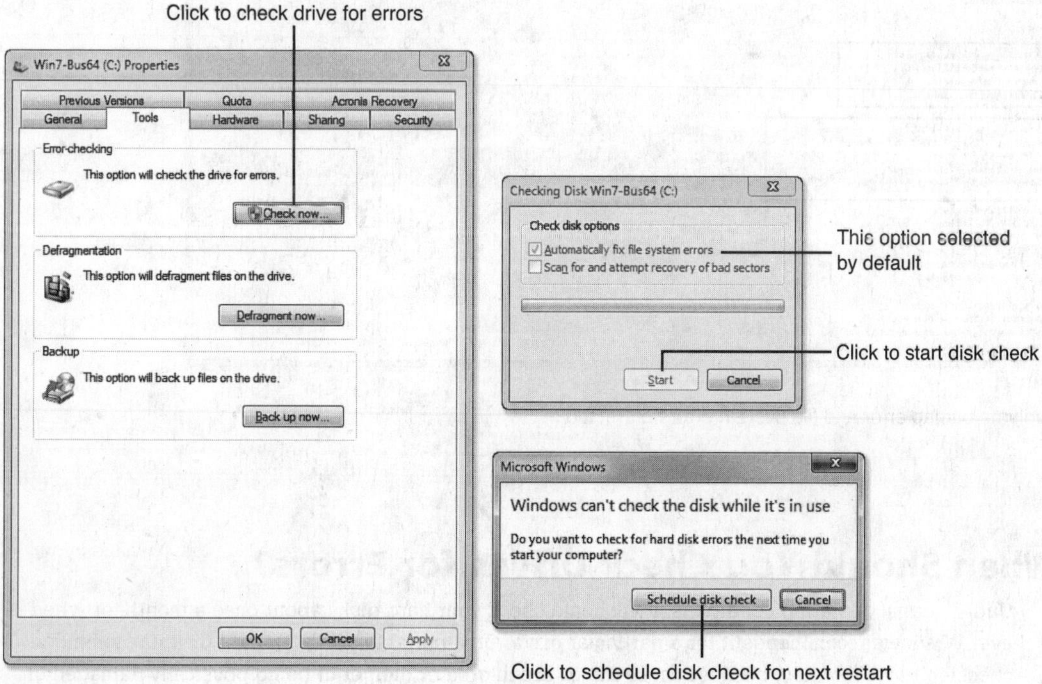

Figure 18.3
Scheduling disk error-checking for C: drive with Windows 7.

You can check drives other than the Windows system drive without restarting your computer. The process is the same, except that the disk test starts after step 5.

During the test, Windows checks a variety of disk structures and looks for errors. If any errors are found, they are displayed at the end of the test (see Figure 18.4).

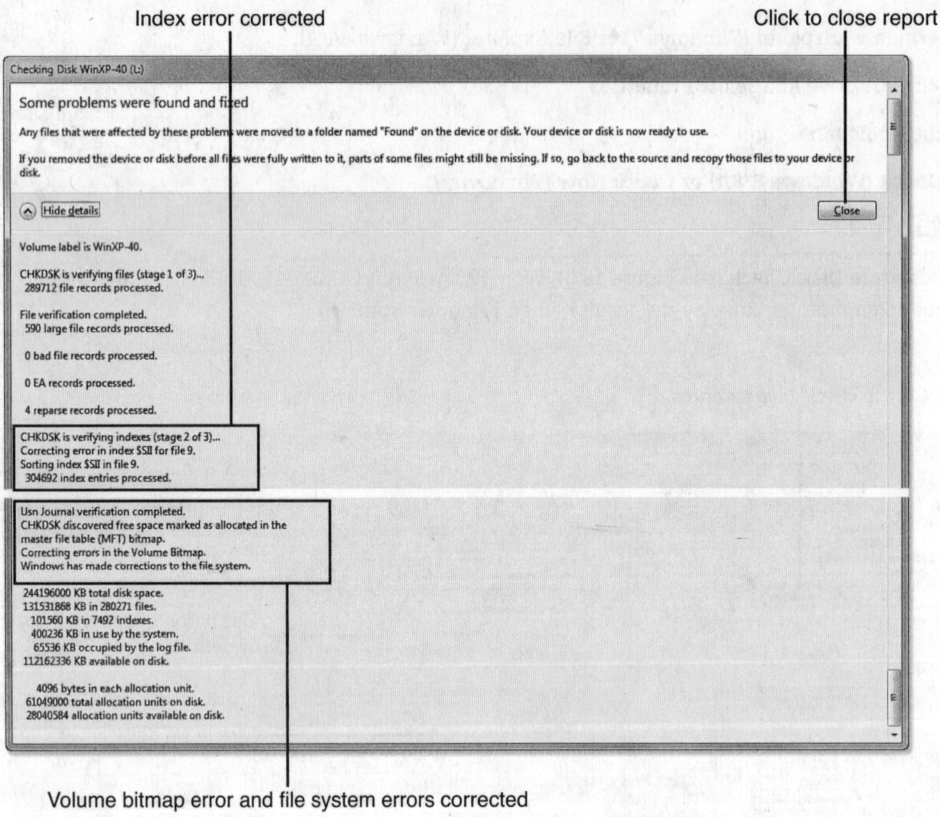

Figure 18.4 Some problems were found on this drive.

When Should You Check Drives for Errors?

Under normal operating conditions, you should check your hard disks about once a month, or whenever Windows recommends it for a particular drive. On a portable or laptop hard disk, I recommend checking twice monthly, because these drives are in greater danger of being physically damaged or overheating.

If a drive has file system errors every time you test it, consider backing it up and replacing it.

Checking USB and Flash Memory Devices for Errors

You can use the same Check/Check Now procedure discussed in the previous section for USB, flash memory, and other external flash and hard disk drives. Windows 8 and 8.1 automatically check external drives for errors when you connect them to your system and will alert you from either the Windows Desktop or the Start menu if testing is recommended (see Figure 18.5).

Figure 18.5 Windows 8 and 8.1 alert you when you connect a drive that might have problems.

You can skip testing or checking the drive, and after the repair process is over determine if any drive problems existed (see Figure 18.6).

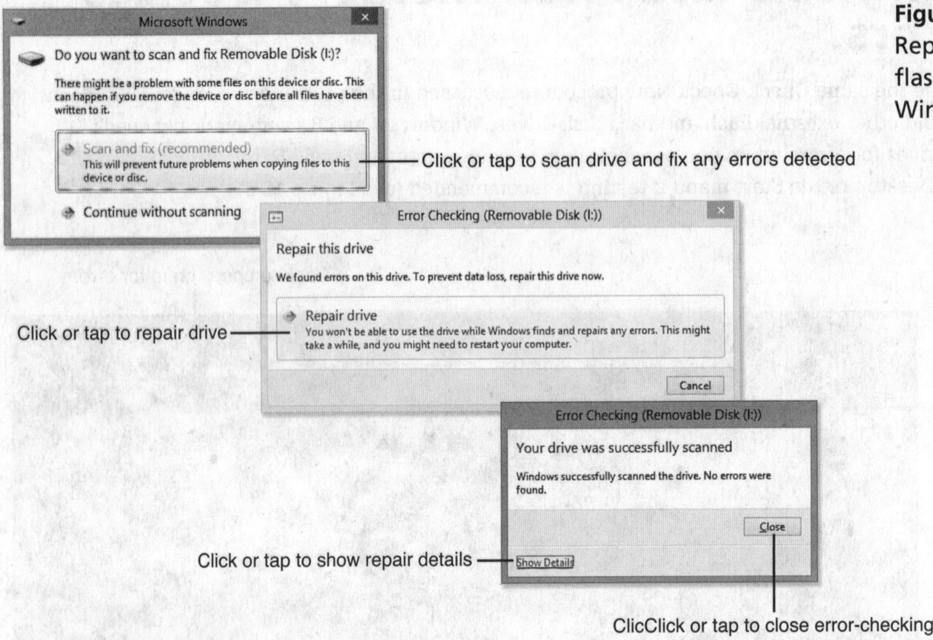

Figure 18.6 Repairing a flash drive with Windows 8/8.1.

When Should You Check USB and Flash Memory Drives for Errors?

Under normal operating conditions, you should check these drives about once a month, or whenever Windows recommends it for a particular drive. If you don't eject the drive before removing it by using the Safely Remove Hardware and Eject Media tool in the notification area of the Windows desktop, you should test the drive the next time you insert it.

If a drive has file system errors every time you test it, consider backing it up and replacing it.

Using Format to Solve Disk Errors

The Format command in Windows is typically run in Quick mode. Quick mode, which takes just a few seconds, erases the drive's root folder (which is where the information about the files on the drive is stored) so the remainder of the space on the drive can be reused. Quick formatting does *not* re-create the drive's logical layout, so a drive that has developed file system errors might still have these errors, even after formatting.

Before replacing a drive, format the drive again without using the Quick option. If you don't use the Quick option, the entire logical layout of the drive is re-created, which can help the drive store information more reliably. Keep in mind that you need to back up the contents of a drive before you perform either type of format. Here's how to use this method:

1. Copy any files you want to keep from the drive you are going to format to a different drive, using drag and drop, copy and paste, or Copy To.
2. Right-click the drive in Windows Explorer or File Explorer and select **Format** (see Figure 18.7).

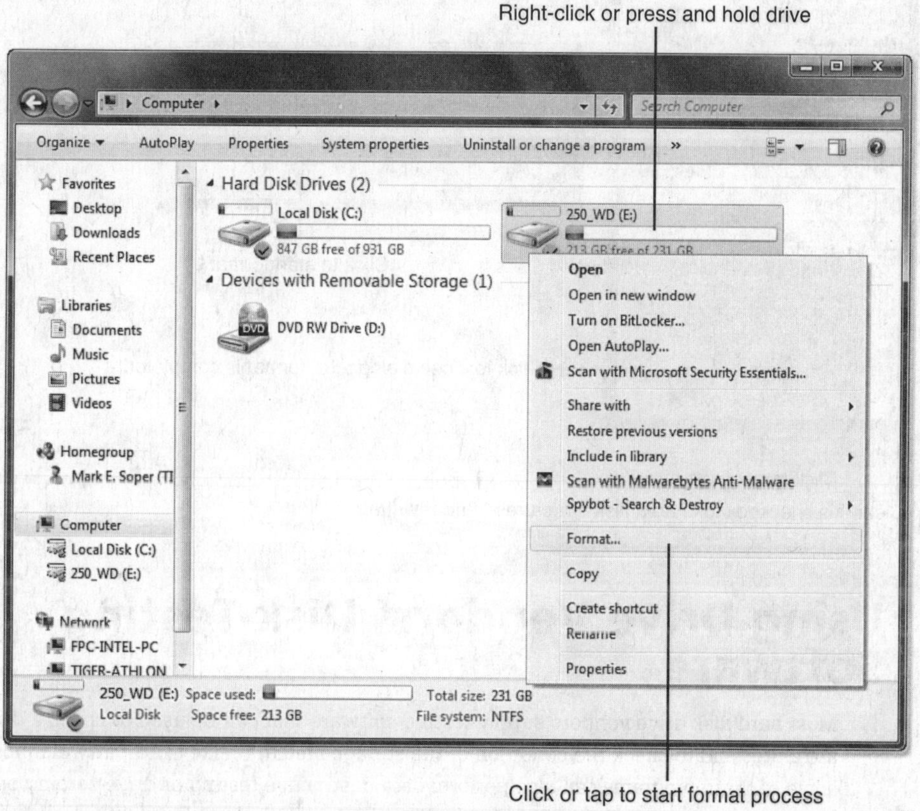

Figure 18.7 Selecting a hard disk for formatting with Windows Explorer (Windows 7).

3. Clear the **Quick Format** check box (it's selected by default).
4. Click **OK** (see Figure 18.8). Prepare to wait a while, especially if you're formatting a hard disk drive. A green progress bar keeps you informed.
5. At the end of the process, close the Format dialog.

Run Error-checking on the drive after you complete the format process, and do so periodically to determine if the drive is more reliable than before. If the drive continues to have problems, replace it.

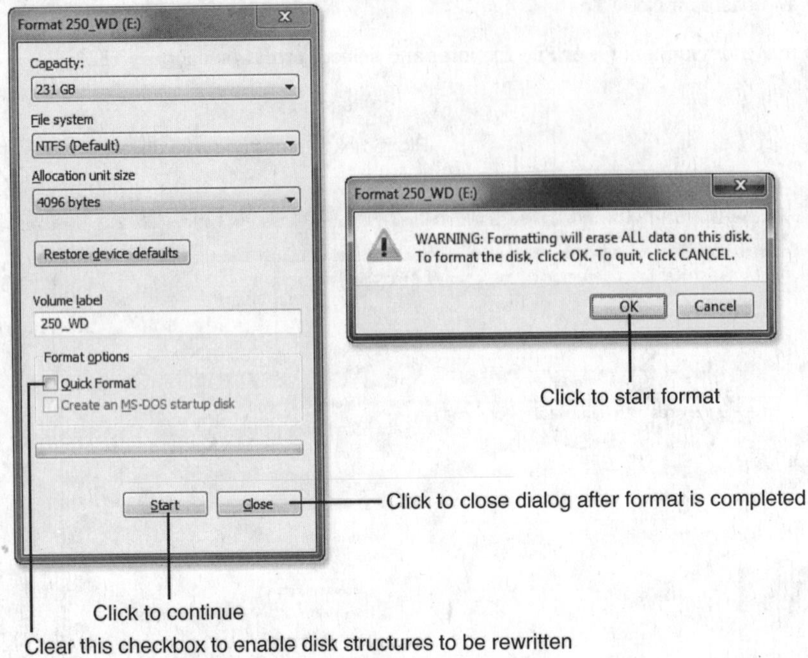

Figure 18.8 Preparing to format a hard disk with Windows 7.

Using Drive Vendors' Disk-Testing Software

Most hard disk drive vendors supply testing software that can be used to check a drive's SMART attributes and to check the condition of the storage media. Unlike third-party diagnostic programs, some of these programs can also perform data-destructive testing or drive-zeroing operations. These programs might be included on a disc supplied with the drive, or they can be downloaded from the drive vendors' websites. See Table 18.2 for a list of the most common tools from major drive vendors.

Table 18.2 Disk-Testing Software from Hard Disk Vendors

Hard Disk Vendor	Program	Website
Seagate (also Maxtor, Samsung)	SeaTools	www.seagate.com
Hitachi Global Storage Technologies	WinDFT	www.hgst.com
Western Digital	Data LifeGuard Diagnostics	www.wd.com

Some of these tools can be used for testing both internal and external drives. Be sure to check the recommendations for testing software for your particular hard disk model.

> **Tip**
>
> To make sure you download a program that is compatible with your hard disk, you need to determine the brand name and model number of your drive.
>
> You can determine the model number of an internal hard disk by opening Device Manager, expanding the Disk Drives section, and looking for drives listed as SATA or PATA drives. The drive model number is usually displayed. Search the model number online to determine the manufacturer of your drive.

In Figure 18.9, Seagate's SeaTools is being used to perform a quick test on an internal hard disk.

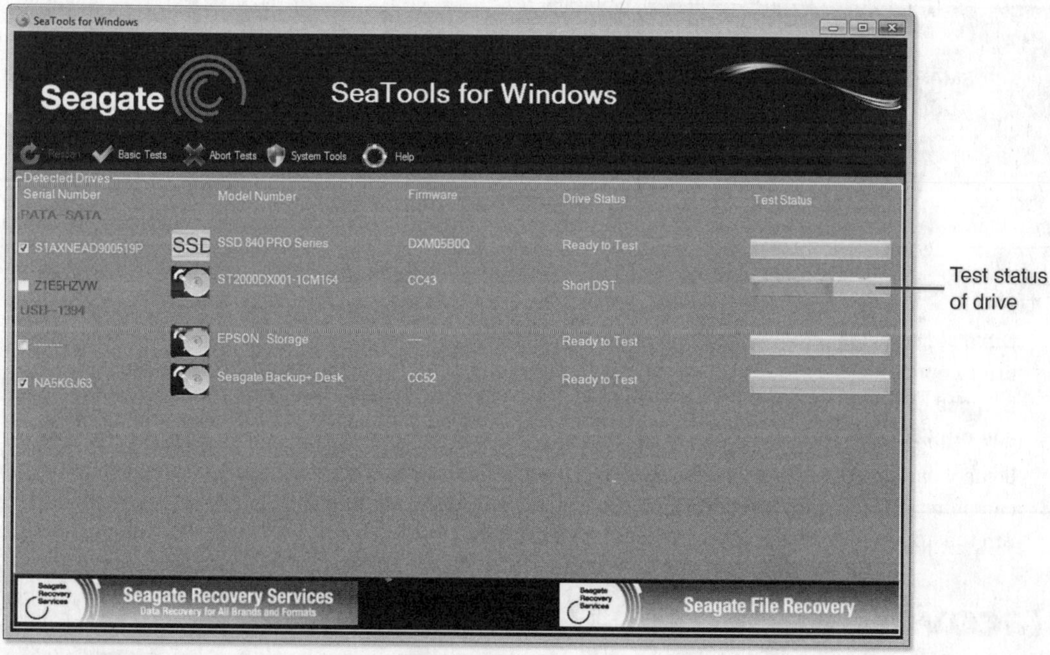

Figure 18.9
Testing a hard disk with Seagate SeaTools.

In Figure 18.10, Western Digital's Data LifeGuard Diagnostics is displaying test results for an installed hard disk.

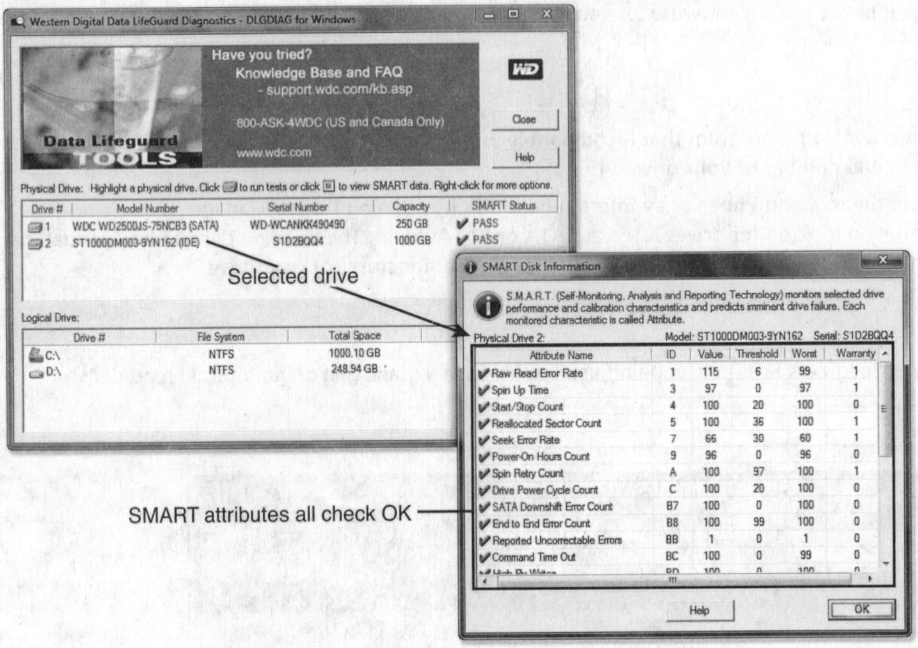

Figure 18.10 Reviewing test results with Western Digital Data LifeGuard Diagnostics.

When Should You Use Drive Vendors' Test Programs?

Drive vendors' test programs should be run every three to six months for both desktop and portable drives under normal conditions, as well as immediately after a serious system problem, such as a dropped computer or drive, a shutdown caused by a power surge, or if the drive displays errors after you run CHKDSK.

Some vendors require that you use their test program to determine if a drive is defective before it can be returned for replacement. So, if you suspect a drive under warranty is defective, you should run the appropriate test program to check its condition.

Recovering "Lost" Data

Did you delete a file by mistake? Did you clear off a flash memory card before you copied its contents to your computer or to an optical disc? What if you resized a photo and saved the small version over the full-sized version? Did you format a drive and then discover it contained vital tax records?

There are a variety of ways to deal with data loss, but before you do anything else, do this:

1. Take a deep breath and let it out slowly.

2. Don't panic.

There are several ways to recover from a data loss. These include the following:

- Restoring items from the Recycle Bin
- Restoring a previous version
- Retrieving a backup copy of the file(s)
- Running data-recovery software to retrieve a file that was not in the Recycle Bin

Tip

If you "lost" files while working in Windows Explorer or File Explorer, the real problem might be that you accidentally dragged a file or folder into another folder. If you think this happened, immediately press Ctrl+Z on your keyboard to undo the move. If you are using a tablet, you can bring up the onscreen keyboard and then click Ctrl+Z on the onscreen keyboard or enable the menu and select Edit, Undo Move.

Restoring Files from the Recycle Bin

When you highlight a file or folder on a hard disk drive or SSD in Windows Explorer or File Explorer and press the Delete (Del) key, or, as in Figure 18.11, you select Delete from the right-click menu) and click Yes (see Figure 18.12), your file or folder and contents are moved from their original location to a special folder called the Recycle Bin.

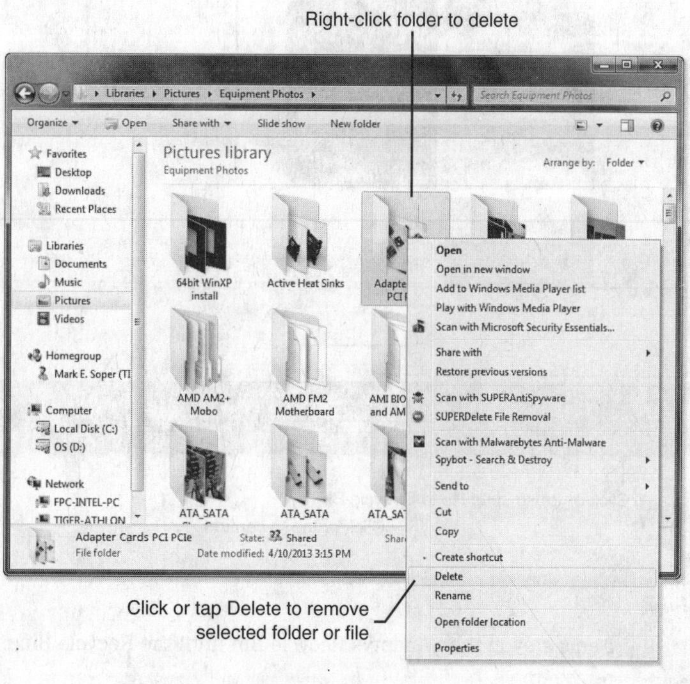

Figure 18.11
Preparing to "delete" a folder in Windows Explorer.

Figure 18.12
Confirming that the folder will go to the Recycle Bin.

If you select a file or folder on a hard disk drive or SSD in This PC from the Windows 8/8.1 Start menu and click or tap Delete (see Figure 18.13), the selected item also goes to the Recycle Bin.

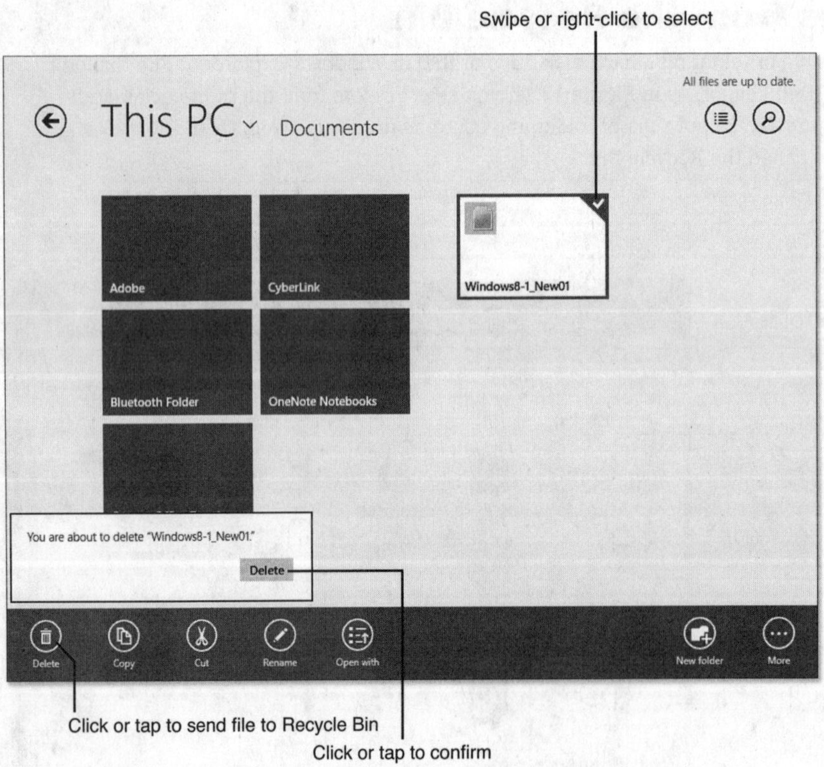

Figure 18.13
Preparing to "delete" a file in Windows 8/8.1.

Items stay in the Windows Recycle Bin until the Recycle Bin is full, and then the oldest files are removed.

Note

To see how much space the Recycle Bin uses on each drive, right-click the Recycle Bin, select Properties, and select a drive. You can adjust the size reserved for Recycle Bin for each drive, disable the Recycle Bin so that files are removed immediately, and disable the default delete confirmation dialog shown in Figure 18.12.

To restore items from Recycle Bin, follow this procedure:

1. Open Recycle Bin from the Windows Desktop.
2. Select the items to restore.
3. Click **Restore This (These) Item(s)** (Windows 7) or **Restore the Selected Item(s)** (Windows 8/8.1). See Figure 18.14.

The items are restored to their original location.

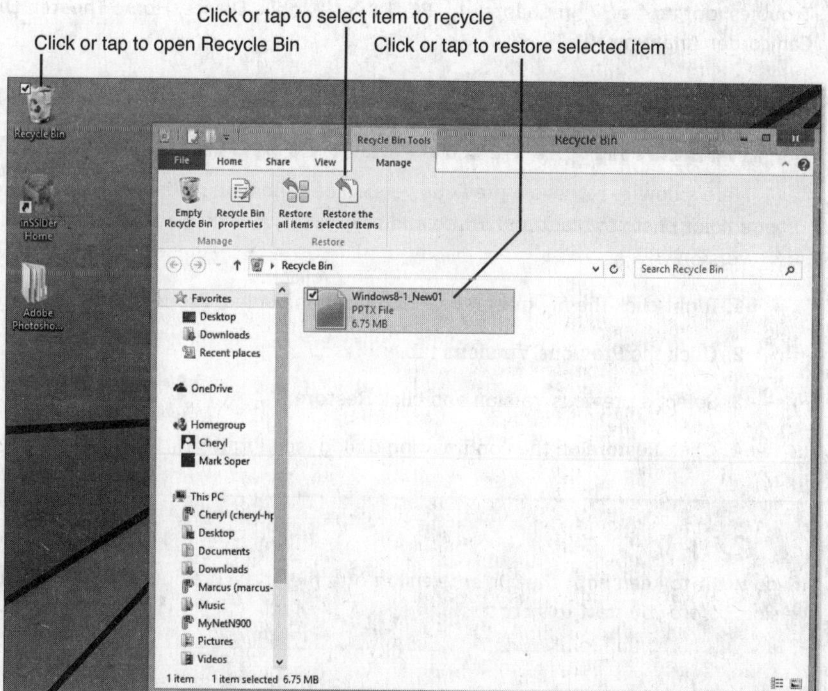

Figure 18.14 Restoring a file from Windows 8/8.1's Recycle Bin.

Note

If you need to free up space on your hard disk, empty the Recycle Bin (see Figure 18.14). If you realize after you empty the Recycle Bin that you need the file, you will need to use data recovery software to retrieve your file.

Restoring a Previous Version

If you accidentally save a changed version of a file using Save rather than Save As, only to realize that you preferred the previous version, you'll appreciate the ability to restore a previous version of a file. However, don't assume that your computer is ready to provide you with this safety net. Here's what you need:

- In Windows 7, you need to enable System Protection for any hard disk other than C: drive (it's enabled on C: drive by default) or use Windows Backup.
- In Windows 8/8.1, you need to set up and use File Protection.

If your system is already configured to support previous versions, you can right-click a file, select Properties, and a Previous Versions tab is available.

> **Note**
> To learn how to set up these options, see, "Preparing a Windows-Based Computer or Tablet for Easier Troubleshooting," p.37, in Chapter 1, "PC, Tablet, Mobile Device, Home Theater, Digital Camera, and Camcorder Anatomy 101."

Restoring a Previous Version in Windows 7

Here's how to retrieve a previous version of a file using Windows 7. In this example, we converted a color photo to black and white and cropped it, and then realized we want to revert to the original version.

1. Right-click the file in Windows Explorer and select **Properties** (see Figure 18.15).
2. Click the **Previous Versions** tab.
3. Select a previous version and click **Restore**.
4. Click **Restore** on the confirmation dialog (see Figure 18.16).

> **Caution**
> If you want to keep both the current version of a file and a previous version, make a copy of the current version *before* you start this process.

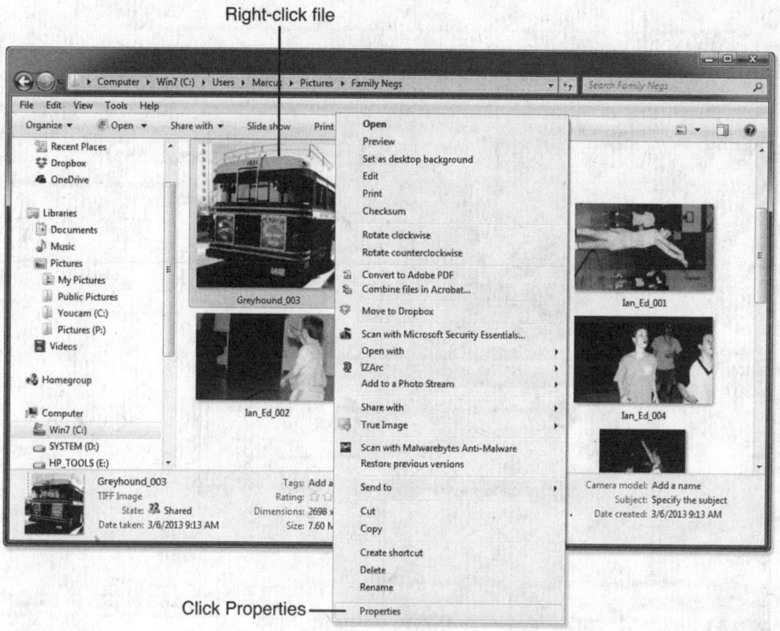

Figure 18.15
Preparing to view the properties sheet for a file in Windows 7.

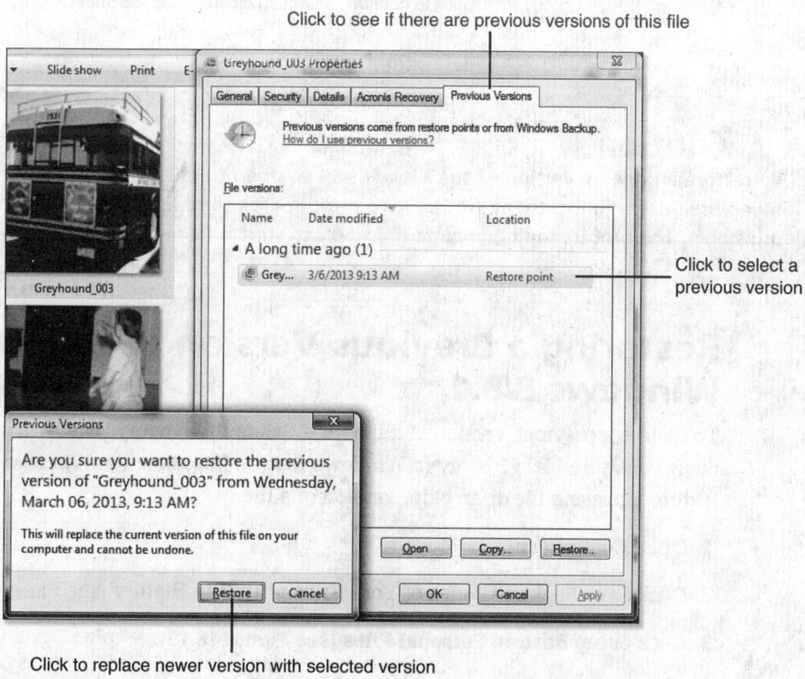

Figure 18.16
Restoring a previous version of a file in Windows 7.

5. Click **OK**. The previous version of the file is restored (see Figure 18.17).

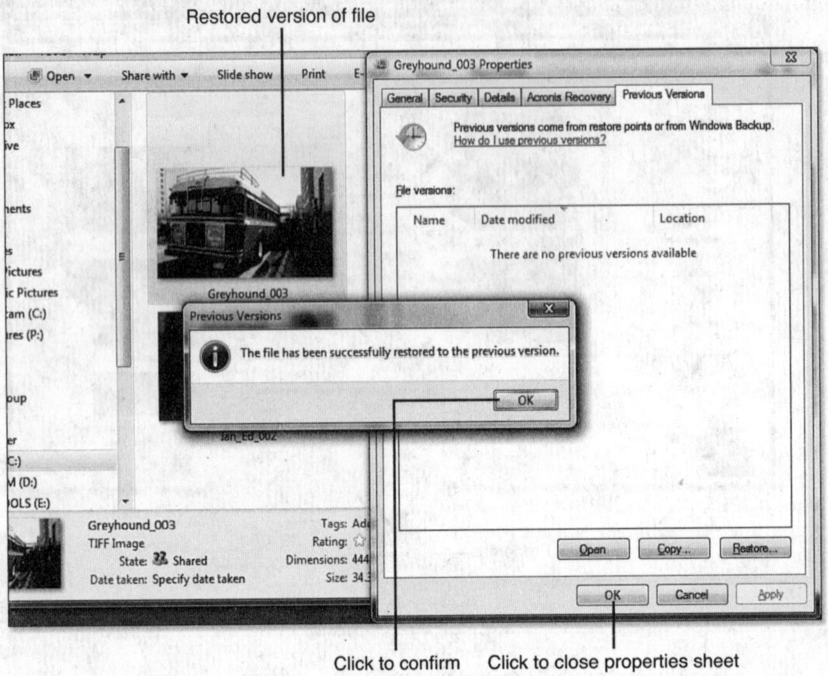

Figure 18.17 The previous version is restored.

Caution

To restore a previous version of the file, be sure to open the file's location and start the process from there. If you use Search to locate the file, be sure to right-click the file and select Open File Location before starting step 1. The process can't complete if you try to start it from Search Results.

Restoring a Previous Version or Deleted File in Windows 8/8.1

To restore a previous version of a file (or a deleted file) using Windows 8/8.1, you must have previously configured File History (a Windows feature introduced in Windows 8). Here's how to use it to restore a missing file or an older version of a file.

1. Open Control Panel.
2. Click **Save Backup Copies of Your Files with File History** (see Figure 18.18).
3. Click or tap **Restore Personal Files** (see Figure 18.19).

Figure 18.18
Preparing to run File History from Control Panel.

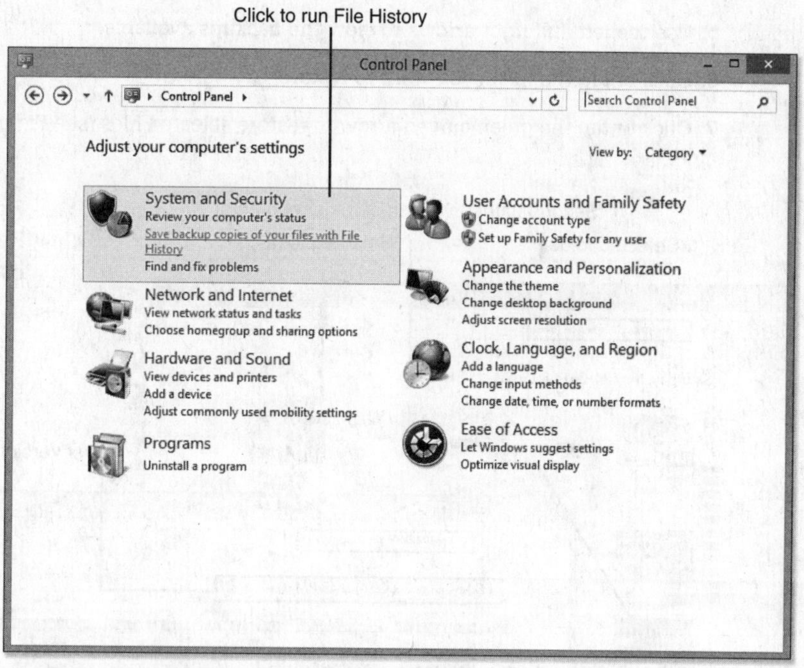

Figure 18.19
The File History dialog.

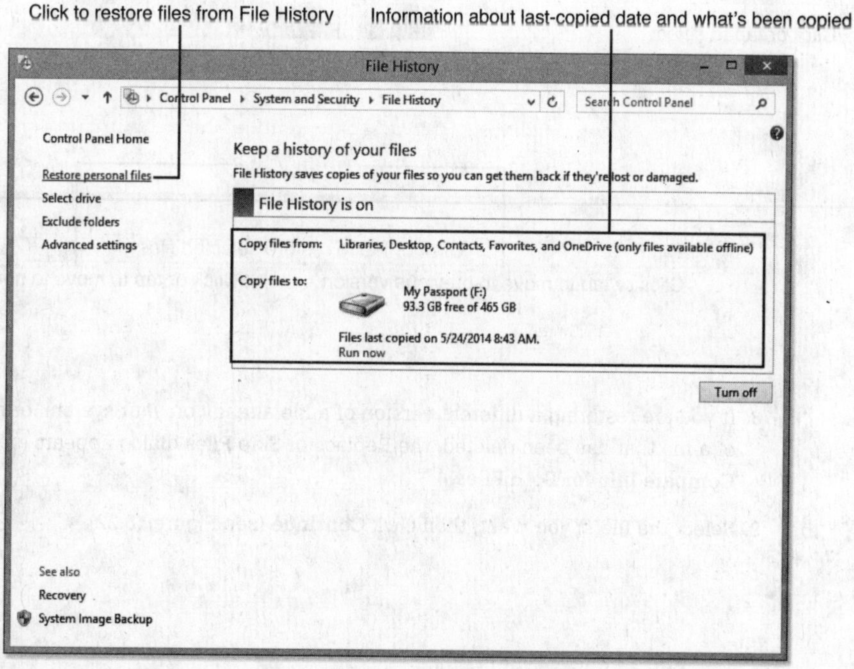

4. Navigate to the folder that contains the file you want to restore.
5. Use the left and right arrows to view the backups available.
6. Click or tap the file(s) you want to restore.
7. Click or tap the green curved arrow to restore selected files (see Figure 18.20).

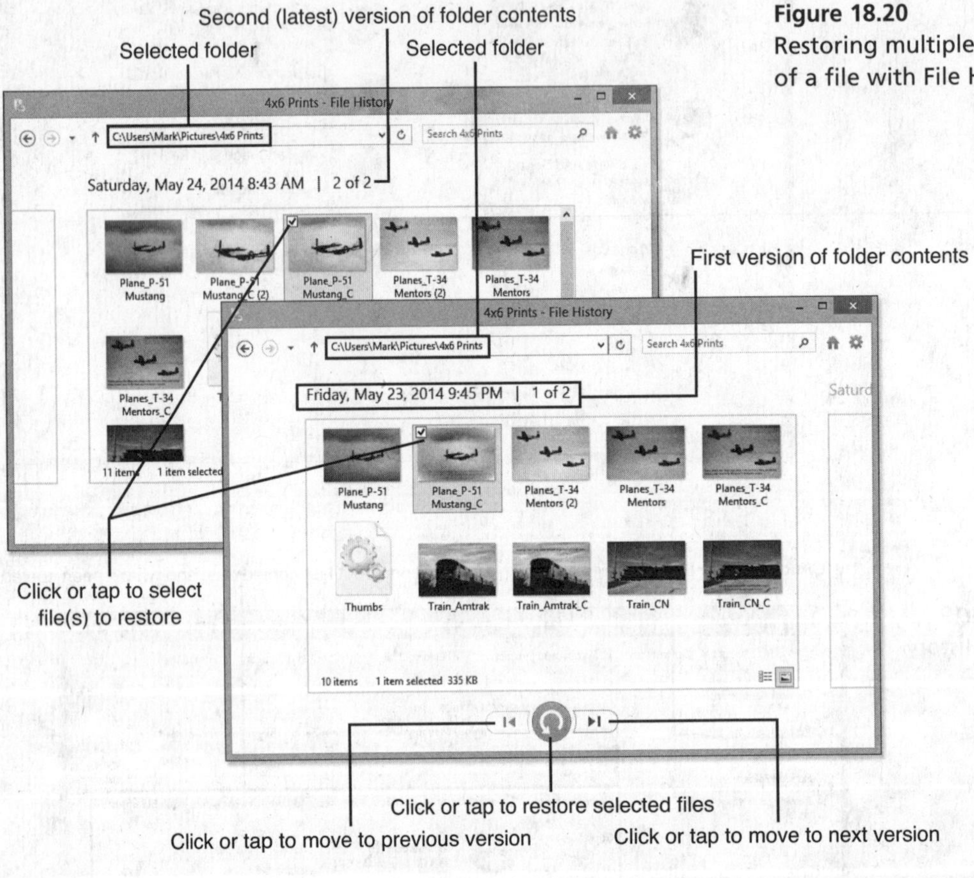

Figure 18.20
Restoring multiple versions of a file with File History.

8. If you are restoring a different version of a file already on your system, or more than one version of a file that has been deleted, the Replace or Skip Files dialog appears (see Figure 18.21). Click **Compare Info for Both Files**.
9. Select the file(s) you want, then click **Continue** (see Figure 18.22).

Figure 18.21 Compare info helps you deal with filename conflicts when restoring files.

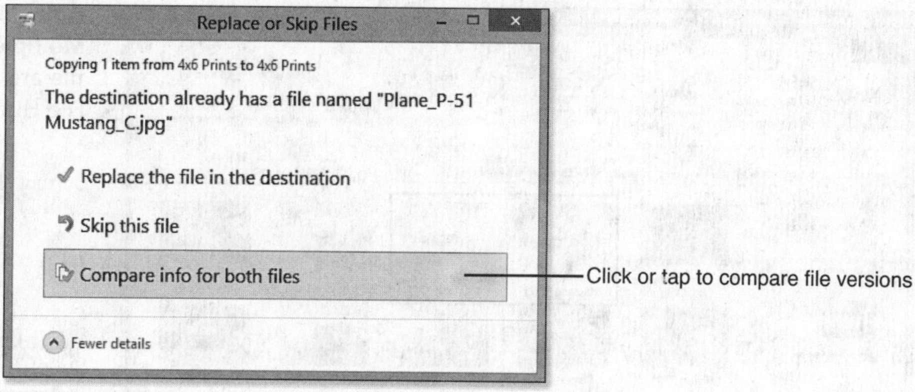

Figure 18.22 Filename conflict? Keep both files, or decide which file you want to keep.

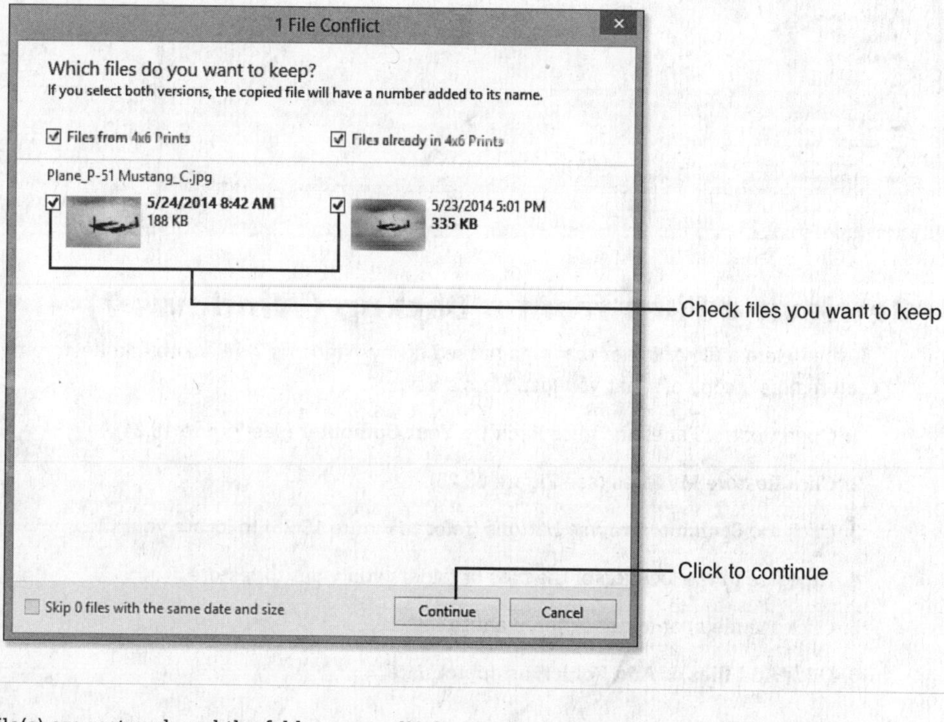

10. The file(s) are restored, and the folder opens displaying the restored files (see Figure 18.23).

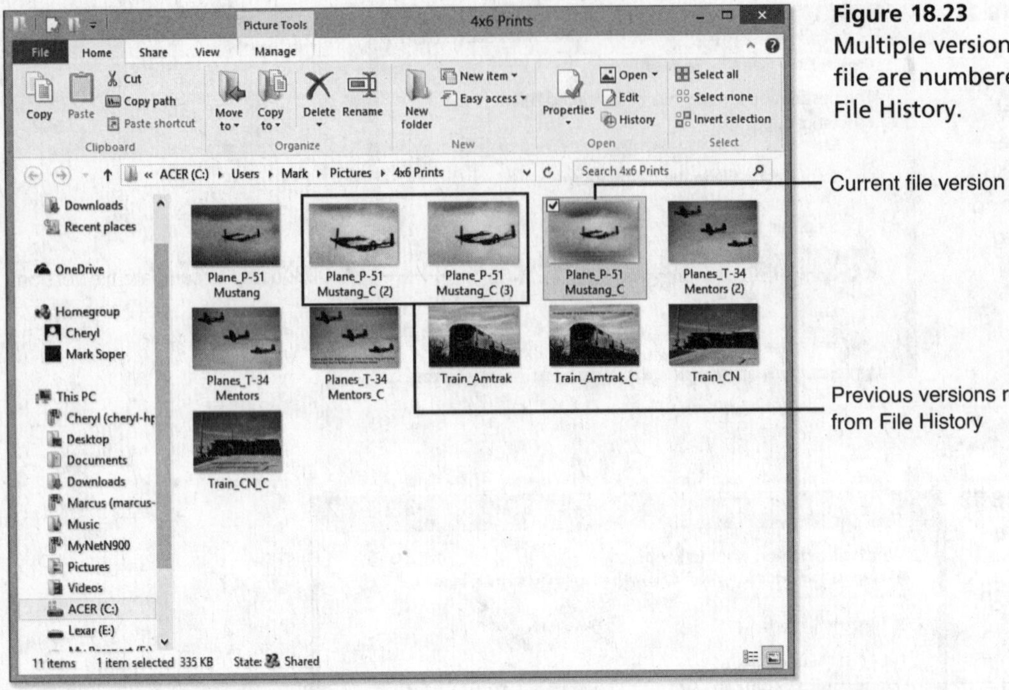

Figure 18.23 Multiple versions of a file are numbered by File History.

Retrieving Files from a Backup (Windows 7)

If you delete a file or folder that was backed up by Windows 7's Backup and Restore program, you can restore a copy of what you lost. Here's how:

1. Open Control Panel and click **Back Up Your Computer** (see Figure 18.24).
2. Click **Restore My Files** (see Figure 18.25).
3. Click the **Search** or **Browse** buttons (refer to Figure 18.26) to locate your files.
4. Navigate to the location of the files or folders you want to restore.
5. Click the file(s) or folder(s) you want to restore.
6. Click **Add files** or **Add Folder**, as appropriate.

Figure 18.24
Starting the restore process from Control Panel.

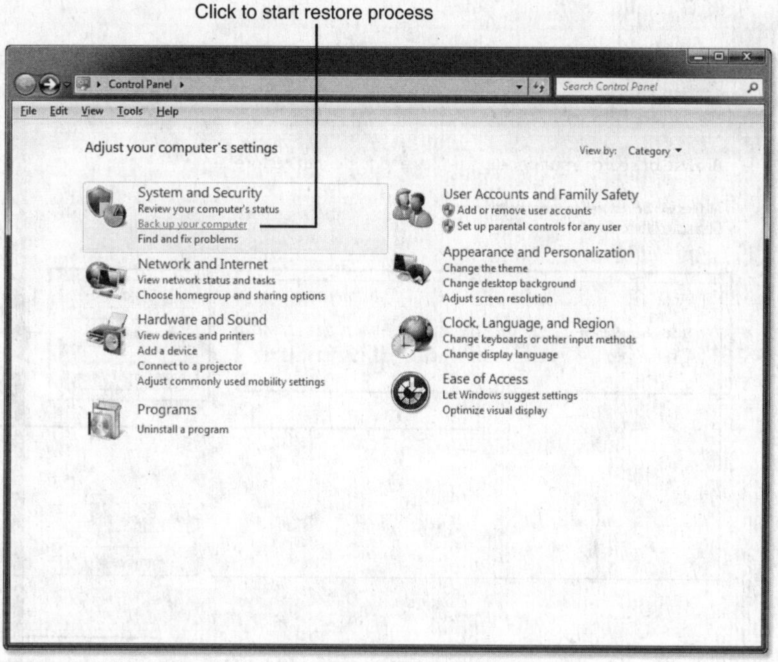

Figure 18.25
The Backup and Restore dialog.

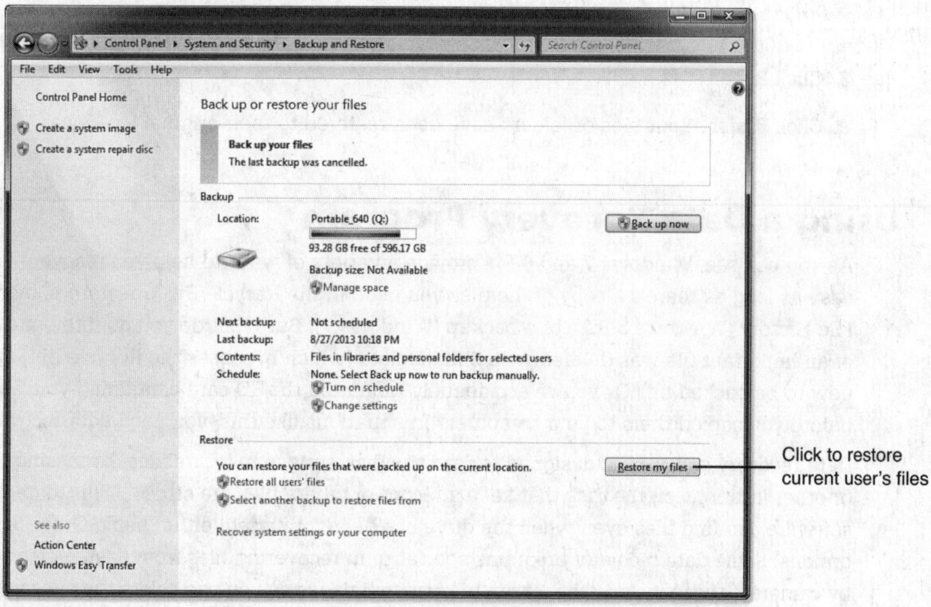

7. Review the file and folders you selected. When you're finished, click **Next** (see Figure 18.26).

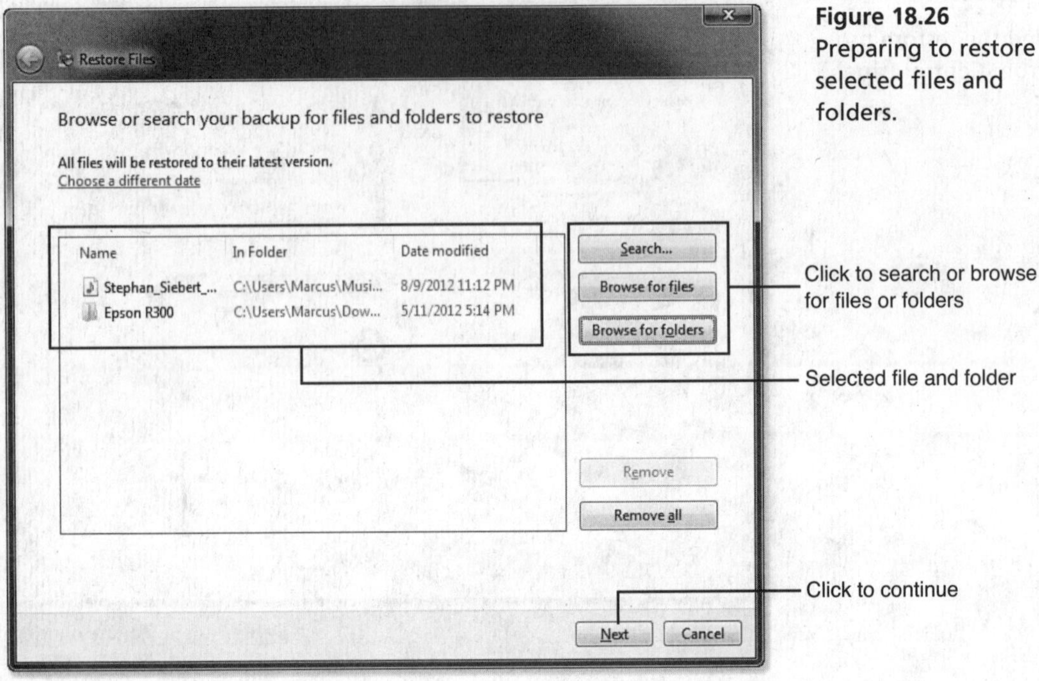

Figure 18.26 Preparing to restore selected files and folders.

8. Click **Restore**.

9. Click **Finish**. Your files or folders have been restored to their original locations.

Using a Data-Recovery Program

As you can see, Windows 7 and 8/8.1 provide a variety of ways to help you recover "lost" data. It's easy as long as there's a copy of the files you need in the Recycle Bin, a restore point (Windows 7), File History (Windows 8/8.1), or a backup (Windows 7). But what do you do if the one and only copy of an important file was deleted with Shift+Delete (which bypasses the Recycle Bin) and it's too new to be backed up? Or you've accidentally formatted the SD card containing your vacation photos before you copied them to your computer? In situations like this, you need data-recovery software.

Data recovery software is designed to read the disk surface to locate files, bypassing the root folder or other locations on the disk that keep a record of where files are stored. Thus, data recovery software can find files even when the drive has been formatted, either using Quick or full format options. Some data recovery programs specialize in recovering files from flash memory cards used by cameras; these include the option to preview images so you can select the ones you want.

Data recovery software should be installed before you delete files from your system. The capability of a data recovery program to locate and restore your files depends on the file space not being overwritten by new programs or other files. To avoid data loss, data recovery programs typically copy retrieved files to a different drive, and some run directly from the program disc rather than requiring installation.

You can find numerous data-recovery programs on the market. Because each data-recovery situation can be different, most vendors offer free versions that can scan for lost data and display the files found. You can then license the program and use it to complete the recovery task.

Some data-recovery programs work with hard disk, flash memory, or SSDs only, whereas others can retrieve data from optical drives as well. Be sure to review the supported drive types, the Windows versions supported, and other information, and try a demo version if available before you buy.

Note

In addition to the programs discussed in this chapter, I have had great success with Ontrack EasyRecovery from www.krollontrack.com.

Retrieving Deleted Files That Bypassed the Recovery Bin

As you saw in Figure 18.12, files that are "deleted" are actually sent to the Recycle Bin, where they are kept until the bin runs out of space or until you empty the Recycle Bin to free up space on the drive. However, if you hold down the Shift key when you press the Del key, the files or folders selected for deletion bypass the Recycle Bin and can be overwritten when the space they occupy is needed.

In this example, I used Iolo Technologies Search and Recover program (www.iolo.com/products/search-and-recover/). It can be launched directly from the CD to avoid overwriting deleted data you want to recover.

To retrieve deleted files, use the option to scan your drive for erased files. In Figure 18.27, the Search and Recover File Rescue Wizard has located all the erased files on the C: drive. Because we're looking for photos, we select Pictures and Photos to narrow the results.

You can select all files or click the check box next to each file to select it. After selecting files, select the option to recover all or selected files.

In Figure 18.28, a new folder on a different drive is being created. This folder will be used as the destination for recovered files.

As each file is recovered, it is copied to the destination folder. At the end of the recovery process, you can view the recovered files. You can copy or move the recovered files to other locations.

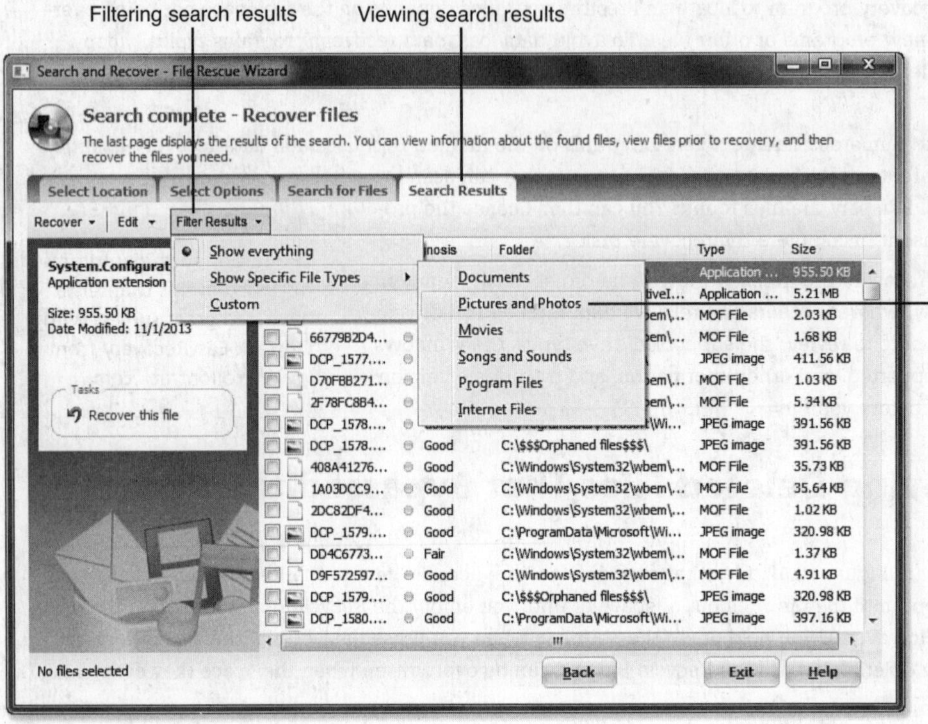

Figure 18.27 Viewing deleted files located with Search and Recover.

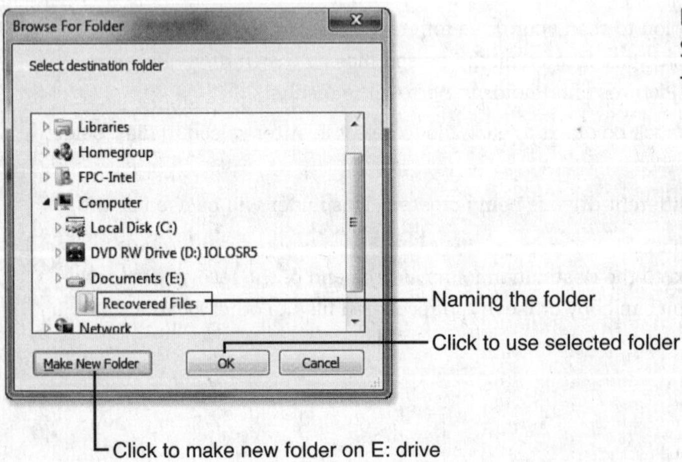

Figure 18.28 Selecting a destination for restored files.

Retrieving Photos from a Formatted Memory Card

Flash memory cards can hold hundreds or thousands of photos, so using a program that can preview recovered files is helpful. In this example, we used MediaRecover (http://freshcrop.com/) to retrieve files from a formatted memory card.

Make sure you use the correct data recovery option when scanning for lost files. MediaRecover's Scan option located no images because it's designed to find erased (deleted) files. However, the Advanced Scan, which scans the disk surface, located several folders, many picture files, and provides a preview (see Figure 18.29).

Figure 18.29 Previewing a lost photo with MediaRecover.

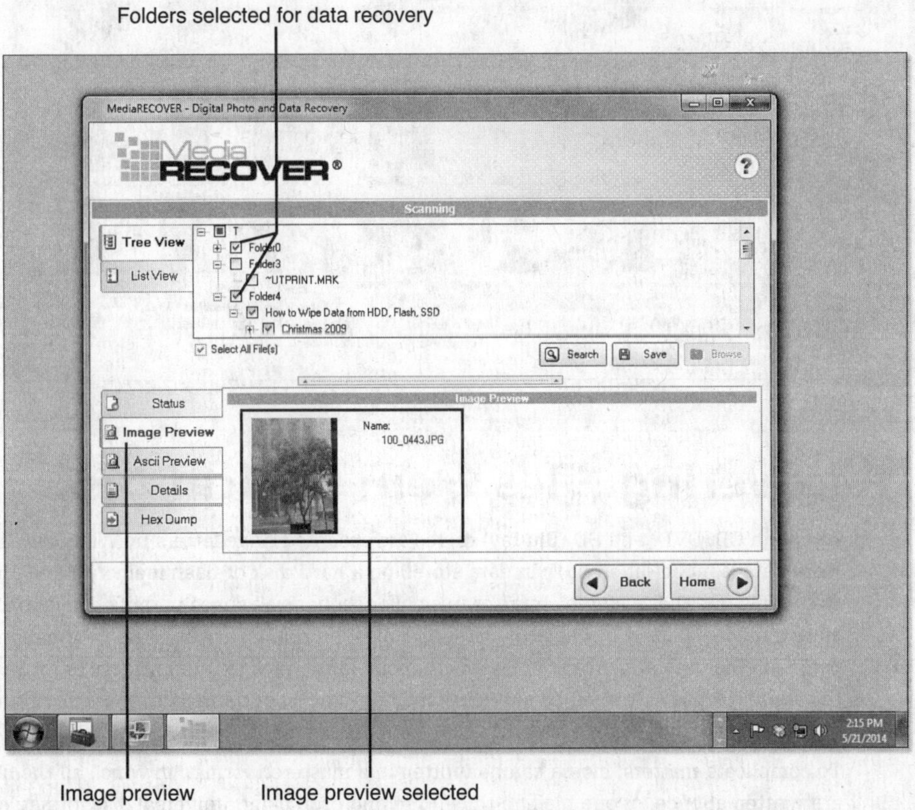

After the files are retrieved to a different folder, open that folder. Select a viewing option that uses medium or larger thumbnails. Images with viewable thumbnails have been recovered successfully. Images displayed with icons were partially or fully overwritten and could not be recovered (see Figure 18.30).

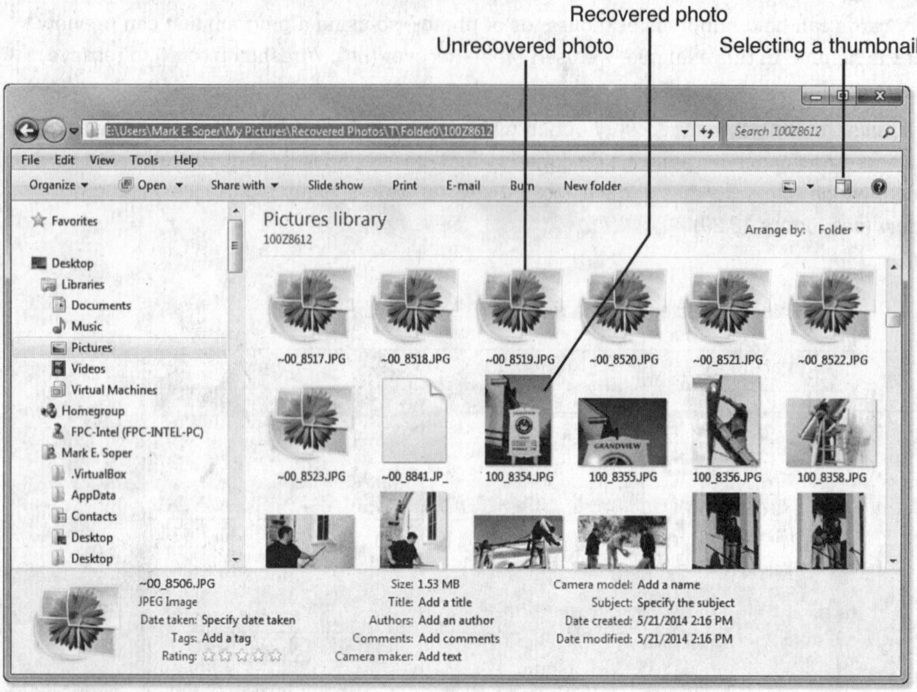

Figure 18.30 Reviewing recovered photos in Windows Explorer.

Recovering Files from Optical Discs

Although CD, DVD, and BD (Blu-ray) drives are assigned drive letters by Windows, the way they store data is much different than data stored on a hard disk or flash memory drive. Hard disks can store a file in either a single chunk or in smaller sections as space permits. Flash memory drives store a file in as many blocks as necessary. However, optical drives write information in a spiral that begins in the data area near the hub, with momentary gaps for audio tracks or for data sessions. If the spiral track is disturbed by surface scratches, cracks, or damage to the reflective coating below the label side, some or all of the data may be inaccessible.

To complicate matters, media can be written in a mastered format, in which all the files in a session are written at once, or one file at a time (drag and drop using universal disc format, or UDF). For these reasons, it can be much more difficult and take much longer to recover data from a damaged optical disc.

Cleaning and Polishing the Disc's Data Surface

If you are unable to read the contents of an optical disc, take a careful look at the data side (the shiny side). Marks and scratches can interfere with the laser used to read the information.

You can use polishing and cleaning materials made especially for optical discs to help remove marks and surface scratches. Figure 18.31 shows the data surface of a marked and scratched CD-R before polishing and cleaning, and Figure 18.32 shows the same disc after polishing and cleaning. In many (but not all) cases, a cleaner disc can be read successfully by Windows or can have more of its data recovered.

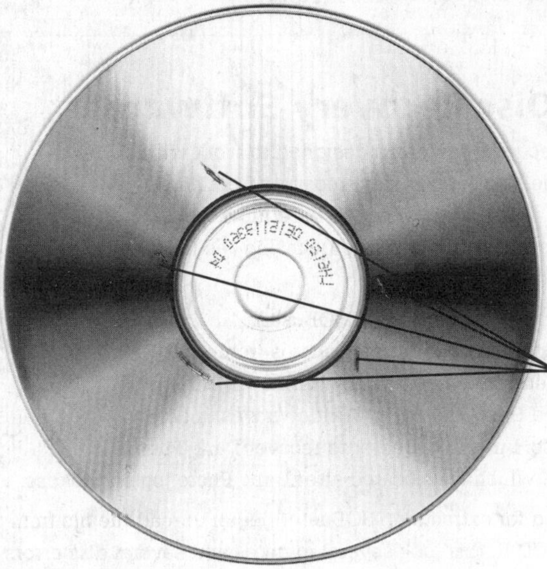

Figure 18.31 A CD-R with (deliberate) surface damage.

Figure 18.32 The same disc after polishing and cleaning has fewer marks.

Caution

Be careful when using optical media. The closer the marks and scratches are to the center of the disc, the more difficult it can be to retrieve information from the disc. Even after cleaning, the information on the disc shown in Figures 18.31 and 18.32 could not be retrieved.

Using Optical Disc Recovery Software

There are many data recovery programs designed to work with optical media, and some also support data recovery from hard disk and flash memory. Use a trial version to determine which files can be recovered successfully before purchasing the full version of the program.

Tip

If you are having problems reading a disc, try the disc in a different drive. You may also have better results recovering data from a disc by using different drives.

In this example, I used the free version of ISOBuster (www.isobuster.com) to attempt to recover photos from a CD-R. Part of the CD-R's contents could be read by Windows, but starting with a picture called Dark_Photo.jpg, Windows was unable to open the rest of the disc. I used ISOBuster to recover Dark_Photo.jpg as well as Dust.jpg, which was located after Dark_Photo.jpg on the disc.

After I selected Dust.jpg for extraction, ISOBuster began to read the file from the CD-R. Because of the condition of the CD-R, this took several minutes and several disc errors were detected (see Figure 18.33).

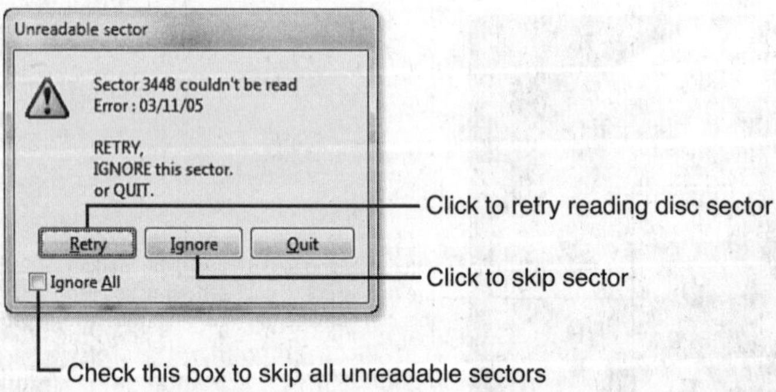

Figure 18.33
A damaged optical disc might have many unreadable sectors.

After trying Retry from the options available in Figure 18.33 without success, I selected Ignore and eventually clicked the Ignore All option. After ISOBuster read the sectors it could read, it created a version of the file in a folder I had created on my hard disk for recovered images.

In Figure 18.34, you can see the results of this and several other optical disc data recovery attempts. Although Dust.jpg and Dark_Photo.jpg were recovered successfully, files on a different disc that were partly overwritten by mistake could not be recovered.

Figure 18.34 Data recovery from two optical discs—some successes, some failures.

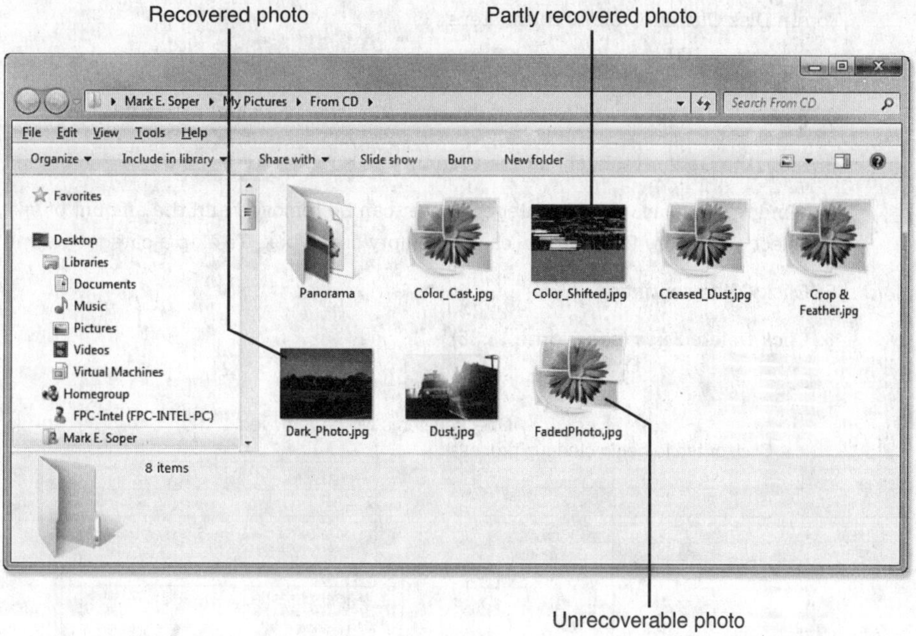

Note

In addition to ISOBuster, take a look at CDRoller (www.cdroller.com).

Freeing Up Storage Space on Your Windows Computer or Tablet

Windows tablets and Ultrabooks rely on limited capacity SSDs (often with capacities as little as 32GB–64GB) instead of hard disk drives for mass storage. However, whether you use a tablet, a laptop, or a desktop hard disk, you might run short of space over time. Windows includes three features that can help you free up storage space: Disk Cleanup, Libraries, and OneDrive (formerly called SkyDrive).

Using Disk Cleanup

Disk Cleanup is available from the drive properties sheet in Window 7 and 8/8.1, as well as older releases of Windows. Disk Cleanup enables you to remove files of limited usefulness from your system and can sometimes free up multiple gigabytes of disk space.

To run Disk Cleanup, follow these steps:

1. Open Windows Explorer or File Explorer.
2. Right-click or press and hold your system (C:) drive icon and select **Properties**.
3. From the **General** tab, click **Disk Cleanup**.
4. Windows displays the file categories that can be removed and the amount of space they use. To select a category for deletion, click an empty check box. To skip a category, clear the check box.
5. Click **OK** to continue.
6. Click **Delete Files** (see Figure 18.35).

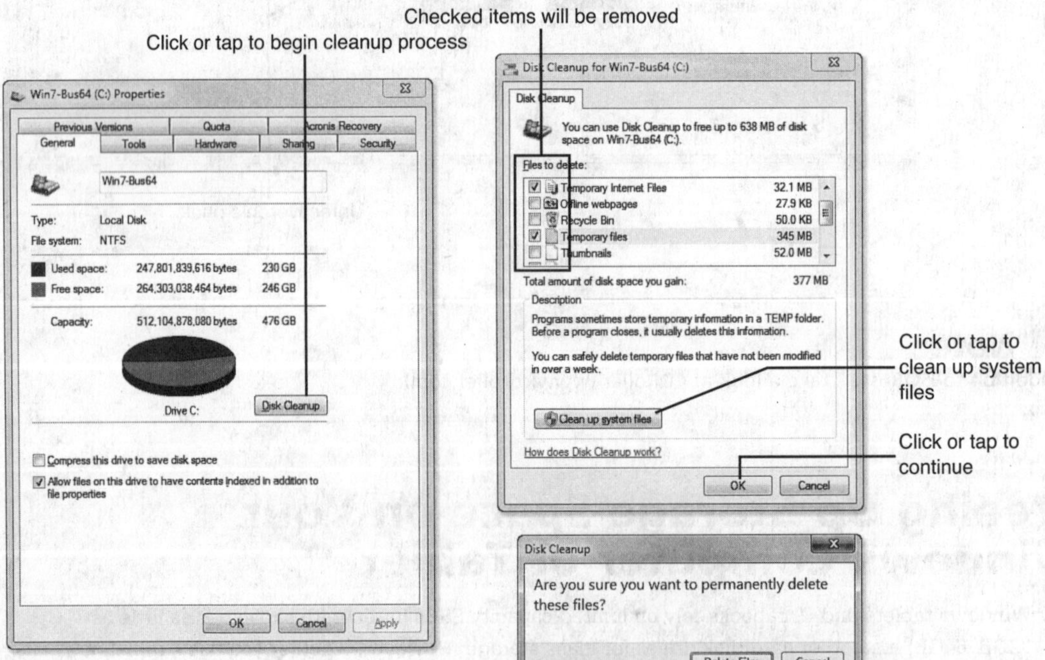

Figure 18.35
Deleting unneeded files with Disk Cleanup.

If you need to recover much more space, click the **Clean Up System Files** button shown in Figure 18.35. You can remove Windows Update and upgrade files and other large files you don't need. Depending on your system's specifics, you might be able to recover 10GB–15GB of space.

Caution

The More Options tab offers two more ways to recover space: removing programs you don't use and removing older system restore points. If you remove older system restore points, you will also lose older versions of files you have edited. As long as at least 15% of your C: drive is available, your system can run properly.

Using Windows Libraries

Windows 7 introduced the concept of libraries, which enables multiple locations with the same content to be viewed as a single logical folder. Rather than clicking your way from folder to folder to see your photos, music, documents, and videos, you can see them all in one place. It's a great feature if you've run out of space on your C: drive and are using external drives for the overflow.

Windows 8/8.1 have libraries turned off by default. To turn on libraries:

1. Open File Explorer.
2. Click or tap the **View** tab.
3. Open the **Navigation Pane** menu.
4. Click or tap **Show Libraries**.
5. To see libraries, scroll down in the left pane to Libraries.

In Windows 7, and in Windows 8/8.1 after you enable Libraries, clicking the Documents library icon displays the contents of the Documents and Public Documents folders. Click Pictures to see the contents of Pictures and Public Pictures, and so on. In Windows 8/8.1, the Documents library also includes the contents of the user's OneDrive (formerly SkyDrive) folder.

You can move file types that consume a lot of disk space, such as digital photos, music files, and videos from your system hard disk (C:) to an external hard disk and still use them as easily as you could when they were stored on your system drive. For example, here's how to use the Libraries feature to free up space occupied by your digital photo collection.

With Windows 7:

1. Connect an external hard disk to your computer.
2. Open Windows Explorer.
3. Click the external hard disk icon.
4. Use the **New Folder** button to create a folder called My Pix on that drive.
5. Open the Pictures library.
6. Select any or all of the folders in the Pictures folder.
7. Drag them to the My Pix folder on the external drive and drop them.

8. Click the **Pictures** library folder.
9. Click or tap the **Includes:** *x* **Locations** link (where x is a number). See Figure 18.36.

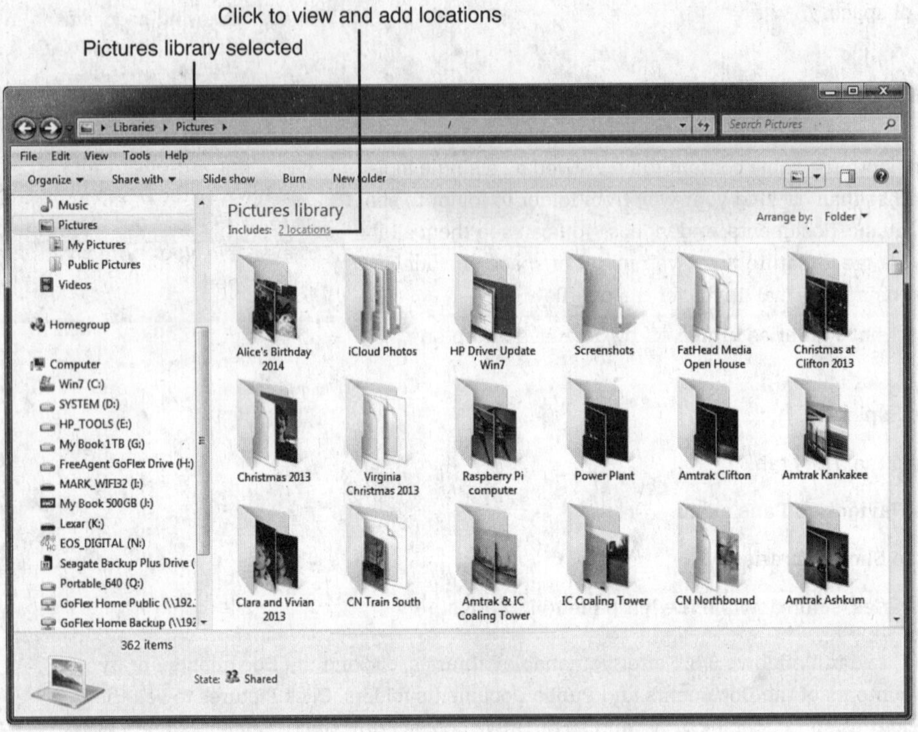

Figure 18.36 The Pictures library.

10. Click or tap **Add** to add an additional location.
11. Navigate to the location you want to add to the library (in this example, the My Pix folder on the external hard disk).
12. Highlight the folder you want to add.
13. Click or tap **Include Folder**. The folder is now listed as part of the Pictures library (see Figure 18.37).
14. Click **OK** to close the dialog.

With Windows 8/8.1:

1. Connect an external hard disk to your computer.
2. Open File Explorer.
3. Click the external hard disk icon.

Figure 18.37 Adding a folder to the Pictures library.

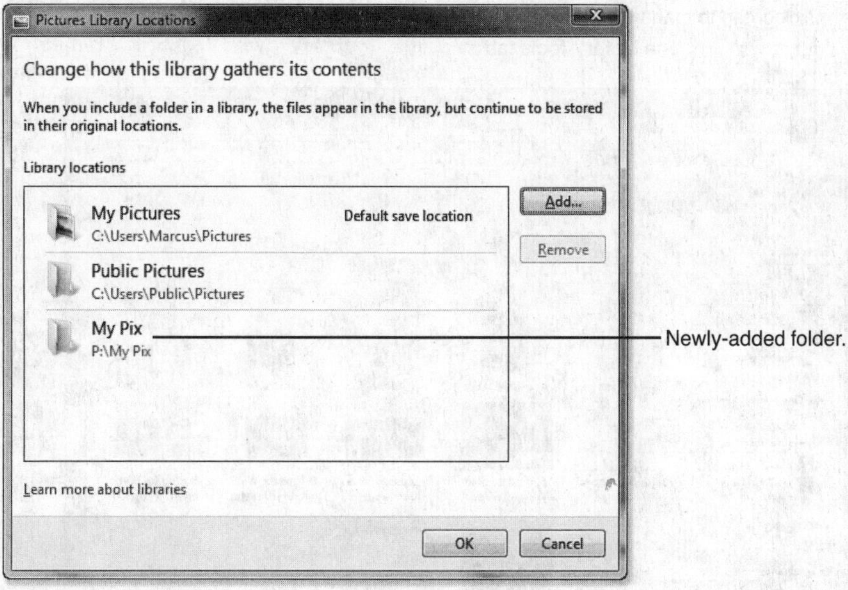

4. Use the **New Folder** button to create a folder called My Pix on that drive.
5. Open the Pictures library.
6. Select any or all of the folders in the Pictures folder.
7. Drag them to the My Pix folder on the external drive and drop them.
8. Click or tap the **Pictures** library folder.
9. Click or tap the **Library Tools** tab.
10. Click or tap **Manage Library** (see Figure 18.38).
11. Click or tap **Add**.
12. Navigate to the location you want to add to the library (in this example, the My Pix folder on the external hard disk).
13. Highlight the folder you want to add.
14. Click or tap **Include Folder**. The folder is now listed as part of the Pictures library.
15. Click **OK** to close the dialog.

Picture files you copy to your computer will continue to go to your computer's system drive unless you change the default Save location. To change the default Save location to the external drive's My Pix folder (or other folder of your choice), follow this procedure:

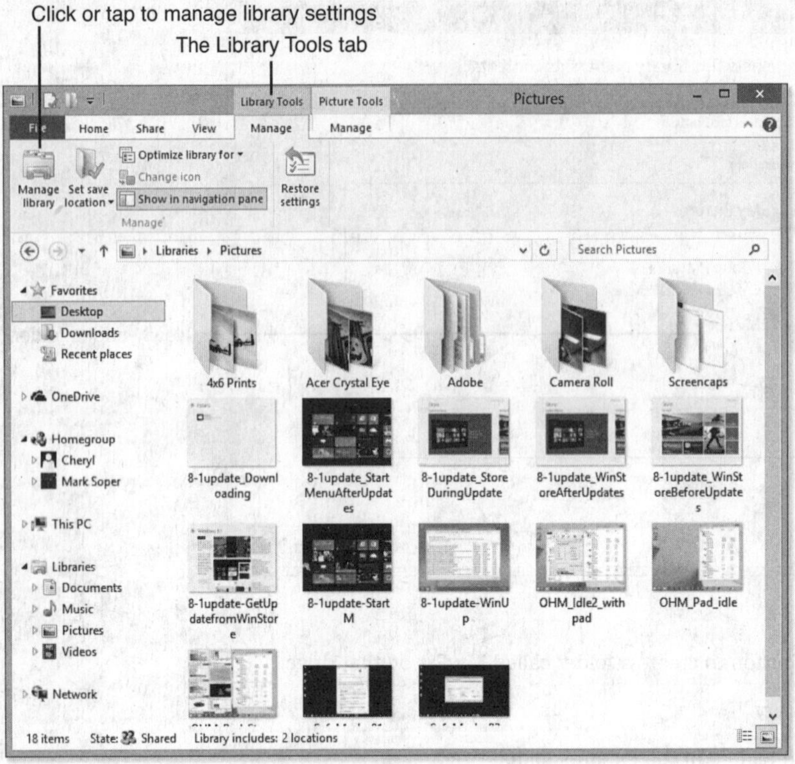

Figure 18.38
The Library Tools tab in Windows 8/8.1.

1. From Windows Explorer or File Explorer, right-click or press and hold the Pictures library folder icon and select **Properties**.
2. Click or tap the folder you want to use as the default Save location (in this example, My Pix).
3. Click or tap **Set Save Location** (see Figure 18.39).
4. Click **Apply**, then **OK**.

Note

A Windows library can use local hard disk, USB flash drive, or network folder locations (network locations must be set for Offline access). It cannot use optical drives.

Windows Backup and Restore (Windows 7) and File History (Windows 8/8.1) will back up all library locations on local drives when you select a library for backup.

Figure 18.39
Setting My Pix as the default save location for the Pictures library.

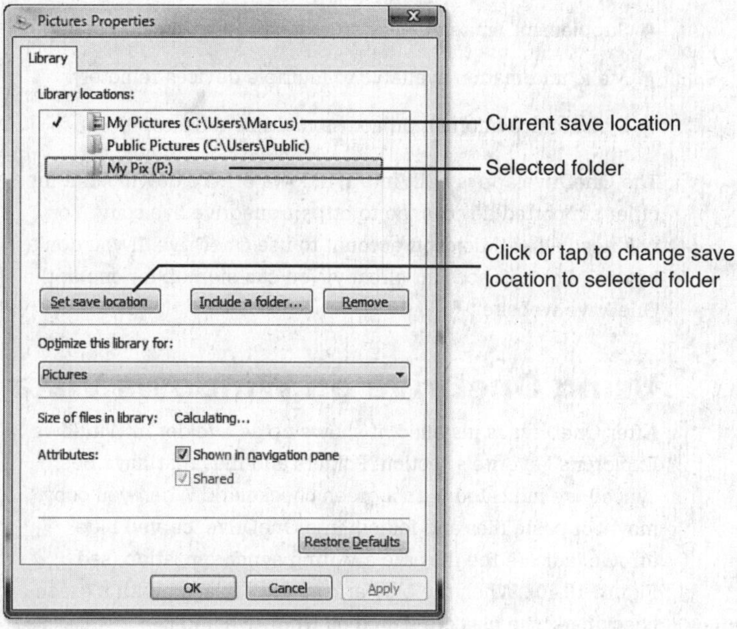

Using Cloud Storage

OneDrive (onedrive.live.com), Dropbox (www.dropbox.com), Google Drive (https://drive.google.com/), and Apple iCloud (www.apple.com/icloud/) are popular cloud storage services that support Windows-based computers. All have web-based services along with a downloadable client. OneDrive, Dropbox, and Google Drive can also be used with MacOS, Android, or iOS devices (Dropbox also works with Linux and BlackBerry), while iCloud can also be used with MacOS and iOS devices.

All vendors offer various amounts of free storage space, with varying price levels for additional space. iCloud does not count Camera Roll storage against its storage limit, while OneDrive offers 5GB additional storage free of charge to iOS users.

To learn more about iCloud, see "Freeing Up Storage Space on Your iOS Device," p.489, this chapter. To learn more about Google Drive, see "Freeing Up Storage Space on Your Android Device," p.496, this chapter. To learn more about Dropbox, see the Dropbox features page at https://www.dropbox.com/features.

Using OneDrive with Windows

OneDrive (formerly SkyDrive) is Microsoft's cloud storage service. It is supported on Windows Vista SP2 and later, Windows 7, and Windows 8/8.1 as well as Android, iOS, Windows Phone, MacOS, and Windows Server. For details, see http://windows.microsoft.com/en-in/onedrive/system-requirements.

By using OneDrive, users can

- Supplement limited device storage space with cloud storage.
- Make information available to multiple devices remotely.
- Synchronize information across multiple devices.

The OneDrive app is built into Windows 8.1. To download it for other supported devices, go to https://onedrive.live.com/. You will need a free Microsoft account to use OneDrive. If you don't have a Microsoft account already, you can sign up for one at the OneDrive website.

> **Note**
> Cloud storage uses remote servers accessed via the Internet to store information. Cloud storage can be accessed via web browsers or via programs or apps installed on desktop, laptop, or mobile devices.

Using OneDrive on Windows Vista or Windows 7

After OneDrive is installed, it shows up as a folder in Windows Explorer's Favorite's section. Folders and files that have been synced are indicated with a green checkmark. When you copy, move, or paste files and folders into OneDrive, curved blue arrows indicate the files are awaiting synchronization (see Figure 18.40). When the blue arrows are replaced with a green checkmark, the files are stored on OneDrive and can be accessed by your other devices.

> **Tip**
> To see which files have been uploaded, click the **Refresh** button in Windows Explorer or press the F5 key.

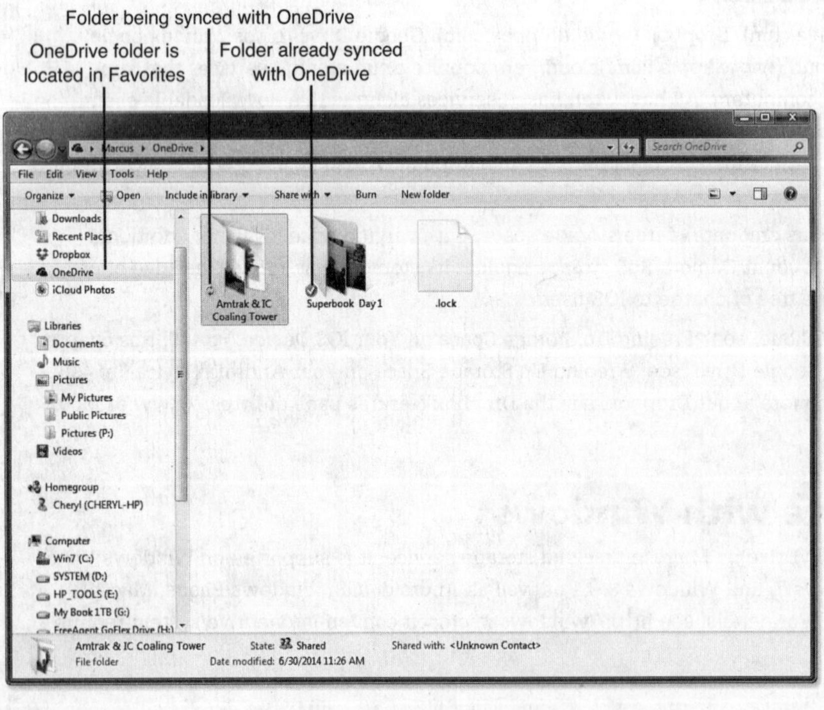

Figure 18.40 The OneDrive folder with a synchronized and unsynchronized folder.

When you use the OneDrive app, you are synchronizing files on your computer and OneDrive cloud storage. In other words, as you update, replace, or delete a file or folder in the OneDrive folder on your PC, the same changes are made to the OneDrive cloud storage version. You can access OneDrive via an app or web browser from another system to view and change these files, and OneDrive will make the same changes to the contents of the OneDrive folder on each device. However, note that the Windows 7 OneDrive app only displays files and folders you uploaded using the app.

If you want to use OneDrive to store files so they don't use space on your Windows 7 system, use one of the following methods:

- Log into the OneDrive website and copy files to it. After the files are copied to OneDrive online, you can delete them from your system, but they will still be available via your web browser.
- Download the SDExplorer program from www.cloudstorageexplorer.com/products.php. It enables access to OneDrive cloud storage from Windows Explorer, so you can copy files to and from OneDrive more easily.

To free up space on your device by using OneDrive with Windows 7:

1. Open your web browser.
2. Go to the OneDrive website (https://onedrive.live.com).
3. Log in if prompted.
4. Click the **Upload** button.
5. Select the files to upload and they are uploaded to OneDrive (see Figure 18.41).
6. After the files are uploaded to OneDrive, delete them from your system. Use **Shift-Delete** to bypass the Recycle Bin, and the files will no longer use space on your device.
7. When you need access to the files, open the OneDrive website.

Note

Microsoft Office files can be opened with Office 2010 and later versions without being downloaded first. To work with other file types, download them to your system.

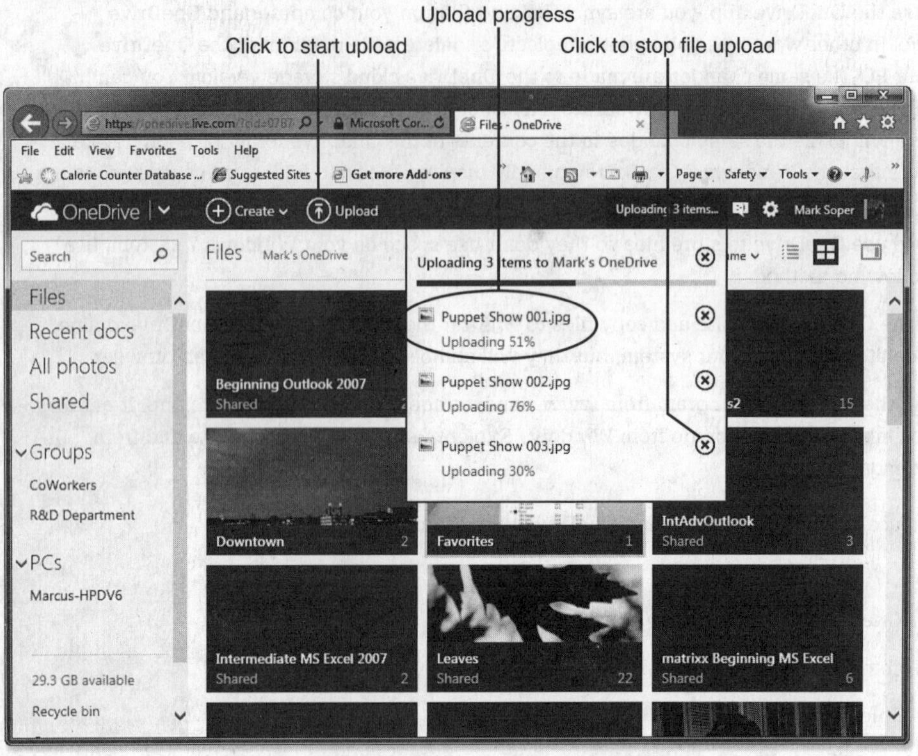

Figure 18.41 Uploading files to the OneDrive website.

Using OneDrive with Windows 8.1

Windows 8.1 includes an enhanced OneDrive app available from both the Start screen and File Explorer. Unlike the Windows 7 version, the Windows 8.1 version lists all files stored on OneDrive, whether they were uploaded with an app or via a web browser. By default, files stored on OneDrive are set as offline, meaning that they are also stored on your computer.

To save space on your computer using OneDrive for Windows 8.1, you need to upload files to OneDrive and make them online-only:

1. Move files you want to remove from your system to the OneDrive folder on your computer.

   Follow these steps from the Start screen:

2. Click or tap **OneDrive**.
3. Navigate to the file or folder you want to remove from your system.
4. Tap and swipe (or right-click) the file or folder to select it.
5. Tap or click the **Make online-only** button (see Figure 18.42).

6. Tap or click **Make online-only** to confirm your choice. Although the file is still listed in your OneDrive folder, it is stored online, so you must be connected to the Internet to access it.

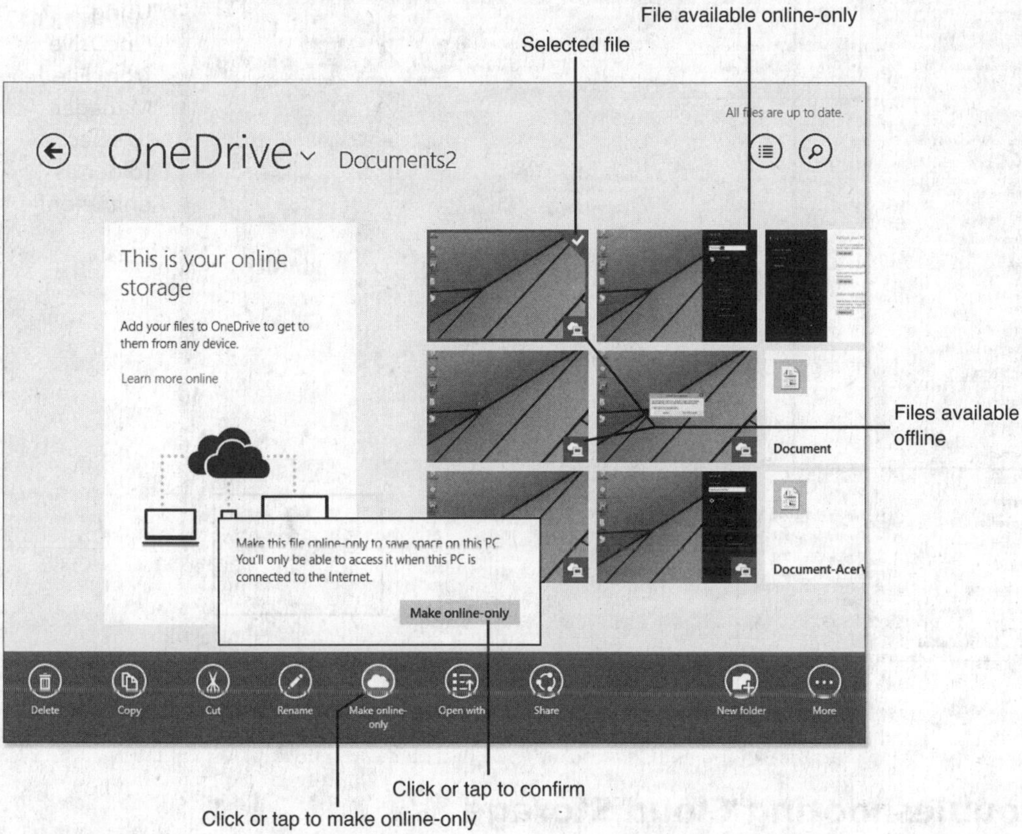

Figure 18.42
Using the OneDrive Start screen app to select a file for online-only access.

Follow these steps from File Manager (Windows Desktop):

1. Click or tap **OneDrive**.
2. Navigate to the file or folder you want to remove from your system.
3. Right-click the file or folder and select **Make available online-only.**
4. To determine if an individual file is available online-only, use **Details** layout from the **View** menu. Scroll to the right to see the Availability column.

Files that are not stored locally are listed as **Online-only** (see Figure 18.43).

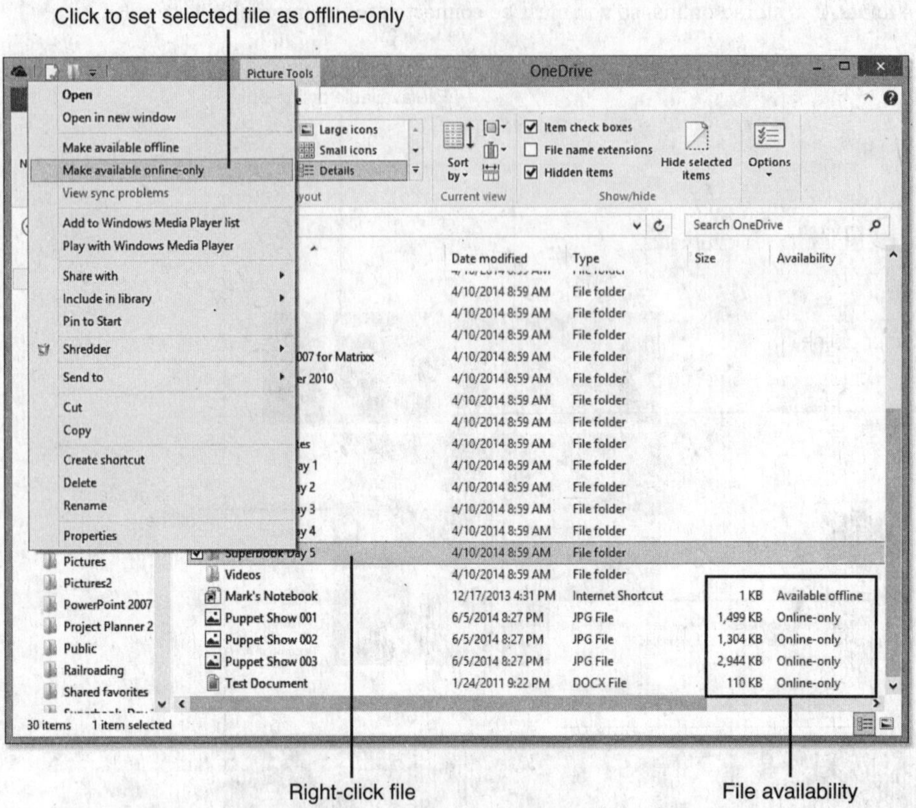

Figure 18.43 Using OneDrive from File Manager to select a folder as online-only.

Troubleshooting Cloud Storage

If you are having problems with cloud storage, check the following:

- **Incorrect login**—With most providers, you have the option to store your login for easier connection. Unless your computer is shared with other users who can access your account, storing your login helps avoid login problems.
- **Can't access files**—Files that are stored only on the service can only be accessed if you have Internet access. If you are going to an area with spotty or non-existent Internet access, download your files to your device or to a wireless device you can access via a peer-to-peer Wi-Fi connection. See "File Sharing with Portable Devices," p.261, in Chapter 9, "Solving File Sharing Problems," for details.
- **Can't access the service**—Make sure you have a working Internet connection and the correct login credentials for the service.

For additional troubleshooting tips, see the following websites:

- **Dropbox forums**—https://forums.dropbox.com/
- **Microsoft OneDrive Help**—http://windows.microsoft.com/en-us/onedrive/onedrive-help
- **Apple iCloud support**—www.apple.com/support/icloud/
- **Google Drive support**—https://support.google.com/drive/

Cloning Your Hard Disk

If you find that you are short of disk space on a Windows desktop or laptop computer, you can clone your hard disk's contents to a larger drive and use it to replace the drive built in to your computer. You can then use the drive you replaced as an additional internal hard disk (if you have an available drive bay) or convert it into an external hard disk with a drive enclosure.

If you are short of hard disk space, we recommend that you do the following:

- Choose a hard disk that has at least twice the storage space of your current hard disk. For example, if you are replacing a 320GB hard disk, select a 750GB or larger drive. If you are replacing a 1TB hard disk, select a 2TB or larger drive.
- Make sure the drive you want to use as a replacement uses the same connection type as your existing hard disk. Refer to "Points of Failure Inside the Computer," p.23, Chapter 1, "PC, Tablet, Mobile Device, Home Theater, Digital Camera and Camcorder Anatomy 101" for details.
- If you are replacing a laptop hard disk drive, keep in mind that some laptops require hard disks that are no more than 7mm thick. Many laptop hard disks are thicker and will not fit it into a narrower space.

To clone your laptop or desktop computer's existing hard disk to a new hard disk, you can:

- Connect your new drive via a drive enclosure that connects to a USB 2.0, eSATA (faster), or USB 3.0 (fastest) port.
- Connect your new drive via a drive dock.
- Connect your new drive to an SATA port inside your computer.

After you connect your drive, you can use software provided by your drive vendor or use commercially available cloning software. In this example, we'll use a version of Acronis True Image.

1. Connect your new hard disk.
2. Download and install the latest version of your drive vendor's cloning software.
3. Start the program and select the **Clone Disk** option.

Note

Seagate distributes a version of Acronis True Image as DiscWizard for use with its drives (including Samsung and Maxtor drives). Western Digital distributes a version of True Image as Acronis True Image for WD Edition. The process is similar with the commercial version of Acronis True Image.

To use the Seagate or WD versions of True Image, you must have at least one drive of an eligible brand installed in your computer.

4. Unless you want to use your new hard disk for more than one operating system, select **Automatic** and continue.
5. With automatic cloning, the partitions on the original hard disk are duplicated on the new drive. If the new drive is larger than the original drive, the partition sizes are adjusted accordingly. In this example, a 1TB hard disk set up as a single partition (C: drive) that is almost full is being cloned to a 2TB drive. Thus, over half of the new drive will be available for new programs or information. Click **Proceed** to continue.

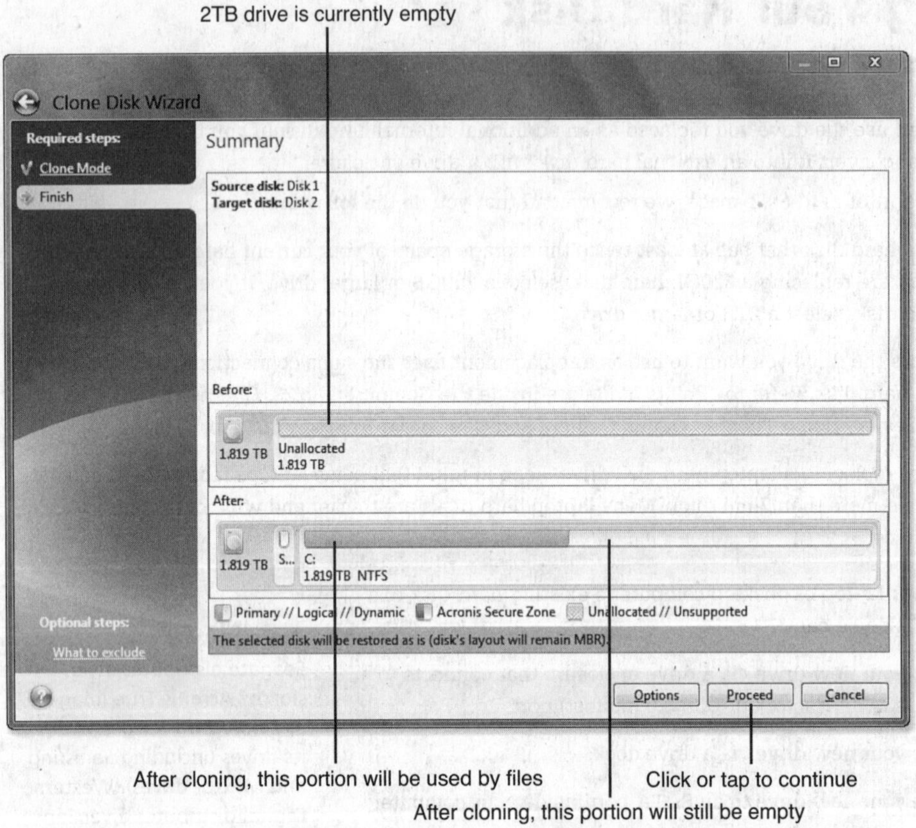

Figure 18.44 The new hard disk (2TB) will have the same layout as the old hard disk (1TB).

6. Restart your computer when requested (this is necessary to enable the operating system to be copied properly).

After the cloning process (see Figure 18.45) is complete, the computer shuts down.

Remove the old hard disk from your computer. Install the new hard disk in its place. When you restart your computer, you can use your computer the same way as before, but with more hard disk space.

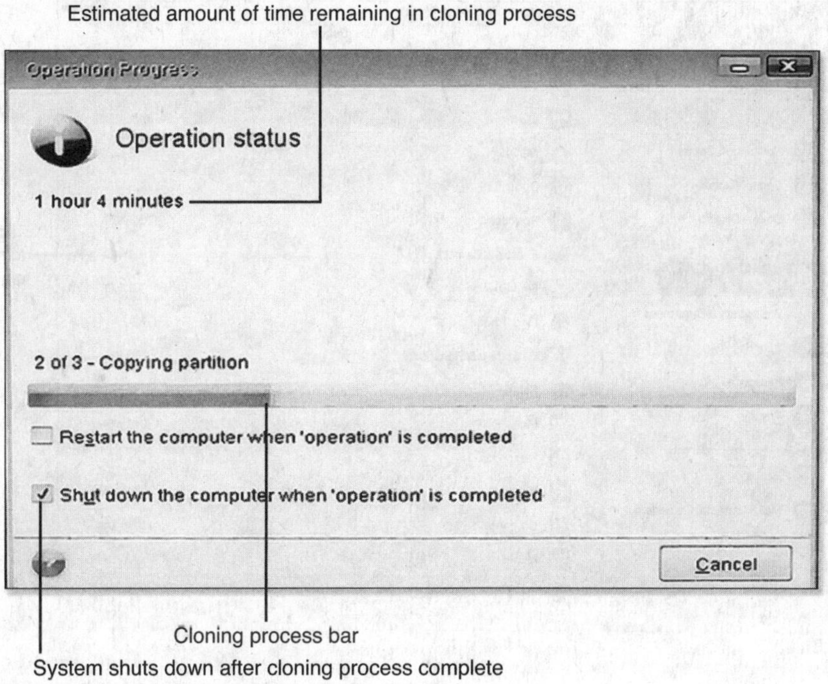

Figure 18.45 Cloning the contents of the old hard disk to the new hard disk can take several hours.

Freeing Up Storage Space on Your iOS Device

Apple iOS devices such as iPads and iPhones have limited, non-expandable storage capacity. It can be used up very quickly with digital photos, music, videos, and games. To see how much space is being used on your device by apps and files:

1. Tap **Settings**.
2. Tap **General**.
3. Tap **Usage**.
4. The most common apps are listed. To see more information, tap **Show All Apps**.
5. Scroll down to view usage for all apps. Tap the right-arrow symbol next to an app to see how much space its files use (see Figure 18.46).
6. The Photos & Camera app uses three storage areas: Camera Roll, Photo Library, and Photo Stream (see Figure 18.47).

Figure 18.46 Viewing the space usage of all apps on a 16GB iPad mini.

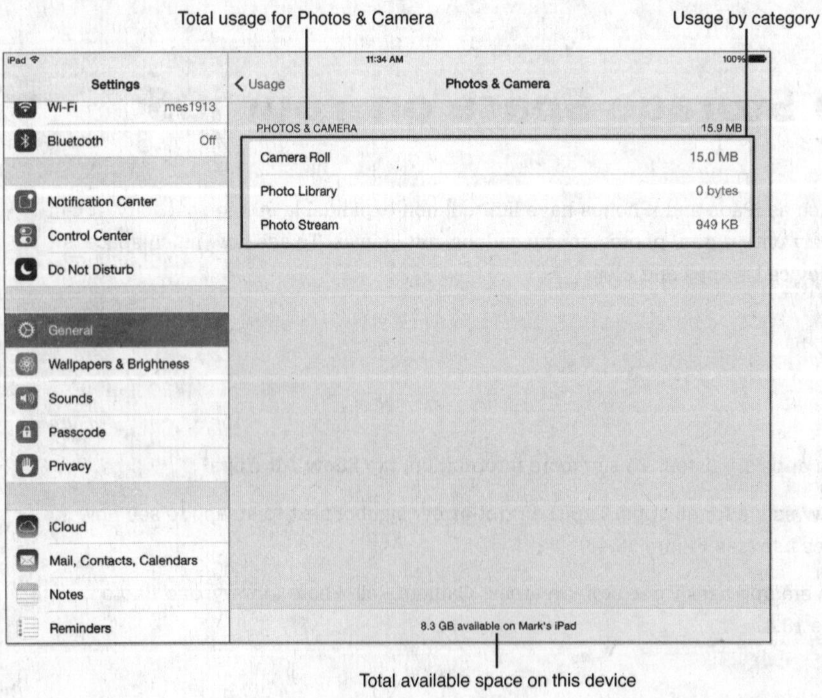

Figure 18.47 Viewing the space usage for Photos & Camera.

Using iCloud to Free Up Storage Space

To free up space used by your digital photos:

1. Set up iCloud on your computer. It syncs photos from your iOS device to other devices with iCloud. Get iCloud from http://www.apple.com/icloud/.
2. After your photos are synced with iCloud, open the iCloud Photos folder on your computer and move the files from iCloud Photos to another folder (see Figure 18.48).
3. The photos will be removed from your iOS devices that are synced via iCloud.

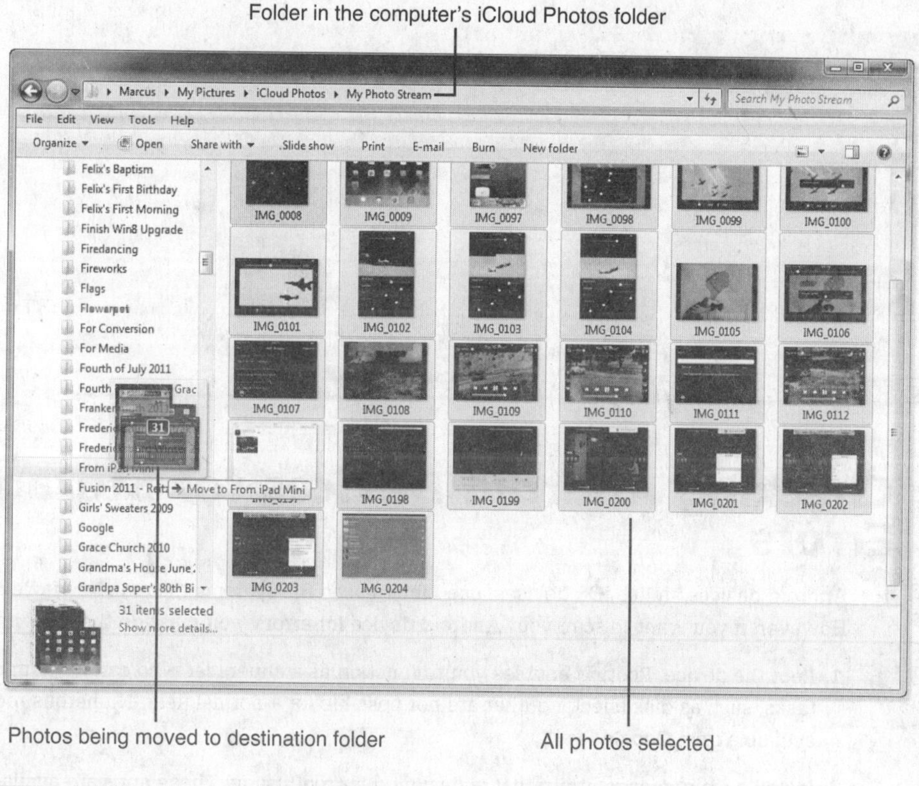

Figure 18.48 Moving photos from iCloud Photos, My Photo Stream to a folder in the Pictures library.

To free up space used by downloaded apps and games you no longer use, follow these steps:

1. Click the right arrow next to the app to see details (refer to Figure 18.46).
2. Click **Delete App** (see Figure 18.49).

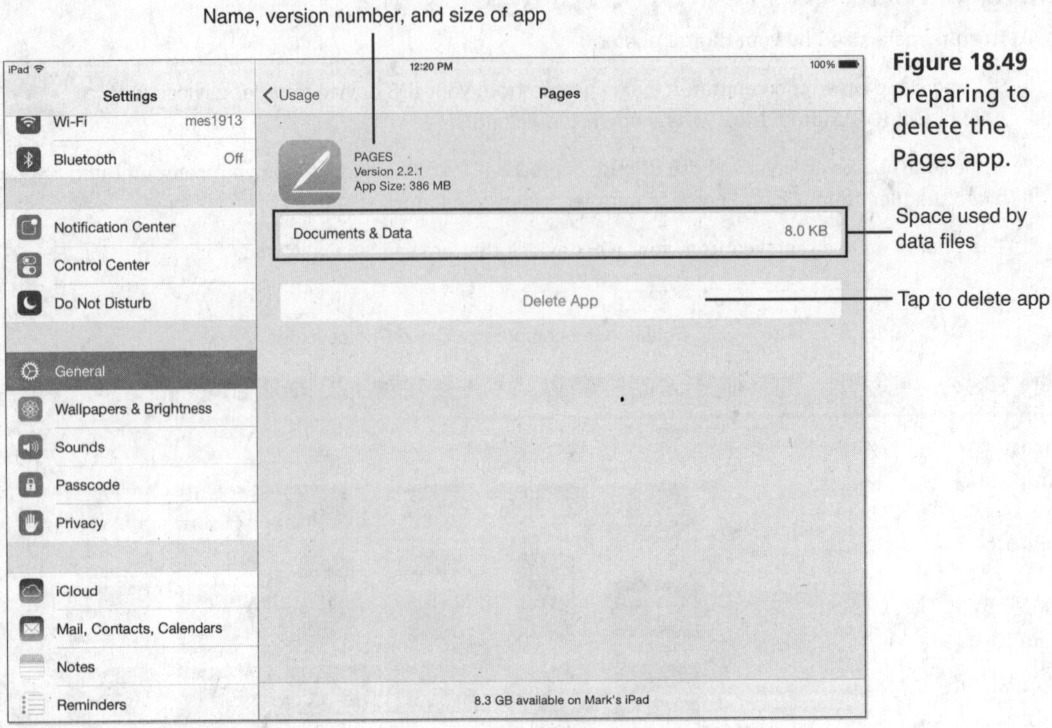

Figure 18.49 Preparing to delete the Pages app.

Checking Android Devices for Storage Errors

Android devices, unlike iOS devices, use Linux-based file systems that can be viewed by Windows. However, if you want to scan your Android device for errors, you must do the following:

1. Root the device. Rooting enables you to function as a superuser who can perform maintenance tasks, such as disk checking, that are not possible for a normal user. Numerous rooting apps are available from Google Play.
2. Install a maintenance utility that is designed for root usage. These apps are available from Google Play and are identified as requiring root access.

However, if you have problems with a microSD card, you can scan it when you receive a notification as a normal user.

Note

Both jailbreaking and rooting give users unrestricted access to a mobile device, but the terms are not interchangeable.

Jailbreaking (or iOS jailbreaking) refers to unauthorized changes to the iOS operating system used on Apple mobile devices. Jailbroken devices often need to be started from a computer for the jailbreak changes to work, and updates to iOS undo or temporarily prevent jailbreaks.

Android rooting, on the other hand, is not prohibited by Google, and is necessary for some Android apps used for system maintenance, backup, and other tasks.

Troubleshooting MicroSD Cards on Android Devices

When you insert a microSD card into your Android smartphone or tablet, it should be recognized as a storage device. You can see details about it from the Storage portion of Settings (see Figure 18.50).

Figure 18.50 This Android smartphone has a microSD card inserted.

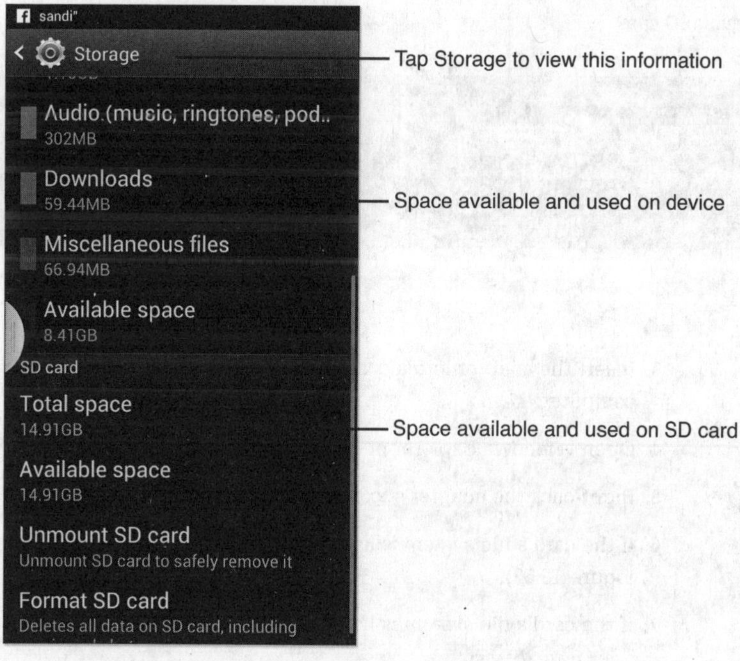

If you need to remove the card, do the following:

1. Close any apps that use the card.
2. Open **Settings**.

3. Open **Storage**.
4. Tap **Unmount SD Card** (refer to Figure 18.50).
5. Tap **OK**.
6. Remove the card.

If a microSD card is not recognized by your Android device, it might be defective or might have been formatted with a file system not recognized by the device (Android recognizes FAT32, but not NTFS).

To see the file system on the memory card, follow these steps:

1. Unmount the card and remove it.
2. If you don't have a microSD slot in a card reader connected to your computer, insert the card into a microSD to SD adapter (see Figure 18.51).

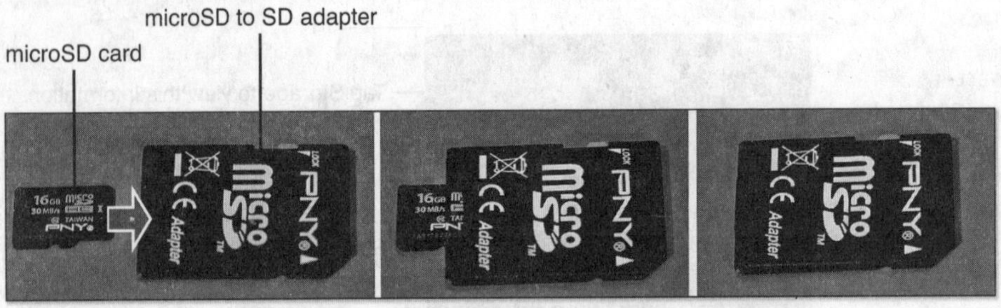

Figure 18.51 Inserting a microSD card into an adapter.

3. Insert the adapter into a compatible SD slot in your computer or a card reader connected to your computer.
4. Open Windows Explorer or File Explorer.
5. Right-click the adapter's icon and select **Properties**.
6. If the card's file system is listed as NTFS, the card needs to be reformatted as FAT32 (see Figure 18.52).
7. If the card's file system is listed as FAT32, click the **Tools** tab.
8. Click or tap **Check Now**.
9. Make sure the **Automatically Fix File System** check box is selected.
10. Click **Start**.
11. At the end of the process, check the results. If there were errors on the drive, reformat the drive (see the instructions later in this section).

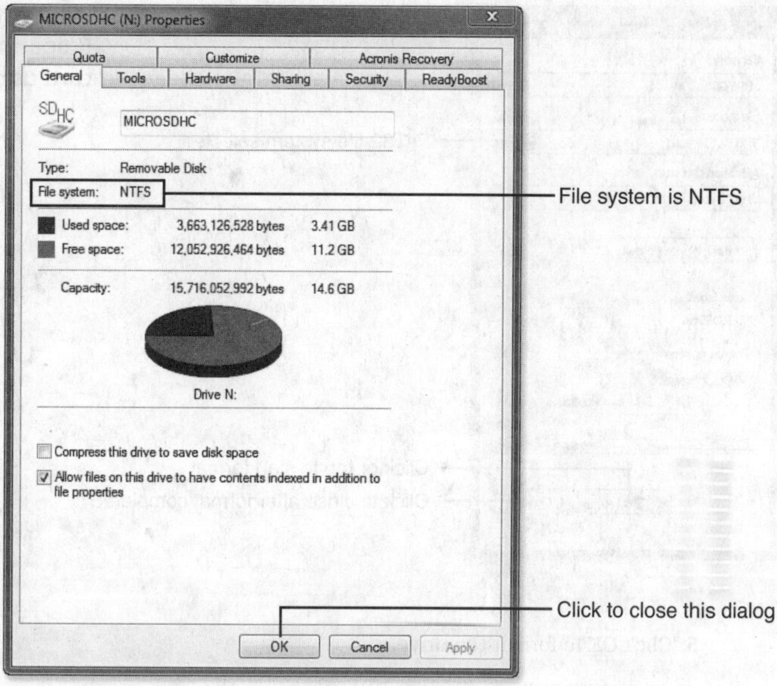

Figure 18.52
A microSD card formatted as NTFS cannot be recognized by an Android device.

12. If there were no errors, use **Eject or Safely Remove Hardware** from the notification area of the Windows desktop to remove the adapter from your computer.
13. Remove the card from the adapter.
14. Reinsert the card into the Android device.
15. Open **Settings, Storage**.
16. If the card was not detected, use the **Remount** option to redetect the card.
17. Verify that the card has been detected.

To reformat the flash memory card, follow these steps:

1. Open Windows Explorer or File Explorer.
2. Double-click the adapter's icon. If there are any files on the card, copy them to another drive. They are removed during the format process.
3. Right-click the adapter and select **Format**.
4. Make sure you select FAT32 as the file system (see Figure 18.53). Click **Start**.

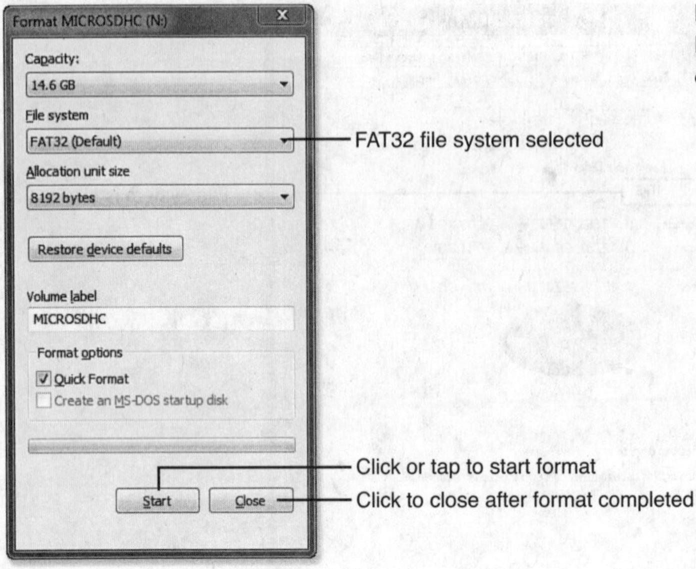

Figure 18.53
Preparing to reformat the microSD card using FAT32.

5. Click **OK** to format the drive.
6. After the drive is formatted, click **Close**.
7. Copy the files from the drive back to the drive.
8. Eject the adapter.
9. Remove the card from the adapter.
10. Reinsert it into your Android device.
11. Open **Settings**, **Storage**, and verify that the card has been detected.

Freeing Up Storage Space on Your Android Device

Android smartphones and tablets have very limited storage space compared to PCs or Windows tablets. If you run out of space in your device, you won't be able to shoot photos or video, download music, or create or edit contacts. However, unlike iOS devices, most Android devices have microSD slots so you can expand your device's available storage.

To determine how much space is being used by apps and data, open **Settings**, tap **More**, and tap **Storage** (see Figure 18.54). To see more information, tap a category, then a subcategory.

On the author's smartphone, about half the 16GB of internal storage is currently in use, but an installed 16GB microSD card is unused.

Figure 18.54
Viewing Android smartphone storage usage.

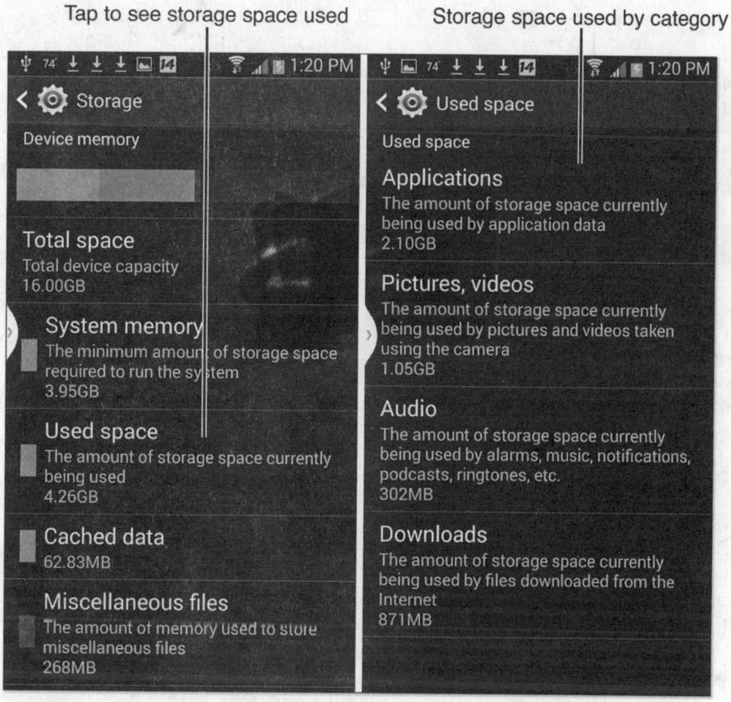

For a faster way to see how space is used, download and install DiskUsage, a free app available from Google Play.

Because I have a microSD card installed, one way to free up more space in my smartphone is to move data and any compatible apps from internal storage to the card.

To move an app to the card, follow these steps:

1. Open **Settings**.
2. In the System Manager section, tap **Application Manager**.
3. Tap an app.
4. Tap **Move to SD Card** (see Figure 18.55).
5. After the app is moved, tap **App Info** (refer to Figure 18.55).
6. Tap **SD Card**. Apps on the card are checked.

Note

When you move an app to the card, a small amount of information is kept in internal storage. This information is used to help the device locate the app. Not all apps can be moved.

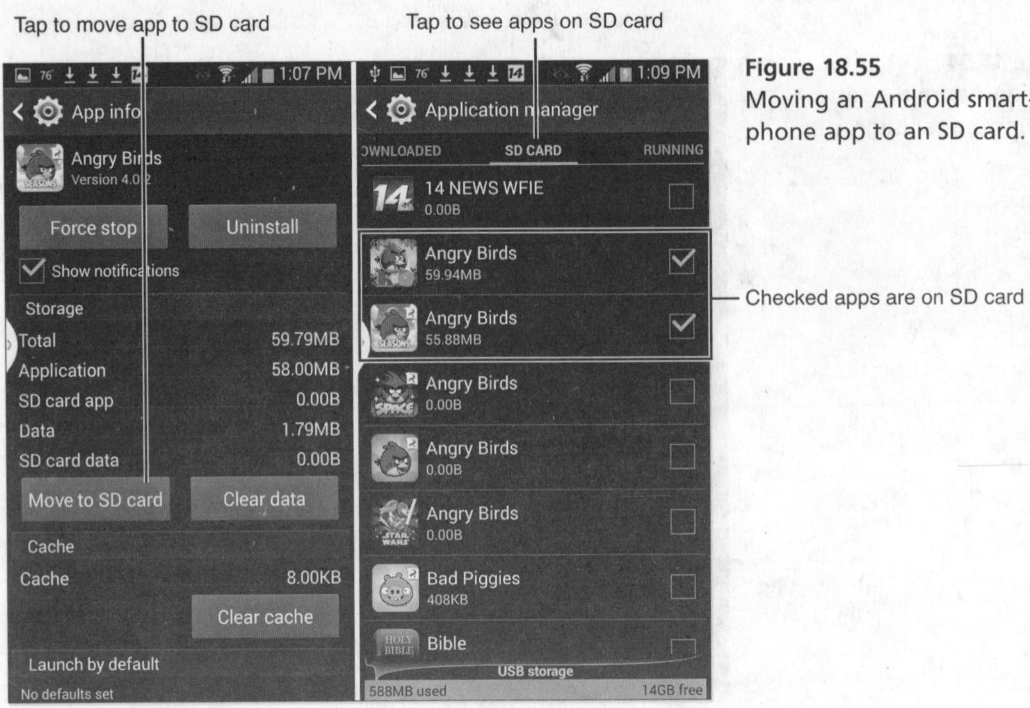

Figure 18.55
Moving an Android smartphone app to an SD card.

Using Google Drive

To save additional space, uninstall apps you don't use, transfer photos and videos to your computer via USB or Wi-Fi (apps available in the Google Play store), or use Google Drive. Google Drive automatically moves files off your mobile device when you upload them with Google Drive.

To save space on your device with Google Drive:

1. Install Google Drive on your Android or iOS device and on your PC.
2. On your Android device, open an app that gives you access to the files you want to upload. In this example, I used the Android Gallery app for photos and screenshots.
3. Select the file(s) you want to upload.
4. After the files are selected, click the **Google Drive** button (see Figure 18.56).
5. The files are listed. Click **OK** to upload them.
6. After the files are uploaded, they are available in the Google Drive folder on your device or your PC.

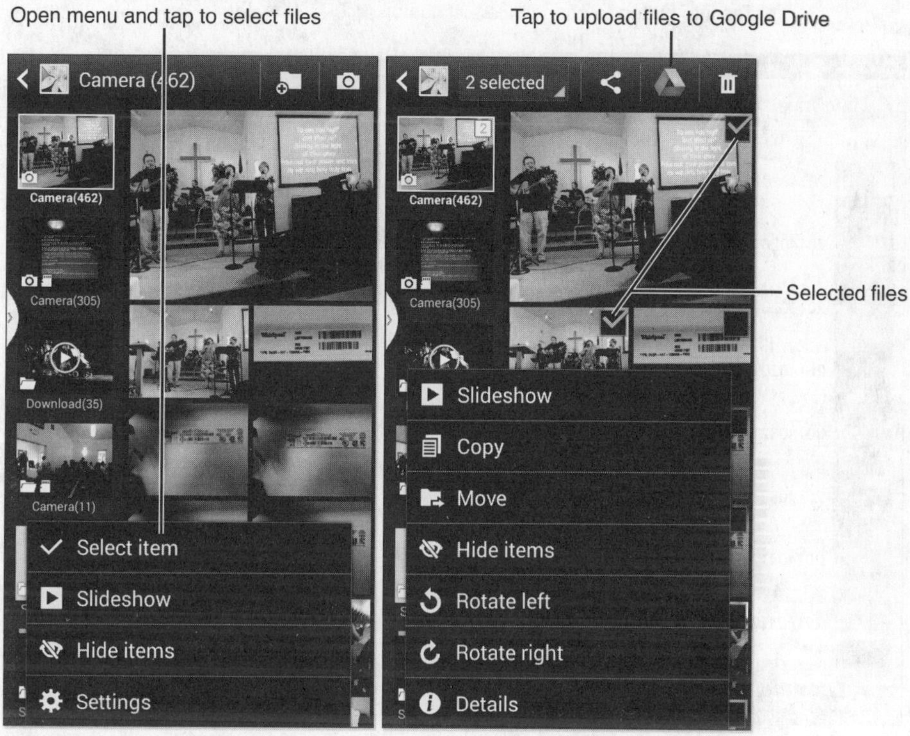

Figure 18.56 Selected files to move to Google Drive.

If you need to access a file in Google Drive whether or not you are connected to the Internet:

1. Make sure your mobile device is connected to the Internet.
2. Open Google Drive on your mobile device.
3. Select a file.
4. Tap the Information (gray i) button.
5. Tap the **Keep on device Off** button and it changes to **On** (see Figure 18.57).
6. The file will be available at all times on your device.

For more information about freeing up space on your device, see www.howtogeek.com/112356/5-ways-to-free-up-space-on-android/.

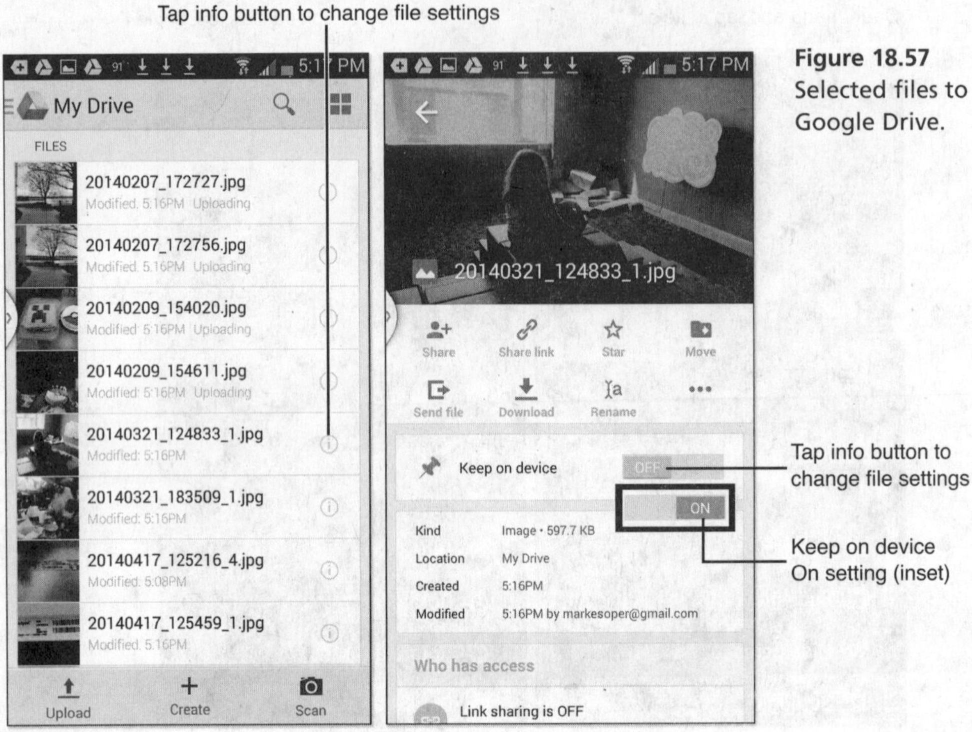

Figure 18.57
Selected files to move to Google Drive.

19

SOFTWARE TROUBLESHOOTING

Fast Track to Solutions

Table 19.1 Symptom Table

Symptom	Flowchart or Book Section	Page #
I can't activate Windows through the Internet.	Problems with Activating Microsoft Programs	504
I installed an app in trial mode, but I now have a license key.	Installing Software in Trial Mode	503
A program that ran on Windows XP doesn't run on Windows 7 or Windows 8/8.1.	Using the Program Compatibility Wizard and Compatibility Tab	514
How do I move an app to a different computer?	Deactivating an App	502
My app (program) has stopped working.	Repairing a Program	512

Solving Software Licensing Issues

Software piracy is a major problem today, and one of the most common ways to deal with it is to enforce software licensing with activation technology. With Microsoft Windows and many Windows programs or apps today, you will lose some or all features if your operating system or app is not properly licensed and activated. To avoid problems, follow these guidelines:

- Unless you have a program or app that can be licensed for multiple computers, you can use it on only one computer at a time.
- Some apps can be moved to a different computer, but only if you de-activate or unauthorize the computer where the app is currently installed.
- If you don't have a software license for an app, some might be installed in a limited feature or demo mode.
- If you purchase a license for an operating system or an app that was already installed, you might be able to add that information to the app or OS without needing to reinstall it.

Tip

Before you retire, recycle, or scrap a computer that contains software you want to reinstall on another device, create a list of license numbers or product keys. The Belarc Advisor program from www.belarc.com generates this information as part of its comprehensive system report.

Let's take a closer look at how to use these solutions.

Deactivating an App

To deactivate or unauthorize an app means that you are removing the license for using the software from a particular computer. Some programs from Adobe, Acronis, and other vendors include this feature. Here are some examples of when to deactivate an app:

- If you need to install a single-user program on more than one computer, but you can use only one installation at a time (for example, a desktop and a laptop computer).
- If you need to test an app that doesn't include a trial version on a different computer.

In these cases, you would do the following:

1. Install the app on the first computer.
2. After using the app, deactivate it.
3. Install the app on the second computer.
4. After using the app, deactivate it.
5. Reactivate the app on the first computer.
6. Repeat the cycle as needed.

The process of deactivating and reactivating an app varies from app to app and version to version. Keep in mind that many apps don't support this feature. Basically, if you install an operating system or an app that requires you to enter a license number before you can use it or to gain full access to its features, don't uninstall it until you find out from the vendor whether and how to deactivate or reactivate it.

Note

Some apps with this feature can automatically deactivate other installations for you when you install the app on a computer that would otherwise exceed the number of allowable installations.

Installing Software in Trial Mode

If you need temporary access to a particular program, you might be able to install it in Trial mode. With data-recovery programs, Trial mode usually limits you to viewing files that can be recovered. However, most other types of programs don't limit available features during the trial period (typically 30 days). Trial versions are often offered separately from the licensed version, but some licensed apps prompt you for a license number and will install in a time-limited trial version if you don't provide a license number (see Figure 19.1).

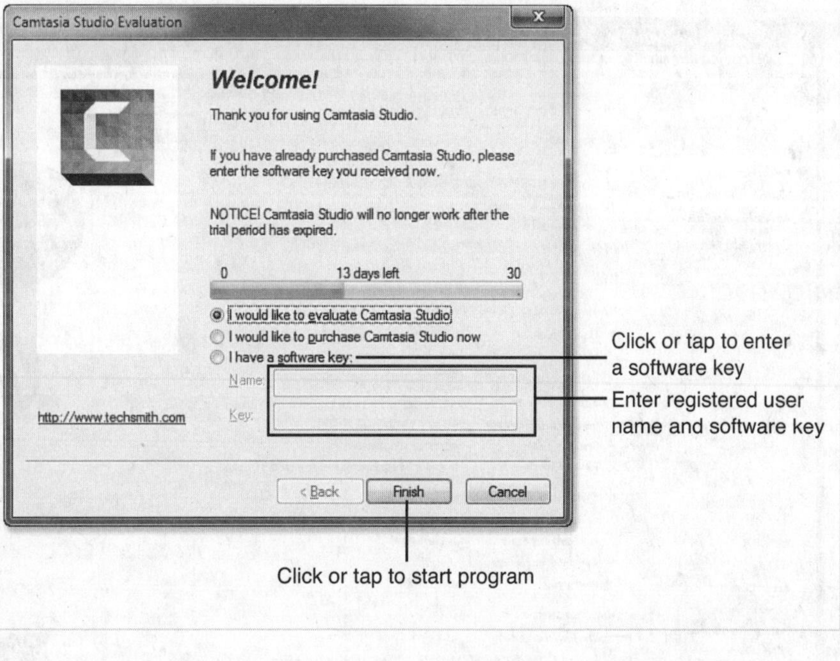

Figure 19.1 A trial version of a program (TechSmith Camtasia Studio) that can be licensed without reinstallation.

With most Windows software vendors offering trial versions today, we don't recommend buying a Windows program or app unless you can try it first. However, with the much lower prices set for Android and iOS apps, you might need to buy an app without having the opportunity to use a trial version first. In those cases, look for a separate Lite or Free version that can be upgraded with in-app purchases.

Problems with Activating Microsoft Programs

Microsoft Windows and Microsoft Office apps must be activated within a specified time (up to 30 days) or some of their features will stop working. Normally, activation is performed through an Internet connection using the Product Activation Wizard. If you did not activate the software the first time you used it, you can access the activation wizard later.

To determine if Windows is activated, open the System properties sheet. In Windows 7, follow these steps:

1. Open the Start menu.
2. Right-click **Computer**.
3. Select **Properties**.
4. Scroll to the bottom of the System properties window to see the activation status (see Figure 19.2).

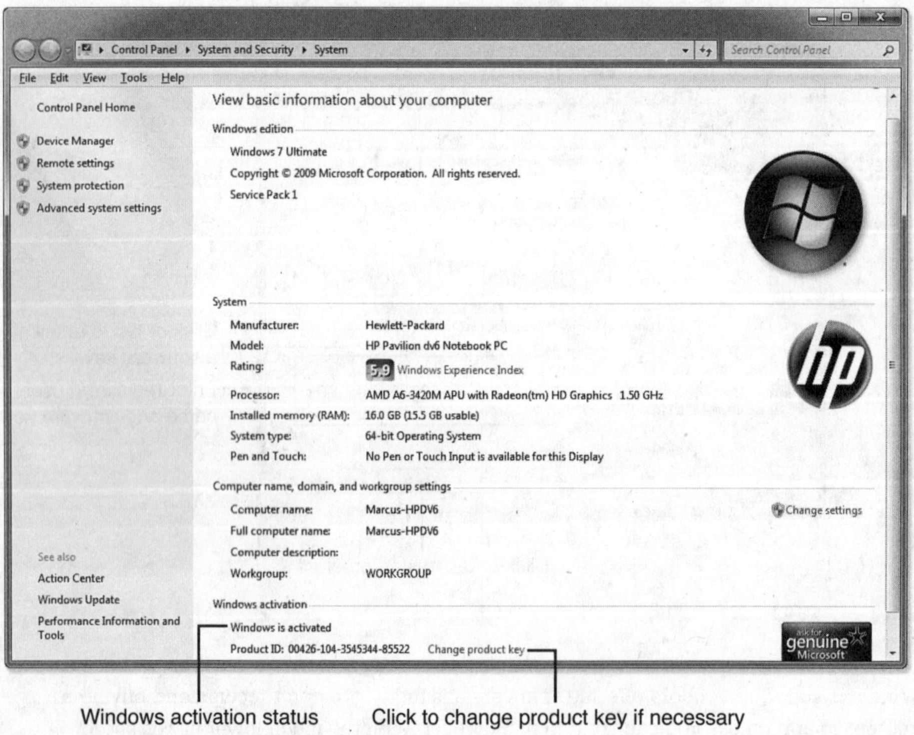

Figure 19.2 Viewing the activation status for Windows 7.

To open the System properties sheet in Windows 8/8.1, follow these steps:

1. Open the Charms menu.
2. Click or tap **Settings**.
3. Click or tap **PC info**.
4. Scroll to the bottom of the System properties window to see the activation status (see Figure 19.3).

Figure 19.3
Viewing the activation status for Windows 8.1.

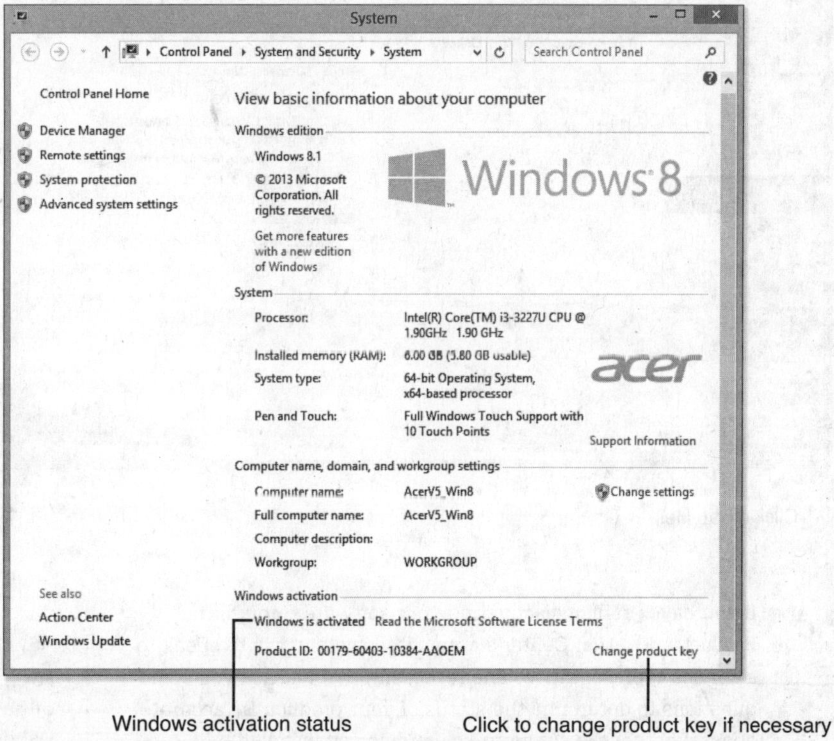

To view the activation status for Microsoft Office 2010 and earlier versions, open the File menu and select **Help** (see Figure 19.4). For Microsoft Office 2013 or Office 365, open the File menu and select **Accounts.**

If you cannot activate via the wizard, or activation via the wizard fails, you can activate your Microsoft software through the Microsoft Product Activation Center.

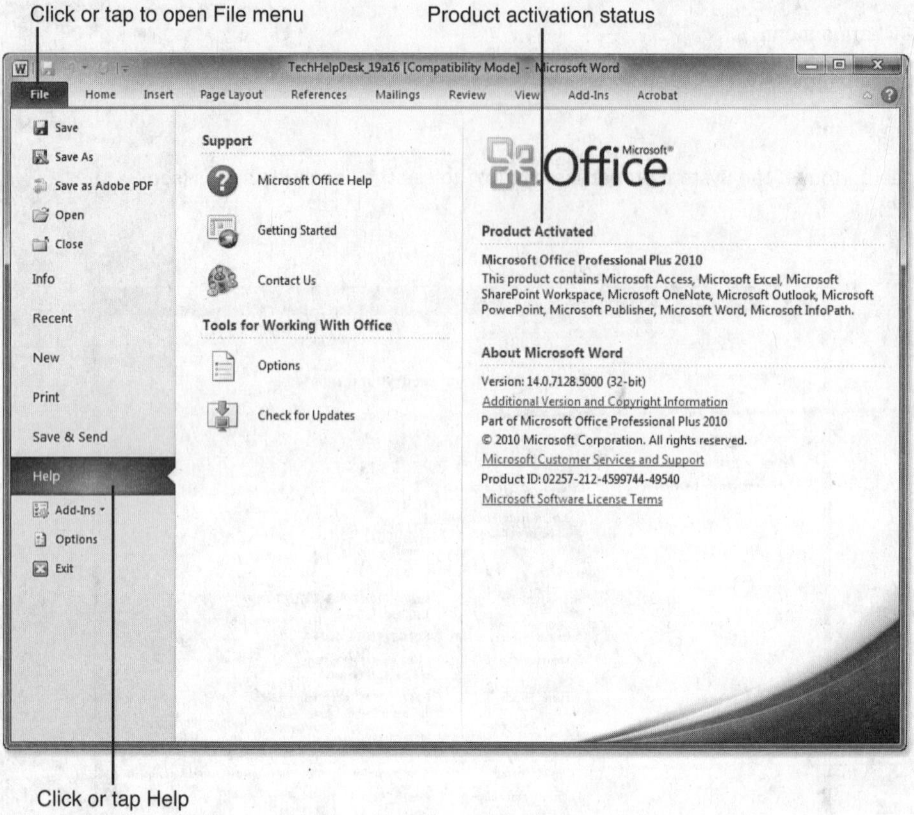

Figure 19.4 Viewing the activation status for Microsoft Office 2010.

If you have problems activating your software through the Product Activation Center's automated system, ask to speak to a service representative. The representative will ask you some questions to determine the status of your product. Be accurate about whether the software was previously installed on a computer (the most common reason for a problem) and if the software is still installed on another PC. If you have removed the software from the other PC, or if it is no longer in use (for example, if it has been scrapped or recycled), you should be able to activate the software using the instructions provided by the service representative.

> **Note**
> For a step-by-step description of how to activate Microsoft Windows and Microsoft Office using the Product Activation Wizard or Product Activation Center, see http://support.microsoft.com/kb/950929.

Tip

If you need multiple copies of Microsoft Office, buying traditional boxed editions is much more expensive than using Office 365. Office 365 is available in versions for home, small business, and large corporation/enterprise settings. After you license it, you install it via the Internet and it works like Office 2013. To learn more about Office 365, visit http://office.microsoft.com/.

Adding or Changing a Product Key or License Number

If you discover that you are using a program that cannot be licensed with the product key or license number you have, you will need to purchase a license for the program. In most cases, you don't need to reinstall the program. Instead, you can change the current product key license number.

In Microsoft Windows, open the System properties sheet (refer to Figures 19.2 and 19.3) and click the Change Product Key link. Figure 19.5 shows the Change Product Key dialog for Windows 7. Figure 19.6 shows the Change Product Key dialog for Windows 8/8.1.

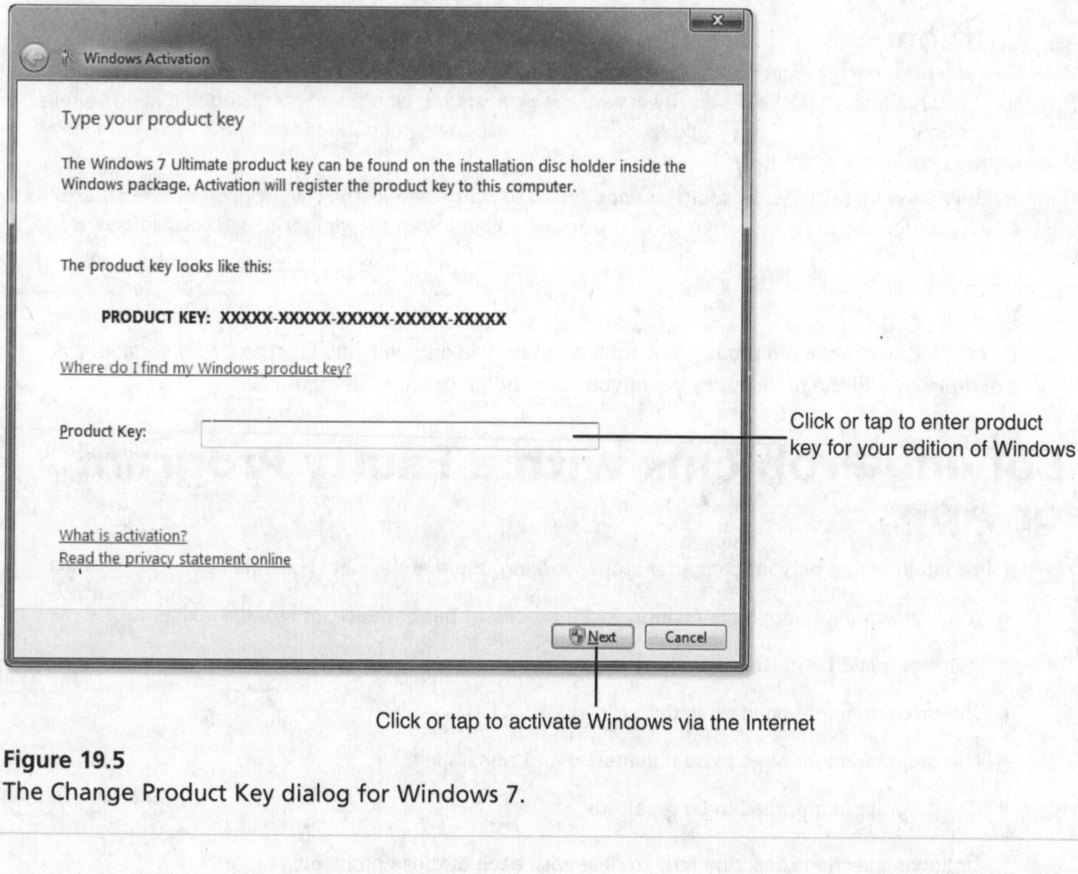

Figure 19.5
The Change Product Key dialog for Windows 7.

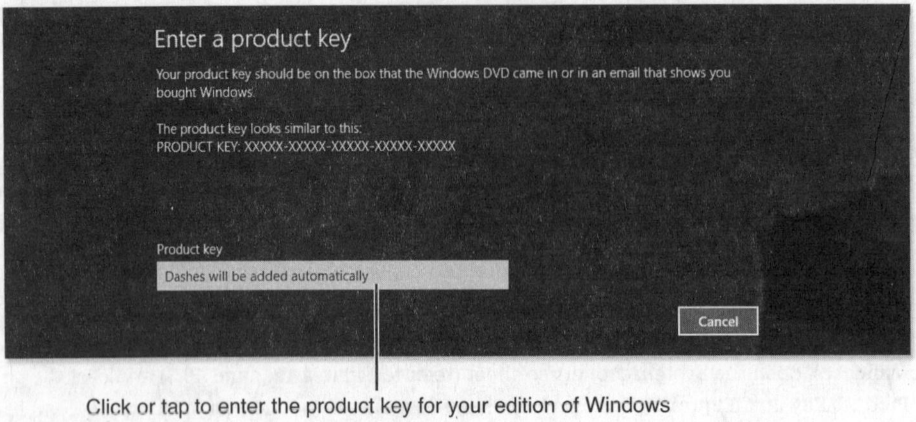

Figure 19.6 The Change Product Key dialog for Windows 8.1.

Caution

Make sure you have purchased a license for the same operating system or app version as the version already installed. If you have purchased a different version, the product key won't work, and you will need to reinstall the version you purchased. This could cause data loss, especially if you are installing a different version of Windows.

Many vendors now store license keys for the apps you have purchased in an account page on their websites. Use the login credentials provided when you set up your account with the vendor to see your software licenses.

If you need to change the product key for a program you originally installed as a trial version, you can typically add the product key when you start the program, as in Figure 19.1.

Solving Problems with a Faulty Program or App

If a program or app on your computer stops working, there are several possible reasons:

- Your system might not have enough RAM, processor performance, or storage space.
- Malware could be present.
- The program might need an update.
- The program might need to be uninstalled and reinstalled.
- The program might need to be repaired.

The following sections describe how to deal with each of these problems.

Freeing Up Memory

A program or app might stop working because your system doesn't have enough RAM or because you are running too many apps at the same time. To free up memory, close apps you are not using:

In Windows 7 or Windows 8/8.1, from the Windows desktop taskbar:

1. Click on an active (highlighted) icon in the taskbar.
2. Click the Close (X) button in the upper right-hand corner of the app window.
3. If prompted, save changes before closing your app.

If an app has two or more instances running (for example, two or more Word documents), follow this procedure to choose what to close:

1. Hover your mouse over the app's icon.
2. Click the live thumbnail for the window you want to close (see Figure 19.7).

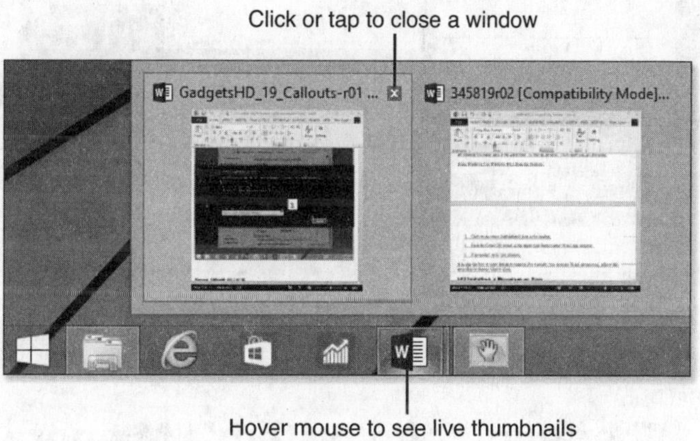

Figure 19.7
Selecting a program (app) window to close from the Windows taskbar.

To close a Start window app in Windows 8/8.1:

1. Press and hold or click and hold on the top of the app window.
2. Drag the app window down until it disappears (see Figure 19.8).

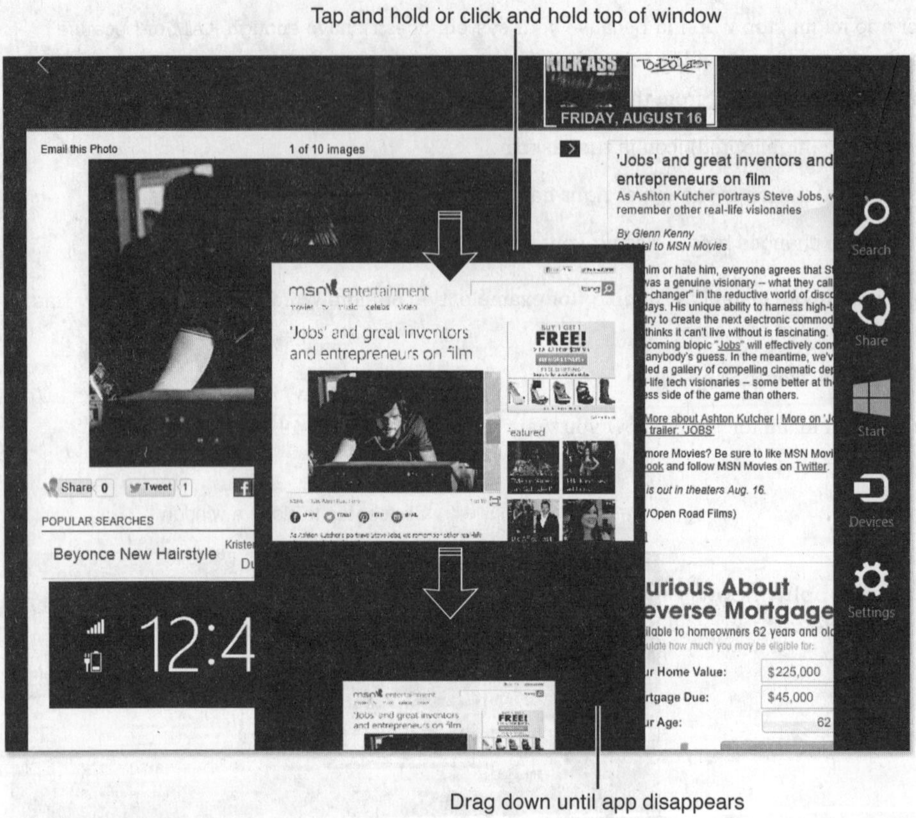

Figure 19.8 Closing a Windows 8.1 Start menu app.

Checking Your System's Memory Size and Processor Speed

Some apps will not install if your computer doesn't have enough RAM (memory) or a fast enough processor. However, some apps can be installed on systems that are not fast enough, and will not run well as a consequence. To determine your computer's processor speed and installed RAM, view the system properties sheet (Windows 7, Windows 8/8.1 desktop) or PC Info (Windows 8/8.1 Start screen).

Note

See "Troubleshooting Slow System Performance," in Chapter 15, "Dealing with Contrary Memory," for details. Chapter 15 also covers how to select and install memory upgrades.

Freeing Up Disk Space

Windows tablets and Ultrabooks use solid state drives (SSDs) rather than hard disks for storage. SSDs are much faster, but are typically much smaller than hard disks, so removing unnecessary information from systems that use SSDs is very important. Use the Disk Cleanup utility in Control Panel to free up space by deleting files and apps you don't use.

Note

See "Using Disk Cleanup," in Chapter 18, "Upgrading and Troubleshooting Storage Devices," for details.

Updating a Program or App

A program or app might stop working because of changes to your system, such as updates to the operating system, hardware, or software (see "Windows System Restore and Problem Apps" later in this chapter). Or, it might work, but not work as well as it should. To solve these problems, update the program or app.

Use these methods to update a program or app:

- Run the program or app's built-in updater. Depending on the program or app, you might find this option in the Help menu or other menus.
- Use Windows Update. With Microsoft Windows or Microsoft Office, use Windows Update to install updates.
- Download and install an update from the vendor's website. With most apps, the update will remove out-of-date components and install replacements.

Note

To learn more about using Windows Update and enabling updates for Microsoft Office, see "Using Windows Update," p.364, in Chapter 14, "Keeping Your Devices Updated."

Uninstall/Reinstall the App

By uninstalling the app, you remove the app's files, and you also remove references to the app in the Windows Registry, the master database of Windows software and hardware settings. When you reinstall the app, the settings are restored to the proper locations in the Windows Registry.

Before you uninstall the app, make sure you do the following:

- Have the license number or license key for the app if it's a commercial app. Without it, you might not be able to install the app, or the app might run in a reduced-feature mode.
- Locate the installation media (CD, DVD, or download file). Some apps require that the installation media be present before the app can be removed.
- Deactivate the app. Some vendors won't allow an app to be reinstalled, even on the same device, unless you deactivate it first. See the app's Help menu or online support website for details.

Tip

To locate your license key, check the following:

For packaged software, check the box or optical media jewel case. For downloaded apps, check your email (we recommend storing a copy of your licensing email in the same folder as your download for safekeeping). Also, many vendors now store license keys for the apps you have purchased in an account page on their websites. Use the login credentials provided when you set up your account with the vendor to see your software licenses.

When you reinstall the app, be sure to follow these guidelines:

- Right-click the app's install program and select **Run as Administrator** (see Figure 19.9). By using this option, you help assure that the app has the permissions needed to make changes to your system so the app will work properly.
- Check for an updated version before you reinstall the app. If you find an update, find out if the update can be installed, or if it must be applied as a patch after you install the version you already have. If it can be installed, download it and install it in place of the version you already have.

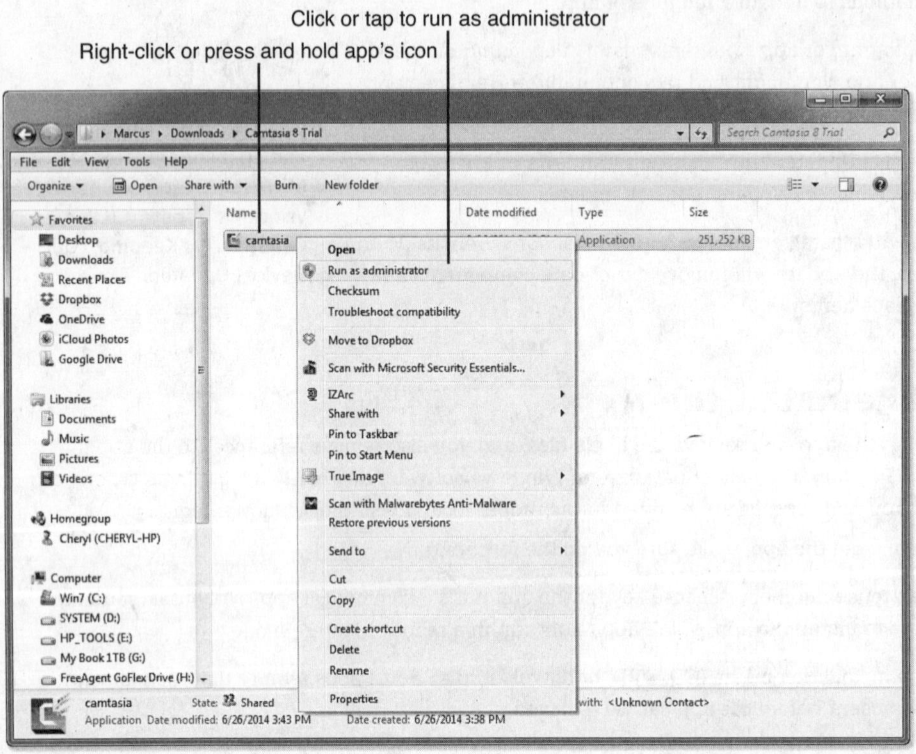

Figure 19.9 Preparing to install an app using the Run as Administrator option.

Repairing a Program

The Programs and Features menu in Control Panel is used mainly for uninstalling (removing) a program. However, some programs might offer two additional options you can use to solve problems:

- Change
- Repair

Use Change to change how a program works. For example, if you did not install all of a program's features, you can use Change to add additional features without reinstalling the program.

Use Repair to fix damaged or defective program components and Windows Registry entries.

To see and use these options, follow these steps:

1. Open Control Panel.
2. Select **Uninstall a Program**.
3. Select the program to change or repair.
4. If either **Change** or **Repair** is listed as an option, click the appropriate button (see Figure 19.10).
5. Follow the prompts to make the changes needed.

Figure 19.10
Modify, Repair, or Remove options on Camtasia Studio's Application Maintenance menu.

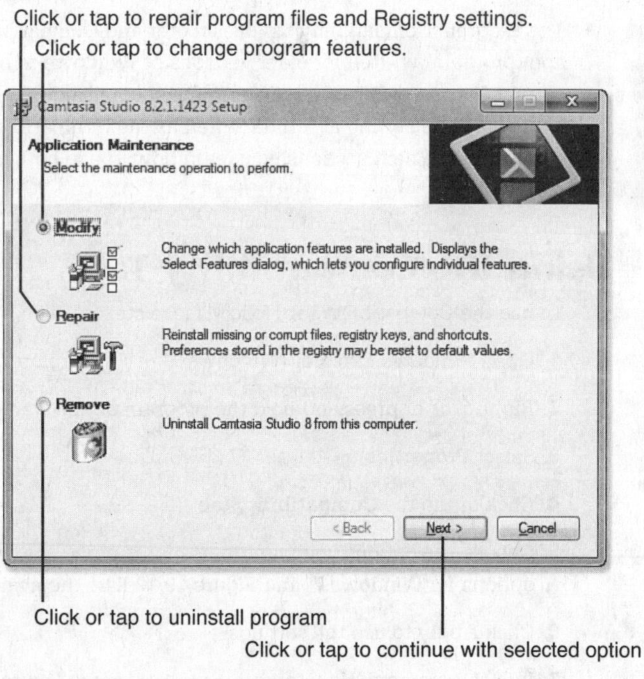

Caution

Some program entries in the Programs and Features menu simply launch an uninstall routine, even if Repair or Change is listed as an option. Be sure to read the dialog carefully after you select **Repair** or **Change**. If Uninstall is the only choice you can make for an app, your only option is to remove the program and reinstall it.

Using the Program Compatibility Wizard and Compatibility Tab

Windows 7 and 8/8.1 can use programs written for many earlier versions of Windows, but these programs might need to be installed in special ways to work properly with current Windows versions. If they are installed using their normal settings, you might see problems such as the following:

- The program won't run after installation.
- The program doesn't use the entire display.
- The program crashes if certain other programs are run.

To solve problems with Windows apps not written specifically for your version of Windows, you can use the Program Compatibility troubleshooter or the Compatibility tab.

The Program Compatibility troubleshooter and Compatibility tab apply compatibility settings to an app (program) written for older versions of Windows to enable the app to run properly under the current version of Windows. The troubleshooter requires you to answer some questions and can apply only one setting at a time, whereas the Compatibility tab lets you apply multiple settings at once. In the next sections, you learn how to use both of these tools to help solve problems with older apps.

Using the Compatibility Tab

To use the Compatibility tab, follow these steps:

1. Open Windows Explorer (Windows 7) or File Explorer (Windows 8/8.1).
2. Right-click or press and hold the program or app.
3. Select **Properties**.
4. Click or tap the **Compatibility** tab.
5. Choose the options you want to use for running the program. Figure 19.11 lists the available options for Windows 7, and Figure 19.12 lists the available options for Windows 8.1.
6. Click **Apply** to use the settings.
7. Run the program. If the program runs properly, you're finished. If the program doesn't run properly, return to step 2 and try other settings.

Tip

The fixes most often needed include the following:

- Selecting the Windows version the program or app was made for.
- Selecting Run as Administrator.
- Changing display settings if the program was written for Windows versions older than Windows XP.

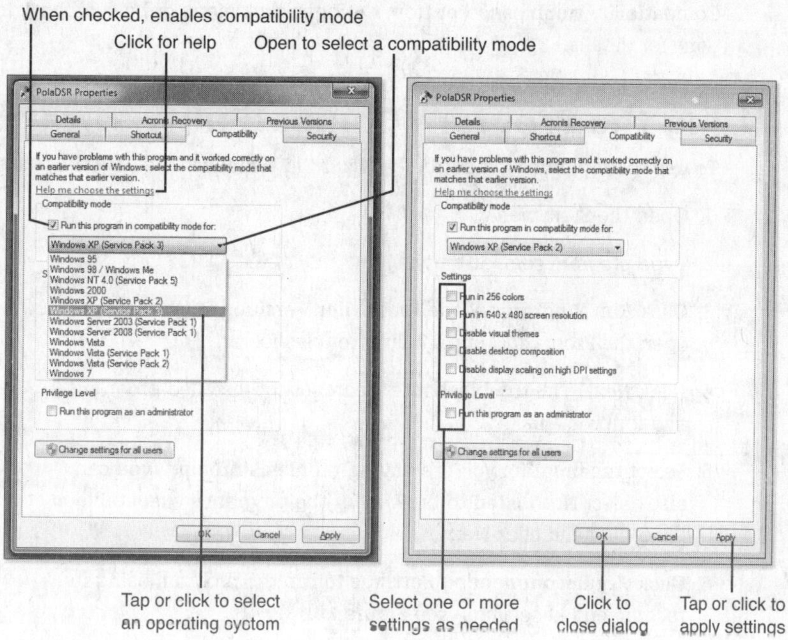

Figure 19.11 Selecting Compatibility mode settings in Windows 7.

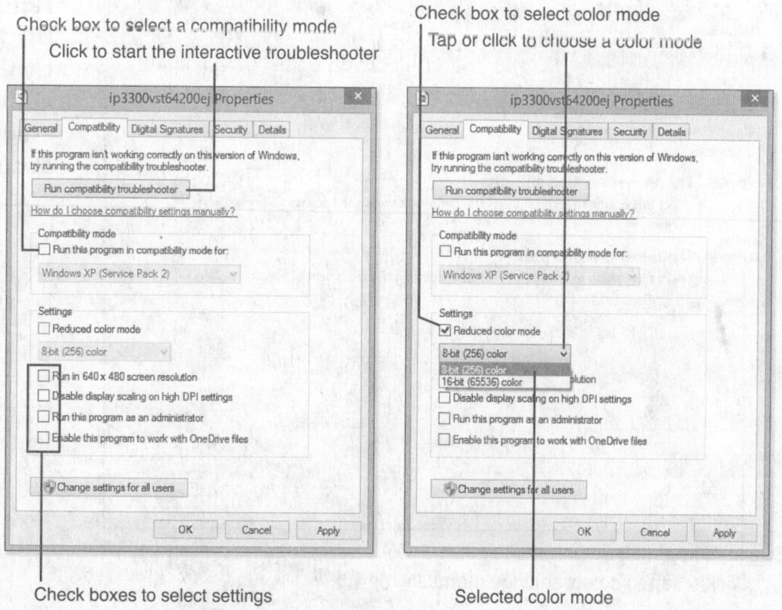

Figure 19.12 Selecting Compatibility mode settings in Windows 8.1.

If you prefer a guided method for setting compatibility options, you can run the Program Compatibility troubleshooter from the right-click menu or by searching for it. See the following sections for details.

Using the Program Compatibility Wizard in Windows 7

To use the Program Compatibility Wizard in Windows 7, follow these steps:

1. Open the Start menu.
2. Type program compatibility.
3. Click **Run Programs Made for Earlier Versions of Windows** to open the Program Compatibility troubleshooter.
4. Click **Next**. The troubleshooter searches for installed programs and for problems.
5. Select the program you are having problems running (you can also select **Not Listed** to browse for the program's executable [.exe] file) and click **Next**.
6. Click **Try Recommended Settings** to run the program using its recommended settings (see Figure 19.13).

> **Note**
> If an app is not compatible, but a compatible upgrade is available, you might see the option **Go to the vendor site and get the upgrade.** Follow the link to get information about the new version.

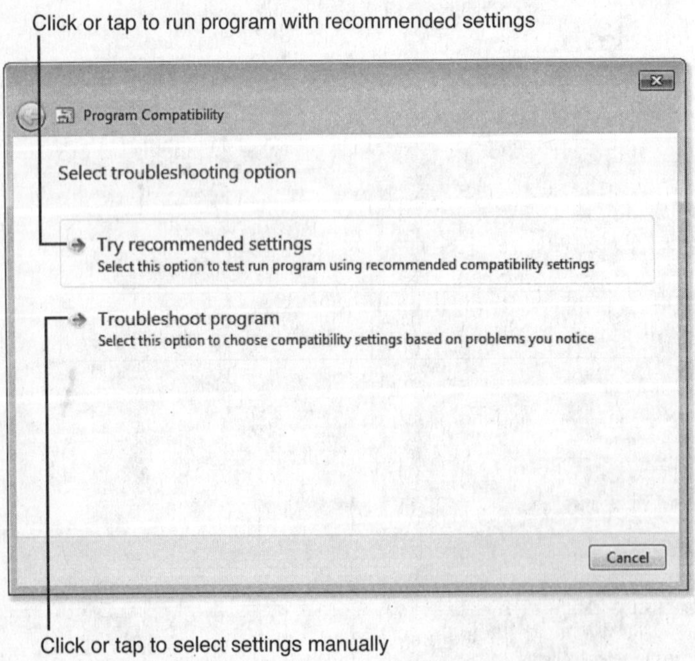

Figure 19.13
Use Recommended Settings to try the troubleshooter's suggestion, or click Troubleshoot Program to answer questions about what's not working.

7. Windows applies recommended settings. Click **Test the Program** to test it.

8. If the Windows Security Shield is displayed in the taskbar, click it to continue to run the program.

9. After the program runs, close it.

10. Click **Next** in the troubleshooter dialog.

11. Choose the appropriate option to end the process (see Figure 19.14).

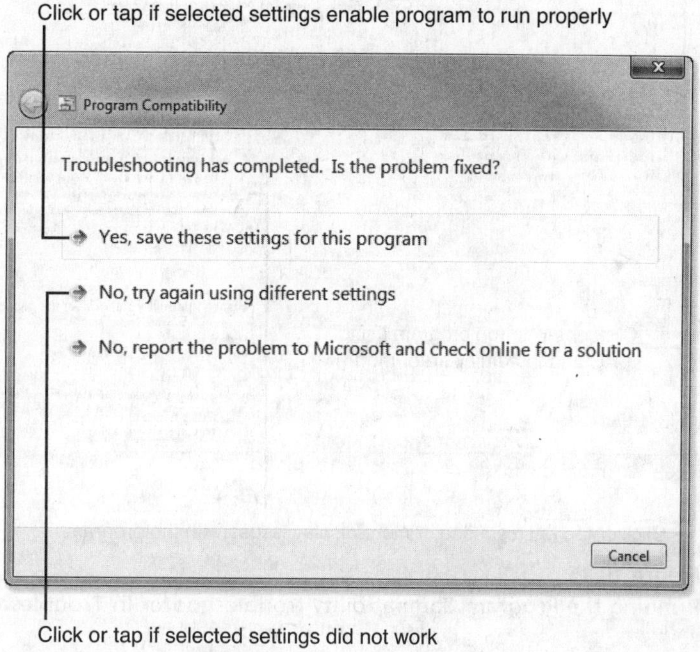

Figure 19.14
Ending the Program Compatibility troubleshooter.

If the program did not run correctly, try this:

1. Click **No, Try Again with Different Settings** in step 11 of the previous procedure. This is the same as selecting **Troubleshoot Program** mode (refer to Figure 19.13).

2. Select the problem you're having, and click **Next** (see Figure 19.15).

3. Choose from the options available (see Figure 19.15).

4. Run the program when prompted. If the program runs correctly, click **Yes, Save These Settings**. Otherwise, return to step 1 and try different options.

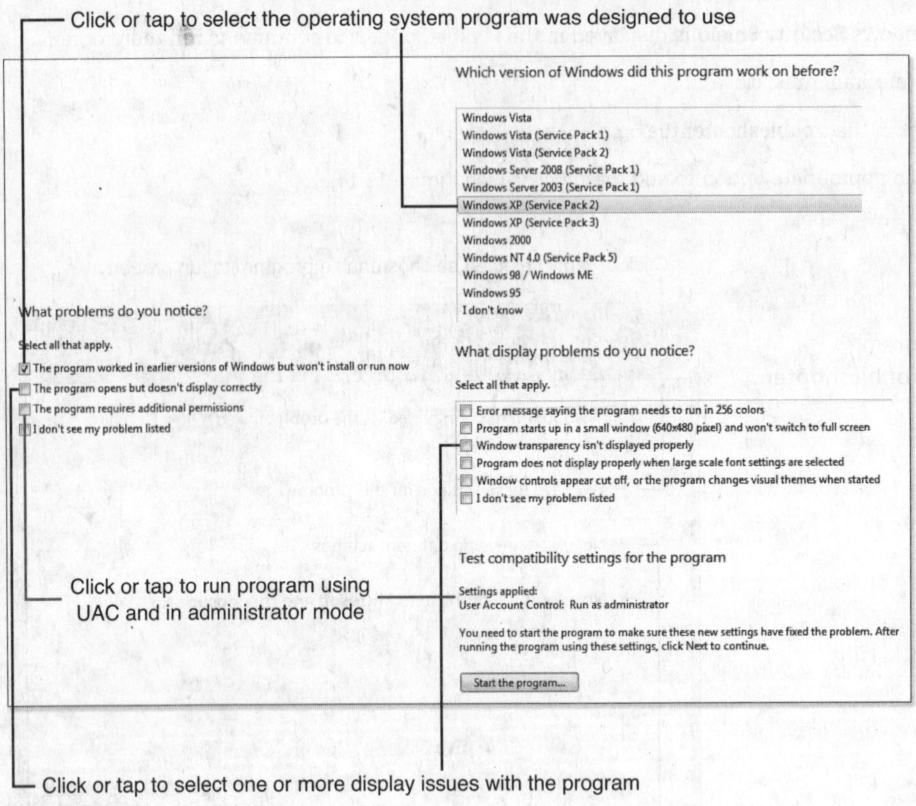

Figure 19.15
Running the Program Compatibility troubleshooter in Troubleshoot Program mode.

Using the Program Compatibility Troubleshooter in Windows 8/8.1

To start the Program Compatibility troubleshooter in Windows 8/8.1, follow these steps:

1. Open the Charms menu.
2. Type **`program compatibility`**.
3. Click **Run Programs Made for Earlier Versions of Windows** to open the Program Compatibility troubleshooter.

After step 3, the steps are the same as in the Windows 7 version.

Fixing Problem Apps with Regedit

In most cases, you should be able to repair or remove a troublesome program or app by using the Programs and Features menu in Windows. However, in a few cases, it might be necessary to manually remove an app or make changes to an app's settings by using the Windows Registry editor, Regedit.

Regedit is a very powerful utility that should not be used unless you have no alternatives: it has no undo option, so any changes you make can't be undone, and it's up to you to make backup copies of your Windows Registry manually.

If you have problems with Windows or with a particular app, many vendors provide preconfigured REG (.reg) files that have appropriate settings needed to make the changes desired.

If you need to use Regedit to remove an app manually or change settings, check these resources for help:

- **Making backups of your system Registry**—http://support.microsoft.com/kb/322756
- **Using Registry Editor and using a REG file**—http://support.microsoft.com/kb/310516

Windows System Restore and Problem Apps

If your software stops working properly after you installed a new program or app (or new hardware), you can return your system to its previous condition with Windows System Restore.

➡ *To learn how to use System Restore, see "Using System Restore," p.218, Chapter 8, "Fixing Windows Devices That Can't Start."*

Using Windows 8/8.1 Refresh

Use Windows 8/8.1 Refresh to fix problems with your system that are caused by incompatible boxed or downloaded software. Refresh removes these programs from your system, but does not remove apps downloaded from the Windows Store.

➡ *To learn more about using Refresh, see "Refresh Your PC," p.226, in Chapter 8, "Fixing Windows Devices That Can't Start."*

Updating Windows Store Apps

In Windows 8, Windows Store apps had to be updated manually by visiting the Windows Store and starting the update process manually. However, in Windows 8.1, Windows Store apps are updated automatically.

20

DIGITAL CAMERA TROUBLESHOOTING

Fast Track to Solutions

Table 20.1 Symptom Table

Symptom	Flowchart or Book Section	Page #
My pictures don't have good color.	Color Problems	526
When I shoot in front of a bright background, my picture is too dark.	Exposure Problems	529
My camera is focusing on the wire barrier not the sports field.	Image Blur (Out of Focus)	531
In dim light, I take pictures that aren't sharp.	Camera Shake	532
I want to find out what settings were used for my pictures.	Viewing Settings Used for a Photo	535
When I get close to people to take pictures, their faces look strange.	Wrong Lens or Zoom Setting	536
I have cleaned my lens, but I see spots in the same place on many of my pictures.	Dirty Image Sensor	538

Symptom	Flowchart or Book Section	Page #
I want to be able to fix bad colors for a group of photos at one time.	Shooting in RAW Mode	539
I can use a 2GB SD card in my card reader, but a 16GB SDHC card won't work.	**Sidebar:** Understanding SD, SDHC, and SDXC Cards	542
I have several memory cards sitting around. I've copied the photos from them, but I don't know how to reuse them.	Emptying the Contents of a Memory Card	549
I'm confused by the terms used by camera lens makers.	Checking Model Numbers and Terminologies	552
I have the same camera as a friend, but my friend's camera is newer and has features I don't have. What can I do?	Installing Firmware Updates	555

Image Quality Problems and Solutions

Whether you're using a smartphone or point-and-shoot camera, a compact system camera, or a digital SLR, the settings you use and the cleanliness of your equipment have a big impact on the quality of photos you create.

Some of the most common problems include the following:

- Using auto settings instead of scenes or manual controls that would get better pictures in some situations.
- Relying on auto white balance instead of choosing the correct white balance settings for a scene.
- Trusting the camera to set the exposure under any circumstances, even when your pictures are too light (overexposed) or too dark (underexposed) photos.
- Choosing the wrong zoom setting for your subject.
- Not cleaning your camera lens or filter.
- Not cleaning your camera's image sensor.
- Assuming that autofocus always works.
- Not getting your subject in focus.
- Subject is moving too fast.
- Shaking the camera during shooting.

Fortunately, there are simple solutions to each of these problems, no matter what type of camera or smartphone you use.

> **Note**
> For much more information and many more before-and-after examples in full color, see my book *The Shot Doctor: The Amateur's Guide to Taking Great Photos*, available in print and electronic form from Que Publishing and major bookstores.

Changing Settings

Digital cameras and smartphones use Auto mode by default. In this mode, the only decision you're making about photography is when to take the picture; your device chooses everything else.

The control dial or menu options in your digital camera or smartphone camera app provide additional options:

- Preset scene modes that can improve photos at sunrise, sunset, when the light is behind the subject, indoors, and more
- Access to manual adjustments for white balance, exposure, and so on

If your camera has a full-fledged control dial like the one shown in Figure 20.1, choose P (Program) mode if you want point-and-shoot ease along with the ability to adjust color and exposure settings. The S or Tv (shutter priority), A or Av (aperture priority), and M (manual) options provide these options and more control over your photo.

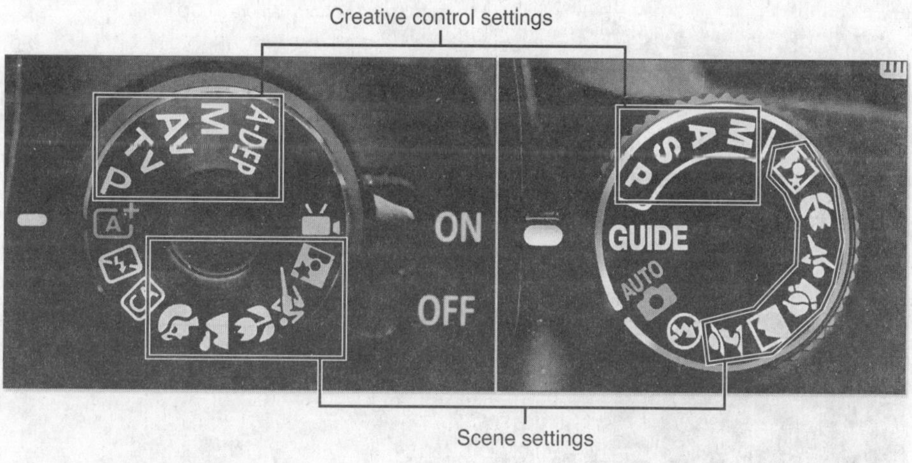

Figure 20.1
Typical DSLR control dials from Canon and Nikon.

Some point-and-shoot cameras have a simplified control dial that emphasizes scene modes (see Figure 20.2). To choose options for color and exposure settings, select P or M.

The Camera app on an Android smartphone also includes many of these options (see Figure 20.3).

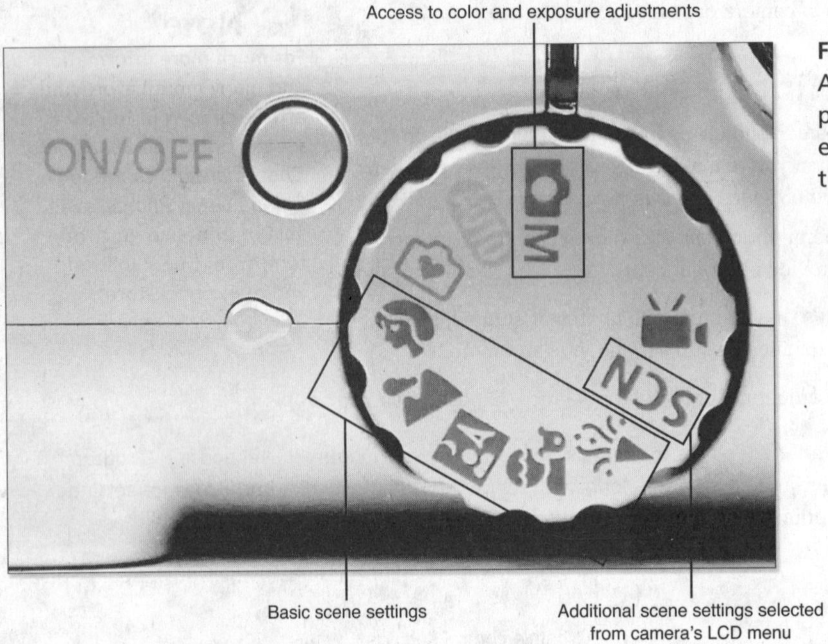

Figure 20.2
A control dial from a point-and-shoot camera features mode settings.

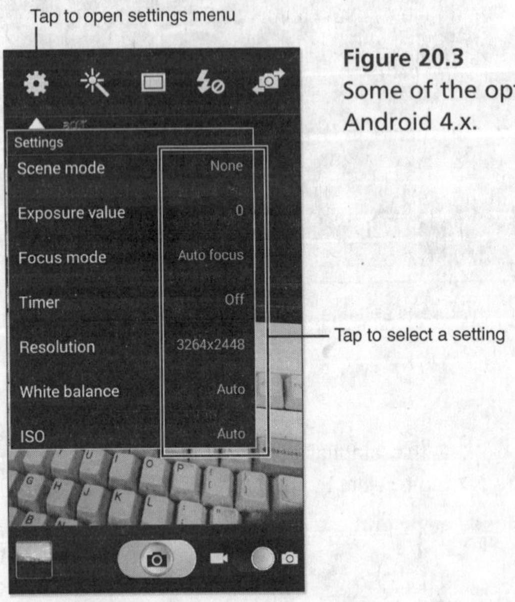

Figure 20.3
Some of the options available in the Camera app included in Android 4.x.

> **Note**
> The Camera app included in iOS is designed to adjust images after you shoot them. If you want more control over the shooting process itself, many iOS camera apps offer more controls, and there are many Android camera apps with additional features beyond those included in the basic Android app. See www.forbes.com/sites/amadoudiallo/2013/06/14/best-camera-apps-ios-android/ for a useful review of iOS and Android camera apps.

Scene Mode

If you want to improve your pictures but don't want to get bogged down in details, try your camera's scene mode. Almost all digital cameras, from cheapies to expensive models, feature several customized settings, as do some smartphone camera apps.

Scene mode provides preset options designed to enhance photos you take in particular situations. Each scene setting has adjustments for settings such as white balance, color, sharpness, shutter speed, lens opening (aperture or f/stop), single-shot or burst mode, and sharpness already included. It's up to you to choose the right scene for a situation.

To use a scene setting, follow these steps:

1. Turn on your device's scene mode. Some cameras feature a few scene modes on the control dial, with additional scenes available from a menu.
2. Look at the list of scene settings (see Figure 20.4).

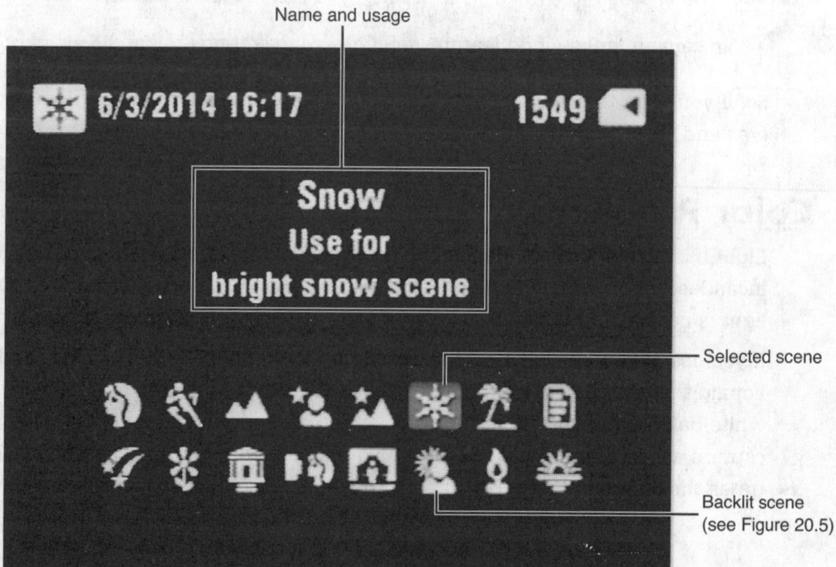

Figure 20.4 Choosing a scene setting on a typical point-and-shoot camera.

3. Compare your subject to the scene settings available.

4. Choose a setting that best matches your subject.

5. Take pictures.

Figure 20.5 illustrates how choosing the right scene setting can enhance your photos.

Figure 20.5 When the light is behind the subject, the Backlit setting brings out details in the subject.

There are two problems with using scene mode:

- If you choose the wrong scene setting, you can make the picture worse.
- No camera in the world features enough scene settings to handle every possible situation.

So, if you want to get even better photos, consider using additional options available in most cameras and some smartphone camera apps.

Color Problems

Light has different colors, depending on when you shoot. At dawn and dusk, and indoors under incandescent or warm-white fluorescent bulbs, the light is yellowish or red. On a sunny day, the light is neutral. But when it's cloudy or overcast, the light becomes bluish.

If you use auto white balance (the default setting on both digital cameras and smartphones), you're hoping that the camera can figure out both the color of the light and the color of the subject. Auto white balance can sometimes do a decent job of rendering a scene, but even at its best, it can't capture all the colors you'd see if you use the best white balance setting available. Figure 20.6 illustrates the difference between auto and daylight white balance on a sunny day.

Figure 20.6 Auto turned red flowers magenta and makes the leaves grayish, whereas daylight white balance provided purer and more accurate colors.

Choosing the Best White Balance Setting

To get the best colors, use the white balance setting on your camera or smartphone and choose a setting that matches the time of day or the lighting in the room

Typical settings include the following:

- **Auto**—Use this if a preset white balance setting doesn't work, or if there's more than one kind of light in the room (for example, window plus incandescent or fluorescent lighting).
- **Incandescent (tungsten)**—Removes excess yellow from indoor lighting, including warm-white CFLs as well as incandescent and halogen bulbs.
- **Daylight**—Use on sunny days after sunrise and before sunset for accurate and vivid color.
- **Fluorescent**—Use with tube-type fluorescent bulbs or similar greenish-white lights. Some digital cameras have two or more fluorescent settings, so try more than one.
- **Cloudy**—Removes excess blue caused by cloudy, overcast days.
- **Open shade**—A stronger effect than cloudy.
- **Electronic flash (speedlight)**—Removes excess blue from electronic flash.
- **Custom**—Uses a white card under the same light as the subject to get the most accurate white balance.

Tip

If you can't use custom white balance, take a picture of the scene using auto white balance and look for an object that is supposed to be white. Take pictures using different white balance settings until the object is as close to pure white as possible (in other words, no blue, red, or yellow cast). If you can't find a white object to shoot, just look at the overall colors and choose the best white balance based on which one produces the colors that most closely match what you see.

Changing White Balance Settings

Look for a button called WB or an onscreen setting called AUTO or AWB. See your camera manual on how to find this setting and change it. Figure 20.7 shows typical white balance settings on digital cameras and an Android smartphone.

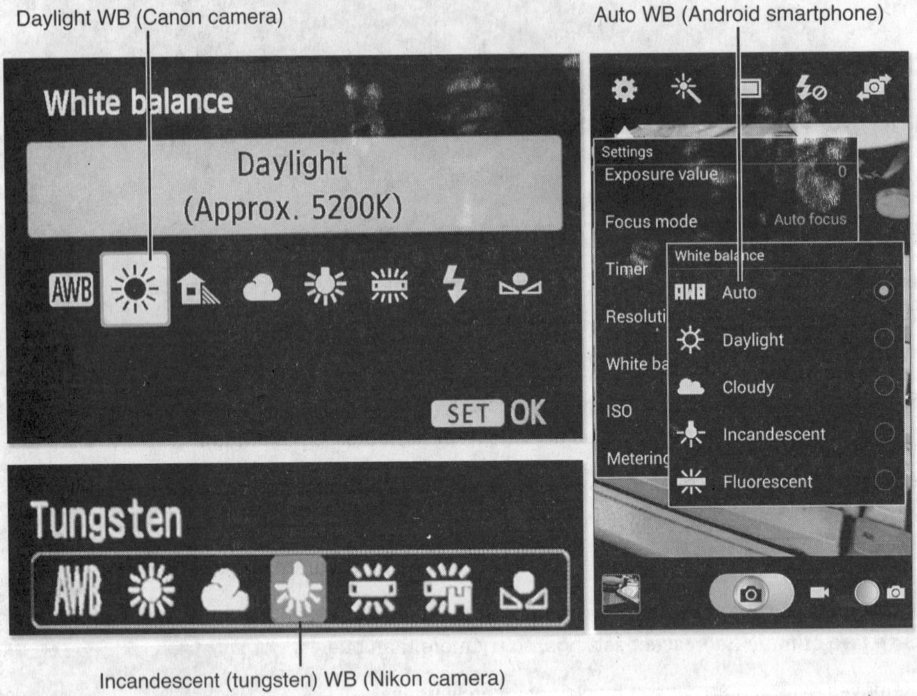

Figure 20.7 White balance menus on a digital SLR, a point-and-shoot camera, and an Android camera app.

Although you might have fewer options when you use your smartphone's front-facing camera for selfies, white balance adjustment, if present, can help you get a more accurate picture of yourself and your friends. In Figure 20.8, we switched from auto white balance (which produced an orange skin tone under indoor light) to Incandescent for more normal colors.

Figure 20.8
Better selfies without flash by using Incandescent white balance.

Exposure Problems

Your digital camera or smartphone sets the exposure for you, but it doesn't always get it right. Bright or dark areas next to or behind the main subject often fool these devices into producing photos that are too dark or too light.

The exposure compensation (EV or AV) adjustment button and menu (Figure 20.9) lets you add light or take away light to help solve these problems. +1 doubles the light, and -1 removes half the light.

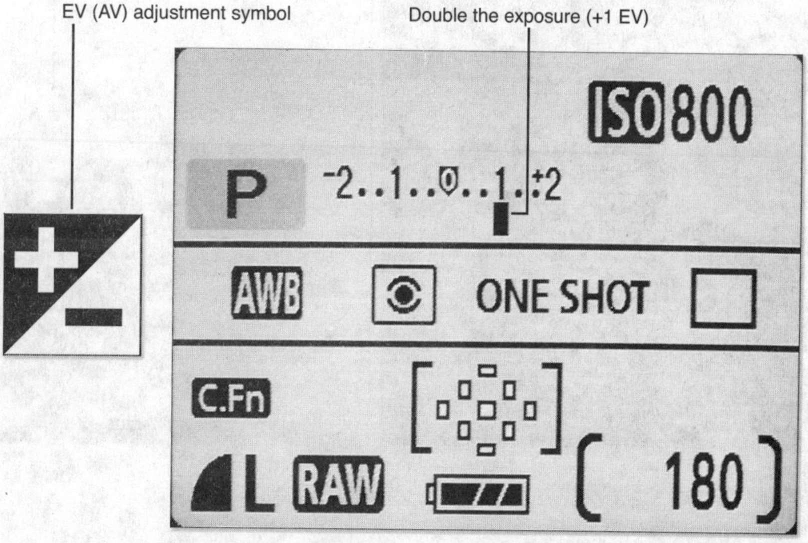

Figure 20.9
After you enable the AV or EV adjustment, use your camera's control wheel or arrows to adjust exposure.

On an Android smartphone or tablet using the built-in Camera app

1. Open the **Options** menu.
2. Select **Exposure Value**.
3. Drag the control toward the top to make the picture lighter, or drag toward the bottom to make the picture darker (see Figure 20.10).

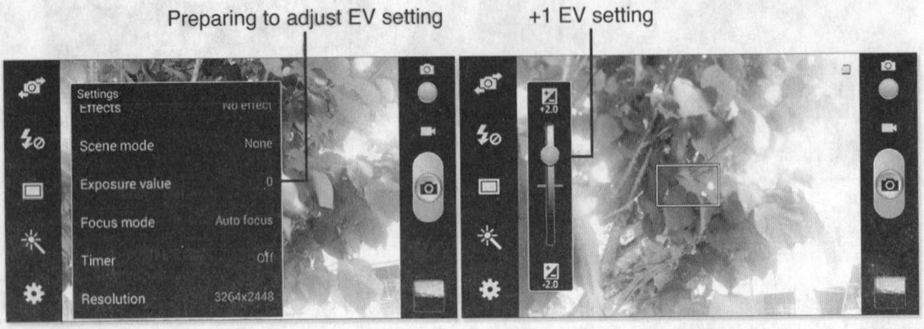

Figure 20.10 Adjusting exposure with an Android smartphone.

Figure 20.11 A selfie against a bright background looks better when +2EV is used.

You can use this feature when shooting in a variety of situations, such as backlit scenes (see Figure 20.11), stage shows or concerts, and more.

Caution

If the subject is within 10 feet of your position, you can also use flash to lighten it up. However, keep in mind that flash can cause glare on glasses and shiny objects, can cause red-eye in dim light, and will run down your camera or smartphone battery faster.

If your flash doesn't fire, change the setting from Auto Flash to Flash (also called forced flash) so it will fire no matter the lighting conditions.

Image Blur (Out of Focus)

Your camera and smartphone have autofocus to help you get sharper pictures. However, shooting through windows, screens, wire, or other objects between you and your subject help guarantee that your device will focus on what you don't want.

If you use a digital SLR or mirrorless (compact system) camera, use manual focus in situations like these. Push the button on the lens and use the manual focus ring as you view your subject (see Figure 20.12).

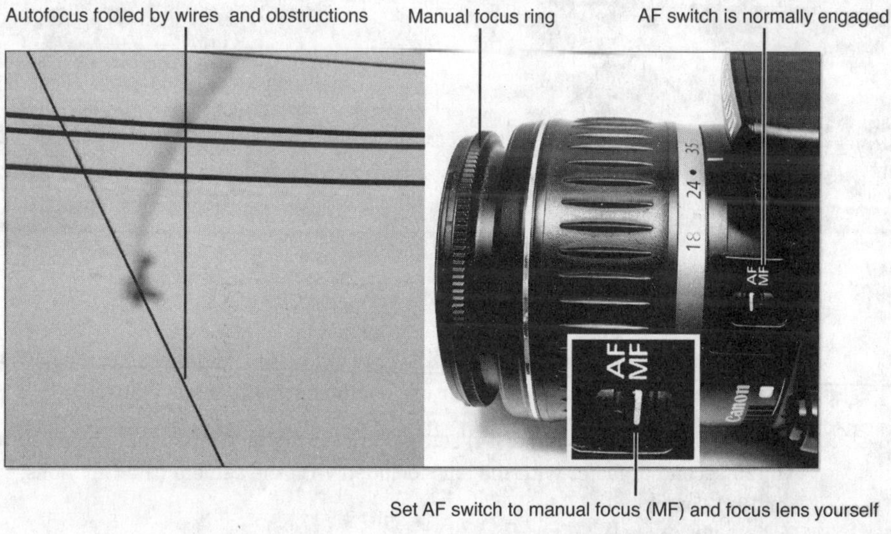

Figure 20.12 Switching to manual focus with a digital SLR camera.

With a point-and-shoot camera, use prefocusing: aim your camera at a point about the same distance as your subject with about the same lighting, hold down the shutter button halfway to lock exposure and focus, frame your photo, and shoot. Some camera apps for smartphones and tablets have the same feature.

What is the simplest way to avoid out-of-focus pictures when there's a fence or wire between you and your subject? Move up to the fence and point your camera through an opening in the fence.

Camera Shake

Camera shake happens when you move your camera during your shot (see Figure 20.13). In this example, you can see the streaks of light indicating the direction of camera movement.

Direction of camera movement

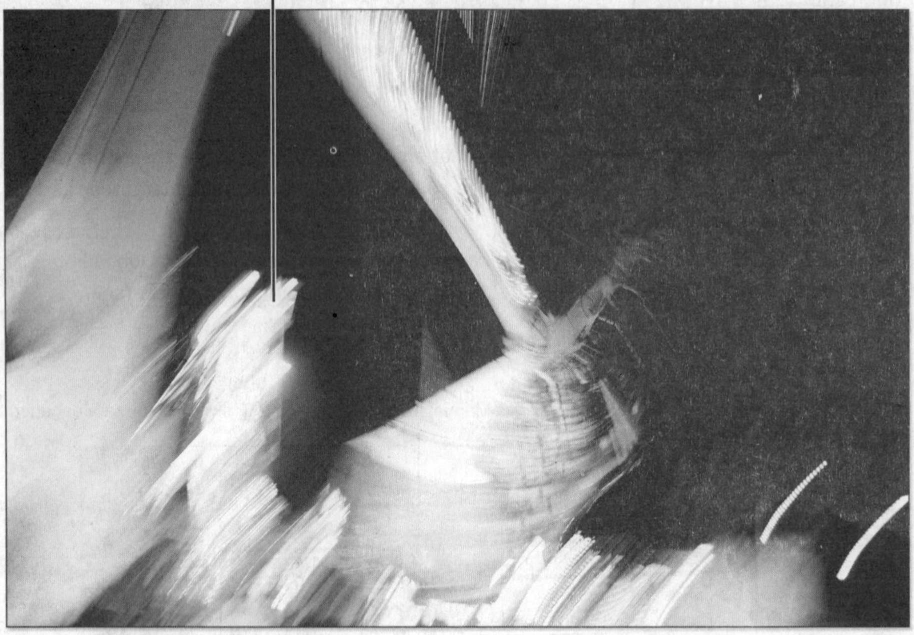

Figure 20.13 An extreme example of camera shake (1/4 second exposure).

There are many ways to avoid camera shake when using a digital camera. One way is to adjust the shutter speed, particularly if you don't use equipment with image stabilization:

- Use the shutter priority (S or Tv) setting on your digital camera and use a shutter speed of 1/125-second or faster with the lens included with the camera (the "kit" lens, typically 18–55mm or 18–135mm).
- Use faster shutter speeds (1/250-second or faster) with longer lenses. Longer lenses bring distant subjects closer and also make camera shake more apparent.
- Make sure you use image stabilization (IS), optical stabilization (OS), or vibration reduction (VR) features when available. This feature compensates for camera shake. It is included with some lenses for Canon and Nikon digital SLR cameras (see Figure 20.15) and is built in to the camera body for other types of cameras.

To adjust shutter speed manually, follow these steps:

1. Turn the camera control dial to S (most brands) or Tv (Canon cameras).
2. For a faster shutter speed, select a smaller value.
3. For a slower shutter speed, select a larger value. See Figure 20.14.

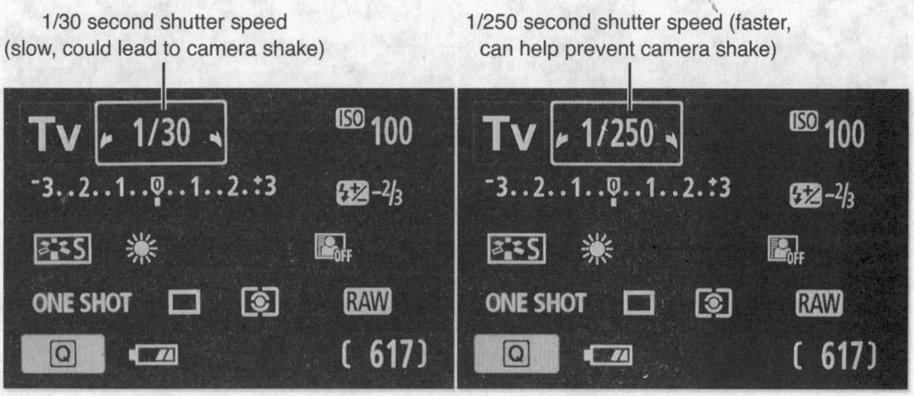

Figure 20.14 Slower and faster shutter speeds on a Canon DSLR.

Figure 20.15 The image stabilization (IS) switch on a Canon telephoto zoom lens.

As you can see from Figure 20.16, image stabilization can significantly improve the sharpness of photos you take using slow shutter speeds.

Figure 20.16 Shots taken with and without IS (1/20-second, 55–250mm zoom lens at 250mm).

- Increase the ISO (higher ISO number) to reduce the amount of light needed to take a picture. Use ISO 100–400 outdoors, ISO 400–800 indoors, and ISO 800 or higher for fast action under dim light.
- Use electronic flash if the subject is less than 10 feet away. Electronic flash "freezes" action.
- Use a tripod in dim light. If you use a tripod, don't enable image stabilization.

> **Caution**
> As ISO increases, image quality declines, especially with smartphones using ISO 400 or higher, point-and-shoot cameras using ISO 800 or higher, and digital SLR or mirrorless cameras above ISO 1600. Take test shots using different ISO settings to see which ISO settings are acceptable for a particular camera or smartphone.

With a smartphone:

- Get a tripod made for a smartphone.
- Brace the phone against a wall or pole.
- Hold the phone with both hands.
- Increase the ISO.
- Use electronic flash if the subject is less than 10 feet away.

Motion Blur

Motion blur, like camera shake, happens when your shutter speed is too slow. The difference is that the subject, rather than the camera, is moving too quickly for a sharp picture.

A little motion blur (see Figure 20.17) can enhance the photo. By shooting subjects at different shutter speeds, you can decide which shutter speed works better.

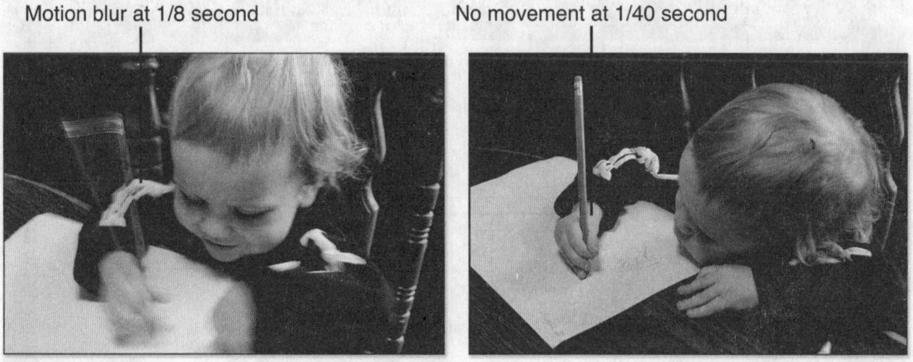

Figure 20.17 To change the amount of motion blur (or to eliminate it), use a faster shutter speed.

Viewing Settings Used for a Photo

Before digital photography, you needed to use a notebook to record your camera's settings. Today, the camera does the job for you. It records information about the shutter speed, aperture (f/stop), ISO, and other settings used by your camera. This information is known as metadata. To see the metadata for a photo, follow these steps:

1. Open Windows Explorer or File Explorer.
2. Navigate to the location where your photo is stored.
3. Right-click or press and hold the picture file, and select **Properties**.
4. Click or tap the **Details** tab.
5. Scroll down to the Camera section (see Figure 20.18).
6. After viewing the metadata, click **OK**.

Note

Smartphones record very little metadata compared with cameras.

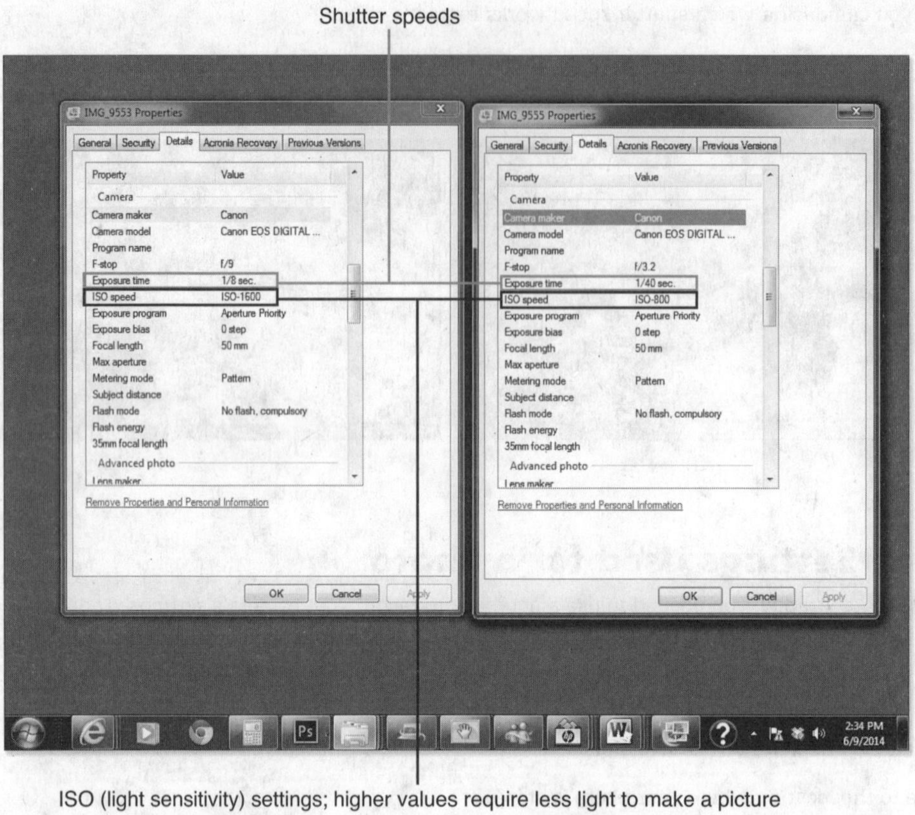

Figure 20.18 Exposure metadata for the photos shown in Figure 20.17.

Wrong Lens or Zoom Setting

Digital SLR and mirrorless (compact system) cameras typically come equipped with a 3× or 4× zoom lens that can be interchanged with other lenses. Point-and-shoot cameras don't have removable lenses, but the zoom range can be up to 30× or longer. You can also add a self-contained lens-style camera that communicates with your smartphone or add-on lenses that fit over your existing smartphone.

Note

To learn more about add-on lenses for smartphones, see ztylus.com, photojojo.com, and Olloclip.com. These and other vendors offer a wide range of add-on lenses. To learn more about Sony's lens-style cameras for smartphones, the Sony QX 10 and QX 100, see www.sony.net/Products/di/en-gb/products/ec8t/.

Table 20.2 lists some basic guidelines for zoom ratios or zoom lenses to help you get better pictures of people.

Table 20.2 Lens Selection Guidelines

Subject	Zoom Lens Ratio	DSLR Lens Zoom Range
Groups	1x–2x	17–36mm
One or two people (full length)	2x–3x	36–55mm
Portrait	3x–5x	50–90mm

What happens if you use a wide-angle lens to photograph a subject at close range? Notice the distortion shown in Figure 20.19.

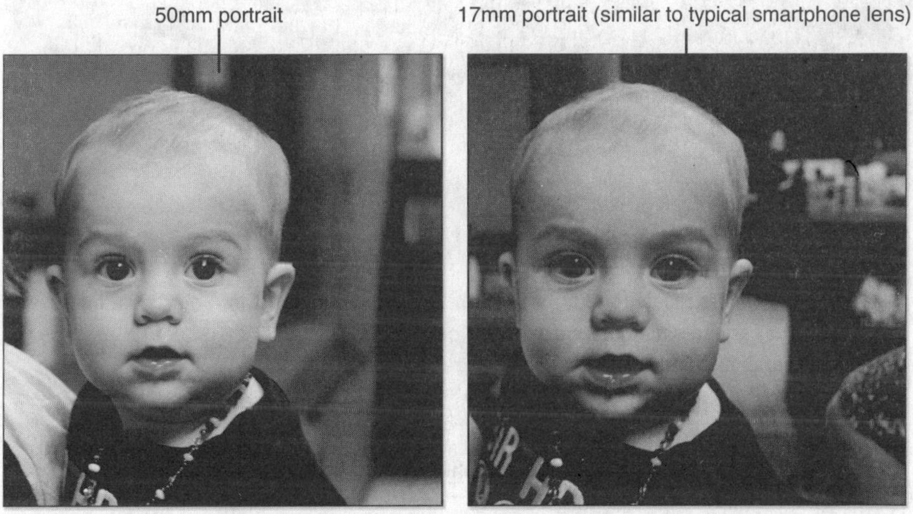

Figure 20.19 50mm (3X) provides a pleasing balance to the face, while moving in closer to shoot at 17mm (1X) exaggerates the size of the nose, cheeks, and chin.

For better portraits, move back and zoom in.

Dirty Lens

A dirty lens on your camera or smartphone reduces sharpness and can cause blurry photos. Figure 20.20 shows the results of shooting with an extremely dirty lens (fingerprints and a bit of smeary moisture) versus a clean lens.

To clean a lens or filter on your camera or smartphone, do the following:

1. Gently remove any loose dirt specks or sand from the surface of the lens.
2. If you use a premoistened lens cleaning cloth, move it gently across the surface of the lens using a rotary motion.

3. If you use a microfiber cloth and lens cleaning fluid, spray one corner of the cloth and then move it gently across the surface of the lens using a rotary motion.
4. Use a dry microfiber cloth to remove any lens fluid residue.

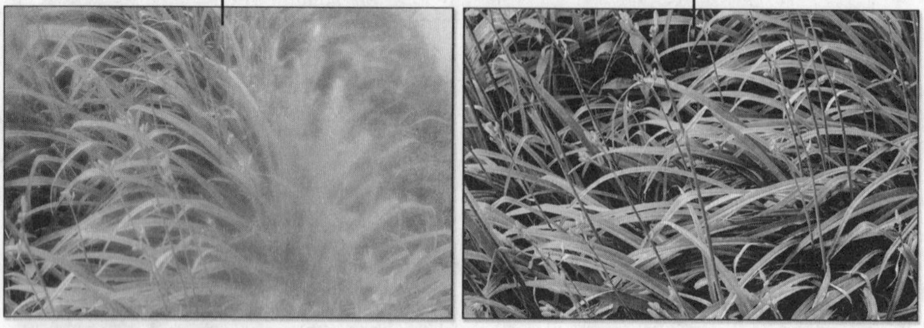

Figure 20.20 Dirty lens versus clean lens.

Dirty Image Sensor

Image sensors receive the light from the lens and convert it into electrical impulses that are stored on your camera's memory card. Image sensors on digital SLR (DSLR) and mirrorless compact cameras can become dirty when you change lenses.

If your image sensor has multiple spots, as in Figure 20.21, the results can ruin your photo, or at the very least require a lot of retouching to fix. Keep in mind that retouching an image can violate photo contest rules and journalism ethics, so it's best to keep your image sensor clean!

Note

To make the spots in Figure 20.21 more visible when reproduced, I reduced the brightness of the photo and increased the contrast.

To remove spots on the image sensor, you can send your camera in for service, or, if your camera has a special mode that moves the mirror and shutter out of the way, you can clean the sensor yourself. Be sure to ask for an estimate before you send your camera in for sensor cleaning. With an older or low-end camera, the service cost might exceed the camera's value.

Tip

The Cleaning Digital Cameras website at www.cleaningdigitalcameras.com provides an outstanding collection of expertise, materials, and methods for cleaning your camera's image sensor.

Figure 20.21 Spots on the image sensor can detract from picture quality.

Shooting in RAW Mode

RAW mode, available on almost all digital SLRs and mirrorless cameras and some advanced point-and-shoot cameras, has many advantages over shooting in the normal JPEG mode:

- **Complete control over white balance**—If you forgot to change white balance before shooting, or the white balance setting you chose didn't match the scene lighting closely enough, you can select the perfect white balance setting after you shoot the picture.
- **Full image quality**—JPEG photos use compression to create relatively small image sizes, but as a consequence, RAW photos are larger andsharper.
- **Greater control over color, contrast, brightness, highlights, shadows, and other image settings**—You can fine-tune every photo to produce the best results (see Figure 20.22).
- **Group photo editing**—Whether you use the RAW image editor included with your digital camera or a third-party program such as Adobe Camera RAW, you can select a group of photos shot under the same conditions and make a single set of edits.

Potential drawbacks to shooting in RAW:

- **RAW photos are about three times larger than the highest-quality JPEG photos**—Thus, you can't take as many pictures per memory card as with JPEG.

- **RAW photos take longer to shoot**—If you want to shoot in burst mode, JPEG is a better choice in terms of speed.
- **RAW photos also need additional software to view and edit them**—Digital cameras that support RAW mode usually include RAW editing software. However, if you want to see thumbnails of your RAW photos rather than icons, you will also need a RAW codec.

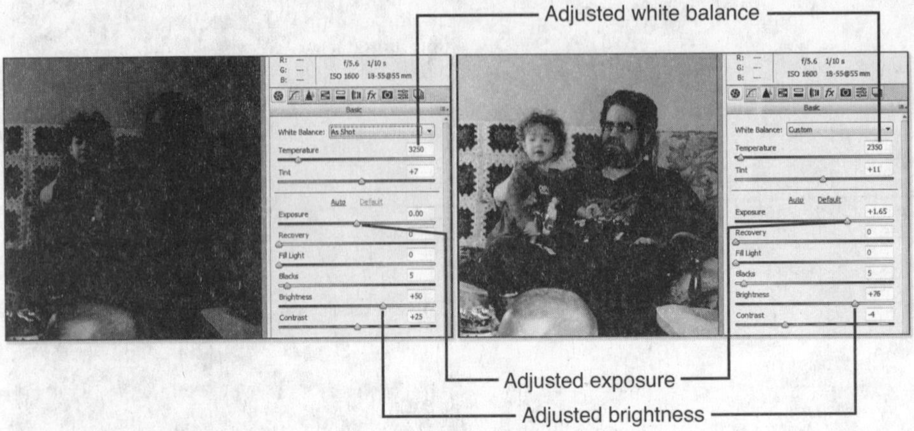

Figure 20.22
Using Adobe Camera RAW (included in Adobe Photoshop Elements and Adobe Photoshop CC) to adjust white balance, color, and brightness settings.

Note

Get RAW codes from the following sources:

- **Your camera vendor**—Check the discs that are included with your camera, or check the website.
- **Third-party sources**—I recommend FastPictureViewer's codec, which works with almost any RAW file type. It's available from www.fastpictureviewer.com/codecs/. I have also used Ardfry's codecs, available from www.ardfry.com.
- **Microsoft**—The Microsoft Camera Codec Pack can be downloaded from the Microsoft website (www.microsoft.com) for Windows 7 as well as Windows Vista SP2. Windows 8/8.1 users can get it from Windows Update.

Some cameras offer the option to save RAW and JPEG versions of a photo at the same time. This uses much more space on the memory card than JPEG or RAW alone but is handy if you need JPEG files for immediate use but want a RAW version for editing later.

Slow Burst Mode

If you use the Sports setting on some cameras, you can shoot multiple pictures by holding down the shutter button. This option, often called Burst mode, can also be selected from a camera or smartphone menu and is helpful when you're trying to capture fast action or the "peak of the moment."

If your camera slows down after shooting a few shots in Burst (continuous) mode, there are several reasons why:

- **Older digital cameras have smaller buffer memory sizes (the buffer holds the photos temporarily until they can be saved to flash memory)**—The only solution to this problem is to replace your camera with one that has a better Burst mode.
- **You're shooting in RAW rather than JPEG mode**—RAW produces better quality photos than JPEG, but if you want more frames per second (fps), shoot in JPEG.
- **Your memory card is too slow**—SD-family (SD, SDHC, and SDXC) cards are speed-rated using either the class or UHS identifiers.

Switching to JPEG from RAW

If you need maximum burst speed (highest frames per second rate), it's time to temporarily put aside RAW and return to JPEG. Be sure to use the highest-quality JPEG setting offered by your camera and set your white balance accurately.

After you're done shooting in Burst mode, you can reset your camera to RAW mode for maximum image quality. See your camera's instruction manual for details.

Choosing Fast Flash-Memory Cards

Class 2, 4, 6, and 10 cards feature read/write speed corresponding to the class rating (2MBps–10MBps).

Some, but not all, Class 10 cards also support UHS Speed Class 1 (10MBps read/write). SDHC and SDXC cards that support UHS Speed Class 1 or Class 3 (30MBps read/write) support the new high-speed UHS bus but will revert to the older Class 10 speed when connected to devices that do not include UHS support.

Figure 20.23 compares SDHC and microSDHC cards with different speed ratings.

If you use a digital SLR or mirrorless compact camera, using Class 10 or UHS1 cards instead of slower cards will improve burst speed. And, if you use your camera to shoot video, these cards will also enable you to shoot smooth 1080p (full HD) video.

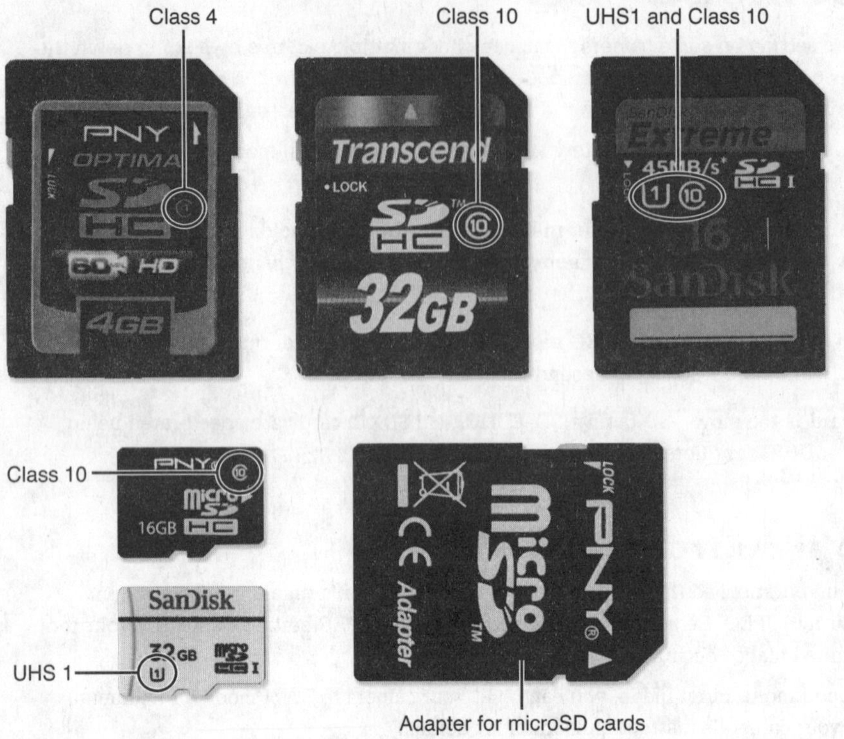

Figure 20.23 SDHC and micro SDHC cards with speeds ranging from Class 4 to UHS Class 1.

Understanding SD, SDHC, and SDXC Cards

SD, SDHC, and SDXC cards have the same form factor and write-protect switch. However, their internal features mean that many older devices can't use all these card types. The following capacities listed here apply to standard-size, mini, and microSD cards.

Secure Digital (SD) cards have capacities up to 2GB. SDHC (SD High Capacity) cards have capacities up to 32GB. SDXC (SD eXtended Capacity) cards have capacities of 64GB and greater. A device compatible with SDXC cards also supports SD and SDHC cards. A device compatible with SDHC cards also supports SD cards, but not SDXC cards. A device compatible with SD cards only cannot use the other types.

If you want to buy a larger memory card for your camera, be sure to check its specifications to find out which types and sizes of cards it can use.

File Transfer Problems

After you take your digital photos, you'll probably want to get them into your computer. You may have been frustrated by issues such as these:

- Your camera shuts down during transfer.
- You keep copying the same pictures over and over if you don't copy all your pictures at the same time.
- Your pictures all wind up in the same folder, making it hard to find the ones you want.
- You're tired of tying up your camera while you transfer pictures.

The following sections provide solutions for you.

Avoiding Camera-to-Computer File Transfer Problems

If you connect your camera to your computer to transfer your photos, you've probably battled one of these problems:

- **Computer won't recognize camera**—To get the computer and camera to "talk" to each other, select the playback option on your camera.
- **Camera shuts off during transfer**—The culprit is the camera's automatic shutoff feature. You can increase the time before the camera shuts off, but it's often just as easy to gently tap the camera's shutter button periodically during the transfer process.

If you've lost your transfer cable, this would be a great time to opt for a card reader if your computer or printer doesn't have one already. However, if you travel with your digital camera, having a transfer cable makes sharing photos with family and friends easier: just copy the photos to their computers rather than emailing them or burning a CD or DVD.

You could order a replacement from the camera vendor, but be prepared for sticker shock. Before you buy a replacement, check the connector on your camera. If your camera uses a five-pin mini-USB or micro-USB connector, you might already have a suitable cable (five-pin mini USB is used by many external USB devices, and micro USB is used by most Android smartphones). If you have two or more digital cameras that use different cables, look for a multi-headed cable.

Tip

If your digital camera uses a proprietary connector, check third-party sources such as Amazon.com, www.dcables.net, or cablewholesale.com.

Using and Troubleshooting a Card Reader

Instead of running down your camera battery and watching as the action passes you by, transfer your pictures by using a card reader. You can switch memory cards and continue shooting and transfer your pictures later.

Note

If your digital camera needs a firmware update, many vendors require you to use a card reader to copy the firmware file from your computer to your camera.

Although many late-model desktop and laptop computers have card readers, you might have discovered that

- The card reader isn't compatible with your memory card form factor (for example, if your camera uses Compact Flash and your card reader works with SD cards).
- The card reader isn't compatible with SDHC or SDXC cards.
- The card reader can't read your memory cards.

Before you buy a new card reader, though, take a look at your inkjet printer or all-in-one device. The card slots on many of these models aren't just for direct printing: they also double as card readers so you can transfer your pictures.

Tip

If you see an error message such as Insert a disk into ____ after you inserted the media, the card reader might not be working properly. If the card can be read by another reader, the reader you tried first is incompatible or defective and should be replaced.

Wondering if your card reader is working? The easiest way is to insert your card and see if the AutoPlay dialog appears (see Figure 20.24).

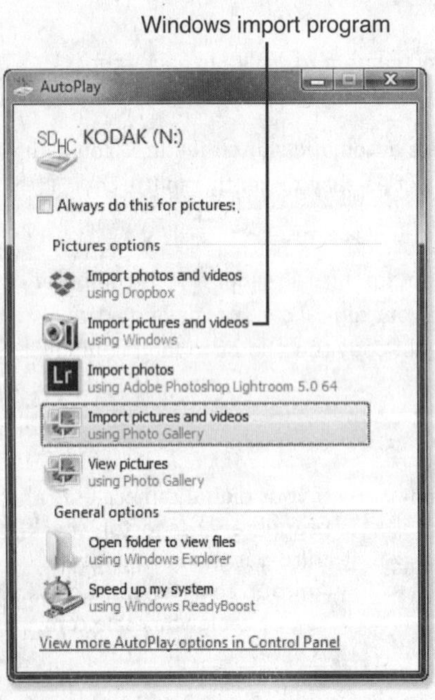

Figure 20.24
A typical AutoPlay menu for a card reader.

Note

You can also use this method to see if your digital camera is recognized by your computer. If the AutoPlay menu does not appear after you set your camera for playback, you might need to install a driver program for your camera.

There are three ways you can connect a card reader to your computer:

- Internal card readers connect to a USB header on your motherboard.
- External readers connect to a USB 2.0 port.
- High-performance external readers connect to a USB 3.0 port.

Figure 20.25 illustrates typical internal and external card readers.

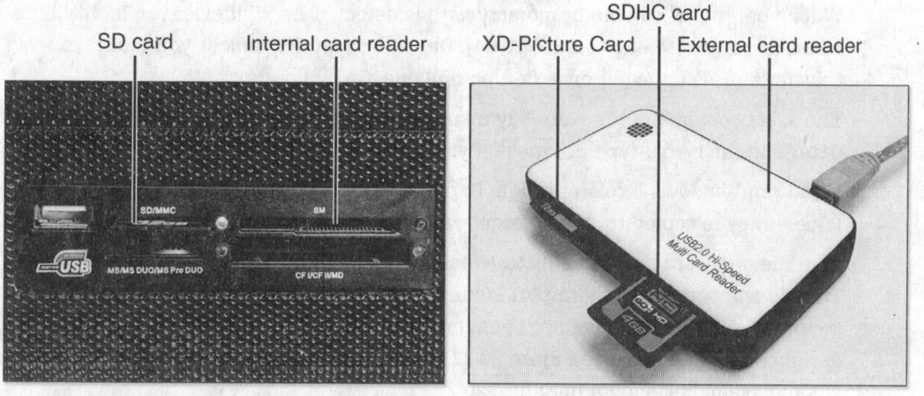

Figure 20.25 Typical multislot internal and external card readers.

I have tried various brands of aftermarket internal card reader-USB port combination devices on several of my desktop computers and have seen most of them fail. Although your results may vary, my experience has convinced me that USB-based external card readers are better. If you have a desktop computer with an internal USB card reader that no longer works, I strongly recommend ignoring it and using an external model instead.

External models are available with support for a single type of card (for example, SD/SDHC/SDXC, Sony MemoryStick, or Compact Flash). I prefer multislot versions because my extended family uses a mixture of memory cards in their cameras. Multislot versions may assign a different drive letter to each card, so you can copy between cards (refer to Figure 20.26), or it may assign one drive letter to the entire reader.

Here's how you can tell which type of multislot card reader you have:

1. If the card reader is already connected, disconnect it.
2. Open Windows Explorer or File Explorer.
3. Note the drive letters shown.
4. Connect the card reader.
5. After Windows recognizes it, note the number of new drive letters. If your reader has multiple slots, but only one additional drive letter is displayed, your reader can use only one card at a time. If you see multiple drive letters, you can use more than one card at a time.

Although USB 2.0 card readers still dominate the market, there are an increasing number of USB 3.0 card readers. USB 3.0 is up to 10 times faster than USB 2.0, and most late-model computers have a mixture of USB 2.0 and USB 3.0 ports.

Even if your current computer lacks USB 3.0 ports, I recommend that you purchase a USB 3.0 card reader. You can plug it into a USB 2.0 port now (it will run at USB 2.0 speeds), but when you have a USB 3.0 port, your card reader will be ready to transfer pictures at much faster speeds.

Better Picture Transfer Without Duplications

When your digital camera or memory card is detected by Windows, you'll typically see an AutoPlay menu displayed (refer to Figure 20.24). Depending on the choices you make, you can make picture transfer a pleasant experience or a painful one.

The exact contents of the AutoPlay menu for a drive depend on the programs installed on your computer and the media type or types on your drive.

If you run Windows Explorer or File Explorer to view your photos, it's up to you to decide which folders they're copied to. If you forget which photos you copied, you could copy them over and over.

Your memory card may have pictures taken at many times and places. If you use the standard Windows import program (Import Pictures and Videos Using Windows—see Figure 20.27), all new pictures (pictures that have not been imported before) are transferred, and any tags you apply are assigned to all photos (see Figure 20.27). To change how folder names are created, you can open the Options menu link shown in Figure 20.26.

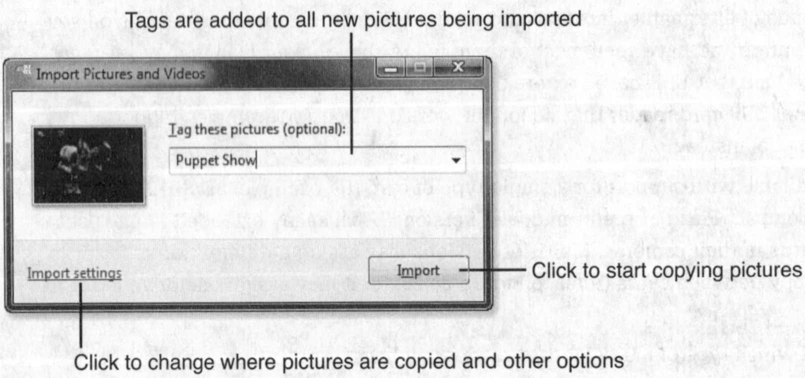

Figure 20.26 Assigning tags to your photos with the Windows built-in import feature.

If you have a photo editing program, its import function might have other options, including the capability to select the photos you want to transfer. That's useful if you use your camera frequently but don't want to erase the card until you've filled it up.

If you don't have a better photo import program already, I recommend the free Microsoft Windows Essentials program (available from http://windows.microsoft.com/en-us/windows-live/essentials). It includes Windows Photo Gallery (which includes import, photo tagging, organizing, and JPEG photo editing) and Movie Maker, as well as other utilities. It works with Windows 7 and Windows 8/8.1.

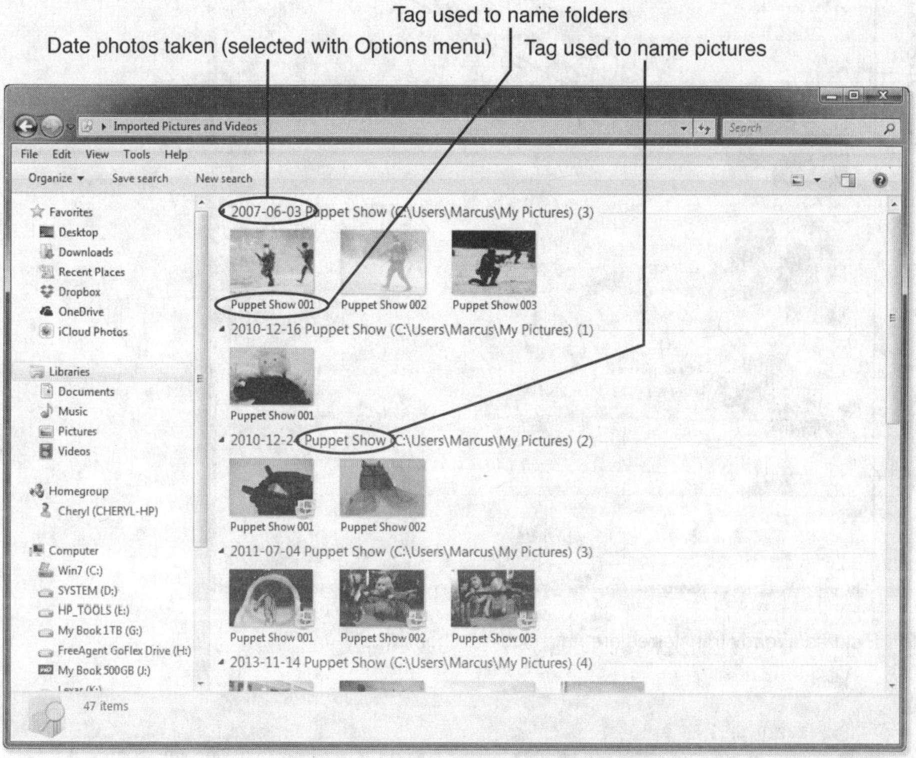

Figure 20.27 The Windows image import program assigns the same tags to all photos.

When you run Windows Photo Gallery's transfer program from AutoPlay, your photos are organized by date and time. You can name each group of photos whatever you like, and the tags you apply to a group apply only to that group (see Figure 20.28). Windows Photo Gallery when used with standard settings will not rename your photos. Windows Photo Gallery does not select already-imported photos by default, but you can select them manually for reimporting.

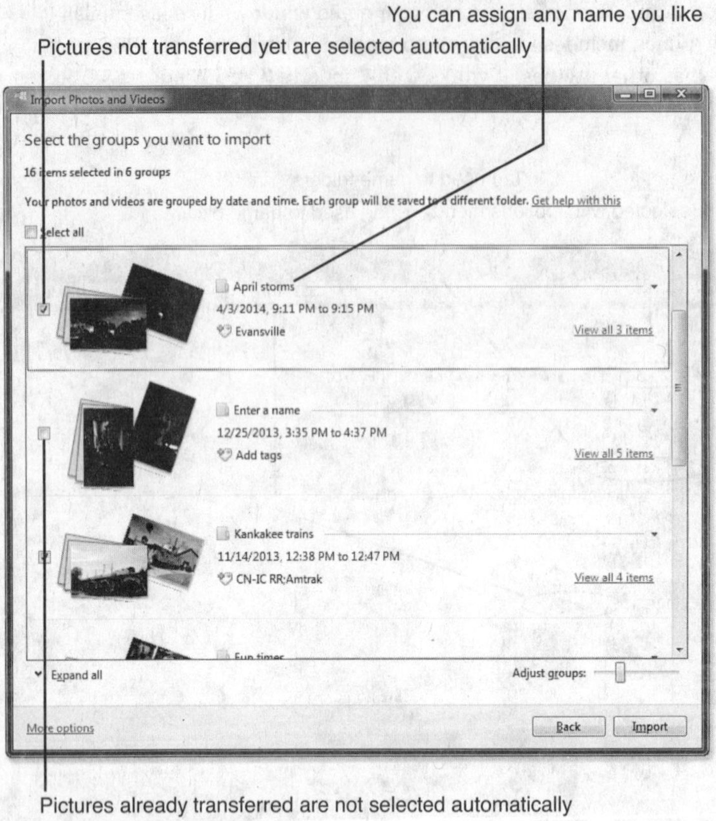

Figure 20.28
Preparing to import photos with Windows Photo Gallery.

Memory Card Problems and Solutions

Almost all digital cameras use flash memory cards for storage, so knowing how to use these cards properly is important. In this section, you'll learn the best ways to prepare a memory card for reuse and what to do if you can't read a card or if you accidentally remove pictures from a card.

Caution

Before you remove a memory card from your camera, make sure you turn off the camera. To remove a memory card from your computer, make sure the card is not being accessed. Following these procedures reduces the possibility of memory card read errors.

Emptying the Contents of a Memory Card

Flash memory cards are designed to be reusable. To do this, you need to remove the photos from the card so you can use it again. There are several ways to do this:

- **Delete the photos after you import them with Windows photo import or Windows Photo Gallery**—If you use this option, you slow down the import process tremendously. And, if you discover that some photos didn't import properly, you would need to use a data recovery program to find them.
- **Delete the photos with Windows Explorer or File Explorer**—You can select all the photos at one time for deletion, but this is slower than using format.
- **Format the card using Windows Explorer or File Explorer**—If you use this option, the camera must re-create the folders it uses for storage (DCIM and subfolders, plus other folders used by the camera).
- **Format the card using your digital camera's format feature**—This is the recommended method; it works quickly, re-creates the necessary folders, and makes sure the card is completely ready for use by the camera.

Tip

To fix any problems with the structure of the memory card, select the low-level format option (if available) when you format your memory card using your camera. If your camera lacks this option, use the Format option in Windows Explorer or File Explorer and clear the Use Quick Format check box. See "Using Format to Solve Disk Errors," p.452, in Chapter 18, "Upgrade and Troubleshoot Storage."

Fixing Data Errors and Recovering Lost Photos

If you are unable to read some or all of the pictures on a card, or if you have accidentally formatted or erased a card, use the data recovery methods discussed in "Recovering 'Lost' Data," p.456, in Chapter 18, "Upgrade and Troubleshoot Storage."

Protecting Your Equipment

Whether you're using or storing your digital camera and accessories, you need to protect your investment in equipment and, even more important, in the photos you've created. Follow these guidelines to help keep your equipment safe.

Protective Filters

You can spend hundreds of dollars on each lens you buy for your digital SLR, mirrorless camera, or smartphone camera, but a few scratches on the front of the lens can turn your investment into junk.

You can protect that investment by using a protective filter (also called a UV filter) on each of your lenses.

How can you get the right size for your lens? The size is listed on the front ring of some lenses or the side of others (see Figure 20.29). Sometimes the front lens cap included with your lens also has the size marking.

To help reduce glare, filters have an anti-reflective coating. The most effective type of coating has two or more layers and is known as multicoating. Multicoated filters reflect light much less than single-coated or uncoated lenses do, which enables your photos to be sharper and have better contrast when direct sunlight enters the lens.

Note

Filters and adapters for Sony QX-100 are available from various vendors, including Amazon.com.

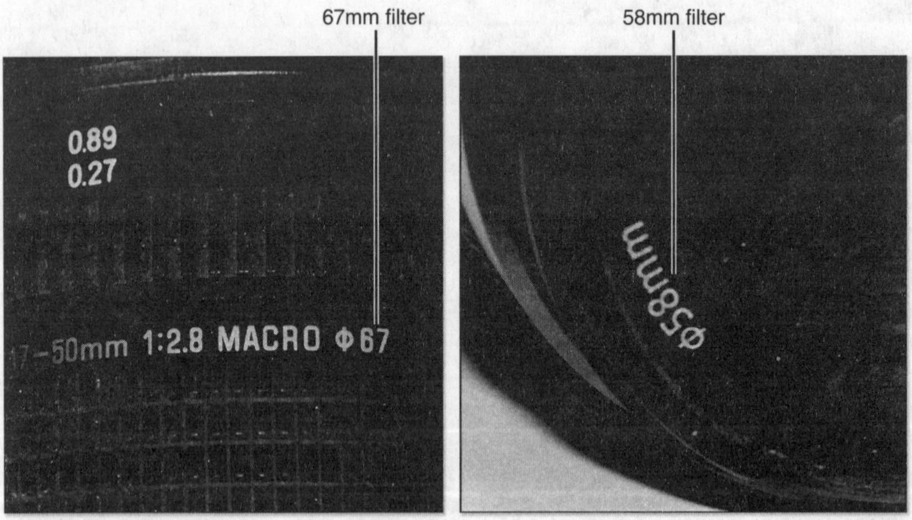

Figure 20.29 Typical filter size markings.

Lens and Body Caps

When you purchase a new digital SLR or mirrorless camera, the lens mount on the camera body is normally protected by a body cap. Remove the body cap to install a lens, but keep the body cap around in case you need to store the body without a lens on it. A camera body without a lens can get dust or spots on the image sensor.

Lenses for your digital SLR or mirrorless camera include a front and rear lens cap. The front lens cap can be snapped over the protective filter or other filters on the front of the lens. The rear lens cap has flanges corresponding to the flanges on the camera body; the rear lens cap is turned to lock it into place.

Changing Lenses

When you change lenses, follow these guidelines to avoid damage to your lenses or your camera:

- Use the rear lens cap from the lens you are installing on the rear of the lens you are removing. Rear lens caps for any lens for the same type of camera body are interchangeable.
- Avoid placing a lens front-end down unless you have a lens cap on it. You could scratch the lens if it has no filter or scratch the filter on the front of the lens.
- Shield the lens opening on your camera body from dust and dirt when a lens is not mounted on the camera.
- Inspect the front and back of your lenses for dust and dirt. Clean them when necessary, as discussed earlier in this chapter.

Cases

Cases are available in a variety of sizes and shapes. To protect your equipment, keep it in a case when you're not using it.

If you want to carry additional lenses or other equipment when you're shooting, look for a case that has room for additional components; is easy to carry; and is easy to access when it's time to switch lenses, memory cards, or cards.

Many users have switched from traditional gadget bags to backpack or sling-type bags. To learn more about the different types of camera bags available, check out vendors such as these:

- **CaseLogic**—www.caselogic.com
- **Domke**—www.tiffen.com/products.html?tablename=domke
- **Lowepro**—www.lowepro.com
- **Tamrac**—www.tamrac.com
- **Vanguard**—www.vanguardworld.com

Lens Compatibility Problems and Solutions

It would be great if you could buy a lens for your camera after trying it on your camera. Unfortunately, with the great decline in brick-and-mortar camera stores and the rise of online and big-box retailers and used sales via eBay, your next lens purchase may be sight unseen. Here are some ways to avoid disappointment as you shop for either new or used lenses.

Checking Model Numbers and Terminologies

Before you can make an intelligent decision about a lens, you need to know the brand, specifications (focal length, aperture, and features), model number, and revision.

Nikon AF Versus AF-S Model Numbers

Nikon digital SLR cameras can use most Nikon-mount lenses manufactured since 1977. However, there are limitations and exceptions. For example, both AF and AF-S lenses are autofocus. AF-S lenses can be used on any Nikon digital SLR but must be used on models that lack a built-in autofocus motor (D40 series, D3XXX series, D5XXX series). These cameras cannot use AF lenses, which use an autofocus motor built in to the camera body.

> **Note**
> For more information on Nikon lens compatibility, see http://www.nikonusa.com/en/Learn-And-Explore/Article/go35b5yp/which-nikkor-lens-type-is-right-for-your-d-slr.html.

Canon Revisions and Lens Types

The revision number indicates changes in the lens design. For example, the (discontinued) Canon 50mm f/1.8 Mark I lens has a metal lens mount, whereas the current Mark II version has a plastic lens mount, making it lighter but less durable.

Canon EF lenses work with both full-frame digital (and all autofocus film) SLRs and with consumer digital SLR models that use smaller image sensors (Canon digital Rebel series, D60, D70, and so on). However, Canon EF-S lenses have a deeper rear lens mount and work only with the Canon DSLR models with smaller image sensors.

> **Note**
> Cameras with smaller-than-35mm film image sensor sizes are often referred to as having an APS-C sensor (this is a now-obsolete consumer film camera size) or as having a "crop" sensor.

What if you're not sure which lenses you can use on your Canon DSLR camera? Check the lens mount on the camera body. If you see a red dot and a white square, your camera can use both EF (red dot) and EF-S (white square) lenses.

Tamron Lens Terminology

Tamron uses many terms as part of its lens model numbers. Understanding these terms can help you choose the lenses that work best for you and your camera. Following are some of the most common:

- **VC**—Lenses with vibration compensation (image stabilization), enabling you to shoot with slower shutter speeds and avoid camera shake.
- **FTM**—Lenses with autofocus and full-time manual focus, enabling manual focus without turning off autofocus.
- **Di**—Lenses compatible with both full-frame and APS-C image sensor sizes.
- **Di-II**—Lenses designed for APS-C (crop) image sensors. Not compatible with full-frame digital SLRs.

- **Di-III**—Lenses designed for mirrorless (compact system) cameras only.

> **Note**
> For more information and additional terms, see www.tamron-usa.com/lenses/technology.asp

Sigma Lens Terminology

Sigma uses many terms as part of its lens model numbers. Understanding these terms can help you choose the lenses that work best for you and your camera. Following are some of the most common:

- **DC**—Lenses designed for APS-C (crop) image sensors. Not compatible with full-frame digital SLRs.
- **DG**—Lenses compatible with both full-frame and APS-C image sensor sizes.
- **DN**—Lenses made for mirrorless (compact system) cameras.
- **OS**—Optically stabilized lenses, so you can shoot with slower shutter speeds and avoid camera shake.
- **HSM**—Lenses with high-speed autofocus motor.
- **APO**—Lenses with two or more elements of special glass designed to minimize chromatic aberration (color fringing).

> **Note**
> For more information and additional terms, see www.sigmaphoto.com/sigma-lens-technology-popup.

Tokina Lens Terminology

Tokina uses many terms as part of its lens model numbers. Understanding these terms can help you choose the lenses that work best for you and your camera. Following are some of the most common:

- **VCM**—Lenses with vibration compensation (image stabilization), enabling you to shoot with slower shutter speeds and avoid camera shake.
- **IF**—Lenses with internal focusing, which enables the lens barrel to stay the same length during focus and have a nonrotating front ring.
- **FC**—Lenses with focus clutch enable you to switch between autofocus and manual focus from the focus ring.
- **FX**—Lenses designed for both full-frame and APS-C (crop) image sensors.
- **DX**—Lenses designed for APS-C (crop) image sensors only.

> **Note**
> For more information and additional terms, see www.tokinalens.com/tokina/technology/.

Lens Re-chipping

Both digital SLR cameras and the lenses they use are computerized, so it's possible to have a situation in which a third-party lens might be mechanically but not electronically compatible with a camera body.

Electronic incompatibility has been a big problem with early Sigma lenses made for Canon EOS film autofocus cameras. Although the EOS (EF) lens mount is mechanically the same for both Canon film and digital SLR cameras, Sigma's original EF-compatible lenses (manufactured up to about 1998) don't work properly with Canon digital SLR cameras. Many of these older lenses are still used.

> **Caution**
> When shopping for used Sigma lenses for Canon autofocus SLR cameras, models identified as for film only will not work with Canon digital SLR cameras.

The most common problem is that the lens will not adjust the aperture (f/stop) when necessary. Some also had problems with incorrect autofocusing. Newer models will work because the electronics have been improved inside the camera lenses.

At one time, Sigma offered re-chipping services for affected lenses. Unfortunately, supplies of these chips have been exhausted because these lenses have not been produced for many years. So, what can you do?

- It is possible to perform a "do-it-yourself" chip replacement. See www.martinmelchior.be/2013/04/conversion-of-old-sigma-lens-to-work.html for the process and parts list.
- If you use your lenses primarily in dim light or indoors (where you'd probably use the lens at its maximum aperture), try shooting in Aperture priority (A or Av mode) and set the aperture to the lenses' maximum aperture.
- Sell these lenses to users still shooting film.

Lens Adapters

If you have a collection of lenses made for 35mm SLR cameras, it is possible to use them with a modern digital SLR. Both Nikon and Pentax autofocus bodies have a high degree of backward compatibility with manual focus lenses.

> **Note**
> For an extensive cross-reference of Pentax camera body and manual and autofocus lens features and compatibility, see www.mosphotos.com/PentaxLensCompatibility.html.

To use manual-focus lenses from these and other vendors (Olympus, Canon FL/FD, and so on) with other autofocus SLRs, you will need specially designed lens adapters.

These adapters are designed to accept the lens as if it's connecting to the original lens mount, and the other end of the adapter is designed to fit into a different camera body.

Lens adapters typically don't support automatic exposure modes and have other limitations. Some include a chip that helps confirm correct manual focus.

The most common sources for adapters designed to enable lenses for one mount to work with another mount are based in China and typically sell through eBay.

Adapters made by the camera vendor to support different camera types, on the other hand, are available from major camera stores. These include Olympus, which makes an adapter for its FourThirds lenses to work with Micro FourThirds mirrorless camera bodies, and Canon, which makes an adapter for its EF lens to fit its EOS-M mirrorless camera bodies.

Installing Firmware Updates

Digital cameras are computers optimized for picture taking. And, just as computers use firmware (software on a chip) to control basic operations, so do digital cameras. Digital SLR and mirrorless cameras have upgradeable firmware, as do some high-end point-and-shoot cameras. Some lenses also have upgradeable firmware.

Why upgrade firmware? To name just a few benefits, upgraded firmware can

- Add features
- Improve connectivity to computers
- Improve shooting performance
- Add support for larger memory cards
- Provide faster electronic viewfinder (EVF) performance
- Improve autofocus
- Improve audio recording in camcorder mode

Firmware updates can be installed in a variety of ways:

- Via a live connection to the Internet via your computer's USB port
- By copying the firmware file to a specially prepared flash memory card
- By copying the firmware file via USB

Before installing a firmware update:

1. Check the current firmware version installed in your camera.
2. Compare the installed firmware version with the latest version.
3. Review the changes in the latest version.
4. Install fully charged batteries in your camera or connect it to an AC adapter.
5. Review the instructions for the update.

Be sure to follow the instructions exactly, and don't shut off your camera until the update is finished.

Note

To find firmware updates for your camera, check your camera vendor's website, or check the DPReview Firmware and Software Updates page at www.dpreview.com/news/category/FirmwareAndSoftwareUpdates.

Battery Failure and Replacement

Battery failure will turn your digital camera into a useless (and expensive) hunk of plastic, metal, and glass. To avoid it, we recommend the following:

- Always have at least one spare fully charged battery or battery set. If you plan to shoot all day, have at least two fully charged spare batteries or battery sets.
- Don't forget your charger! If you travel with your camera, consider buying a universal charger you can carry with you so you don't need to worry about losing your primary charger in a hotel room somewhere. Universal chargers that work on both AC and 12V DC outlets enable you to charge your batteries while you're on the go.
- If your camera or electronic flash uses AA batteries, don't use cheap batteries. Buy top-of-the line alkaline or, for maximum life, lithium batteries.
- If your camera or electronic flash uses AA batteries, consider using rechargeable batteries if the unit supports them.

Note

For more information about battery replacement issues, see "Replacing Your Device's Battery," p.162, in Chapter 6, "Keep Devices Powered Up."

21

HD CAMCORDER AND VIDEO TROUBLESHOOTING

Fast Track to Solutions

Table 21.1 Symptom Table

Symptom	Flowchart or Book Section	Page #
I'm not sure what resolution to use for my video.	Selecting the Best Resolution	558
I'll save space by using a lower quality setting. What will I lose in video quality?	Improving Low Video Quality	560
What recording speed do I need to shoot a sequence in slow motion?	Choosing the Best Recording Speed	561
I'm not sure which type of stabilization to use when I shoot video.	Image Blur Caused by Camera Shake	562
I need more light when I shoot video. What should I use?	Adding Additional Light	563
How do I control my camcorder's microphone?	Adjusting Microphone Gain	566

Video Quality Problems and Solutions

Whether you shoot video with a camcorder, some type of digital camera, a smartphone or tablet, or an action camera, you can have problems with video quality, color, exposure, image blur, and sound. In the following sections, we'll help you find the answers you need.

> **Note**
>
> Understanding camera types:
>
> **Camcorder**—A camera designed to shoot video. It might take still photos, but as a secondary use.
>
> **HD camcorder**—A camcorder that shoots video at 720p, 1080i, or 1080p resolutions.
>
> **4K camcorder**—A camcorder that shoots video at 4K resolutions.
>
> **Digital SLR**—Interchangeable-lens still camera with a fixed or moving mirror inside. Most recent models can also shoot 720p or 1080p video.
>
> **Compact system camera**—Interchangeable-lens still camera that uses an electronic viewfinder or LCD display rather than an optical prism viewfinder. Lighter and smaller than a digital SLR. Almost all models can also shoot 720p or 1080p video.
>
> **Digital camera**—Fixed-lens still camera. Most late-model versions can also shoot 720p or 1080p video.
>
> **Action camcorder (also known as a sport camera or action camera)**—An HD camcorder with an ultra wide-angle (120–180 degree viewing angle) lens. Action cameras are very light in weight, can be mounted to vehicles, helmets, or body harnesses, and are optimized for capturing fast action in a point-of-view mode.
>
> Most action camcorders include support for Wi-Fi (standard or as an option) and can use a smartphone or a tablet to control the camera and show you what the camera lens sees.

Selecting the Best Resolution

The number of pixels (dots) that your camcorder captures is directly related to the quality of your videos. If you shoot video with a higher resolution (more dots), you get better quality video than with a lower resolution.

Devices that shoot video typically offer two or more resolution settings (see Figure 21.1). The tradeoff is higher quality equals shorter recording time. We recommend that you shoot at the highest quality or resolution your camera can produce, especially if you plan to view the recording on an HDTV or use it in a video project. Remember, you can always reduce quality or resolution for specific needs, but you can't restore quality that was lost during the initial recording.

Figure 21.1 shows the resolution selection dialog on a Samsung Galaxy SIII Smartphone.

> **Caution**
>
> The multimedia messaging standard (MMS) video setting available on some smartphones creates very blurry, very low-resolution videos that are suitable for use with messaging services. The resulting video is too poor quality to use in any other way. Refer to Figure 21.2.

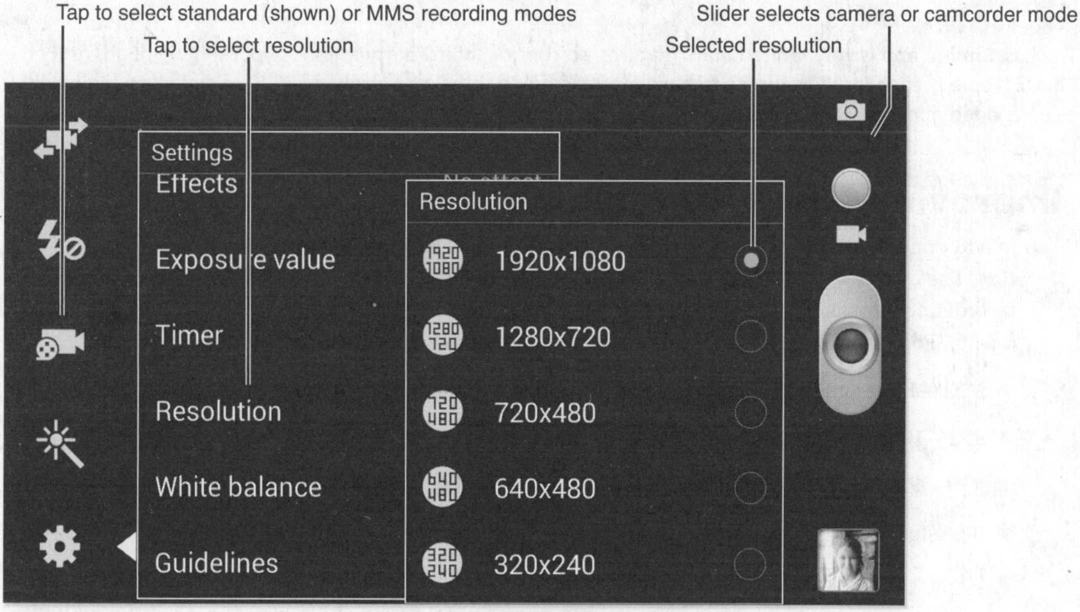

Figure 21.1
Selecting resolution on a Samsung Galaxy SIII Android smartphone.

Figure 21.2 compares a screen grab of video shot at MMS (176x144), 320x240, 720x480, and 1080HD using a Samsung Galaxy SIII smartphone. High-resolution images were adjusted in size to match low-resolution images. As you can see, high-resolution video looks better than lower-resolution video.

Figure 21.2
Details from video shot at different resolutions from MMS to 1080p on a smartphone.

> **Note**
> The iOS Camera app is very limited in its features, so consider third-party apps for your iPhone, iPad, or iPod Touch. Apple is enabling developers to have more access to camera controls in iOS 8, so expect to see better camera/video apps for iOS devices after iOS 8 is released.

Improving Low Video Quality

In addition to resolution, the second factor affecting the sharpness of your video is the quality setting. The quality setting controls the level of compression used to shoot video. On a camcorder, recording quality is usually expressed in terms of bandwidth: the higher the value, the better the quality. For example, on a Canon VIXIA camcorder, bandwidth options include the following:

- **MXP**—High quality, 24Mbps
- **FXP**—High quality, 17Mbps
- **XP+**—High quality, 12Mbps
- **SP**—Standard play, 7Mbps
- **LP**—Long play, 5Mbps

As lower bandwidth (recording quality) selections are made, the amount of space needed to store the recording drops because less detail is stored in the video. Figure 21.3 compares detail from a video recorded at MXP (24Mbps) quality versus LP (5Mbps) quality. The difference in detail and sharpness is obvious.

Less detail (LP quality)

More detail (MXP quality)

Figure 21.3 Video recorded in LP mode doesn't capture fine details of the brickwork and leaves in the way that video recorded in MXP mode does.

On a smartphone, tablet, or digital camera with video capability, different quality settings might be expressed in terms of bandwidth or as superfine, fine, and normal. Superfine provides the highest quality at a selected resolution, but uses more space than fine. Fine provides better quality than normal and uses more space than normal, but is lower quality and uses less space than superfine. Normal provides the lowest quality but uses the least space.

We recommend using the maximum quality setting for recording, particularly if you plan to show the recording on an HDTV or incorporate it into a video project. You can always reduce quality from a maximum-quality recording, but you can't restore lost quality to a recording made at lower quality.

Choosing the Best Recording Speed

Recording speed is another important factor in video quality. Normal recording speeds of 24 or 30 frames per second (fps) can be increased by some video recording apps and devices to 60fps or higher for slow-motion analysis or can be decreased below 24fps for special effects or to save space on the recording media.

With some devices, such as many action cameras, the recording quality and speed settings are grouped into combinations rather than being selected separately.

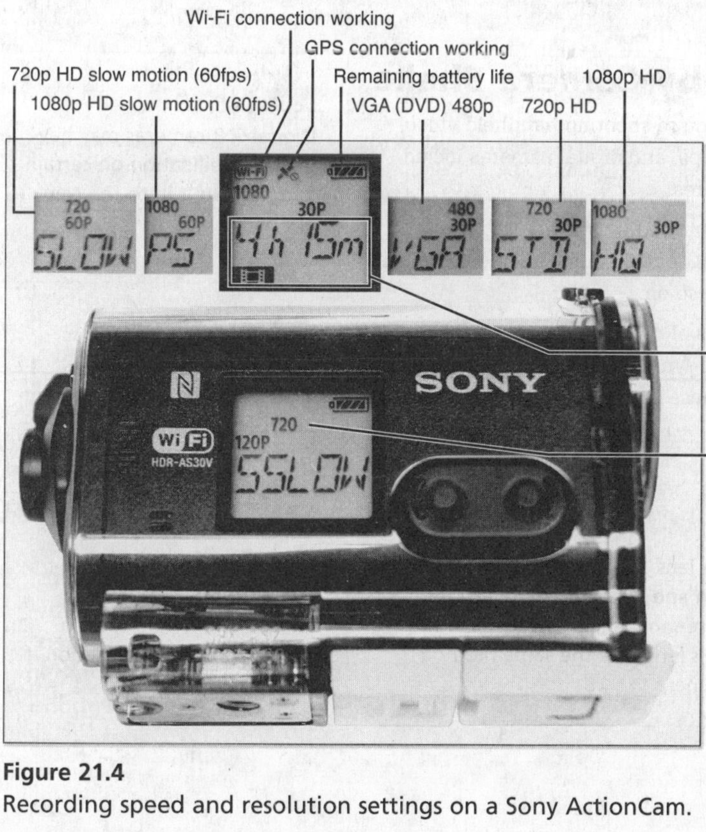

Figure 21.4
Recording speed and resolution settings on a Sony ActionCam.

Improving Color in Your Videos

Most camcorders and camcorder apps provide options for color adjustment, including white balance settings. However, some camera apps support white balance and exposure adjustments only in still-photo mode, not in camcorder mode. The default auto white balance setting can provide good results (varies by lighting and device quality), but for maximum quality under indoor or theater lighting, using the correct white balance preset provides better results. The adjustments (when present) are performed in the same way as white balance adjustments on digital cameras.

> **Note**
> For details, see "Color Problems," p.526, in Chapter 20, "Digital Camera Troubleshooting."

Improving Exposure in Your Videos

Just as with digital cameras and camera apps, camcorders and camcorder apps can be fooled by differences between the lighting on the subject and the lighting of the foreground or background in view of the camera. Many, but not all, camcorders and apps also include exposure EV adjustments to help you shoot better video.

> **Note**
> For details, see "Exposure Problems," p.529, in Chapter 20.

Image Blur Caused by Camera Shake

To help improve results when you're shooting handheld video, many camcorders, camcorder apps, and digital cameras include video (image) stabilization features.

Image stabilization might be identified by a hand icon or a term such as vibration reduction (VR), optical stabilization (OS), image stabilization (IS), antishake, and so on.

Some cameras include two types of image stabilization: single-shot is used for still photos, and dynamic is used for shooting videos. Figure 21.5 illustrates these choices.

> **Note**
> Digital SLR cameras may have image stabilization on certain lenses or built in to the camera body.

> **Note**
> For details, see "Camera Shake," p.532, in Chapter 20, "Digital Camera Troubleshooting."

> **Tip**
> Dust, dirt, water, and fingerprints on a lens can have a big impact on video quality. Use a microfiber cloth and lens fluid (applied to the cloth, not directly to the lens) or pre-moistened lens tissue and a microfiber cloth to clean your device's lens. Use the same method to clean the lens cover on an action camera.

> **Note**
> Use a tripod for maximum image stability. Be sure to turn off image stabilization if you use a tripod.

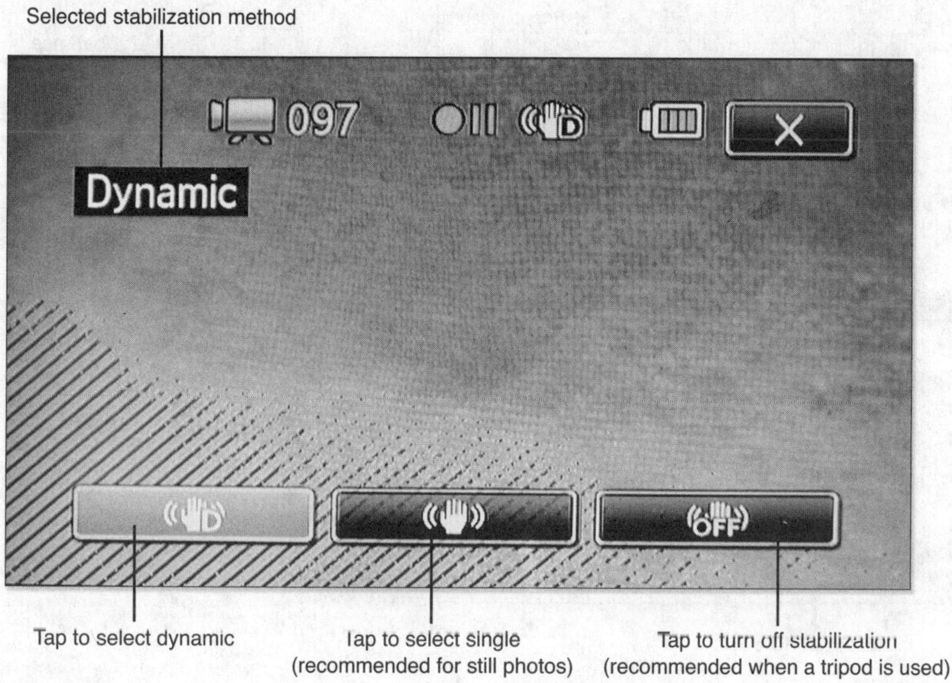

Figure 21.5
Selecting dynamic image stabilization on a Canon HD camcorder.

Adding Additional Light

Some camcorders include a video light you can use in dim light. The light can help you focus or improve exposure. Figure 21.6 illustrates a built-in video light.

If you shoot video with a digital SLR or compact system camera, many third-party vendors make camera video lights that can be attached to the camera's accessory shoe, a light stand, or a tripod (see Figure 21.7). These typically use LED arrays and many are dimmable. Prices start at under $20 U.S.

Caution

Most add-on video lights provide light that mimics daylight (5200–5600K). Some low-cost models recommend that you use a filter over the light to improve the quality of the light. Using a filter reduces the effective amount of light the unit produces. Check reviews before purchasing.

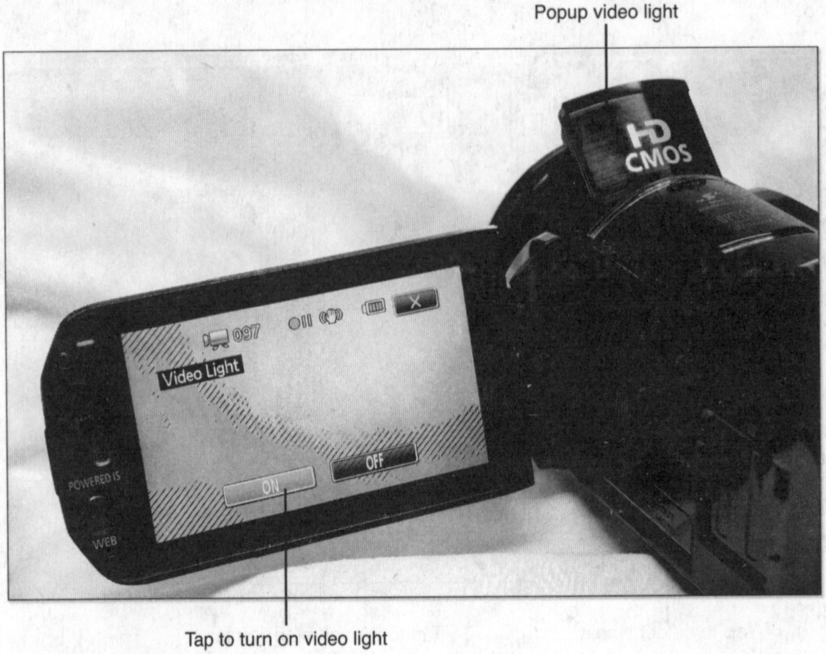

Figure 21.6
Using a built-in video light on a Canon VIXIA camcorder.

Figure 21.7
A typical add-on video light LED array.

Poor-Quality Sound

If you have problems with poor-quality audio recording (muffled audio, pops, wind noise, low volume, and so on) with your camcorder, digital camera, or app, you have a variety of options to help get better audio next time:

- Use an external microphone.
- Adjust the microphone gain.
- Use a wind shield.
- Change the housing on an action camera.

The next sections take a closer look at these solutions.

Using an External Microphone

If your camera or camcorder's autofocus or other mechanisms are too loud in your videos, or your camera's microphone is picking up your breathing instead of your subjects' speaking, check your device's specifications to see if you can connect an external microphone. An external microphone can connect via the stereo input mini-jack found on many camcorders and digital cameras with camcorder features (see Figure 21.8) or a special accessory shoe found on some camcorders.

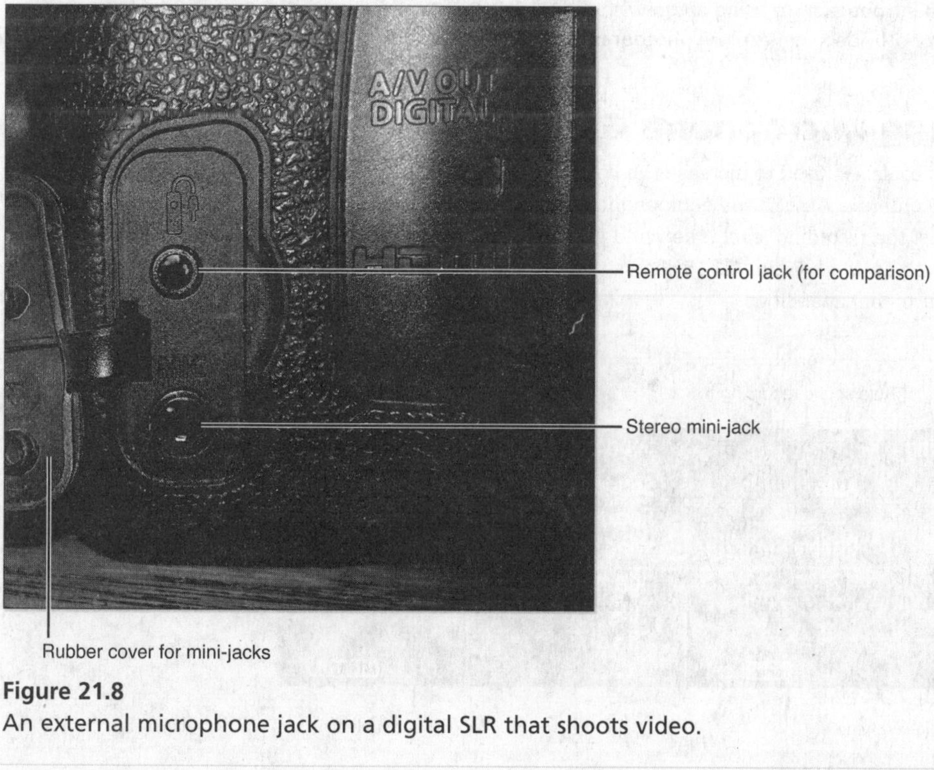

Figure 21.8
An external microphone jack on a digital SLR that shoots video.

A shotgun microphone points in the same direction as the camera to make it easier to pick up distant conversations (see Figure 21.9), whereas a handheld or lapel microphone is good for interviews.

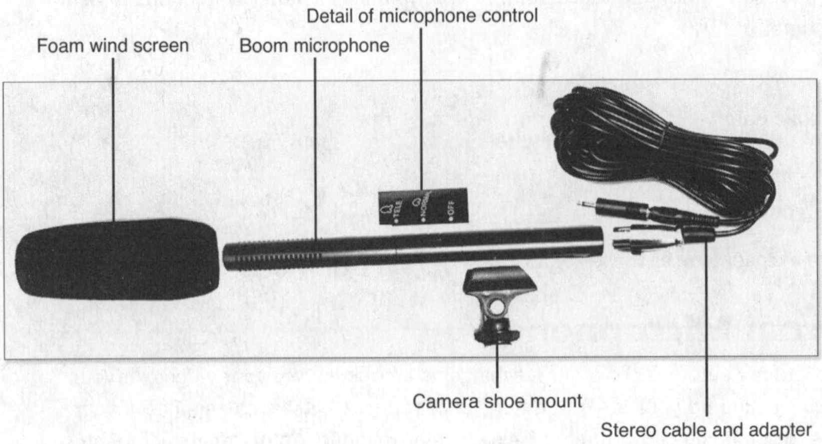

Figure 21.9
A typical shotgun microphone with wind screen.

> **Note**
> For a very good introduction to using audio with digital SLR cameras with camcorder capability, I recommend www.bhphotovideo.com/explora/photography/buying-guide/hdslr-guide-chapter-13-audio

Adjusting Microphone Gain

The gain control is used to increase the volume of recorded audio. The default setting on cameras and camcorders is Auto. If the microphone is picking up too much ambient noise, set it to Manual and adjust the recording level. The Wind Filter setting, when available, reduces low-frequency noises such as wind. Figure 21.10 shows typical Auto and Manual settings for audio on a digital SLR with camcorder capabilities.

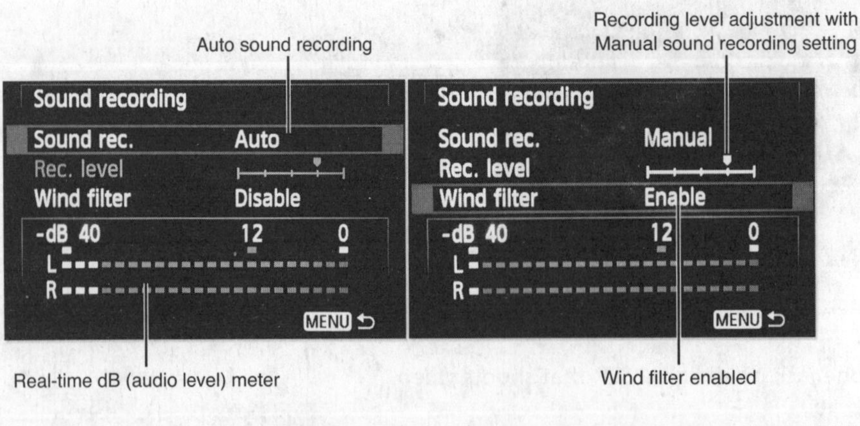

Figure 21.10
Adjusting audio settings on a Canon T3i digital SLR.

Protecting Your Microphone from Wind Noise

A wind shield helps minimize wind noise during audio recording. As you saw in Figure 21.9, a foam wind shield is a common accessory for shotgun microphones. Many other types of microphones also include wind shields, and they can be purchased separately.

You can create a low-cost, effective wind shield for a built-in microphone by using a small piece of fake fur with hook-and-loop (Velcro or equivalent) material. By making the wind shield removable, you can replace it if anything happens to it.

> **Note**
> See http://youtu.be/PpECH4K5eow for an example of how to make your own wind shield.

Removing or Changing Housings on an Action Camera

Most action cameras include a water-resistant housing to protect the camera. However, the housing can interfere with the onboard microphone. If you don't need to use the protective housing on an action camera, remove it. Some models of the GoPro HERO feature an interchangeable protective plate so you can optimize the device for greater water resistance or better audio recording.

Can't Play or Edit Video

Digital video is usually stored in two formats: AVHCD and MP4. If you have problems playing back or editing your video, you can

- Install additional codecs to support your video type.
- Convert to a different file format that is supported by your devices and playback software.
- Install a compatible video editing program. You might have received one with your camcorder or digital video device, but third-party products are widely available.

Popular third-party titles include Adobe Premiere Elements (available alone or bundled with Adobe Photoshop Elements), Corel VideoStudio Pro, Microsoft Photo Gallery/Movie Maker, and Cyberlink PowerDirector.

> **Note**
> Get a trial version of Adobe Premiere Elements from www.adobe.com/downloads.html. Learn more about Corel VideoStudio Pro from www.videostudiopro.com/en/. Download Microsoft Photo Gallery/Movie Maker as part of Windows Essentials from http://windows.microsoft.com/en-us/windows-live/essentials. Learn more about the Cyberlink PowerDirector at www.cyberlink.com/products/creative-director-family/creative-director-family_en_US.html.

Figure 21.11 illustrates Microsoft Movie Maker.

Figure 21.11
Publishing options for a movie clip in Microsoft Movie Maker.

> **Note**
> To learn more about troubleshooting playback issues with videos, see Chapter 5, "Solving Problems with Viewing Your Photos and Videos."

Skipping Frames During Recording

Some camcorders and digital cameras with camcorder capability have built-in flash memory (older DV camcorders used tape). However, flash memory cards (typically SD, SDHC, or SDXC types) are used for primary or additional storage by most consumer camcorders and digital cameras with camcorder functionality.

If you have problems with skipping frames during recording to a flash memory card, the memory card is too slow for continuous recording. Some SD and all SDHC and SDXC cards are marked with a speed class rating. For shooting standard-definition video (720/640x480 resolution or lower), a card with a speed class rating of 2 is sufficient. For shooting 720p HD video, look for cards with a minimum speed class rating of 6. If you shoot 1080p or higher resolutions, look for cards with a speed class rating of 10 or a UHS rating of 1 or higher.

Note

To learn more about memory card speeds and to see card markings, see "Choosing Fast Flash-Memory Cards," p.541, in Chapter 20, "Digital Camera Troubleshooting."

22

iOS TROUBLESHOOTING

Fast Track to Solutions

Table 22.1 Symptom Table

Symptom	Flowchart or Book Section	Page #
I can't receive a phone call.	iPhone Configuration Issues	572
My iPad or iPhone can't connect to cellular data services.	4G Issues	574
My Wi-Fi connection is weak, but my device won't switch to the cellular network.	Wi-Fi Issues	573
I don't want to use the cellular network for some of my apps	Figure 22.1	575
My iOS device isn't responding.	Restarting an iOS Device	577
I changed my home screen layout, but want to change it back to normal.	Resetting iOS Settings to Defaults	578
I want to move my apps and data to a new device.	Backing Up Your iOS Device	579

Symptom	Flowchart or Book Section	Page #
My iOS device is being replaced with a new one. How can I make sure that my information will not be available to my device's new user?	Erasing All Contents and Settings	580
What should I do if my device is not recognized by iTunes?	Restarting Your Device in Recovery Mode	582

Can't Make or Receive Phone Calls

Despite everything else it can do, an iPhone is primarily a cell phone. Problems with cell phone operation can be caused by the following:

- Incorrect phone configuration
- Software updates needed
- SIM card and carrier-related issues

Use the solutions in the following sections to help.

iPhone Configuration Issues

If Do Not Disturb or Call Forwarding is enabled, you cannot receive phone calls. If Airplane Mode is enabled, you can't make phone calls. Change these options through your iPhone's Settings menu.

If you are expecting a call from a phone number that is blocked, you won't be able to receive a call from that number until you unblock it. See http://support.apple.com/kb/HT5845 for details.

iPhone Updates

Check for iOS software updates. These can be made wirelessly or via iTunes. See http://support.apple.com/kb/ht4623 for details.

Cell phone carriers periodically issue updates you need to install. To check for updates, go to the Settings, General, About menus and install any update listed. See http://support.apple.com/kb/HT1970 for details.

Hardware- and Carrier-Related Issues

Make sure your phone's SIM card is properly installed. To do so, remove and reseat it. Details vary by model, so see http://support.apple.com/kb/HT5163 for illustrations and details.

If you are unable to receive or make calls on a phone that supports multiple networks, disable one of the networks and see if you can make and receive calls on the other network.

Check with your carrier for outages or account issues.

iPhone 4/4s-Related Issues

On Verizon-network phones only, update the preferred roaming list (PRL). Dial *228 and select option 2. Your iPhone uses the PRL to identify the cell towers with the best signal.

If you have an iPhone 4 (not 4s) and have not received a free black iPhone 4 Bumper, contact AppleCare, an Apple Retail Store, or your local Apple provider. See http://support.apple.com/kb/HT4389 for contact information. The bumper prevents you from touching the antenna, which is built in to the outer shell of the phone. Third-party cases can also prevent you from touching the antenna.

If you're not sure which model phone you have, look at the model number on the back of the phone. You can then do a web search for the model number for more information.

Can't Connect to a Bluetooth Headset or Keyboard

Bluetooth headsets make hands-free operation of your iPhone or iPod Touch easy and wire-free, and Bluetooth keyboards provide a better typing environment for iPad users. If you are unable to connect, check the following:

- Make sure the Bluetooth device's battery is fully charged.
- Make sure Bluetooth is enabled on your iOS device.
- Make sure your Bluetooth device will work with iOS.

> **Note**
> For more information about troubleshooting Bluetooth connections on iOS, see "Bluetooth Keyboard (iOS)," and "Troubleshooting Problems with Bluetooth Devices," both in Chapter 17, "Troubleshooting Touchscreens, Keyboards, and Mice."

Wi-Fi Issues

If you're worried about exceeding the data allowance for your iPhone or cellular-equipped iPad, Wi-Fi is an excellent alternative to using your cellular network.

If you are unable to connect to a Wi-Fi network, assuming that a Wi-Fi network is available, check the following:

- Make sure Wi-Fi is enabled. If you have enabled Airplane Mode, Wi-Fi, cellular, and Bluetooth connections are disabled. See "Airplane Mode Versus Wi-Fi Mode" in Chapter 3, "Troubleshooting Internet Problems," for details.
- Make sure you know the SSID and encryption key (if necessary) to make the connection.
- If you can choose from multiple SSIDs (as in a hotel, conference center, or large building), use the SSID with the strongest signal.
- As you travel throughout an area using Wi-Fi, it might be necessary to switch to a different SSID with a stronger signal.
- If your device doesn't automatically switch from Wi-Fi to cellular data when the Wi-Fi signal is too weak to use, disable Wi-Fi. This also has the benefit of improving battery life. See "Switching Connection Types Manually" in Chapter 3 for details.

- If you cannot connect in all parts of your home or office, install signal repeaters or replace routers with more antennas. See "Installing and Using a Signal Repeater" in Chapter 3 for details.

4G Issues

Your iPhone or iPad's connection to a 4G network can be affected by many of the same issues that prevent making or receiving phone calls because both telephone and data connections use the cell phone carriers' networks. If you can't get a reliable connection, check the following:

- Make sure Airplane Mode is not enabled.
- Make sure that iOS and carrier service updates are installed.
- Remove and reinstall your device's SIM card.
- Check with your carrier for outages or account issues.

> **Note**
> For more information about these procedures, see "Can't Make or Receive Phone Calls," p.572, this chapter.

FaceTime Issues

FaceTime, which enables voice and video chatting in real-time, can be affected by iOS update issues, device certificate issues, device configuration issues, network issues, and cellular provider limitations. Here's how to keep it working for you:

- Use a Wi-Fi network instead of a cellular network when possible. Although cellular providers in the United States and Canada now support FaceTime over their networks, heavy FaceTime usage could use up smaller data plans.
- To enable FaceTime over cellular, use Settings, Cellular and select Use Cellular Data for FaceTime by moving the slider next to FaceTime (see Figure 22.1).
- Make sure both ends of the connection are using devices with the latest iOS updates.
- Make sure date and time are being set automatically on both ends of the connection (use Settings, General, Date & Time to verify or change time settings).
- If either or both ends of the connection are using Wi-Fi and a firewall program or appliance, make sure the firewall is configured to permit FaceTime traffic. See http://support.apple.com/kb/HT4245 for details.
- If you make changes to your device's configuration, turn it off and back on again.

For more information, see http://support.apple.com/kb/TS3367.

If you want to use FaceTime or other apps on a cellular network, or block them from running when you connect via cellular, here's how:

1. Open **Settings**.
2. Tap **Cellular**.

3. Scroll down the apps list. Each app (including FaceTime) that can use cellular connections lists the amount of bandwidth it has used via cellular connection since the last time the statistics were reset.
4. Use the slider next to an app to disable cellular access; the app can still use your Wi-Fi connection when available.
5. To see when the last time stats were reset, scroll to the bottom of the list.
6. To reset the stats, tap **Reset Statistics** (see Figure 22.1).

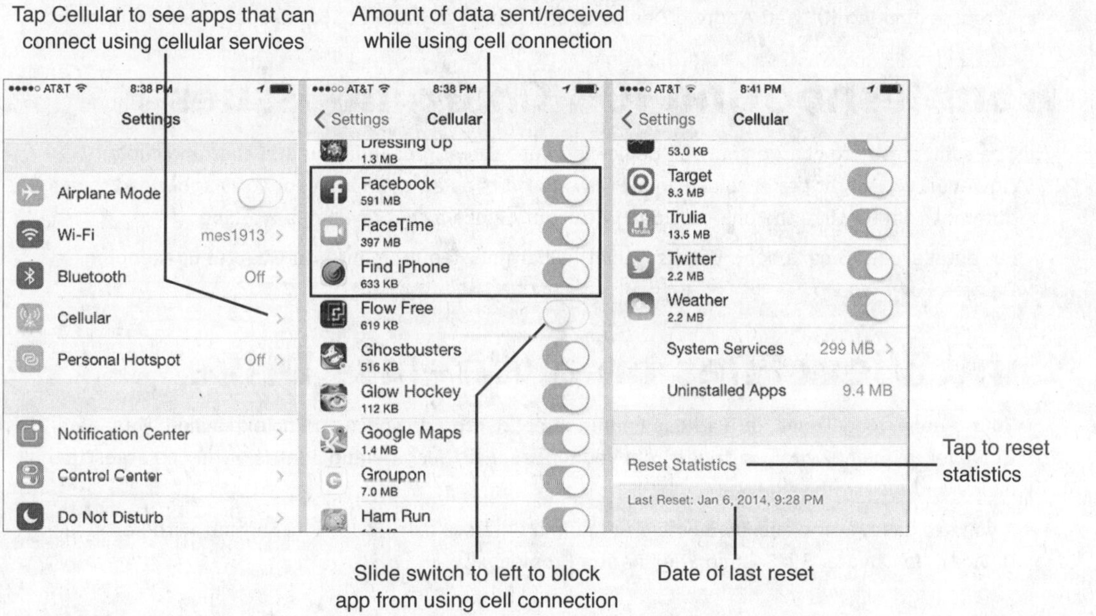

Figure 22.1
Viewing and changing the apps that use cellular connections.

Tip

Reset your statistics monthly (preferably on the same schedule as your cellular billing) to determine if FaceTime over cellular or other cellular-enabled apps threaten to exceed your data plan limits. Disable cellular usage for apps you don't need to use when you're not connected to Wi-Fi.

Can't Print from Your iOS Device

To use a printer with your iOS device, you must have a printer that supports wireless printing, the appropriate client program for your device, and a working network connection. For details, see "Troubleshooting iOS and Android Printer Support" in Chapter 11.

Dealing with an Overheated iOS Device

If your iOS device is overheating, that's not good for the device nor for its battery. To learn some simple ways to help prevent overheating and to deal with an overheated device, see "Troubleshooting iOS and Android Device Overheating" in Chapter 16, "Keeping Devices Cool."

Troubleshooting iOS Charging Issues

The easiest way to charge your iOS device is to use the original adapter and charging cable. However, you might prefer to use your PC's USB ports as an alternative, or you might need to use a different adapter than the one provided with your device if that one stops working.

For details, see "Smartphone Versus Tablet—Charging Requirements" in Chapter 6, "Keeping Devices Powered Up."

Can't View Files on a Wireless Drive

Your iPhone, iPod Touch, or iPad has limited onboard storage space and no expansion slots. However, by using wireless drives from vendors such as Seagate and SanDisk, you can access documents and media files via Wi-Fi.

If you are having problems connecting or using a wireless drive, see "File Sharing with Portable Devices" in Chapter 9, "Solving File Sharing Problems."

Can't Play or Sync Media

Your iOS device can use direct USB or mini-jack connections, Bluetooth, Wi-Fi, or Apple TV to play media on your home theater system.

If you are having problems playing music, see "I Want to Play Music on My iOS Device Through My Receiver" in Chapter 12, "Troubleshooting Home Theater, HDTVs, and Projectors."

If you are having problems playing a movie, see "I Want to Play a Movie on My iOS Device Through My Receiver" in Chapter 12.

If you are having problems syncing your existing music files to an iOS device, see "Troubleshooting Syncing to an iOS Device" in Chapter 12.

Updating Your iOS Device or Apps

One of the first steps recommended by Apple for most iOS problems is updating your device. You can update via Wi-Fi (default setting) or via your cellular network. For details, see "Updating iOS Devices" in Chapter 14, "Keeping Your Devices Updated."

Running Short of Space on Your iOS Device

Unlike Android devices, which usually feature Micro SD expansion slots, Apple's iOS devices have no expandable storage. So, sooner or later, you might run out of space and need to houseclean your device to make room for a must-have app or go-anywhere content.

To learn what's chewing up your capacity and how to give your device some free space, see "Freeing Up Storage Space on Your iOS Device" in Chapter 18, "Upgrading and Troubleshooting Storage Devices."

Stopping Malware in its Tracks

Although Windows-based devices are the most common target for malware attacks, iOS devices need protection, even if for no other reason than to prevent their being used as a means of infection for other devices they connect to.

To learn more about anti-malware apps you can use on your iOS device, see "Preventing and Removing Malware on iOS Devices" in Chapter 4, "Curing Malware and Stopping Scams."

To learn more about third-party browsers that can help protect your system from scams and threats, see "Google Chrome" in Chapter 4.

Troubleshooting an iOS Device That Stops Responding

If an iOS device won't respond when you press the Home button, won't sleep, or is slow to respond to your commands, it's time to take action. To solve problems with an unresponsive device, you can restart it or reset it. Neither of these actions does anything to your information, so they're safe to use.

Restarting an iOS Device

To restart your device, follow these steps:

1. Press and hold down the Sleep/Wake button on the top of the device.
2. When the Slide to Power slider appears, use it to turn off your device.
3. Press and hold the Sleep/Wake button again to restart the device.

Resetting an iOS Device

If you are unable to restart your device, you need to perform a hard reset:

1. Press and hold the Sleep/Wake button and the Home button for at least 10 seconds.
2. Release both buttons when the Apple logo appears.

Resetting iOS Settings to Defaults

Problems with network connections, the custom dictionary, the home screen layout, and location and privacy settings can be solved by resetting these options to their defaults. Here's how:

1. Open **Settings**.
2. Tap **General,** and then scroll down and tap **Reset**.
3. Choose a reset option. To reset the network, dictionary, home screen layout, and location and privacy settings, tap **Reset All Settings**. Or you can choose what to reset (see Figure 22.2).
4. Follow the confirming prompts to finish the process.

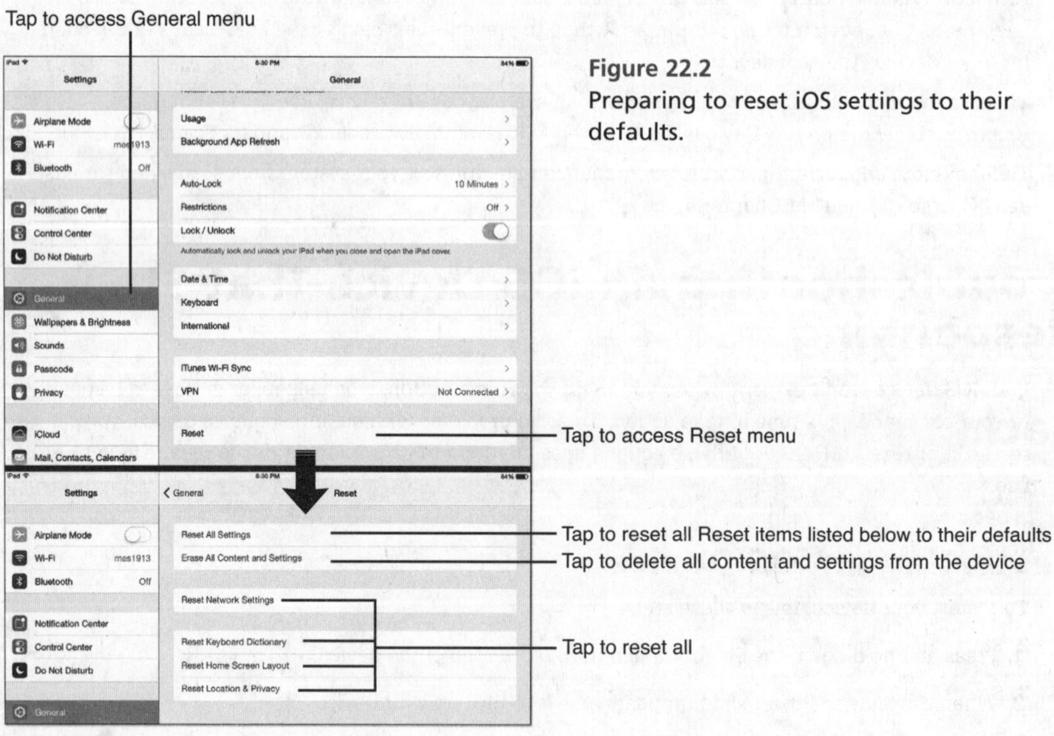

Figure 22.2
Preparing to reset iOS settings to their defaults.

Caution

You will lose the current settings for whatever you reset. For example, if you reset your network settings, you will need to reenter any wireless encryption keys or hidden SSIDs the next time you want to use those networks.

The Erase All Contents and Settings button is also in this menu. It should be used only if you are preparing a device for service, if you need to restore the device from a backup for troubleshooting, or if you are planning to stop using the device. Don't use this option unless you have backed up your device first!

Troubleshooting an iOS Device That Can't Start

If you can't turn on your iOS device, check the following:

Make sure your charger and charging cable are working. Whether you use an original Apple charging cable or one of the innumerable third-party versions, charging cables often fail. Swap cables, plug in your device for at least 20 minutes, and see if it comes on. If it does, your cable was to blame.

If changing cables makes no difference, try connecting your device to a USB port on your computer. A standard USB 2.0 port puts out 500mA, which is enough to charge your iPhone or iPod Touch. If the charge indicator (a lightning bolt through the battery indicator) comes on when the device is plugged into a USB port, but not your charger, it's time to replace your charger.

Note

To see the recommended charging amperage for your device, see "Smartphone Versus Tablet—Charging Requirements" in Chapter 6.

For a step-by-step troubleshooting process, see "Smartphone or Tablet Cable or Charger?" in Chapter 6.

If you want to charge your iPad with your computer, you will need to enable your computer's USB ports to output more amperage than normal. For details, see "Setting Up Your PC's USB Ports for Full-Time Charging Support" in Chapter 6.

Backing Up Your iOS Device

The best way to protect from future problems with your iPhone, iPad, or iPod Touch is to use iTunes to back it up. By doing so, you make it possible to restore your system in case you need to reset it. Here's how.

1. Connect your iOS device to your PC via its USB/charging cable.
2. Start iTunes on your PC.
3. Select your device from the Devices category in the left pane.
4. Tap **Summary**.
5. Tap **This Computer** in the Backups section of the Summary tab.

6. To start the backup, tap **Back Up Now** (see Figure 22.3).

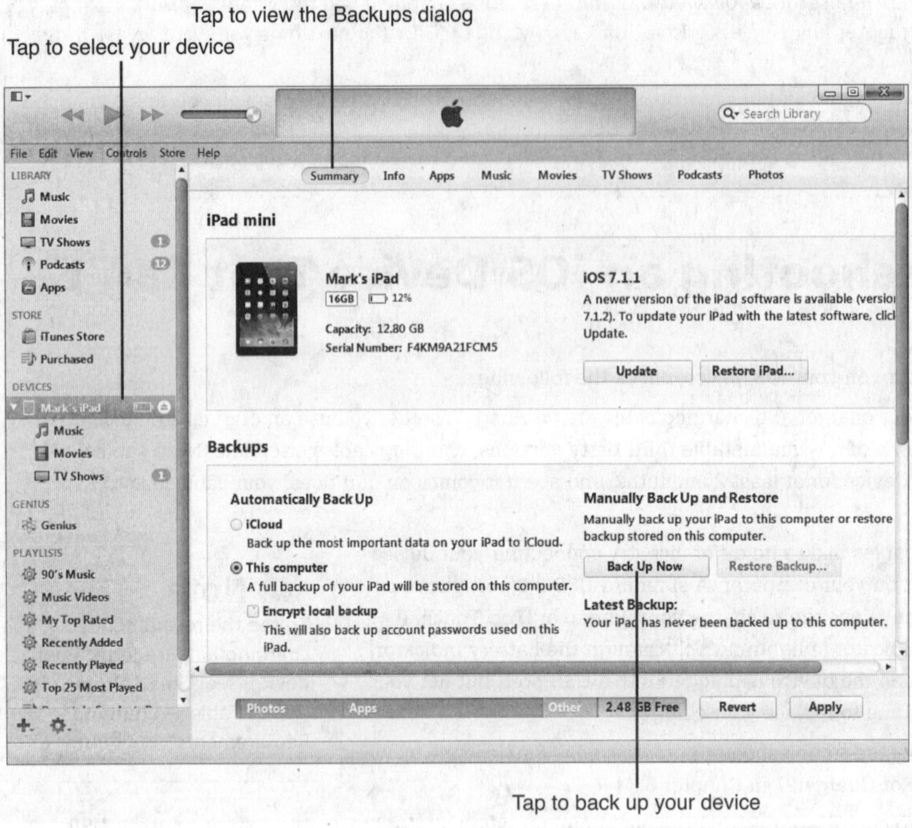

Figure 22.3 Backing up an iPad.

7. If prompted to back up apps that are not in your iTunes library, tap **Back Up Apps.**

8. The backup process runs. At the end of the process, the Latest Backup section of the Summary tab lists the date of the backup.

Erasing All Contents and Settings

If your iOS device stops working, the backup process we described in the previous section becomes very important. Having a recent backup means that you can erase all content and settings from your device and restore them.

The erasing process (without restoring the backup) is also how you prepare an iOS device you no longer plan to keep. Whether you're giving it away, selling it, or recycling it, you don't want your information on it. Here's how to clean it up.

1. Open **Settings**.
2. Tap **General**.
3. Tap **Reset.**
4. Tap **Erase All Contents and Settings** (refer to Figure 22.2).
5. If you use a passcode, enter it when prompted.
6. Tap **Erase** twice when prompted.
7. Enter your Apple ID password and tap **Erase**.
8. The Apple icon with a progress indicator is displayed during the erasure process.
9. When the Apple icon disappears, the process is complete. The device is ready for a new user or to have its contents restored from an iTunes backup.

> **Note**
> For more information about using Erase All Contents and Settings, see http://support.apple.com/kb/HT2110.

Restoring from a Backup

If you use Erase All Files and Settings to reset your iOS device to solve problems, you can use your iTunes backup to restore its contents. You can also move your apps and data from an old iOS device to a new one. Here's how:

1. Connect your device to your PC with the charging cable.
2. Start iTunes.
3. Click your device.
4. On the Welcome to Your New (device) dialog, select **Restore from This Backup**.
5. Click or tap **Continue** to restore from your latest backup (see Figure 22.4).
6. The restore process begins. A progress bar appears along with an estimate of the remaining time for each step.
7. At the end of the restore process, the progress bar disappears. Close iTunes, and your device is ready to use.

If some of your apps are not restored, you can install them manually from iTunes or download them again from the iTunes store.

> **Note**
> You might hear a chime coming from your device during the restore process. The chime repeats periodically until you set up the passcode on your device. Go to the device and enter a passcode. Confirm it when prompted.

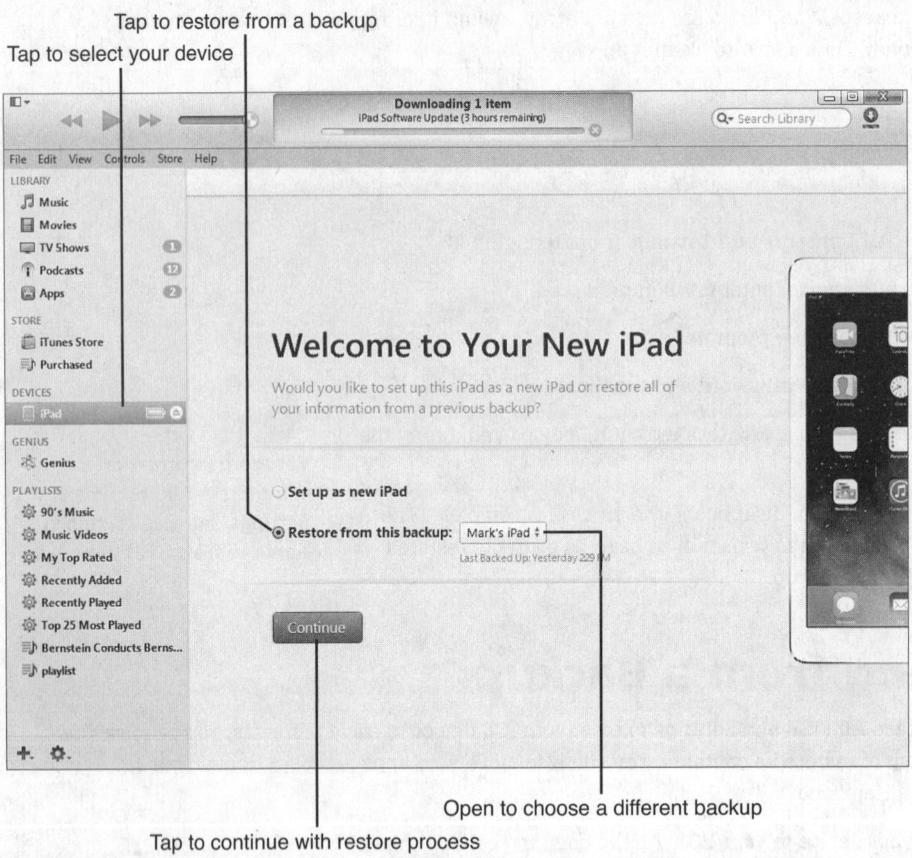

Figure 22.4 Preparing to restore an iPad's contents from an iTunes backup.

Resetting Your Device to Like-New Condition

After you use Erase All Files and Settings, you can use iTunes to set up your device as new. Select **Set Up as New (Device)** from the Welcome to Your New (device) dialog shown in Figure 22.4.

Restarting Your Device in Recovery Mode

Use Recovery Mode if your device is not recognized by iTunes, if iTunes reports that your device is in Recovery Mode, if the Apple logo does not have a progress bar, or if your device tells you to connect to iTunes.

Recovery Mode performs two tasks: it erases your device (similar to Erase All Files and Settings) and restores your device to like-new condition. You can then restore your latest iTunes or iCloud backup to it.

If you need to run Recovery Mode, follow these steps:

1. Turn off your device. Press the Sleep/Wake and Home buttons at the same time, and in a few seconds, your device will turn off.
2. If your device is connected to your computer with your charging cable, unplug the cable from your device. Leave the cable plugged into your computer's USB port.
3. Hold down the Home button on your device while you plug the charging cable into it. Do not release the Home button until the Apple logo is replaced by the iTunes logo and charging cable image (see http://support.apple.com/kb/HT1808 for an illustration of this image and more details).
4. When iTunes opens, it displays a dialog indicating that your device is in Recovery Mode. Click **OK** to run the restore process.

23

ANDROID TROUBLESHOOTING

Fast Track to Solutions

Table 23.1 Symptom Table

Symptom	Flowchart or Book Section	Page #
I have an "Process com. Android.Phone Has Stopped Unexpectedly" error message.	Can't Make or Receive Phone Calls	586
I need help connecting a Bluetooth device.	Can't Connect to a Bluetooth Device	586
I'm having problems using Wi-Fi.	Wi-Fi Issues	587
My device is not working correctly. What should I do?	Performing a Factory Reset/Restore	590
I want to make sure I back up everything before I do a factory reset.	Backing Up Your Android Device's Data	589

Can't Make or Receive Phone Calls

Android smartphones depend on the com.Android.Phone process for making telephone calls and connecting to 4G cellular data services. If you see this error message: Process com.Android.Phone Has Stopped Unexpectedly, follow these steps until you reach a solution:

1. If you see this error after installing a new app or installing an app update, uninstall the app. If the error no longer occurs, don't reinstall the app until an updated version is available.
2. Check for an update for your phone. The update might come from the vendor's website or be listed in Settings.
3. If an update is available, install it. If the error reappears, go to step 4.
4. If no app was installed or updated, and if no phone updates are available, check the battery. If the battery won't hold a charge, replace it.
5. If the problem recurs, power down your smartphone.
6. Remove its battery.
7. Remove its microSD card.
8. Remove its SIM card.
9. Wait a minute or two, reinstall the battery, microSD card, and SIM card and power it back up again.
10. If the error message occurs again, perform a factory reset (see "Performing a Factory Reset/Restore" later in this chapter page 590). If the problem persists, the phone needs to be serviced.

Tip

The androidforums.com website is an excellent resource for Android troubleshooting.

Can't Connect to a Bluetooth Device

Bluetooth headsets make hands-free operation of your Android smartphone easy and wire free, and Bluetooth keyboards and mice provide a better input environment for Android tablet users. If you are unable to connect, check the following:

- Make sure the Bluetooth device's battery is fully charged.
- Make sure Bluetooth is enabled on your Android device.
- Make sure your Bluetooth device will work with Android.

Note

For more information about troubleshooting Bluetooth connections on Android, see "Bluetooth Mouse (Android)," "Bluetooth Keyboard (Android)," and "Troubleshooting Problems with Bluetooth Devices," all in Chapter 17, "Troubleshooting Touchscreens, Keyboards, and Mice."

Wi-Fi Issues

If you're worried about exceeding the data allowance for your Android smartphone or cellular-equipped Android tablet, Wi-Fi is an excellent alternative to using your cellular network.

If you are unable to connect to a Wi-Fi network, assuming one is available, check the following:

- Make sure Wi-Fi is enabled. If you have enabled Airplane Mode, Wi-Fi and cellular and Bluetooth connections are disabled. See "Airplane Mode Versus Wi-Fi Mode," Chapter 3, "Troubleshooting Internet Problems," for details.
- Make sure you know the SSID and encryption key (if necessary) to make the connection.
- If you can choose from multiple SSIDs (as in a hotel, conference center, or large building), use the SSID with the strongest signal. An app such as the free Wi-Fi Analyzer can help you choose the best SSID. To learn more about using Wi-Fi Analyzer, see "Solving Signal Strength Problems," in Chapter 3, "Troubleshooting Internet Problems."
- As you travel throughout an area using Wi-Fi, it might be necessary to switch to a different SSID with a stronger signal.
- If your device doesn't automatically switch from Wi-Fi to cellular data when the Wi-Fi signal is too weak to use, disable Wi-Fi. This also has the benefit of improving battery life. See "Switching Connection Types Manually," Chapter 3, for details.
- If you cannot connect in all parts of your home or office, install signal repeaters or replace routers with more antennas. See "Installing and Using a Signal Repeater," Chapter 3, for details.

Can't Print from Your Android Device

To use a printer with your Android device, you must have a printer that supports wireless printing, the appropriate client program for your device, and a working network connection. For details, see "Troubleshooting iOS and Android Printer Support" in Chapter 11, "Troubleshooting Printing."

Dealing with an Overheated Android Device

If your Android device is overheating, that's not good for the device or its battery. To learn some simple ways to help prevent overheating and to deal with an overheated device, see "Troubleshooting iOS and Android Device Overheating" in Chapter 16, "Keeping Devices Cool."

Troubleshooting Android Charging Issues

If your Android device is charging slowly or won't charge at all, the problem could be caused by a faulty charger, charging cable, or using a connection that doesn't provide enough amperage for the device's power requirements.

To see the recommended charging amperage for your device, see "Smartphone Versus Tablet—Charging Requirements," in Chapter 6. To determine whether the charging cable or charger is at fault, see "Smartphone or Tablet Cable or Charger?" in Chapter 6, "Keeping Devices Powered Up."

Can't View Files on a Wireless Drive

Most Android devices have Micro-SD expansion slots and a few have USB ports. However, you can access large amounts of information wirelessly, and by using wireless drives from vendors such as Seagate and SanDisk you can access documents and media files via Wi-Fi.

If you are having problems connecting or using a wireless drive, see "File Sharing with Portable Devices," in Chapter 9, "Solving File Sharing Problems."

Can't Play or Sync Media

Your Android device can use direct USB or mini-jack connections, Bluetooth, Wi-Fi, or streaming media devices to play media on your home theater system.

If you are having problems playing music, see "I Want to Play Music on My Android Device Through a Home Theater System" in Chapter 12, "Troubleshooting Home Theater, HDTVs, and Projectors."

If you are having problems playing a movie, see "I Want to Play a Movie on My Android Device Through a Home Theater System" in Chapter 12.

If you are having problems syncing your existing media, see "Troubleshooting Syncing to an Android Device" in Chapter 12.

Updating Your Android Device or Apps

Want to solve problems with your Android device? Want better-behaved Android apps? Understanding how to keep your Android device and apps updated is a big part of the answer. You can update via Wi-Fi or via your cellular network. For details, see "Updating Android Devices" in Chapter 14, "Keeping Your Devices Updated."

Running Short of Space on Your Android Device

Unlike iOS devices, most Android devices have expandable storage, thanks to Micro SD card slots. However, your device won't use the card automatically: you need to specify which apps can be stored there and what types of files the card can use. To learn how, see "Freeing Up Storage Space on Your Android Device" in Chapter 18, "Upgrading and Troubleshooting Storage Devices."

Preventing Malware Attacks

Android devices are common enough that they've become popular malware targets, and part of the problem is that the Google Play store doesn't do a good enough job of stopping infected apps from being distributed there. So, if you want to stop malware on your Android, it's up to you. For anti-malware app features to look for, see "Preventing and Removing Malware on Android Devices" in Chapter 4, "Curing Malware and Stopping Scams."

Backing Up Your Android Device's Data

Google's automatic backup does not back up everything on your Android device (see http://www.howtogeek.com/140376/htg-explains-what-android-data-is-backed-up-automatically/) for a list of what Google does, and does not, back up automatically. If you use non-Google email services and contacts and other content not listed as being backed up by Google's automatic backup, use an additional backup program. Many free and low-cost backup programs are available from Google Play. Some device vendors also offer their own backup utilities, such as Samsung's Kies and Kies 3.

If you decide to use a third-party backup program, be sure to install and use it to make a backup before performing a factory reset.

When using a backup program, be sure to select all items to back up on both your device's built-in storage and the device's micro-SD card (if installed),

Figure 23.1 illustrates the process of backing up a Samsung Android smartphone with Samsung's Kies 3 app.

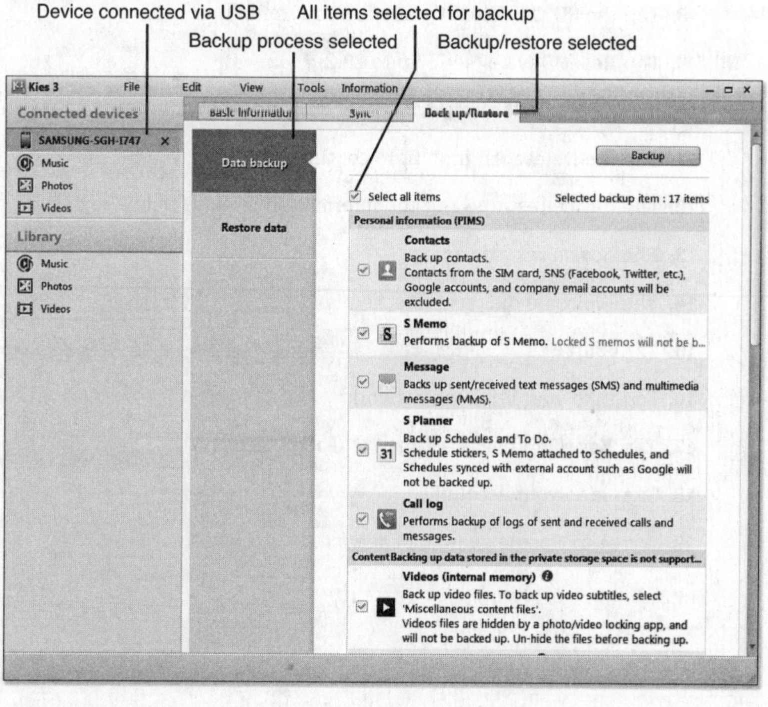

Figure 23.1
Using the Samsung Kies 3 app to back up a Samsung smartphone.

Performing a Factory Reset/Restore

A factory reset returns your Android device to "out of the box" condition. It deletes all user data and settings. However, the version of Android running on your device remains the same as it was before the factory reset.

Use a factory reset as a last resort before servicing a device or when you're ready to sell, give away, or scrap your device.

Here's how to perform a factory reset from the Android Settings menu:

1. Run your preferred third-party backup app (refer to Figure 23.1), selecting all items for backup.
2. Open **Settings**.
3. Navigate to Backup Options, Backup and Reset (recent Android versions) or Privacy, Backup and Reset (older Android versions).
4. If you want to restore your information after running Factory Reset, make sure that **Back Up My Data** and **Automatic Restore** are checked.
5. Make sure you have the password for the Backup Account email address listed.
6. Tap **Factory Data Reset** to continue.
7. Scroll down to the bottom of the accounts list.
8. Tap the SD Card box if you want to format your card.
9. Tap **Reset Device** (see Figure 23.2).
10. If you use a PIN to restrict access to your system, enter it when prompted.
11. Tap the **Delete All** prompt to continue.
12. The device restarts, and the information on your phone is deleted.
13. The device restarts again.
14. The Welcome dialog appears.
15. Tap **Start**.
16. Log in to your wireless network.
17. Tap **Yes** (if you have a Gmail or Google account).
18. Sign in to your account.
19. Agree to Google's terms of service.

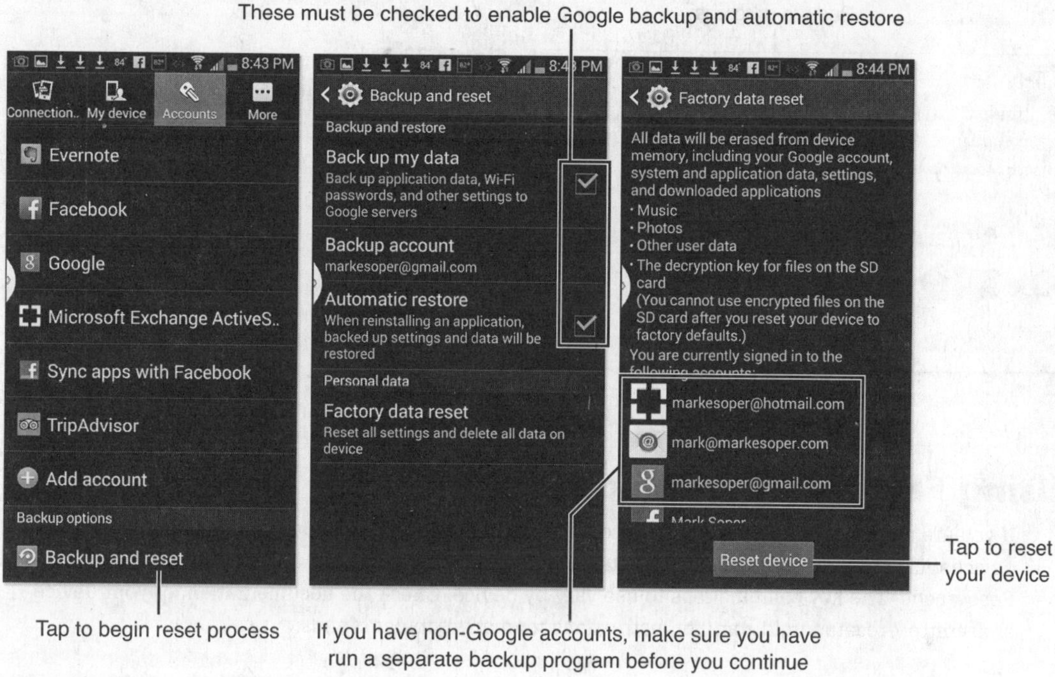

Figure 23.2
Preparing to reset an Android smartphone.

20. Google services such as Backup, Location, and Communication are pre-selected. Use the right-arrow button onscreen to click through.

21. The restore process starts.

22. Confirm your name. Use the right-arrow button onscreen to click through.

23. Tap **Finish**.

24. Your device connects automatically to the Google Play Store to reinstall apps you previously downloaded/purchased there.

25. If you made a backup with another app, you can restore it now (see Figure 23.3).

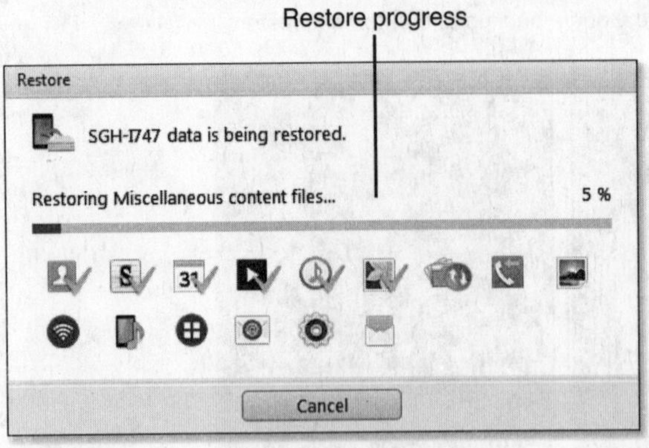

Figure 23.3
Restoring data using Kies 3.

Using Factory Reset Mode

If you are unable to start the Factory Reset process from your Android device (for example, if your device will not start properly), you can start Factory Reset by powering up your device in Factory Reset mode. The key combinations to use vary by device. Check the documentation for your device, or see http://resetandroid.com/ for instructions for many popular brands.

24

TROUBLESHOOTING FLOWCHARTS

Troubleshooting Methodology

If you don't service technology devices for a living, it might seem scary to talk about the troubleshooting process. But, believe me, it's worth the effort to follow a process that can find problems in a hurry, whether you earn your living at it or just want to save a few bucks and be the hero of your office or home.

To become a successful troubleshooter, you need to:

- Learn as much as you can about what went wrong.
- Evaluate the environment where the computer problem took place.
- Use testing and reporting software to gather information about the system.
- Form a hypothesis about the nature of the problem and how to resolve it (a theory you will try to prove or disprove).
- Use the troubleshooting cycle to isolate and solve the problem.

The First Step—Finding Out What Happened

Whether you're troubleshooting your own computers or helping out a co-worker, a friend, your spouse, your kids, or your parents with a computer problem, the first task is to find out *what happened*. Unless you know what was happening when the problem first showed up, you're going to have a very hard time finding and solving the problem.

Here's what you need to find out—or remember:

- What software was being used?
- What hardware was being used?
- What error messages were displayed?
- What was the computer user working on?
- What type of environment (electrical and otherwise) was in the work area at the time of the problem?

Using the preceding questions, you want to find the answer to this question: "What changed since the last time it worked?" Let's look at the first question from the list: What software was being used? You want to find out the following:

- **The name of the program and the version**—Restart the program and click Help, About to see this information.
- **The operating system**—Open the Windows Device Manager or the Settings menu on a mobile device to see this information.
- **Any other programs that were also in use at the time.**

The second question, What hardware was being used? should reveal what add-on hardware (printer, scanner, DVD burner, network) was in use.

The third question is simple: What error messages were displayed? You might need to try to reproduce the problem to display a complex error message such as a Blue Screen of Death.

The fourth question, What was the user working on? is designed to determine the specifics of the task. For example, trying to print a multipage document with lots of graphics to a laser printer is a different task than printing a single-page letter to the same printer or to a different printer. You should also find out what programs the user was running because some programs might conflict with others running at the same time.

Sometimes, after you learn the answers to these questions, the solution to the problem will jump out at you. But sometimes, you'll need to look around your computer space (if it's your problem) or go to the problem's central location, put on your deerstalker cap, and play detective.

How to Check Out the Computing Environment

Even if you're trying to solve a problem with your own computer, and especially if you're assisting somebody else, you need to find out some facts about the environment where the computer is located.

What kinds of information are you looking for? Use Table 24.1 to provide a quick checklist of what to take with you or what you'll need access to, depending on what you learned from your initial questions.

Table 24.1 Troubleshooting Tests and Requirements

Test	Requires
Power	Multimeter, circuit tester
BIOS beep and error codes	List of BIOS codes from system documentation
Printer self-test	Printer and paper
Windows logs	Run Manage Windows
Hardware and software installed	System information

Which test or diagnostic routine is the best one to start with? Before you perform any specific tests, review the clues you got asking the initial questions. For example, if you found out that you could print simple documents to a laser printer with Microsoft Word, but you had problems printing graphics-rich publications with Adobe Reader, the problem isn't with Windows (which controls the printer), and probably not with the printer, but it could be with the documents themselves. To learn more about the printer, you should use the printer's self-test.

A laser printer's self-test usually indicates the amount of RAM onboard, emulation (HP or PostScript), and firmware revisions. The amount of RAM onboard is critical because laser printers are page printers: The whole page must fit into the laser printer's RAM to be printed.

Thus, there are two variables to this printing problem: the amount of RAM in the printer and the size of the document. If, for example, the self-test reveals the printer has only the standard amount of RAM onboard, then it's adequate for text, but an elaborate page can overload it. If a look at the document reveals that it has a large amount of graphic content, you're likely to have problems. There are two easy solutions to this type of problem:

- Add more memory to the printer.
- Reduce the graphics resolution.

It's easier (and cheaper!) to reduce the graphics resolution to see whether the documents will print. If this works, you can check with a memory vendor for a printer memory upgrade if you need the full graphics quality or print documents using reduced resolution.

On the other hand, if the problem you're experiencing centers around the computer locking up frequently (and randomly), you'd want to check the electrical power. The first step here is to see whether the power the computer uses is good. A low-cost wall outlet analyzer is a useful tool. This device has signal lights indicating whether the wiring is correct or if faults exist with grounding, reversed polarity, and the like. Random lockups, crashes, and other types of mysterious computer problems can be traced to bad power. If the problem happens only after the computer's been on for a while, it's time to look at the computer's hardware monitor to check the internal temperature or voltage settings. They system could be overheating.

Conversely, if the system locks up only when you're using a specific application, it's more than likely that the problem is with the application and not your computer. In that case you should check the application vendor's website to see whether it's a common problem and if a patch is available to fix it.

Your Diagnostics Toolbox

If you like to be prepared for any computing disaster, it's helpful to have the tools you need ready at all times. Here are the tools I recommend:

- Hex drivers
- Phillips and straight-blade screwdrivers
- Torx drivers
- 3-claw parts retrieval tool
- Hemostat clamps
- Needle-nose pliers
- Eyebrow tweezers
- Penlight and magnifier

For diagnosing power issues and working safely with equipment, I recommend you have the following:

- An AC/DC multimeter with Ohm and Continuity options
- A grounded AC circuit tester
- An antistatic mat and wrist strap

Any set of cleaning and maintenance tools should include these:

- Compressed air
- Keyboard key puller
- Computer-rated minivacuum cleaner
- Wire cutter and stripper
- Extra case, card, and drive screws (salvage or new)
- Extra card slot covers (salvage or new)
- Antistatic cleaning wipes and spray

Replacement cables should include the following:

- SATA data cable
- Molex to SATA power adapter
- USB 2.0 standard, mini, and micro
- USB 3.0 standard, mini
- HDMI

- VGA
- Extra card slot covers (salvage or new)
- Antistatic cleaning wipes and spray

If you think that you might need to reinstall or repair Windows, you'll need:

- The original operating system disc **or**
- A repair disc for that version of Windows

For solving problems with mobile devices, you should also have:

- A microSD card for making backups
- Tools for opening iOS devices and removing their SIM cards

Use these tools to help you perform the steps you need to follow during the troubleshooting cycle.

The Troubleshooting Cycle

The troubleshooting cycle is a method that you can use to determine exactly what part of a complex system, such as a computer, is causing the problem.

The first step, as we've seen previously, is to determine the most likely source of the problem. The questions you ask the user (or yourself) will help determine which subsystem is the best place to start in solving the problem. In the previous example, the printing subsystem was the most likely place to start.

To help you focus on the likely cause for a computer problem, use the Symptoms Table at the beginning of each chapter to look up the most likely solutions for the symptoms of the computer problem. Follow the recommendations, and you're on the road to the solution.

Sometimes, you might discover that a particular symptom seems ambiguous: it points to more than one possible solution. In cases like this, it's helpful to realize that any computer is a collection of subsystems. What's a subsystem?

A subsystem is the combination of components designed to effect a particular task, and it can include both hardware and software components. Use Table 24.2 to better understand the nature of the subsystems found in any computer.

Table 24.2 Computer and Peripheral Subsystems and Their Components

	Components		
Subsystem	*Hardware*	*Software*	*Firmware*
Printing	Printer, cable, parallel or serial port	Printer driver in Windows, Application	BIOS configuration of port

	Components		
Subsystem	*Hardware*	*Software*	*Firmware*
Display	Graphics card, monitor, cables, port type, cables, motherboard (integrated video)	Video drivers in Windows	Video BIOS, BIOS configuration of video type, boot priority
Audio	Sound card, speakers, cables, motherboard (integrated audio)	Audio drivers in Windows	BIOS configuration of integrated audio
Mouse and Pointing Device	Mouse or pointing device, serial or mouse port, USB port	Mouse driver in Windows	BIOS port configuration, USB legacy configuration
Keyboard	PS/2 or USB port	Keyboard driver in Windows	BIOS keyboard configuration, USB legacy configuration
Storage	Drives, data cables, power connectors, USB, IEEE-1394 cards or built-in ports	Storage drivers in Windows	BIOS drive configuration, BIOS configuration of built-in USB or other ports
Power	Power supply, splitters, fans	Power-management software (Windows)	BIOS power-management configuration
CPU	CPU, motherboard	System devices	BIOS cache and CPU configuration
RAM	RAM, motherboard	(none)	BIOS RAM configuration
Network	NIC, motherboard, USB port (for USB devices)	Network configuration files and drivers	BIOS PnP and power management, BIOS configuration of integrated network port or USB port
Modem	Modem, motherboard or serial port or USB port	Modem drivers, application	BIOS PnP, power management, BIOS port configuration

You can see from this list that virtually every subsystem in the computer has hardware, software, and firmware components. A thorough troubleshooting process will take into account both the subsystem and all its components.

As you use the Symptoms Table in each chapter and the flowcharts, keep the subsystems inside your computer in mind. The flowcharts and chapter write-ups are designed to cover the different components of each subsystem. However, in some cases, you might need to check more than one subsystem to find the solutions you're looking for.

Testing a Subsystem

Whether you troubleshoot to save money or to make money, and whether you're operating on your own computer or a friend's, you should take the computer user's version of the Hippocratic oath: "First, do no harm (to the computer)."

Before you change anything, record the current configuration. Depending on the item, this may include one or more of the following:

- Recording jumper or cable settings on the motherboard or an add-in card
- Printing the complete report from the Windows Device Manager
- Printing a complete report from a third-party diagnostic or reporting program such as SiSoftware Sandra
- Recording device settings on a tablet or smartphone
- Recording BIOS configurations

Use a digital camera to make this easier.

After you have recorded the configuration you are going to change, follow this procedure:

1. Change one hardware component or hardware/software/firmware setting at a time.
2. Try the task the user was performing after a single change, and evaluate the results.
3. If the same or similar problem reoccurs, reinstall the original component or reset the software to the original settings and continue with the next item.
4. Repeat until the subsystem performs normally. The last item changed is the problem; repair, replace, or reload it as appropriate to solve the problem.

Best Sources for Replacement Parts

To perform parts exchanges for troubleshooting, you need replacement parts. Use known-working parts from a spare system to save money and to avoid problems with brand-new, out-of-the-box defective parts.

Where to Start?

As the preceding subsystem list indicates, there's no shortage of places to start in virtually any subsystem. What's the best way to decide whether a hardware, software, or firmware problem is the most likely cause?

Typically, hardware problems come and go, and software and firmware problems are consistent. Why? A hardware problem is often the result of a damaged or loose wire or connection; when the connection is closed, the component works, but when the connection opens, the component fails.

On the other hand, a software or firmware problem will cause a failure under the same circumstances every time.

Another general rule that's useful is known as Occam's Razor, or the least hypothesis. English Philosopher William of Occam suggested centuries ago that the simplest (or least complex) explanation that fits the known facts is usually the accurate one. While TV shows such as the late, lamented *X-Files* are enjoyable to watch, their "trust no one" paranoia and incredibly complicated explanations for everything are exactly the wrong approach to take when you're trying to fix a computer problem. Instead, look at the least-expensive, easiest-to-replace item first. In most cases, the cable connected to a subsystem is the first place to look for problems. Whether the cable is internal or external, it is almost always the least-expensive part of the subsystem, can easily come loose, and can easily be damaged.

If a cable is loose; has bent pins; or has a dry, brittle, or cracked exterior, replace it. Although it may sound overly simplistic, good cables usually look good and bad cables often look bad.

When new software or new hardware has been introduced to the system and a problem results immediately afterward, that change is often the most likely cause of the problem.

To confirm whether new hardware or software is at the root of a PC problem, you should remove it and reboot your PC. If all functions normally again, you have your answer (or at least part of it). The System Restore feature is a very useful tool for determining if the software or hardware you added is at fault; it automates the process of returning your computer to a previous condition before a given software or hardware installation.

Where to Go for More Information

After you've gathered as much information as possible, you may find that you still need more help. User manuals for components often are discarded, software drivers need to be updated, and some conflicts don't have easy answers. There's one "place" to go to find the information you need: the World Wide Web. Fire up your browser and check out the websites suggested in this book, use search engines such as Google (www.google.com) to search for solutions, and also try these: the manufacturers' websites; CNet's http://download.com.com (for drivers); and online computer magazines such as PCMagazine (www.pcmag.com), PCWorld (www.pcworld.com), and others.

Keeping Track of Your Solutions

If you hate solving the same problems over and over again (and who wouldn't?), keep detailed notes about the problems you solve. Be sure to note symptoms, underlying problems, workarounds, and final resolutions. Use the copy and paste feature in Windows to store website URLs, and use File, Save as Web Archive in Internet Explorer to save useful web pages and their graphics in the documents you write up.

Summarizing the Troubleshooter's Philosophy

The troubleshooter's philosophy can be summarized this way:

- Discover what really was happening when trouble happened.
- Find out what changed.
- Use the troubleshooting cycle to reproduce the problem and discover a solution.
- Record the solution in case you need it again.

Use this philosophy and this book to become a troubleshooting hero to your family, friends, and co-workers.

Ethernet Performance Troubleshooting

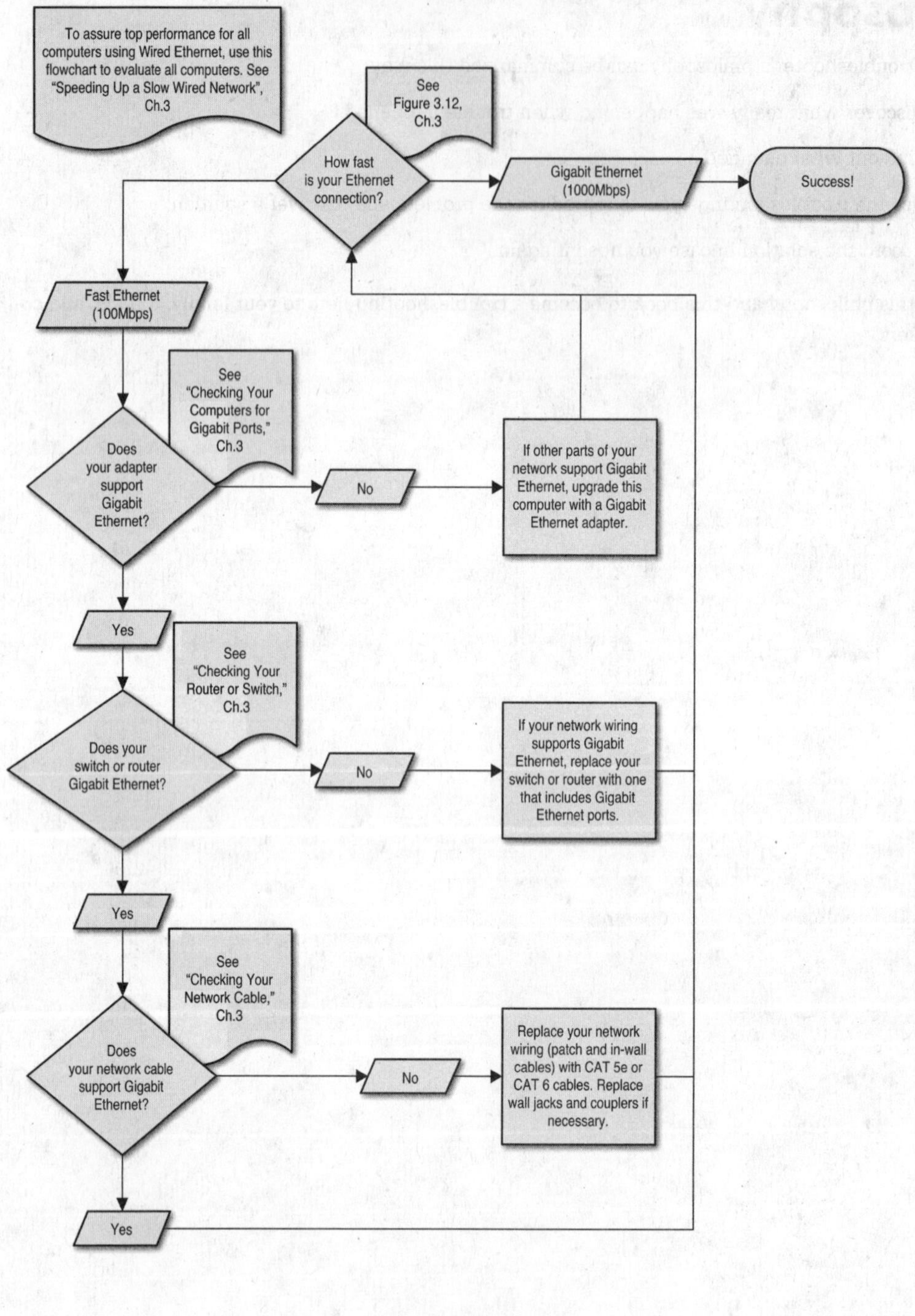

Troubleshooting a System That Won't Start

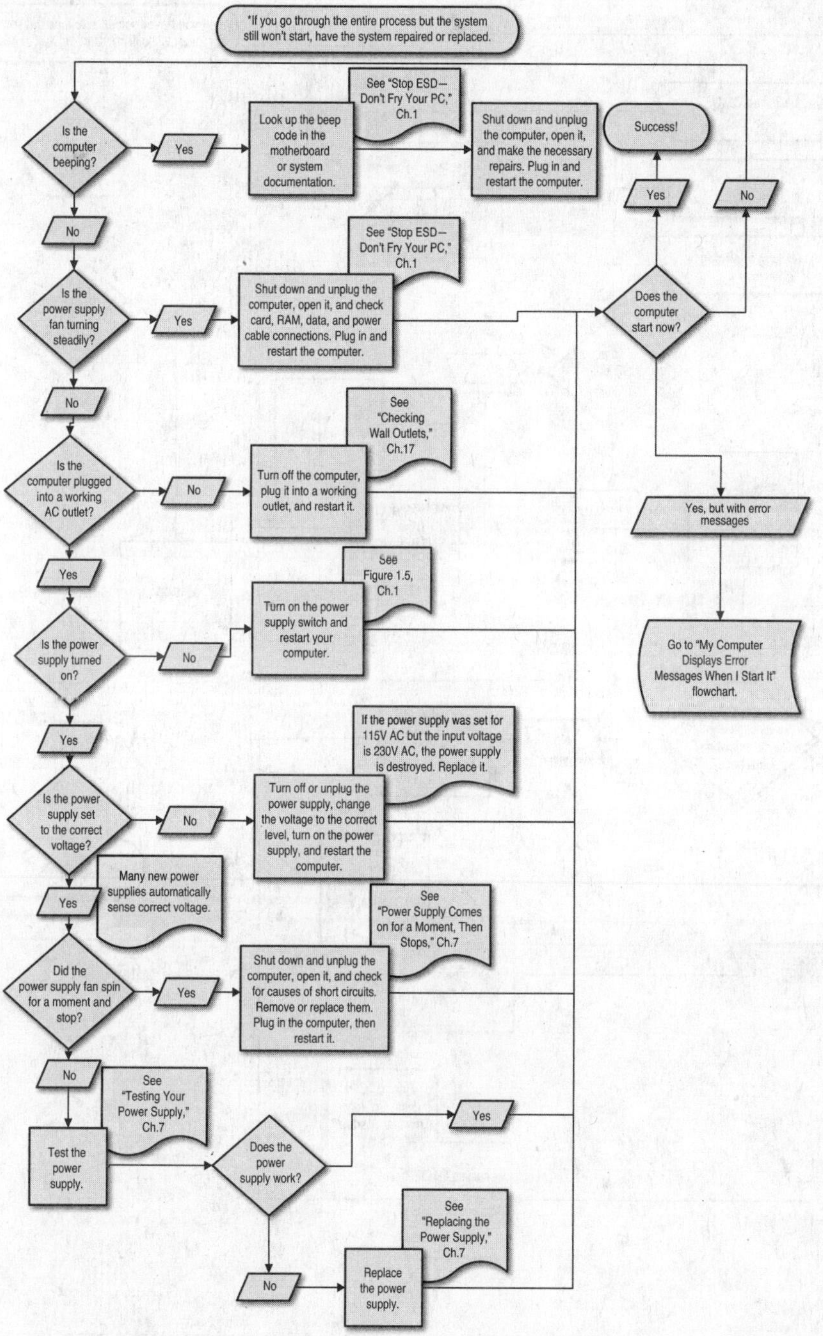

Troubleshooting a System That Displays Errors at Startup

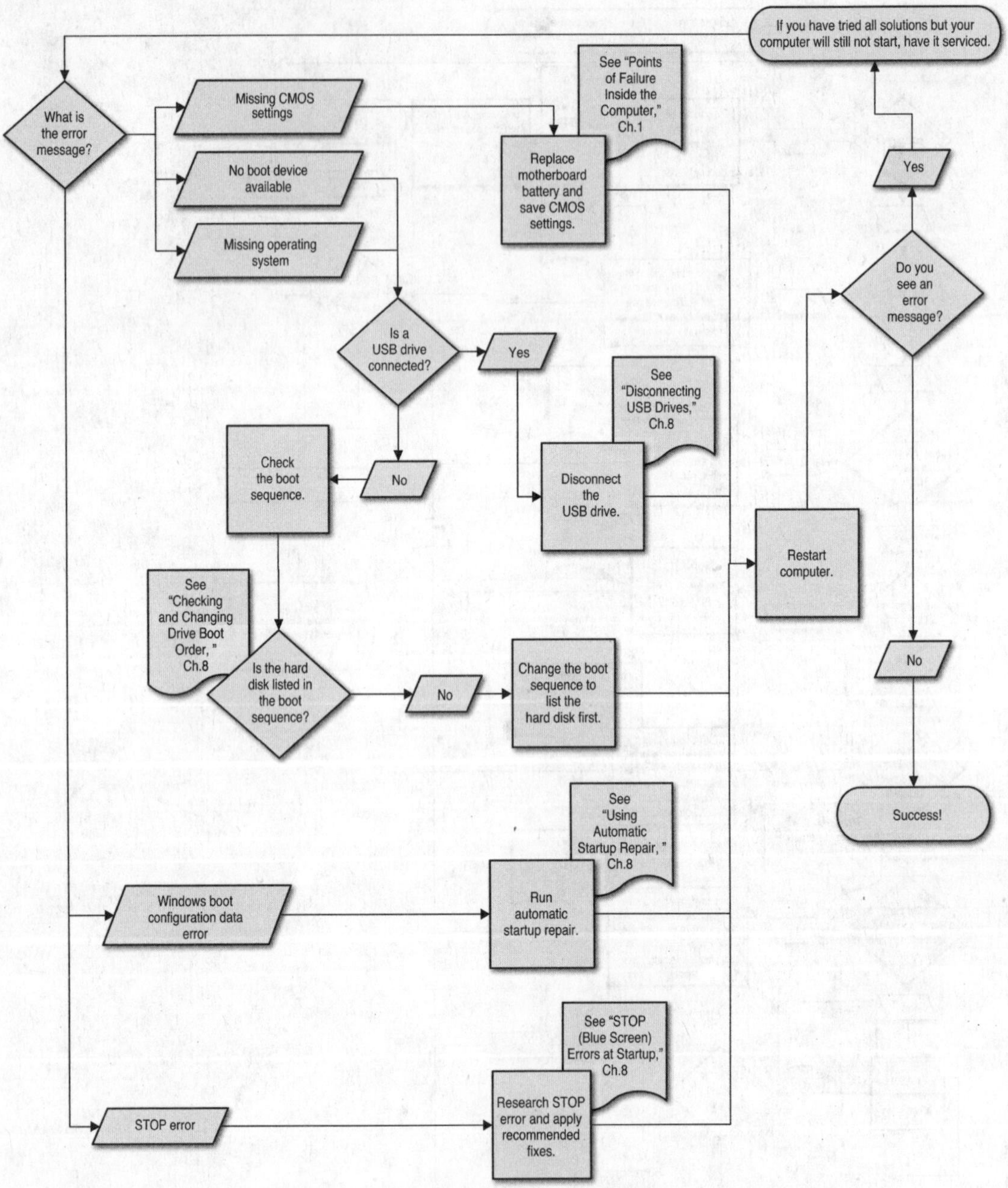

Can't Join or Create a HomeGroup

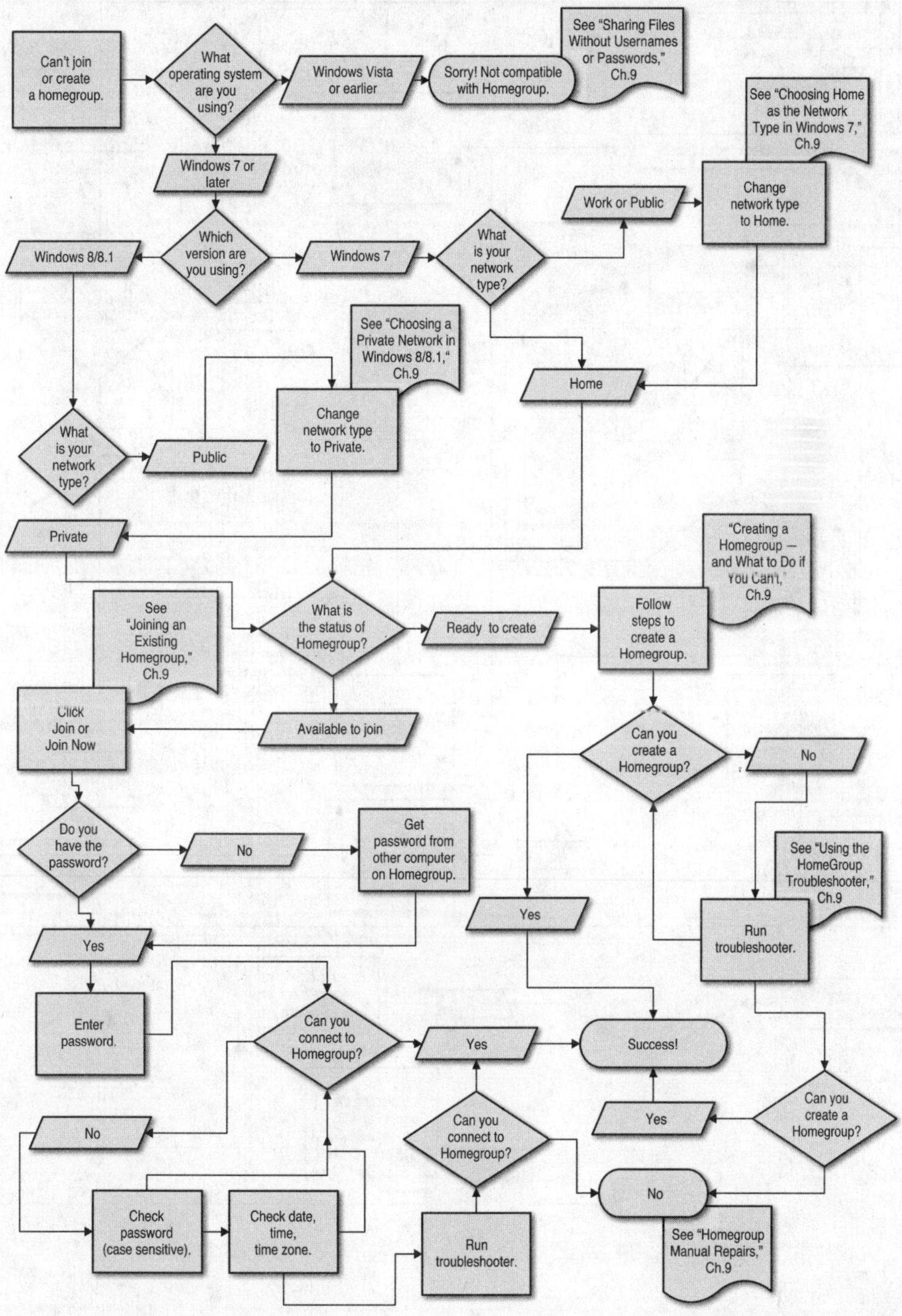

Troubleshooting Inkjet Print Quality

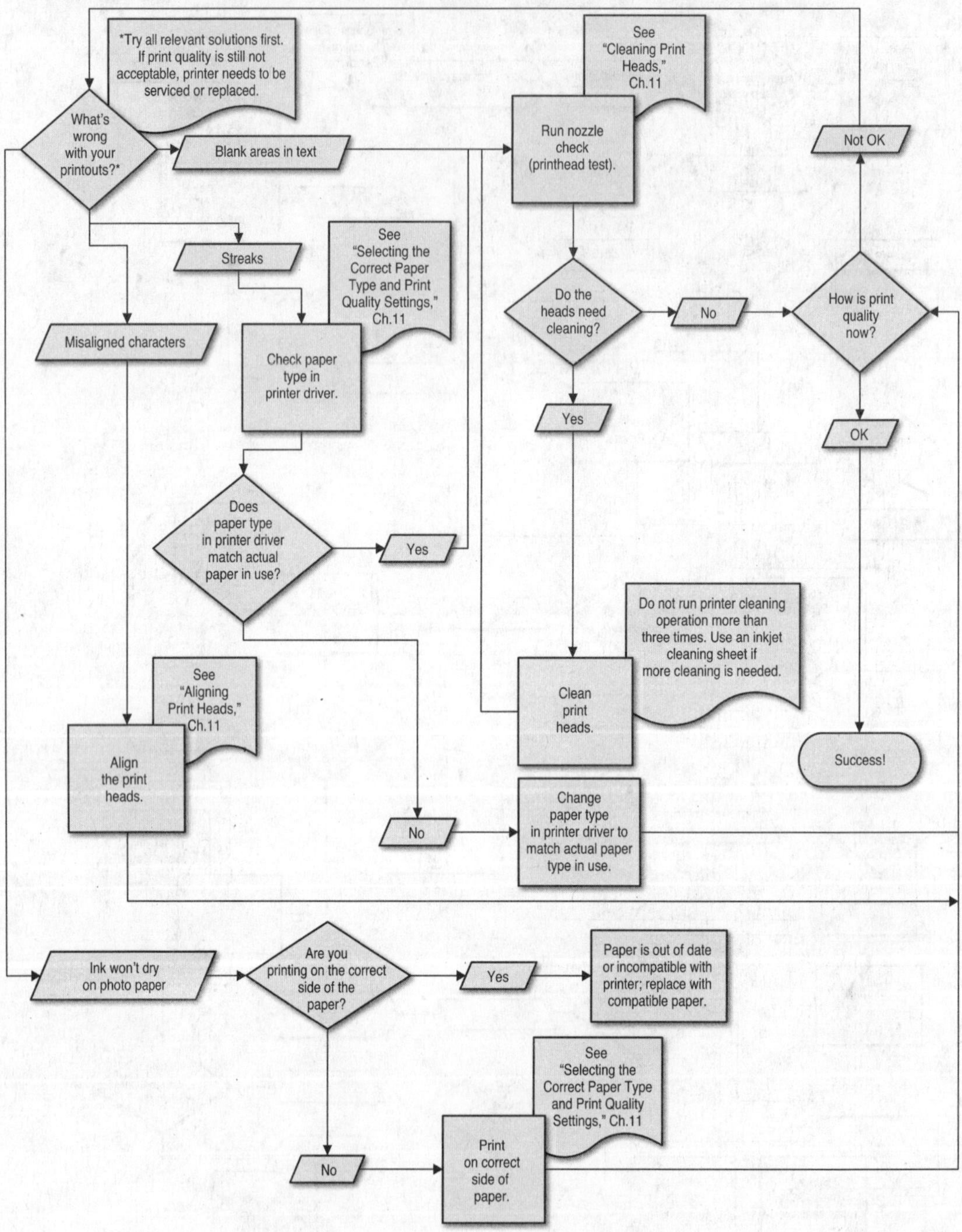

Determining Whether a Power Supply Should Be Replaced

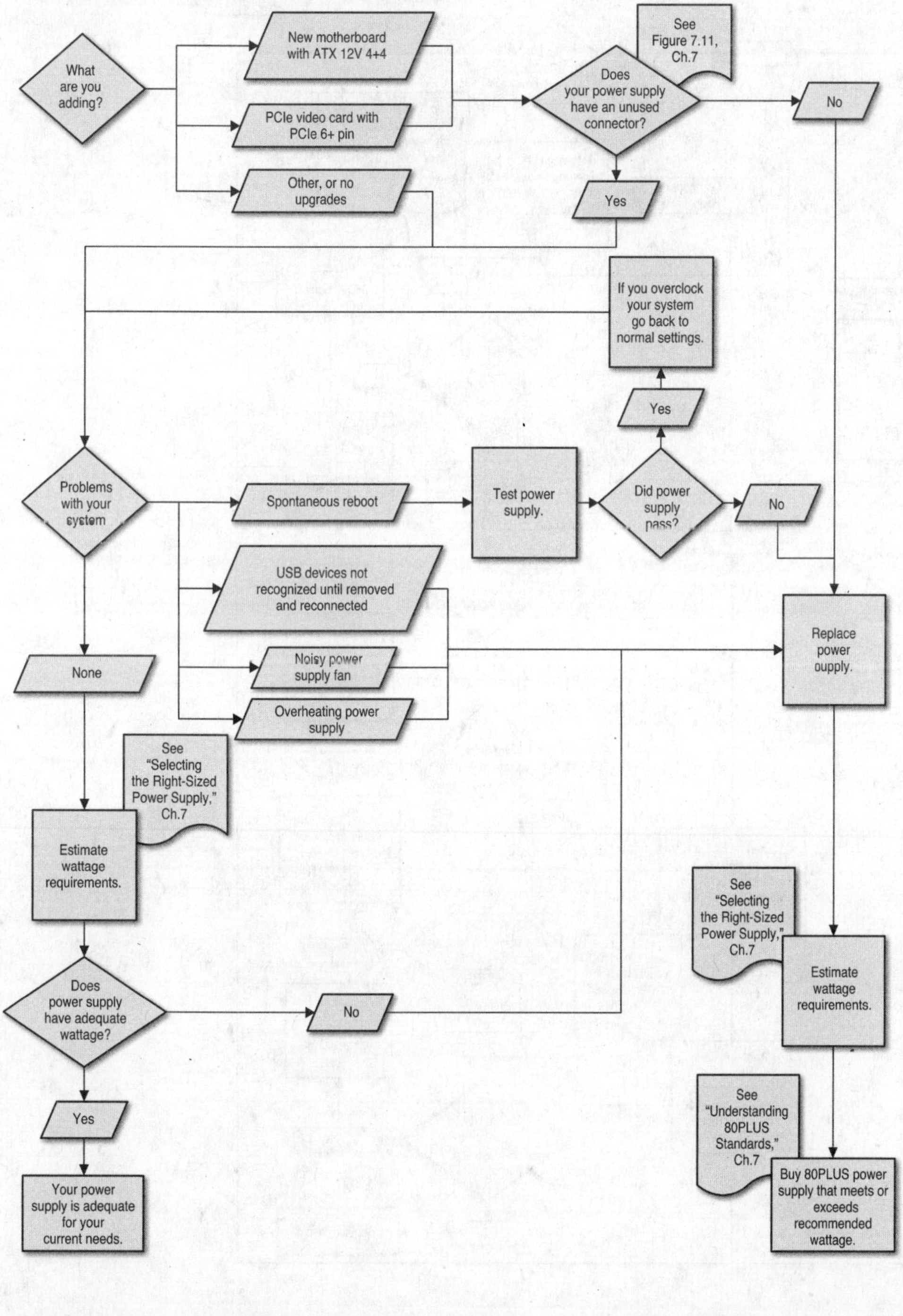

Troubleshooting Blu-ray Playback Quality

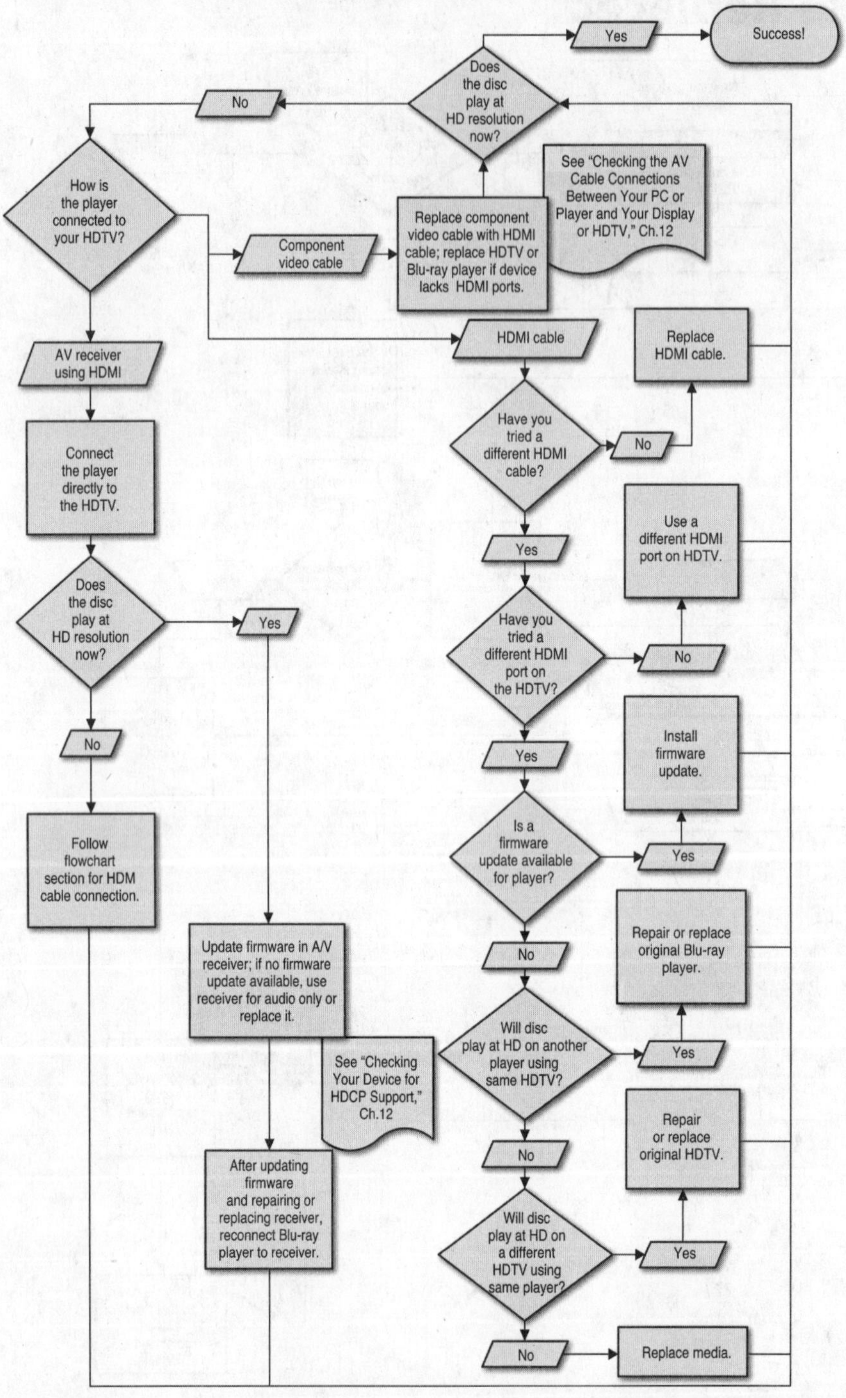

Troubleshooting Noises Inside Computer

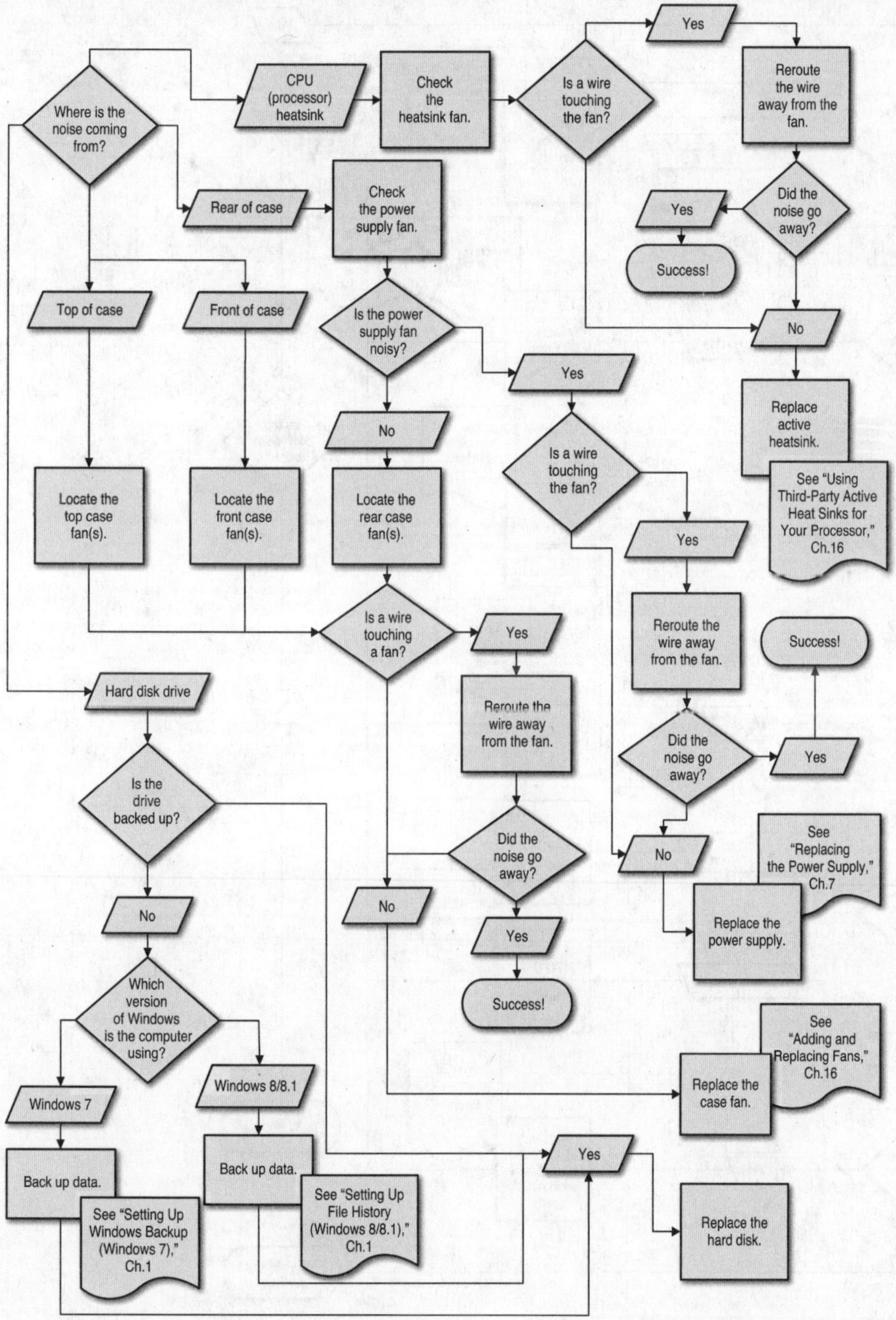

Troubleshooting Laptop Crashes

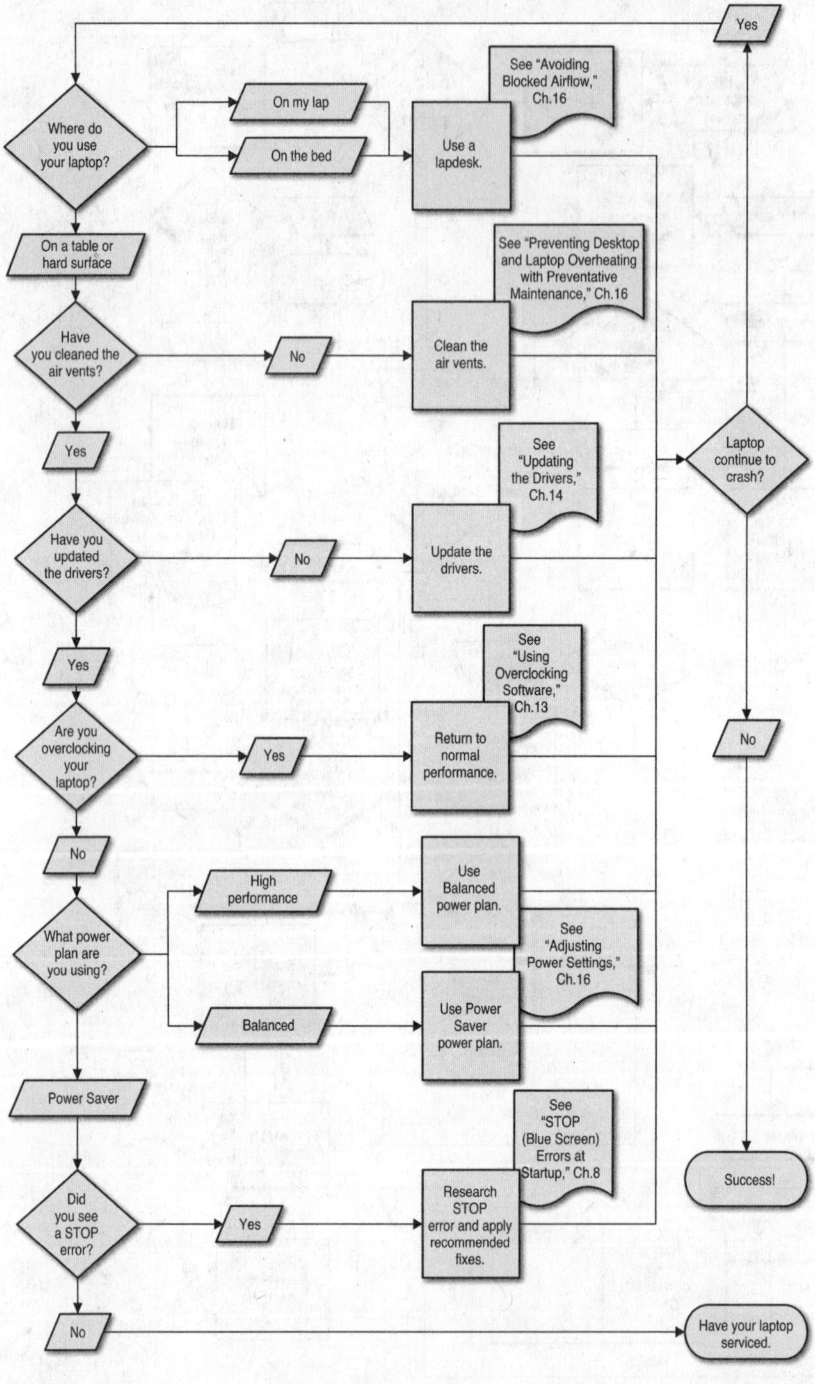

Troubleshooting Wireless Keyboards

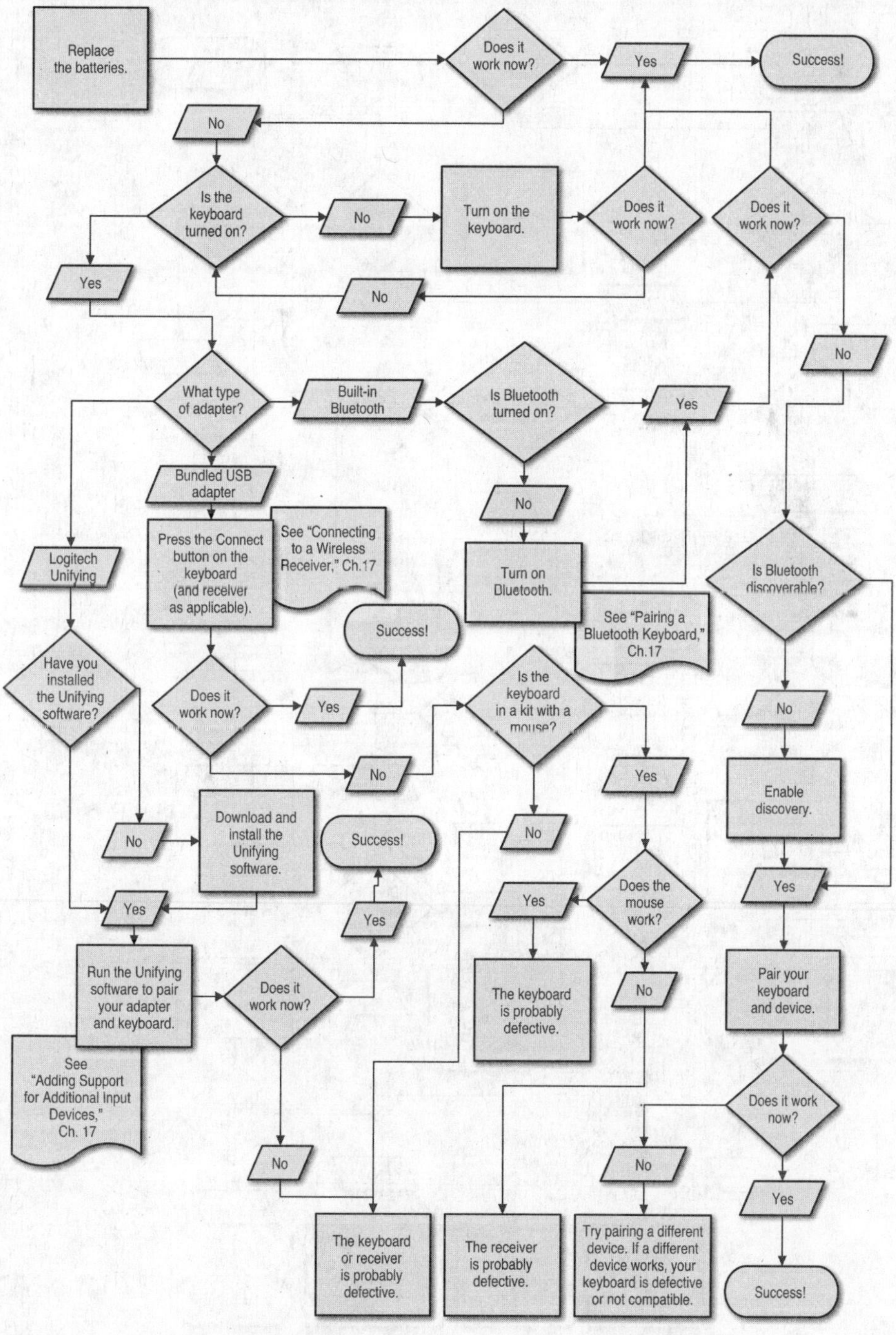

Troubleshooting Wireless Mice

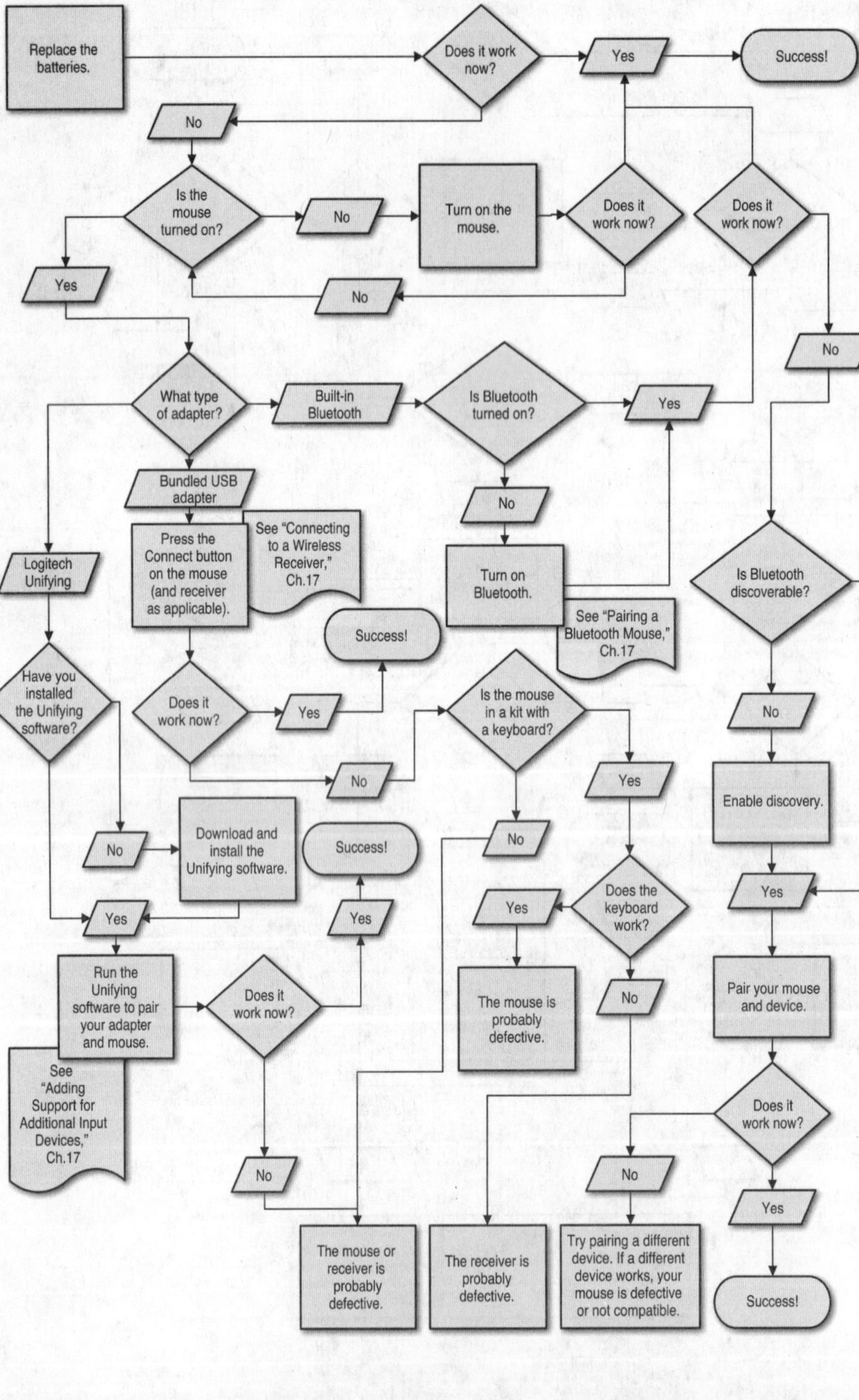

GLOSSARY

104-key keyboard Keyboard layout with Windows and right-click keys added to the old 101-key layout.

802.11a A wireless Ethernet standard that uses 5GHz radio signals and provides performance at rates from 6Mbps up to 54Mbps. It is not compatible with other 802.11-based wireless networks unless dual-band access points are used.

802.11b A wireless Ethernet standard that uses 2.4GHz radio signaling for performance from 2Mbps to 11Mbps. It is compatible with 802.11g-based wireless networks, but not with 802.11a-based networks unless dual-band access points are used.

802.11g A wireless Ethernet standard that uses 2.4GHz radio signaling for performance up to 54Mbps. It is compatible with 802.11b-based wireless networks, but not with 802.11a-based networks unless dual-band access points are used.

802.11n A wireless Ethernet standard that uses 2.4GHz and 5GHz radio signaling for performance up to 600Mbps.

A

AC Alternating current; the type of electrical current used to run homes and businesses.

AC '97 version 2.3 audio An analog audio codec standard that supports 96kHz sampling and 20-bit stereo playback. Most implementations support jack sensing.

Accelerator A feature of Internet Explorer 10 and 11 that enables you to highlight text in a web document and map, search, or perform other activities using that text without opening up a separate browser window.

accelerometer A combination of hardware and software that measures velocity in mobile devices; accelerometers detect rotation, shaking of the device, and so on.

access point Device on a Wi-Fi network that provides a connection between computers on the network. Can be combined with a router and a switch. See *Windows Action Center.*

Action Center See *Windows Action Center.*

active heat sink Heat sink with attached fan.

ActiveX Microsoft technology for interactive webpages; used with Internet Explorer.

administrator Windows term for the manager of a given computer or network; only users in the administrator's group can perform some management tasks. Other users must provide an administrator's name and password for tasks marked with the Windows security shield icon.

ADSL Asymmetric Digital Subscriber Line. A form of DSL that enables faster downloads than uploads. Can be provided over high-quality existing phone lines and is well suited for residential and small-business use.

AHCI Advanced Host Controller Interface. SATA setup option in BIOS that supports native command queuing (NCQ) and all other advanced features.

App Program designed for touchscreen operating systems, such as iOS, Android, and Windows 8.x. In Windows 8.x, an app is a program that runs from the Modern UI (Start screen) in Windows 8 and 8.1.

aperture The iris-like opening inside the lens barrel that determines how much light passes through the lens. See also f-stop.

Aperture Priority mode (A, Av mode) The user sets the aperture, and the camera sets the shutter speed. The user can also adjust the white balance, ISO, focus methods, EV compensation, and other settings. Recommended for portraits, group, and landscape photography.

application program Program used to create, modify, and store information you create. Microsoft Word, Adobe Photoshop, and CorelDRAW are all application programs.

ATA AT Attachment. A family of standards for PATA and (in ATA-7 and above) SATA interfaces.

ATX Advanced Technology eXtended. Motherboard form factor with integrated port cluster at left rear of board, basis for most mid-size to full-size desktop systems.

audio minijack 3.5mm (1/8-inch) jacks used for stereo and surround audio, microphones, and line in/line out connections.

Auto mode The camera sets the aperture, shutter speed, and most other settings. The user has limited or no ability to override the default settings. Some cameras include a simple mode that allows no overrides and an Auto mode with limited overrides.

Auto white balance The default white balance setting; the camera attempts to determine the white balance setting. Selecting the correct preset white balance usually provides more accurate and vivid color.

B

backup A copy of a file made for safekeeping, especially with a special program that must be used to restore the backup when needed; backups can be compressed to save space. Full backup backs up the entire contents of the specified drive or system; a differential backup backs up only the files that have changed since the last full backup.

battery backup A device that provides temporary power to connected units until they can be shut down; UPS and SPS devices are two types of battery backups.

BD Blu-ray disc. Media used by Blu-ray drives. Is the same physical size as CD and DVD media but has a capacity of 25GB (single-layer) or 50GB (dual-layer).

BD-R Blu-ray recordable. Contents of BD-R can be added to but not changed. BD-R DL media is dual-layer.

BD-RE Blu-ray rewriteable. Contents of BD-RE can be erased and rewritten.

Belarc System Advisor A third-party ActiveX web-based program that identifies the computer's operating system, hardware, Windows version, and security status.

biometrics Biometrics fall into the category of "something a person is." Examples of physical-body characteristics that are measured include fingerprints, retinal patterns, iris patterns, and even bone structure.

BIOS Basic Input Output System. It controls and tests basic computer hardware at the beginning of the boot procedure.

BitLocker A full disk encryption feature available in the Enterprise and Ultimate editions of Windows Vista and Windows 7 and in Windows 8/8.1 Pro.

Blu-ray An optical medium originally developed for HD movies; capacity of 25GB single-layer and 50GB in dual-layer; also referred to as BD.

Bluetooth A short-range wireless networking standard that supports non PC devices such as mobile phones and PDAs, as well as PCs. Bluetooth uses frequencies ranging from 2.402GHz to 2.480GHz with a range up to about 30 feet. Data transmission runs at 1Mbps or 2Mbps, depending on the version of the technology supported by the devices. Windows 8/8.1 includes Bluetooth support.

Boot Configuration Data BCD; the configuration information used by Windows Vista and Windows 7 to determine how to start (boot) the system.

boot disk A disk with operating system files needed to start the computer. Windows 7, 8, and 8.1 DVDs are bootable, as is the Repair Disc you can make with Windows 7 and the Recovery Drive you can create with Windows 8.1.

boot sequence The procedure followed by the system during the startup process; also called bootstrapping.

broadband Internet Internet connections with rated download speeds in excess of 256Kbps. Most common types include cable modem and DSL, but fixed wireless, FIOS, and satellite Internet services are also broadband services.

browser A program that interprets HTML documents and allows hyperlinking to websites. Windows includes various versions of Internet Explorer (IE) as the default browser. Other popular browsers include Mozilla Firefox and Google Chrome.

BSOD Blue Screen of Death. This is a fatal system error in Windows that stops the system from starting; it is also called a STOP error and is named after the blue background and the white text error message. See *STOP error*.

bus-powered hub Receives power from upstream USB port; limits power to 100mA per device.

C

cable select A PATA jumper setting that enables the 80-wire cable to determine primary and secondary drives.

calibration Adjustments to improve print quality on inkjet or color laser printers.

camera shake An overall blur with streaks caused by the user moving the camera during a shot; indicates too slow a shutter speed for hand-holding.

card reader A single-slot or multislot device for reading from and writing to flash memory cards.

CCFL backlight Backlight for conventional LCD displays.

CD Compact Disc. The oldest optical disc format; DVD and BD drives can also use CD media.

CDFS Compact Disc File System.

CD-R Recordable CD. Contents of CD-R can be added to but not changed.

CD-ROM Compact Disc-Read-Only Memory. Standard optical drive. Most can read CD-R media, but drives require MultiRead capability and a UDF reader program to read CD-RW media.

CD-RW Compact Disc-Rewritable. Rewritable CD. The contents can be changed. A CD-RW drive can also use CD-R media.

Charms bar Windows 8/8.1 interface that appears on the right side of the display. Includes charms for search, share, Start screen, devices, and settings.

clean boot Starting Windows without startup services or programs. Windows 8/8.1 uses Safe Mode boot options from the Advanced Startup option to boot with only essential drivers.

client Computer that uses shared resources on network.

client/server Network using dedicated servers such as Novell NetWare or Windows Server.

cloudy white balance Removes excess blue color cast under open shade or overcast skies to provide more accurate color. A weaker effect than Open Shade white balance.

CMOS Complimentary Metal-Oxide Semiconductor. Refers to low-power chip design; also a common term for Real-Time-Clock/Non-Volatile RAM chip (RTC/NVRAM).

CMYK Cyan, Magenta, Yellow, Black. Refers to a four-color model for graphics and printing; these are the ink colors used by most inkjet printers; compare to RGB (Red, Green, Blue), a three-color model used for onscreen graphics.

cold color Color that has a bluish cast. Indicates that white balance is incorrect.

color mode Settings that adjust the intensity of color or replaces colors in photos with sepia or black-and-white tones.

color temperature Daylight is about 5000–5200° Kelvin; fluorescent is about 4000° Kelvin (although some fixtures are warmer or colder); incandescent (tungsten) is about 3000–340° Kelvin; cloudy (overcast) light is about 6000° Kelvin; open shade is about 7000° Kelvin. Some cameras display the °Kelvin value when you select the corresponding white balance setting.

COM See *serial port.*

Computer Management Windows XP/Vista/7/8/8.1 interface for managing tasks, events, users, performance, storage, and services. Snap-in for the Microsoft Management Console (MMC).

constant aperture A zoom lens with a maximum aperture that does not change as the lens is zoomed from minimum to maximum magnification. Often marked on the lens barrel. Example: 1:2.8 (lens maximum aperture remains at f/2.8 at any zoom setting). Constant-aperture lenses are bulkier and more expensive but provide the same exposure at any zoom setting.

continuous reboots Symptom of Power Good power supply problem or STOP (BSOD) error if system is configured to restart on BSOD.

Control Panel A Windows feature that sets Windows hardware options. It can be accessed from the Start or Start, Settings menu in most versions of Windows.

CONVERT.EXE Windows command-line utility for converting a FAT32 drive to NTFS.

COPY Windows internal command for copying files between one location and another.

CPU Central processing unit. An electronic circuit that can process data and execute computer programs (Intel Core i7, AMD FX, and so on).

CPU fan connector Connection on motherboard to power CPU fan and monitor speed.

CPU-Z A third-party CPU identification program that provides extensive technical information on a CPU's features and revision level.

cropping factor The difference between the angle of view and the magnification between a lens used on a 35mm SLR and a digital SLR (most of which have smaller image sensors than 35mm film). Most Nikon DSLRs have a 1.5× cropping factor; most Canon DSLRs for consumers have a 1.6× cropping factor. Olympus and other FourThirds DSLRs have a 2.0× cropping factor.

custom system configuration A computer configuration that is not a stock or standard configuration to better fit the computer to a specified task.

D

daylight white balance Provides accurate, vivid color in daylight or with electronic flash.

DC Direct current. The type of electrical current supplied by batteries or by a PC or laptop's power supply.

dead short Short circuit on motherboard that makes the system appear to be dead.

defragment Reorganizing the files on a drive to occupy contiguous sectors to improve retrieval speed; a defragmenting utility is included in all recent Windows versions.

depth of field An area of the photo behind and in front of the point of sharpest focus that is also acceptably sharp; smaller apertures at the same focal length produce greater depth of field.

desktop Windows uses the desktop for program shortcuts, access to components such as the Recycle Bin, and for program windows.

Device Manager A Microsoft Windows utility that displays detailed information about the computer hardware in the system, including status and driver information.

Devices and Printers A Windows 7/8/8.1 feature that displays all devices and printers in a single window for quick access to the management features for each device.

DHCP Dynamic Host Configuration Protocol. A typical router feature that provides IP addresses as required; allows a limited number of IP addresses to service many devices that are not connected at the same time.

digital camera A camera that uses a digital image sensor instead of film. Most use flash memory cards for storage.

DIMM Dual Inline Memory Module. These are available in 168-pin, 184-pin, and 240-pin versions. *Dual* refers to each side of the module having a different pinout.

directory Older term for a folder in Windows.

Disk Management Windows interface for managing hard drive and SSD storage.

DisplayPort Primarily used to transmit video but can also send audio and USB signal. Designed as a replacement to VGA and DVI.

DLL Dynamic Link Library. Binary files used by Windows and Windows programs.

DMZ Demilitarized zone. In network computing it is a subnetwork that provides external services. It is often between the LAN and the Internet but is controlled by the organization that also controls the LAN.

DNS Domain name service or domain name server. Translates domain names into IP addresses.

docking station Enables laptop computers to use devices not built in, such as card slots, high-end audio and video ports, and others; requires a proprietary, dedicated external bus connector.

domain name Unique alphanumeric identifier for websites.

dpi Dots per inch. The resolutions of a printer, scanner, or monitor are commonly defined in dpi. Higher values provide sharper images and text but use more memory or disk space to store.

drag and drop Windows term for clicking and holding an object, such as a file or a tile on the Start screen; dragging it to another location; and releasing it.

drive array Two or more drives used as a single logical unit.

DSL Digital Subscriber Line. A type of broadband Internet service that uses telephone lines to carry Internet traffic at speeds as high as 6Gbps or more while allowing you to use your phone for normal functions at the same time. Two major types of DSL are ADSL and SDSL. See those entries for details.

DualView Windows standard for supporting extended desktop or cloned desktop with external video port on laptop computers.

DUN Dial-Up Networking. Using an analog (phone line) modem to connect to other computers.

DVD Digital Versatile Disc. The most common optical disc format.

DVD-R Digital Video Disc-Recordable.

DVD-RAM Digital Versatile Disc-Random Access Memory. A rewritable DVD standard developed by Panasonic and supported by the DVD Forum. Not as common as other DVD standards.

DVD-ROM Digital Video Disc-Read Only Memory. Retail and upgrade editions of Windows are distributed on DVD-ROM media, as are many other application and utility programs from major publishers.

DVD-RW Digital Video Disc-Rewritable. A rewritable DVD standard developed by Pioneer Electronics and supported by the DVD Forum. These drives also support DVD-R write-once media.

DVD+/-RW Refers to drives that support both DVD-R/RW and DVD+R/RW media.

DVD+RW A rewritable DVD standard supported by the DVD+RW Alliance and sold by HP, Philips, Sony, and other vendors. Most of these drives also support DVD+R write-once media.

DVI Digital Visual Interface. Replaced DFP as the standard for support of LCD displays on desktop computers. DVI-D is for digital displays only; DVI-I supports digital and analog displays. Sometimes this is also referred to as Digital Video Interface.

E–F

electrostatic discharge (ESD) The release of static electricity when two objects with varying electrical potentials come into contact with each other.

email Electronic mail. The contents of email can include text, HTML, and binary files (such as photos or compressed archives). Email can be sent between computers via an internal computer network, a proprietary online service such as AOL, or via the Internet.

eSATA External SATA, a version of SATA for use with external drives.

EV adjustment Overrides the exposure selected by the camera. +1EV doubles the recommended exposure; -1EV halves the recommended exposure. The typical range is +2 to -2EV in 1/2- or 1/3-step increments.

exFAT (FAT64) File system designed to support high-capacity removable storage media, such as flash drives.

expansion slots Slots in motherboard for video, network, mass storage, and other types of cards. Types include PCIe, PCI, and others.

exposure lock When the shutter button is pressed down part-way, the camera sets the exposure according to the scene. Most cameras also set the focus at the same time, but some offer separate exposure and focus lock options.

ExpressCard High-performance expansion slot for laptops; available in 34mm-wide (/34) and 54mm-wide (/54) versions.

Extended partition Windows disk partition that can be divided into one or more logical drives. Cannot be made bootable.

external command Programs run from the command line, such as XCOPY.EXE.

FAT32 32-bit file allocation table. Formatting method optionally available with Windows 8.1 and older versions. It allows for drive sizes up to 2TB (terabytes). It is used primarily for USB flash memory and memory cards.

File Explorer File management interface for Windows 8/8.1 desktop. Similar to Windows Explorer in Windows XP/Vista/7.

file extension Up to four alphanumeric characters after the dot in a filename; indicates file type, such as .html, .exe, .docx, and so on. Windows does not display file extensions by default, but you can make them visible through the Control Panel's Folder Options utility.

file system How files are organized on a drive; FAT16, FAT32, and NTFS are popular file systems supported by various versions of Windows.

filter A transparent optical glass or plastic device that attaches to the front of the lens to protect the lens or change the characteristics of light passing through the lens.

firewall A network device or software that blocks unauthorized access to a network from other users. Software firewalls, such as the Windows Firewall, Zone Alarm, and Norton Internet Security, are sometimes referred to as personal firewalls. Routers can also function as firewalls.

FireWire 400 See *IEEE 1394.*

FireWire 800 See *IEEE 1394.*

firmware A middle ground between hardware and software, it is a software program that has been written for read-only memory (ROM).

flash memory Memory that retains its contents without electricity.

FlexATX Small version of ATX motherboard designed for low-profile or small form factor systems.

fluorescent white balance Removes color cast to provide more accurate color under fluorescent lights. Some cameras offer two or more settings in this category because of the wide variety of fluorescent tubes and CFLs in use.

Fn key Special key on laptop keyboards that, when pressed, enables other keys to perform an additional task, such as adjusting screen brightness, toggling the Windows desktop to an external display, and so on. On a few laptops, the function keys along the top of the keyboard are configured to provide special tasks and the user must press the Fn key to access traditional function key tasks such as F1 for Help.

focus lock When the shutter button is pressed down part-way, the camera sets the focus on the subject in the focus framing or detection area. Most cameras also set exposure, but some offer separate exposure and focus lock options.

font A particular size, shape, and weight of a typeface. 12-point Times Roman Italic is a font; Times Roman is the typeface. Windows 8/8.1 includes a number of typefaces, and you can select the desired font with programs such as WordPad, Paint, and others.

form factor Physical size and shape of motherboard, power supply. See www.formfactors.org for specifications for common motherboard and power supply standards.

format Can refer to document layout or the process of preparing a disk drive for use.

FORMAT A Windows program to prepare a drive for use; hard disks must be partitioned first.

front-panel connectors Connections on front or side of motherboard for power switch, indicator lights, reset, and other features on the front of the computer.

f-stop Aperture setting. Typical f-stops include f/2.8, f/4.0, f/5.6, f/8, and so on. See also *Aperture* and *Aperture Priority mode (A, Av mode).* The wider the aperture, the smaller the f-stop (f-number): f/2.8 allows twice as much light as f/4.0, and so on.

FTP File Transfer Protocol. File transfer to or from a special server site on the World Wide Web.

G

GB Gigabyte. 1 billion bytes.

generic hub USB hub that plugs in to a USB port or USB root hub.

geotracking The practice to track and record the location of a mobile device over time.

GHz Gigahertz.

Global positioning system (GPS) A worldwide system of satellites that provide information concerning the whereabouts of mobile devices and anything else with a GPS receiver.

GUI Graphical user interface. Windows is a GUI.

gyroscope In addition to the accelerometers, this adds the measurements of pitch, roll, and yaw to mobile devices, just like in the concept of flight dynamics.

H

hard drive A storage device with rigid, nonremovable platters inside a case; also called hard disk or rigid disk.

hardware Physical computing devices such as hard disk, mouse, keyboard, power supply, and so on.

hardware-assisted virtualization Features in CPU and BIOS that enable virtualization to perform faster.

HD Audio An Intel standard for High Definition Audio (also known as HDA or Azalia). It supports 192kHz 32-bit sampling in stereo and 96kHz 32-bit sampling for up to eight channels.

HDMI High-Definition Multimedia Interface. A compact audio/video interface for transmitting uncompressed digital data. HDMI is used by HDTVs, receivers, and most recent desktop and laptop computers.

header cable Connects to motherboard header pins connected to integrated I/O ports.

heat sink Device that draws heat away from a component (CPU, GPU, and memory).

Hi-Speed USB USB 2.0 ports and devices.

HID Human interface device; a mouse or keyboard.

high-level format A type of format performed by the Windows Format program on hard drives; it rewrites file allocation tables and the root directory but doesn't overwrite existing data on the rest of the disk surface.

home server PC A PC optimized to provide file, print, and backup services on a home or SOHO network.

HomeGroup A Windows network feature that enables two or more Windows 8/8.1 or Windows 7 systems to belong to a secure, easy-to-manage network. Requires the Home setting in the Windows Firewall.

HTML Hypertext Markup Language. A standard for markup symbols that enables hyperlinking, fonts, special text attributes, graphics, and other enhancements to be added to text files for display with web browsers such as Microsoft Internet Explorer, Mozilla Firefox, and Google Chrome. The official source for HTML standards is the World Wide Web Consortium (W3C).

HTTP Hypertext Transfer Protocol. The basis for hyperlinking and the Internet; it is interpreted by a web browser program.

HTTPS Hypertext Transfer Protocol Over Secure Sockets Layer. HTTPS connections are often used for payment transactions on the World Wide Web and for sensitive transactions in corporate information systems.

hub A device used to enable multiple USB devices to connect to a single USB port.

hyperthreading (HT Technology) Intel CPU technology that enables a single processor core to work with two execution threads at the same time.

I

IEEE 1394 A high-speed serial connection. IEEE 1394a (FireWire 400) runs at 400Mbps, and IEEE 1394b (FireWire 800) runs at 800Mbps. i.LINK is Sony's name for a four-wire version of IEEE-1394a.

i.LINK See *IEEE 1394*.

icon An onscreen symbol used in Windows that links to a program, file, or routine.

image noise Splotches and small dots of false color in images shot at ISO ratings of 800-1600 or higher, or when a very dark (underexposed) photo has its exposure corrected.

image backup System backup that stores all information on the system, including the operating system, programs, settings, and data. Windows 7 Backup and most third-party backup programs such as Acronis True Image and others create image backups. Most recent image backup programs also support restoration of individual files.

image stabilization Cameras or lenses with the capability to counteract camera movement and enable hand held shooting at slower shutter speeds. Also known as IS, VR, or OS. Used in both still cameras and camcorders.

imaging device How Microsoft Windows identifies devices such as digital cameras or scanners in My Computer/Computer.

IMAP Internet Message Access Protocol. Second most common protocol used to download email.

incandescent white balance Removes excess yellow or orange color cast under incandescent light bulbs to provide more accurate color. Do not use if electronic flash is the light source.

install The process of making a computer program usable on a system, including expanding and copying program files to the correct locations, changing Windows configuration files, and registering file extensions used by the program.

integrated GPU GPU (graphics processing unit) incorporated in the CPU.

integrated I/O ports Ports built in to the motherboard port cluster or internal headers such as USB, Ethernet, FireWire, and others.

internal command Windows command-line operations built in to the Windows command interpreter, CMD.EXE, such as COPY, DEL, and DIR.

Internet The world wide "network of networks" that can be accessed through the World Wide Web and by Telnet, FTP, and other utilities.

inverter Converts DC current into AC current to power CCFL backlight in LCD displays.

I/O port A generic term for ports used for input or output, such as USB, PS/2 mouse and keyboard, and FireWire. Storage device ports (PATA, SATA, and eSATA) are not categorized as I/O ports.

IrDA Infrared Data Association. Defines physical specifications and communications protocol standards for the short-range exchange of data over infrared, used in personal area networks (PANs).

ISO image A single file that contains the layout of an optical disc.

ISO rating A measurement of how sensitive the camera is to light; the equivalent to film ISO settings. ISO up to 200 is recommended for bright light. ISO 200–400 is recommended for flash, outdoor action, or dim light. ISO 800 and above are recommended for very dim light without flash or very fast action. ISO 200 requires half the light of ISO 100, and so on.

J–K

jailbreaking The process to remove limitations on Apple devices, give the user root access and allows a person to install unauthorized software.

JPEG A compressed file format used as the standard file format for digital cameras. Smaller image size than RAW, but the image quality is not as high. Most cameras offer two or more quality settings that affect the level of compression.

jump list A Windows 7/8/8.1 feature that enables programs, documents, and common tasks to be started from taskbar shortcuts.

jumper Group of two or three pins on a motherboard or card; used for configuration.

jumper block Fits across two jumper pins to enable or disable a feature.

Kelvin A measurement of the color temperature of light. See also *color temperature*. The higher the degree Kelvin, the bluer the light.

KVM switch Keyboard-video-mouse. A device that enables a single keyboard, video display, and mouse to work with two or more computers.

L

LAN Local area network. A network in which the components are connected through network cables or wirelessly; a LAN can connect to other LANs via a router.

Land grid array (LGA) Intel CPU socket technology that uses small metal lands in the CPU socket instead of pins on the CPU.

landscape mode A print mode that prints across the wider side of the paper; from the usual proportions of a landscape painting.

laser printer Type of nonimpact page printer that quickly produces quality text and images. Most use the electrophotographic (EP) printing process.

LCD Liquid crystal display. Type of screen used on portable computers and on flat-panel desktop displays.

LDAP Lightweight Directory Access Protocol. Maintains distributed directory information services. Examples include email and Microsoft Active Directory.

LED Light-emitting-diode backlit LCD display. It is similar to an LCD display but uses LED backlighting instead of a cold cathode fluorescent lamp (CCFL).

Level 1 (L1) cache Cache memory read by CPU first when new memory information is needed; smallest cache size.

Level 2 (L2) cache Cache memory read by CPU if L1 cache does not have wanted information; much larger than L1 cache.

Level 3 (L3) cache Cache memory read by CPU if L2 cache does not have wanted information; much larger than L2 cache; used on high-performance CPUs.

LGA775 First LGA socket from Intel; used by late-model Pentium 4, Pentium D, others; 775 lands.

LGA1155 LGA socket used by second- and third-generation Core i-series processors; 1155 lands.

LGA1156 LGA socket used by first-generation Core i-series processors; 1156 lands.

LGA1366 LGA socket used by Extreme Core i7 CPUs; 1366 lands.

Library A Windows 7/8/8.1 feature that enables multiple locations to be viewed in a single Windows Explorer window.

liquid cooling Cooling system for CPU, GPU, and other components that replaces air cooling with heat blocks, a heat exchanger, and liquid-filled hoses; used for extreme overclocking.

Live File System Microsoft's implementation of the Universal Disc Format (UDF) for writing to recordable or rewriteable CD or DVD media in Windows Vista and Windows 7.

lock screen This screen appears when Windows 8/8.1 is started or locked. The user must press the spacebar, click a mouse, or press the touch interface to see the login screen. This screen displays the date, time, and a full-screen image.

logging Recording events during a process. Windows creates logs for many types of events; they can be viewed through the Computer Management Console.

logical drive Drive created inside of an extended partition.

M

macro lens A lens that can focus up to 1:1 (life-size) magnification at close distances (less than 1 foot). Macro lenses can be prime or zoom lenses.

malware Malicious software designed to infiltrate a computer system and possibly damage it without the user's knowledge or consent. Malware is a broad term used by computer people to include viruses, worms, Trojan horses, spyware, rootkits, adware, and other types of unwanted software.

Manual mode (M mode) On cameras with aperture and shutter priority options, the user sets both the aperture and the shutter speed. The user can also adjust the white balance, ISO, focus methods, EV compensation, and other settings. Recommended for experimental photography, photos in very dim light, or when the camera's light meter cannot make accurate settings. On cameras that lack aperture and shutter priority, M mode enables the user to adjust the white balance, ISO, focus methods, EV compensation, and other settings; however, the camera sets the aperture and shutter speed automatically.

master Jumper setting for primary PATA drive on a 40-wire cable.

mastering Creating a CD or DVD by adding all the files to the media at once. This method is recommended when creating a music CD or a video DVD. Windows' built-in CD and DVD creation feature supports mastering.

media Anything used to carry information, such as network cables, paper, CD or DVD discs, and so on.

megapixel (MP) Mega = million; refers to the number of millions of pixels in the camera's image sensor. Most digital cameras can also shoot photos at lower MP ratings using only a portion of the sensor's pixels.

memory module Memory chips on a small board.

metadata Exposure and other data about the photograph embedded inside the image file. This data can be viewed within Mac OS X, Windows Vista/7/8.x, without special software. You must install third-party programs with Windows XP or with iOS or Android devices.

Microsoft account Account setup option supported by Windows 8/8.1. Log in with a Microsoft account (for example, *name@live.com* or *name@outlook.com*), and your settings are synchronized between systems. This was previously known as a Windows Live ID.

Microsoft Knowledge Base The online collection of Microsoft technical articles used by Microsoft support personnel to diagnose system problems. Can also be searched by end users by using the http://support.microsoft.com website.

MIDI Musical Instrument Digital Interface. A standard developed for the storage and playback of music based on digital sampling of actual musical instruments.

Mini-ITX VIA Tech-originated ultracompact motherboard design; used in computing appliances (media servers, and so on).

MLC Multi Level Cell; faster but more expensive than SLC flash memory; used in SSDs.

MMC Microsoft Management Console. The Windows utility used to view and control the computer and its components. Disk Management and Device Manager are components of MMC.

modem Short for modulate-demodulate, a modem converts signals to and from a computer-usable form. Modems are used to send and receive information from dial-up telephone lines, DSL networks, and cable TV networks.

monitor A TV-like device that uses either a CRT or an LCD screen to display activity inside the computer. Attaches to the video card or video port on the system. Windows supports multiple monitors.

motherboard The logical foundation of the computer; all components connect to it.

motion blur Blur in part of the subject caused by the subject moving too fast for the shutter speed.

mouse A pointing device that is moved across a flat surface; older models use a removable ball to track movement; recent models use optical or laser sensors.

MP3 Moving Picture Experts Group Layer 3 Audio. A compressed digitized music file format widely used for storage of popular and classical music; quality varies with the sampling rate used to create the file. MP3 files can be stored on recordable or rewritable CD or DVD media for playback and are frequently exchanged online. The process of creating MP3 files is called *ripping*. Windows Media Player and Windows Media Center can create and play back MP3 files.

MPEG Motion Picture Experts Group; creates standards for compression of video (such as MPEG 2) and audio (such as the popular MP3 file format).

multicore Processor with two or more cores; some desktop processors have as many as eight cores.

multimeter An electrical testing device that can test amperage, AC and DC voltage, continuity, and other items.

multitouch touchscreens A display that can sense the presence of two or more contact points; enables icons and windows on touch-sensitive screens to be dragged, resized, and adjusted. Used by all-in-one computers and laptops with touch screens as well as Apple (iOS) and Android mobile devices.

N–O

netbook A mobile computing device that is smaller than a laptop and has a folding keyboard and screen (usually no more than about 10 inches diagonal measurement). Netbooks have lower-performance processors, less RAM, and smaller hard disks (or solid state drives) than laptop or notebook computers. Windows 7/8/8.1 run on netbooks as well as more powerful types of computers.

network Two or more computers that are connected and share a resource, such as folders or printers.

Network and Sharing Center The Windows control center for wired, wireless, and dial-up networking functions.

network drive A drive or folder available through the network; usually refers to a network resource that has been mapped to a local drive letter.

nozzle check Inkjet printer maintenance option that uses all nozzles to print a pattern that indicates whether some nozzles are clogged.

NTFS New Technology File System. Preferred file system for Windows XP and all newer versions.

objects Items that can be viewed or configured with File Explorer, including drives, folders, computers, and so on.

OneDrive A Windows online file and photo storage and sharing site formerly known as SkyDrive. Requires a free Microsoft account (formerly known as a Windows Live ID). Windows 8.1 provides access to OneDrive from the Start screen and Windows desktop. Windows 7 and 8 can access OneDrive from the Windows desktop by installing the OneDrive desktop app from http://windows.microsoft.com/en-us/onedrive/windows-app-faq.

open shade white balance Removes excess blue color cast under open shade or overcast skies to provide more accurate color. A stronger effect than cloudy white balance.

optical Storage such as CD, DVD, and BD drives, which use a laser to read data.

OS Operating system. Software that configures and manages hardware and connects hardware and applications. Windows, iOS, and Android are the operating systems covered in this book.

overclocking Running CPU, memory, and other components at faster-than-normal speeds. May require adjustments to component voltage and improved air cooling or a switch to liquid cooling.

P–Q

packet writing A method for writing data to an optical disc in small blocks (packets). This method is used by UDF programs. Packet-written media requires a UDF reader, unlike media created with a mastering program, which can be read without any additional software. Windows CD and DVD writing feature can use packet writing (UDF formatting).

paging file (virtual memory) The file stored on the hard drive used by the paging process as virtual memory, also known as a swap file. In Windows it is a file called pagefile.sys.

passive heat sink Heat sink that relies on outside air flow for cooling.

password A word or combination of letters, numbers, and symbols that is matched to a username or resource name to enable the user to access a computer or network resources or accounts.

PATA Parallel ATA; term used for drives that use the 40-pin interface formerly known as IDE or ATA-IDE.

PC99 system design guide A series of computer specifications originally developed by Intel and Microsoft in the late 1990s. Most of its recommendations are obsolete, but the port color coding it contains continues to be largely followed by the industry. See http://en.wikipedia.org/wiki/PC_System_Design_Guide#Color-coding_scheme_for_connectors_and_ports.

PCI Peripheral Component Interconnect. 32-bit I/O bus providing a shared 33MHz or 66MHz data path between the CPU and peripheral controllers.

PCI Express (PCIe) A high-speed set of serial bus communication channels used by adapter cards.

peer server A client PC that also shares drives or other resources on a Windows network.

peer-to-peer network A network in which some or all of the client PCs also act as peer servers.

personal firewall Software that blocks unauthorized access to a computer with an Internet connection. Can also be configured to prevent unauthorized programs from connecting to the Internet. The free Shields Up! service at Gibson Research (http://grc.com) tests the protection provided by personal firewalls and recommends specific products. Windows includes a personal (software) firewall.

phishing The attempt to gain such information as personally identifiable information and credit cards using fraudulent email, websites, or other electronic communications.

Photo Viewer A Windows utility for photo viewing and printing.

PIN Personal identification number. Windows 8/8.1 supports PIN numbers as an optional login method.

pin grid array (PGA) CPU socket design in which pins in the rear of the CPU are inserted into holes in a socket and clamped into place.

pinning The act of locking a program or document to the Windows taskbar or Start menu. Use this feature along with jump lists to create shortcuts to your most commonly used programs in either location.

plasma Type of display that uses small cells that contain ionized gas. This type of display is used by some HDTVs.

pointing device General term for any mouse-type device.

pointing stick Generic term for IBM/Lenovo TrackPoint, Toshiba AccuPoint, or other eraser-head pointing devices located in the middle of the keyboard.

POP3 Post Office Protocol 3. Email protocol used by client computers to download or receive email.

port replicator Provides a single connection for various types of I/O ports for portable computers; the port replicator connects to the external devices and then connects to the portable computer through an external proprietary expansion bus or through a USB port.

portrait mode The default print option that prints across the short side of the paper; it gets its name from the usual orientation of portrait paintings and photographs.

POST Power-On Self-Test. BIOS test of basic hardware performed during cold boot.

power management BIOS or OS techniques for reducing power usage by dropping CPU clock speed, turning off the monitor or hard disk, and so on during periods of inactivity.

Power plan Windows Vista/7/8/8.1 power management setting.

power supply Converts high-voltage AC to low-voltage DC.

primary partition Bootable disk partition created with Disk Management or with Diskpart.

prime lens A lens that does not zoom, such as a 50mm f/1.8 lens.

print queue List of print jobs waiting to be sent to the printer.

print spooler Windows service responsible for receiving print jobs and sending them to the printer.

printer preferences Printer settings such as quality, paper type, and monochrome or color; details vary with printer.

printer properties Printer management options such as sharing, port usage, security, spooling options, and availability.

Program mode (P mode) The camera sets the aperture and shutter speed. The user can adjust the white balance, ISO, focus methods, EV compensation, and other settings. Recommended for general photography.

properties sheet A Windows method for modifying and viewing object properties. Accessible by right-clicking the object and selecting Properties or by using Control Panel.

PS/2 port A 6-pin Mini-DIN port used for mice or keyboards.

R

RAM Random access memory. Volatile memory whose contents can be changed.

RAW A file format that retains all exposure and image quality information. Supported by digital SLRs and some advanced point-and-shoot digital cameras. Can be converted to JPEG or other formats by vendor-provided or third-party software. Each camera manufacturer's version of RAW is proprietary and uses its own file extension (Canon's is CR2, Nikon's is NEF, and so on).

ReadyBoost Windows Vista/7/8/8.1 feature that uses flash memory as a disk cache. Not supported on systems with SSDs.

Recycle Bin Windows holding area for deleted files, allowing them to be restored to their original locations; files in the Recycle Bin are deleted after a specified period of time or disk usage to free up disk space. You can also empty the Recycle Bin manually.

Refresh New Windows 8/8.1 system recovery feature; enables system and Windows Store software to be reset to their original configuration without losing personal settings or files.

Registry Database of all hardware, software, and system settings in Windows.

Reset New Windows 8/8.1 system recovery feature; resets Windows to its as-installed state. All user changes (new programs, files, and settings) are also wiped out.

resolution The number of dots per inch (dpi) supported by a scanner or printer, or the number of pixels supported by a display.

restore point File that stores configuration information for the system. Created automatically. Used by System Restore. Also stores older versions of data files in Windows Vista/7/8/8.1.

RGB Stands for red, green, and blue, the three additive primary colors used in electronic systems and monitors.

root access Enables a user of a mobile device to have unlimited access to the device's hardware and features. Required by some programs.

root hub Hosts USB ports on a PC.

rooting The process of adding a root user (superuser) to a device. Many rooting programs are available for Android devices.

rootkit Malware designed to gain administrative-level control of a computer.

router Device that routes data from one network to another. Often integrated with wireless access points and switches.

RPM Revolutions per minute.

S

safe mode Windows troubleshooting startup mode; runs the system using BIOS routines only. Can be selected at startup on Windows 7 and earlier versions by pressing the F8 key repeatedly and then selecting it from the startup menu that appears. In Windows 8/8.1, it can be run by using Advanced Startup options.

SATA Serial ATA; this version of ATA uses thin data and power cables to transmit data serially at rates of 1.5Gbps, 3.0Gbps, and 6.0Gbps.

screen calibration A program on a mobile device that verifies the three axes (left to right, up and down, and back to front) are calibrated properly.

screenlocks A pattern drawn on the display, a PIN (passcode), or a password used to make a mobile device inaccessible to other people.

SD card Secure Digital card. Popular flash memory card format for digital cameras and other electronic devices; capacity up to 2GB. See also *SDHC card.*

SDHC card Secure Digital High Capacity card. Popular flash memory card format for digital cameras and other electronic devices. Devices that use SDHC cards can also use SD cards; however, devices made only for SD cards cannot use SDHC cards. Capacity up to 32GB.

SDSL Synchronous DSL. A type of DSL connection in which upload and download speeds are the same. SDSL connections are marketed to business users rather than to home users and almost always require a newly installed circuit to the location and professional installation. See also *DSL* and *ADSL*.

SDXC card Secure Digital eXtended Capacity card. Popular flash memory card format for digital cameras and other electronic devices. Devices that use SDXC cards can also use SD and SDHC cards; however, devices made only for SD or SDHC cards cannot use SDXC cards. Capacity up to 2TB (2048GB).

self-powered hub Uses AC adapter; provides full power specified for USB port type(s) supported.

server Computer that shares drives and other resources over a network. Peer servers can also be used as workstations; dedicated servers provide services such as file, print, email, and so on to other computers.

Shadow Copy Windows Vista/7 feature that uses restore points to store older versions of files. Replaced in Windows 8/8.1 by File History.

shared resource A drive, printer, or other resource available to more than one PC over a network.

shortcut A Windows icon stored on the desktop or in a Windows folder with the .lnk extension; double-click the icon to run the program or open the file.

Shutter Priority mode (S, Tv mode) The user sets the shutter speed; and the camera sets the aperture. The user can adjust the white balance, ISO, focus methods, EV compensation, and other settings. Recommended for sports and action photography.

SkyDrive Former name for Windows OneDrive. See *OneDrive*.

SiSoftware Sandra A third-party system analysis program that provides extensive technical information on a computer's hardware.

slave Jumper setting for secondary PATA drive on a 40-wire cable.

SLC Single level cell. Flash memory type most often used in SSDs.

slow shutter speed Shutter speeds of 1/60 second or slower.

SMTP Simple Mail Transfer Protocol. A common Internet standard for uploading or sending email.

social engineering The act of obtaining confidential information by manipulating people.

SODIMM Small Outline DIMM. A compact version of the standard DIMM module, available in various pinouts for use in notebook computers and laser/LED printers.

software Anything that can be stored electronically, known as data, instructions, programs, or applications.

sound card An add-on card designed for digital sound recording and playback. Plugs into a PCI or PCIe x1 or wider slot.

SPDIF Sony/Philips Digital Interface; digital audio standard for interfacing sound cards or onboard sound hardware to a digital amplifier.

SPS Standby Power Supply. A battery backup technology that switches to battery power in the event that AC power is lost.

spyware A type of malware that collects computer and user information without the owner's consent or knowledge.

SSD Solid state drive; a hard drive that uses flash memory instead of magnetic storage platters.

SSID Service Set Identifier is a user-friendly name that identifies the wireless network. It is usually set on a wireless router device.

SSL Secure Sockets Layer. Predecessor of TLS. Used for securing online transactions.

start page The webpage that is first displayed when you open a web browser; can be customized to view any webpage available online or stored on your hard disk.

Start screen The default Windows 8/8.1 user interface that uses tiles for apps and is designed for touchscreens but can also be navigated with a keyboard, mouse, or touchpad.

startup event File loading and other activities during the startup of Windows.

STOP errors Also known as Blue Screen of Death (BSOD). An error that forces the system to halt until resolved. Systems can be configured to restart automatically after a STOP error or to leave it onscreen.

SVGA Super Video Graphics Array or Super VGA. May refer to 800×600 VGA resolution or to any VGA display setting that uses more than 16 colors or a higher resolution than 640×480.

S-Video S-Video (known as Separate Video) is an analog video standard used in many VCR and DVD products for input and output of video signals. Many older video cards use S-video for their TV output. Can be down-converted to composite video by using an adapter.

SuperSpeed USB USB 3.0 ports and devices.

surge suppressor A device that absorbs overvoltage conditions such as spikes and surges to prevent damage to connected devices.

suspend The power-saving mode that shuts down the monitor and other devices; it saves more power than standby. Called sleep mode in Windows 8/8.1.

switch Network device that sets a direct path for data to run from one system to another; can be combined with a router or wireless access point; faster than a hub because it supports the full bandwidth of the network at each port, rather than subdividing the bandwidth among active ports as a hub does.

synchronization The matching up of files and other data between one computing device and another.

system fan connectors Connectors on the motherboard that provide power and speed monitoring to case fans and sometimes the power supply fan.

System Information A Microsoft Windows application that displays information about a computer's operating system, hardware, and environment (MSInfo32.exe).

system lockups System is completely unresponsive; usually caused by overheating leading to corrupted memory contents. Shut down and turn off computer, wait a couple of minutes, and restart the computer to retry your operation. Check the system cooling if the problem persists.

System Restore A feature built in to Windows that enables the user to revert the system back to a previous state in case of a crash or other system problem. System Restore points can be created by the user and are created automatically by Windows when new hardware or software is installed or by a predefined schedule.

T

taskbar A Windows feature that displays icons for running programs, generally at the bottom of the primary display. In Windows 7 and later versions, the taskbar also contains jump list shortcuts to frequently used programs, documents, and tasks.

Task Manager Windows XP/Vista/7/8/8.1 interface for viewing and managing running programs, processes, services, and other information.

TB Terabyte. 1 trillion bytes.

TCP/IP Transmission Control Protocol/Internet Protocol. The Internet's standard network protocol that is now becoming the standard for all networks.

temp file Temporary file. A file created to store temporary information, such as a print job or an application work file. It may be stored in the default Temp folder (such as \Windows\Temp) or in a folder designated by the application. Temp files may use the .tmp extension or start with a tilde (~).

theme Windows term for the combination of desktop wallpaper, color scheme, screensaver, and sound effects.

thermal compound A material sandwiched between a device and a heat sink to provide the best possible heat transfer from the device to the heat sink. Also called thermal grease.

tile The Windows 8/8.1 term for the icons on the Start screen. They can be moved to different places on the Start screen by using drag and drop. Live tiles display up-to-date photos, news, email, and social network updates.

touchpad Most common type of pointing device installed in laptops. All emulate mice, but some recent models also support multitouch.

touchscreen A touch-sensitive screen built in to some desktop and most tablet computers. Windows 8/8.1's Start screen is designed for touchscreens but can also be navigated with a mouse or touchpad.

TLS Transport Layer Security. Successor of SSL. A cryptographic protocol that provides security and data integrity for communications over networks such as the Internet.

tripod A three-legged support for cameras. Most tripods have adjustable legs and an adjustable center column, and most also permit the camera to be mounted horizontally or vertically.

tripod socket A threaded hole in the bottom of the camera body that enables a tripod or monopod to be attached to the camera.

Trojan horse A malware program that appears legitimate but has a harmful action when triggered. It is similar to a computer virus but cannot spread itself to other computers, although some Trojan horses can be used to install a remote control program that allows an unauthorized user to take over your computer. Antivirus programs can block Trojan horses as well as true viruses.

tungsten white balance See *incandescent white balance*.

TV tuner A device that can receive analog or digital TV from over-the-air or cable TV sources for live playback or storage for later viewing.

U–V

UAC User Account Control. A security component of Windows Vista and later that controls how users gain access to resources.

UDF Universal Disk Format. A standard for CD and DVD media to drag and drop files to compatible media using a method called packet writing. Windows 8/8.1 supports various UDF versions.

uninstall The process of removing Windows programs from the system.

Universal Disk Format See *UDF*.

Universal Serial Bus (USB) High-speed replacement for older I/O ports USB 1.1 has a peak speed of 12Mbps. USB 2.0 has a peak speed of 480Mbps; USB 2.0 ports also support USB 1.1 devices. USB 2.0 devices can be plugged into USB 1.1 devices but run at only USB 1.1 speeds. USB 3.0 (supported in Windows 8/8.1) runs at 5Gbps; supports older USB devices at the native speeds of those devices.

upgrade Replacing an old version of software or hardware with a new version.

upgrade version A version of a program (such as Windows 8) that requires proof of ownership of a previous version before it can be installed.

UPS Uninterruptible Power Supply. The term for battery backup that uses a battery at all times to power the system.

URL Uniform resource locator. The full path to any given webpage or graphic on the Internet. A full URL contains the server type (such as http://, ftp://, or others), the site name (such as www.markesoper.com), and the name of the folder and the page or graphic you want to view (such as /blog/?page_id=38). Thus, the URL http://www.markesoper.com/blog/?page_id=38 displays the "About Mark" page on the author's website.

username Used with a password to gain access to network resources.

utility program A program that enhances day-to-day computer operations but doesn't create data.

variable aperture A zoom lens with a maximum aperture that gets narrower as the lens is zoomed from minimum to maximum magnification. Often marked on the lens barrel. Example: 1:4.0–5.6 (the lens maximum aperture changes from f/4.0 to f/5.6 as the lens is zoomed). Reduces the cost and bulk of the lens, but makes shooting in low light more difficult.

VGA Video Graphics Array. First popular analog video standard; basis for all current video cards.

video capture The process to capture live video from analog or digital sources and store it as a computer file.

video card A video card (also known as display adapter or graphics card) is an expansion card that generates video signal and displays it on a monitor.

virtual memory Disk space used as a substitute for RAM.

virtualization Creating an environment in which operating systems or applications run on a software-created simulation of a computer rather than directly on the computer hardware.

virus Computer program designed to infect a computer and make unwanted modifications to the operating system. If executed, the virus can replicate itself; in this way it resembles a Trojan horse that can also replicate itself to other computers.

VoIP Voice over Internet Protocol. Delivery of voice communications over IP networks such as the Internet.

W–Z

WAN Wide area network. Network that spans multiple cities, countries, or continents. Network sections might be linked by leased line, Internet backbone, or satellite feed; routers connect LANs to WANs and WAN segments to each other.

WAP Wireless access point. A device that enables connectivity between computers with wireless network adapters to create a wireless network.

warm boot Restarting a computer with a software command; no memory or hardware testing.

warm color Color that has a yellow, red, or orange cast. Indicates that white balance is incorrect.

WAV A noncompressed standard for digital audio. Some recording programs for Windows can create and play back WAV files. However, WAV files are very large and are usually converted into other formats for use online or for creating digital music archives.

wavetable A method of playing back MIDI files with digitized samples of actual musical instruments.

webcam A video camera designed for live chat sessions. Resolutions range from sub-VGA to 1080p HD.

WEP Wired Equivalent Privacy. A now-obsolete standard for wireless security. Replaced by WPA.

white balance A preset or custom setting that produces neutral white and correct colors in various types of light. For best results, match the white balance setting to the lighting type used in the photo. See also *auto white balance*, *fluorescent white balance*, *daylight white balance*, *incandescent white balance*, *tungsten white balance*, *cloudy white balance*, *open shade white balance*, and *custom white balance*.

Wi-Fi The name for IEEE-802.11a, IEEE-802.11b, IEEE-802.11g, or IEEE-802.11n wireless Ethernet devices that meet the standards set forth by the Wi-Fi Alliance.

Wi-Fi tethering When a mobile device shares its cellular Internet connection with other Wi-Fi–capable devices.

wildcard A character used to replace one or more characters as a variable in DIR, Windows Find/Search, and File Explorer. * = multiple characters; ? = a single character.

Windows 7 Microsoft's seventh-generation desktop operating system.

Windows 8/8.1 Microsoft's most recent operating system.

Windows Aero Windows Vista/7 3D desktop with translucent windows.

Windows Explorer File management interface for Windows desktop. Known as File Explorer in Windows 8/8.1.

Windows Recovery Environment Windows Vista/7/8/8.1 collection of automatic and user-operated repair and diagnostic tools for fixing problems with systems that won't start.

Windows Action Center A Windows 7/8/8.1 feature that combines security and system warnings and notifications into a single interface.

Windows Essentials 2012 An optional addition to Windows 7/8/8.1 that provides support for photo management and light editing, blogging, family safety, instant messaging, email, and video editing. These programs run from the Windows desktop.

wireless network The general term for any radio-frequency network, including Wi-Fi. Most wireless networks can be interconnected to conventional networks.

WLAN Wireless local area network. Instead of wires, stations on a WLAN connect to each other through radio waves. The IEEE 802.11 family of standards guide the development of WLANs.

WMA Windows Media Audio. This is the native compressed audio format created by Windows Media Player. Unlike MP3, WMA files support digital rights management.

worm A self-replicating type of malware similar to a virus but without the need for a user to execute it. It often uses a network to spread itself.

WPA Wi-Fi Protected Access. A security protocol developed by the Wi-Fi Alliance to secure wireless networking. Takes the place of WEP. Uses the TKIP encryption protocol.

WPA2 Wi-Fi Protected Access version 2. A security protocol developed by the Wi-Fi Alliance to secure wireless networking using the AES encryption protocol. Takes the place of WPA.

WWW World Wide Web. The portion of the Internet that uses the Hypertext Transfer Protocol (http://) and can thus be accessed via a web browser, such as Microsoft Internet Explorer, Google Chrome, and Mozilla Firefox.

WXGA Wide XGA. A common widescreen graphics resolution for laptops and some displays.

x64 64-bit extension to x86 processor architecture; backward compatible; supports more than 4GB of RAM.

x86 32-bit processor architecture used by AMD and Intel CPUs.

XCOPY Command-line utility for copying files and folders.

XGA eXtended Graphics Array. 1024×768 display standard that is a minimum requirement for most Windows programs.

Zip The archive type (originally known as PKZIP) created when you use Send To Compressed (Zipped) folder. A Zip file can contain one or more files and can be created, viewed, and opened in Windows Explorer or File Explorer. Formerly also referred to the Iomega Zip removable-media drive.

zoom lens A lens that adjusts the magnification to change the angle of view and bring objects closer or farther away. Also called optical zoom, because lens elements inside the lens barrel move as the zoom control is used.

zoom ratio The difference between minimum and maximum zoom magnification, such as 4×, 8×, and 12×.

Enhance your IT skills
PC Repair and Troubleshooting Guide
ISBN: 9788183335096
Price: 499/-
Mastering HTML, CSS & JavaScript Web Publishing
ISBN: 9788183335157
Price: 450/-
Project Management Study Guide
ISBN: 9789386551009
Price: 399/-
C++ Study Guide
ISBN: 9788183335324
Price: 360/-
JavaScript Study Guide
ISBN: 9789386551016
Price: 399/-
Advance Excel 2016 In Depth
ISBN: 9788183335980
Price: 498/-
Microsoft Visual Studio 2015 Unleashed
ISBN: 9788183334174
Price: 699/-
How Computers Work
ISBN: 9788183335997
Price: 498/-
Oracle PL/SQL Training Guide
ISBN: 9788183334518
Price: 180/-
WordPress Study Guide
ISBN: 9788183335331
Price: 495/-
Windows 10 In Depth
ISBN: 9788183335164
Price: 498/-
Available at amazon
www.bpbonline.com